GREEK HISTORY

GREEK HISTORY

Advisory Editor:

W. R. CONNOR

CHAIRMAN, DEPARTMENT OF CLASSICS
PROFESSOR OF GREEK
PRINCETON UNIVERSITY

ATHENIAN STUDIES

PRESENTED TO

WILLIAM SCOTT FERGUSON

ARNO PRESS
A New York Times Company

New York / 1973

Reprint Edition 1973 by Arno Press Inc.

Reprinted from a copy in
The University of Illinois Library

Greek History
ISBN for complete set: 0-405-04775-4
See last pages of this volume for titles.

Manufactured in the United States of America

回厄回

Library of Congress Cataloging in Publication Data
Main entry under title:

Athenian studies.

    (Greek history)
    Reprint of the 1940 ed., which was issued as
supplementary v. 1 of Harvard studies in classical
philology.
    Includes bibliographical references.
    CONTENTS: Blegen, C. W. Athens and the early age
of Greece.--Mylonas, G. E. Athens and Minoan Crete.--
Daux, G. Athènes et Delphes. [etc.]
    1. Athens--History--Addresses, essays, lectures.
I. Ferguson, William Scott, 1875-1954. II. Title.
III. Series: Harvard studies in classical philology,
supplementary v. 1.
DF285.A86 1973   913.8'5'03   72-7883
ISBN 0-405-04777-0

HEAD OF NIKE FROM THE ATHENIAN AGORA

PAGES 183–210: FIGURE 1

ATHENIAN STUDIES

PRESENTED TO

WILLIAM SCOTT FERGUSON

HARVARD STUDIES IN CLASSICAL PHILOLOGY

SUPPLEMENTARY VOLUME I

CAMBRIDGE

HARVARD UNIVERSITY PRESS

LONDON : HUMPHREY MILFORD

OXFORD UNIVERSITY PRESS

1940

PRINTED AT THE HARVARD UNIVERSITY PRESS
CAMBRIDGE, MASS., U. S. A.

FOREWORD

THIS volume in honor of Professor William Scott Ferguson is published separately as a Supplementary Volume of the *Harvard Studies in Classical Philology*. The history and institutions of Athens have been his chosen field, and it has seemed proper that this volume of essays presented to him should center upon that subject. Naturally, to achieve some unity of content, sacrifices had to be made. Several scholars who were invited to contribute have written regretfully to say that they found themselves unable at the moment to present an essay related to that subject.

Publication of the volume has been made possible by a substantial grant from the American Council of Learned Societies, and by generous gifts from Mr. Philip R. Allen, Mr. Robert W. Bliss, Mr. John Nicholas Brown, Miss Mary H. Buckingham, Mr. William H. Buckler, Mr. Lawrence Coolidge, Mr. Gardiner H. Fiske, Mr. Edward W. Forbes, Mr. Claude M. Fuess, Mr. Frank B. Jewett, Miss Bettina J. Kahnweiler, Mr. Carl T. Keller, Mr. Thomas W. Lamont, Mr. Walter Lichtenstein, Mr. A. Lawrence Lowell, Mr. Stephen B. Luce, Mr. Henry S. Morgan, Mr. William B. Munro, Mr. Paul G. Pennoyer, Mr. Ralph Barton Perry, Mr. Edward M. Pickman, Mr. W. K. Richardson, Mr. Paul J. Sachs, Mr. William T. Semple, Mr. Alfred M. Tozzer, Mr. Robert Walcott, Mr. Charles Warren, Mr. K. G. T. Webster, and others.

The editors are the former students of Professor Ferguson, who completed under his direction their studies for the Degree of Doctor of Philosophy. Their own essays appear in the regular Volume LI (1940) of *Harvard Studies in Classical Philology*. For helpful collaboration in the task of preparing both volumes for the press, they are grateful to the Editorial Committee of the Department of the Classics.

CONTENTS

ATHENS AND THE EARLY AGE OF GREECE   1
    Carl W. Blegen

ATHENS AND MINOAN CRETE   11
    George E. Mylonas

ATHENES ET DELPHES   37
    Georges Daux

THE PRO-PERSIAN PARTY AT ATHENS FROM 510 TO 480 B.C. . . .   71
    Malcolm F. McGregor

DIE KÄMPFE AM EURYMEDON   97
    Werner Peek

THE PEACE OF KALLIAS   121
    H. T. Wade-Gery

THE TRIBAL CYCLES OF THE TREASURERS OF ATHENA   157
    William Bell Dinsmoor

A GOLDEN NIKE FROM THE ATHENIAN AGORA   183
    Homer A. Thompson

THE OLD OLIGARCH   211
    A. W. Gomme

ATHENS AND CARTHAGE   247
    Benjamin D. Meritt

THE UNITY OF THUCYDIDES' HISTORY   255
    John H. Finley, Jr.

THE USE OF HEMLOCK FOR CAPITAL PUNISHMENT   299
    Robert J. Bonner

STUDIES IN HISTORICAL LITERATURE OF THE FOURTH CENTURY B.C. .   303
    Herbert Bloch

Contents (*continued*)

TWO ATTIC TREASURE-RECORDS 377
    Arthur M. Woodward

THE DATE OF ISOCRATES' AREOPAGITICUS AND THE ATHENIAN OPPO-
SITION 409
    Werner Jaeger

ATHENAEUS AND THE SLAVES OF ATHENS 451
    William Linn Westermann

LES RAPPORTS D'ATHÈNES ET DE L'AITOLIE AU IIIᵉ SIÈCLE AVANT J.-C. 471
    R. Flacelière

PHTHIA — CHRYSEIS 483
    W. W. Tarn

ARCHON DIOMEDON 503
    Johannes Kirchner (deceased June 27, 1940)

ΑΜΦΙΘΑΛΗΣ 509
    Louis Robert

JULIA DOMNA AS ATHENA POLIAS 521
    James H. Oliver

INDEX LOCORUM 531

ATHENIAN STUDIES

ATHENS AND THE EARLY AGE OF GREECE

By Carl W. Blegen

ATHENS plays only a minor role in the Homeric poems, whether or not there ever was a Peisistratid recension of the text. Although the city is recorded in the Catalogue as having provided a substantial contingent of ships and men to participate in the Trojan expedition, it gained little glory beyond a mere passing mention in the dispatches, so far as the Epic itself is concerned. Athenian share in the greater cycles of Hellenic traditions and myths is also meagre, and in this respect Attica takes a very modest place in comparison with Argolis, Boeotia and other districts more richly endowed with folk-memories. It has become almost a truism to say that the volume of folk tales and traditions clustering about a city affords a convenient and fairly close measure of the antiquity of the settlement's history.

The existence of Cyclopean walls and the survival of bare traces of a Mycenaean "palace" on the Acropolis have of course long ago been duly noted[1] together with the occurrence of a single tholos tomb, apparently representing a relatively late type, near Menidi somewhat remote from the citadel. Mycenaean sites and cemeteries of chamber tombs have likewise been found in various parts of the Attic countryside. But in spite of much excavation and extensive exploration in Athens and Attica, archaeological material pertaining to the Bronze Age and earlier has until very recent times been scanty, not to say undistinguished.

It is not surprising therefore that attempts to reconstruct the "history" of prehistoric Greece have generally dealt for the most part with the abundant evidence from Knossos, Mycenae, Tiryns, Thebes and other sites, and have neglected, or passed lightly over, Athens and Attica. But a sober consideration of the whole matter in the light of our knowledge today, it seems to me, leads to the conclusion that the Athenian birthright in this connection has not received the recognition that is its due.

---

[1] The regal magnificence of the walls themselves, which places them on a qualitative level with those at Mycenae, has seldom been adequately recognized.

The very name of the city is surely not without significance in its bearing on the early history of the site. Athenai must mean, as so ably argued by Professor Nilsson, the town of Athena, the place enjoying the special protection of the goddess herself; and there can be no doubt that the city was named after her and not vice versa. Athena and her origins have formed the subject of much discussion which has revealed not a little diversity of opinion. Among philologists it is now generally held that Ἀθήνη belongs to a group of words, chiefly place-names, characterized by their ending -ηνη-, which may be associated with other groups, like those with the elements -νθ- and -σσ-, that are almost universally regarded as being of pre-Greek origin. This statement is quoted almost verbatim from Nilsson who gives the appropriate references.[1] A dogmatic conclusion may still be somewhat unsafe, but I think in his further discussion of the problem, dealing with survivals in the cult of the goddess, Nilsson has succeeded in making out a satisfactory case for his theory that Athena is a direct descendant of the Minoan palace goddess. Perhaps it would be more accurate to say that she is not a descendant but the same deity in a different environment, since her migration to Attica must almost surely be ascribed to a date far earlier than the best known phases of the Palace cult. For her association with the place-names mentioned unmistakably assigns her to the linguistic layer that seems to belong to the Early Bronze Age. We are therefore justified in concluding provisionally that Athens, under that name, already existed before 2000 B.C.

The problem of the myths is not susceptible of easy explanation. It is not that Athens is actually devoid of a real mythology, for there is a considerable body of folk tales and traditions that seem to have sprung, like Kekrops himself, from Attic soil. But the long genealogies and the more elaborate cycles have the appearance of being relatively late and artificial inventions or compositions, as for example, the tales of Theseus, which for the most part undeniably reflect the greater exploits of Herakles; and on the other hand Attic heroes are conspicuously absent in the great Hellenic sagas, such as that of the Trojan expedition we have already men-

[1] M. P. Nilsson, *The Minoan-Mycenaean Religion*, Lund, 1927, pp. 419–420.

tioned, the Voyage of the Argonauts, the Caledonian Boar Hunt, and many others. Professor Nilsson has, however, called attention to certain elements in the Theseus cycle that may have formed the original kernel of the myth, which are evidently native to Attica and must go back to a time when the Palace of Minos at Knossos still flourished; and, as he points out,[1] it is noteworthy that the only strong mythological links between the mainland of Greece and Minoan Crete are preserved in the stories of Theseus and Ariadne and perhaps of Minos, Scylla and Nisos at home in neighboring Megara. Some of the Attic myths, therefore, appear to pertain to a period not much if at all later than the middle of the second millennium B.C.; and it is surely of some significance for the role at that time played by Athens that Minoan contacts with the Greek mainland were made through Attica. Athens seems then to have stood as a buffer between Minos and the rest of the mainland world. Later when the Cretan palaces were destroyed, it was no doubt to an expedition from Argolis that they fell victims, and it was to Argolis that the booty was brought home. Some parts of the Athenian myths would thus appear to be earlier than the Argive and Theban cycles of story, and it may well be that in the later period Athens had lost much of her power and Attica had become to some extent isolated from the Achaean states, and was consequently excluded from participation in most of their myths.

When we turn to the archaeological side we find that exploration in recent years has vastly increased the material available and has greatly amplified our understanding of preclassical Athens. The brilliant discoveries of the German Archaeological Institute in the vicinity of the Dipylon and of the Greek Archaeological Society at Vari have revealed an astonishing wealth of pottery of the orientalizing period and have placed our knowledge of this phase of Athenian culture on a new footing. We see now that Attica of the seventh century was not a crude and backward region, but a lively progressive centre, perhaps not her equal in delicacy and finesse, but hardly falling short of Corinth in inventive power, originality and sturdy vigor. Athens of the Geometric Age, already fairly well

---

[1] M. P. Nilsson, *The Mycenaean Origin of Greek Mythology*, Berkeley, 1932, p. 180.

known, has been further illuminated through discoveries in the
Agora and outside the Dipylon; and the same researches, especially
in the latter place, have brought to light much new evidence for
the evolution of civilization in the Proto-geometric and sub-
Mycenaean periods.

Mycenaean remains are still far from copious in comparison with
those found in Argolis, but in quality they are beginning to show a
parity that cannot be ignored. The excavations of the Agora and
on the north slope of the Acropolis have made this clear. The fine
rock-hewn chamber tomb unearthed in the Agora in the campaign
of 1939[1] yielded a series of vases of excellent style from the beginning of Late Helladic III, together with exquisitely carved ivories
in no way inferior to the best of their kind from Peloponnesus.
The chance survival of this tomb on the slope north of the Are-
opagos, in a spot constantly occupied and disturbed by building
and rebuilding in later times, is sufficient to establish beyond doubt
the wealth and importance of Mycenaean Athens, and to give an
idea of how much has been destroyed and lost to us through the
activities of the later habitants. Construction of modern houses
on the lower slope of the Philopappos Hill in 1930 led to the finding
and destruction of another Mycenaean tomb, the shape of which
is unfortunately not now known.[2] Of its contents, evidently rather
rich, some gold jewelry was saved and ultimately reached the
National Museum. The beads and plaques seem to point to the
fifteenth rather than the fourteenth century as the date of the
burial, and we are thus carried back to Late Helladic II. Still
earlier Mycenaean objects are certainly not common in Attica,
but among the sherds from the Acropolis are some from pots of
quality and style that can definitely be attributed to Late Helladic
I. All three phases of the Late Helladic Period are thus represented
in Athens. The pottery from the cemeteries in the Mesogaea, all
of Late Helladic III, including much new material lately brought
to light by the Ephor of Attica, N. Kyparissis, has recently been
subjected to a careful study by F. H. Stubbings of Cambridge, following out a suggestion of Professor Wace. His paper has not yet

[1] T. L. Shear in *Illustr. London News*, July 22, 1939, 161–163.
[2] *Arch. Anz.* 1931, 213 (*Jahrbuch* XLVI, 1931).

been published; but he has succeeded in distinguishing some interesting elements of a local Mycenaean ceramic style; and it seems
clear that the Attic potters of this period had attained a position
of no little distinction. Their work suffers not at all by comparison
with that of the contemporary craftsmen of Argolis, and I think
the blossoming of a distinctive Attic style in the Late Mycenaean
period may fairly be regarded as an expression of creative genius
parallel to the similar and better known phenomena that have
already been mentioned as occurring later in the Geometric and
Orientalizing phases. How much farther back we shall ultimately
be able to trace such manifestations of a peculiarly Attic individuality it is not yet possible to say. In the meantime, however, it
may be noted that the Acropolis and its slopes and the region of
the Agora have yielded a considerable quantity of Middle Helladic
and Early Helladic remains, permitting us to assert that the settlement flourished throughout the whole of the Bronze Age. Indeed,
we can say more, for recent explorations on the south[1] and the
north slopes and in the Agora have also produced not a little pottery of the Neolithic Period closely akin to that found in northeastern Peloponnesus and in Central Greece. It is, therefore, obvious that the site was already inhabited in the late Stone Age; and
Athens thus shows the same succession of strata that have been observed at other old mainland centres where the sequence is complete.

Much has been written concerning the racial and cultural
origins of the Greeks; and the problem, already sufficiently complex
in itself, has often been made more intricate by interpretations,
prejudices, and preconceived theories regarding the migrations of
peoples from one direction or another. If, for the moment, the possible sources of these folk-movements may be left out of consideration, the whole question is greatly simplified. It is becoming increasingly more certain from the archaeological evidence that we
must recognize three main cultural, and presumably also racial,
layers in Early Greece.

---

[1] A detailed publication of the pottery recovered in the Italian excavations on
the south slope of the Acropolis between the Stoa of Eumenes and the Asklepieion
has been written by Dr. Doro Levi and will appear in the next number of *Annuario*
(Vol. XIII).

The first belongs to the Neolithic Period, when a more or less nearly homogeneous civilization of long duration may be postulated throughout the whole of continental Greece from Northern Thessaly to Southwestern Peloponnesus. The remains indicate an agricultural population living in fixed abodes in settled communities, possessing domesticated animals and using implements of stone and bone. The ceramic handicraft reached a relatively high stage of development, and characteristic figurines of crude and obese types, both male and female, of stone and terra-cotta, were produced in abundance. Almost no graves have been found and human skeletal material is too scanty to permit anthropological generalizations. However, it may safely be said that no relationship with contemporary culture in Crete and the Cyclades can be shown. If one allows imagination some scope in interpreting these remains one may conclude that the people who left them were a superstitious folk who expressed themselves with rude, unrestrained exuberance, sometimes taking the form of coarse humor, not to say vulgarity.

The second layer falls in the Early Bronze Age, when the working of metal — mainly copper — becomes widespread. In this period it is clear that the cultures of the mainland from the Peloponnesus to Thessaly, the Aegean Islands and Crete were closely akin, the dominating elements in the population in the three areas probably representing collateral offshoots from a common parent stem. It is likely that the relationship extended even to the use of an essentially common language characterized by its numerous words with the elements -$\nu\theta$- and -$\sigma\sigma$-. Some skeletons have been recovered and studied, though the evidence is still far from adequate, and anthropologists generally hold the view that we have here a branch of the Mediterranean race. In Crete a long period of uninterrupted peace and prosperity permitted a gradual evolution from a seafaring and agricultural phase into what we may fairly call an urban stage of society in which civilization blossomed and the arts flourished. A similar development on the Aegean Islands and on the mainland seems to have been cut short prematurely by violence when a new wave of migration rolled over these regions, but failed to reach Crete. The character of the population mainly responsible for the second layer naturally finds its best expression, so far as we can grasp it, in Minoan culture, and I think one is justified in recognizing among its dominant traits a delicacy of feeling and a sobriety of judgment that, without limiting imaginative power, led to orderliness and a deep love of beauty.

The third layer, as already implied, marks the violent advent of the Middle Bronze Age. This culture, which has been called Middle Helladic, primarily at home in Continental Greece, but soon spreading to the adjacent Cyclades, introduces a new type of house, a new kind of tomb, and a characteristic pottery of its own, and it is apparently familiar with the technique of making bronze. Although at first seemingly responsible for a recession of civilization, it gradually forges ahead as it absorbs what it had conquered and comes into closer contact with Minoan Crete, and finally it evolves into the culture we call Mycenaean. For its earlier phases skeletal remains have not yet been widely examined and anthropological data are insufficient; but the current view regards the new arrivals as being of Aryan stock and as bringing with them Indo-European speech, more specifically an early form of Greek. Judged by their monuments, especially of the later phases of their period, these people might be viewed as a vigorous warlike folk, pervaded with an epic spirit of adventure, and with a singularly straightforward directness of outlook.

The three strata, thus briefly and inadequately sketched, unquestionably constituted the soil that nourished the roots from which classical civilization grew to maturity and flower, and one cannot doubt that it was a rich soil. I think it may be taken for granted that the successive waves of invasion were not in any case wholly destructive of what had gone before. It was certainly not a total extermination. Much damage was surely done and many men were doubtless slain. But a considerable body of the population must each time have survived, and in the course of many generations that followed a gradual fusion of elements came about. Some folk-knowledge must always have been remembered, and not all the advances and achievements that had been made in arts and crafts can have been forgotten. Each folk-layer thus lived on in the layer that succeeded, and something of its contributions may have become a permanent heritage. Some of the fundamental characteristics of the diverse human elements are particularly likely to have been transmitted in the fusion. I do not mean to insist too seriously on the specific origins of those qualities that have been mentioned in the foregoing paragraphs as distinctive of the three layers; but all are outstanding traits in the character of the classical Greeks themselves, and it is perhaps not wholly vain to speculate on their possible sources.

Early Greece was clearly a melting-pot, a crucible in which elements of diverse origins were melted together and fused into a new alloy. Its quality presumably varied somewhat from place to place in accordance with differing proportions in the mixture; but the three chief ingredients were essentially the same and the resultant metal was of fairly uniform consistency and intrinsic worth. The numerous and rather striking local differences that meet us among the Greeks of classical times may perhaps best be explained as due to variations in the processes of refinement and tempering which were slowly worked out in the troubled times of the later Aryan migrations culminating in the Dorian invasion. The latter movement is well enough attested archaeologically, mainly through the scar it caused, but the preceding waves have left almost no visible traces that can be recognized as peculiarly Ionian or Achaean. The Achaeans in particular are highly elusive when one attempts to fix the time of their arrival. Yet in view of their established place in Greek tradition, it can hardly be doubted that they were real. The first Aryans, who came at the beginning of the Middle Bronze Age, may perhaps be regarded as Ionians; between their coming and that of the Dorians is ample room for the appearance of an Achaean strain even if it is not yet possible on archaeological evidence to determine the exact time of its advent.

The material remains that have been brought to light for this early period are not in themselves sufficient to explain the outstanding position held by Athens among the city states in classical times. One among them, yet standing apart, she must surely owe her special and peculiar individuality in large measure to her particular heritage from the past. But just what there was in this heritage, unique and different from that which was handed down elsewhere, can only form the subject of speculation. We may conjecture that one important factor is that recorded in Hellenic tradition, namely that the Dorians never succeeded in establishing a foothold in Attica. The process of fusion here must thus have had a longer time to work itself out to the end, free from disturbance and interruption, than was possible in most other districts; and the bright Ionic tempering was not dulled through the later application of a coat of Doric plating.

The original ingredients of the classical alloy are becoming somewhat more perceptible and distinguishable. But we must acknowledge in conclusion that the mysterious combination of forces and processes and time that led to the splendid flowering of classical Greek civilization both in Attica and elsewhere still remains essentially as impenetrable and miraculous as ever.

ATHENS AND MINOAN CRETE

By George E. Mylonas

AMONG the many traditional theses which are accepted by scholars axiomatically is the Cretan domination if not conquest of Athens in prehistoric times. It was developed before the epoch-making discoveries of Sir Arthur Evans at Knossos, it was strengthened by the same discoveries, and it has appeared in one form or another in many of our history books.[1] Since this tradition was created, however, our knowledge of the prehistoric period of Greece in general and of Athens in particular has been increased considerably and it may prove of some interest and perhaps of some importance to survey our evidence and see whether it proves or disproves this popular thesis. We may begin with a brief discussion of the archaeological evidence, which perhaps offers the most concrete data on the problem.

The earliest remains thus far uncovered in Athens belong to the Neolithic Period. Along the southern slope of the Acropolis and behind the stoa of Eumenes, the Italian Archaeological School brought to light in 1922 remains belonging to the Stone Age.[2] In 1931–1932 Dr. Oscar Broneer found some neolithic sherds in his excavations of the North Slope of the Acropolis and more remains were uncovered in the same area in the spring of 1932.[3] Professor T. L. Shear and his collaborators uncovered a neolithic grave in 1935 about "two meters east of the façade of the 'Metroön.'" A marble neolithic statuette was also found in the Agora district as well as numerous neolithic sherds.[4] Beyond Athens neolithic remains are known to me from two sites near Eleusis. And it is possible to assume that a steatopygous figurine now in the museum at

---

[1] Cf. besides: J. L. Myres, *Who Were the Greeks*, Berkeley, 1930, 325, 348; J. D. S. Pendlebury, *The Archaeology of Crete*, London, 1939, p. 230.

[2] *Bolletino d'Arte* III (Dec. 1922) figs. 7–10; *Annuario* IV–V (1921–22) 490; Γ. 'Ε. Μυλωνᾶς, 'Η νεολιθικὴ ἐποχὴ ἐν 'Ελλάδι, Athens, 1928, p. 76.

[3] *Hesperia* II (1933) 357; VI (1937) 540–542.

[4] *Hesperia* V (1936) 20–21; VIII (1939) 235.

Eleusis comes from one of these two sites.[1] The neolithic culture represented by these few remains seems to be related to that existing in the northeastern half of the mainland of Greece and certainly has nothing in common with the stone age culture revealed in Crete.[2]

Characteristic sherds of the Early Helladic Period have been found in the neighborhood of the Erechtheum, on the North and South Slopes of the Acropolis, and in the Agora region.[3] In the vicinity of Athens, Early Helladic remains are known from Haghios Kosmas, Peiraeus, Eleusis, and Minoa, and at least five sites dating from the same period are known to me in more distant parts of Attica.[4] These Early Helladic remains are in every respect similar to those discovered on other contemporary mainland sites.

The Middle Helladic Period is better represented at Athens. Minyan and matt-painted wares were found on the North Slope in such abundance as to justify the belief in the existence on that site of a "fairly long Middle Helladic Period."[5] More remains are known from the South Slope where the late Andreas Skias uncov-

---

[1] Γ. ᾿Ε. Μυλωνᾶς, Προϊστορικὴ ᾿Ελευσίς, Athens, 1932, pp.138–140. To this must be added the marble figurine now in the Ashmolean Museum reported to have been found north of Athens: cf. A. J. B. Wace and M. S. Thompson, *Prehistoric Thessaly*, Cambridge, 1912, p. 225.

[2] Cf. Sir Arthur Evans, *The Palace of Minos at Knossos*, I, London, 1921, pp. 32–55; Pendlebury *Archaeol. of Crete* 35–45; Μυλωνᾶς, Νεολ. ἐποχή 102–112.

[3] C. W. Blegen, *Korakou, A Prehistoric Settlement Near Corinth*, Boston, 1921, p. 110; Broneer *Hesperia* II (1933) 358–359 n. 1; *Bolletino d'Arte* IV (1924–25) fig. 8; B. Graef, *Die antiken Vasen von der Akropolis zu Athen*, I, Berlin, 1909, pl. 1 nos. 2–3; Hansen *Hesperia* VI (1937) 542–546 figs. 3–4.

[4] G. E. Mylonas, "Excavations at Haghios Kosmas," *American Journal of Archaeology*, XXXVIII (1934), pp. 258–271; Προϊστ. ᾿Ελευσίς 59–62; I. Θρεψιάδης καὶ I. Τραυλός, "᾿Ανασκαφικαὶ ἔρευναι ἐν Μεγάροις," Πρακτικὰ τῆς ἐν ᾿Αθήναις ᾿Αρχαιολογικῆς ῾Εταιρείας, 1934, p. 51 n. 1 and fig. 11, 6. D. Fimmen, *Die Kretisch-Mykenische Kultur*, Berlin, 1924, p. 136, illustrates a "sauce-boat," now in the National Museum at Athens, and he states that the vase was found at Phaleron. Apparently he derived this information from the catalogue of Collignon-Couve, p. 25 no. 135. But it seems that Collignon and Couve were misled by the inscription on the show-case ("Phaleron") in which the vase is kept. The Museum inventory states that the vase is from Chalandriane on the island of Syra; there is no connection with Phaleron.

[5] *Hesperia* VI (1937) 546–557, 568; II (1933) 359–363; Graef *Ant. Vasen* I plates 1–2 nos. 10, 11, 15, 27, 28, 29.

ered a "premycenaean" (= Middle Helladic) tomb.[1] We have no Middle Helladic remains at Haghios Kosmas, but a large settlement has been uncovered at Eleusis.[2] Minyan and matt-painted pottery were also found at Thorikos and sherds can be obtained from three unexcavated sites in Attica.[3] The Middle Helladic remains of Athens and of Attica with their local variations are similar to Middle Helladic remains found on other mainland sites.

Thus far only two stratified sites of the Late Helladic Period have been excavated, Eleusis and Haghios Kosmas.[4] The latter has yielded remains of the Late Helladic II and III Periods. Remains of Late Helladic I are comparatively rare in Attica. The best deposit was found at Eleusis and sherds were obtained from the Acropolis and its North Slope. However, Late Helladic II and III are represented by a great many graves uncovered in various places, proving that Attica was well populated in Late Helladic III times and indicating that it then enjoyed a certain degree of prosperity.[5] From the Acropolis itself we have a good deal of pottery belonging to Late Helladic II and III. The remains of the megaron and of the fortification wall of the Acropolis, belonging to Late Helladic III times, are too well known to call for further description.[6] A rich deposit of Late Helladic III pottery was un-

---

[1] "Τύμβος προϊστορικὸς ὑπὸ τὴν Ἀκρόπολιν," Ἐφ. Ἀρχαιολ. 1902, 128. The Middle Helladic date of the grave is proved by its contents, which included "Lydian," i.e. "Minyan," ware.

[2] Μυλωνᾶς, Προϊστ. Ἐλ. 17–29, 36–57, 62–107.

[3] Β. Στάης, "Προϊστορικοὶ συνοικισμοὶ ἐν Ἀττικῇ καὶ Αἰγίνῃ," Ἐφ. Ἀρχ., 1895, pp. 221–234. I found Minyan and matt-painted sherds at Thorikos a little below the present surface of the site.

[4] Μυλωνᾶς, Προϊστ. Ἐλ. 29–36; 57–58; 108–138; Mylonas *AJA* XXXVIII (1934) 258–271.

[5] For the graves cf.: Spata: Ἀθήναιον VI (1877) 167 pl. 6; *Bulletin de Correspondance Hellénique* II (1878) 185–228; Menidi: Lolling, *Das Kuppelgrab bei Menidi*, Athen, 1880; Vravron, Steiria, Lighori, Kopreza, Thorikos: Ἐφ. Ἀρχ. 1895, 193–235; Pikermi, Velanideza, Vourvasti: Ἀρχαιολογικὸν Δελτίον XI (1927–28) Παράρτημα 60–66. For sherds and other smaller articles from various parts of Attica cf. Fimmen *Kret.-Myk. Kultur* 6–9. For sherds from Minoa cf. Θρεψιάδης-Τραυλός, Πρακτικὰ 1934, 51–52.

[6] Graef *Ant. Vasen* plates 2–6; P. Cavvadias and G. Kawerau, *Die Ausgrabung der Akropolis*, Athen, 1907, plates A, Γ.

covered by Broneer on the North Slope, remains of a settlement were discovered at Kerameikos, and a few graves of the period have been found in the Agora district and on the hill over the location known today as Σφαγεῖα.[1] These remains of the Late Helladic Period present a culture gradually and normally developed from the one existing in the region in an earlier period,[2] and in spite of their local variations and poorer quality present many similarities to the remains found in other contemporary sites on the mainland.

It is to be noted that thus far not a single object has been unearthed which could link Attica to Crete and which could indicate, even by a great stretch of the imagination, a Cretan domination over Attica in Minoan times. Conceivably the ring found in the Late Helladic grave of the Agora is of Cretan origin. But Professor Shear has proved that it belongs to the closing years of the Late Helladic III period, to about 1200 B.C.,[3] a time when a Cretan conquest or domination of the mainland would be impossible. The prehistoric remains of Attica, the Neolithic, Early, Middle, and Late Helladic, with their local peculiarities, are in every respect similar to the remains found in the rest of the mainland of Greece, and consequently indicate the existence in Attica of the same social, cultural, and political conditions as existed in other parts of the mainland. These conditions are different from those existing in Crete in Minoan times and do not indicate a Cretan conquest or domination. Of course for the Late Helladic remains of Mycenae and Tiryns a Cretan origin has been claimed, indicating a Cretan conquest. This claim is by no means proved as yet and I personally believe that the existing evidence proves that

---

[1] *Hesperia* I (1932) 35; II (1933) 363–372; IV (1935) 318–321; V (1936) 21–23; VI (1937) 557–566; VIII (1939) 212 and 317–433; *AJA* XLIII (1939) 578–588 (the last two articles appeared after the present study was completed); Kraiker-Kübler *Kerameikos* I 109. The finds from the graves of "Σφαγεῖα" have not been published as yet, but cf. *Arch. Anz.* 1931, 213.

[2] Cf. Μυλωνᾶς, Προϊστ. Ἑλ. 159–162.

[3] *Hesperia* IV (1935) 318–320 and figures 7–8. The destruction of Knossos and of the other Minoan towns at the end of Late Minoan II, or ca. 1400 B.C., will of necessity form the *terminus ante quem* for any Minoan domination of any part of the mainland.

such a conquest never occurred.[1] However, the lack of refinement, of exceptional artistic or intrinsic value, and of outside influence on the Late Helladic I and II remains uncovered in Attica, the complete absence of any Cretan remains in the district, and the purely local color of the remains, definitely prove that no archaeological basis exists for an assumption of a Cretan hegemony over Attica in Middle or Late Helladic times, even if this was the case for the northeastern corner of the Peloponnesus, which is doubtful.

All scholars agree that during the Middle Helladic Period the mainland of Greece had few relations with Minoan Crete and consequently no claims could be raised for a conquest or domination of any part of the mainland by the Cretans during that period. In the Early Helladic Period we find a community of cultural and racial elements in the mainland and in Crete, but again these have been attributed to a common racial stock from which the inhabitants of both areas were derived. As a matter of fact, in the Early Helladic Period Crete itself seems to be under the influence of the Cycladic world especially.[2] We have seen that in Neolithic times the mainland and Crete exhibit no cultural or other relations. It should be admitted that the remains of certain periods are not so numerous, but what we have to date seem to indicate definitely that the assumption of a domination or conquest of Athens by the Minoan Cretans is not justified. On the contrary the remains indicate that Attica in general and Athens in particular had no direct relations with Crete during the Middle and Late Helladic I and II Periods, i.e. during the time when such a dependence of Athens on Crete could be assumed.

We may now pass on to the consideration of the indirect archaeological evidence which has been used in support of the Cretan

---

[1] Evans *Palace of Minos* IV 283, 754, 887; H. R. Hall, *The Ancient History of the Near East*,[4] 1919, p. 61; M. P. Nilsson, *The Minoan-Mycenaean Religion and Its Survival in Greek Religion*, Lund, 1927, pp. 11–23; *Homer and Mycenae*, London, 1933, pp. 71–82; J. P. Harland, "The Peloponnesos in the Bronze Age," *Harvard Studies in Classical Philology*, XXXIV (1923), pp. 28–30; Γ. Μυλωνᾶς, "Οἱ προϊστορικοὶ κάτοικοι τῆς Ἑλλάδος καὶ τὰ ἱστορικὰ ἑλληνικὰ φῦλα," 'Αρχ. 'Εφ., 1930, p. 3.

[2] Cf. Cycladic figurines from Early Minoan graves in St. Xanthoudides, *The Vaulted Tombs of Messara*, London, 1924, plates VII 122; XV 224, etc.

conquest. Lately Professor Picard in discussing the struggles between Athens and Eleusis in prehistoric times seems to take it for granted that Athens in the time of Cecrops was under Minoan control.[1] He seems to base his thesis on two considerations. 1) According to the legends Cecrops introduced the worship of Zeus Hypatos. This worship is taken to be a cult of the "peak-sanctuary" type imported from Crete to Athens. 2) When Cecrops died the Athenians built his tomb on the Acropolis and this later is referred to as the ἱερὸν Κέκροπος.[2] The Minoan ossuary of Kato-Chrysolakkos near the Middle Minoan Palace of Mallia is taken as an exact parallel, and the inference is that the tomb of Cecrops is of a Cretan type and therefore points to a Cretan origin.

Perhaps one could remark that the attribution of the cult of Zeus Hypatos to Cecrops is legendary, that Cecrops himself according to the legend was not a Cretan, and that our information of the so-called ἱερόν comes from a very late date. But even if we assume that fact underlies these legends, still we cannot accept the conclusions which Professor Picard bases on them. Peak sanctuaries were established by the Cretans on mountains at a distance from the settlements,[3] while the altar or sanctuary established by Cecrops was in the settlement of prehistoric Athens itself. This settlement happens to be on the top of a hill, but this will not make the sanctuary a "peak sanctuary." The altar could be considered as part of the Palace complex, as seems to have been the case at Mycenae,[4] and in this respect the situation at Athens is similar to that which we find in contemporary Mycenae. Everyone admits that Mycenae was a citadel; so was Athens in prehistoric times; and its legendary altar could have nothing to do with the "peak sanctuaries" of Crete.

The tomb of Cecrops cannot be compared with the remains of Kato-Chrysolakkos. These are found at some distance from the

---

[1] Ch. Picard, "Les luttes primitives d'Athènes et d'Eleusis," *Revue historique*, CLXVI (1931), pp. 25–28.

[2] Cf. J. M. Paton and others, *The Erechtheum*, Cambridge, 1927, pp. 127–137.

[3] Cf. the sanctuary of Juktas near Knossos, Evans *Palace of Minos* I 154–159.

[4] A. J. B. Wace, "Excavations at Mycenae. The Palace," *The Annual of the British School at Athens*, XXV (1921–1923), pp. 223–226.

palace, and perhaps from the settlement; they belong to an ossuary where for generations various families were interred; they do not belong to the grave of a single person or a single royal family, as is the case with the tomb of Cecrops.[1] And then one has still to prove that the ossuary of Chrysolakkos was a ἱερόν as the term was understood in later times. The grave of Cecrops placed in the citadel itself, and apparently at a short distance from his palace, has its exact parallel in the shaft graves of Mycenae, where we have even our ἱερόν in the circular enclosure, and evidence for hero-cult in later years.[2] It is evident that our parallels are with Mycenae and not with Crete and that the evidence which led Professor Picard to consider the Athens of Cecrops as a Minoan outpost is not sufficient and according to our interpretation seems to prove the opposite of what has been assumed. It is rather interesting to remark that the traditional date for Cecrops agrees with the date of the period to which belong the shaft graves of Mycenae. Professor Wace has proved that the shaft graves "were dug during the course of the sixteenth century" and "that they date from the end of the Middle Helladic Age and do not quite reach the end of Late Helladic I" while the grave circle dates from the beginning of Late Helladic III.[3] The Parian marble places the reign of Cecrops at about 1580 B.C.[4] This agreement of dates and of burial customs obtained from widely different sources perhaps will indicate that there is some fact behind the legend of the first king of Athens.

[1] Pendlebury *Arch. of Crete* 102.

[2] 'Α. Κεραμόπουλλος, "Περὶ τῶν βασιλικῶν τάφων τῆς ἀκροπόλεως τῶν Μυκηνῶν," 'Αρχ. 'Εφ., 1918, pp. 52–60. It is to be noted that the circular wall dates from Late Helladic III times, from a period when the Cretan domination, if we accept one, had been overthrown, and that the offerings found by Professor Keramopoullos date from the end of the period. It certainly is very doubtful whether the Mycenaeans would have continued to reverence the graves of foreign rulers after they had overthrown their rule, as would be the case if we accept a Cretan conquest and Cretan rulers in Mycenae in Late Helladic I and II times. We believe that this hero-cult at Mycenae and at Athens is another definite indication that those cities were ruled by mainland families (Hellenic in race and tradition) and not by Cretans in Late Helladic I and II times.

[3] Wace *BSA* XXV (1921–1923) 119, 122, 391.

[4] F. Jacoby, *Das Marmor Parium*, Berlin, 1904, p. 3, lines 3 and 4.

One of the most important religious festivals of Athens in historic times was the annual celebration of the mysteries at Eleusis. The details of the ritual have remained unknown and the origin of the mysteries has been the subject of many a learned paper. In the latest monograph on the subject Professor Magnien maintains that the cult was introduced from Crete in Minoan times.[1] This may be taken as an indication of a Cretan domination over Attica and consequently will require our consideration. Magnien bases his belief on the conclusions of Professor Persson for the earlier remains at Eleusis, published before the excavations of 1931.[2] Persson rightly has pointed out that the earliest remains in the "telesterion area" go back to Late Helladic times and that the cult was established in Eleusis in prehistoric times. However, the latest excavations have proved that what can be taken to be the earliest telesterion at Eleusis is mainland in type and has nothing in common with the Cretan palaces to which Persson compares the historic telesteria.[3] Furthermore in the prehistoric filling of the "telesterion area" not a single object was found which could be conceived as Cretan or as directly derived from Cretan prototypes. And the evident conclusion is that at least the pre-

---

[1] V. Magnien, *Les mystères d'Eleusis*, Paris, 1938, p. 51.

[2] A. W. Persson, "Der Ursprung der eleusinischen Mysterien," *Archiv für Religionswiss.* XXI (1922), p. 308. Perhaps the most important reason for the Cretan origin given by Persson is the following: "Die Form des Telesterions ist vielleicht eine Entwicklung der minoischen sogenannten Theaters; das Anaktoron ist identisch mit den Kretischen Repositorien." The comparison of course is with the classical telesterion, but the earliest temple which could have been derived from the Cretan forms mentioned by Persson is of an entirely different type than that represented by the classical telesterion. And that type definitely is not Cretan. As for the nature goddess worshipped in Crete, we could remark that Crete is not the only place where such a goddess was worshipped. A great many other primitive religions are based on her cult. The use of the kernoi in both districts is interesting, but before any weight could be placed on their evidence bearing on the origin of the mysteries we have to prove the existence of the kernoi at Eleusis in prehistoric times. As far as we know to date "a thousand years intervene between the Minoan and the Greek specimens" from Eleusis (Nilsson *Min. Myc. Relig.* 390).

[3] Cf. K. Κουρουνιώτης, 'Αρχ. Δελτίον XIV (1931–32) Παράρτημα 2 and fig. 3; *Archiv für Religionswiss.* XXV (1935) 52–63 and plates I–II; Mylonas-Kourouniotes *AJA* XXXVII (1933) 271–286.

historic sanctuary at Eleusis and its cult could not be used as evidence for a Cretan domination of Attica. Perhaps here we may mention the oft-quoted passage of the Homeric Hymn to Demeter in which the goddess herself states that she came to Eleusis from Crete by way of Thorikos.[1] When we assume from this passage a Cretan origin we forget that the goddess is telling a story to cover up her real identity and her provenience. The use of Crete in this way is not unique in epic poetry and we find in the *Odyssey* again and again Odysseus mentioning Crete as his birthplace. Certainly we cannot assume that Odysseus was from Crete because he said so to Eumaeus.[2] It seems therefore safe to assume that in such stories Crete stands for the far-away country whose inhabitants are apt to be entirely unknown to the hearers of the story. Consequently no importance should be placed on the passage of the Homeric Hymn in which Crete is mentioned.

Beyond Eleusis with its sanctuary and across Nisaia, the harbour of Megara, we have Minoa, now a hill surrounded by the beds of dry streams and alluvial soil, in antiquity an island. The name of the island has been taken as an indication of a Cretan occupation[3] and this was strengthened by the reports of a Cretan expedition against Megara mentioned by ancient authors. The explorations and excavations carried out in that district have failed thus far to produce a single Minoan sherd or other Minoan object that would give support to that assumption and it is impossible to prove from the remains uncovered that a Minoan settlement did exist on the island.[4] The available archaeological evidence therefore definitely indicates that the reputed Minoan hold on the island is based only on its name and has no real basis. If we turn to the

---

[1] Εἰς Δήμητρα 123–134.

[2] *Odyssey* ξ 199–200; π 62; etc.

[3] Evans *Palace of Minos* I 2–3; W. Ridgeway, "Minos the Destroyer Rather than the Creator of the So-called 'Minoan' Culture of Cnossus," *Proceedings of the British Academy*, IV (1909), p. 17; Pendlebury *Arch. of Crete* 286.

[4] Μυλωνᾶς, Νεολ. ἐπ. 77; Θρεψιάδης-Τραυλός, Πρακτικὰ 1934, 51–52 and fig. 11. The pottery from Minoa is composed entirely of the known varieties of the Early, Middle, and Late Helladic wares. In the summer of 1934 and after the recent excavations of Threpsiades and Travlos I had the chance to examine the site again. I could find no remains which in any way resemble Cretan varieties.

tradition we find that it also offers no support to the assumption
of a Cretan settlement on Minoa. We learn from Pausanias that
the fleet of the Cretans was anchored at Minoa when Minos besieged Nisaia where Nisus the king of Megara had taken refuge.[1]
We further read that Nisus was killed and that the Cretans were
successful in their war, but there is not a single statement to the
effect that the Cretans left a garrison at Minoa, as the Athenians
did later,[2] or that they transformed it into a commercial post.
In fact there is some indication that the opposite was true, that
the Cretans left immediately after their objective, the destruction
of Megara, was accomplished. Pausanias, after a brief excursion
into the genealogies of the Megarians, concludes: Φαίνεται δὲ τε-
λευτήσαντος Νίσου καὶ τῶν πραγμάτων Μεγαρεῦσιν ἐφθαρμένων ὑπὸ
τοῦτον ᾿Αλκάθους ἀφικόμενος τὸν καιρὸν ἐξ ῞Ηλιδος· μαρτύριον δέ μοι·
τὸ γὰρ τεῖχος ᾠκοδόμησεν ἐξ ἀρχῆς ἅτε τοῦ περιβόλου τοῦ ἀρχαίου καθαι-
ρεθέντος ὑπὸ τῶν Κρητῶν. In that work we hear he had the assistance
of Apollo.[3] No mention is made of renewed successful efforts to oust
a garrison or destroy a settlement of the old enemies on Minoa,
which would have been the case if such did exist there; what is
mentioned is simply the task of rebuilding the walls of Megara.
In fact the impression gathered from these vague reports of the
struggle between Crete and Megara is that it was not a real war,
but a raid on the Megarian cities by roving Cretans. It seems very
likely that they are part of the cycle to which belongs the story of
the wars of Minos against Athens, and that both belong to post-
Minoan times as I shall try to suggest later. Meanwhile we may
conclude that no remains have been found to prove a Cretan hold
on the island in Minoan times, and that the traditional War of
Minos against Megara fails to give support to the assumption of a
Cretan domination over Minoa and the Megarid.[4] On the other
hand there is no doubt that the island opposite Nisaia was called
Minoa in antiquity and there must be some reason for this appella-
tion. We may propose that the name was given to the island be-

---

[1] I 19. 4, 44. 3; cf. also Apollodorus III 15. 8.
[2] Thuc. III 51, IV 118.
[3] I 41. 6. For Apollo's contribution to the work cf. I 42. 2 and Frazer *ad loc.*
[4] The date of this war also will support the suggestion of a later raid: cf. *infra.*

cause the fleet of Minos anchored there during his siege of Nisaia. As a parallel to this we may cite the Areopagus at Athens, which according to Pausanias Ἄρειος πάγος καλούμενος, ὅτι πρῶτος Ἄρης ἐνταῦθα ἐκρίθη and according to Aeschylus received the name because of the sacrifices held there by the Amazons:

> Ἄρει δ'ἔθυον, ἔνθεν ἔστ' ἐπώνυμος
> πέτρα, πάγος τ' Ἄρειος.[1]

The brief survey of the direct and indirect archaeological evidence available to date proves, we believe, that no real foundation exists for the assumption of a Cretan conquest or domination of Attica in Minoan times. The survey of the linguistic, literary, and traditional evidence will lead us to the same conclusion. In Attica we have a considerable number of place names which are pre-Indo-European and which have parallels in Minoan Crete.[2] Professor Blegen, however, has definitely proved that these pre-Hellenic place-names go back to the Early Helladic Period[3] and consequently cannot be construed as evidence for a Cretan conquest.

The literary evidence worth the name is limited to the single well-known passage of Thucydides (I 4), Μίνως γὰρ παλαίτατος ὧν ἀκοῇ ἴσμεν ναυτικὸν ἐκτήσατο ·καὶ τῆς νῦν Ἑλληνικῆς θαλάσσης ἐπὶ πλεῖστον ἐκράτησε καὶ τῶν Κυκλάδων νήσων ἦρξέ τε καὶ οἰκιστὴς πρῶτος τῶν πλείστων ἐγένετο.[4] It is to be noted that Thucydides does not

---

[1] Pausanias I 28. 5. So also Euripides *Electra* 1258–1263; Aeschylus *Eumenides* 685–690. For a derivation from *ara* cf. Frazer *ad* Paus. *l.c.* V. Bérard, *Ithaque et la Grèce des Achéens*, Paris, 1927, p. 38, maintains that Minoa is a Semitic word and means "station," "stop-over" place.

[2] Λυκαβηττός, Ὑμηττός, Ἀρδηττός, Ἰλισσός, Κηφισός, Προβάλινθος, Τρικόρινθος, etc. A. Fick, *Vorgriechische Ortsnamen*, Göttingen, 1905, pp. 129–130. J. B. Haley, "The Coming of the Greeks, I," *AJA*, XXXII (1928), pp. 141–145.

[3] "The Coming of the Greeks, II," *AJA*, XXXII (1928), pp. 146–154. Cf. also Harland *Harv. St. C. P.* XXXIV (1923) 10–11.

[4] When this thalassocracy was established is a debatable matter. The Parian Chronicle places the first Minos at about 1462/1 (Jacoby *Mar. Par.* 6) and Sir Arthur Evans (*Pal. Min.* I 12) remarks that the date "is well within the limits of the last Palace Period of Knossos." However, it is doubtful whether the conditions which this thalassocracy was to remedy, *viz.* piracy, could have existed with the Mycenaean power so strong and the Mycenaean commercial activities over the

state that Minos conquered and controlled any other part of Greece beyond the Cyclades and certainly he would not have omitted that information if it had been current during his time or if he had known of any foundation for it. Diodorus repeats the tradition. Minos, he states, κτήσασθαι δὲ καὶ δύναμιν ναυτικὴν μεγάλην, καὶ τῶν τε νήσων τὰς πλείστας καταστρέψασθαι καὶ πρῶτον τῶν Ἑλλήνων θαλαττοκρατῆσαι.[1] No indication of a Cretan conquest or domination of Athens is contained in this statement of Diodorus.

It seems that the assumption of the Cretan domination over Attica was created by the well-known story of Theseus' successful ἆθλos against the Minotaur. Apparently the Minotaur episode, to be referred to as the *mythos*, was the last in a series of events which marked a conflict between Athens and Crete. All our sources agree as to the cause of the conflict. It was the death of Androgeus, the son of Minos. Most of them indicate that the Athenians agreed to the terms of Minos especially because of the famine and pestilence with which their city was afflicted as a result of Minos' prayers to his father Zeus.[2] Our authorities again agree in one important point, that Minos was unable to capture Athens. Apollodorus (III 15. 8) is very specific on the matter: χρονιζομένου δὲ τοῦ πολέμου, μὴ δυνάμενος ἑλεῖν Ἀθήνας εὔχεται Διί, etc. Furthermore the statement of Diodorus (IV 61. 3–4): διελθόντων δὲ ἐτῶν ἐννέα πάλιν ὁ Μίνως ἦλθεν εἰς τὴν Ἀττικὴν μετὰ μεγάλου στόλου καὶ τοὺς δὶς ἑπτὰ κόρους ἀπαιτήσας ἔλαβε and that of Plutarch (*Theseus*

Aegean so numerous (cf. Pendlebury *Arch. of Crete* 223–224). Perhaps it will be better to disregard the date of the Parian Chronicle, which after all is a later compilation, and to accept the view that the thalassocracy was established in Middle Minoan times. The close contact of Crete and Melos and the influx of Cretan artistic ideas in the mainland furnish a strong argument in support of the statement of Thucydides.

[1] Diodorus Siculus V 78.3. Cf. also Pausanias I 27.9.

[2] Apollodorus III 15. 8. Diodorus IV 61. 1 (connects it with the general λιμός in the time of Aeakos). Plutarch *Theseus* 15. 1. But Pausanias, I 27. 10, does not mention the pestilence, but states that Minos harassed the Athenians until they agreed to pay the tribute. For the latest account of Theseus cf. Hans Herter, "Theseus der Jonier," *Rheinisches Museum für Philologie*, LXXXV (1936), p. 177, and "Theseus der Athener," *Rhein. Mus.*, LXXXVIII (1939), pp. 244–286; F. H. Wolgensinger, *Theseus* (Diss.), Zürich, 1935.

15. 1): ὀλίγῳ δ' ὕστερον ἧκον ἐκ Κρήτης τὸ τρίτον οἱ τὸν δασμὸν ἀπά-
ξοντες, indicate very definitely that no permanent Cretan authority was established at Athens. In fact these statements, and the
account of Minos' war against Megara and the cities of the Megarid
which occurred at the same time, would lead one to believe that
these stories are echoes of piratical raids on the shores of Attica
rather than organized campaigns for conquest and domination.
The Cretans depart after capturing their booty, which included a
good number of youths who could be carried into slavery, and then
they return again after a while for the same purpose.[1]

Perhaps we are on more definite grounds when we turn to the
consideration of the date of this conflict. The *mythos* places it
within the reign of Aegeus and in the early years of Theseus, in
other words around the beginning of the thirteenth century.[2]
Was Crete at that time in a position to carry out a war or a series
of raids against Attica? The evident answer is negative, because
in that period the Mycenaean powers dominated the seas and
because the great centers of Knossos and Phaestos were a mass of
ruins and their peoples and rulers were not in a position to carry
out such expeditions. Lately Professor Myres expressed the view
that the issue is not so definitely settled. He states: "It is not yet
certain whether the deliverance (of Athens) from Cretan dominance belongs wholly to the generation of 1260–1230 (i.e. to the

---

[1] The fate of the people who were carried to Crete is not so definite as the *mythos*
would lead us to believe. Plutarch's efforts to record the various traditions on the
matter is very instructive (*Theseus* 15. 2–17). He distinguishes very definitely the
τραγικώτατος μῦθος from the other traditional accounts. Without committing himself definitely, he allows his reader to understand that he did not believe in the
mythos so much when he defends the cause of Minos against the tragedians (*Theseus*
16. 3). With this we may compare the statement of Socrates (Plato *Minos* 318 D)
'Αττικόν, ὦ βέλτιστε, λέγεις μῦθον καὶ τραγικόν and again (320 E) ἐξήμαρτεν ὁ
Μίνως, πολεμήσας τῇδε τῇ πόλει, ἐν ᾗ ἄλλη τε πολλὴ σοφία ἐστὶ καὶ ποιηταὶ παντοδαποὶ
τῆς τε ἄλλης ποιήσεως καὶ τραγῳδίας. (321 A) ἐν ᾗ δὴ καὶ ἐντείνοντες ἡμεῖς τὸν Μίνων
τιμωρούμεθα ἀνθ' ὧν ἡμᾶς ἠνάγκασε τοὺς δασμοὺς τελεῖν ἐκείνους.

[2] Jacoby *Marmor Parium* 8–9 (1307/6 and 1259/8). The reign of Nisus, King of
Megara, will be placed in the same era, since he was a younger brother of Aegeus
to whom he gave up Athens and in return received the kingship of Megara. Pausanias I 29. 4; Strabo IX 1. 6.

generation of Theseus) or incorporates memory of the collapse of the 'palace regime' when the Athenian dynasty was still young." [1] And perhaps to strengthen this suggestion we have the evidence of the Parian marble where it is recorded that the Minos who exacted the tribute from Aegeus flourished ca. 1294/3 B.C. [2] Fortunately we have the archaeological evidence which is definite on this problem. The remains of the Late Minoan III period uncovered thus far are numerous and very illuminating. They prove that with the destruction of 1400 B.C. the concentration of power in the hands of the ruler of one center ceased, and that the people of Crete "with their trade in the hands of others" turned to the exploitation of the "wild country west of Ida." The location of these remains further proves that the inhabitants of the island in Late Minoan III period had a tendency to scatter, and certainly could not undertake raids or wars against mainland cities, however small. [3] It seems certain that the traditional conflict between Athens and Crete, if it ever occurred, could not have occurred in the days of Aegeus, Nisus, and Theseus. And the possible conclusion is that the later Atthidographers in their efforts to create a national hero for Athens attributed to Theseus events and exploits with which he could have no connection. The entry in the Parian marble must be attributed to a similar effort on the part of its compilers.

We may now attempt to determine the times during which occurred the events attributed to the period of Aegeus and Theseus. Since our evidence is not concrete and definite we have to proceed on the principle of the greatest probability. There are two possible answers to our problem. The attributed events either were older or were later than the period of Aegeus and Theseus. It has been suggested before this that they were older, [4] but I want to

---

[1] *Who Were the Greeks* 348.

[2] Jacoby *Marmor Parium* 8.

[3] Cf. Pendlebury *Arch. of Crete* 237–238, whence the quotations. Apparently towards the end of the period and as a result of the coming of the Achaean and Dorian inhabitants of the island a centralization of power in rulers of cities again occurred.

[4] Picard *Rev. hist.* CLXVI (1931) 53; M. Nilsson, *The Mycenaean Origin of Greek Mythology*, Berkeley, 1932, p. 176.

suggest that they occurred long after the days of Theseus and even
after the Trojan wars.

If we assume that the first answer is the correct one, i.e. if we
believe that the events attributed to the reign of Aegeus and
Theseus did occur long before their reign, then necessarily we shall
have to place them at least in Late Minoan I times or even a little
earlier. In that period Athens was one of the many πόλεις whose
power apparently did not go much beyond the Acropolis area,[1]
while Crete and especially Knossos were experiencing one of
their most prosperous periods. The reported expedition of Minos
against Athens can be conceived either as a regular military campaign or, as we have suggested, as a raid. If it were the former
it is strange that such a powerful empire, that of Knossos as pictured by our leading Cretan scholars, was unable to capture the
rather small town of Athens. We must further recall that Minos
ravaged the Megarid and captured Nisaia during his war against
Athens.[2] Now that the event is assumed to have taken place long
before the days of Aegeus and Nisus, long before the sons of the
same family ruled over the two towns, how can we explain Minos'
attack not only on Athens but on Megara and also on the other
cities of the Megarid?[3] Could it be attributed to a war of con-

---

[1] That communities in Attica were independent of each other is definitely indicated by the conflicts reported between Athens and Eleusis; cf. Picard *Rev. hist.*
CLXVI (1931) 1–76.

[2] Apollodorus III 15. 8.

[3] We cannot assume that Megara and the Megarid were under the control of
Athens at that time. The wars of Eleusis and Athens in the days of Erechtheus
(Thuc. I 15. 2) will definitely prove that the area west of Eleusis was independent
at that time at least. The claims of the Athenians on Megara and the Megarid are
rather late in date. The earliest evidence seems to go back to Sophocles (Nauck
frgm. 19). Plato, *Critias* 110 D, mentions the legendary information that Athens'
domain included the area to the Isthmus. But since Critias is creating an imaginary
kingdom, that of Atlantis, we have a right to think that whatever he says of
Athens is not the real truth. It is also to be noted that in the Homeric Catalogue of
Ships no city of Attica other than Athens is included. This might indicate that
under the name of Athens the poet included the other communities of Attica, and
this apparently was the favorite explanation of the ancient Athenians. However,
this is contrary to the general practice of the poet who names separately the communities which form a given district, and therefore the suggestion that Attica was

quest? But this is incompatible with the character of the Cretan mind and life as revealed by the Cretan remains and with the tradition itself as preserved in ancient authors.[1] It is evident that these warlike events must be interpreted as raids on the coast of Attica.[2] But then it will be difficult to assume that a king of Knossos in Minoan times was making piratical raids on others when the extinction of piracy meant so much to the commercial activities of the Cretan people on which directly their welfare depended. We cannot assume it for Minos, at any rate, who according to the Athenian Thucydides, our best ancient authority, wiped out piracy from the Greek seas and made piratical raids impossible. We cannot assume that Athens was a center for pirates which had to be cleared out for the safety of the seas, because we have the

---

ignored by the poet is more plausible. Again it seems that the settlement of Νῖσα, mentioned with the communities of Boeotia (B 508), is the Νίσαια of later times and if this is so then that part of the Megarid was under Boeotian control in the times pictured by the Catalogue. The tradition of the coming of Megareus from Onchestus to help dispel the attack of Minos (Apollod. III 15; Paus. I 39. 5) seems to reflect such a relation. (Cf. T. W. Allen, *The Homeric Catalogue of Ships*, Oxford, 1921, pp. 57-58.)

[1] The Cretans seem not to have been warlike people who delighted in battle and conquest. This is indicated by the rarity of combat scenes represented in their art. Pendlebury, *Arch. of Crete* 277, remarks: "A curious gap in the Minoan mentality is the lack of historical sense. No picture exists of any scene which can be described as a record of an historic event." This gap can be explained very easily. Perhaps the Cretans had no "historic events" of any consequence to immortalize. They certainly represented often enough the experiences of their sea-faring lives. The ancient authors, especially Thucydides, do not know of any Cretan conquests beyond the Cyclades.

[2] Additional support to this interpretation is, we believe, given by the fact that Eleusis was not molested by Minos. We may assume that Eleusis escaped because it was a religious center which Minos did not dare attack. This cannot be the case, however, if we accept a war of conquest conducted in Late Minoan I times or earlier, since our earliest possible sanctuary at Eleusis does not go beyond 1400 B.C. There is another and more plausible explanation. The approach to Eleusis from the sea is guarded by the island of Salamis. A raiding party would avoid the almost closed and very calm bay of Eleusis for fear of getting trapped in its quiet waters; but following the coast-line of Salamis could attack the next point on the main coast. This was the harbour-town Nisaia. In case of a reverse, a retreat would have been possible. It seems logical to believe that her position saved Eleusis from the raids in Minoan as later on in mediaeval times.

definite statement of Plutarch: μηδέπω τότε τῶν ᾿Αθηναίων προσεχόντων τῇ θαλάσσῃ.[1] However, if the raids were not made in Minoan times when the safety of the seas was of paramount importance, but in much later years, then they could be admitted as possible events. Of course it has been suggested that these wars between Minos and Athens, as well as the Androgeus tale, were "a later invention made in order to rationalize and historicize the earlier myth" (the myth of the Minotaur).[2] But we could maintain equally well that the myth was made as a further embellishment of the historic events.

Before we can accept a later date for the raids of Minos against Athens and the Megarid, we have to prove first that Crete was strong enough to attempt such raids after the days of Theseus and second that the conditions which existed in the Aegean then were such as to make possible Minos' attempts. Our evidence for this quest is literary and archaeological. In the Homeric Catalogue of the Ships, Crete, called ἑκατόμπολις, contributes 80 ships, equalling the contingent of the Argive section which was the third largest contingent of the Greek συναγερμός. The Athenian contingent numbered 50 ships.[3] In the *Odyssey* Crete is

καλὴ καὶ πίειρα, περίρρυτος ἐν δ᾽ἄνθρωποι
πολλοί, ἀπειρέσιοι, καὶ ἐννήκοντα πόληες.[4]

In both the *Iliad* and the *Odyssey* we find that Knossos again is the first city and its ruler, Idomeneus or Minos, is the leading chieftain of the island. At the same time we can adduce that the glories of the Minoan past were not entirely forgotten since the rulers of Knossos, in true heroic fashion, tried to trace their an-

---

[1] *Theseus* 17. 7. So much so that Theseus had to take a κυβερνήτης from Salamis to be able to sail his boat to Crete.

[2] Nilsson *Myc. Origin of Greek Myth.* 177–178.

[3] *Iliad* B 645–652; for Argos, B 559–568; for Athens, B 546–556.

[4] *Odyssey* τ 173–174. On the passage and its discrepancy with *Iliad* B 649, cf. Strabo X 4. 15. During the Late Minoan III times, as we have seen, the inhabitants of the island, pure Minoans still, had the tendency to scatter and to create small independent communities. The concentration of power in the hands of the ruler of Knossos and the establishment of so many cities once more was the result of the Achaean and later of the Dorian occupations of the island.

cestry to the mythical ruler Minos.[1] When we turn to the archae-ological remains we find that the sub-Minoan, proto-Geometric, Geometric, and Early Archaic periods are well represented in the island. We shall find further that Knossos itself was inhabited in Geometric times.[2] To equate the literary with the archaeological evidence will be rather a long and difficult task and beyond the scope of this paper and consequently we may limit our discussion to the statement that in the years which followed the reign of Theseus and of the Trojan war, Crete is proved both by our literary and by our archaeological evidence to have possessed sufficient power to attempt raids against the mainland, if conditions were appropriate. That conditions favorable for such raids did exist in the Aegean area after the era of Theseus can be proved very easily.

It is well known that the Trojan war was followed by the col-lapse of the Mycenaean power and that this collapse brought about chaotic conditions in the Aegean, as a result of which piracy grew up once more.[3] It is natural to believe that the sea-faring Cretans were not behind the rest of the Greeks in this profitable enterprise and the story of Odysseus to the swineherd Eumaeus gives val-uable support to this belief.[4] During these unsettled times the Cretans could have made their raids against Athens and the Megarid and could have carried back with them to Knossos their booty and their captives. The ruins of the great palace were still standing and it is safe to assume that some of the wall frescoes were still to be seen. Sir Arthur Evans in discussing his restoration of the painted relief fresco of the charging bull in the west portico remarks: "From the high ground level ön which the remains had fallen, it may be inferred that this monumental work was still in position on the wall of the portico at the time when the first men of Greek stock made their way through the old Sea Gate of the

---

[1] Evans *Palace of Minos* I 10, "By the new comers, Achaean as well as Dorian, the old hierarchical tradition attaching to the name of Minos was invoked as a sanction for their own claim."

[2] Pendlebury *Arch. of Crete* 302–344; Evans *Palace of Minos* IV 18.

[3] Cf. *Odyssey* ι 39, 254, ο 425–429, π 426, ρ 425, φ 18–19; *Homeric Hymn to Demeter* 123–125; Thuc. I 5.1.

[4] *Odyssey* ξ 245–359.

Palace."[1] These remains naturally excited the imagination not only of the captives but also of the inhabitants of Knossos, among whom was then a great number of late comers to the island — Achaeans and Dorians — and their efforts to explain these ruins, now that the Minoan tradition was becoming weaker and weaker, gave rise to the stories of the labyrinth and of the Minotaur.[2]

The story of the Minotaur is often assumed to reflect memories of the "palace" regime of Knossos, but why?[3] This assumption presupposes that the mainlanders of Late Helladic III times were ignorant of the conditions which existed in Crete in Late Minoan times and were ignorant of Minoan ways; this is highly improbable. Whether we believe in Sir Arthur Evans' theory of the Cretan conquest of Greece in the Bronze Age or not, we have to admit that Crete and the mainland, at least its southeastern side, were in very close contact during Late Helladic times. As Professor Nilsson very aptly remarked, in ca. 1600 B.C. "the mainland of Greece, or to put it more correctly, its eastern districts, became saturated with Minoan culture";[4] and this of course will not permit the assumption of ignorance. Furthermore representations of scenes from the bull ring could be seen on the walls of the Late Helladic III palace of Tiryns, on the dromos of the so-called "treasury of Atreus," and perhaps on the walls of other mainland

---

[1] Evans *Palace of Minos* IV 16.

[2] The painted relief fresco of the charging bull was still *in situ* in Late Minoan III times (Evans *Palace of Minos* III 160; Pendlebury *Arch. of Crete* 239) and there is every reason to believe that it remained in place long after those times. It is to be noted that the original meaning of the name "labyrinth" could not have been forgotten in Late Minoan times, but it could have become unintelligible to the Greek settlers of a later period. From personal experience, derived from the destruction of my home town Smyrna in 1922, I could state that a building in ruins looks more like a maze than one standing complete, and certainly the Palace of Knossos when in ruins would have created that impression. Furthermore some of its areas on the ground floor covered with debris could have been used very successfully for imprisoning slaves. The occasional discovery of seal-stones with representations of human beings with a bull's head would strengthen the reputation of the *mythos*. That the Cretans of the historic period were familiar with such seal-stones is proved by the "late Greek bead-seal" illustrated by Evans (*Palace of Minos* IV fig. 9).

[3] Nilsson *Mycen. Or. Grk. Mythol.* 176–177; Myres *Who Were the Greeks* 348, etc.

[4] *Min. Mycen. Relig.* 24.

palaces, while the activities of the bull ring were reflected on smaller works of art like the Vapheio Cup, and Mycenaean gems.[1] That the Athenians of the times of Theseus were not only familiar with the sport but also with the "human beings with a bull's head" (perhaps human beings wearing the mask of a bull for ritualistic purposes) not uncommon on Minoan seals is proved by the ring discovered by Professor Shear in the Mycenaean grave of the Agora.[2] We have to go down to a later period than the date of the ring (ca. 1200 B.C.) to find the confused ideas about the meaning of the Cretan bull representations which could have given rise to the myth of the Minotaur.

Professor Nilsson has suggested that the other myths in which Minos and Attica are brought together should be accepted as post-Mycenaean.[3] Why not accept the same date for the myth of Theseus and the Minotaur? The former presupposes "even the war of Minos against Athens"; but so does the latter also. Certainly the Athenians would not have sent their tribute, granting that they did send tribute, if they had not been compelled to. It should be noted that the *mythos* is not known to Homer, who knows even the latest exploits of Heracles.[4] Certainly he could have used it to advantage in the long story which Odysseus made up to cover his identity and in which he included whatever he knew about Crete and its people. Yet not a line about this exploit and even the war of Minos against Athens is ignored. We could assume that this war is referred to in the well-known passage in the Νέκυια [5] where Theseus and Ariadne the daughter of the "baleful-

---

[1] *JHS* XLI (1921) 249 fig. 3; 259 figs. 11–12; Sir Arthur Evans, *The Shaft Graves and Bee-Hive Tombs of Mycenae*, London, 1929, pp. 77–80; Evans *Palace of Minos* III 180–182; figs. 150, 158, 162, 164A; A. J. B. Wace, *Chamber Tombs at Mycenae*, Oxford, 1932, p. 85; pl. XXXVIII 61; Otto Frödin–Axel W. Persson, *Asine*, Stockholm, 1938, p. 371, fig. 241.

[2] *Hesperia* IV (1935) 318–320 figs. 7–8. "A group of three persons, two women and a man" and a column apparently standing for a building are represented on this signet ring. The man, bull-headed, is leading the two women who have their hands perhaps bound behind their backs.

[3] *Myc. Or. Grk. Myth.* 179.

[4] The bringing of Cerberus from the lower world: *Odyssey* λ 623–626.

[5] *Odyssey* λ 322.

hearted" Minos are mentioned, but before we do that we have to prove that the passage was not introduced much later. The only other passage in the *Odyssey* where the name of Theseus is introduced aroused the suspicion even of ancient authors,[1] and the term ὀλοόφρων given to Minos by Odysseus certainly does not agree with the character of the great judge Minos, whom shortly afterwards and in the same story he calls Διὸς ἀγλαὸν υἱόν. We may get around the difficulty, if indeed a difficulty does exist, if we accept the explanation suggested by the late Professor Ridgeway that two figures called Minos exist in the Greek tradition.[2] The term ὀλοόφρων is applied to Minos II who lived shortly before the Trojan war and who was responsible for the Athenian misfortunes, while that of Διὸς ἀγλαὸς υἱός is applied to Minos I the great law-giver of Knossos in the times of Cretan supremacy over the Aegean. But if we accept that view we shall be unable to explain another reference to Minos again voiced by our hero Odysseus. In his tale to Penelope he described Crete and claimed that he was the brother of Idomeneus the grandson of Minos. Now this Minos who lived two generations before the Trojan war is the Minos II of Ridgeway and he is not ὀλοόφρων but Διὸς μεγάλου ὀαριστής.[3] How can we explain this sharp difference in the statements of Odysseus? This coupled with the name of Theseus could only mean one thing, that the passage where Theseus and the ὀλοόφρων Minos are mentioned is a later addition.[4] We may repeat safely then that the *mythos* is unknown to Homer.

[1] E.g., Plutarch *Theseus* 20. 2 on *Odyssey* λ 631. In the *Iliad*, Theseus is mentioned but once, A 265, and the verse in which he is mentioned is regarded as doubtful. Professor Scott's arguments against any additions introduced by the Athenians in the times of Peisistratus (*Classical Philology* VI (1911) 419–428) are very convincing, but the poems were known to the inhabitants of the mainland in general, including the Athenians, before the times of Peisistratus (cf. *Herod.* V 67), and it would have been possible to introduce into the poems references to national heroes in pre-Peisistratean days. The way in which the tragedians tried to force Theseus and his sons into the poems is of course well known (cf. Euripides *Iph. Aul.* 248). Minos is called Διὸς ἀγλαὸς υἱός in *Od.* λ 568.

[2] *Minos the Destroyer* 14–17.

[3] *Odyssey* τ 178–181.

[4] It is to be noted that in his discussion of Minos, in Plato's *Minos* 318 D–321 B, Socrates ignores completely the passage of the Νέκυια where Theseus and the

In literature the myth appears in post-Homeric times, and to the closing years of the seventh century B.C. are attributed the earliest representations in art.[1] Another argument in favor of the later date of the myth could be based on the rôle which Daedalus played in the story,[2] but we believe that our discussion thus far has brought forth enough reason to justify the belief that the story of the Minotaur and the events which preceded it must be placed in the post-Minoan era. Consequently they could not serve as proof or even as indication for a Cretan domination of Attica in Minoan times. On the contrary they seem to prove that such domination never existed.

The myth of the Minotaur and the events which preceded it have been accepted thus far as based upon some historic fact. Professor Nilsson, as we have seen, has suggested that the events were created to "rationalize and historicize the earlier myth" of the Minotaur. And we could add that perhaps the myth of the Minotaur itself was created to explain the remains of the palace of Knossos by visitors or people who had forgotten their significance and at a time when the Minoan tradition was weak and coloured with the imagination of generations. These of course are possible

---

ὀλοόφρων Minos are mentioned. To him the Διὸς ἀγλαὸς υἱός (*Od.* λ 568) and the Διὸς μεγάλου ὀαριστής (*Od.* τ 179) is the same person whom the Athenian poets represent as ἄγριόν τινα καὶ χαλεπὸν καὶ ἄδικον. It may be argued that Socrates uses only the passages which would help out his point. But is it possible to assume that the learned youths of Athens were ignorant of the few Homeric passages in which their city and their national hero were mentioned?

[1] Cf. Roscher's *Lexikon s.v. Theseus* 690–707. H. Couch, "The Illinois Minotaur," *AJA*, XXXVI (1932), p. 42. T. L. Shear, "A Terra-Cotta Relief from Sardes," *AJA*, XXVII (1923), pp. 131–150.

[2] According to Diodorus, IV 76, Daedalus was the first to make statues ὁμοιότατα τοῖς ἐμψύχοις. . . . πρῶτος δ' ὀμματώσας καὶ διαβεβηκότα τὰ σκέλη ποιήσας ἔτι δὲ τὰς χεῖρας διατεταμένας ποιῶν, εἰκότως ἐθαυμάζετο παρὰ τοῖς ἀνθρώποις, κλπ. But it is a well-known fact that the Minoan artists did not attempt to create life-sized statues in the round, in spite of Sir Arthur Evans' suggestions (*Palace of Minos* III 522–525). On the other hand our earliest specimens of historic sculpture seem to come from Crete (cf. G. M. A. Richter, *The Sculpture and Sculptors of the Greeks*, New Haven, 1930, p. 35 and figs. 14, 347, 262) and our earliest sculptors in the mainland acknowledge Daedalus as their master. It seems that Daedalus the ἀνδριαντοποιός has no place in the Minoan era.

assumptions which if accepted will not alter our main conclusion. Our primary purpose is to determine whether we have any evidence which would justify the generally accepted thesis of the Cretan domination of Attica in Minoan times. And if the myth is "aetiological" then it cannot be used as evidence for this thesis as it has been used in the past.

There remain two considerations to which we have to give brief attention. The first is the assumption that a bull-cult existed in Athens and that it was introduced from Crete.[1] Professor Nilsson, however, has definitely proved that there "is no evidence for a bull-cult among the Minoans"[2] and consequently it could not have been introduced into Athens from a place in which it did not exist. Furthermore it seems unreasonable to accept the story that a bull-cult existed in Athens in the days of Erechtheus simply because it is stated in the *Iliad* (B 550–551)

> ἔνθα δέ μιν ταύροισι καὶ ἀρνειοῖς ἱλάονται
> κοῦροι Ἀθηναίων περιτελλομένων ἐνιαυτῶν.

Since lambs are also mentioned along with the bulls we should also provide for a lamb-cult in Athens![3]

The second consideration has to do with the introduction of the cult of Athena. Professor Myres has recently repeated that in the days of Cecrops (ca. 1582 or 1560) "the great contest occurred between Athena and Poseidon for the patronage of Attica."[4] In this he follows Apollodorus who states τούτων (τῶν δώδεκα θεῶν) δικαζόντων ἡ χώρα τῆς Ἀθηνᾶς ἐκρίθη, Κέκροπος μαρτυρήσαντος ὅτι πρώτη τὴν ἐλαίαν ἐφύτευσεν.[5] It must be remembered, however, that the representation of the contest on the west pediment of the Parthenon must have influenced the tradition considerably, and that consequently any statements dating from a later period

---

[1] Cf. C. N. Deeds in *The Labyrinth* (edited by S. H. Hooke), London, 1935, Chapter I, p. 28, based on J. E. Harrison, *Themis, A Study of the Social Origins of Greek Religion*, Cambridge, 1927, p. 169.

[2] *Min. Mycen. Relig.* 322 and 327.

[3] This regardless of the possible objections about the pedigree of the passage.

[4] *Who Were the Greeks* 326.

[5] III 14. 1.

could not be accepted at their face value. Certainly no one would accept a sculptured composition of the fifth century as a documented translation into stone of Athenian tradition, especially when we have the definite statement of Plato ταύτῃ δὴ τὰ τῶν παλαιῶν ὀνόματα ἄνευ τῶν ἔργων διασέσωται.[1] The older references to Athena as the patron Goddess of Athens are to be found in the *Iliad* and in the *Odyssey*. In the former we find that Athena was settled on the sacred rock in the reign of Erechtheus; in the latter she is on the Acropolis in the early days of Theseus. However, we doubt that these passages could be taken seriously as evidence for what was happening in Athens in the days of its mythical kings. Certainly they could not be used before they were proved as genuine and before they were cleared of all doubt as to their date. In spite of the brilliant efforts of Professors Scott and Allen we may still doubt whether they formed part of the original poem.[2] And so we may conclude that our literary evidence is not sufficient to prove that the contest occurred during the reign of Cecrops or during that of the other mythical kings of Athens.

It is universally believed that the story of the contest simply indicates that the cult of Athena supplanted that of Poseidon at Athens some time before the historic period. Athena again is accepted as a non-Indo-European divinity, perhaps a Cretan Goddess, and her cult introduced into Athens may indicate Cretan domination. But the date when her cult was introduced cannot be definitely determined, and this date is the crux of the whole problem. It should be noted that this expulsion of Poseidon from Athens

---

[1] *Critias* 110 A. Cf. Harrison *Themis* 267 "Cecrops is the projection of the Cecropidae, Erechtheus of the Erechtheidae; neither is a real actual man, only an ancestor invented to express the unity of a group."

[2] *Iliad* B 546–551; *Odyssey* λ 322–324; Scott *Class. Phil.* VI (1911) 419–428; Allen *Cat. Ships* 55. For the passage in the *Odyssey* cf. *supra* pp. 39–31 and references. I plan to discuss in a special paper the passage in the *Iliad*: it may be noted here that the length of the passage and the praise lavished on Menestheus are incompatible with the conduct of the latter in the struggles which followed and with the contingent contributed by Athens. No argument could be based on *Odyssey* ʒ 78–81 because the date of the event cannot be determined and because the name could have been the traditional name of a much later building (cf. the historic Erechtheion).

was not a unique experience for the god. We know that he lost Argos to Hera, Aegina to Zeus, perhaps Naxos to Dionysos, while he was forced to share with Athena the allegiance of the people of Troezen, to give up Delphi and Delos in exchange for Calauria and Taenaron and to be satisfied with the Isthmus and the parts adjoining while Helios took possession of the height above the city of Corinth.[1] But in no instance have we definite evidence as to the date of the event. Professor Harland, who has discussed lately the cult of Poseidon in connection with Aegina, has proved that this cult was supreme in the area of the Saronic Gulf until about 1400 B.C.[2] It seems to me, however, that the evidence offered by the Calaurian amphictyony and by the ἱερόν of Poseidon there, which seems to have been established in Late Helladic III times and by people whose leading deity was Poseidon, indicates that the cult of Poseidon persisted in the cities forming the amphictyony during these Late Helladic III times and after 1400 B.C.[3] Athens was a member of that amphictyony and her cult of Poseidon must have existed at the time when the amphictyony was formed and was flourishing. Whether we accept the beginning of the fourteenth century or the end of the twelfth as the *terminus* for the supremacy of the cult of Poseidon in the area of the Saronic Gulf as indicated by the Calaurian Amphictyony, the fact remains that the substitution of this cult by that of Athena so dramatically depicted on the west pediment of the Parthenon does not indicate a Cretan dominance over Athens in Minoan times.[4]

All possible indications and sources dealing with the relations of Athens and Crete in Minoan times have now been considered. It has become evident that the assumption of a Cretan domination over

[1] For the contest at Athens: Pausanias I 24. 5, 26. 5; Aegina and Naxos: Plutarch *Quaest. Conv.* 9. 6 (p. 741 ab); Schol. to Pindar *Isth.* 13. 92; Argos: Pausanias II 22. 4; Troezen: *ib.* 30. 5, 32. 8; Delphi and Delos: Strabo VIII 6. 14; Corinth: Pausanias II 1. 6.

[2] *Prehistoric Aegina*, Paris, 1925, pp. 51–56.

[3] *Ibid.* 102–103. The earliest relics found in the area of the sanctuary of Poseidon at Calauria belong to about 1400 B.C., cf. *Ath. Mitt.* XX (1895) 275.

[4] We have already seen that a Cretan conquest after the destruction of the palaces and of the power of the Minoan rulers of Knossos and of Phaestos at about 1400 B.C. is not justified by the existing archaeological evidence.

Attica is not justified. The examination of the evidence — the archaeological, such as it is to date; the linguistic, the non-Indo-European names of Attica; the literary, the well-known passage of Thucydides; the traditional, the *mythos* of the Minotaur and the wars of Minos against Athens and Megara; the religious, the bull-cult and the cult of Athena — has proved, I believe, that such a conquest or domination of Athens never occurred in Minoan times. It has furthermore indicated that the *mythos* and the other traditions, if conceived as based on historic facts, probably refer to events and experiences which occurred after the fall of the Mycenaean Empire.

ATHENES ET DELPHES

Par Georges Daux

’Εγὼ δέ, Παλλάς, τἄλλα θ’ ὡς ἐπίσταμαι,
τὸ σὸν πόλισμα καὶ στρατὸν τεύξω μέγαν. . . .

Apollon (Eschyle *Eum.* 667–8)

ENTRE Athènes et Delphes les premiers rapports historique-
ment attestés remontent à la tentative de Cylon, les plus
récents descendent jusqu’à la fin du IIème siècle après J-C. Avant
de passer en revue et d’interpréter quelques-unes des données que
nous possédons sur ce sujet, il importe de dissiper un certain
nombre d’équivoques. L’historien de l’antiquité est trop souvent
porté à exagérer l’importance de faits isolés; privé de grandes
idées directrices par la nature même des sources, souvent tendan-
cieuses, toujours fragmentaires ou sommaires, dont il dispose, il
est sans cesse en quête de considérations générales, destinées à
élargir un exposé aride. Le problème qui s’offre à lui est en principe
le problème même de la science historique et de la science tout
court: interprétation des faits, passage de l’analyse à la synthèse.
Mais ce problème unique offre, pour chaque moment de l’histoire,
pour chaque catégorie de documents, des aspects particuliers.
Les remarques préliminaires que je voudrais faire à propos des
rapports d’Athènes et de Delphes sont conformes à l’esprit de
doute méthodique; en exposant les difficultés qui l’arrêtent, l’auteur
a chance d’atteindre un double but: échapper lui-même aux pièges
d’une généralisation hâtive, et, s’il y succombe parfois, éveiller
du moins l’attention et la méfiance du lecteur.

Les deux réalités entre lesquelles se situe notre enquête ne sont
ni simples, ni faciles à définir. Etudier les rapports d’Athènes et
de Delphes, ce n’est qu’une formule; aussitôt qu’on essaye de la
transformer en programme, les questions se multiplient. A chacun
de ces deux noms en effet répondent des activités diverses et
complexes.

Sous celui de Delphes on entend souvent une doctrine religieuse
et morale, dont les membres sont épars dans la littérature grecque,

de Pindare à Plutarque. Il est difficile de tirer, de tant d'indications et d'allusions, un système; mais il est clair que, mis à part
les cultes orgiastiques, c'est à Delphes, autour d'Apollon Pythien,
que s'est cristallisé peu à peu le seul noyau doctrinal commun à
toute l'Hellade. Sont-ce les rapports d'Athènes avec Delphes,
métropole du paganisme grec, que nous étudierons?

Delphes est aussi le siège d'un oracle, le plus célèbre du monde
grec. De toutes parts on vient consulter le dieu; sa renommée
s'étend au delà des limites de l'hellénisme. La Pythie, prophétesse
d'Apollon, se prononce sur les sujets les plus graves: elle préside à
la fondation des villes nouvelles, elle prédit la chute des empires;
tantôt elle encourage les états à la résistance, tantôt elle avertit
que toute lutte est vaine. S'agit-il d'examiner les relations
d'Athènes et de l'oracle?

Avec l'oracle, d'ailleurs, nous glissons vers la politique. Le
clergé de Delphes est sensible à la menace, à l'or. Il est recruté
parmi les Delphiens, qui sont comme d'autres — plus que
d'autres, disait-on — vénaux; comme ailleurs, des clans se par-
tagent souvent la cité. Bref la vie du minuscule état delphique
est affligée des mêmes passions et des mêmes luttes que nous
retrouvons dans toutes les cités grecques. Notre sujet est-il:
l'état athénien et l'état delphique?

Mais l'état delphique, à la frontière de la Phocide et de la
Locride, au cœur de la Grèce centrale, n'est autonome que de nom.
Maintenir à Delphes la prépondérance phocidienne, ce sera pour
Athènes, à plusieurs reprises, un moyen de lutter contre des cités
rivales. La politique d'Athènes à Delphes n'est qu'un aspect de
sa politique générale dans le monde grec.

Il y a plus. Delphes est le siège d'une amphictionie dont le rôle
est en principe religieux et administratif, mais d'où les intrigues
politiques ne sont certes pas absentes. Le conseil international
peut favoriser un groupe d'états contre un autre. Sa tribune permet d'atteindre, à travers les représentants des douze ἔθνη,
l'opinion publique d'une grande partie de la Grèce. Athènes et
l'amphictionie delphique, ce serait encore un aspect de notre
sujet.

Moins incohérent que le complexe delphique, l'autre terme —

Athènes — n'est pas si simple qu'il peut paraître d'abord. Je n'en donnerai qu'une preuve. La littérature athénienne est d'une richesse incomparable. Si nous nous avisions de réunir, dans les écrits grecs qui nous ont été conservés, toutes les mentions qui témoignent du prestige singulier de Delphes, ce sont les auteurs athéniens qui l'emporteraient évidemment par le nombre et l'importance des citations. Toutefois cette masse ne prouve rien par elle-même; elle demande à être critiquée et analysée; parmi ces documents, il en est qui révèlent une sympathie particulière, un lien moral ou politique entre les deux cités; d'autres n'ont rien de proprement "athénien": ils attestent seulement la primauté spirituelle d'Apollon Pythien dans le monde grec, et leur étiquette athénienne n'a pas de signification propre; ils appartiennent à l'histoire de Delphes et de la pensée religieuse en Grèce; ils sont le fait, non de citoyens d'un état particulier, mais bien d'Hellènes. La suprématie littéraire d'Athènes risque de fausser toute conclusion qui serait fondée sur une statistique nue.

Ici donc un état minuscule, en butte à la convoitise de ses voisins, siège d'un conseil international, d'un culte panhellénique et d'un oracle plus consulté et plus influent qu'aucun autre; là un état puissant, qui a exercé à deux reprises une manière d'hégémonie sur le monde grec et qui n'a pas cessé d'en être, du Vème au IIIème siècle, la métropole intellectuelle. Il faut prendre garde à ces différences et à cette complexité avant de s'engager plus avant. Athènes et Sparte, Athènes et Corinthe, Athènes et Thèbes, le problème est relativement simple, même si les faits sont obscurs. Mais entre Athènes et Delphes il n'y a ni guerres, ni traités d'alliance ou de paix, il n'y a pas rivalité commerciale, et la géographie physique ou humaine ne donne pas les éléments essentiels du problème.

Il en est un que l'historien néglige trop souvent: la foi. Sa qualité, sa profondeur n'importent pas ici. Le fait est que, pour les Grecs, il existait à Delphes un pouvoir surhumain, capable de guider, de purifier, de sauver les individus et les peuples. Que cette croyance ait été parfois offusquée par la passion politique ou par le rationalisme, peut-être; latente ou explicite, elle n'en demeure pas moins un mobile puissant, pour les particuliers comme pour les nations. Non seulement, dans les moments de détresse ou d'inquiétude, elle peut — l'histoire du monde est pleine de tels exemples — balayer toutes les autres considérations; elle est aussi un facteur permanent: Apollon Pythien n'est pas de ces divinités locales qui s'inféodent à un état et en suivent le sort; c'est un dieu panhellénique, envers lequel Athènes a des obligations régulières, et les magistrats qui ont la responsabilité du pouvoir ne peuvent pas l'oublier.

Il pourrait sembler, après l'analyse qui précède, que la meilleure méthode consisterait à traiter successivement de chacun des domaines que nous avons définis, et pour le moins à essayer de distinguer entre les questions proprement religieuses et les questions politiques qui se posent à propos des rapports d'Athènes et de Delphes. Mais l'enchevêtrement des unes et des autres nous conduit à observer d'abord l'ordre chronologique, quitte à dégager ensuite certains aspects particuliers.

Si l'on essaye de remonter à l'origine, on est frappé d'abord par la date relativement récente où des contacts suivis sont attestés entre Athènes et Delphes. Laissons de côté tout ce qui appartient à la préhistoire, refaite après coup, de la religion grecque et à la mythologie.[1] Le premier événement historique où nous voyons l'oracle de Delphes intervenir à Athènes est la tentative de Cylon. Il est inutile de raconter une fois de plus cet épisode célèbre. Trois faits nous interdisent d'en tirer parti pour notre propos: d'abord la date n'en est pas assurée (VIIème ou VIème siècle?); ensuite le texte même de l'oracle reste inconnu; enfin la signification politique de la tentative de Cylon nous échappe.[2] Ainsi vidé de toute substance, dépouillé de toute précision, le fait même de la consultation — d'ailleurs mal assuré — perd beaucoup de son intérêt.

Le nom de Solon est attaché à une mesure qui intéresse Delphes. Il avait établi que les neuf archontes, au moment de leur entrée en charge, prêteraient serment de "consacrer une statue d'or s'ils

[1] C'est à Delphes que Thésée consacre sa chevelure, etc. . . .

[2] Cf. par ex. G. Glotz et R. Cohen, *Hist. grecque* I (1925), 418–9 et J. Beloch[2] I 2 (1913), 304 sqq.

transgressaient l'une quelconque des lois,"[1] et cette règle était encore en vigueur au temps d'Aristote. Or, selon Platon et Plutarque,[2] la statue devait être consacrée à Delphes. Nous ne savons pas si la clause jurée par les archontes a jamais reçu un commencement d'application.[3] Mais elle est un témoignage du prestige de Delphes, dès l'époque de Solon, à Athènes;[4] Apollon Pythien est dès lors, il restera le dieu *moral* par excellence, celui qui *organise* la vie sociale, politique et religieuse des Grecs.

A l'époque de Solon encore se rapporte l'intervention d'Athènes dans la première guerre sacrée, au côté des Thessaliens. Le rôle personnel de l'homme d'état athénien, à cette occasion, fut considérable, selon Plutarque;[5] ses arguments auraient décidé les Amphictions à intervenir contre Cirrha et en faveur de Delphes.[6]

Le texte de Plutarque semble indiquer qu'Athènes faisait partie, avant même la guerre sacrée, de l'amphictionie pyléo-delphique. Vers cette époque en tout cas dut se produire une réorganisation des Pythia, qui deviennent pentétériques à partir de 582, et de l'amphictionie, dont le centre de gravité se trouve, et se trouvera de plus en plus, reporté des Thermopyles à Delphes. On con-

---

[1] Aristote, ᾿Αθ. πολ. 7. 1: ἀναθήσειν ἀνδριάντα χρυσοῦν.

[2] Platon *Phèdre* 235 d; Plutarque *Solon* 25. Il s'agit d'une statue représentant le coupable (εἰκών, ἀνδριάς). Dans le dialogue de Platon, Phèdre s'engage plaisamment à dédier, dans le sanctuaire de Delphes, non seulement sa propre statue, mais aussi celle de Socrate. Plutarque reproduit le texte d'Aristote, mais ajoute le mot ἰσομέτρητον qui se trouve chez Platon.

[3] Diels a voulu reconnaître une allusion à cet usage dans une strophe mutilée du péan de Philodamos (vers 137); son interprétation et la restitution qu'elle entraînait ont été écartées avec raison par W. Vollgraff: cf. *BCH* 1927, 441–2, et 1931, 353–4.

[4] Wilamowitz pense que la clause imposant l'offrande d'une statue est bien antérieure à Solon et remonte à un temps où la monnaie n'était pas encore en usage: la statue n'était donc que l'équivalent d'une amende considérable. Mais nous ne nous occupons ici que de la mention de Delphes, et nous n'avons aucune raison de supposer qu'elle soit antérieure à Solon; bien plus, on aimerait que l'autorité d'Aristote vînt confirmer la mention de Delphes par Platon et Plutarque.

[5] *Solon* 11 (chapitre remarquable par l'étalage de l'érudition critique); cf. Pausanias X 37.

[6] Faut-il rappeler que Solon figure parmi les sept sages associés de tant de manières à Delphes?

sidère parfois[1] qu'Athènes entra seulement alors dans le conseil international. Ce qu'il faudrait savoir surtout, c'est quand le siège athénien devint permanent, et si ce fut en fait seulement ou en droit. Lorsque l'on suit l'histoire de l'amphictionie, on constate que, les états limitrophes mis à part, Athènes est la seule grande cité grecque qui soit représentée de façon presque continue à l'assemblée pyléo-delphique.

Jusqu'à la fin du VIème siècle aucun document littéraire ni archéologique ne nous livre le moindre renseignement sur les rapports d'Athènes et de Delphes. Mais en 513/2 — date approximative[2] —, à Delphes, les Alcméonides exilés se rendent adjudicataires des travaux d'achèvement du temple d'Apollon. Bien loin de chercher à s'enrichir dans cette entreprise ils n'y voyaient qu'un moyen de séduire les amphictions et la Pythie.[3] De Delphes en effet, et par l'entremise de la Pythie, ils sollicitent l'appui de Lacédémone contre les Pisistratides; en 510 Hippias capitule sur l'Acropole et s'exile. L'Alcméonide Clisthène[4] jette les bases de la constitution athénienne; il soumet à la Pythie cent noms d'archégètes parmi lesquels elle en désigna dix, qui devinrent les éponymes des tribus entre lesquelles Clisthène avait réparti les citoyens de l'Attique.[5]

D'autre part on a pu attribuer récemment[6] à l'année 497/6 l'archontat de Pisistrate le Jeune et du même coup la dédicace citée par Thucydide[7] et retrouvée en 1877:

Μνῆμα τόδ' ἧς ἀρχῆς Πεισίστρατος ῾Ιππίου υἱὸς
Θῆκεν ᾿Απόλλωνος Πυθίου ἐν τεμένει.

Deux gloses tardives attribuent à un Pisistrate la construction du temple d'Apollon Pythien à Athènes.[8] S'agit-il dans les deux cas

---

[1] Beloch[2] I 1, 338 et note 2.

[2] C'est celle que reproduit Glotz *l.l.* 465: je ne la cite que comme point de repère. Sur l'ensemble de la question cf. Homolle *BCH* 1902, 597–627.

[3] Cf. Hérodote V 62–63.

[4] ὅσπερ δὴ λόγον ἔχει τὴν Πυθίην ἀναπεῖσαι, Hérodote V 66.

[5] Aristote ᾿Αθ. πολ. 21.

[6] Meritt *Hesperia* 1939, 64.

[7] VI 54; cf. *IG*[2] I 761.

[8] Suidas *s.v.* Πύθιον; Hésychius *s.v.* ἐν Πυθίῳ.

du grand Pisistrate? Une confusion ne s'est-elle pas produite très tôt pour attribuer au grand-père ce qui revenait au petit-fils? Ou plutôt celui-ci, en consacrant l'autel dont la dédicace nous est parvenue, ne faisait-il que renouer une pieuse tradition de famille? Tant d'incertitudes nous interdisent d'épiloguer,[1] mais le culte d'Apollon Pythien semble, dès avant 490, s'imposer indistinctement à tous les partis qui se disputent le pouvoir en Attique.

Si nous nous tournons maintenant vers les monuments et les inscriptions de Delphes antérieurs aux guerres médiques, nous n'en trouvons point qui puisse être attribué sans conteste à l'initiative d'Athènes. Aucune statue archaïque ne paraît être d'origine attique, à l'exception des frontons du temple reconstruit par les Alcméonides: Athéniens, ils firent appel à un Athénien, Anténor.[2] Pour le portique des Athéniens la date de 506, proposée par Wilamowitz, est défendue par les archéologues français;[3] mais une étude systématique des profils et des proportions de la colonnade, et aussi de l'écriture[4] de la dédicace reste à faire. Un trésor archaïque de tuf, dont "quelques misérables restes"[5] nous ont été conservés s'élevait à peu près à l'endroit où se dresse aujourd'hui le trésor reconstruit par J. Replat; on l'attribue généralement, par conjecture et presque par prétérition, à la ville d'Athènes; mais il n'y a en faveur de cette hypothèse et de cette identification aucun document positif.

Ainsi, lorsqu'on fait le bilan des rapports athéno-delphiques

[1] Certes on imaginerait volontiers Pisistrate s'efforçant de contrebattre les intrigues menées à Delphes par les Alcméonides en exil, et rivalisant avec eux de flatteries envers le culte pythien: d'où la fondation du Pythion athénien, avant que décidément l'or ou la diplomatie des Alcméonides ne l'emporte. Diptyque séduisant peut-être, mais tout imaginaire.

[2] Cf. en dernier lieu P. de La Coste-Messelière, *BCH* 1938, 285–8 et surtout 286 n. 3. Des compléments seront apportés prochainement à cet article pour ce qui concerne les caryatides ioniques; l'unité stylistique du fronton est et son origine athénienne sont des faits acquis.

[3] Cf. les références données par Daux, *Pausanias à Delphes* (1936) 132; *contra*: Pomtow *RE* Suppl. IV 1299 sqq.

[4] Il faut se féliciter qu'E. Löwy ait, dans son étude *Zur Datierung attischer Inschr.* (1937), remis en question des dates trop facilement acceptées; mais la partie positive de son travail est fragile.

[5] J. Audiat, *FD* II, *Le Trésor des Athéniens* (1933), 55.

jusqu'au début du Vème siècle, on est frappé de voir combien rares sont à Delphes les témoignages tangibles et assurés de la présence athénienne. Le fait est susceptible d'explications diverses. La plus désabusée, la plus sage peut-être, consiste à soutenir que le hasard seul est responsable de cet état de choses. Pourtant le nombre des dédicaces archaïques, individuelles ou collectives, trouvées à Delphes (quelques-unes, fort mutilées, sont encore inédites) est assez considérable pour que l'on ne renonce pas à une interprétation moins paresseuse: l'intérêt d'Athènes pour le culte d'Apollon Pythien ne s'est développé qu'au cours du VIème siècle et n'a pas eu le temps de se manifester à Delphes même par une série d'œuvres importantes avant la crise des guerres médiques.

Celle-ci marque dans l'histoire de Delphes un tournant. Compromis par son attitude pour le moins équivoque, le clergé delphique sut promptement rétablir la situation. Dès lors et pendant tout le Vème siècle va se manifester dans le hiéron oraculaire la rivalité de Sparte et d'Athènes.

Les monuments athéniens à Delphes se multiplient. Enuméronsles rapidement. Ce sont d'abord le trésor d'Athènes et son socle, dîmes de Marathon, et les boucliers mèdes accrochés à l'entablement du grand temple; puis, vingt ou trente ans plus tard, pour commémorer la même bataille, le groupe des dieux, des héros athéniens et de Miltiade, œuvre de Phidias;[1] entretemps Athènes avait participé à l'offrande commune des Grecs après les batailles de Salamine[2] et de Platées,[3] elle avait consacré le palmier de bronze supportant la statue dorée d'Athéna comme dîme de la victoire de l'Eurymédon. Voici de plus deux dédicaces de particuliers: Callias, fils de Lysimachidès, qui s'était enrichi à l'occasion des guerres médiques a offert un cheval;[4] Alcibiade, père de Cleinias et grand-père de son glorieux homonyme, a remporté aux Pythia une vic-

---

[1] Pausanias X 10. 1–2. Les statues d'Antigone, de Démétrios et de Ptolémée furent ajoutées après 307 et après 229.

[2] Statue d'Apollon: Hérodote VIII 121; Pausanias X 14. 5.

[3] Trépied: Hérodote IX 81.

[4] Pausanias X 18. 1.

toire à la suite de laquelle il a consacré dans le sanctuaire une base.[1]
A cette liste il faut peut-être ajouter le trésor dorique qui s'élevait
dans le sanctuaire d'Athéna Pronaia: postérieur de quelques
années au trésor du grand sanctuaire, il en serait la réplique —
avec les variantes que comporte toujours chez les Grecs une
œuvre d'art — et aurait été consacré à la suite de la victoire de
Salamine, à Athéna.[2]
Ainsi, dans la période qui suit les guerres médiques, nous voyons
s'affirmer à Delphes le nom athénien. Avec la seconde guerre
sacrée la rivalité d'Athènes et de Lacédémone y devient éclatante.[3]
Le nom de Périclès est attaché à cette politique;[4] elle est donc
vraiment représentative des ambitions athéniennes, dans ce
moment unique de l'histoire grecque où la grande démocratie a
pu légitimement aspirer à l'hégémonie sur le monde grec. Plutarque ajoute un détail précis: sur la partie antérieure du loup de
bronze offert par Delphes dans le sanctuaire,[5] les Lacédémoniens
avaient fait graver la promantie que leur avaient accordée des
Delphiens; Périclès obtint le même privilège pour les Athéniens
et le fit graver sur le flanc droit du loup.

Le mot promantie, attesté par des centaines de textes, est clair;
mais on voit mal comment, dans la pratique, était exercé le privilège qu'il exprime: dans quel ordre ceux qui, états ou particuliers,
avaient été honorés de la promantie étaient-ils admis à consulter
l'oracle? La question n'a d'importance que s'il existe une rivalité
d'amour-propre ou de prestige entre deux des consultants; de sorte
qu'elle se confond en somme avec celles-ci: quelle est la signification politique et quelle est la durée de la promantie? une fois
accordée à un état est-elle valable sans limite de temps? Le décret

[1] *BCH* 1922, 439–445.
[2] Daux *Pausanias à Delphes* 64 n. 1.
[3] Thucydide I 112: Λακεδαιμόνιοι δὲ . . . τὸν ἱερὸν καλούμενον πόλεμον ἐστράτευσαν καὶ κρατήσαντες τοῦ ἐν Δελφοῖς ἱεροῦ παρέδοσαν Δελφοῖς· καὶ αὖθις ὕστερον
Ἀθηναῖοι ἀποχωρησάντων αὐτῶν στρατεύσαντες καὶ κρατήσαντες παρέδοσαν Φωκεῦσι.
Les restes d'un traité d'alliance athéno-phocidien nous ont été conservés, *IG*[2] I 26.
Dans le décret athénien de proxénie *IG*[2] I 27, la restitution de l'ethnique [Δελ]φός
n'est pas assurée.
[4] Plutarque *Périclès* 21.
[5] Pausanias X 14. 7.

du IVème siècle octroyant aux Thouriens la promantie "avant tous les Italiotes, sur le même rang que les Tarantins"¹ donne une indication précieuse, quoique insuffisante: on prend soin de respecter la susceptibilité des Tarantins, déjà munis de ce privilège.² Toutes proportions gardées, puisqu'il s'agit cette fois des deux plus grands états de la Grèce, le problème qui se pose après la deuxième guerre sacrée est du même ordre. Mais il faut avouer que nous ne sommes pas en état de mesurer exactement la portée de la promantie successivement octroyée à Lacédémone, puis à Athènes; et il n'est pas sûr que, dans une question de ce genre, la perspective de Plutarque soit bien exacte: il n'est, comme nous, qu'un *historien*, non un *témoin*; la promantie est devenue peu à peu honneur banal et, l'oracle se mourant, presque vide de sens; si Plutarque a raison d'en marquer au Vème siècle l'importance politique et la valeur en quelque sorte symbolique, il le fait, répétons-le, en historien, et peut-être a-t-il tendance à dramatiser, à schématiser, à magnifier les anciennes coutumes.

Au début de la guerre du Péloponnèse Delphes se montra favorable à Sparte. Il n'est pas question de réfuter cette affirmation, qui rallie tous les suffrages,³ mais peut-être faut-il en préciser et en restreindre le champ. Elle se fonde avant tout sur l'oracle pro-laconien que rapporte Thucydide: ὁ [θεὸς] ἀνεῖλεν [τοῖς Λακεδαιμονίοις], ὡς λέγεται, κατὰ κράτος πολεμοῦσι νίκην ἔσεσθαι, καὶ αὐτὸς ἐφῆ ξυλλήψεσθαι, καὶ παρακαλούμενος καὶ ἄκλητος.⁴ Nous

---

¹ *REA* 1919, 77. Le texte, après les mots π[ρὸ 'Ιτ]αλιωτᾶν [πάν]των, n'est pas établi de façon définitive, mais le sens paraît assuré. Je ne puis accepter pour l'archonte Θησαγόρας, éponyme du décret, la date proposée par E. Bourguet (c'est un autre nom, à mon sens, qu'il faut restituer dans les documents *FD* III 5, 23–25); et les considérations politiques qui accompagnent son analyse du décret me paraissent appeler des réserves. Mais ce n'est pas le lieu de reprendre un problème qui touche cependant à notre sujet par un point: quelle est la portée de ce privilège?

² Comparer Démosthène 9. 32, 19. 327; cf. *BCH* 1899, 517 (= *SIG*³ 176): Δε[λφοὶ ἔδωκαν] Θηβαίο[ις τὰν] προμα[ντείαν] μετὰ Δ[ελφοὺς] πράτο[ις].

³ Citons, par exemple, H. Donner *Klio* 1923, 35: "Ganz offen tritt die Parteinahme Delphis für Sparta bei Ausbruch des peloponnesischen Krieges hervor."

⁴ I 118. Il faut dire que la substance et la forme de cet oracle sont inouïes et justifient la réserve de Thucydide lui-même, qui se refuse à prendre position: "ὡς λέγεται"; on ne doit considérer ni les propos d'une population affolée (II 54),

devons nous garder d'attribuer aux contemporains de Périclès
l'attitude critique que nous adoptons à bon compte: à leurs yeux
l'hostilité du dieu ne résulte pas de quelque marché honteux avec
Lacédémone; et ce n'est pas en boudant le sanctuaire pythique
qu'on a chance de l'apaiser. En outre il convient de ne pas pré-
senter comme attitude délibérée de l'oracle ce qui a pu n'être que
complaisance d'un moment. Aux historiens qui se laissent tenter
par l'extrapolation, si commode pour combler les lacunes des
documents, mais si funeste, rappelons que le sujet s'y prête mal;
car l'oracle est opportuniste. Ne nous étonnons point par consé-
quent de rencontrer plusieurs indices qui témoignent dans les années
suivantes que les relations entre Athènes et Delphes sont normales.

En 429 à la suite de la campagne de Phormion dans la région du
Rhion, des trophées maritimes et des boucliers sont déposés à
Delphes dans le portique d'Athènes. Le pilier messénien, qui
supportait, à Delphes comme à Olympie, une Niké de Péonios,
date peut-être de 425 environ.[1] Vers le même temps plusieurs inscriptions trouvées à Athènes attestent que les contacts sont
fréquents avec le sanctuaire pythique.[2] La fondation des Délia
par Athènes,[3] après la purification de Délos, ne représente pas
nécessairement une tentative contre Delphes, une manifestation
ionienne et anti-dorienne; mais elle a pour résultat de maintenir
une sorte d'équilibre entre les deux grands sanctuaires apolliniens:
Athènes est à mi-chemin entre le Cynthe et le Parnasse et partage
sa piété entre les deux divinités. La politique d'apaisement et de

---

ni le discours des Corinthiens (I 123) comme une confirmation directe ou indirecte
de l'authenticité de l'oracle; Thucydide fait simplement prononcer à l'orateur περὶ
τῶν . . . παρόντων τὰ δέοντα (cf. I 22. 1).

[1] Le débat sur la date n'est pas clos (455 ou 425 environ?); j'ai eu l'occasion d'y
revenir à propos d'une autre base messénienne, récemment reconnue à Delphes:
BCH 1937, 71-72. De toute façon l'offrande de la Niké est une manifestation de
prestige, faite sous l'égide d'Athènes et dirigée contre Sparte.

[2] Elles sont publiées *IG*² I 76-80 (cf. aussi le fragment 135 avec une mention des
amphictions; mais sont-ce bien ceux de Delphes?). La plus importante est le décret
sur les prémices d'Eleusis; la dernière partie de ce texte, relative au Pélargicon,
nous ramène aux textes littéraires: cf. Thucydide II 17. Sur le rôle de Lampon
dans cette politique, je renvoie, non sans réserve, à Glotz-Cohen II (1929) 427.

[3] Thucydide III 104.

modération pratiquée par l'oracle delphique, lorsque les intérêts immédiats et mesquins de ses représentants ne sont pas en jeu, se manifeste par l'intervention du dieu qui amena les Athéniens à réintégrer en 421/0 la population délienne, expulsée l'année précédente.[1] La mention expresse du sanctuaire de Delphes dans la trêve de 423 et le traité de 421[2] atteste l'importance internationale du sanctuaire: pour assurer la paix on s'efforce de neutraliser ce point névralgique.

Pendant une partie au moins du IVème siècle, l'histoire de Delphes est un peu mieux connue, et les faits que l'on peut grouper autour de la question qui nous occupe sont plus nombreux. Avec la troisième guerre sacrée Delphes devient comme l'enjeu de la liberté grecque et le centre des intrigues politiques. Nous n'avons pas à résumer cette étape décisive de l'histoire grecque; ce qui s'y trouve en cause, ce sont moins les rapports d'Athènes et de Delphes que ceux d'Athènes et des Phocidiens, de Philippe, etc. . . . Mais quelques points particuliers doivent être signalés ici.[3]

Le parti athénien à Delphes, quelques années avant la guerre sacrée, a pour chef Astycratès,[4] et un décret athénien, confirmé par une série de documents delphiques, fournit de précieuses indications sur ce sujet.[5] Toutefois la chronologie des archontats delphiques pour cette période est loin d'être assurée: l'étude devra en être reprise.

La faveur que semble trouver à Athènes le culte d'Ammon vers les années 367–363 implique-t-elle un mécontentement des Athéniens envers l'oracle de Delphes? Je crois que l'on se hâte trop d'établir un lien de cause à effet entre des événements tout-à-fait indépendants. Les rapports entre Athènes et l'oracle d'Ammon

---

[1] Thucydide V 32. 1.

[2] Thucydide IV 118 et V 18.

[3] Certains épisodes sont si mal connus qu'ils perdent beaucoup de leur intérêt: vers 345 les Déliens firent appel aux amphictions de Delphes pour recouvrer l'autonomie; malheureusement nous n'avons, du discours d'Hypéride qui fit triompher contre Délos la thèse athénienne, que des fragments insignifiants.

[4] Cf. Homolle *CRAI* 1923, 316–317, et *BCH* 1926, 25 sqq.

[5] *IG*² II 109 (= *SIG*³ 175); cf. *FD* III 5, *index, s. v.* 'Αστυκράτης.

remontent au Vème siècle;¹ en 363 le δῆμος fait une série de dons au dieu Ammon dans son sanctuaire du Pirée. L'auteur ([- - -]ινος) de la proposition gravée en tête de cette liste est peut-être le même que celui (Κρατῖνος) qui, la même année, a fait voter le décret ou du moins un amendement au décret en faveur d'Astycratès, chef du parti athénien à Delphes, exilé par ses compatriotes. Mais quatre années plus tôt un document attique mentionne déjà des offrandes faites à Ammon: à ce moment le parti athénien est puissant à Delphes. Bornons-nous donc à constater que le culte d'Ammon, établi au Pirée, reçoit à plus d'une reprise au cours du IVème siècle le tribut de la piété athénienne. Isis, plus tard, recevra des hommages plus nombreux; mais Ammon est venu le premier: "Why Ammon, alone of all Egyptian gods, should have succeeded thus early is no mystery: he had an oracle, and he had Greek intermediaries."² C'est simplifier indûment les faits que d'écrire: "Les Athéniens envoyaient consulter l'oracle d'Ammon au fond du désert chaque fois qu'ils étaient brouillés avec Delphes."³ Je ne crois pas qu'Athènes ait jamais "boycotté" l'oracle d'Apollon Pythien.

En revanche les documents du IVème siècle font ressortir un autre fait. La ferveur de la foule athénienne ne s'est jamais portée vers Delphes; le culte pythien n'est pas populaire en Attique, alors que les Doriens du Péloponnèse et la Grèce centrale le considèrent presque comme un culte national. De fait il est frappant de voir combien les Athéniens tiennent peu de place dans les listes de souscriptions pour la reconstruction du temple d'Apollon; on n'en trouve que deux: l'un a versé 1 drachme et 3 oboles d'argent attique; l'autre a donné 70 drachmes, somme considérable, mais il s'agit d'un acteur, Théodoros, de renommée internationale et dont la générosité n'allait pas peut-être sans ostentation.⁴ Les nouvelles listes découvertes en 1938 et 1939 ne nomment aucun

---

¹ Les textes essentiels sont cités par A. Dain, *Inscr. grecques du Musée du Bardo* (1936), 20–21; c'est dans cette brochure qu'est publiée la liste dont il va être question.
² S. Dow, "The Egyptian Cults in Athens," *Harv. Theol. Rev.*, 1937, p. 184.
³ Glotz-Cohen III 425; cf. déjà Glotz *Revue hist.* CXXI (1916, I) 111.
⁴ *FD* III 5, 4, ll. 6–8, et 3 ll. 67–69 avec le commentaire de Bourguet. Les donateurs sans indication d'ethnique groupés autour de Théodoros sont peut-être ses συναγωνισταί (hypothèse de Nikitsky signalée *SIG*³ I p. 350 n. 11).

Athénien. Athènes, en tant que cité, a certainement versé sa contribution, et le hasard seul nous prive d'en connaître le montant. Mais les offrandes modestes, témoignages d'une piété vivante et spontanée font jusqu'ici, à une exception près, complètement défaut. S'agit-il au contraire d'une question cultuelle? On ne manque pas de s'adresser à Apollon Pythien, seul compétent. C'est ce que font les Acharniens, comme en témoigne un décret *stoichedon* récemment publié; le dieu qui a recommandé de construire des autels d'Arès et d'Athéna Areia est évidemment l'Apollon de Delphes.[1] De même plusieurs Pythaïdes, théories dont le caractère est aristocratique ou officiel, se sont rendues à Delphes au cours du IVème siècle.[2]

Pendant la plus grande partie du IIIème siècle aucun des deux états dont nous étudions les rapports n'est vraiment lui-même; Delphes est sous la domination étolienne; les Macédoniens sont maîtres d'Athènes. Ainsi les rapports entre les deux villes sont largement fonction de l'histoire générale.[3]

Nous retiendrons trois faits. D'abord Démétrios Poliorcète fait célébrer à Athènes les Pythia de 290. Ensuite aucun hiéromnémon athénien ne figure dans les listes conservées du IIIème siècle, si ce n'est de 277 à 264 environ et à partir de 216 environ. Enfin, en 242, lorsque les Etoliens réorganisent sous leur nom la fête des Soteria, Athènes loue leur piété et agrée cette transformation, officiellement qualifiée de "fondation."

Rappelons le texte de Plutarque relatif à l'initiative inouïe, πρᾶγμα καινότατον, de Démétrios: Ἐπεὶ γὰρ Αἰτωλοὶ τὰ περὶ Δελφοὺς στενὰ κατεῖχον, ἐν Ἀθήναις αὐτὸς ἦγε τὸν ἀγῶνα καὶ τὴν πανήγυριν,

---

[1] L. Robert *Etudes épigr. et philol.* (1938) 294–295: "le culte est introduit par un oracle, sans doute de Delphes." Cela me paraît incontestable. *Ibidem* 295 n. 4, un lapsus: la restitution proposée repose sur une forme qui n'est pas grecque (participe ἐπιτετελεκάσι).

[2] Cf. Daux *Delphes au IIème siècle* 528–531; H. W. Parke, *JHS* 1939, 82, date de 355 la Pythaïde à laquelle a pris part Thrasyllos, le client d'Isée (VII). Le calendrier sacrificiel *IG²* II 1357b, republié par Oliver *Hesperia* 1935, 24, remonte aux toutes premières années du IVème siècle.

[3] R. Flacelière, *Les Aitoliens à Delphes* (1937), donne les indications essentielles: cf. son index.

ὡς δὴ προσῆκον αὐτόθι μάλιστα τιμᾶσθαι τὸν θεόν, ὃς καὶ πατρῷός ἐστι
καὶ λέγεται τοῦ γένους ἀρχηγός.[1] Démétrios affirme ainsi ses droits
sur les Pythia et dénonce l'usurpation étolienne. Pourquoi choisit-il
Athènes, et non plutôt les Thermopyles, par exemple, où siège
aussi le conseil international et qui est, des deux centres amphictioniques, le plus ancien? La réponse est simple: célébrant par un
coup d'audace les Pythia hors de leur siège traditionnel, Démétrios
devait veiller à ce que l'éclat de la fête ne fût pas amoindri, et c'est
à Athènes que son entreprise avait les meilleures chances de succès.
L'argument rapporté par Plutarque et dont Démétrios en effet fit
vraisemblablement usage constitue surtout un prétexte et repose
sur une équivoque. Au IVème siècle il y a beau temps que, grâce
à la philosophie religieuse, un Apollon commun s'est dégagé de
toutes les appelations particulières, mais quant au culte, Apollon
Patrôos ne saurait être assimilé à Apollon Pythien. Voici posé
une fois de plus le problème si complexe des ἐπικλήσεις divines.
Il y avait à Athènes un temple et un clergé d'Apollon Πύθιος
distincts de ceux d'Apollon Πατρῷος, considéré comme ἀρχηγὸς τοῦ
γένους. Rien en principe n'opposait ces deux cultes; même, leur
rapprochement était favorisé par l'épiclésis Πατρῷος qui se trouve
avoir d'autre part un sens banal. C'est ainsi que Démosthène,
dans un texte célèbre et souvent mal interprété,[2] où il invoque
d'une part les dieux proprement attiques (ὅσοι τὴν χώραν ἔχουσι τὴν
Ἀττικήν) et *d'autre part* Apollon Pythien, ajoute à propos de ce
dernier: ὃς πατρῷός ἐστι τῇ πόλει. Combien en ce sens n'y a-t-il pas
de dieux πατρῷοι! A l'époque de Démosthène, Apollon Pythien
est certes devenu en Attique un dieu ancestral. Mais dans l'expression Ἀπόλλων Πατρῷος, il s'agit d'une épithète de culte. Le jeu de
mots, qui reste discret dans les textes de Démosthène et de Plutarque, se précise et devient complet chez Platon, qui a l'habitude
de ces fantaisies et de ces subtilités: cf. l'*Euthydème* 302 b-d.[3] La

---

[1] *Démétrius* 40. 8.

[2] 18. 141. On y voit, à tort, une preuve de l'identité d'Apollon Patrôos et
d'Apollon Pythios.

[3] Dans le livre de H. Jeanmaire, *Couroi et Courètes*, paru tout récemment, je
trouve, pp. 143-4, sur l'épithète patrôos, des remarques auxquelles je suis heureux
de pouvoir renvoyer; elles confirment le point de vue exposé ci-dessus.

fusion entre les deux cultes se fera tardivement, à la faveur de
l'équivoque créée par le mot πατρῷος et de l'amitié athéno-del-
phique: on peut tenir pour vraisemblable la restitution ἱερεὺς
Ἀπόλλωνος [Πυθί]ου καὶ Πατρώιου dans un texte de l'époque
impériale.[1]

Après la guerre de Chrémonidès, on ne trouve plus, pendant 40
ans et davantage, de hiéromnémon athénien dans les listes amphictioniques.[2] Or en 243/2, Polyeuctos étant archonte, les Athéniens
agréent les Soteria étoliennes et louent la piété de la confédération,
au moment précis où elle met la main sur une fête amphictionique
et se charge désormais de l'organiser au mieux de sa propre gloire.
Cette double donnée — non-représentation d'Athènes à l'amphictionie et reconnaissance des Soteria — crée un problème qui ne
se posait pas aussi longtemps que l'on datait l'archonte Polyeuctos
de 275 ou d'une année voisine. La solution admise aujourd'hui est
celle que Bikerman formule ainsi (*REA* 1938, 373): "La con-
currence politique n'empêchait pas, en général, de cultiver les relations d'ordre religieux. . . . Sous la domination d'Antigone
Gonatas, les Athéniens s'abstenaient de se faire représenter au
conseil amphictionique dominé par les Etoliens. Mais ils recon-
nurent, en 242, la fête des Soteria, instituée à Delphes par les mêmes
Etoliens en souvenir de la victoire sur les Galates." Une telle
interprétation ne satisfait pas pleinement. La distinction entre
le domaine religieux et le domaine politique vaut-elle bien ici?
Les deux faits opposés par E. Bikerman me paraissent du même
ordre (où d'ailleurs il est assez difficile de mesurer la part de la
politique et celle de la religion). On comprendrait très bien
qu'Athènes, soit sous la pression d'Antigone, soit d'elle-même, se
refusât à entretenir des relations avec une amphictionie vassale

---

[1] *FD* III 2, 63. Cf. aussi *IG* III 720*a*.

[2] On admet que le siège d'Athènes par Antigone Gonatas n'empêcha pas les
hiéromnémons athéniens de remplir leurs fonctions: cf. Beloch[2] IV 2, 394 (au moins
jusqu'au milieu de l'année 263, cf. p. 396); Klaffenbach *Klio* 1939, 208. De son côté
Flacelière, *l.l.* 415 n° 49, accepterait de placer en 264/3 ou 263/2 une liste qui comporte un Athénien (une partie du commentaire repose d'ailleurs sur une confusion,
cf. *Klio* 1939, 208), et il restitue la mention d'un Athénien dans une liste qu'il date
de 264; mais sa note 2, p. 195, est en contradiction avec ce point de vue.

ou une Etolie sacrilège;[1] mais un peuple qui, de gré ou de force, adoptait cette attitude et ce point de vue pouvait-il, sans se déjuger, louer la piété des Etoliens et agréer la fête des Soteria? Comment pouvait-il en même temps approuver cette nouvelle fête et refuser sa collaboration à l'organisation des traditionnelles Pythia? Il faut, je le crains, laisser la réponse en suspens.

Il n'y a pas à faire figurer dans une étude sur les rapports de Delphes et d'Athènes le péan composé par Aristonoos de Corinthe dans le courant du IIIème siècle en l'honneur d'Apollon Pythien.[2] On le proclama d'abord d'inspiration attique, parce que le texte en est gravé sur un cippe que l'on crut, au moment de la découverte, appartenir au trésor d'Athènes; et le rôle important qui y est attribué à Pallas semblait s'accorder avec une telle origine. Alors que le point de départ s'est révélé faux, on continue d'accorder créance à la conclusion qu'il avait provoquée.[3] En réalité il est bien établi maintenant que ce cippe ne fait pas partie des dépendances du trésor,[4] et d'ailleurs aucun des textes qu'il porte n'a le moindre rapport avec Athènes. D'autre part l'hymne lui-même ne fait pas allusion à la déesse athénienne; Tritogeneia et Pallas, épithètes courantes et poétiques, n'orientent pas vers une ville particulière; la tradition qu'Aristonoos est seul à nous faire connaître est fort curieuse, mais il n'est pas besoin, pour en rendre compte, de chercher bien loin; la donnée du problème dont le poète corinthien nous offre une solution[5] est purement delphique; la place qu'il fait à Athéna[6] correspond exactement à l'état de choses

---

[1] Je cite par exemple R. Flacelière *l.l.*: "La domination aitolienne à Delphes était généralement considérée en Grèce comme un sacrilège permanent."

[2] *FD* III 2, 191, cf. 190.

[3] *FD* III 2, p. 185 et p. 214; Flacelière *l.l.* 272.

[4] *FD* II, *Le trésor des Ath.*, p. 68.

[5] "Une fois purifié dans la vallée de Tempé . . . Pallas te ramena à Pythô. . . . C'est pourquoi, sous le nom de Pronaia, Tritogénès reçoit, au siège sacré de ton oracle, des honneurs immortels; tu gardes le souvenir éternel des services qu'elle te rendit en ces temps éloignés, et tu ne cesses de lui accorder les hommages les plus élevés" (traduction de G. Colin, à peine modifiée). Est-ce la forme officielle de la légende à Delphes? Est-ce celle que connaissait Eschyle déjà, *Euménides* 21: Παλλὰς Προναία δ'ἐν λόγοις πρεσβεύεται?

[6] Importance du sanctuaire de la Pronaia; intervention de la déesse dans la querelle du trépied (fronton du trésor de Siphnos); etc.

attesté par les monuments et au rang qu'occupe à Delphes la déesse: le premier après Apollon.

Pour le IIème et le Ier siècle av. J-C. jusqu'à l'avènement d'Octavien Auguste, j'ai présenté les faits dans un chapitre et dans deux appendices d'une étude publiée en 1936: je me permets de renvoyer à ces quelques pages,[1] où j'ai essayé de mettre en valeur l'amitié de Delphes et d'Athènes. Au début de l'empire appartiennent les dodécades, théories analogues aux Pythaïdes, mais moins brillantes; les textes qui les concernent ont été publiés et commentés par G. Colin.[2] Il n'y a point de faits particuliers à signaler ensuite dans les rapports entre les deux villes. Je voudrais seulement attirer l'attention sur la lettre d'Hadrien publiée par E. Bourguet;[3] on y trouve la mention des Athéniens à propos d'une réorganisation de l'amphictionie. Hadrien a rêvé d'établir à Delphes, sur une base rationnelle, un conseil des nations grecques. Athènes y aurait joué à coup sûr un rôle de premier plan. Mais des temps obscurs approchaient.

La revue à laquelle nous venons de procéder est loin d'être complète; le serait-elle, l'aspect de notre exposé ne serait guère différent: des indications fragmentaires et isolées ne permettent pas de reconstituer un tableau d'ensemble, avec une perspective nette. L'état actuel des questions que nous avons examinées ou signalées comporte plus d'incertitudes que de faits.[4]

[1] *Delphes au IIème et au Ier siècle* 521–583, 625–628, 708–729; cf. aussi l'index. Au dossier des Pythaïdes on joindra maintenant le fragment publié par J. Bousquet *BCH* 1938, 362–369.

[2] G. Colin *Le culte d'Apollon Pythien à Athènes* (1905), pp. 146 sqq. = *FD* III 2, 59–66; cf. *SIG*^{3} 772–773 et A. Boëthius *Die Pythaïs* (1918). Les deux ouvrages de Colin et de Boëthius touchent de près à notre sujet et constituent vraiment, comme l'indique le sous-titre du second, une contribution à l'histoire des relations entre Delphes et Athènes. Autre étude d'ensemble à signaler: *Die Exegeten und Delphi*, par Axel W. Persson (1918).

[3] *De rebus delph. imp. aetatis* (1905), 74–5, 78–9; les fragments de la page 74–5 font suite à la partie de la 2ème colonne publiée p. 79: cf. F. Courby *FD* II p. 33, fig. 31.

[4] L'objet de notre recherche nous a conduit, dans les pages précédentes et dans l'appendice, à recueillir des indications même insignifiantes. Une contre-épreuve

En ce qui concerne le rôle d'Athènes dans l'amphictionie, si les lacunes de notre information restent considérables, l'épigraphie delphique a permis du moins de poser un certain nombre de jalons auxquels d'autres, on peut l'espérer, viendront s'ajouter. Un fait est maintenant bien établi, grâce aux listes amphictioniques réparties sur plus de deux siècles, de 343 à 125 environ av. J-C.: Athènes est le seul état grec important qui ait occupé de façon permanente un siège au conseil international, sauf une éclipse de quelques décades pendant la domination étolienne sur Delphes. Le contraste est frappant avec le cas de Sparte,[1] qui n'est représentée que deux fois au conseil pendant tout ce laps de temps: en 329 et vers le milieu du IIIème siècle.

Contentons-nous de cette observation statistique. Par son rôle international l'amphictionie ressortit à l'histoire générale, et les réactions que provoquèrent à Athènes les guerres sacrées, l'intervention de Philippe, l'usurpation étolienne n'intéressent pas directement l'objet de notre recherche. Cet objet, qu'il était difficile de définir *a priori*, nous sommes mieux en mesure de le résumer, après avoir poussé notre enquête dans différentes directions: quel est en face du culte de Delphes, oraculaire et panhellénique, la position particulière d'Athènes? Il n'est guère possible de répondre que par des approximations; plusieurs des points que je vais indiquer appellent corrections et réserves; je prie que l'on y voie seulement des suggestions.

1° Les relations entre Delphes et Athènes ne semblent pas remonter à une haute antiquité. Sur les origines et les premiers temps de l'oracle on peut orienter la recherche de différents côtés: la Crète, l'Asie mineure, la Thessalie, la Thrace, la Béotie, les Doriens; à chacun de ces noms peuvent s'attacher quelques faits et des hypothèses plus ou moins vraisemblables. Athènes, elle, n'a pas contribué à la naissance et à l'établissement du culte

---

permet de remettre les choses à leur juste place; elle consiste à se reporter aux monographies qui étudient non les rapports d'Athènes et de Delphes, mais l'un des deux termes. Dans *The Delphic Oracle* (1918), de T. Dempsey, Athènes tient fort peu de place, et de même Delphes dans le livre magistral de W. S. Ferguson, *Hellenistic Athens* (1911). A bon droit: nos sources sont pauvres.

[1] Cf. provisoirement Daux *l.l.* 329–335; j'aurai à revenir sur cette question.

oraculaire qui après avoir appartenu à différentes divinités, est devenu le bien d'Apollon. A un moment donné, vers la fin du VIIème siècle ou le début du VIème, elle s'est trouvée en face d'un oracle et d'un dieu dont le prestige était bien établi. C'est alors que leurs relations commencent. Elles mettront quelque temps à se développer: parmi les dédicaces et les monuments archaïques retrouvés à Delphes, il n'en est pas jusqu'à la fin du VIème siècle que l'on puisse attribuer à Athènes.

2° Ce culte ne semble pas avoir joui à Athènes d'une véritable popularité, s'étendant à toutes les classes sociales. Apollon Pythien n'a jamais été pour l'état athénien un dieu national. Le peuple ne paraît pas empressé à souscrire pour la reconstruction du temple de Delphes au IVème siècle. D'autre part, quel que soit le rayonnement de son oracle, le culte pythique n'est pas de ceux qui enthousiasment les foules; c'est un culte formaliste et raisonnable, sans ὄργια; le dieu conseille et dirige de haut les hommes; il ne s'empare pas de l'esprit ni des sens,[1] et la Pythie est seule bouleversée par son inspiration. Ses propagandistes ont été des poètes, des prêtres, des aristocrates, une manière d'élite intellectuelle ou sociale.[2] Les traditions relatives à la Pythaïde de la Tétrapole marathonienne et l'organisation des Pythaïdes de 137, 127, 105 et 97 av. J-C. montrent qu'une aristocratie sacerdotale et politique présidait au développement des relations entre les sanctuaires attiques et celui de Delphes. Le culte d'Apollon Pythien à Athènes garde, de Pisistrate à Sarapion, un caractère officiel ou "distingué":[3] il est promu par des hommes d'état et par des écrivains.

3° Il y a eu probablement de la part d'Athènes des moments de méfiance envers Apollon Pythien. Athènes est la pointe extrême et militante de l'ionisme sur un continent dorien (au sens large du

---

[1] L'élément dionysiaque, malgré son importance, reste à l'arrière-plan; il ne parvint pas à prendre le dessus.

[2] Soit dit sans ironie, le μικροφιλότιμος de Théophraste (21), qui emmène son fils à Delphes pour consécration de la chevelure, est un ἱππεύς.

[3] Disons même, si cet autre néologisme ne paraît pas déplacé, que l'engouement dont témoignent les Pythaïdes de 127, 105 et 97 touche au snobisme. Cf. d'ailleurs déjà Théophraste, cité tout à l'heure.

mot) ou fortement dorisé. Dans la mesure où Delphes est restée,
à ses débuts, sous l'influence de ses origines non-ioniennes, dans la
mesure où elle a continué pendant un certain temps à doriser et à
laconiser, Athènes pouvait se méfier d'elle. Peut-être aussi la
faiblesse — ou la vénalité — du clergé de Delphes au moment des
guerres médiques fit-elle fâcheuse impression. Mais sur les consé-
quences, en tout cas passagères, de ce "médisme" ou de ce "la-
conisme" de la Pythie, nous en sommes réduits aux conjectures;
et je ne puis souscrire à une affirmation comme celle-ci: "A l'ap-
proche de Xerxès Athènes [interrogea] la Pythie; la réponse fut
d'une ambiguité qui sentait déjà la trahison. Désormais, quand
elle avait besoin d'une consultation politique, Athènes se tira
d'affaire par se propres moyens [et recourut aux devins]."[1]

4° Il y a eu peut-être comme une rivalité spirituelle entre les
deux villes. Pour le monde grec tout entier, Delphes est en quelque
manière au sommet de la hiérarchie religieuse; dans la mesure où
les différentes cultes recourent à une autorité suprême, le rôle
d'arbitre et de législateur est dévolu au dieu pythien. D'autre
part dès le milieu du Vème siècle la primauté littéraire et artistique
d'Athènes est un fait acquis; la ville aspire à l'hégémonie politique.
Un état fort, conscient de ses mérites envers la Grèce, un état qui
par la bouche de ses hommes d'état proclame qu'il représente une
forme supérieure de culture, s'accomodera-t-il d'une sorte de
vassalité envers Delphes? N'y a-t-il pas antinomie entre la mission
de Delphes et la mission d'Athènes, toutes deux panhelléniques?
Il ne s'agit pas seulement d'un épisode de la lutte entre l'état et
l'église, entre le spirituel et le temporel. Sur certains points les
conceptions athéniennes et delphiques ne s'opposent-elles pas?
"Que Delphes [au Vème siècle] reste attachée au vieux dogme de
la responsabilité héréditaire, libre à elle; Athènes, qui ne reconnaît
pas la famille comme un groupe intermédiaire entre l'Etat et les
individus, tous égaux, fait prévaloir, fût-ce aux dépens de la
puissance publique, la responsabilité strictement personnelle."[2]
"Delphi's Ansehn und Reichtum imponierte, erregte auch wohl
Neid und Rivalität; Athen wenigstens hätte gern auf sich den

[1] Glotz-Cohen II 426.   [2] Glotz-Cohen II 421.

religiösen Nimbus übertragen, welchen seit alter Zeit die Weih-
stätte Gäa's und ihrer Erben umkleidete; man suchte zu über-
bieten, man erborgte."[1] Je cite ces phrases à titre d'indication,
sans les prendre à mon compte, mais il est certain, *a priori*, que
l'extraordinaire développement d'Athènes, depuis la fin du VIème
siècle, entraînait une sorte de rivalité, consciente ou inconsciente,
avec le culte de Delphes.

5° Pourtant l'accord se fait; les ambitions des deux villes se sont
plutôt conjuguées qu'opposées. Les raisons de cette entente sont
multiples, mais claires. Au clergé delphique il apparaît vite que
l'agent de propagande le plus efficace — par la parole, par la poésie
et par l'art — est Athènes: écrivains et potiers de l'Attique portent
au loin la gloire d'Apollon Pythien. D'ailleurs, en fin de compte, le
dieu ne gêne en rien les ambitions athéniennes; il se contente d'un
honnête profit et d'un rôle plus honorifique qu'actif; il ne menace
pas, comme d'autres le feront, l'ordre social ni l'autorité de l'état.
Ainsi Delphes et Athènes ont mieux fait que se tolérer mutuelle-
ment; elles ont uni leurs forces morales. J'écartais en commençant
certains témoignages littéraires parce qu'ils me paraissaient moins
athéniens que grecs. Il n'en reste pas moins que des écrivains
athéniens sont devenus en fait les apôtres zélés du culte delphique:
la confiance que Platon témoigne à Apollon Pythien, le rôle qu'il
lui attribue dans sa république idéale (voir la *République* et surtout
les *Lois*), montrent assez que le dieu de Delphes est au-dessus de
toute discussion, quelles que puissent être parfois les faiblesses
de ses mandataires. Le rapprochement spirituel d'Athènes et de
Delphes se poursuit à partir d'Eschyle pour aboutir à une entente
parfaite sous la domination romaine et s'exprime clairement dans
deux décrets, votés par les Amphictions et par Athènes vers 125
et 97 av. J.-C.[2] Le malheur, au cours de ces trois siècles, est que le
rôle de Delphes va s'amoindrissant; si, comme on l'a soutenu, la
période la plus florissante de l'oracle est le VIème siècle, il faut
bien dire que les relations entre les deux villes commencent à se

---

[1] A. Mommsen *Delphika* (1878) 291. Il ajoute même (n. 4.): "Schliesslich siegte
Athen in diesem Wettkampf; es wurde gewissermassen Delphi's Nachfolgerin."
[2] *FD* III 2, 69 et 48; cf. Daux *Delphes au II*[ème] *siècle* 369.

développer au moment même où apparaissent, à Delphes, les premiers germes de décadence. Et leur entente parfaite, sous la domination romaine, est un symptôme ou une conséquence de l'affaiblissement de la Grèce.

6° La part d'Athènes dans ce que l'on peut appeler, avec un peu d'exagération, la doctrine et l'éthique de Delphes ne saurait être déterminée. Le rôle de l'oracle est essentiellement cathartique. Il semble qu'Athènes ait reçu et loué les bienfaits d'une religion qui était née sans elle; mais elle l'a sans doute enrichie, approfondie, humanisée. Les *Euménides* nous montrent un droit nouveau triomphant d'un droit ancien (les Erinyes) grâce à Apollon (Delphes) et à Athéna (Athènes); dans cette collaboration, le poète revendique pour sa patrie la meilleure part; nous ne sommes pas obligés de le suivre, mais il est clair que dans ce domaine comme dans tant d'autres Athènes a été un centre de maturation et de diffusion.

APPENDICE

Le tableau qui suit énumère par ordre chronologique tous les textes épigraphiques trouvés à Delphes, antérieurs à l'empire romain,[1] qui concernent Athènes ou des Athéniens. Il est à peine besoin de rappeler que la division par siècle est arbitraire: pour trois proxénies, j'ai indiqué un jeu s'étendant sur la fin du IVème et le début du IIIème siècle. D'autre part, étant donné que la date de beaucoup de textes reste imprécise, il a semblé préférable d'établir à l'intérieur de chaque siècle un classement par catégories (dédicaces, représentants à l'amphictionie, etc. . .). Ont été laissés de côté les noms des Athéniens participant au concours des Soteria (IIIème siècle), les textes relatifs aux quatre Pythaïdes qui s'échelonnent de 137 à 97 av. J.-C., et les noms des technites dionysiaques qui paraissent dans des textes contemporains de ces Pythaïdes (*FD* III 2, 68, 69 et 70).[2] Tous les autres noms d'Athéniens signalés dans des inscriptions antérieures à 31 av. J.-C. sont reproduits ici (en ce qui concerne les entrepreneurs du IVème siècle, je n'ai pas renvoyé aux textes où leur nom figure sans ethnique: cf. dans ce cas les références de l'index *FD* III 5). — Pour le IVème siècle j'ai reproduit, sans les considérer comme toujours assurées, les dates données dans *FD* III 5, 318 sqq.; cependant j'ai tenu compte d'un fragment découvert en 1939 qui prouve que la liste amphictionique *FD* III 5, 58 (cf. *SIG*³ 252 O) appartient au printemps de l'archontat de Κᾶφις (330 av. J.-C.), et non à l'automne (331 av. J.-C.) comme le croyait E. Bourguet. Pour le IIIème siècle, j'ai tenu compte des dates proposées par Flacelière dans son livre sur *Les Aitoliens à Delphes*, appendices I et II, mais j'ai insisté sur les réserves faites par l'auteur lui-même et marqué mes doutes ou mes objections en indiquant un jeu très large pour certaines dates et en refusant même d'en proposer aucune dans plusieurs cas; sur la chronologie du IIIème siècle (dont je n'ai dit que quelques mots dans deux articles de la *Revue de philologie* 1938 et du *Journal des savants* 1939), je me permets de renvoyer à un article qui paraît au *Bulletin de correspondance hellénique* 1939. Pour le IIème et le Ier siècle av. J.-C., cf. Daux *Delphes au IIème et au Ier siècle*.

Je remercie vivement J. Bousquet, P. Amandry et H. Metzger, grâce à

---

[1] Les textes datant de l'empire et relatifs à Athènes sont peu nombreux (pour les dodécades, cf. ci-dessus), et la chronologie de l'épigraphie delphique pour cette période reste à étudier.

[2] Les textes relatifs aux Pythaïdes et aux technites athéniens ont été étudiés par G. Colin, G. Klaffenbach (*Symbolae ad historiam colleg. artif. bacch.*), A. Boëthius. Il faudra les publier à nouveau en tenant compte des corrections qui ont été proposées au cours de ces dernières années. De même les catalogues des Soteria (IIIème siècle) appellent une publication et une étude particulières (cf. provisoirement le tableau de U. Kahrstedt *Hermes* 1937, 370–4; mais l'article lui-même ne saurait être recommandé).

qui j'ai été tenu sans délai au courant des découvertes épigraphiques de
1938 et 1939.

VIÈME SIÈCLE

506(?)		dédicace du portique	*SIG³* 29; de La Coste-Messelière *A u Musée de Delphes* 49 n.3.

VÈME SIÈCLE

490		dédicace du trésor	*BCH* 1930, 296 sqq.
479		dédicace du trépied, ligne 5: Ἀθαναῖο[ι]	*SIG³* 31.
1ère moitié		signature: Διοπείθες ἐποίεσεν Ἀθεναῖο[s]	*FD* II *Terr. Temple* p. 283.
2ème moitié		lex sacra	*FD* III 2, 194; *FD* II *Trésor des Ath.* p.76
"	"	autre lex sacra	*FD* III 2, p. 224 n. 2 fr. *a*
"	"	autre lex sacra	*FD* III 2, p. 224 n. 2 fr. *b* + *c*.

IVÈME SIÈCLE

?	signature: Ἀριστόδημος Ἀθηναῖος ἐ[ποίησε]ν	*FD* II *Terr. Temple* p. 151.
	hiéromnémons athéniens:	cf. *FD* III 5, pp. 324–325.
343 automne	Μνησ[ι]λό[χ]ου	
342 printemps	Μνησιλόχου	
342 automne	[Π]ρωτάρχ[ου]	
340 automne	Διογν[ήτου]	
339 automne	[10 lettres]	
335 printemps	Ἀρχιδή[μ]ου	
334 printemps	[12 lettres environ]	
332 automne	Ἀπημάν[του]	
331 printemps	Ἀπημάντου	
330 printemps	Ἀπημάντου	
329 printemps	Λυσιστράτου	
328 automne	[Εὐθυ]κλέος	
327 printemps	Εὐ[θ]υκλέους	
?	liste géogr. des naopes, Ἀθηναίων:	

Κλεινόμαχος, Εὐκτήμων Χαρίου,
Πυθόδωρος Πύθων[ος], Εὐθυκράτης
Εὐθυ[κράτους], Ἐπιτέλης Σωινόμ[ου],
Λεόφρων Εὐθύφρον[ος],[1] Κάλλαισχρος
Φιλα[ίου]   *FD* III 5,91,ll. 21–29.

---

[1] Cf. *FD* III 5, 91, commentaire de la ligne 27, et *SIG³* 237 n. 7.

356 printemps	naope: Τηλοκλέας	*FD* III 5, 19, l. 34 et l. 39.
356 automne	" : Κύδιμος	*ibid.*, l. 43.
355 printemps	" : Νικιάδης	*ibid.*, l. 53.
346 automne	" : Εὐκτήμων, Ἐπικράτης	*ibid.*, l. 74
343 automne	" : Εὐκτήμων	*ibid.*, l. 96.
341 automne	" : Ἐπικράτης	*FD* III 5, 20, l. 3.
338 automne	" : [Εὐ]κτήμων, [Πυθόδ]ωρος, Εὐθυκράτης	*FD* III 5, 48, l. 13-14.
331 automne	" : [Ἐπ]ιτέλης Σωινόμου, [Π]υθόδωρος Πύθωνος	*FD* III 5, 58, l. 22 et l. 29.
329 printemps	" : Πυθόδωρος, Ἐπιτέλης, Θεόφρων	*FD* III 5, 20, l. 33 et l. 38.
327 printemps	" : Ἐπιτέλ[ης Σωινόμου], [Λεόφρων] Εὐ(θύ)φρονο[s] [1]	*FD* III 5, 61 II B, l. 25 et l. 26.
339 automne	trésorier: Θουκυδ[ίδης Κηφισο]δ[ό]τ[ου]	*FD* III 5, 47 I, l. 46.
342	entrepreneur: Ἕρμων (ethnique douteux)	*FD* III 5, 26, l. 10.
341	" : Πυθόδημος Ἀθηναῖος	*FD* III 5, 20, l. 5.
340	" : Μ[ο]λοσσὸς Ἀθηναῖος	*FD* III 5, 20, l. 10.
338	" : Ἀθήνηθεν Φιλ[ι]σκος, [Ν]ικοκράτης, Φίλων, Μο[λοσσός], Λαθοῖος; Ἀγλαό[θυμος] Ἀθηναῖος, [ϙ lettres] Ἀθηναῖος, Φίλων Ἀθηναῖος	*FD* III 5, 48, ll. 24-34.
331	" : Ἐπιτέλης Ἀθηναῖος	*FD* III 5, 58, l. 38.
330	" : [Χάρ]ης Ἀθηναῖος	*FD* III 5, 59B, l. 2.
?	" : [Ἀγ]λαόθυμος Ἀθηναῖος	*FD* III 5, 62, l. 9.
début	théarodoque(?): [Κλ]ειτοφῶν [ἐν Ἀθ]άναις	*SIG*[3] 90.
2ème moitié	texte amphictionique (fragment)	Inv. 3606, inédit.
fin	dédicace: Χαιρέφιλος Φείδωνος Ἀθηναῖος	*SIG*[3] 301.
"	dédicace: (mention des Athéniens)	Inv. 1656, inédit.
334	dédicace: Ἀθηναίων ὁ δῆμος ὁ ἐν Σάμωι	*BCH* 1899, 536; *SIG*[3] 276A.
?	dédicace: [ὁ δῆμο]s ὁ Ἀθηνα[ίων ὁ ἐ]s Σάμωι	*SIG*[3] 276B.
vers 330-324	dédicace: [ὁ δ]ῆμος ὁ Ἀθηναίων; noms des hiéropes οἱ τὴν Πυθαΐδα ἀγαγόντες· Φανόδημος Διύλλου, Βόηθος Ναυσινίκου, Λυκοῦργος Λυκόφρονος, Δημάδης Δημέου, Κλέαρχος Ναυσικλέους, Γλαυκέτης Γλαύκου, Νεοπτόλεμος Ἀντικλέους, Κλεοχάρης Γλαυκέτου, Ἱπποκράτης Ἀριστοκράτους, Νικήρατος Νικίου	*SIG*[3] 296; *FD* III 1, 511.

[1] Cf. la note précédente.

vers 330–324	proxénie: Δημάδει Δη[μέου] ’Αθηναίωι	*SIG*³ 297*A*; Daux *Delphes au II*ᵉᵐᵉ 529 n. 4.
" "	proxénie: Γλαυκέτε[ι Γλαύκο]υ ’Αθηναίω[ι]	*SIG*³ 297*B*.
320(?)	proxénie: [’Επιτέλ]ει Σωινόμου [’Αθηναί]ωι, φυλῆς ’Ερε[χθηίδο]s, δήμου Περ[γασῆθε]ν	*SIG*³ 308; *FD* III 1, 408.
fin	proxénie: Νεο [*7 lettres*] Νικί[ου ’Αθηνα]ίωι, φυλ[ῆς ’Ιππ]οθωντί[δος, δή]μου ΔΕΕΙ [*4 l.*]	*BCH* 1882, 230; *GDI* 2656.¹
"	proxénie: [*7 lettres*] τει Φιλ [*4 l.* ’Αθη]ναίωι, δ[ήμου Περγ]ασῆθε[ν]	*BCH* 1899, 503.
fin IVᵉᵐᵉ–début IIIᵉᵐᵉ	proxénie: ’Αλκαίωι Τεισιάδου ’[Α]θηναίωι, δήμου Θριασίωι	*FD* III 2, 206.
fin IVᵉᵐᵉ–début IIIᵉ ᵐᵉ	renouvellement de proxénie: Χαριδήμωι Χαριδήμου ’Αθηναίωι, φυλῆς Πανδιονίδος, δήμου Παιανιεῖ	*BCH* 1928, 217.
fin IVᵉᵐᵉ–début IIIᵉᵐᵉ	décret attique: ne subsistent que des formules	Inv. 2473, inédit.
363	souscriptions pour la reconstruction du temple: Θεόδωρος ’Αθηναῖος ὑποκρίτας, Κλεογένης (?), Πείσιος (?), Κτήσων (?), Εὐτέλης (?), ’Ηγήμων (?)	*FD* III 5, 3, l. 67 et ll. 57–74; cf. *ib.*, p. 41 n. 1 et *SIG*³ 239*B* n. 11.
361	autre souscription: [*5 l.*] ρος ’Αθηναῖος	*FD* III 5, 4, l. 6.

¹ Baunack, d’ordinaire si minutieux, n'a pas reproduit les justes remarques d’Haussoullier, et il restitue, sans point d’interrogation, δήμου δὲ ’Ερ[ωέος], forme qui manque d’autorité (les inscriptions ne connaissent que le démotique ’Εροιάδης ou, tardivement ’Ερυάδης); d’ailleurs Haussoullier indique que la lettre qui suit le second E ne peut être P, mais plutôt K; la photographie F97 de l’Ecole française confirme sa remarque. Le texte est *stoichedon*. Aucun démotique connu ne répond à ces données; en désespoir de cause, au lieu de δήμου δὲ ἐκ[. . . .] ou δήμου δὲ Εκ[. . . .], on songerait à écrire δήμου Δε(κε)[λεεῖ] — avec interversion de deux lettres par le lapicide —, si le texte n’était très soigneusement gravé. Une faute comme ἐκ [Οἴου] serait encore plus barbare.

IIIᵉᵐᵉ SIÈCLE

hiéromnémons athéniens:

cf. Flacelière *Ait. à Delphes* 386 sqq. et Bousquet *BCH* 1938, 361.

277 printemps	Φωκίωνος	
277 automne	Ἀριστοκλέους	
276 printemps	Ἀριστοκλέους	
274 automne	[5 l. env.]ιος	
273 automne	Φαλα(ί)κου	
272 printemps	Φαλαίκου	
272 automne	Ἀσωποδώρου	
271 automne	Ἱερωνύμου	
?	Ἱερωνύμου	
?	Περιάνδρου	
?	Φιλοκτήμονος	
266(?) printemps	Χαιρεστράτου	
265(?) automne	Εὐθυδίκου	
vers 215	Μενάνδρου	
vers 210	Εἰρανίωνος	
vers 210	Εὐδάμου	
vers 205	Ἀμύκλα	
vers 202	Ἀριστοκλέος	
?	liste géographique des naopes, Ἀθηναίων: [Κ]αλλίας Λυσιμάχου, Πάναιτος Παντακλ[έος]	*FD* III 5, 91, ll. 29-30.
vers 270–268(?)	naope: Καλλίας Λυσιμάχου Ἀθηναῖος	*FD* III 5, 93 I, l. 11.
?	dédicace: [- - - -] [- - -]υς Ἀθηναῖος	Inv. 6212, inédit.
?	couronne: ὁ δῆμος ὁ Ἀθηναίων Πυθίοις	*CIG* 1687; *Klio* 1915, 301.
300–280	proxénie: Πλ[ά]τωνι Κελε[υ]σίου Ἀθηναίωι, φυλῆς Ἱπποθωντίδος, δήμου ἐξ Οἴου	*FD* III 2, 198.
300–280	proxénie: Λυκόφρονι Κελευσίου Ἀθηναίωι, [φυλ]ῆς Ἱπποθωντίδος, δήμου ἐξ [Οἴ]ου	*FD* III 2, 199.
300–280	proxénie: Βαθύλλωι Ἀρχεβούλου Ἀθηναίωι, φυλῆς Ἱπποθωντίδος, δήμου Πειραεῖ	*FD* III 2, 200.
290–280	proxénie: [Ἱπ]ποστράτωι Καλλιπ(π)ίδου, [- - - -] [- - - -] [Ἀθηνα]ίοις, φυλῆς Πανδιονίδος, [δήμου - - - -]	*FD* III 2, 71; *BCH* 1930, 310.
290–280	décret honorant Γλαύκων Ἐτεοκλέους Ἀθην[αῖο]ς	*FD* III 2, 72.

278	décret amphictionique en faveur des technites athéniens	FD III 2, 68, ll. 61 sqq. = IG² II 1132, ll. 1 sqq.
278/7	proxénie: [- - - -], [- - - -] [- -]τρείδου ʼΑ[θην]αίοις	FD III 2, 203.
274/3	proxénie: Τιμοκράτει ʼΑσκληπιοδώρου ʼΑθηναίωι οἰνοποιῶι	FD III 2, 210.
255/4(?)	décret amphictionique honorant Μενάλκης Σ[πεύ]σωνος ʼΑθηναῖος κιθαρωιδός	SIG³ 431.
255–245(?)	proxénie: Κυβέρνιδι Κυδίου ʼΑθηναίωι, φυλῆς Λεωντίδος, δήμου ʻΑλιμουσίωι	FD III 2, 159.
255–245(?)	proxénie: Παυσίαι [ʼΕ]ξηκίου ʼΑθηναίωι, δήμου [ʼΑ]χαρνέως, φυλῆς Οἰνεῖδος	FD III 2, 163
255–245(?)	proxénie: Φιλ[οχά]ρει Φιλ[οκρ]άτους ʼΑθηναίωι	FD III 2, 196.
255–245(?)	proxénie: [- - - - - - - - - - - - - ʼΑθηναίωι]	FD III 2, p. 231 n. 2, texte a; cf. FD II, Trésor des Ath., p. 78.
?	proxénie: ʻΙερωνύμωι ʼΑ[ρί]στωνος ʼΑθηναίωι, φυλῆς ʼΙπ[ποθ]ωντίδος, δήμου ʻΕλαι[ουσίωι]	FD III 2, 197.
243/2	décret amphictionique honorant Καλλικλῆς Καλλικλέος ʼΑθηναῖος οἰκῶν ἐν Αἰτωλίαι, hiérokéryx des amphictions	SIG³ 444.
243/2	proxénie: Καλλικλεῖ Καλλικλέους, etc. . . .	SIG³ 445.
241 sqq.	4 décrets amphictioniques honorant le même	GDI 2509, 2508, 2511, 2512.
242–225	proxénie: Εὐκλεῖ Εὐκλέους [. . . . .]ει ʼΑθηναίωι, φυλῆς Κεκροπίδος, [δήμ]ου ʼΑλαιεύς (sic)	FD III 2, 77.
250–225	proxénie: Σωγένει Καλλιάδου ʼΑθ[ην]αίωι, φυλῆς ʼΑντιγονίδος, [δή]μου ʼΙκαριέως (sic)	FD III 2, p. 232.
250–215	proxénie:[- - - - - - - - ο . . . . . .ʼΑθηναίωι], [δήμου Λαμ]πτ[ρεῖ], [φυλῆς ʼΕρεχθηίδος]	FD III 2, 81.
235–225	proxénie: ʼΑριστοτέλει Λυσιμαχίδου ʼΑθηναίωι, δήμου Κειριαδῶν, φυλῆς ʻΙπποθωντίδος	FD III 2, 79.
235–225	proxénie: ʼΕρατοξένωι Στρα[το 5–6 l.] [ʼΑθ]ηναίωι, ποιητῆι ἐπῶν, [φυλῆς Λεων]τίδος, δήμου ʻΕκαλῆθεν	FD III 2, 158.

230–220   décret honorant Κλεοχάρης Βίωνος Ἀθηναῖος, φυλῆς Ἀκαμαντίδος, δήμου Κι-
κυν(ν)έως (sic), ποιητὴς μελῶν   FD III 2, 78.

230–220   proxénie: Καλλίαι Καλλιάδου Ἀθηναίωι,
φυλῆς Ἀ[ν]τιοχίδος, δήμου Αἰγιλιέως
(sic)   FD III 2, 74.

225–215   proxénie: Ἀπολλοφάνει vacat Ἀθηναίωι   FD III 2, 82.

225–215   proxénie: [Κυδίπ?]πωι Κυδίππου [Ἀθη-
ναίωι], [φυλῆς Αἰαντ]ίδος, δήμου Οἰ-
νο[αίωι]   FD III 2, 166.

220–205   proxénie: Σωσικράτει Ἀλ[κ]αμένου, δ[ή-
μ]ου[1] Φλυέων, φ[υλῆς Π]τολεμαιίδος,
Καλλιστράτωι Καλλικτήτου, δήμου
[Ἀ]λωπεκῆθεν, [φ]υλῆς Ἀντιοχίδος,
Δημοφίλωι Θεοκλέους, δήμου ἐκ Μυρ[ρ]ι-
νούττης, φυλῆς Αἰγεῖδος, Ἀθηναίοις   FD III 2, 76.

vers 210   décret amphictionique honorant Εὔδαμος
Ἀπολλωνίου Ἀθηναῖος, hiéromnémon   FD III 2, 86.

"   proxénie: [? Εὐδάμωι Ἀπολλωνίου] [Ἀθη-
ναίωι], [δήμου] [Ἀ]νακαιέων, φ[υλῆς]
[Ἱππο]θωντίδος   FD III 2, 87.

?   proxénie: Χαιρέαι Ἀθηνοδώρου Ἀθηναίωι,
δήμου Εἰτεαίωι, φυλῆς Ἀντιοχίδος   FD III 2, 80.

?   proxénie: [- - - - - - - - - Ἀθηναίωι?]   BCH 1930, 397; cf.
    FD II, *Trésor des*
    Ath., p. 74.

?   proxénie: Θεο[- - -] [- - -]ωνος Ἀθηναίωι,
φυλῆς Π[αν]διονίδος, δήμου [Πα]ι-
ανιεῖ   BCH 1930, 397.

?   proxénie: [Θ]ε[ο]ξεν[ίδηι] Δειν[- - -],
[ὁ l. env.]ντι Διοδόρου, δήμου Ἑρμε[ί-
οις]   FD III 2, 201.

?   proxénie: Φιλάγρωι Ἀθηνοδώρ[ου] [Ἀθ]η-
ναίωι, δήμου Περιθοίδει, φυλῆς Ο[ἰνηί-
δ]ος   FD III 2, 85.

?   proxénie: Ἀγαθάρχωι Ἐπικύδου Ἀθηναίωι,
δήμου Ε[ἰτ]εαίωι, φυλῆς Ἀντιοχίδος   FD III 2, 73.

?   proxénie: [- - - - - - - - - - - - - Ἀθηναίωι?]   FD III 2, 195.

?   proxénie: [- - - - - - - - - - - Ἀθηναίω]ι,
δήμου Ἀχα[ρνεῖ, - - - - - - - - -]   FD III 2, 204.

2ème moitié   2 décrets honorant les Τετραπολεῖς   FD III 2, 18 et 19.

fin   proxénie étolienne: Γόργιππος Ἀντιγόνου
Ἀθηναῖος   FD III 2, 90.

---

[1] Colin: Ἀλ[κ]αμένους, [δήμου]; mais cf. la photographie, planche III 2.

décret attique: mention des Σωτήρια et de
[Μικίων?] [Εὐ]ρυκλείδου Κηφισιεύς,
(de Μικί[ων] et de [- - - - -] [- -]ντιά-
δου   FD III 2, 140 (cf.
                                                      141).

274 automne   voleur ou recéleur dénoncé: Χαιρένεος (?)
               'Αθη[ναῖος]; cf. aussi [.]με[.]α[.]ος[1]
               'Αθην[αῖος]   FD III 1, 83, l. 12 et
                                                      l. 23.
273 automne   recéleur dénoncé: Διοπείθης 'Αθηναῖος   FD III 2, 205; SIG³
                                                      416.

IIème ET Ier SIÈCLES

hiéromnémons athéniens: cf. Daux *Delphes au*
                                                      IIème siècle 650
                                                      sqq.

186 automne   Μενέδημος
vers 178   [Εὔ]χειρ Εὐβουλί[δου]
178 automne   'Ερμαγόρας Λυσιστράτου
134(?) automne Διονυσογένης 'Αθηνοδώρου
128/7   [. .]οσ[- - - -]
vers 125   'Ασκληπιάδης 'Ικεσίου
106/5   'Ασκλαπίων Κίττου
98/7   Κτησικλῆς Δημοτέλου
58   [Α]ἰνείας Διοπείθου Αἰθαλίδης
42(?)   'Α[π]ολλοφάνης 'Απολλοφάνους Σφήττιο[ς]
IIème siècle   décret attique (restes de 8 lignes)   Inv. 6694 inédit.
178   ἄρχοντος ἐν 'Αθήναις Φίλωνος, décret hon-
               orant les Τετραπολεῖς et leurs ambas-
               sadeurs Διόφαντος, Καλλισθένης, Λυσί-   FD III 2, 20.
               θεος
avant 138   décret honorant les Τετραπολεῖς et les   ⎰ FD III 21 et 22 +
               théores 'Ηρόδ[οτ]ος Προβαλίσιος,   ⎪ fragments iné-
               [- - - - - -]   ⎬ dits découverts
   "   "   décret honorant les Τετραπολεῖς et   ⎪ en 1939.
               [- - -]φυλέα Οἰν[οαῖον], [- - -] [Τρικ]- ⎭
               ορύσιον, 'Αρτεμ[- - -]
153–143   affranchissement, ἐν 'Αθήναις στραταγέον-
               τος Ξενοκλέος, vendeur Ξένων Φιλισ-
               τ[ου] 'Αθηναῖος   GDI 2089; cf. Daux
                                                      l.l. 626–7.

[1] Si la lecture est exacte, je proposerai ['Ι]με[ρ]α[ῖ]ος.

196	proxène: Ξένων Διονυσίου Ἀθηναῖος	*SIG*³ 585, n°2.
191	" : Εὐβουλίδας Εὐχήρου Ἀθηναῖος	" " , n°28.
189	" : Ἄβρων Καλλίου Ἀθηναῖος	" " , n°41.
183	" : Ὀλυμπιόδωρος Ὀλυμπίχου Ἀθηναῖος	" " , n° 89.
179(?)	décret honorant Ἀπολλόδωρος Ὀλυμπιοδώρου Ἀθηναῖος	*FD* III 2, 89; cf. Daux *l.l.* 277 sqq.
175 sqq.	théarodoque ἐν Ἀθήναις [.]ίων Κλεο[- - -]	*BCH* 1921, p. 5, l. 31.
167/6	décret honorant Ἀ[ρισ]τόμαχος Ἀριστομάχου Ἀθηναῖος	*FD* III 2, 91.
165	proxène: Πυθῆς Ἀπολλωνίου Ἀθηναῖος	*SIG*³ 585, n° 131.
153–143	décret honorant Λεόντης Ἀντιγόν[ου] Ἀθηναῖος, poète ou musicien	*FD* III 2, 92 + Inv. 6726, inédit.
milieu IIème	couronnes de - - - η - - - - - - γησ - - - - υ, Ἀθηναῖος	*FD* III 2, 135; cf. L. Robert *Coll. Froehner* 31.
153–143	décret honorant Λέων Κιχησίου Ἀθηναῖος	*FD* III 2, 93.
150–125	décret relatif à des juges athéniens	Daux *l.l.* 480.
"	arbitrage athénien(?): frontières Delphes-Ambryssos	*FD* III 2, 136.
"	fragment: mention d'Ambryssos et d'Athènes	*FD* III 2, 142; cf. *FD* II, *Trésor des Ath.*, p. 24–5.
137	décret honorant Κλέαρχος Ξάνθου Ἀθηναῖος	*FD* III 6, 4.
134	décret amphictionique en faveur des technites dionysiaques d'Athènes	*FD* III 2, 68 = *IG*² II 1132, ll. 52 sqq.
vers 125	décret amphictionique en faveur des technites dionysiaques d'Athènes	*FD* III 2, 69 = *IG*² II 1134.
129–124	proxénie: Πραξ[- - -] [- - - - -] [δήμου] [- - -]-ρίδηι, φυλῆς (- - - -)	*FD* III 2, 95; cf. *Klio* 1923, 274 n. 1.
vers 125	décret honorant le peuple athénien et ses ambassadeurs [Δε]ινοκράτης, Διοκλῆς, Πραξικλῆς	*FD* III 2, 94.
112	dossier relatif à une contestation entre technites de l'Isthme et d'Athènes	*FD* III 2, 70.
fin IIème	mention de jugements athéniens dans la contestation Thronion-Scarphée	*FD* III 4, 38 et 39.

fin IIème	décret amphictionique relatif au tétra-drachme attique	*FD* III 2, 139.
102	décret honorant 'Αμμώνιος 'Αμμωνίου 'Αθη-ναῖος	*FD* III 1, 228; cf. Daux *l.l.* 571.
après 86	décret honorant Δημήτριος 'Αριστοξένου 'Αθηναῖος, ἱερεὺς τοῦ 'Απόλλωνος τοῦ Πυθίου	*FD* III 2, 55.
après 86	décret honorant 'Απολλώ[νιος 'Αρ]χία 'Αθηναῖος	*FD* III 2, 249b.
?	théorie athénienne aux Pythia	*FD* III 2, 56c, cf. Daux *l.l.* 562.

58 théorie athénienne aux Pythia ἐν 'Αθή-
[να]ις ἄρχοντος [Κα]λλιφῶντος τοῦ
[Κ]αλλιφῶν[τος Π]ανβωτά[δου; [- - - -]
Αρι[- - -] 'Αχαρ[νε -]; [ἱ]ερομνη-
[μο]νοῦντος [Α]ἰνείου [τοῦ] Διοπείθου
Αἰθαλίδου

FD III 2, 56 + 56a
+ 56b, cf. Daux *l.l.*
562.

42 théorie athénienne aux Pythia ἐπὶ Εὐθυ-
δόμου ἄρχοντος; 'Α[π]ολλοφάνης 'Απολλοφάνους Σφήττιο[ς], [Εὐ]κλῆς Μαρα-
θώνιος, [Κρ]ιτόλαος [Φλυεύς], [Πα]μμέ-
[ν]ης Λαμπτρεύς, ['Αρί]στ[αρ]χος
Λαμπτρεύς, ['Αντι]κλῆς ['Αντι]κλέους
'Αζηνιεύς, [. . .]όστρατος Φηγ[α]ιεύς

FD III 2, 57.

? théorie athénienne aux Pythia ἐπὶ ἱερέως
[τοῦ Πυθίου 'Απόλλωνος] Εὐκλέους τοῦ
'Ηρώδου Μαρ[αθωνίο]υ; [- - - -] [- - - -]
[Φ]λυεύς, 'Αργαῖος 'Αριστ[. . . . o]υ
Φλυεύς, [- - - -] [- -]ράτου 'Ιωνίδης,
'Απ[ολλοφάνης 'Απο]λλοφάνους Σφήτ-
τιος, Μενεκράτης Με[νεκρά]τους Πα-
[- - -]

FD III 2, 58.

Date inconnue
fragment sans n° d'inventaire que je ne
connais que par une copie rapide:
l. 2 ['Α]θηναῖος, l. 3 'Απόλλων[ι], l. 4
ἀκροθιν[- -]

THE PRO-PERSIAN PARTY AT ATHENS FROM 510 TO 480 B.C.

By Malcolm F. McGregor

C. A. ROBINSON'S recent stimulating article, "The Struggle for Power at Athens in the Early Fifth Century," has aroused among students of Greek history a renewed interest in party politics at Athens from 510 to 480 B.C. Robinson was actuated, apparently, by differences of opinion with Walker and Munro. Since Robinson's analysis of the Athenian situation, though correcting Walker and Munro in certain particulars, does not appear to me to proceed far enough and is not always cogent, no apology is needed for a fresh review of the already well known evidence. In addition to the work of the scholars cited here, students of this involved but fascinating period in the history of Athens will find essential Meritt's important commentary on an epigraphical fragment found in the Athenian Agora in 1937.[1]

Walker, insisting on the close relation of Athenian internal and foreign problems, believes that the Alkmaionidai were the original medizers (at the time of the first embassy to Persia, in 508/7 B.C.), that at the beginning of the Ionian revolt the party of the tyrants in Athens was joined by the Alkmaionidai to oppose the sending of aid to Ionia. Munro agrees in criticism of the Alkmaionidai, imputing the shield signal of Marathon to them and affirming that the Alkmaionidai, to avoid the disaster that awaited them as the inevitable result of an Athenian alliance with Sparta, were ready to seek better terms from Persia, to sacrifice the form in order to preserve the substance of democracy. Robinson denies the coalition between the Alkmaionidai and the friends of the tyrants, absolves the Alkmaionidai of pro-Persian sentiment, and decides that the aristocrats[2] formed the natural pro-Persian faction at

---

[1] C. A. Robinson, *American Journal of Philology*, LX (1939), 232–237; E. M. Walker, *The Cambridge Ancient History*, IV (Cambridge, 1930), 138–140, 151–153, 157–159, 163, 167–172, 265–267; J. A. R. Munro *CAH* IV 230–232, 249–250; B. D. Meritt, "An Early Archon List," *Hesperia*, VIII (1939), 59–65.

[2] I use the term "aristocrats" to denote the conservative or oligarchical nobles, as opposed to the liberal, though by birth aristocratic, Alkmaionidai.

Athens; further, he separates foreign policy from domestic strife, more especially in dealing with the trial of Miltiades in 493/2 B.C. Reference will be made in the course of this study to the incidental arguments of Walker, Munro, and Robinson.

I shall attempt to show, by a survey of the ancient evidence as a whole, (1) that the Alkmaionidai were always hostile to the tyrants and so must be called anti-Persian, and that after 510 B.C. they were also anti-Spartan; (2) that the aristocrats, the friends of Sparta, were anti-Persian (decidedly so after 510), despite their apparent tolerance of the active tyranny at Athens; (3) that no strong pro-Persian element existed at Athens after ca. 510; (4) that, although in the years of peace with Persia domestic politics were influenced by foreign policy, when Persia threatened Hellas (in 498, 490, and 480) domestic quarrels were by common consent postponed in favour of a unified foreign policy.

The chief point at issue concerns the attitude of the Alkmaionidai towards Sparta, towards the tyrants and their sympathizers, and therefore towards Persia, whose expressed wish at Athens was the restoration of Hippias.[1] A survey of the relations between the Alkmaionidai and the tyrants, then, will be of the utmost pertinence to the present enquiry.

The Alkmaionidai and Peisistratos were hostile to one another from the beginning. Megakles and his kin fled upon Peisistratos' entrance into Athens as tyrant, and Peisistratos' first expulsion was due to the united efforts of the *pediakoi* and the *paralioi* (i.e., Alkmaionidai). The Alkmaionidai, however, never remained on good terms with any group or power for very long and in 560 (or 559), when the coalition at Athens disintegrated, Peisistratos returned to Athens at the invitation of Megakles, the Alkmaionid leader. This temporary political union, weakly bound by Peisistratos' unproductive marriage to Megakles' daughter, ended in the second expulsion of the tyrant, engineered by the disappointed and incensed Megakles. The restoration of Peisistratos in 546 B.C. was the signal for the withdrawal of the Alkmaionidai, who, during their long exile, must have progressed considerably

---

[1] Herodotos V 96. 2 (ca. 501 B.C.): ὁ δὲ ᾽Αρταφρένης ἐκέλευέ σφεας, εἰ βουλοίατο σόοι εἶναι, καταδέκεσθαι ὀπίσω ῾Ιππίην.

towards earning the title μισοτύραννοι applied to them by Herodotos.[1]

Until recently there has existed no reason for doubting that the Alkmaionidai were forced to remain away from Attica from 546 to 511/0 B.C.; in the latter year Hippias and the active Peisistratidai were driven from the state and the exiles came home.[2] Epigraphical studies, however, have again supplemented the literary sources, for a fragment of a sixth century archon list (inscribed about 425 B.C.) from the Agora excavations, in which [h]ιππία[s], [K]λεισθέν[es], and [M]ιλτιάδες are certain entries for the years 526/5, 525/4, and 524/3 B.C., now provides indisputable evidence of an unsuspected reconciliation between Hippias and the Alkmaionidai.[3] Once more the friendship was temporary, as we know that in 513 B.C. the Alkmaionidai resorted to arms at Leipsydrion in an unsuccessful effort to dislodge Hippias.[4] Sometime between 524 and 513 the Alkmaionidai had found Athens unhealthy. As Meritt infers, the change in their fortunes should most likely be connected with the assassination of Hipparchos in 514 B.C. and the increasingly harsh tyranny which followed;[5] the attempt at Leipsydrion in the next year thus represents an immediate retaliation.

The Alkmaionidai now ingratiated themselves at Delphi and soon (in 511/0 B.C.) we find them, with Sparta as their ally and after an initial Spartan failure, driving Hippias and his immediate supporters from Athens.[6]

---

[1] Herodotos I 60–64; Plutarch *Solon* 30; Aristotle Ἀθηναίων Πολιτεία 14–15; Herodotos VI 121. 1, 123. 1 (Alkmaionidai called μισοτύραννοι); for the exiles and tyrannies of Peisistratos, I accept the chronology of F. E. Adcock, "The Exiles of Peisistratus," *The Classical Quarterly*, XVIII (1924), 174–181, especially 181.

[2] Herodotos V 64–66. 1; Aristotle Ἀθ. Πολ. 19, 22. 4.

[3] Meritt *Hesperia* VIII 60–62; the general reconciliation among Miltiades (the younger), Kleisthenes, and Hippias should be placed directly after the death of Peisistratos. Hippias clearly attempted to begin his rule in a harmonious atmosphere, and was willing to overlook the past.

[4] Herodotos V 62. 2; Aristotle Ἀθ. Πολ. 19. 3.

[5] Herodotos V 55, 62. 2; Aristotle Ἀθ. Πολ. 19. 1; Thucydides VI 59. 2.

[6] Herodotos V 62. 2 – 65; Aristotle Ἀθ. Πολ. 19; cf. 22. 4. Since Hippias' movements have much influence on the history of Athens in the next 20 years, I shall trace them here. The Peisistratids fled to Sigeion, where Hegesistratos, son of

Despite the fact that Kleomenes himself, with a Spartan force, supplied the military persuasion, it was the scheming of the Alkmaionidai, as Herodotos relates,[1] that banished tyranny from Athens for all time. Nevertheless, the Alkmaionidai did not immediately attain their goal, the leadership of Athens. The aristocrats, directed in the ensuing factional strife by Isagoras, offered stout resistance,[2] for Isagoras, after conducting a revision of the citizenship rolls[3] and besting Kleisthenes, was elected archon for 508/7 B.C.[4] This revision of the census struck directly at the former *diakrioi*, residents of metic and impure Athenian descent, who, with the poorer classes, had formed the bulk of Peisistratos' support.[5] We may observe that Kleisthenes was astute enough to attach to himself the loyalty of this drifting popular element, to whom his new democratic programme most appealed.[6] Kleisthenes' partnership with the *demos* meant that the mass of those whose favour the tyrants had courted could hope for civic security only by rallying about the standard of the Alkmaionid; this manoeuvre really marks the first step in the history of the Alkmaionidai as the professed champions of democracy (προστάται τοῦ δήμου). Their initial adherence to the democratic cause was motivated by their own driving ambition to attain political supremacy at Athens. The immediate effect of Kleisthenes' policy was to

---

Peisistratos, had ruled (Herodotos V 65. 3, 94. 1; Thucydides VI 59. 4), no doubt with Persian consent. Thence Hippias went to Lampsakos, where he had prepared a safe refuge (Thucydides VI 59. 2 – 4), travelled to Sparta in 504 to plead at the Peloponnesian congress (Herodotos V 91–94), only to return to Sigeion when his case proved unattractive (Herodotos V 94. 1). We next find him (ca. 501 B.C.) maligning the Athenians to the satrap Artaphrenes (Herodotos V 96. 1). It must have been soon after this that he reached Dareios at Sousa, whence he set out for Marathon with the invaders (Thucydides VI 59. 4). Upon the accession of Xerxes there were still members of the house of Peisistratos at the Persian court (Herodotos VII 6. 2).

[1] Herodotos VI 123; cf. Aristotle 'Αθ. Πολ. 20. 4.
[2] Aristotle 'Αθ. Πολ. 20. 1.
[3] Herodotos V 69. 2; Aristotle 'Αθ. Πολ. 13. 5.
[4] Aristotle 'Αθ. Πολ. 21. 1.
[5] Aristotle 'Αθ. Πολ. 13. 5, 14. 1, 16. 2; Plutarch *Solon* 29-30.
[6] Herodotos V 66. 2; Aristotle 'Αθ. Πολ. 20. 4, 21. 1; *Politics* III 1. 10 (1275b).

remove from the ranks of those who might have welcomed the return of Hippias, despite the general unpopularity of his last few years as tyrant, a large number who now accepted Kleisthenes as their spokesman. Later, many of them swung behind Themistokles. These exchanges of loyalties explain, partially at least, why there never did exist in Athens after the expulsion of Hippias any considerable body of sympathy with the cause of the tyrants. Kleisthenes had destroyed the tyranny, appropriated its supporters, and had rendered a restoration of the tyranny, from within at any rate, almost impossible of achievement.

Sparta now (in 508/7 B.C.) took a further hand in Athenian affairs, at the invitation of Isagoras. The Athenian aristocrat and the Spartan king joined forces against the Alkmaionidai, the recent allies of Sparta, with the intention of consolidating Isagoras' position as director of Athenian policy.[1] We need do no more than recall the discomfiture of Kleomenes' expedition, the failure of the plan for invasion a year or so later,[2] and the similar failure at the congress of Sparta in 504 B.C. of the proposal to restore Hippias to Athens.[3] We must digress, however, to discuss the motive behind the remarkable change of Spartan front displayed in 504.

It is true that Peisistratos had maintained friendly relations with Sparta, it is equally true that the Spartans, after the attempted coup of 508/7 had failed and the projected invasion of Attica had collapsed, affected a belated disgust at learning of the Alkmaionid lobbying at Delphi and suddenly remembered, rather self-righteously, their ancient friendship with Peisistratos.[4] All these protestations, however, were no more than camouflage and did not deceive the Peloponnesian delegates at Sparta, of whom the Korinthian spokesman was representative, in the slightest degree.

Spartan policy had changed since the days of Peisistratos, the Peloponnesian League was an actuality, and Hippias had proved by no means the able diplomat that his father had been before him.[5]

---

[1] Aristotle 'Aθ. Πολ. 20. 2–3; Herodotos V 70, 72. 1–2; Thucydides I 126. 12; Pausanias III 4. 2; scholiast (ed. Dübner) on Aristophanes *Lysistrata* 273.

[2] Herodotos V 74–75.   [3] Herodotos V 91–94.

[4] Herodotos V 63. 2, 90. 1; Aristotle 'Aθ. Πολ. 19. 4.

[5] See Adcock *CAH* IV 77–79.

Sparta, by 511/0, was recognized as the champion of free Greeks against tyrants.[1] Athens had won alliance with Plataia in 519 B.C.[2] and was too friendly with Thessaly and Argos to suit Sparta.[3] Hippias' relations with Persia after the assassination of Hipparchos furnished more grounds for suspicion at Sparta, for he soon married his daughter to Aiantides, tyrant of Lampsakos and client of Persia, thus providing himself with a safe refuge in case trouble should develop at home.[4] The Spartans, while fulfilling their mission to crush tyranny in mainland Greece, had expected as usual to usher an aristocratic (oligarchic) government into a freed and grateful Athens, that is, a government that would show a proper deference to Sparta. The pressure exerted upon Delphi by the Alkmaionids provided Sparta with a convenient excuse for her professedly disinterested interference; but she was anti-tyrant, not pro-Alkmaionid. Her coöperation with the Alkmaionidai was unnatural and transitory. Any alliance of the moment was satisfactory to Sparta in 511/0, provided only that it promised her a footing in prospering Athens. Such a footing was normally supplied by a pro-Spartan aristocracy, and that Sparta had not entirely miscalculated may be deduced from the immediate rise of Isagoras, even though the latter's eventual fate disappointed his Peloponnesian friends and taxed the ingenuity of Kleomenes for some years.

In view of the share taken by Sparta in the expulsion of Hippias in 511/0, her reversal of policy in 504 B.C. needs explanation. It is not sufficient to state with Walker[5] that Sparta, still striving to establish a government subservient to herself at Athens, looked to her bygone friendship with the tyrants and anticipated a repatriated and obligated Hippias as a means of obtaining her will. This may not even be a contributing factor; the easier method of secur-

---

[1] Plutarch *de malignitate Herodoti* 21; scholiast on Aischines 2. 77 (p. 56 Dindorf); A. S. Hunt, *Catalogue of the Greek Papyri in the John Rylands Library* (Manchester, 1911), no. 18; cf. Thucydides I 18. 1; Adcock *CAH* IV 74.

[2] Thucydides III 68. 5; Herodotos VI 108.

[3] Herodotos V 63. 3, I 61. 4; Aristotle 'Αθ. Πολ. 17. 4, 19. 4; Plutarch *Cato* 24. 8.

[4] Thucydides VI 59. 2–3.

[5] *CAH* IV 163.

ing pro-Spartan government would still have consisted in full support for the Athenian aristocrats, who were far more acceptable to most Athenians than was the already discredited tyrant. Sparta's lack of success on behalf of her natural allies, Isagoras and the conservatives, had been and continued to be a blow to Spartan prestige, a blow which must at all costs be avenged. So after two failures, one in Athens and one on the borders of Attica, Sparta now resorted to more desperate measures and proposed to the delegates gathered at Sparta in 504 B.C. the restoration of Hippias. The dominating figure present was Kleomenes, a Spartan king unique for personal independence of thought, notorious for his tenacity of purpose, and possessed of a peculiarly unforgiving spirit; he was in a large measure responsible for the powerful Sparta of the fifth century, with its solid confederation. Now Athens, with the Alkmaionidai directing her course, was becoming too strong,[1] and worse still, Sparta and her ambitious king had twice been foiled in attempts to oust these same Alkmaionidai. Kleomenes' first thought at the congress was, by any means at hand, to discipline the Alkmaionidai. He had failed twice, now he must propose a new plan. And the most effective weapon that could be brandished against the Alkmaionidai was a threat to restore the tyranny. With Hippias in Athens the Alkmaionidai must be elsewhere, as they well realized. Other factions in Athens would tolerate the presence of the Alkmaionidai, a ruling tyranny could never do so.

In 508/7 B.C., after Kleomenes' failure, the Athenians, anticipating Spartan reprisals, sent an embassy to Persia seeking alliance. Walker's view[2] is that Kleisthenes himself was responsible for the despatch of this embassy, preferring "to secure the cause of democracy even at the cost of submission to Persia." But how would submission to Persia (and with it the certain restoration of Hippias[3]) secure the cause of democracy? Discussing the passage of Herodotos Walker writes, "It is an obvious inference from the phrasing that the embassy was sent soon after the recall of Cleisthenes; that is, it was sent at a moment when his influence was at

---

[1] Herodotos V 66. 1.
[2] *CAH* IV 157–158.
[3] For the movements of Hippias see pp. 73–74, note 6.

its height." Herodotos says,[1] . . . Ἀθηναῖοι δὲ μετὰ ταῦτα Κλει-
σθένεα καὶ τὰ ἑπτακόσια ἐπίστια τὰ διωχθέντα ὑπὸ Κλεομένεος μετα-
πεμψάμενοι πέμπουσι ἀγγέλους ἐς Σάρδις, συμμαχίην βουλόμενοι
ποιήσασθαι πρὸς Πέρσας. Is the inference really obvious? The
Athenians, upon Kleomenes' ignominious departure, make two
decisions: (1) they send for Kleisthenes and the other exiles, and
(2), having sent word of recall to Kleisthenes, they despatch envoys to Persia. Both resolutions were probably voted at a single
meeting. This analysis does no violence to the tenses of Herodotos
and is more logical historically. The Athenians expected invasion
from the Peloponnese and so entertained hopes of a Persian alliance
to hold off the Spartans. There are two significant factors which
militate against the view that Kleisthenes was responsible for the
embassy. One is that a Persian alliance meant the restoration of
Hippias. The second is implied by Walker himself. "That Cleisthenes, . . . who was possibly better acquainted with the circumstances of the Persian empire than most people at Athens, should
have imagined that Persian aid could be obtained on any other
condition than that of giving earth and water, the symbols of
homage to the Great King, is incredible. . . . It is not less incredible
that he should have sent the envoys without instructions on the
question of earth and water. . . . No doubt Cleisthenes was careful
not to explain to the Assembly the conditions on which the alliance of Persia was to be obtained." With all this there is no arguing; but what is really most incredible of all is that Kleisthenes for
one moment imagined that the Athenian Assembly would think of
accepting an alliance on such terms. Kleisthenes could have evaded
the initial explanation to the Assembly, but the complete dis-
closure could scarcely have been avoided upon the return of the
embassy, when awkward questions must have arisen. And well
as Kleisthenes may have been acquainted with the circumstances
of the Persian empire, he was far better acquainted with his own
people. The history of the Alkmaionidai is stormy, but they never
hastened to commit political suicide with their eyes open. No
matter how the embassy to Persia may be explained, Kleisthenes
must be absolved from all connexion with it.

[1] Herodotos V 73. 1.

Nor need Kleisthenes' sudden disappearance from the political scene be construed as inexplicable except as the result of disgrace incurred among the Athenians because of the embassy.[1] We do not know the year of Kleisthenes' birth but the marriage of his parents, Megakles and Agariste, is generally dated about 570 B.C.;[2] it can scarcely be placed later. Kleisthenes, the eldest son, was not a young man when he opposed Isagoras; a natural death soon after 507 B.C. should not be considered untimely — and the resultant sudden disappearance is anything but inexplicable. The silence of our sources is not alarming or suspicious, for a great man's death is far less likely to earn comment than is his disgrace.[3]

Shortly after the congress of Sparta the Athenians sent a second embassy to Sardes.[4] This suggests not, as Meritt claims,[5] that Athens was on good terms with Persia (which was impossible after the earlier embassy), but that she was most anxious to defend her own conduct, and thus to *establish* friendly relations and free herself from the menace of which she had been conscious for some years. That menace became all the more vivid when the envoys were rebuffed and Persia loomed in Athenian minds as rather more than a potential enemy.[6] We hear nothing of Athenian politics for the next few years, during which the city probably experienced comparative peace.[7] When Aristagoras reached Athens in 498 on

---

[1] Walker *CAH* IV 167–168.

[2] Wade-Gery, *CAH* III 555. According to Adcock's chronology (see p. 73, note 1) Peisistratos married Megakles' daughter about 559 B.C.; if this is correct the marriage of Megakles and Agariste must have occurred several years earlier than 570.

[3] A passage in Aristotle ('Αθ. Πολ. 22. 1–4; cf. 28. 2) suggests that Kleisthenes' disappearance was not so sudden as Walker thinks. The democratic reforms of the Alkmaionidai, associated by Aristotle with Kleisthenes himself, the leader of the party, must have covered several years; one measure is actually dated in 504/3. The programme stood or fell with its proponent and could scarcely have progressed as it did had Kleisthenes, the champion of the people after Isagoras' defeat, fallen from favour. That the Alkmaionidai did not lose popularity after 508/7 is also implied by the fact that Alkmaion was archon in 507/6 B.C. (Pollux VIII 110).

[4] Herodotos V 96.

[5] *Hesperia* VIII 63.

[6] Herodotos V 96. 2.

[7] After the debacle of 508/7 the aristocrats were without a leader. Isagoras

behalf of the Ionians, however, the question of foreign policy once more arose.

Walker builds a coalition between the Alkmaionidai and the party of the tyrants at the time of Aristagoras' presence in Athens.[1] "There are three facts to be taken into account in this connection. A fleet is sent to the aid of the Ionians; it consists of only 20 vessels; and it is recalled on the first reverse to the insurgents." On these three facts Walker bases his reconstruction of the power and policies of the parties in Athens. But are these the facts? After Aristagoras had won over the Athenians, says Herodotos,[2] Ἀθηναῖοι μὲν δὴ ἀναπεισθέντες ἐψηφίσαντο εἴκοσι νέας ἀποστεῖλαι βοηθοὺς Ἴωσι, στρατηγὸν ἀποδέξαντες αὐτῶν εἶναι Μελάνθιον, ἄνδρα τῶν ἀστῶν ἐόντα τὰ πάντα δόκιμον. αὗται δὲ αἱ νέες ἀρχὴ κακῶν ἐγένοντο Ἕλλησί τε καὶ βαρβάροισι. Here there is no belittling of the Athenian squadron; "*only* 20 ships" is a modern version.[3] Its rightness or wrongness will be examined below; but it must not be read into Herodotos. The simple facts, according to the ancient account, are thus reduced to two: the Athenians sent 20 ships to aid the Ionians; they were withdrawn after the first reverse. The question that now arises is, did 20 ships constitute a half-hearted effort, that is, was the despatch of 20 ships a victory for the pro-Persian faction at Athens?

The best evidence of Athenian power by sea comes from Herodotos' account of the feud between Aigina and Athens. Before considering the Aiginetan war we may allude briefly to other campaigns of the period. Nothing is known of Athenian naval operations in the year of Marathon,[4] but it is perhaps significant of

---

was probably in exile (Herodotos V 74. 1) and Miltiades had not yet been compelled to leave the Chersonese. The friends of the tyrants were not important as a political force (see pp. 92–93 below).

[1] *CAH* IV 168–169.

[2] Herodotos V 97. 3.

[3] That the Athenians made their decision "after considerable debate" (Robinson *AJP* LX 232) is also unrecorded by Herodotos, who gives just the opposite impression of Aristagoras' success (V 97. 2): πολλοὺς γὰρ οἶκε εἶναι εὐπετέστερον διαβάλλειν ἢ ἕνα, εἰ Κλεομένεα μὲν τὸν Λακεδαιμόνιον μοῦνον οὐκ οἷός τε ἐγένετο διαβάλλειν, τρεῖς δὲ μυριάδας Ἀθηναίων ἐποίησε τοῦτο.

[4] Munro *CAH* IV 237, suggests that the Athenian fleet was stationed at Oro-

Athenian naval weakness that, even when the Persians appeared off Phaleron, there is still no mention of the possibility of Athenian maritime opposition. In the next year Miltiades persuaded the Athenians to equip 70 ships for his Parian adventure.[1] This was an extraordinary expedition, however, and the success of Miltiades' request was due to his personal prestige won at Marathon and to the willingness of the victory-flushed Athenians to listen to his optimistic promises.

We now return to the Aiginetan episode. The intricacies of the chronological and other problems do not affect the present investigation.[2] The pertinent fact from the Unheralded War, whether it is assigned to ca. 506 or ca. 488 B.C., is that the Aiginetans were able to raid the Attic coast with impunity and wreak considerable damage.[3] The Athenians offered no adequate defence against the islanders; "nor had the Athenians as yet any fleet to resist them."[4] After the seizure of the sacred vessel off Sounion (ca. 488), Athens and Aigina clashed by sea. Athens appreciated the fact that her navy was no match for that of Aigina and a plot to take the island from within misfired because the Athenian ships did not dare move until reinforced by 20 unpunctual Korinthians; apparently Athens needed all the ships she could muster before confronting the power of Aigina. In the battle which followed the Aiginetans were opposed by a squadron of 70, this figure including the 20 Korinthians; that is, Athens herself manned 50 vessels in her vigorous effort to crush Aigina, who, on this occasion, merely matched the allied fleet.[5]

---

pos (or Chalkis) to maintain communications. Later (*op. cit.* 241), he places it at Chalkis and assumes that the Persian squadron was in command of the channel between Oropos and Eretria; if so, the Persians had manoeuvred into a position between the Athenian ships and Athens, a presumption which is not entirely convincing.

[1] Herodotos VI 132.
[2] I follow Munro's account, *CAH* IV 254–259, 263–265.
[3] Herodotos V 81. 2–3.
[4] George Grote, *A History of Greece* (new edition, London, John Murray, 1888), III 390.
[5] Herodotos VI 87–93, see especially 89: οὐ γὰρ ἔτυχον ἐοῦσαι νέες σφι ἀξιόμαχοι τῇσι Αἰγινητέων συμβαλεῖν.

The triumph of Aigina led to her thalassocracy, which is assigned to the decade between the Persian invasions.[1] The future policy of Athens corroborates the tradition, for it was in an attempt to break this supremacy (theoretically at least) that Themistokles persuaded the Athenians (in 482 B.C.) to build 200 new triremes,[2] "an effort out of all proportion to anything that Athens had yet attempted. In the greatness of the effort we may find some measure of the success of Aegina and the humiliation of Athens."[3] These 200 ships formed the Athenian navy when Xerxes descended upon Greece,[4] at a time when Athens had to man every available vessel. To summarize: the Athenians commenced the building of their 200 triremes in 482, after humiliation on the sea at the hands of Aigina; in 480 the entire navy, 200 ships, was ready for action. Of course, Athenian warships were afloat before 482; but their number and prestige, compared to the later fleet, must have been negligible beside the sea-power of any state that boasted naval aspirations worthy of respect.

This survey of naval operations reveals that not once during the period did the Athenians muster as many as 100 ships, in fact the largest force manned down to the year of Salamis was 70 (for Miltiades' Parian expedition), and this was a special venture.[5] It is perhaps more revealing that only 50 Athenian ships were engaged in the crucial battle of the Aiginetan war. It was only through an extraordinary effort and as the result of an opportune stroke of economic luck that she could raise 200 triremes to meet her most severe test. If this is the case, then the 20 ships sent to

---

[1] Cf. Munro *CAH* IV 264.

[2] Herodotos VII 144. Before the Aiginetan war Athens was not a naval power: οὗτος γὰρ ὁ πόλεμος συστὰς ἔσωσε τότε τὴν Ἑλλάδα, ἀναγκάσας θαλασσίους γενέσθαι Ἀθηναίους.

[3] Munro *CAH* IV 265.

[4] Herodotos VIII 1, 14. 1; note that 20 of these were manned by the inhabitants of Chalkis, others by inexperienced Plataians.

[5] When Athens risked the expedition to Paros she had just emerged triumphant from a David and Goliath struggle against Persia; and Paros was within easy hailing distance in case of emergency. The sending of 20 ships all the way to Asia Minor in 498, before Athens had made her mark at home, was a very different matter.

aid the Ionians should not be dismissed so lightly. They must in reality have represented an appreciable percentage of Athens' sea-power, even if in 498 she could count as many as 70 ships, an assumption that would be hazardous. Attempts to belittle this squadron arise from an unconscious comparison with Athenian maritime strength later in the century. The criterion for judgment should rather be the number of vessels at Athens' command in the generation before Salamis. Thus the Athenians, as they saw the problem, aided Ionia very considerably. When the Ionians took to the sword against Persia there was every reason for concern at Athens. Aside from the fact that Athens was recognized as the metropolis of the Ionians[1] and so was open to claims of kinship, there existed commercial and political ties to account for Athenian sympathy with Ionia. The Athenian merchants naturally favoured Ionia, whose once flourishing prosperity was falling into ruins under Persia; Athenian commercial bonds were with the east and not with the west. Hippias was still a Persian pensioner and Athens had twice defied the empire of Dareios after embassies had travelled into Persian territory to seek friendship. Every realistic Athenian statesman knew by now that Athenian boundaries lay not in Attica but in Ionia; if Persia could be beaten back before reaching Athenian soil, so much the better. In consequence Aristagoras experienced less difficulty than has sometimes been supposed, less perhaps than he had anticipated, in securing Athenian assistance.[2] To aid Ionia was only common sense and a unit of 20 ships, representing as great a force as Athens could spare (she was not free from menace at home; Aigina was probably unfriendly), was despatched to the Ionians, who were fighting Athens' war in the east.

We now meet Walker's affirmation that, upon receipt of the news of the first reverse in Ionia, the anti-Ionian coalition effected the withdrawal of the Athenian contingent from the war zone. It has already been urged that far-sighted statesmen in Athens realized that the Ionian cause was Athens' cause; hence the 20

[1] Herodotos V 97. 2.
[2] See p. 80, note 3. It is not even necessary to invoke "the Greek habit of caution" to explain the number of ships sent to Ionia (Robinson *AJP* LX 233, where "Persia" must be a slip for "Ionia").

ships. The burning of Sardes and the defeat of a combined Athenian-Eretrian-Ionian force at Ephesos was followed by the retirement of Athens from the war.[1] Now when the Athenians, at the behest of the persuasive Aristagoras, voted to assist Ionia, they did so in the expectation (optimistic indeed) of finishing on the winning side, in the hope, perhaps, of turning the scale against Persia. Instead, the first engagement brought defeat. In addition, Ionian conditions as described by Aristagoras were very different from the actual disunity and confusion that was probably apparent to the Athenian commanders. It was not so much the shock felt by the Athenians at the burning of Sardes as the utter hopelessness of eventual victory that influenced the return from Ionia. For the Athenians, who had already exasperated the Great King, it was, as Robinson says,[2] the merest common sense to withdraw before becoming involved in the inevitable crushing of Ionia. That Athens might live to fight another day, the city's policy must be one of polite appeasement to Persia. Just as, a few years ago, Athens had first affronted Persia (ca. 507) and then had professed friendship (ca. 501), so now she backed water in her efforts to convince the Great King that her hostile act had been a mistake, voted in an absent-minded moment of folly. This retreat was both military and diplomatic, consisting of the withdrawal of troops from Ionia and the election, possibly in two successive years, of archons who could be pointed to as friendly to Persia.

Perhaps Athens, who had for years distrusted and feared Persia, found it difficult to stomach a policy of appeasement. There could be no question of another embassy, but she could publicly profess an absence of hostility to Persia's suspected friends in the city. A method lay conveniently ready and here was the opportunity for a coalition, not of the type assumed by Walker or Robinson, but a coalition among all the parties for the sake of Athens' safety in the near future. There still resided in Athens members of the Peisistratid house, and if one or more of these should hold the chief magistracy, the city could support her claim that no oppression of Persia's friends in Athens existed. We have always known that

---

[1] Herodotos V 101–103. 1.
[2] *AJP* LX 233.

Hipparchos, son of Charmos and a Peisistratid, was archon eponymous for 496/5 B.C.[1] But perhaps Athenian reaction set in even more quickly, for Meritt's recent argument in favour of placing the archonship of Peisistratos, son of Hippias, in 497/6 is attractive historically and epigraphically; tentatively, it may be accepted. Meritt's sound analysis of the situation in Athens just after the battle of Ephesos has helped to bring comprehension and order to a hitherto confusing period.[2] The Athenians were thoroughly alarmed by the unfortunate turn of events in Ionia and the prompt election of Peisistratos to the archonship reflects their emotions in what seemed very properly[3] a critical hour.

According to this interpretation Walker's evidence for a coalition at the beginning of the century does not exist. Robinson also rejects Walker's conclusion, only to substitute for it a political alliance between the friends of the tyrants and the aristocrats, an even more incomprehensible theory and one to which we shall return in due course.

The next few years witnessed the rise of Themistokles; and just as the Alkmaionidai had once appealed to the previous admirers of the tyrants, so now Themistokles outbid the Alkmaionidai for the support of the same popular element. The Alkmaionidai seized the opportunity offered by the return of Miltiades (in 493), but their effort to convict him and simultaneously to discredit Themistokles, who was usurping their democratic leadership, failed when reasons of both domestic and foreign policy persuaded the *novus homo* and the aristocratic chief to combine their political resources.[4]

We pass on to the year of Marathon. A glance at the previous history of the Alkmaionidai leaves the critical reader extremely reluctant to accept the story current in the time of Herodotos, that

---

[1] Dionysios of Halikarnassos *Antiquitates Romanae* V 77. 6, VI 1. 1.

[2] *Hesperia* VIII 62–65; but I cannot agree that the burning of Sardes was the primary motive for the withdrawal from Ionia. (It should be observed that the placing of Peisistratos' archonship in 497/6 is not essential to the historical argument; the certain magistracy of Hipparchos in the following year is sufficient.)

[3] Herodotos V 105.

[4] Herodotos VI 104. 2; cf. Walker *CAH* IV 170–172; Munro *CAH* IV 230–232. The charge (tyranny in the Chersonese) is of no significance.

they were responsible for a treacherous signal to the Persians after the battle. The best defence of the Athenian family is still to be found in the pages of Herodotos, who considers the story absolutely incredible.[1] His opening remark deserves more credence than it has apparently received: Θῶμα δέ μοι καὶ οὐκ ἐνδέκομαι τὸν λόγον, 'Αλκμεωνίδας ἄν κοτε ἀναδέξαι Πέρσῃσι ἐκ συνθήματος ἀσπίδα, βουλομένους ὑπὸ βαρβάροισί τε εἶναι 'Αθηναίους καὶ ὑπὸ 'Ιππίῃ. (He then sketches the record of the Alkmaionidai, emphasizing that they were μισοτύραννοι and had been chiefly responsible for the expulsion of the tyrants.) Herodotos realized that capitulation to Persia meant the return of tyranny to Athens, and that the latter spelled ruin for the Alkmaionidai. Herodotos, therefore, in referring at once to the barbarians and Hippias, has grasped the essential absurdity of the story; unfortunately the rejection of Herodotean evidence has been overdone and the wheat is often discarded with the chaff.[2] The most recent treatment of the incident is by Hudson,[3] who, while discounting the probability of Alkmaionid guilt under any circumstances, concludes that no signal at all was displayed by conspirators in Athens. The story took root, one may surmise, in the days when Perikles met bitter opposition, first from Kimon and then from Thucydides, son of Melesias. "The Athenians knew their Alcmaeonidae, and readily believed the accusation which Herodotos treats as incredible."[4] Quite so; anything could be ascribed to the Alkmaionidai and be sure of finding credulous ears. The opponents of the Alkmaionidai and Perikles were as resourceful as they were politically unscrupulous.

If the Alkmaionidai had been guilty of treason during the Persian invasion, then surely the Athenians, in the full flush of successful patriotism, would have been quick to turn upon them;

[1] Herodotos VI 121, 123–124.

[2] A. T. Olmstead, in another connexion, accepts the shield story and ignores Herodotos' criticism of it: *Classical Philology*, XXXIV (1939), 312.

[3] Harris Gary Hudson, "The Shield Signal at Marathon," *The American Historical Review*, XLII (1936–37), 443–459, especially 458–459. See also Grote *History of Greece* IV 44–45 for a defence of the Alkmaionidai which appreciates the competence of Herodotos.

[4] Munro *CAH* IV 250, a flimsy case against the Alkmaionidai.

obviously the story was unknown in Athens at just the time when it should have been most vivid. In the year after Marathon, however, two facts confirm the innocence of the Alkmaionidai: Aristeides was archon[1] and Miltiades the Philaid fell victim to party strife, prosecuted by Xanthippos.[2] The Alkmaionidai were clearly in high favour and Themistokles, playing his own individualistic game, no longer felt it expedient to support their opponents. In 488/7 occurred the first of several ostracisms suffered by the friends of the tyrants, when Hipparchos, son of Charmos, was compelled to leave the city.[3] The Athenians had lost much of the awe that they had once possessed for Persia and had decided to settle their tyrant question once and for all by removing all possible sympathizers with the Peisistratidai. This they could do by putting into active service the weapon, forged by Kleisthenes against potential tyranny specifically,[4] which they had so far not had the courage to employ.

In 487/6 Megakles, son of Hippokrates and head of the Alkmaionid house, was ostracized. That Aristotle includes him among the friends of the tyrants is not significant, for with the defeat of Megakles should be associated very closely another event of the same year, the application of the lot to the archonship. In each case we can detect the hand of Themistokles. He was the first to recognize the political value of ostracism, and by merely shouting "tyrant," disposed of a formidable opponent. Now Themistokles had the upper hand. Miltiades was dead and his son Kimon had neither the years nor the dignity as yet to assume the leadership of the Philaidai; the Alkmaionidai had also lost the head of their house. It comes as no surprise to learn that in the next few years first the alleged friends of the tyrants and then Xanthippos (485/4) and Aristeides (483/2)[5] followed their chiefs into ostra-

---

[1] Plutarch *Aristides* 5. 10.
[2] Herodotos VI 136.
[3] For the ostracisms of the decade and for the application of the lot to the archonship see Aristotle 'Αθ. Πολ. 22. 3–8.
[4] Aristotle 'Αθ. Πολ. 22. 3–4: θαρροῦντος ἤδη τοῦ δήμου τότε πρῶτον ἐχρήσαντο τῷ νόμῳ τῷ περὶ τὸν ὀστρακισμόν. . . .
[5] Plutarch *Aristides* 7. 2.

cism. These moves, however, arose entirely from domestic politics, as is shown by the amnesty passed in 481 in the face of a fresh Persian invasion and the consequent return of Aristeides and Xanthippos, both of whom proceeded to work with Themistokles against the Persian. The fall of Miltiades and the ostracisms of the decade (except perhaps in the case of Hipparchos and his close friends) should not be connected with foreign policy at Athens.

Having tried the Alkmaionidai and found them not guilty of medism, we shall next investigate the similar charge laid against the Athenian aristocrats by Robinson. The same method may be followed, that is, we shall review aristocratic relations with the tyrants and with Sparta, briefly indeed, since some of the ground has already been covered. We should also, as Meritt has suggested, appraise Aristotle's judgment of Isagoras as φίλος ὢν τῶν τυράννων. To this we may add his earlier remark, that most of the notables and *demotikoi* wanted Peisistratos: ἐβούλοντο γὰρ καὶ τῶν γνωρίμων καὶ τῶν δημοτικῶν οἱ πολλοί.[1] Are these statements, which apply to the period before 510, sufficient to justify us in painting the aristocrats with a Persian brush in 498 B.C.?

First let us note that originally Peisistratos formed his party of landless malcontents against the *pediakoi* specifically.[2] There was a natural and bitter opposition between the aristocrats, who, true to aristocratic tradition, held most of the land and meant to maintain their privileged position, and the motley group whom we know as the *diakrioi*, whose position in the state was tenuous; it is the usual class war between the "haves" and the "have nots." Peisistratos, in distributing land to these newcomers, attacked the very root of aristocratic principle. It is most enlightening that upon the expulsion of Hippias in 511/0 Isagoras' first act was to revise the citizen list and thus deprive of the franchise many who had looked upon the tyrants as their saviours.[3]

Shortly after Peisistratos' first appearance as tyrant the *pediakoi* and *paralioi* united to expel him (560); then Megakles invited him back to aid the Alkmaionidai against the aristocrats (560/59). A

---

[1] Aristotle 'Αθ. Πολ. 20. 1, 16. 9; Meritt *Hesperia* VIII 62.
[2] Aristotle *Politics* V 4. 5 (1305a).
[3] See p. 74 above.

few years later (556), only the assistance of the aristocrats can explain Megakles' success in forcing Peisistratos from Athens a second time. In all this shifting of sides the aristocrats do not once appear in combination with Peisistratos. This was natural enough, for the aristocrats, though disapproving of the Alkmaionidai, had far more in common with them, their social peers, than with the radical Peisistratid family and its policies, whatever the origins of Peisistratos himself. When the tyrant was finally established in Athens (546) the Alkmaionidai left Attica. Herodotos reports that some Athenians accompanied the Alkmaionidai into exile, and that Peisistratos took hostages from the Athenians who remained in the city and did not flee immediately.[1] Perhaps certain of the aristocrats are included in these groups; with the Alkmaionidai in flight, against what element other than the aristocratic did the tyrant need to take precautions?

There is nothing conjectural about the ill feeling which existed between the tyrants and the important Philaid family of Miltiades. Early in the tyranny Miltiades (the elder) sailed off to the Chersonese, glad to get away from a rule that irked him (... ἀχθόμενόν τε τῇ Πεισιστράτου ἀρχῇ καὶ βουλόμενον ἐκποδὼν εἶναι);[2] Peisistratos must have witnessed his departure with delight. Kimon, half brother to Miltiades, was not so fortunate. He was banished by Peisistratos, was allowed to return later when he surrendered the victor's glory at Olympia to the tyrant, and was slain finally by the sons of Peisistratos.[3] The latter sent Miltiades the younger to the Chersonese, οἵ μιν καὶ ἐν Ἀθήνῃσι ἐποίευν εὖ ὡς οὐ συνειδότες δῆθεν τοῦ πατρὸς αὐτοῦ Κίμωνος τὸν θάνατον.[4] Of Miltiades' later hostility to Persia and to the restoration of Hippias there is no doubt.

That the nobles were not entirely reconciled to the tyranny at Athens may also be implied by Aristotle's sentence concerning disclosures made by Aristogeiton (514 B.C.) under torture: κατηγόρησεν δ' ἐν ταῖς ἀνάγκαις πολλῶν οἳ καὶ τῇ φύσει τῶν ἐπιφανῶν καὶ φίλοι τοῖς τυράννοις ἦσαν.[5] There is perhaps more historical fact in this charge than has heretofore been supposed.

---

[1] Herodotos I 64.
[2] Herodotos VI 35.
[3] Herodotos VI 103. 1–3.

[4] Herodotos VI 39. 1.
[5] Aristotle Ἀθ. Πολ. 18. 4; cf. 5.

Isagoras, called a friend of the tyrants by Aristotle, was nevertheless, according to the same author, able in 508/7 to seek the aid of Kleomenes, ὄντα ἑαυτῷ ξένον.[1] A similar remark is found in Herodotos, who says that Isagoras summoned Kleomenes, γενόμενον ἑωυτῷ ξεῖνον ἀπὸ τῆς Πεισιστρατιδέων πολιορκίης.[2] Spartan conduct during this decade has already been examined.[3] It is sufficient here to emphasize that as soon as Isagoras' position in Athens was threatened, Kleomenes responded to his appeal for assistance, and that the projected invasion of 506 was undertaken on behalf of the now exiled Athenian. There can be no question of the natural sympathy existing between Sparta and the Athenian aristocrats from the last decade of the sixth century. This friendship continued as an important factor in fifth century Athenian politics. It is a mistake, however, to apply to the period after 510 the alleged friendship with the Peisistratid family (which was more an expedient tolerance) of the years when the tyrants were actually in power.

This summary treatment of aristocratic history in the sixth century should serve as a warning that Aristotle's φίλος ὢν τῶν τυράννων is not to be construed as connoting a political sympathy with tyranny, especially after 510 B.C. Even if in 546 most of the notables and *demotikoi* preferred Peisistratos to the violent turmoil that seemed so often to accompany the Alkmaionidai, Aristotle's two statements[4] must not be transferred to the years after Hippias' expulsion, when Kleisthenes (and later Themistokles) won over the tyrants' popular support and the aristocrats became intimate with Sparta. The most that can be granted is that during the latter half of the century aristocratic hostility to the tyrants was at first expediently quiescent; but that it gradually increased is implicit in the ancient accounts. Aristocratic murmurings, however, were quite overshadowed by the feud between the tyrants and the Alkmaionidai. This does not imply aristocratic satisfaction, only that the conservative element proved more diplomatic

---

[1] Aristotle ᾿Αθ. Πολ. 20. 2.
[2] Herodotos V 70. 1.
[3] See pp. 75–77 above.
[4] See p. 88 above.

than the Alkmaionidai. Even so, the fortunes of Miltiades and his family are indicative of aristocratic discontent. That the Alkmaionidai took the lead in expelling Hippias is not surprising, for they had most to win — a safe return to their native city. Yet it was the aristocrats who made the immediate gain from the successful intrigues of the Alkmaionidai, and in so doing they severed all friendly relations (genuine or assumed) with the Peisistratidai and consolidated their merger with Sparta. And no Athenian group could entertain pro-Spartan and pro-Persian feelings simultaneously.

After Isagoras' fatal error in 508/7 we hear little of the aristocrats for a few years, during which the democracy developed and the Alkmaionidai directed Athenian policies, domestic and foreign; the aristocratic eclipse, with Isagoras in disgrace and Miltiades still in the Chersonese, contributes to the comprehension of Kleomenes' proposal at the congress of Sparta. When the Ionian question became an issue at Athens, aristocratic views were undoubtedly pro-Ionian; no incident can be cited, before or after 498, which affords evidence of aristocratic leanings towards the tyrants or Persia. Aristocrats and Alkmaionidai, for the moment at any rate, saw eye to eye.

As we glance over the history of the years from 560 to 490 we notice a more or less latent hostility between aristocrats and tyrants, followed by an increasingly close coöperation between Sparta and the aristocrats; the irritation of Miltiades the elder, the death of his half-brother Kimon, and the violent hatred for Persia displayed by Miltiades the younger. To this add the indisputable fact that a sound aristocratic tradition stands behind the pronounced anti-Persian policy of the Philaid Kimon in the fifth century.

It is now time to gather the conclusions to which this investigation of Athenian policy leads. The evidence adduced above is sufficiently strong for us to deny that the Alkmaionidai were ever pro-Persian or that they could have favoured a restoration of the tyranny. At the time of the Ionian revolt the Alkmaionidai were firm in their anti-Persian convictions. The same is true in the year of Marathon, and the absurdity of the charge laid against them later is obscured only by the years that had elapsed. Of the situation in Athens just before Marathon, Munro writes:[1] "A war against Persia would be madness without Spartan assistance. But the Alcmaeonidae had good reason to apprehend what might be the price eventually to be paid for an alliance with Sparta — their own expulsion and the repeal of the new Constitution. Better come to terms with Hippias, restore the monarchy, and by sacrifice of the form preserve the substance of the democracy." Yet Athens, under the new democracy, had successfully coped with Sparta since 510 B.C., and the actual aftermath of Marathon proved that Sparta's interference in Athens was not inevitable. I see no valid reason for assuming Alkmaionid timidity before the Persian invasion. Of the two enemies Persia was certainly the more formidable. Thus the Alkmaionidai were hostile both to Sparta and to the tyrants, and (partly as a result) to the Athenian aristocrats and to Persia.[2] Alkmaionid ambitions and a lust for personal power, coupled with an utter lack of scruples, left the Alkmaionidai without enduring political friendships in Athens, and bitterly detested abroad.

The aristocrats, on the other hand, found a natural sympathy in Sparta and so may be justly termed pro-Spartan. Ample evidence vouches for their antipathy to the tyrants and to Persia, which after all conformed to Hellenic aristocratic tradition. And whereas a faction in Athens might be anti-Spartan and anti-Persian, it is next to impossible to label any group pro-Persian and pro-Spartan simultaneously.

If both the Alkmaionidai and the aristocrats realized the potential menace of Persia and accordingly were anti-Persian, then the alleged coalition of 498 B.C. has disappeared. If any opposition to the proposal to aid Ionia was heard in Athens it could have originated only with the friends of the tyrants in the city. Yet there is no evidence of party strife at this time and it is hazardous to create it by conjecture and theory. Some of the friends of the tyrants had been allowed to remain in Athens when Hippias was expelled, but only those who had taken no active part in the

---

[1] *CAH* IV 231.

[2] Cf. Hudson *AHR* XLII 459 note 79: ". . . but to be anti-Spartan at this juncture would mean to lean toward Persia." The error needs no further refutation

disorders of that year.[1] This forms no good reason for assuming a strong pro-tyrant group in Athens between 510 and 490. These inactive friends of Hippias were well aware of Athenian emotions towards Persia; of the commons who had looked kindly upon Hippias, the majority soon owed allegiance to the Alkmaionidai or to Themistokles. The friends of the tyrants were in Athens because they had rendered no aid to Hippias at a crisis in his career; now they had no popular support and they were on probation, so to speak. The situation was delicate and a careless move would have placed them in considerable jeopardy. We may perhaps go further and question whether these friends (with the possible exception of Hipparchos, Peisistratos, and one or two more) were seriously interested in the restoration of Hippias. We know of no activity on the part of the Peisistratidai in the *stasis* of 508, we are told nothing of support from Athens when Kleomenes threatened to restore Hippias in 504. It is true that the archon of 496/5 — perhaps also of 497/6 — was a Peisistratid, when a disturbed and uncomfortable Athens wished to assure Persia that she regretted her participation in the ill-organized Ionian revolt. But this was a move agreed upon by all the parties. In the year of Marathon every Athenian must have known that a Persian victory meant far more than the mere restoration of Hippias. The so-called supporters of the tyrants were Athenians, a fact which is often neglected and never properly stressed. Their choice was not between Athenian tyranny and Athenian democracy, but between Athenian democracy and Persian domination. The friends of Hippias had not been a powerful force in recent Athenian politics and the pressure to restore him had been applied from beyond the borders of Attica, not from within Athens. When the Persians approached Marathon and the friends of the tyrants could weigh the issues and make their choice, which cause did they choose?[2]

The presence of a pro-tyrant (or pro-Persian) faction inside Athens after 510, a quarry hunted for years by historians,[3] is not

---

[1] Aristotle ᾽Αθ. Πολ. 22. 4.

[2] Hudson presents a well-argued case against the shield signal emanating from Athenian traitors; see p. 86, note 3.

[3] E.g., Walker *CAH* IV 138.

supported by ancient testimony and such a faction makes no appearance in Athenian controversies between 510 and 490. My conclusion is that no appreciable pro-Persian or pro-tyrant party existed after the expulsion of Hippias and his closest adherents. Tyranny had rendered its service to the young city; politically, Athens had grown up.

Finally, we may advance certain proposals concerning the influence of party politics on Athenian foreign policy during the period with which this paper deals. It has already been shown that the supposed pro-Persian coalition of 498 B.C. is fictional, that the aid sent to Ionia, its speedy recall, and the resultant election of Peisistratidai to the archonship were moves supported by both the conservative aristocrats and by the Alkmaionidai. These two groups were traditionally bitter political enemies in the sixth and fifth centuries. Yet there is no ground for believing that their foreign policies, in 498, differed appreciably.

The next strange political alliance occurred in 493/2 B.C., when Miltiades' return as a fugitive from Persia was followed by his union with Themistokles and his prosecution by the Alkmaionidai. Miltiades, head of the proud Philaidai, was not a natural associate for Themistokles, a *novus homo*, with whom he had but one emotion in common, a deep hatred for Persia. Themistokles was the rising man at Athens, with no background to be sure, but enjoying the support of many who had previously followed the Alkmaionidai, and with the vision to perceive the approaching Persian cloud; his enmity to Persia is undisputed. Themistokles, therefore, had a double motive in gaining Miltiades as his ally: the latter would prove a perfect partner for his foreign policy, while in domestic circles he was well aware of the political prestige to be gained from association with the name Miltiades. The prosecution by the Alkmaionidai was wholly a matter of domestic politics and the charge, that of tyranny in the Chersonese, is important only insofar as it was the crime most likely to bring a conviction. Miltiades' conduct was also governed by considerations of both domestic and foreign policy, for Themistokles saw the foreign situation as clearly as he did himself, and Themistokles would prove a convenient helper against the initial onslaught of the

Alkmaionidai, his family's traditional political rivals. Thus the whole incident is not entirely a domestic matter, as Robinson claims, for only the Alkmaionidai were influenced by internal policies alone.

Party politics appear to have been more or less shelved now until after Marathon, for in the year of the campaign the only evidence for serious domestic disunion has grown from the story of the shield signal and its attribution to the Alkmaionidai, a signal which, as has been demonstrated, should not be construed as proof of medizing by the Alkmaionidai; its very historicity is questionable. With the departure of the Persians the old rivalries broke out anew. In the archonship of Aristeides, 489/8 B.C., Miltiades, the recent hero of Marathon, fell from grace, prosecuted by Xanthippos (husband of the Alkmaionid Agariste). The triumph of the Alkmaionidai was short-lived, however, for Themistokles, with his possibly awkward ally out of the way, proceeded to secure the ostracism of the Alkmaionid leaders and Hippias' kin. With the foreign threat temporarily checked Themistokles must have abandoned his support of Miltiades and allowed his natural political opponents, the two great families, to fight one another. The disgrace of Miltiades left Themistokles only one hostile party with which to cope.

For several years Themistokles stayed at the Athenian helm. Nevertheless, as soon as he realized that a second Persian invasion was imminent, a political amnesty was declared, Aristeides and Xanthippos (to name the leaders) returned to Athens to aid in the Greek defence, and in the campaigns that followed the Alkmaionid chiefs were prominent on the Athenian board of strategy.

The conclusion is obvious. We must recognize that policies at Athens were dictated by the international situation and its possible effect on the city. In the intervening years, with Athens free from actual danger from abroad, the division of party politics frequently split the citizens; and of course domestic and foreign affairs could not be entirely divorced. But when the Persian threat menaced the Athenians, the ranks could close and present a united front to the foe. Athens, in her crises, learned and appreciated the blessings of Nationalist government.

DIE KÄMPFE AM EURYMEDON

Von W. Peek

SEITDEM Eduard Meyer die Verworrenheit und Unglaubwür-
digkeit des auf Ephoros zurückgehenden Berichts über die
Doppelschlacht am Eurymedon bei Diodor XI 60 ff. eindrück-
lich dargelegt hat,[1] galt es lange Zeit als ausgemacht, dass neben
dem kurzen Hinweis bei Thukydides I 100 einzig die von Plutarch
im Leben des Kimon Kap. 12 f. gegebene Darstellung als zuver-
lässig gelten darf; E. Meyer hatte sie auf Kallisthenes zurückgeführt und auch damit allgemein Zustimmung gefunden.[2] Eine
eingehende Nachprüfung der Meyerschen Thesen hat erst W.
Graf Uxkull-Gyllenband in seinem Buch über "Plutarch und die
griechische Biographie" (1927), 45 ff. vorgenommen. Uxkull-
Gyllenband ist dabei zu Ergebnissen gekommen, die ihn zu einer
ganz neuen Auffassung über den Hergang der Schlacht geführt
haben: Die Erzählung des Plutarch "weicht von Thukydides vollständig ab und trägt auf den ersten Blick mehr abenteuerliche als
wahrscheinliche Züge," sie wird deswegen abgelehnt und der Verlauf der Schlacht hauptsächlich auf Grund des mit Diodor (XI 62
Ende) auf die Eurymedonkämpfe bezogenen Epigramms Ἐξ οὗ
τ' Εὐρώπην Ἀσίας δίχα πόντος ἔνειμεν so rekonstruiert, dass die Landschlacht der Seeschlacht vorausgeht; die Erbeutung der von Cypern nachkommenden 80 phönikischen Trieren (Plut. 13, 3) wird
überhaupt gestrichen. Soviel ich sehe, hat zu diesen Aufstellungen
im einzelnen noch niemand ausführlich Stellung genommen;[3]

[1] Forschungen z. alten Gesch. II 1 ff. Das Referat über Diodor ist nicht in
allem genau. Thukydides: "Die Athener nahmen und vernichteten zusammen
ungefähr 200 phönikische Trieren." Diodor nennt aber nicht nur "hundert
Schiffe ... , während die übrige Flotte leer in die Hände der Athener fiel" (M.
9), sondern sagt 60, 6 ausdrücklich πολλὰς μὲν τῶν ἐναντίων ναῦς διέφθειραν, πλείους
δὲ τῶν ἑκατὸν σὺν αὐτοῖς τοῖς ἀνδράσιν εἷλον (60, 6).

[2] Beloch, Gr. G. II 2, 161 f.; L. Weber, Philologus N. F. 28, 1917, 251; Will,
Kallisthenes' Hellenika, Diss. Würzburg 1913, 25 ff.; Jacoby, FGH II Kommentar S. 422 f.; E. M. Walker, CAH V 54 f.

[3] Im allgemeinen zustimmend V. Ehrenberg, DLZ 50, 1929, 1921 ff. Ableh-
nend H. T. Wade-Gery, JHSt 53, 1933, 86 Anm. 65. Als Zustimmung darf

und doch sind die Folgerungen, die sich aus der veränderten Auffassung vom Hergang dieser Schlacht nach den verschiedensten Seiten hin ergeben, so erheblich, dass eine Untersuchung der Fundamente, auf die sie sich gründet, zur Pflicht wird.

Uxkull-Gyllenband glaubt, die Überlieferung über die Schlacht in zwei Hauptstränge zerlegen zu können. Hauptzeugen für die erste, nach ihm thukydideische Version, sind neben Thukydides selbst das Epigramm der Anthologie VII 258 und das von Diodor (Ephoros) für die Kämpfe am Eurymedon zitierte, von E. Meyer auf Kimons kyprischen Feldzug bezogene Gedicht 'Eξ οὗ τ' Εὑρ-ώπην. . . .[1] Die zweite Reihe, die "ephoreische," ist vertreten durch den Papyrus von Oxyrhynchos XIII 1610 (*FGH* II 70 F 191) und die mit ihm übereinstimmende, längst auf Ephoros zurückgeführte Erzählung bei Diodor;[2] daneben (trotz einzelner Besonderheiten) hauptsächlich durch Plutarch (s. o.). Ephoros und die von U. postulierte hellenistische Vorlage Plutarchs gehen nach U. letztlich auf eine gemeinsame Quelle zurück, die Persika des Ktesias, die bei Ephoros direkt, bei Plutarch in Deinons Bearbeitung benutzt sind (67 ff.).

Das unterscheidende Merkmal liegt bei dieser Aufteilung in der Abfolge der Kämpfe: Landschlacht-Seekampf bei Thukydides, Seeschlacht-Landkampf bei Ephoros. Wäre diese Ableitung richtig, so könnte über die Frage, welcher Zeuge als der vertrauens-

---

wohl auch das kurze Referat von Ammon, *Ph. Woch.* 49, 1929, 162 ff. verstanden werden.

[1] Es sei gleich hier bemerkt: dass auch Lykurg *gegen Leokr.* 72 hierhergezogen wird (46, 57), ist bare Willkür. Die 100 genomenen Schiffe stimmen gerade zu Ephoros-Diodor. πεζομαχοῦντες καὶ ναυμαχοῦντες ἐνίκησαν beweist für die Reihenfolge der Kämpfe so wenig wie πεζομαχία καὶ ναυμαχία bei Thukydides (s. unten). Es ist mir auch unverständlich, wieso Lykurg für die Einheit des Epigramms 'Eξ οὗ τ' Εὑρώπην . . . zeugen soll. Aber Uxkull glaubt ja auch allen Ernstes, dass in einem Zusammenhang, wo hintereinander Eurymedon, Salamis, Kalliasfriede erscheinen, dies Salamis auf "das berühmte Salamis" zu beziehen sei.

[2] Der Papyrus bestätigt die von E. Meyer bestrittene Angabe über die Zahl der persischen Schiffe bei Diodor. Was erhalten ist, deckt sich fast wörtlich mit dem Text des Diodor, nur der Kampf bei den Schiffen (24 ff.) war augenscheinlich genauer erzählt.

Die Kämpfe am Eurymedon 99

würdigere zu gelten hat, kein Zweifel sein. Wir dürften dann alle
bei Plutarch erhaltenen Angaben ebenso beiseitelegen wie den
Bericht des Diodor.[1] Es lässt sich aber zeigen, dass das von
Uxkull hervorgezogene Distinktiv in der Überlieferung gar nicht
ursprünglich gegeben, sondern von ihm erst künstlich in sie
hineingedeutet ist. Zwar, dass bei Diodor (Ephoros) und Plutarch
der Landkampf auf die Seeschlacht folgt, ist eindeutig. Mit-
nichten aber bezeugt der Wortlaut für Thukydides und die mit
ihm zusammengestellten Zeugnisse die umgekehrte Folge.

Der Bericht des Thukydides lautet: ἐγένετο δὲ μετὰ ταῦτα καὶ ἡ
ἐπ' Εὐρυμέδοντι ποταμῶι ἐν Παμφυλίαι πεζομαχία καὶ ναυμαχία 'Αθηναίων
καὶ τῶν ξυμμάχων πρὸς Μήδους καὶ ἐνίκων τῆι αὐτῆι ἡμέραι ἀμφότερα
'Αθηναῖοι Κίμωνος τοῦ Μιλτιάδου στρατηγοῦντος καὶ εἷλον τριήρεις
Φοινίκων καὶ διέφθειραν τὰς πάσας ἐς διακοσίας. Diese Sätze stehen
in dem skizzenartigen Überblick über die Ereignisse seit den
Kämpfen um Eion, Kapitel 98–117. Sie geben keine historische
Erzählung, keinen Bericht über die Abfolge der Operationen,
sondern begnügen sich, die Hauptpunkte des Geschehens heraus-
zuheben: Land- und Seeschlacht, die Teilnehmer, Doppelsieg der
Athener am gleichen Tag unter Kimons Führung, die Beute an
eroberten und zerstörten Schiffen. Wie die Kämpfe aufeinander
folgten, die Anlage der Operationen als solcher war in diesem Zu-
sammenhange ganz gleichgültig. Wenn Thukydides ναυμαχία
hinter πεζομαχία stellt, so folgt er damit zunächst nur griechischem
Sprachgebrauch, dem κατὰ γῆν καὶ κατὰ θάλασσαν das Natürliche ist,
wie uns umgekehrt die Folge "zu Wasser und zu Lande."[2] Die
historische Frage, ob damit das wirkliche Zeitverhältnis der
Kämpfe wiedergegeben ist, ist für Thukydides nicht zu entscheiden.
Man darf aber sagen: hätte Thukydides die zeitliche Folge fest-

[1] Über ihn vgl. ausser E. Meyer a. O. 7 f. noch De Sanctis *Riv. di fil.* 21,
97 ff.
[2] Das meint wohl auch V. Ehrenberg a. O. 1922, wenn er die Reihenfolge
πεζομαχία καὶ ναυμαχία bei Thukydides für "sprachpsychologisch selbstver-
ständlich" erklärt. — Auch E. Meyer misst fälschlich dem Nacheinander von
πεζομαχία und ναυμαχία eigene Bedeutung bei (7 Anm. 1, vgl. 22 oben), betont
aber mit Recht, dass die Landschlacht im Epigramm 'Εξ οὗ τ' Εὐρώπην ganz
zurücksteht (19). — Auch für die kyprischen Kämpfe folgt aus Thuk. I 112
ἐναυμάχησαν καὶ ἐπεζομάχησαν ἅμα für ihre Abfolge nichts.

legen wollen, so hätte er sich, eben weil sie aus πεζομαχία καὶ ναυμαχία nicht abzulesen war, anders ausgedrückt: schon einfache
Gliederung mit πρῶτον μὲν . . ., ὕστερον δέ hätte jedes Missver-
stehen ausgeschaltet. Ganz das Gleiche wie für Thukydides gilt für das Epigramm
Anth. Pal. VII 258, die Grabschrift der in der Schlacht am Eurymedon Gefallenen, die jetzt mit Recht allgemein für echt gehalten
wird.[1]

Οἵδε παρ' Εὐρυμέδοντα ποτ' ἀγλαὸν ὤλεσαν ἥβην
μαρνάμενοι Μήδων τοξοφόρων προμάχοις
αἰχμηταί, πεζοί τε καὶ ὠκυπόρων ἐπὶ νηῶν·
κάλλιστον δ' ἀρετῆς μνῆμ' ἔλιπον φθίμενοι.

"In der Schlacht mit den bogentragenden Persern gaben diese
Männer ihre herrliche Jugend dahin, Lanzenkämpfer zu Fuss und
auf den schnellen Schiffen." Der Oberbegriff αἰχμηταί, an betonter

[1] Vgl. zuletzt Wade-Gery a. O. 79 ff. Eine Konjektur, die ποτ' ἀγλαὸν ὤλεσαν
ἥβην in ἀπὸ τίμιον ὤλεσαν ἥβην "bessert," nur um das nach Εὐρυμέδοντα überlieferte
ποτε loszuwerden, braucht kaum erst widerlegt zu werden (τίμιος ist überhaupt
kein für ἥβην in Betracht kommendes Epitheton). Wade-Gery ist diesen Weg
auch nur gegangen, um das Epigramm der von ihm aufgestellten Regel gefügig
zu machen, nach der ποτε nur auf Denkmälern stehn soll, die einige Zeit nach
dem auf ihnen gefeierten Ereignis errichtet worden sind. Warum nimmt er
dann dasselbe nicht auch für das Eurymedonepigramm an? Ich glaube aber
garnicht, dass die Regel, von der ihr Entdecker selbst Ausnahmen zugeben
muss, in dieser Form gültig ist. Das ποτε der Epigramme ist weder "Flickwort," noch darf es so rational-logisch verstanden werden, wie es Wade-Gery
tut. ποτε legt nicht die wenigen Jahre fest, die vielleicht zwischen der Errich-
tung des Denkmals oder der Stiftung der Aufschrift und dem historischen
Ereignis liegen, sondern betont die Distanz, die den späteren Betrachter — und
für ihn ist die Mitteilung doch bestimmt — von den Taten der Vergangenheit
trennt. Wie weit solche Beziehung auf die Nachwelt gehen kann, zeigt ein-
dringlich das Gedicht auf die vor Potidäa Gefallenen (Hiller v. Gaertringen,
Hist. gr. Epigr. 53)

Ἀθανάτόμ με θα[νōσι πολῖται σε͂μ' ἀνέθεκαν.]
σε͂μαίνεν ἀρετ[ὲν τōνδε καὶ ἐσσομένοις]
καὶ προγόνōσθέν(ο)s [ἐσθλόν - - -

Auch hier hat Wade-Gery unglücklich eingegriffen und aus Fauvels offenbar
unzuverlässiger Abschrift das monströse Epitheton προγονοσθενὲς (ἔπαρ)
"hergestellt."

Stelle nachgebracht (im Gegensatz zu der für die Perser charakteristischen Fernwaffe), wird in πεζοί und ἐπὶ νηῶν untergeteilt.[1] Wie will man aus der einfachen Aufzählung auf die Reihenfolge der Operationen rückschliessen, wenn auch hier wieder πεζοί voransteht? Ist die Abfolge der Kämpfe, in denen die Gefeierten gefallen sind, für das Epigramm irgendwie wesentlich? Ist sie es für Pausanias in den Sätzen (I 29. 14) κεῖνται δὲ καὶ οἱ σὺν Κίμωνι τὸ μέγα ἔργον πεζῇ καὶ ναυσὶν αὐθημερὸν κρατήσαντες und (X 15. 4) ἀπὸ ἔργων ὧν ἐπ᾽ Εὐρυμέδοντι ἐν ἡμέρᾳ τῇ αὐτῇ τὸ μὲν πεζῇ, τὸ δὲ ναυσὶν ἐν τῷ ποταμῷ κατώρθωσαν? oder Lykurg (*gegen Leokr.* 72) ἐπ᾽ Εὐρυμέδοντι δὲ καὶ πεζομαχοῦντες καὶ ναυμαχοῦντες ἐνίκησαν? Es bedarf nach dem zu den Hauptzeugen der "thukydideischen Version" Dargelegten des Beweises nicht mehr, dass alle Versuche, die stereotype Abfolge πεζομαχία καὶ ναυμαχία im Sinne eines zeitlichen Nacheinander auszudeuten, in die Irre führen, weil sie als sachliche Absicht des Schriftstellers deuten, was auf Gesetzen der Sprache und des Stils beruht.

Somit bleibt für die "thukydideische Version," die Abfolge: Landschlacht-Seeschlacht, als einziges Zeugnis das von Diodor angeführte Gedicht übrig, denn was immer man vor Μήδων πολλοὺς ὀλέσαντες Φοινίκων ἑκατὸν ναῦς ἕλον lesen mag (s. u.), hier ist das Nacheinander von Land- und Seeschlacht gesichert. Aber gerade dies Gedicht ist in seiner historischen Einordnung wie in seiner Interpretation umstritten. Wenn Uxkull es mit Diodor (Ephoros) auf die Schlacht am Eurymedon, nicht, wie Ed. Meyer auf Cypern bezieht, so ist zu prüfen, ob die Gründe, die ihn zu diesem Ansatz geführt haben, Stand halten. Da das Gedicht neuerdings auch von Wade-Gery wieder — wie mir scheint, nicht befriedigend — behandelt worden ist (a. O. 83 ff.), wird es gut sein, dabei etwas weiter auszuholen, als für den vorliegenden Zweck zunächst erforderlich scheinen könnte.

Das Epigramm ist an folgenden Stellen und in folgenden Fassungen überliefert:[2]

---

[1] Uxkull interpretiert dies allzu "sachlich" dahin, "dass griechische Lanzenkämpfer gegen persische Kerntruppen gefochten haben" (46).

[2] Preger, *Inscr. Gr. metr.* 269; Diehl *Anth. lyr.* II 99, 100; Hiller v. Gaertringen, *Hist. gr. Epigramme* 49. — Die Verse standen nach Diodor auf

Diodor XI 62. 3:

'Εξ οὗ γ' Εὐρώπην 'Ασίας δίχα πόντος ἔνειμε
καὶ πόλιας θνητῶν θοῦρος "Αρης ἐπέχει,
οὐδέν πω τοιοῦτον ἐπιχθονίων γένετ' ἀνδρῶν
ἔργον ἐν ἠπείρωι καὶ κατὰ πόντον ἅμα.
οἵδε γὰρ ἐν Κύπρωι Μήδους πολλοὺς ὀλέσαντες
Φοινίκων ἑκατὸν ναῦς ἕλον ἐν πελάγει
ἀνδρῶν πληθούσας· μέγα δ' ἔστενεν 'Ασὶς ὑπ' αὐτῶι
πληγεῖσ' ἀμφοτέραις χερσὶ κράτει πολέμου.

Aristides orat. 28. 64 (= II 162 Keil); or. *pro quatt.* II 209, 210
Dindorf Schol. Arist. III 209 Dindorf:

'Εξ οὗ τ' Εὐρώπην 'Ασίας δίχα πόντος ἔκρινεν
καὶ πόλιας θνητῶν θοῦρος "Αρης ἐφέπει,
οὐδενί πω κάλλιον ἐπιχθονίων γένετ' ἀνδρῶν
ἔργον ἐν ἠπείρωι καὶ κατὰ πόντον ὁμοῦ.
οἵδε γὰρ ἐν γαίηι Μήδων πολλοὺς ὀλέσαντες
Φοινίκων ἑκατὸν ναῦς ἕλον ἐν πελάγει
ἀνδρῶν πληθούσας· μέγα δ' ἔστενεν 'Ασὶς ὑπ'αὐτῶν
πληγεῖσ' ἀμφοτέραις χερσὶ κράτει πολέμου.

Anthol. Pal. VII 296: Σιμωνίδου τοῦ Κήου· εἰς τοὺς μετὰ Κίμωνος
στρατευσαμένους ἐν Κύπρῳ 'Αθηναίους, ὅτε τὰς ἑκατὸν ναῦς τῶν Φοινίκων
ἔλαβεν.

'Εξ οὗ γ' Εὐρώπην 'Ασίας δίχα πόντος ἔνειμε
καὶ πόλεμον λαῶν θοῦρος "Αρης ἐφέπει,

dem Weihgeschenk, das die Athener nach der Schlacht am Eurymedon τῷ
θεῷ stifteten, also nach Delphi; eine Weihung dort auch bei Pausanias X 15. 4.
Das Lemma der Anthologie εἰς τοὺς μετὰ Κίμωνος στρατευσαμένους ἐν Κύπρῳ κτλ.
passt nur auf das Grabdenkmal im Kerameikos, das Pausanias I 29. 13 erwähnt.
Mir scheint οἵδε keine andere Beziehung zuzulassen als die auf eine Verlustliste,
genau wie im Epigramm auf die Gefallenen der Eurymedonschlacht, der
Chersonneskämpfe (Hiller 52), in Sizilien (ebd. 55). Für die Marathongedichte
hat sie eben J. H. Oliver gegen A. Wilhelm erneut sichergestellt, auch mit
Recht den nichtigen Einwand zurückgewiesen, dass an dem Ruhm nicht nur
die Gefallenen Anteil hätten (*Am. Journ. Phil.* 56, 1935, 193 ff., *Hesperia* 5,
1936, 225 ff.). Hillers Ausweg, dass das Kyprosepigramm für die Grabschrift
und gleichzeitig für ein delphisches Weihgeschenk verwandt worden wäre (zu
Hist. Epigr. 49), scheint mir zu gekünstelt.

οὐδαμά πω κάλλιον ἐπιχθονίων γένετ' ἀνδρῶν
ἔργον ἐν ἠπείρωι καὶ κατὰ πόντον ἅμα.
οἵδε γὰρ ἐν Κύπρωι Μήδων πολλοὺς ὀλέσαντες
Φοινίκων ἑκατὸν ναῦς ἕλον ἐν πελάγει
ἀνδρῶν πληθούσας· μέγα δ' ἔστεν[ε - - - -
πληγεῖσ' ἀμφοτέραις χερσὶ κράτει πολέμου.

Dazu kommen als indirekte Überlieferung die Nachahmungen
auf der Stele von Xanthos (Hiller v. Gaertringen *Hist. gr. Epigr.*
56):

['Ε]ξ οὗ τ' Εὐρώπην ['Α]σίας δίχα πόν[τ]ος ἔνεμ[ε]ν,
[ο]ὐδές πω Λυκίων στήλην τοιάνδε ἀνέθηκ ⟨ε⟩ν
. . . .

und auf dem attischen Stein *IG* II² 1141:

'Εξ οὗ Κέκροπα λαὸς 'Αθηναίων ὀνομάζει
καὶ χώραν Παλλὰς τήνδ' ἔκτισε δήμῳ 'Αθηνῶν,
οὐδὲς Σωσιβίο καὶ Πύρρο μείζονα θείην
φυλὴν Κεκροπίδων ἔργα ἔδρασε ἀγαθά.

'Εξ οὗ τε und ἔνειμε auf der Stele von Xanthos sichern beide
Lesungen für das Original. Dasselbe gilt nicht auch wegen οὐδείς
πω . . . für οὐδενί πω, denn bei dem lykischen Dynasten ist der
Singular durch die Persönlichkeit des Gefeierten gefordert, während
in dem hier zur Erörterung stehenden Gedicht οὐδενί neben
dem Plural οἵ δε befremden könnte; οὐδαμά πω κάλλιον empfiehlt
sich schon als lectio difficilior, der Komparativ wird ausserdem
durch οὐδείς . . . μείζονα . . . ἔργα ἔδρασε im attischen Stück
geschützt. πόλεμον λαῶν θοῦρος "Αρης ἐφέπει (dies sicher besser als
ἐπέχει) klingt gegenüber dem anschaulichen Bild πόλιας θνητῶν
θοῦρος "Αρης ἐφέπει wenig überzeugend, und die Städte erscheinen
neben den Erdteilen natürlicher als das farblose πόλεμος λαῶν.
Schwieriger ist über ὑπ' αὐτῶν und ὑπ' αὐτῶι zu urteilen, "schwer aufstöhnte Asis unter ihnen (αὐτῶν auf οἵδε zurückbezogen), getroffen
vom Doppelschlag in des Krieges Entscheidung," will mir aber
stilistisch besser und im Ablauf gefälliger erscheinen als "schwer
aufstöhnte Asis von des Krieges Entscheidung selbst getroffen
im Doppelschlag." Doch über die Verbindlichkeiten solcher Wer-

tungen mag man streiten. Wichtig ist allein, dass Aristides in einem Fall, dem stümperhaften ἔκρινε (1) sicher, in einem anderen, οὐδενί πω (3) sehr wahrscheinlich eine falsche Lesung bietet.

Mit dieser Feststellung ist von vorherein die einzige sachlich gravierende Abweichung im Text des Aristides, ἐν γαίηι Vers 5 für ἐν Κύπρωι schlecht empfohlen. Und doch hat gerade auf ihr Uxkull seine Beweisführung aufgebaut. Uxkull (S. 55/6) verteidigt die Lesart ἐν γαίηι mit zwei Argumenten. Einmal aus dem Aufbau des Gedankens: γαίη und πέλαγος seien gewählte Gegensätze, die mit ἐν ἠπείρωι und κατὰ πόντον korrespondierten; dann mit dem Nachweis, dass ἤπειρος im fünften Jahrhundert "ausgesprochen der Kontinent" bedeute: "unverantwortlich ist die Behauptung, dass ἤπειρος eine Insel sein könne, weil in der Odyssee (ε 57) die Insel der Kalypso so genannt würde." Ich halte diese Beweisführung nicht nur für nicht durchschlagend, sondern auch für verfehlt. Gewiss ist es richtig, dies Gedicht in die Gedanken- und Anschauungswelt des fünften Jahrhunderts zu stellen: Uxkull weist für die Vorstellung von der Teilung der Erde mit Recht auf die Tragiker,[1] für die personifizierte Ἀσίς (7) auf Aisch. *Perser* 181 ff. und besonders 549: στένει γαῖ' Ἀσιὰς ἐκκενουμένα — aber die Argumentation, dass ἤπειρος, weil es im fünften Jahrhundert "Festland" heisst, nicht auf Cypern bezogen werden könne, schiesst über das Ziel hinaus, sie zäumt sozusagen das Pferd von hinten auf, denn sie verlangt vom Dichter, dass er den Gegensatz Landschlacht-Seeschlacht mit κατὰ γῆν — κατὰ θάλασσαν wiedergibt, weil er weiss, dass er gleich darauf von Kypros sprechen wird.

"Seit die Erde steht und Ares die Städte der Menschen heimsucht, ist keine schönere Tat getan auf dem Festland und auf dem Meer zugleich (als die Männer sie vollbrachten, die hier bestattet sind, oder: denen dieses Denkmal errichtet ist)." Dies der erste

---

[1] Es hätte aber auch Herodot I 4 herangezogen werden sollen, wo entwickelt wird, wie in der uranfänglichen Scheidung der Erdteile der Konflikt zwischen Griechen und Persern gewissermassen vorausbestimmt ist. Diese Auseinandersetzung, dessen erste Phase die Kämpfe vor Ilion sind, führt über Marathon, Salamis, Eurymedon zu Kypros. Die Doppelschlacht von Kypros ist die Krönung des hellenischen Sieges, der Abschluss dieses Ringens: so will es der Dichter, so wollte es, dürfen wir hinzufügen, die offizielle Meinung in Athen, trotz des Kalliasfriedens oder gerade seinetwegen.

Gedanke, mit feierlichen Worten umkleidete Einleitung, Verkündung des Themas, zugleich höchster Preis der ruhmvollen Tat. Welcher? Es ist klar: diese zwei Disticha allein können niemals auf einem Denkmal gestanden haben. Wer irgend Sinn hat für Ablauf und Aufbau eines griechischen Epigramms, muss empfinden, dass ein so allgemeiner Satz nicht in der Luft hängen kann: selbst dann nicht, wenn das ἔργον etwa durch eine Prosainschrift Erklärung und Beziehung erhielt. Es ist schwer verständlich, dass sich E. Schwartz und neuerdings wieder Wade-Gery diesem einfachen Schluss entzogen haben.[1] Müsste nicht unvoreingenommene Interpretation, wenn die beiden Distichen für sich allein überliefert wären, folgern, dass mindestens ein weiteres verloren ist? Wenn die Überlieferung einstimmig eine Fortsetzung bietet, kann die Frage nur lauten: erfüllt sie das, was man dem Gedanken nach erwartet? oder, wenn sie in sich geteilt ist: welche Lesart erfüllt diese Forderung besser?

Im Einleitungssatz waren Land und Meer ganz allgemein als die Schauplätze kriegerischer Taten nebeneinander gestellt. Auf beiden Kriegsschauplätzen zugleich ist das ἔργον getan, das hier als das schönste gefeiert wird. Muss man nicht verlangen, dass im

[1] E. Schwartz, *Hermes* 35, 1900, 106 ff. Schon das hätte warnen sollen, dass doch auch Ephoros-Diodor das vollständige Gedicht voraussetzt. Tut es nicht auch die Stele von Xanthos? Wade-Gery greift eine von Domaszewski, *SBAk Heidelberg* 1914, 10.16 ff. vorgetragene These wieder auf, nach der V 1–4 auf die Eurymedonschlacht, 5–8 auf die kyprischen Kämpfe zu beziehen wären, gibt aber wenigstens zu, dass dann der Anfang des zweiten Gedichts nicht herzustellen ist. Selbst wenn er es wäre (warum nicht: Οἵδε ποτ' ἐν γαίηι? vgl. Anth. Pal. VII 256, 270; herzustellen auch *IG* II 1676): ist der pathetische Schluss μέγα δ' ἔστενεν Ἀσὶς ὑπ' αὐτῶν . . . tragbar, wenn nichts vorausging als "diese erschlugen viele Feinde und erbeuteten 100 Schiffe"? — An Unechtheit wird trotz Wilamowitz' Skepsis (*Hell. Dicht.* I 128 Anm. 4 zu S. 127) heute niemand mehr denken (vgl. bsd. E. Meyer a. O. 11 f.). Gewiss ist die Form merkwürdig: die Tat wird in pathetischen Worten gepriesen, ehe sie überhaupt genannt ist, man würde einen Anfang erwarten wie in den Marathonepigrammen (zuletzt *Hesperia* 5, 1936, 232 ff.) "dieser Männer Tat wird ruhmvoll durch alle Zeiten leuchten denn sie erschlugen . . . und erbeuteten. . . ." Aber eben diese Weiträumigkeit der Anlage hat ihren eigenen Sinn: der geschichtliche Moment des Abschlusses der Perserkriege sollte bewusst gemacht werden, verklärt durch den letzten Sieg, den hellenische Waffen errangen (vgl. oben 104 Anm. 1).

Folgenden nicht nur das ἔργον, sondern auch das Lokal näher bestimmt wird? Bei Aristides aber fährt das Epigramm fort: "denn diese haben auf dem Lande viele Perser erschlagen und auf dem Meer hundert Schiffe von den Phönikern erbeutet." Erläutert wird also nur die Kampfhandlung selbst, der Schauplatz bleibt genau so unbestimmt wie im Vordersatz: ἤπειρος — πόντος, γαῖα — πέλαγος korrespondieren, ein leeres Nebeneinander synonymer Ausdrücke, ein Spiel mit Worten. Und weiter: γαῖα ist gegenüber ἤπειρος der allgemeinere Begriff, und doch soll, wie γάρ zeigt, ἐν ἠπείρωι durch ἐν γαίηι illustriert werden. Heisst aber nicht überhaupt ἐν γαίηι nicht vielmehr "auf der Erde" oder "in der Erde"? Solche Unklarheiten und Allgemeinheiten widersprechen dem Stil des echten Epigramms zu allen Zeiten: die Inschrift dient, gerade auch wenn sie metrisch stilisiert ist, immer in erster Linie der prägnanten Mitteilung von Tatsachen. Was darüber hinaus ins Dichterische vorstösst, ist der geformte Ausdruck eines Gefühls — das Epigramm auf die Gefallenen von Koroneia ist dafür jetzt das sprechendste Beispiel—Allgemeinheiten und leere Wiederholungen haben hier, mindestens im fünften Jahrhundert, keinen Raum.

Was der Gedanke wie der Stil des Epigramms in gleicher Weise fordern, bietet die durch Diodor und die Anthologie vertretene Überlieferung. "Denn auf Cypern haben sie viele Perser erschlagen und den Phönikern auf dem Meer hundert Schiffe abgenommen." Hier ist der Kriegsschauplatz für Land- und Seeschlacht (denn auch ἐν πελάγει wird durch ἐν Κύπρωι erläutert) klar bestimmt, der allgemeine Satz durch den untergeordneten γάρ-Satz illustriert. Der Einwand: heisst denn aber nicht ἤπειρος im fünften Jahrhundert immer der Kontinent? verfängt nicht. Gewiss wird ἤπειρος gewöhnlich nicht von einer Insel gesagt, wenn auch Homer zweimal (ε56 und κ56) ἤπειρόνδε bzw. ἐπ' ἠπείρου βαίνειν braucht, wo es sich um das Anlandgehen auf einer Insel handelt (Kalypso, Phäaken).[1] Das ist ja aber auch hier gar nicht geschehen. Man darf nicht von ἐν Κύπρωι ausgehen und dies in ἐν ἠπείρωι wiederfinden wollen — um dann einzuwenden, dass Κύπρος keine ἤπειρος ist — sondern muss anerkennen, dass der allgemeine Satz "kein schönerer Sieg zu

[1] Wade-Gery meint (84): "the only two cases . . . are magic islands." War das für Homer ein Unterschied?

Wasser und zu Lande zugleich errungen" den folgenden Tat-
sachenbericht in keiner Weise ausschliesst.

Das auf dem Wege der Interpretation gewonnene historische
Ergebnis ist dies: Da die Lesung ἐν Κύπρωι als die allein sinnvolle
erwiesen ist, entfällt jede Möglichkeit, das Gedicht auf die Kämpfe
am Eurymedon zu beziehen[1] — es sei denn, man verstehe (mit
Gleichordnung der Partizipien) ἐν Κύπρωι fälschlich so wie Ephoros
es verstanden zu haben scheint: "sie haben bei Cypern (im Seekampf) viele Perser getötet und hundert Schiffe genommen"
(wobei dann der Landschlacht nach V 4 nicht weiter gedacht
worden wäre);[2] die Konsequenz wäre die Anerkennung des nun

---

[1] Über die angeblich andere Folge der kyprischen Kämpfe bei Thukydides
s.o. 99, Anm. 2. Wie es dazu kam, dass das Gedicht auf die Doppelschlacht am
Eurymedon bezogen wurde, hat E. Meyer 11 f. aus der Stimmung des vierten
Jahrhunderts psychologisch verständlich gemacht. Die Übertragung lag um
so näher, als der Eingang auf die Eurymedonkämpfe tatsächlich sehr gut passte;
wer nur die ersten Verse las, musste zunächst an diese Schlacht denken: dies
gebe ich Wade-Gery (83 f.) zu.

[2] Nach Uxkull hätte auch Ephoros ἐν γαίηι gelesen (55), obwohl bei Diodor
ἐν Κύπρωι im Text steht. Dann kann er aber nur verstanden haben "nachdem
sie auf dem Land viele Perser erschlagen hatten, nahmen sie den Phönikern
hundert Schiffe weg"; seine Darstellung stände also in offenem Widerspruch
zum Epigramm, denn in ihr folgt die Landschlacht der Seeschlacht. Eine
solche Unsinnigkeit traut denn auch Uxkull dem Ephoros nicht zu und erklärt
folgerichtig "Ephoros hat das Epigramm (überhaupt) nicht in der bei Diodor
erhaltenen Form gelesen" (54). In welcher aber dann? Ist es nicht evident,
dass er Cypern eben aus dem Epigramm entnahm, das er zitierte? Dagegen
ist mit der Möglichkeit zu rechnen, dass Ephoros 5/6 allein auf die Seeschlacht
bei Kypros bezogen, die partizipialen Bestimmungen also gleichgeordnet hat:
nach den Eingangsversen (ἐν ἠπείρωι καὶ κατὰ πόντον ἅμα) und dem pathetischen
Schluss (ἀμφοτέραις χερσὶν) allerdings sinnlos. So hat E. Meyer (10) erklärt:
"den Landkampf bezeichnet dann nur V 4" (von Uxkull offenbar missver-
standen) und damit einen Weg gezeigt, der die Anlage der ephoreischen
Schilderung und die Erfindung des Stratagems verständlich macht: wenn
Ephoros auf Grund des Epigramms die Seeschlacht nach Cypern verlegte,
musste er um eine Verknüpfung mit der immer nur am Eurymedon lokali-
sierbaren Landschlacht bemüht sein. — Nach Uxkull soll die Lesung ἐν γαίηι
für Ephoros durch die "der des Diodor gleichwertige" des Aristides gesichert
sein. Er beruft sich dafür auf den Nachweis von E. Beecke, *Die hist. Angaben
in. Ael. Arist. Panath.* 47 ff., dem zufolge "Ephoros dem Aristides an jener
Stelle vorliegt." Dieser Nachweis gilt aber nur für den Panathenaikos. Uxkull

mit dem Gedicht so ziemlich in Einklang stehenden Berichts, den doch auch Uxkull für verkehrt hält. Es kann in Wahrheit keine Frage sein, dass die Verse vielmehr die kyprischen Kämpfe von 449 feiern und das Lemma der Anthologie εἰς τοὺς μετὰ Κίμωνος στρατευσαμένους ἐν Κύπρῳ das Richtige bewahrt hat. Damit ist auch das letzte Zeugnis für die angeblich thukydideische Version, nach der die Landschlacht der Seeschlacht vorausgehen soll, als nichtig erwiesen. Es bleibt die Frage, wie es um die Zuverlässigkeit der zweiten, "ephoreischen Version" steht. Uxkull hat hierher neben sekundären Zeugnissen, von denen hier abgesehen werden kann,[1] auch Plutarch gezogen, Ephoros und Plutarch als Ableitungen aus demselben Urbericht nebeneinander gestellt. Die Berechtigung dieser Gleichordnung ist, nachdem sich ein Distinktiv in der Folge von Land- und Seeschlacht als gar nicht vorhanden erwiesen hat, mithin aus einer "Gleichheit" in dieser Beziehung keine engere Verwandtschaft dieser Berichte gegenüber anderen gefolgert werden kann, zuerst zu untersuchen. Es ist für den unvoreingenommenen Leser nicht zu übersehen, dass dieser Teil von Uxkulls Beweisführung auf besonders schwachen Füssen steht.

Uxkull findet nach dem Vorgang von Kirchhoff (*Hermes* 11, 20 f.) neben auch von ihm nicht in Abrede gestellten Unterschieden gleichwohl gewisse Ähnlichkeiten in den Berichten bei Ephoros und Plutarch und folgert, bei beiden sei die gleiche Quelle benutzt, "aber zweifelsohne von Ephoros recht willkürlich umgestaltet worden" (S. 52). In Wahrheit gehen die behaupteten Ähnlichkeiten nicht über selbstverständliche, mit den Voraussetzungen der geschichtlichen Situation selbst gegebene Züge hinaus. Sie betreffen allein die vorausliegenden Operationen in Karien, Lykien, Pamphylien, und auch hier sind Abweichungen nicht wohl zu übersehen: nur

---

übersieht, dass gerade Beecke, so sehr auch er für ἐν γαίηι bei Ephoros eintritt, es für unwahrscheinlich hält, dass Aristides in den Quatt. — im Panathenaikos ist das Epigramm nicht zitiert — den Bericht des Ephoros eingesehen hat, und ausdrücklich feststellt: "woher er das Epigramm hat, ist nicht zu bestimmen." — Woher die Konjektur ἐν γαίηι kommt, muss also unbestimmt bleiben.

[1] Aristodemos ist von Uxkull fälschlich auf Ephoros zurückgeführt, denn bei ihm fehlt gerade das für Ephoros charakteristische Cypern.

Plutarch nennt Knidos als Operationsbasis, während er im übrigen von einer Tätigkeit Kimons in Karien nichts weiss, nur *er* erzählt ausführlicher die Gewinnung von Phaselis. Gewichtiger sind die Unterschiede in der Schilderung der Kämpfe selbst; die hier von Uxkull hervorgezogenen gemeinsamen Züge erledigen sich von selbst: dass die Landschlacht bei beiden auf die Seeschlacht folgt, ist, wie wir erkannten, kein Kriterium, da eine abweichende Darstellung in unserer Überlieferung gar nicht nachzuweisen ist; die These, dass bei beiden, "allerdings in verschiedener Anwendung (!) das höchst unwahrscheinliche Cypern" erscheint, beruht auf der willkürlichen und sicher falschen Konjektur Κύπρῳ für Ὕδρῳ im Text des Plutarch.[1] Und selbst wenn diese Übereinstimmungen noch bestünden: was könnten sie besagen gegen das völlige Auseinandergehen der beiden Autoren bei der Erzählung der Schlacht selbst: Schiffskampf am Eurymedon, Landung, Angriff auf das persische Landheer, Landschlacht, Vernichtung der achtzig nachgekommenen phönikischen Schiffe bei Plutarch — Schiffskampf bei Cypern, Fahrt mit den als Persern verkleideten Mannschaften auf persischen Schiffen zum Eurymedon, nächtlicher Überfall auf das persische Lager, Flucht der überraschten Perser, (die an einen Angriff der Pisidier glauben) zu den griechischen (vermeintlich persischen) Schiffen, Verwirrung, Blutbad: — bei Ephoros-Diodor. Und wenn es bei Plutarch heisst (12. 6) "man sieht, wie zahlreich die persische Flotte gewesen sein muss, wenn man in Rechnung stellt, dass viele Schiffe doch entkommen sein müssen, viele aber auch vernichtet worden sind, und trotzdem noch 200 Schiffe von den Athenern erbeutet wurden," Ephoros-Diodor aber sagt (XI 60. 6-7) "viele gegnerische Schiffe zerstörten die Athener, mehr als 100 aber eroberten sie mitsamt der Mannschaft, die übrigen aber flüchteten sich nach Kypros": kann man da wirklich noch behaupten, "noch ein Satz lässt, wenn auch schwach (!), eine gemeinsame Vorlage durchschimmern" (S. 51)? Mit dergleichen ähnlichen Unähnlichkeiten lässt sich doch wohl nichts beweisen. Wer diese Berichte unvoreingenommen nebeneinanderhält, wird an die Benutzung einer gemeinsamen Vorlage nicht glauben können. Es kann nicht zweifelhaft sein: Ephoros stellt

[1] S. 113, Anm. 1.

gegenüber der von Plutarch repräsentierten Tradition eine selb-
ständige Version dar; über ihren Wert bedarf es nach den über-
zeugenden Darlegungen von E. Meyer keines Wortes.[1] So
bleibt schliesslich das Verhör des letzten "ephoreischen" Zeugen,
Plutarchs.

Plutarch kommt bei Uxkull schlecht weg. Sein Bericht "weicht
von Thukydides vollständig ab und trägt auf den ersten Blick
mehr abenteuerliche als wahrscheinliche Züge" (S. 47). Die erste
Bemerkung stützt sich allein auf das angebliche Nacheinander von
Land- und Seekampf bei Thukydides, für das, wie wir sahen, jeder
Anhalt fehlt; die zweite Behauptung bleibt unbewiesen; wir werden
diese Frage später noch zur Entscheidung stellen (s. u. S. 114).
Weiter glaubt Uxkull aber, die Vertrauenswürdigkeit der plu-
tarchischen Erzählung durch den Nachweis erschüttern zu können,
dass ihre vor allem von Ed. Meyer verfochtene Rückführung auf
Kallisthenes nicht zu halten sei. Die Anführungen des Kallisthenes
bei Plutarch stehen für U. auf *einer* Stufe mit andern unwesent-
lichen Variantzitaten: im wesentlichen sei ein unbekannter
Grundbericht benutzt — vermutlich Ktesias bzw. dessen Überar-
beitung durch Deinon —, der mit einer rhetorisch gefärbten
Quelle zusammengearbeitet worde. Erneute Analyse wird zu
überprüfen haben, ob diese Aufstellungen Bestand haben.

Plutarch beginnt seine Darstellung der Eurymedonschlacht mit der
programmatisch vorangestellten These (Kap. 12): Keiner hat den
Sinn des Grosskönigs so gedemütigt wie Kimon. Es folgt: Denn von
Anfang an liess er ihm keine Ruhe und ruhte selbst nicht eher, als
bis er ganz Kleinasien von Jonien bis Pamphylien von den Persern
gesäubert hatte. Nach diesem zusammenfassenden Überblick wird
der letzte und wichtigste Abschnitt der Offensive selbst erzählt:
"Als er erfuhr, die Feldherrn des Königs hätten in der Nähe von
Pamphylien grosse Streitkräfte zu Wasser und zu Land zusammen-

---

[1] Die Frage nach den Quellen des Ephoros braucht hier nicht neu gestellt
zu werden. Selbst wenn die Benutzung des Ktesias so feststände, wie Uxkull
im Anschluss an Mess, *Rh. Mus.* 61, 390 ff. glaubt, folgt natürlich keineswegs,
dass Ephoros ihn bei den Eurymedonkämpfen zugrundegelegt hätte. Mir ist
mit Ed. Meyer gewiss, dass seine Hauptquelle vielmehr eben das Epigramm
Ἐξ οὗ τ' Εὐρώπην . . . gewesen ist.

gezogen, fasste er den Entschluss, αὐτοῖς ἄπλουν καὶ ἀνέμβατον ὅλως ὑπὸ φόβου τὴν ἐντὸς Χελιδονίων ποιήσασθαι θάλατταν und stach von Knidos aus in See." Das in diesem Satze bezeichnete Vorhaben wird durch die siegreiche Schlacht erreicht und der Erfolg ist: dieses ἔργον demütigte den Sinn des Grosskönigs so sehr, dass er aus Furcht wegen jener Niederlage, διὰ φόβον τῆς ἥττης ἐκείνης, sich soweit von Griechenland zurückzog, dass, als Perikles und Ephialtes über die Chelidonischen Inseln hinausfuhren (ἐπέκεινα πλεῦσαι Χελιδονίων), ihnen kein feindliches Schiff begegnete:[1] Wenn irgend etwas, so ist klar, dass Einleitungs- und Schlusspassus eng zusammengehören; klar auch, dass in diesem letzteren der diesen einfachen Zusammenhang zerreissende Satz von ἔργῳ δὲ ποιεῖν bis zurück zu (ὥστε) συνθέσθαι — hier im Referat ausgelassen — störender Einschub ist. Hier steht, die Niederlage habe den König zum Abschluss des Kalliasfriedens veranlasst; Kallisthenes aber hätte diesen Friedensschluss bestritten und nur zugeben wollen, dass der in ihm festgelegte Zustand de facto damals allerdings schon eingetreten wäre, ἔργῳ δὲ ποιεῖν διὰ φόβον . . . Gleichgültig, ob Kallisthenes überhaupt auf die Frage eingegangen ist und ob er die Existenz eines formellen Vertrages oder nur seine Verbindung mit der Eurymedonschlacht geleugnet hat:[2] die Wiederaufnahme des φόβος-Motivs in Verbindung mit dem Namen des Kallisthenes in diesem Zusammenhang lässt keinen Zweifel darüber, dass Ed. Meyers Schluss, der Bericht Plutarchs gehe auf Kallisthenes zurück, mindestens für die Rahmenabschnitte bündig ist. Und weiter: wenn der das Geschichtswerk des Kallisthenes einleitende Abschnitt die Zeit nach dem Antalkidasfrieden an der Lage nach dem Doppelsieg an Eurymedon mass:[3] steht mit der Tendenz dieser Einleitung die Haltung der oben zitierten Sätze nicht auf das beste im Einklang? So gewiss es übertrieben ist, hier mit

---

[1] Über die Zeit dieser Fahrten des Ephialtes und Perikles vgl. W. Judeich, *Hermes* 58, 1923, 12 Anm. 2.

[2] Über die verbreitete Anschauung, die den Kalliasfrieden unmittelbar an die Eurymedonschlacht anschliesst, Ed. Schwartz, *Hermes* 35, 111 ff., Walker *CAH* V 469 ff.

[3] E. Meyer hat diese Partie a. O. 4 f. nach Plutarch rekonstruiert; zustimmend Jacoby *RE* X 1695 und im Kommentar zu *FGrHist* II 124 F 15-16.

Uxkull von Rhetorik zu sprechen,[1] so richtig ist es die Beobach-
tung, dass der Stil an diesen Stellen gegenüber dem Tenor der
eigentlichen Schlachtbeschreibung gesteigert scheint; man wird
nicht verkennen, dass die gleiche Stilisierung aber auch bei den
Höhepunkten des Schlachtverlaufs spürbar wird, in 13. 1 nicht
weniger als in 13. 3. Wird durch den Rahmen und die Einheit des
Stils die Rückführung auf eine einheitliche Schilderung nahegelegt,
so muss ein weiterer dem Text unmittelbar zu entnehmender
Hinweis den letzten Zweifel über ihre Identifizierung beseitigen.
Der Name des Kallisthenes erscheint noch einmal in 12. 5. Hier
wird erzählt, Ephoros hätte als Befehlshaber der Flotte Tithraustes
genannt, für die Landmacht Pherendates; bei Kallisthenes aber
hiesse der Oberbefehlshaber der gesamten Streitkräfte Ariomandes.[2]
Es ist falsch, diese Angaben als Variantzitate auf eine Stufe zu
stellen mit den aus Phanodemos und Ephoros notierten Schiffs-
zahlen. Denn während hier augenscheinlich nur zusätzliche
Bemerkungen vorliegen, die auch fehlen könnten, für den Verlauf
der Schlacht jedenfalls von sekundärer Bedeutung sind,[3] ist der

---

[1] Über rhetorische Züge bei Kallisthenes Jacoby a. O. 1691 f.

[2] Dass Kallisthenes nur den Oberbefehlshaber gekannt hätte (E. Meyer 2),
ist damit nicht gesagt: Plutarch 12. 2 spricht von τοὺς βασιλέως στρατηγούς.

[3] Nach E. Meyer (6) ist der ganze Satz οἱ δὲ πρῶτον μὲν . . . εἰς τὸν ποταμὸν
εἰσωρμίσαντο, προσφερομένων δὲ τῶν Ἀθηναίων ἀντεξέπλευσαν, ὡς μὲν . . ., ὡς
δ᾽ Ἔφορος (12.6) ein "Einschub, der die Zahlen der anderen Berichte einfügen
will." Ausserdem soll hier mit den Kampf auf offener See ein Moment der
Schilderung des Ephoros eingedrungen sein, das zu Kallisthenes, der die
"eingeschlossene Flotte ohne ernstlichen Kampf bewältigt werden lässt"
nicht passt (vgl. auch S. 21 unten "der Seekampf . . . war nur ein Sieg, keine
Schlacht"). Ich glaube, Ed. Meyer macht die Dinge komplizierter als sie sind.
Es ist an sich mindestens nicht wahrscheinlich, dass die Perser Kimons Angriff
vor der Mündung des Eurymedon, also in strategisch ungünstiger Lage, einfach
abgewartet haben sollten, und bei Plutarch steht nichts von einer Einschlies-
sung der Flotte. Dass wirklich ein Kampf auf dem Meere stattfand, zeigt das
samische Epigramm auf Maiandrios, der in dieser ναυμαχίη, wie sie hier ausdrücklich heisst, . . . Schiffe erbeutete (*Ath. Mitt.* 51, 1926, 26 ff.; *Philologus* 86,
1931, 424 ff. S. d. Beilage unten S. 116). Wenn es hier zum Schluss von diesen
Schiffen heisst ὑπεδέξατο πόντος, so können die Perser nicht kampflos in die
Mündung des Flusses zurückgedrängt und hier überwältigt worden sein. Das
Epigramm, so wie es jetzt auf dem Stein steht, gehört zwar erst der Mitte des
dritten Jahrhunderts an, aber es kann die Erneuerung eines älteren Gedichts

Schlachtbericht bei Plutarch, wie E. Meyer mit Recht hervorhebt, auf das engste mit der aus Kallisthenes entnommenen Tatsache verbunden, dass Ariomandes als Oberbefehlshaber sich nicht eher zur Schlacht stellen will, bis die erwarteten Verstärkungen von Cypern eingetroffen sind, während Kimon alles daran liegen muss, so schnell wie möglich loszuschlagen. Diese Verknüpfung kann auch Uxkull nicht bestreiten; umso weniger versteht man, dass er sich der Folgerung daraus verschlossen hat.

Nach einem offenbar von Plutarch selbst herrührenden Zusatz, der noch einmal die Zahl der Schiffe diskutiert (Kallisthenes hatte darüber augenscheinlich keine detaillierten Angaben), und der schon von E. Meyer als Fremdkörper aus der eigentlichen Schlachtbeschreibung ausgeschieden worden ist (12. 6), geht die Erzählung mit Kapitel 13 zu den Landkämpfen über. Die Landtruppen der Perser ἐγγὺς κατατεταγμένον (12.6) stellen die Verbindung mit den an Land flüchtenden Schiffsbesatzungen her und sichern ihren Rückzug auf das feste Lager: die Perser befürchten augenscheinlich eine sofortige Landung der Griechen. Sie scheint ursprünglich nicht in Kimons Absichten gelegen zu haben, er entschliesst sich erst dazu, als die Truppen ῥώμῃ καὶ φρονήματι τοῦ κρατεῖν ἐπηρμένοι selbst verlangen, gegen den Feind geführt zu werden. Schneidiges Vorgehen der Griechen, es kommt zur Schlacht, in der sich die Perser tapfer schlagen, viele angesehene Athener fallen. Schliesslich weichen die Perser, können auch ihr Lager nicht halten: viele Gefangene und reiche Beute fallen den Siegern in die Hände. Inzwischen bringen die von Kimon ausgesandten Spähschiffe die Nachricht, dass die von Cypern her erwarteten phönikischen Trieren bei Hydros vor Anker gegangen sind. Der Platz, bisher nicht identifiziert, ist offenbar an der pamphylischen Küste, nicht allzu weit von der Eurymedonmündung zu suchen.[1] Die Griechen

---

vorliegen und es spricht an sich alles dafür, dass sich die Erinnerung an diese Schlacht gerade auf Samos lebendig erhalten hat; ein noch unpubliziertes Gedicht, das im Heraion von Samos gefunden wurde, rühmt von einem samischen Historiker, dass er geschrieben hat πόσα ναυσὶν ῥέξαντες σκύλοις ἱερὸν ἀγλά-ισαν (die Samier).

[1] Ich kann Schäfers Ἴδυρος (nördl. v. Phaselis) an sich nicht für so unmöglich halten wie Beloch II 2, 161. Aber die Stadt liegt mit fast 60 km Luftlinie

besteigen sofort die Schiffe, überraschen die völlig Ahnungslo-
sen und vernichten τὰς ναῦς ἁπάσας, καὶ τῶν ἀνδρῶν οἱ πλεῖστοι
συνδιεφθάρησαν. Es braucht nicht vieler Worte um darzutun, dass die Erzählung
Plutarchs, wie sie hier paraphrasiert worden ist, Vertrauen weckt.
Der Bericht des Plutarch, den wir nun wieder auf Kallisthenes
zurückführen dürfen, bleibt, nachdem alle vermeintlichen Zeugnisse
gegen ihn sich als nicht stichhaltig erwiesen haben, neben Thukydides unsere einzige verlässliche Quelle. Dass er Thukydides in
keiner Weise widerspricht, ist zur Genüge dargelegt worden.
Auch Uxkull hat keinen Versuch gemacht, den Beweis dafür
anzutreten, dass er "auf den ersten Blick mehr abenteuerliche
als wahrscheinliche Züge" trägt. Wohl aber gilt dies Urteil für
seine eigene, auf die angeblich thukydideische Version zurückge-
hende Rekonstruktion (52). In ihr landet Kimon in der Mündung
des Eurymedon oder westlich von ihr und marschiert dann auf
Aspendos, wo das persische Landheer lagert. Aspendos liegt gute
10 Kilometer landeinwärts: traf unterdessen die persische Flotte
ein, die Uxkull bei Kypros stationiert sein lässt, so war das griechische Schiffslager, von der Besatzung entblösst, verloren, Kimon
der Rückzug abgeschnitten. Weiter: Kimon siegt und vernichtet
das persische Lager mitsamt den Transportschiffen,[1] die, wenn
ich Uxkull recht verstehe, identisch sein sollen mit den achtzig
nachkommenden Trieren bei Plutarch. Angenommen, der Fluss
sei überhaupt soweit schiffbar: müssen erst Schiffe bemüht werden,
um die Truppen nach Aspendos zu bringen? Und ist es nicht

doch etwas weit vom Eurymedon und man wird den Platz auch mit Rücksicht
auf den Kurs der phönikischen Schiffe, die von Cypern her erwartet werden,
lieber östlich als westlich vom Eurymedon suchen. W. Vischer hat Σύεδρα
vorgeschlagen (vgl. Busolt, *Gr. G.* III 1, 150 Anm.), das 100 km Küstenfahrt
östlich liegt: das ist wieder zu weit. So unbequem es ist, dass wir Hydros nicht
kennen, so misslich bleibt in jedem Fall das Konjizieren. Bürchners törichte
Gleichsetzung mit dem Vorgebirge Hydria in der Aeolis hat Uxkull 47 Anm.
26 gebührend gekennzeichnet.

[1] Was Uxkull aus der Überlieferung zu beweisen versucht, steht in den
Hauptzügen schon bei Beloch *Gr. G.* II 2, 161; auch Beloch stützt sich für
die Reihenfolge Landschlacht-Seeschlacht auf das angebliche Zeugnis des
Thukydides.

höchst inkonsequent und methodisch bedenklich, aus einer Erzählung, die man im übrigen verwirft, einen einzelnen Zug herauszunehmen, um ihn für die eigenen Zwecke zurechtgemacht dort einzusetzen, wo er sich dem Bilde einzufügen scheint? Schliesslich das allerunwahrscheinlichste: jetzt erfährt Kimon, dass die persische Flotte von Cypern aus unterwegs ist und fährt ihr entgegen — wozu er erst von Aspendos zurückmarschieren muss. Es kommt zur Schlacht, die Athener siegen, erbeuten hundert Schiffe und vernichten ebensoviele. Aber die Schlacht, auch die Seeschlacht, heisst doch ἡ ἐπ᾿ Εὐρυμέδοντι ποταμῷ? Also muss er "sehr bald auf sie (die Perser) gestossen sein, damit auch die Seeschlacht noch so bezeichnet werden konnte." Wer diese Konstruktion gegen den Bericht des Plutarch hält, wird nicht lange zu überlegen brauchen, welchem Gewährsmann er zu folgen hat.

Damit dürfte der Beweis geschlossen sein. Die Überlieferung über die Doppelschlacht ist bis auf den romanhaften Bericht des Ephoros in allem wesentlichen einheitlich. Wir haben neben den kurzen Andeutungen bei Thukydides und dem nicht mehr bietenden Epigramm Anth. Pal. VII 258 nur Plutarch. Seine Erzählung geht auf Kallisthenes zurück, ist aus einem Guss und in sich durchaus glaubwürdig. Sie ist mangels besserer Zeugen solange für uns verbindlich, wie sie nicht durch schlagende Gründe widerlegt ist. Diese Widerlegung ist Uxkull nicht gelungen. Seine Rekonstruktion ruht auf falschen Voraussetzungen und willkürlichen Interpretationen, sie ist auch für sich betrachtet unhaltbar. Das Fundament, das Ed. Meyer vor nun fast vierzig Jahren gelegt hat, hat sich in fast allen Stücken tragfähig erwiesen. Das gilt, wie für die Kämpfe am Eurymedon, so auch für den Kyprischen Feldzug, nachdem das Epigramm Ἐξ οὗ τ᾿ Εὐρώπην . . . wieder an die Stelle gerückt ist, die Ed. Meyer ihm zugewiesen hat. Gerade hier behalten seine Ausführungen über die Lage, wie sie nach Kimons Tode wirklich war, ihr volles Gewicht: das Gedicht rühmt die Erfolge der Athener um so lauter, je weniger die tatsächlichen Erfolge den Hoffnungen entsprachen, mit denen Kimon ausgezogen war. Die Kräfte waren erschöpft. Perikles handelte folgerichtig; er liquidierte die kimonische Politik und

schloss den Frieden, den Athen brauchte, wenn es seinen Aufstieg
zur Thalassokratie vollenden wollte.

BEILAGE

MAIANDRIOS

Die im Heraion von Samos gefundenen Gedichte auf den Führer des samischen Kontingents in der Schlacht am Eurymedon liest
Wilamowitz bei Klaffenbach, *Ath. Mitt.* 51, 1926, 27:

[Ἦρξε νεῶν Σαμίων] Μαιάνδριος, εὖτ᾽ ἐπὶ καλῶι
ἐστήσαντο μάχην Εὐρυμέδο[ντι κλυτήν]
[τὸν δὲ πόλις τίμησεν· ἀριστ]εύσας γὰρ ἐκείνηι
ναυμαχίηι πάντων κλέος ἔθετ᾽ ἀθάν[ατον].

5　[Δώδεκα νῆας ἕλεν Μαιάν]δριος, ὧν ἀπ᾽ ἑκάστης
ἀσπὶς πρύμναν ἔχει χείρ τ᾽ ὑποδεξ[αμένη],
[τὰς δὲ βαθὺς τηλεκλε]ιτὰς ὑπεδέξατο πόντος
κρυφθείσας Μήδων συμμαχ[ίδας ψαμάθωι].

Schon der Herausgeber hat eingewandt, dass diese Ergänzungen
ungleiche Zeilenanfänge ergeben: vor ΕΤΣΑΣ Zeile 2 der Inschrift =
V. 3 dürfen nicht mehr Buchstaben eingesetzt werden als in der
darüber stehenden Zeile vor Μαιάνδριος (V. 1), und das gleiche gilt
Z. 3 = V. 5 und Z. 4 = V. 7. (vgl. die Zeichnung bei Klaffenbach).
Der Versuch von Hiller v. Gaertringen,[1] durch die Annahme von
scriptio continua einen Ausgleich herbeizuführen (die vorn über-
schüssigen Buchstaben werden an die Zeilenenden gesetzt), muss
so lange als missglückt gelten, als er durch keine Analogie gestützt
werden kann. Auch E. Buschor ist für die einzig natürliche
Anordnung, nach der je ein Distichon eine Zeile füllt, nachdrück-
lich eingetreten; er berechnet die Zahl der vorn fehlenden Buchstaben nach den Massen des Steins auf 18–19.[2]

---

[1] *Ath. Mitt.* 51, 1926, 155 f.
[2] *Philologus* 86, 1931, 424 ff. — Die Erscheinung ist für diese Zeit unge-
wöhnlich und offenbar auf archaistische Tendenzen zurückzuführen; vgl. die
Marathongedichte.

Von diesen Erwägungen abgesehen unterliegen die Ergänzungen
von Wilamowitz auch stilistischen Bedenken: (1) Am Ende des ersten Pentameters hinkt κλυτήν unschön nach; erwartet man aber in
der Verbindung ἐστήσαντο μάχην "sie begannen den Kampf" überhaupt ein Epitheton zu μάχην? Wilamowitz hat dann (bei Hiller v.
Gaertringen a. O.) ποτε eingesetzt: als Flickwort von vornherein
verdächtig, vollends an so später Stelle.

(2) Dass die phönikischen
Schiffe noch nachträglich als "weithin berühmt" gekennzeichnet
sein sollen (7), ist ganz unglaubhaft; und richtet sich nicht eine
Ergänzung, die in einem hellenistischen Gedicht die Zäsur des
dritten Versfusses zerstört, selbst? (3) βαθύς, wieder ein Verlegen-
heitswort — der πόντος braucht kein Epitheton — zwischen τὰς
und τηλεκλείτας gestellt stösst sich an τηλεκλείτας und lässt dieses
unnötig scharf hervortreten. (4) ψαμάθῳ hat in Φ 319 keine ausrei-
chende Parallele, συμμαχίς ist für uns nur in Prosa nachzuweisen;
auch die Stellung von ψαμάθωι, das doch zu κρυφθείσας gezogen
werden muss, weckt wenig Vertrauen.

Eine Ergänzung, die äusserlich den Anforderungen entspricht,
die aber inhaltlich wie formal gleich wenig befriedigen kann, hat
für das erste Gedicht neuerdings Wade-Gery, *JHS* 53, 1933, 97 ff.
versucht. Wade-Gery nimmt an, dass Maiandrios in der Seeschlacht gefallen ist und liest:

[Σκληρὰ παθεῖν Τυρίοις] Μαιάνδριος, εὖτ' ἐπὶ καλῶι
  ἐστήσαντο μάχην Εὐρυμέδο[ντι πόρων]
[εὖ ζωὴν ἤμειψεν· ἀριστ]εύσας γὰρ ἐκείνηι
  ναυμαχίηι πάντων κλέως ἔθετ' ἀθάν[ατον].[1]

Es dürfte einleuchten, dass der Satz "denn indem er sich in der
Schlacht auszeichnete, machte er aller (Samier) Ruhm unsterb-
lich" als Erläuterung zu dem von Wade-Gery Ergänzten nicht
passt, πόρων durch einen ganzen Vers von seinem Objekt getrennt,
stilistisch nicht tragbar ist. Die von Wade-Gery weiterhin in
Betracht gezogene Variante πόρεν ἐν πᾶσι ζηλωτός lässt dies Missver-
hältnis nicht weniger grell hervortreten.

---

[1] Auf dem Stein steht, wie ich aus Autopsie bezeugen kann, in V. 4 wirklich
ΚΛΕΟΣ. Wade-Gery hat irrtümlich auf der Photographie ΚΛΕΩΣ zu erkennen
geglaubt.

An dem zweiten Gedicht hat sich dann A. Wilhelm, *Anzeiger AkWien* 1934, 117 f., versucht. Er hat [τηλεκλε]ιτάς als Beiwort der erbeuteten Schiffe mit Recht abgelehnt. Ich kann aber seinen eigenen Vorschlag [Παμφυλ]ίτας nicht für glücklicher halten. Abgesehen von der Bildung und der dorischen Form: dass der πόντος hier durch das unterscheidende Adjektiv ausdrücklich als pamphylischer gekennzeichnet sein sollte, scheint mir nicht stilgemäss und entbehrt jeder inneren Notwendigkeit: ohne Zwang aber wird kein hellenistischer Dichter den Versbau durch ein die Zäsur überspringendes viersilbiges Wort zerstören.

Es mag nach solchen Fehlschlägen und angesichts der Tatsache, dass an den fraglichen Stellen meist mehr als die Hälfte der Verse fehlt, aussichtslos erscheinen, eine Ergänzung überhaupt noch zu versuchen. Wenn im folgenden gleichwohl neue Vorschläge gemacht werden, so geschieht es in der Überzeugung, dass nur solchem Suchen nach den Möglichkeiten der poetischen Form Aufbau und Haltung des Gedichts sich erschliessen.

Der sicherste Ausgangspunkt für eine Ergänzung ist die Bestimmung der Lücke im Beginn des zweiten Gedichts. Hier hat schon Buschor bemerkt, dass δώδεκα die Zahl der erbeuteten Schiffe unnötig hoch ansetzt; ihm folgend hat Wade-Gery [ὀκτὼ νῆας ἕλεν Μαιάν]δριος hergestellt: das ergibt 16½ Buchstaben, das nur teilweise erhaltene Δ nicht eingerechnet. Eine andere Möglichkeit wäre [ἐξ κατέδυσε νέας Μαιάν]δριος (Maas) mit 18½ Buchstaben. Unter fünf Schiffe wird man wegen ἑκάστης nicht gern heruntergehen, [πέντε νέας κατέδυσε M.] würde aber den Raum schon übermässig weiten (21½ Bchst.). Mit ὀκτὼ νῆας ἕλεν gewinnt man vor Μαιάνδριος im ersten Gedicht 17–18 freie Stellen, mit ἐξ κατέδυσε νέας 19–20; genau die gleichen Zahlen gelten für Vers 3 und 7. Soweit die äusserlich erreichbaren Indizien.

Der Satz, mit dem das erste Gedicht schliesst, sagt aus, dass Maiandrios durch sein Verhalten in der Schlacht allen Samiern Ruhm gebracht hat; wenn er mit γάρ angeschlossen ist, war vorher die Anerkennung, der Dank der Gesamtheit, die an diesem Ruhme teilhatte, ausdrücklich bezeichnet:[1] v. Hillers [ὅν δῆμος τίμησεν· ἀριστ]-

---

[1] Deswegen kann ich an [λάϊνος ὦδ᾽ ἔστηκεν . . .] (mit dem Folgenden = 19 Bchst.), das Maas für V. 3 vorschlug, nicht glauben: πάντων verlangt, dass

εὔσας γάρ . . . füllt mit 18 Buchstaben (2 Iotas) die ὀκτὼ νῆας ἕλεν entsprechende Lücke. Für den Schluss des Pentameters bietet sich νέες, oder, wenn die Samier vorher genannt waren, νεῶν, 'den Schiffs-kampf.' Bei der Bestimmung des vor Μαιάνδριος Fehlenden ist in Betracht zu ziehen, dass nach Buschors Darlegungen das erste Gedicht erst nachträglich auf den Stein gesetzt ist, also wohl an die Stelle einer Prosainschrift vom Typus ὁ δῆμος ὁ Σαμίων Μαιάνδριος τοῦ δεῖνα . . . Ἥρηι trat. Man wird danach hier in Ergänzung des zweiten, älteren Epigramms, allgemeinere Angaben erwarten: die Benenn-ung der Schlacht, die Rolle des Maiandrios, die Tatsache der Weihung. Nach homerischem Gebrauch von κοσμεῖν liesse sich der Anfang dann etwa mit [Τοὺς Σαμίους κόσμησε] Μαιάνδριος herstellen (17½ Buchst.).[1] Die Ergänzung setzt voraus, dass Maiandrios der Führer des samischen Aufgebots in der Schlacht war. Das ist gewiss wahrscheinlich, aber keineswegs sicher. So möchte ich mit [Πλεῖστα τρόπαια φέρεν]M.[2] einen Vorschlag zur Erwägung geben, der von dieser Annahme absieht oder sie doch nicht besonders ausdrückt (18 Bchst.): er erzielt, für den Anfang des Gedichtes besonders willkommen, einen volleren Klang, und eine so allge-meine Bezeichnung der Taten des Maiandrios nimmt weder die Angaben des zweiten Gedichts voraus noch das hier mit V. 3 folgende ἀριστεύσας . . ., das gerade wenn es für sich stände, als Auftakt für das stark betonte πάντων κλέος ἔθετ᾽ ἀθάνατον etwas matt wirken würde.

Besondere Schwierigkeiten stellen sich der Ergänzung von Vers 7 entgegen. Wenn man die Zäsur erhalten will, ist man gezwungen, entweder τας mit einer vorausgehenden langen Silbe (I kann wohl auch H oder N gewesen sein) zu einem Wort zusammenzunehmen, oder man muss τάς als Relativum bzw. Demonstrativum fassen

---

der δῆμος oder die πόλις ausdrücklich genannt war. Es dürfte auch schwerhalten, in V. 1 das nun erforderliche Partizip unterzubringen.

[1] Bei der etwas nüchtern-"prosaisch" anmutenden Ergänzung Ἦρξε νεῶν Σαμίων Μαιάνδριος wird Wilamowitz der Eingang des Simonideischen Gedichts auf Demokritos, Bergk 136 = Diehl 65 vor Augen gestanden haben Δημόκριτος τρίτος ἦρξε μάχης, ὅτε . . .

[2] Vgl. Hiller v. Gaertringen, *Hist. gr. Epigr.* 66. 2 Ζηνὶ τρόπαια φέρειν und andererseits Kaibel 62. 1 ἕστηκεν . . . πλεῖστα τρόπαια.

und in -]ι einen Dativ, eine Präposition, eine Konjunktion suchen.
Alle Versuche, den ersten Weg zu gehen, scheitern. Maas hat
[σημάινουσα βροτοῖς ὅτ]ι . . . vorgeschlagen (18 Bchst.). Ohne
diese Ergänzung für unmöglich zu halten, möchte ich zu bedenken
geben, ob nicht der Gedanke, die ἀσπίς oder die χείρ mit den
πρύμναι einen Hinweis auf den *Untergang* der Schiffe sein zu
lassen, etwas weit hergeholt scheint; natürlicher wäre jedenfalls,
wenn sie für die Tat des Maiandrios zeugen würden, die Eroberung
der Schiffe. Es kommt hinzu, dass der Bau des ersten Gedichts die
Annahme einer einzigen Periode nicht empfiehlt. Wenn man
[ἀλ]ι[1] einsetzt — der Dativ würde gerade zu κρυφθείσας gut pas-
sen —, liesse sich etwa [πάσας δ᾽ αὐτάνδρους ἀλ]ι τὰς ὑπεδέξατο πόντος
denken (18 Bchst.) oder nach dem Epigramm auf die kyprischen
Siege (7) [πληθούσας δ᾽ ἀνδρῶν ἀλ]ι τὰς ὑ. π. Weniger könnte [βυσσῶι
δ᾽ αὐτάνδρους ἔν]ι τὰς ὑ. π. (18½ Bchst.) befriedigen: ἔνι klappt nach
und κρυφθείσας hängt vollends in der Luft. Sonst käme wohl auch
[πάσας δ᾽ αὐτάνδρους κα]ι τὰς ὑ. π. in Betracht: auch sie verschlang
wie die übrigen damals eroberten oder versenkten Schiffe das
Meer. αὐτάνδρους empfiehlt sich in jedem Fall wegen des folgenden
Μήδων συμμαχ[ίαν . .], das nur als Apposition zu τὰς . . . verstanden werden kann. Hier hat Maas das diese Beziehung störende
und auch an sich anstössige ἐν ψαμάθωι durch den schönen Schluss
Μήδων συμμαχ[ίην ἄλιον] (= "vanam") glücklich beseitigt.
Ich würde also vorschlagen zu lesen:

[Πλεῖστα τρόπαια φέρεν] Μαιάνδριος, εὖτ᾽ ἐπὶ καλῶι
    ἐστήσαντο μάχην Εὐρυμέδο[ντι νέες·] |
[ὃν δῆμος τίμησεν, ἀριστ]εύσας γὰρ ἐκείνηι
    ναυμαχίηι πάντων κλέος ἔθετ᾽ ἀθάνατον. |

['Οκτὼ νῆας ἕλεν Μαιάν]δριος, ὧν ἀπ᾽ ἑκάστης
    ἀσπὶς πρύμναν ἔχει χείρ τ᾽ ὑποδεξ[αμένη·] |
[πάσας δ᾽ αὐτάνδρους ἀλ]ι τὰς ὑπεδέξατο πόντος
    κρυφθείσας, Μήδων συμμαχ[ίην ἄλιον.]

---

[1] Vergleichen liesse sich homerisches πόντος ἀλός, ἀλὸς πέλαγος.

THE PEACE OF KALLIAS[1]

By H. T. Wade-Gery

THE Peace of Kallias, between Athens and Persia, is recorded by Diodoros under the year 449/8 as an immediate consequence of Kimon's last campaign in Cyprus, XII 4.

4: Ἀρταξέρξης δὲ ὁ βασιλεὺς πυθόμενος τὰ περὶ τὴν Κύπρον ἐλαττώματα, καὶ βουλευσάμενος μετὰ τῶν φίλων περὶ τοῦ πολέμου, ἔκρινε συμφέρειν εἰρήνην συνθέσθαι πρὸς τοὺς Ἕλληνας. ἔγραψε τοίνυν τοῖς περὶ Κύπρον ἡγεμόσι καὶ σατράπαις, ἐφ' οἷς ἂν δύνωνται συλλύσασθαι πρὸς τοὺς Ἕλληνας. (5) διόπερ οἱ περὶ τὸν Ἀρτάβαζον καὶ Μεγάβυζον ἔπεμψαν εἰς τὰς Ἀθήνας πρεσβευτὰς τοὺς διαλεξομένους περὶ συλλύσεως. ὑπακουσάντων δὲ τῶν Ἀθηναίων καὶ πεμψάντων πρέσβεις αὐτοκράτορας ὧν ἡγεῖτο Καλλίας ὁ Ἱππονίκου, ἐγένοντο συνθῆκαι περὶ τῆς εἰρήνης τοῖς Ἀθηναίοις καὶ τοῖς συμμάχοις πρὸς τοὺς Πέρσας, ὧν ἐστὶ τὰ κεφάλαια ταῦτα·

(i) αὐτονόμους εἶναι τὰς κατὰ τὴν Ἀσίαν Ἑλληνίδας πόλεις ἁπάσας

(ii) τοὺς δὲ τῶν Περσῶν σατράπας μὴ καταβαίνειν ἐπὶ θάλατταν κατωτέρω τριῶν ἡμερῶν ὁδόν

(iii) μηδὲ ναῦν μακρὰν πλεῖν ἐντὸς Φασήλιδος καὶ Κυανέων· ταῦτα δὲ τοῦ βασιλέως καὶ τῶν στρατηγῶν ἐπιτελούντων

(iv) μὴ στρατεύειν Ἀθηναίους εἰς τὴν χώραν ἧς βασιλεὺς Ἀρταξέρξης[2] ἄρχει.

---

[1] I have used the following special abbreviations frequently:

ATL   Meritt, Wade-Gery, and McGregor, *The Athenian Tribute Lists*, Vol. I, Harvard University Press, 1939.

J.   Jacoby, *Die Fragmente der griechischen Historiker*, I–II, Berlin, 1923–30. The historians are numbered serially: "115 F 153" means "Theopompos (historian no. 115) fragment 153."

This essay, based on papers I have read before the Oxford Philological Society, the Classical Club at Harvard, and elsewhere, owes much to the discussions on these occasions, and in its final form to the help of my wife and Mr. A. Andrewes.

[2] So the *Patmius*: Vogel brackets Ἀρταξέρξης: the inferior mss. give Ἀρταξέρξης βασιλεύς. If the name is genuine (and the variation of order is of course no proof of its intrusion), it indicates that the treaty was "with Artaxerxes" and would need renewal with Dareios.

(6) συντελεσθεισῶν δὲ τῶν σπονδῶν 'Αθηναῖοι τὰς δυνάμεις ἀπήγαγον ἐκ τῆς Κύπρου.

Thucydides in his sketch of the years 476–439 (I 98–117) does not mention the treaty: when, after the rather shameful Peace of Antalkidas in 386, it became by contrast a favourite theme of the Attic orators, Theopompos (J. 115 F 153) undertook to prove it was a myth. Kallisthenes (J. 124 F 16) appears to have accepted this proof: but Krateros, who later published extensive extracts from the Athenian archives, included a copy of it, of which a fragment perhaps survives.[1]

The contention of this paper is that Diodoros' account, like much of what he took from Ephoros, is true so far as it goes,[2] but a bit bowdlerized and unrealistic: and I seek to determine the actual terms more precisely and put the event in its historic context.

I

THE LITERARY PROBLEM

"Der Vertrag mit Persien oder der sogenannte Kalliasfrieden ist kein Problem der politischen, sondern der litterarischen Geschichte." By these impatient words (*Hermes* XXXV 111) Eduard Schwartz meant that the historical event is plain enough, what needs explaining is the way Kallisthenes and others wrote about it: in an acute footnote he adds that the (then) position of European settlements in the dominions of the Sultan, or in China, gives a good analogy. And though neither he nor anyone else has made the historical event plain enough for my taste, nor, I fancy, for the shrewd and uncompromising eyes of the great scholar whom we are honouring, yet Schwartz did well to distinguish the two problems, and it is convenient to take the literary problem first.

The crux of the literary problem is not that Thucydides does not mention the treaty with Persia (he has other no less strange omissions) nor that Theopompos declared the inscribed treaty to be a

---

[1] See pp. 155–156, *Appendix*.

[2] The date, as usual in narrative derived from Ephoros, is not more than approximate. I believe the treaty was sworn early in 449: see pp. 149–152.

forgery (though this is a matter of some interest): the crux lies, as both Schwartz and Ed. Meyer saw, in the words of Kallisthenes as quoted by Plutarch, *Kimon* 13. 4. Schwartz and Meyer give different solutions of this crux and neither solution is quite satisfactory. Plutarch, having given a description of the victory of the Eurymedon (evidently Kallisthenes' description: see Jacoby's note on 124 F 15–16) concludes: "This achievement so humbled the King's pride that he subscribed to the terms of the famous Peace, that he should keep a horse's ride distant from the Greek sea nor let his ships of war sail to the Greek side of Kyaneai and Chelidoniai. Kallisthenes says indeed that the King did not actually subscribe to these terms (οὔ φησι ταῦτα συνθέσθαι τὸν βάρβαρον), but observed them in fact through fear of that defeat, keeping indeed so far from Greece that Perikles sailed with 50 ships beyond the Chelidoniai, and Ephialtes with only 30, and no Persian fleet encountered them."[1] It is perhaps arguable that Plutarch need not be understood as recording a definite denial of the treaty's existence: the words οὔ φησι, etc., might mean only that Kallisthenes did not mention it. This is, in effect, Meyer's contention: that Kallisthenes did not mention it in this context.[2] The difficulty here (apart from the fact that οὔ φησι commonly means *negat*) is that the context,

[1] Plutarch's statement, *Kim.* 19. 4, that οὐδὲ γραμματοφόρος κατέβαινεν οὐδ' ἵππος πρὸς θαλάσσῃ τετρακοσίων σταδίων ἐντὸς ὤφθη στρατηγοῦντος Κίμωνος, is no doubt from this passage of Kallisthenes, since the famous clause (see p. 133 n. 2) is here put as a *de facto* result of Kimon's victories.

[2] Meyer, *Forschungen* II 4–5, who however thinks Plutarch is just wrong. Kallisthenes illustrated his point by two instances (Plut. *Kim.* 13. 4): Perikles sailed beyond the Chelidoniai with 50 ships, and Ephialtes with only 30, and neither met an enemy fleet. Ephialtes was killed in 461, so that his voyage must certainly belong to the years immediately following the Eurymedon, before the Egyptian revolt. Perikles is mentioned first, which may suggest that he went first and therefore his voyage also belongs to those years. But Perikles was then very young: I suspect the order is rhetorical ("P. with 50 ships, E. with only 30") and that Kallisthenes refers to the voyage which Thucydides records (I 116. 3) in 440 B.C. — Perikles sailed from Samos with 60 (not 50) ships, towards Kaunos and Karia (not beyond the Chelidoniai): such inexactnesses in a fourth-century historian should not surprise us. The central fact, that no enemy fleet ventured to show itself, is what matters. If this is right, then Kallisthenes' two instances are taken from very wide apart, and indicate that he conceives the situation created by the Eurymedon to extend right down to

as Meyer so persuasively shows, was a digression from the Peace of
Antalkidas: if Kallisthenes contrasted that shameful treaty, not
with the earlier treaty but merely with the situation produced by
the Eurymedon, this suggests very strongly that he did not believe
in the earlier treaty's existence. Schwartz, accepting Plutarch's
statement that Kallisthenes denied its existence, infers that Kallisthenes must have known Theopompos' arguments against it, and
further, that the passage must come from the only work of Kallisthenes which Schwartz believed later than the publication of
Theopompos' arguments, viz. the *History of Alexander*.[1] No one,
I think, has followed Schwartz in this: it is indeed hardly con-
ceivable that the account of the Eurymedon and its effects which
lies behind Plutarch's *Kimon* 12–13, formed a digression on Alexander's march. Unless Plutarch has managed to change the whole
tone, Kimon is there glorified by contrast to his successors, and his
achievement is still unparalleled.

It looks, then, as if Kallisthenes denied the treaty in his *Hellenika* I, before the publication of Theopompos' *Philippika* XXV.
He evidently admired the Athenian achievement; had he perhaps
some reason for denial more cogent than Theopompos' imputation
of forgery? *Omne ignotum pro magnifico*: the unknown arguments
which may have moved Kallisthenes remain among the most
potent weapons in the armoury of doubt. We move here amongst
unknowns. Yet I would urge the possibility that Kallisthenes,
writing his *Hellenika* in Philip's reign, could know of Theopompos'
argument, although Book XXV of the latter's *Philippika* (where
the argument finally stood) cannot have been published before
Philip's death. It appears to me almost certain[2] that the two anti-
Athenian "pamphlets" which Theopompos inserted into *Philippika*

---

440 (and no doubt beyond); and this will explode Meyer's hypothesis that
Kallisthenes not only did not deny the treaty, but actually recorded it a few
pages on.

[1] *Hermes* XXXV 109: "Kallisthenes knüpfte die Leugnung des Vertrages an
eine Schilderung der Schlacht am Eurymedon: für ein solche Schilderung ist
kein leichterer Anlass denkbar, als Alexanders Marsch durch Pamphylien im
Jahr 333. Damals, vermutlich schon vor 334, müssen von Theopomps philippi-
schen Geschichten mindestens die ersten 25 Bücher veröffentlicht gewesen sein."

[2] Cp. *AJP* LIX 132 n. 7.

X and XXV had done service as propaganda (i.e. had been in some form "published") long before the publication of the complete history. Speusippos' complaint to Philip about Theopompos' malicious utterances (*Epist. Socrat.* 30.14, see J. 69 F 1) was written in the late 'forties (τοσαύτην ἡμῖν σπάνιν βυβλίων βασιλεὺς Αἴγυπτον λαβὼν πεποίηκεν, *ibid.*): and unless Theopompos was known as a vitriolic pamphleteer, Anaximenes could not have fathered upon him his *Trikaranos*, no doubt in Philip's lifetime (Paus. VI 18. 5: for the date see Jacoby's note on 72 F 20–21, *sc.* the fragments of the *Trikaranos*). I conceive then that Kallisthenes, aware that the treaty's authenticity had been questioned, preferred to contrast the Spartan treaty not with the earlier treaty but with the *de facto* situation after the Eurymedon. On that occasion he would be right in saying the king swore to no covenant, but observed its terms (or some of them) in fact.

My working hypothesis, then, is that Ephoros published his earlier fifth-century books (VIII–XII), with an account of the Treaty,[1] between 350 and 345: that in the middle 'forties Theopompos declared the Treaty a forgery: that in the later 'forties Kallisthenes retorted that that did not affect the magnitude of Athens' achievement, since Athens in fact broke Persia's power at the Eurymedon, and Persia only recovered when Athens had fallen and Sparta betrayed the Greek cause. This statement of the case misled Plutarch into dating the Treaty immediately after the Eurymedon (*Kim.* 13. 4), since by his time the authenticity was no longer questioned: it has been alleged that already the orator Lycurgus, writing in 331, drew the same false inference, *in Leocr.* 72–73 (τὸ κεφάλαιον τῆς νίκης [but this νίκη is not the Eurymedon?] - - - - συνθήκας ἐποιήσαντο). But this concerns fourth-century history more than fifth: such propaganda commonplaces tell us very little of the actualities of 450 B.C. I come back to Theopompos.

Theopompos in *Philippika* XXV undertook to expose the vanities of Athenian historic claims, including αἱ πρὸς βασιλέα Δαρεῖον

---

[1] And also the Ἑλληνικὸς ὅρκος: Diodoros, XI 29. 3, gives it practically *verbatim* the same as Lycurgus *in Leocr.* 81, and no doubt both have it from Ephoros, since it is in ripe fourth-century style (e.g. no hiatus: contrast Hdt. VII 132. 2). This too Theopompos undertook to explode (J. 115 F 153).

Ἀθηναίων †πρὸς Ἕλληνας† (?περὶ Ἑλλήνων) συνθῆκαι (J. 115 F 153).
His argument is preserved in two further fragments (J. 115 F 154,
155): the stele on which it was inscribed bore Ionic letters, not
Attic, and the Ionic alphabet was not introduced till 403/2 B.C.
Theopompos' conclusion (*ibid.* 154) that the Treaty was therefore
a forgery (ἐσκευωρῆσθαι) goes far beyond this evidence and is in
itself incredible: fourth-century Athens was anything but totali-
tarian and a public forgery of that kind (I submit) quite impossible. It is indeed very possible that the stele was inscribed in the
fourth century. The publication of a document from the archives
was frequently ordered; especially in the early years of the fourth
century, when previous publications had perished in the troubles
at the end of the fifth century (e.g. *IG* II² 6). If, as seems most
likely, this publication was ordered about 380 B.C., it will not be,
like those just mentioned, a publication of something still valid,
but a piece of sentimental diplomacy, comparable to Isokrates'
Panegyrikos of that date. Isokrates had there said (4. 120):
μάλιστα δ' ἄν τις συνίδοι τὸ μέγεθος τῆς μεταβολῆς εἰ παραναγνοίη τὰς
συνθήκας τάς τ' ἐφ' ἡμῶν γενομένας καὶ τὰς νῦν ἀναγεγραμμένας: if the
world was to compare the two treaties, the earlier one had to be
published. I am assuming that Theopompos was right in contending that the inscription he knew was of the fourth century: but the
fact though probable is not certain. Could it not have been inscribed as soon as the Treaty was concluded? The only Attic
decree in Ionic letters which is anywhere near the date of the Peace
of Kallias is *IG* I² 16: that was inscribed at the expense of the Phase-
lites, who might use a foreign workman, whereas the publication
of the treaty with Persia was a matter for the Poletai, who would
surely use an Athenian. But it is too little observed that Theopompos is reported as speaking of "the treaty of the Athenians
with King Dareios": such a treaty was certainly concluded (Andok.
3. 29: see the following section) and would belong to the year 423.
At that date Ionic writing was getting commoner in Attic decrees;
IG I² 25 is of the same year and in some ways an analogous document: it was no doubt commissioned by the Poletai: it was begun
in Attic, but continued in Ionic, script.[1]

[1] See pp. 129-130, (d).

Our evidence is, then, that the stele which Theopompos knew contained the treaty with Dareios. It would be foolish to press this too far, since the citation may be in error: but it looks as if the headline of the stele read συνθῆκαι 'Αθηναίων πρὸς βασιλέα Δαρεῖον, much like the slightly more elaborate heading of the treaty of 412/1 transcribed by Thucydides VIII 37. 1: ξυνθῆκαι Λακεδαιμονίων καὶ τῶν ξυμμάχων πρὸς βασιλέα Δαρεῖον καὶ τοὺς παῖδας τοὺς βασιλέως καὶ Τισσαφέρνην. If so, the possibilities are many: I suggest a few, not to be exhaustive but to indicate the uncertainty of any one hypothesis:

(a) The stele contained the original Treaty with Artaxerxes, inscribed in 449, with a new headline inscribed *in rasura* in 423 (cf. *IG* I² 51, 52), the headline only being in Ionic script.

(b) The stele contained the Treaty with Artaxerxes on one face, that with Dareios on the other (cf. *IG* I² 24, 25), the latter face being in Ionic script. In cases both (a) and (b), the Ionic letters may be from the same hand as *IG* I² 25: in case (a) Theopompos must be presumed to have satisfied himself with reading the headline only.

(c) The stele contained only the Treaty with Dareios, inscribed in 423, in a hand similar to *IG* I² 25.

(d) The stele contained only the Treaty with Dareios, inscribed (as being the more recent) in 380 for comparison with the Peace of Antalkidas.

(e) The stele contained both treaties (cf. *IG* I² 57, II² 1), inscribed in 380 for comparison with the Peace of Antalkidas.

It is evident that a good deal turns on whether the Treaty with Dareios was a mere ratification of that with Artaxerxes [as implied in case (a)], or was something quite new. We probably cannot answer this question for certain, but at least we can get it formulated. That is our next concern.

II

THE TREATY WITH DAREIOS

The Treaty with Dareios (the Bastard, not the Great) is recorded by Andokides, 3. 29. Speaking in favour of the peace negotiations of 390 (see below, p. 148) he says, "I fear we shall make our usual mistake, and give up our strong friends and choose weak ones. Remember how we made a treaty and covenanted friendship forever[1] with the King of Persia (and Epilykos my uncle was your ambassador to him), and later, persuaded by Amorges, a slave of the King and a runaway slave, we threw away the King's strength, as if it was no use to us, and chose Amorges' friendship: wherefore the King was indignant and made alliance with Sparta and gave them 5000 talents for the war and finally brought our power to ruin." Andokides does not expressly say that the King in question was Dareios: but he tells us elsewhere that when his uncle Epilykos was killed in Sicily in 414 he left as issue two young daughters, and this suggests that his mission to Sousa is not likely to have been very many years before that.[2] The date can be fixed precisely to 424/3, sc. Dareios' first year, by a comparison of the following documents.

(a) *IG* II² 8 (*Syll.*³ 118): decrees in honour of Herakleides of Klazomenai. Of the main decree, which perhaps conferred Attic citizenship on him, only the last line survives; the bulk of the extant inscription is taken up by a presumably earlier decree which had made him a proxenos.

$$[\epsilon]\delta o\xi \epsilon \nu \ \tau \eta \iota \ \beta o\lambda \eta \iota \ [\kappa \alpha \iota \ \tau \omega \iota \ \delta \eta \mu \omega \iota \ \Pi \alpha \nu \delta \iota o]$$
$$[\nu]\iota \sigma \ \epsilon \pi \rho \upsilon \tau \alpha \nu \epsilon \upsilon \epsilon \nu \ \Sigma [\iota \mu \omega \nu ? \ \epsilon \gamma \rho \alpha \mu \mu \alpha \tau \epsilon \upsilon \epsilon \nu]$$
$$5 \ \ [N]\epsilon o\kappa \lambda \epsilon \iota \delta \eta \sigma \ \epsilon \pi \epsilon \sigma \tau [\alpha \tau \epsilon \ . . . . . ^{13} . . . .]$$
$$[\epsilon \iota]\pi \epsilon \nu \cdot \ H \rho \alpha \kappa \lambda \epsilon \iota \delta \eta \nu \ [\tau o\gamma \ K\lambda \alpha \zeta o\mu \epsilon \nu \iota o\nu \ \alpha \nu]$$
$$[\alpha \gamma \rho]\alpha \psi \alpha \iota \ \tau o\gamma \ \gamma \rho \alpha \mu \mu [\alpha \tau \epsilon \alpha \ \tau \eta \sigma \ \beta o\lambda \eta \sigma \ \pi \rho o\xi]$$
$$[\epsilon \nu o]\nu \ \kappa \alpha \iota \ \epsilon \upsilon \epsilon \rho \gamma \epsilon \tau \eta [\nu \ \kappa \alpha \theta o\tau \iota \ \alpha \nu \ \tau \omega \iota \ \delta \eta \mu \omega]$$
$$[\iota \ \delta o]\kappa \eta \iota \ \kappa \alpha \iota \ \theta \epsilon \nu \alpha \iota \ \epsilon [\nu \ \pi o\lambda \epsilon \iota \ \epsilon \pi \epsilon \iota \delta \eta \ \epsilon \upsilon \ \epsilon \pi]$$

[1] Σπονδὰς ποιησάμενοι καὶ συνθέμενοι φιλίαν εἰς τὸν ἅπαντα χρόνον.

[2] Epilykos and his three sisters (who married, one the strategos Glaukon, one Andokides' father Leogoras, one Perikles' son Xanthippos) appear all to have been born c. 460–450: he, as we shall see, was secretary of the first prytany in 424/3. Son of Teisandros, grandson of Epilykos, no doubt he was a member of the *genos* of Philaidai (like the elder Miltiades), since both Epilykos and Teisandros are among the descendants of Philaios in Marcell. *vit. Thuc.* 3. For the evidence for these relationships (not always quite conclusive) see *PA* under these names, and especially the *stemma s.v.* 'Ανδοκίδης, no. 828.

10 [οησ]εν τασ Αθηναιω[ν πρεσβειασ και εν π]
    [ασι α]νηρ εστι αγαθ[οσ περι τον δημον τον]
    [Αθην]αιων. Θοκυδιδ[ησ ειπε· τα μεν αλλα κ]
    [αθα]περ τηι βοληι ε[πειδη δε οι πρεσβεσ]
    [οι πα]ρα βασιλεωσ ηκ[οντεσ αγγελλοσι Η]
15 [ρακλ]ειδην συμπρατ[τεν εαυτοισ προθυ]
    [μωσ ε]σ τε τασπονδασ [τασ προσ βασιλεα ε]
    [σ τε α]λλο οτι επαγγε[λειαν, etc.]

Lines 13–16 make it certain that *spondai* have been made with the King. The supplements in 3–4 are suggested and explained by West *AJP* LVI 73–76.[1] Neokleides, who is here epistates for his own tribe Pandionis, was (presumably earlier the same year, as member of the same Boule) secretary for the tribe Aigeis: as such he appears in perhaps three extant decrees, *viz.*:

(b) *IG* I² 145

    Σωτιμο Ηερα[κ]λειοτο κ
    αι εκγονον προχσενο κ
    αι ευεργετο Αθεναιον
    [εδοχσεν τει] βολει κα[ι] τοι [δεμ]
5   [οι Αιγεισ επρυτανε]υε Νε[οκλε]
    [ιδεσ εγραμματευε, etc.]

Neokleides' name was first supplied here by Ferguson, *Ath. Sec.* 15, 17: cf. West *AJP* LVI 72 for the length of the line.

(c) *IG* I² 87, Treaty between Athens and Haliai: cf. Meritt *AJP* LVI 65–71.

    [Νε]οκλειδ[εσ — 6 or 7 — εγρα]μματευε
    εδοχσεν τει [βολει και τοι δεμοι Αιγει]σ επρυτανευε
    Νεοκλειδησ [εγραμματευε — 7 — επεσ]τατε Λαχεσ ε
    ιπε· χσυνθεκα[σ, etc.]

That this year is 424/3 is demonstrated by Meritt *loc. cit.*

(d) *IG* I² 25: provision for the Priestess of Nike.

---

1 I write περι in line 11, since εισ conflicts with the spellings in line 16.

εδοχσεν τει βολει και τοι δε
μοι Αιγεισ επρυτανευε Νεοκ
λειδησ εγραμματευε Αγνοδε
μοσ επεστατε Καλλιασ ειπε· τ
5   ει ḫιερεαι, etc.

This is the inscription which was begun in Attic script but continued (lines 7 ff.) in Ionic. It is doubtless consequent on the news of the Treaty, being a renewal of 24 which itself was doubtless consequent on the news of the Treaty with Artaxerxes.

(e) *IG* I² 324 lines 25–26: text from Meritt *AFD* 138:

25   [ταδε παρεδ]οσαν ηοι ταμιαι Θ[οκυ]διδεσ¹ Αχερδοσιοσ και χσυ-
ναρχοντεσ επι Ισ[αρχο αρχοντοσ κα]
[ι επι τεσ βολεσ] h[ει Επι]λ[υ]κοσ [προ]τοσ εγραμματευε, etc.

This is the year 424/3.

May we assume that Epilykos of (e), the secretary of the first prytany of 424/3, is the same as Epilykos who went on the embassy? That Neokleides, secretary of the prytany of Aigeis in 424/3 (b c d), is the same as Neokleides, epistates on the day when Herakleides was honoured for his services to the embassy (a)? That Laches who moved (c) is the same as the Laches who moved the decree for the armistice in 424/3 (Thuc. IV 118. 11)? That Thucydides of (e), the tamias of 424/3, is the same as Thucydides who moved the amendment in (a), in which the Treaty with the King is mentioned? The case for these identifications (at least the first three) has been put by West *AJP* LVI 72–76, to whom I refer: they provide a notable confirmation of the *a priori* arguments of Koehler,² that (a) belongs to the year 423. If we accept them, Epilykos went to Sousa in his capacity as bouleutes, since his fellow bouleutes Neokleides is still in office when the embassy has returned, cf. (a) line 14. It is of course possible (see West *l. c.* 74 n. 7)

¹ This restoration is made certain by lines 34–35. Cf. Marcell. *vit. Thuc.* 28.
² *Hermes* XXVII 68–78, accepted (before the further evidence of the names was known) in *Syll.*³ 118.

that the bouleutes Neokleides in (b c d) is not the same man, or does not belong to the same year, as the bouleutes of the same name in (a): but the name is rare, the evidence is coherent: the economical hypothesis is that Epilykos went to Sousa, and came back, before midsummer 423. The statement of Andokides, that he had made a treaty with the King, is unequivocally confirmed by (a) line 16, τασπονδασ [τασ προσ βασιλεα]. In 424/3, Dareios the Bastard began his reign.

It is very remarkable that Thucydides does not mention this treaty. In IV 50, he tells how in the winter of 425/4 the Persian Artaphernes had been captured in Thrace, on his way from King Artaxerxes to Sparta: and how an Attic embassy was sent with him as far as Ephesos, but no further, since on the news of Artaxerxes' death they returned home. To have recorded this abortive embassy, and then said nothing of the embassy which a year later made a treaty with the new King, is something of quite a different order from his silence on the Treaty with Artaxerxes. In 424/3 he is in the main stream of his proper subject, and the attitude of Persia is part of the story (as IV 50, and again VIII 5. 5, 6. 1, 16. 3, etc., show). No doubt this extraordinary silence is partly due to the unfinished state of the history. In this winter of 424/3, the historian was commanding in Thrace, failed to save Amphipolis, and was exiled: and the narrative from then onwards was perhaps due for more revision than the earlier years of the ten-year war. But this silence is evidence of the reality of the treaty with Artaxerxes. If Athens had not before been in treaty with Persia, the treaty of 423 becomes so cardinal an event that no lack of revision really explains its absence from a narrative which devotes twenty-eight chapters to the winter of 424/3, and seventeen chapters to the summer of 423 (IV 89–116 and 117–133). But if the treaty of 423 was no more than a reaffirmation, with the new king, of the treaty which had existed with his predecessor,[1] it becomes less momentous.

I conceive, then, that the Treaty of 424/3 was in essentials a renewal of that of 450/49: possibly a verbatim renewal [as suggested on p. 127, under (a)]. But this is not proved; and in our attempts

[1] See p. 121 n. 2.

to recover the terms of the treaty of 450/49, that of 424/3 will perpetually obtrude itself. The *status quo* which was upset in the last ten years of the Peloponnesian War was of course that of 424/3: the treaty which Theopompos saw inscribed on a stele was very probably that of 424/3. Are the terms which Isokrates and the orators report (see pp. 134–135) those of 450/49 or of 424/3 ? Was the document which Krateros transcribed (pp. 122, 155) that of 450/49 or of 424/3 ? It is never easy to say: and though I conceive the two treaties to have been in essentials identical, let us remember that this is not proved.

III

The Terms of the Treaties with Artaxerxes and Dareios

I have called Diodoros' account of the Treaty "bowdlerized and unrealistic": this applies especially to his summary of the terms. Of his four heads (see p. 121), the first two may be classed as "autonomy clauses," the last two as "non-aggression clauses." It is true, I believe, that the Treaty prescribed autonomy for the Greek cities, and non-aggression between Athens and Persia: it will be convenient, then, to examine the further evidence under these two heads.

A. Autonomy clauses (and tribute)

In the *Panegyrikos*, published in 380, Isokrates invited the world to compare τὰς συνθήκας τάς τ' ἐφ' ἡμῶν γενομένας καὶ τὰς νῦν ἀναγεγραμμένας (4. 120). Whether "the treaty made in our time," which he wishes to compare with the Peace of Antalkidas, is the treaty with Artaxerxes or with Dareios, is not clear: but I am assuming there was little essential difference between the two Athenian treaties.[1] From the Athenian treaty, he then cites three clauses: τότε μὲν γὰρ ἡμεῖς φανησόμεθα

    (i) τὴν ἀρχὴν τὴν βασιλέως ὁρίζοντες

    (ii) καὶ τῶν φόρων ἐνίους τάττοντες

    (iii) καὶ κωλύοντες αὐτὸν τῇ θαλάττῃ χρῆσθαι.

---

[1] The most striking of the clauses which Isokrates here cites is (ii), the fixing

Of these (i) and (iii) are "non-aggression clauses," see below p. 134. The clause which concerns the conditions of autonomy is (ii). Athens fixed the scale of certain tributes payable to the King. What tributes could these be except those from the Greek cities of Asia Minor? A famous sentence of Herodotos (VI 42. 2) tells us how the scale was fixed: the tribute payable was that laid down by Artaphernes after the reduction of the Ionian revolt. A mild assessment, based on area,[1] and containing no punitive advances: κατὰ δὴ τούτους μετρήσας φόρους ἔταξε ἑκάστοισι, οἳ κατὰ χώρην διατελέουσι ἔχοντες ἐκ τούτου τοῦ χρόνου ἔτι καὶ ἐς ἐμὲ ὡς ἐτάχθησαν ἐξ Ἀρταφρένεος. The King then was entitled to certain limited revenues from the Greek cities, but had no further authority over them. Diodoros' "autonomy clauses" say that the Greek cities were left autonomous, and that the satrap covenanted not to move to the west of Sardis:[2] the latter is one of the most constantly reported terms.

Walker in *CAH* V 470 says: "as Persia never resigned her claim to the tribute of the Greek cities in Asia, she cannot possibly have recognized their autonomy." Ancient diplomacy thought otherwise. Substitute Artaphernes for Aristeides, and the terms could be expressed in the words of the Peace of Nikias (Thuc. V 18. 5): τὰς δὲ πόλεις φερούσας τὸν φόρον τὸν ἐπ' Ἀρταφέρνους αὐτονόμους εἶναι. The Peace of Nikias was between two Greek powers: that the concept is equally possible between a Greek power and Persia, may

---

of the tribute payable to the King. Herodotos implies such a clause for the Artaxerxes treaty (VI 42. 2), Thucydides for the Dareios treaty (VIII 5. 5).

[1] Not, therefore, tapping the industrial or mercantile wealth of Ionia.

[2] I take this to be the sense of Diodoros' μὴ καταβαίνειν ἐπὶ θάλατταν κατωτέρω τριῶν ἡμερῶν ὁδόν: cf. Hdt. V 54. 2; Xen. *Hell.* III 2. 11. Sardis to Ephesos was 540 stades (Hdt. *l. c.*), the distance forbidden to Persian officials is given by Plut. *Kimon* 19. 4 (presumably from Kallisthenes, see p. 123 n. 2) as 400 stades. These 400 stades may be the distance to Smyrna (for fifth-century Smyrna see *ATL* 560 n. 2: for the possibility of a road, Xen. *Hell.* I 1. 10): more likely perhaps they indicate a covenanted point on the Ephesos road some miles SW of Sardis. The same distance is called a day's journey on horseback by Dem. 19. 273, Plut. *Kim.* 13. 4, Suidas Κίμων. In Aristodemos, J. 104 F 13.2, we should perhaps read ἐντὸς τριῶν ἡμερῶν ὁδόν, ⟨ἣ⟩ ἣν ἂν ἵππος ἀνύσῃ διωκόμενος, μὴ κατιῶσιν. The Halys boundary (Isok. 7. 80, 12. 59) is part of the non-aggression clause, quite another matter: see below.

be seen in Xen. *Hell.* III 4. 25. Tithraustes there conveys to Agesilaos the terms which Artaxerxes II proposes:[1] βασιλεὺς ἀξιοῖ . . . τὰς ἐν τῇ Ἀσίᾳ πόλεις αὐτονόμους οὔσας τὸν ἀρχαῖον δασμὸν αὐτῷ ἀποφέρειν.

I would summarize the autonomy clauses thus:

The Greek cities shall pay a fixed yearly sum to the satraps, but the Satrap and his officers shall not come beyond a certain point westward and, provided they receive their money, shall have no authority beyond that point.

This rather precarious balance was materially steadied by the "bilateral demilitarization" which accompanied the non-aggression clauses.

B. Non-aggression clauses (and de-militarization)

Diodoros says (p. 121 *supra*) that the King covenanted that no Persian ship of war should come west of "Phaselis and Kyaneai," and Athens on her side covenanted, if the King observed his obligations, not to attack "the land over which King Artaxerxes rules." The former of these clauses is very frequently mentioned, in slightly varying form:

(1) Isokr. 12. 59, οὔτε (*sc.* ἐξῆν) μακροῖς πλοίοις ἐπὶ τάδε πλεῖν Φασήλιδος (cf. *id.* 7. 80, 4. 118, and more vaguely, 120).

(2) Dem. 19. 273, ἐντὸς δὲ Χελιδονίων καὶ Κυανέων πλοίῳ μακρῷ μὴ πλεῖν.

(3) Lycurg. *in Leocr.* 73, μακρῷ μὲν πλοίῳ μὴ πλεῖν ἐντὸς Κυανέων καὶ Φασ⟨ήλ⟩ιδος.

(4) Diod. XII 4. 5, μηδὲ ναῦν μακρὰν πλεῖν ἐντὸς Φασήλιδος καὶ Κυανέων.

(5) Plut. *Kim.* 13. 4, ἔνδον δὲ Κυανέων καὶ Χελιδονίων μακρᾷ νηὶ καὶ χαλκεμβόλῳ μὴ πλέειν.

(6) Aristodemos J. 104 F 13.2, ἐντὸς Κυανέων καὶ Νέσσου ποταμοῦ καὶ Φασήλιδος (ἥτις ἐστὶν πόλις Παμφυλίας) καὶ Χελιδονέων μὴ μακροῖς πλοίοις καταπλέωσι.

This is a proposal to restore the Kallias terms: see p. 147, and note 1 *ibid.*

(7) Suidas *s.v.* Κίμων, ἐκτὸς Κυανέων καὶ Χελιδονέων καὶ Φασήλιδος (πόλις δὲ αὕτη τῆς Παμφυλίας) ναῦν Μηδικὴν μὴ πλεῖν
νόμῳ πολέμου.

These points are in south or east Lykia (*pace* Aristodemos and
Suidas): Kyaneai is the southernmost point;[1] the Chelidonian
islands are off the south-east point; Phaselis is on the east coast; the
River Nessos is unknown.[2] Of the latest writers, Aristodemos gives
all four names, Suidas three: the intermediate writers give two
apiece: Isokrates, the earliest, gives Phaselis only. What is the
meaning of this variety? "If the inscription contained the limits
by sea and land," asks Walker in *CAH* V 471, "how can we account
for such discrepancies in our authorities? They had only to use
their eyes, and to see what stood written on the stone." I do not
know what answer he intends to the rhetorical question. He does
not, presumably, suggest that Theopompos was wrong in saying
that the Peace was engraved on stone: forgery or no, the alleged
terms were on public view.

I am inclined to think that all these places were named in the
Treaty, and the writers chose such as took their fancy, or as they
remembered. No doubt the accumulation of names in the latest
writers is due to their love of erudition. Isokrates was content
with the furthest limit, Phaselis, which gave the essential fact: if
the King's warships might not approach Phaselis, *a fortiori* they
might not Kyaneai. Why then were so many places named? If
the limit were inclusive, it might well be laid down that the King's
warships could sail "as far as Phaselis and Chelidoniai and Kyaneai." But I find this incredible: can Phaselis have been left
exposed to such visits? The limit was surely exclusive. It could no
doubt even so be laid down that the King's ships must not approach
either Phaselis or the Chelidoniai; i.e. they could move south of

---

[1] See Pauly-Wissowa, *s.v.* Kyaneai (2), and cf. Robert *Études anatoliennes*
ch. XIX. But see p. 136 n. 1.

[2] See Müller's note in *FHG* V pp. 15–16. In the list of rivers in Hesiod
Theog. 337 ff., Νέσσον in 341 is usually understood as the Nestos in Thrace,
which is called Νέσος in a few passages (e.g. Theophr. *hist. plant.* III 1. 5:
cf. schol. Thuc. II 96). But in 450 B.C. the Nestos as a boundary would concern
the rising Odrysian power, not Persia.

Phaselis if they kept east of the Chelidoniai. But Kyaneai cannot be thus explained.[1] Possibly Phaselis-Chelidoniai was the limit in 449, Kyaneai in 423,[2] and Demosthenes contaminated the two treaties. Far more likely the clause was reciprocal, and Kyaneai-Chelidoniai-Phaselis defined the zone into (and beyond) which neither party should send ships of war. A demilitarized zone: this would help to explain the growth of piracy in these waters: Thuc. II 69 says that in 430, Peloponnesian pirates based on Lykia were interfering with cargoes from Phaselis and the east. Was there a similar demilitarized zone on land? Isokrates 7. 80 says οὔτε μακροῖς πλοίοις ἐπὶ τάδε Φασήλιδος ἔπλεον οὔτε στρατοπέδοις ἐντὸς Ἅλυος ποταμοῦ κατέβαινον: cf. 12. 59, οὐκ ἐξῆν αὐτοῖς οὔτ' ἐντὸς Ἅλυος πεζῷ στρατοπέδῳ καταβαίνειν οὔτε μακροῖς πλοίοις ἐπὶ τάδε πλεῖν Φασήλιδος. Walker (CAH V 470) appears to regard this Halys line as a variant of the three days' limit of the autonomy clause. It is no such thing: the three days' limit, or the "Sardis line," is the eastern limit of Greek autonomy; the "Halys line" is the eastern limit of demilitarization. As such, Isokrates properly brackets it in both passages with Phaselis.

The King covenanted not to move west of the Halys with a land army. — We have probably to distinguish three elements in the army of the Persian empire:[3] (1) what I will call the "Palatine Army"; that is, the King's own army, consisting primarily of the

---

[1] Could Kyaneai be Kyaneai (3) in Pauly-Wissowa, sc. the mouth of the Bosporos? So Walker assumes, CAH V 470, and finds it ridiculous: but such a limit might be meant to deny the Black Sea to Athenian (rather than allow it to Persian) ships: and if so, Perikles' expedition in the middle 'thirties was a breach of treaty. But the explanation in the text is a lot simpler.

[2] But Phaselis paid tribute to Athens in 418/7 or later: ATL p. 153, no. 37. I 17.

[3] I am conscious how superficial this account is. E. Herzfeld, Altpersische Inschriften, Berlin, 1938, pp. 51–54, makes suggestions about the feudal organization, which he believes the pseudo-Smerdis sought to abolish (Hdt. III 66. 3) and Dareios restored (Behistun §14). The system he infers seems to me intrinsically probable, but I cannot estimate his evidence: see R. Zaehner's criticisms in "Aparmānd," in the forthcoming JRAS. — I have not followed Ed. Meyer's view that the satrap commanded all the troops of his satrapy, but I recognize that, of the evidence I use, Xenophon's Cyropaedia is romance and his Oikonomikos largely unintelligible.

10,000 Immortals: (2) the native levies of the provinces, under command of the satraps: (3) the royal garrisons in the provinces, under phrourarchs immediately responsible to the King. The "Palatine Army" is what Isokrates in the *Panegyrikos* (4. 145) calls τὴν στρατιὰν τὴν μετὰ τοῦ βασιλέως περιπολοῦσαν: what Xenophon, in a difficult passage of the *Oikonomikos* (4. 6) calls τοὺς μὲν ἀμφὶ τὴν ἑαυτοῦ οἴκησιν, which at the annual inspection the King himself inspects, in contrast to τοὺς πρόσω ἀποικοῦντας to which he sends inspectors. Its ideal institution by Kyros the Great is described in Xen. *Cyrop.* VII 5. 66–70. It is this Palatine Army of whose maintenance Herodotos speaks, when he says, I 192. 1, βασιλέϊ τῷ μεγάλῳ ἐς τροφὴν αὐτοῦ τε καὶ τῆς στρατιῆς διαραίρηται γῆ πᾶσα ὅσης ἄρχει:[1] this was a charge additional to the tribute (πάρεξ τοῦ φόρου), and one third of it was borne by the Satrapy of Babylonia. When Ktesias and Deinon are quoted for the astounding figures (Athen. IV 146c) that the King would dine with 15,000 men and his dinner would cost 400 talents, these are of course exceptional and outside figures, and the second is taken from Herodotos VII 118, where it is part of a petulant anecdote and anyway includes the whole of the apparatus of gold and silver plate which was a capital and not a routine expense. But for both figures the army's dinner is included in the King's: and in the 400 talents, the dinner of the whole Army of Invasion. The first figure, 15,000 diners, no doubt includes the 10,000 Immortals and is the Palatine Army; it is to this peace-time "dinner" that Theopompos refers in J. 115 F 113: "when the King comes to any of his subjects, twenty and sometimes thirty talents is spent on the dinner, sometimes indeed much more. For each city has had apportioned to it from of old the tribute it must pay and the dinner it must provide."

Such was the Palatine Army. Herodotos says it was maintained by the peoples of Asia; and, comparing this with his careful phras-

[1] But in the next sentence it is Babylonia and ἡ λοιπὴ πᾶσα 'Ασίη, Babylonia paying for four months, "the rest of Asia" for eight: so Egypt is not included (cf. III 96). The passage of Theopompos quoted below (J. 115 F 113) suggests that the four months represent four months' actual sojourn of the King and his army (ὅταν βασιλεὺς εἴς τινας ἀφίκηται τῶν ἀρχομένων). Herodotos writes of the Kallias period; Theopompos, though he writes presumably of the Antalkidas period, says ἐκ παλαιοῦ.

ing in III 96, we may conclude it did not normally move into Egypt. I suggest that neither did it move into Asia Minor, but stayed at the heart of the Empire east of the Euphrates. This was *de facto* true; and Herodotos and Theopompos speak of the routine provision for something which looks like a fixed annual royal progress (see p. 137 n. 1). The simplest meaning of the famous Halys clause in the treaty with Athens is, that the King covenanted not to move this Palatine Army into the western satrapies, ἐντὸς "Ἀλυος πεζῷ στρατοπέδῳ μὴ καταβαίνειν. By covenanting this, the Persian Empire was converted from an offensive power, treating the world as its prey, into a defensive power, living on terms with its neighbours.

It is possible that the western satrapies were even further de-militarized, having neither native levies at the satrap's command, nor royal garrisons.

Xenophon (*Cyrop.* VIII 6. 1) ascribes to Kyros the Great the institution of a system whereby satraps did not command the "garrisons" in their satrapies: he decides to send out satraps, τοὺς μέντοι ἐν ταῖς ἄκραις φρουράρχους καὶ τοὺς χιλιάρχους τῶν κατὰ τὴν χώραν φυλακῶν οὐκ ἄλλου ἢ ἑαυτοῦ ἐβούλετο ἀκούειν. He makes a speech to the satraps designate, and explains he does not wish to super-sede the phrourarchs (6.3), ἄλλους δὲ σατράπας πέμψαι μοι δοκεῖ οἵτινες ἄρξουσι τῶν ἐνοικούντων καὶ τὸν δασμὸν λαμβάνοντες τοῖς τε φρουροῖς δώσουσι μισθὸν καὶ ἄλλο τελοῦσιν ὅ τι ἂν δέῃ. Such "garrisons" possibly include the feudal establishments which Kyros had charged those Persians to maintain who owned property in the conquered prov-inces (*Cyrop.* VII 5. 72 ff., esp. 85–86: cf. VIII 1. 1 ff.). The *Cyropaedia* is not history, but Xenophon knew the Persian military system well, and these two categories appear in Herodotos: the feudal landowners in V 102. 1, οἱ Πέρσαι οἱ ἐντὸς "Ἀλυος ποταμοῦ νομοὺς ἔχοντες, and the fortress garrisons in his account of Egypt; they had stations at Elephantine and Daphnai (II 30. 3) and at Memphis (III 91. 3), they are composed of Persians and ἐπίκουροι (presumably not natives), and elaborate measures are taken for their commissariat. They do not appear to have accompanied Xerxes to Greece: Egypt only provided sailors, who served under the satrap Achaimenes. When Aeschylus in the *Persae* talks of the governors of Memphis and Thebes (lines 36 to 38) no doubt he has in mind the phrourarchs: that they were not in fact with Xerxes would be no matter. We shall meet another "royal garrison" in Syria (Xen. *Anab.* I 4. 4, see below). These royal troops in the provinces are no doubt οἱ πρόσω ἀποικοῦντες whose annual inspection Xenophon distinguishes from that of the Palatine army, *Oikon.* 4. 6. — The satrap Achaimenes, on the other hand, commands his Egyptian sailors; and where we can control it, the army list of Xerxes shows satraps regularly in command of the native levy of their provinces.

We have no specific information about royal fortresses or garrisons in the western satrapies. Certainly none were allowed in the autonomous zone, and I take Isokrates' "Halys clause" to indicate that none was allowed west of the Halys. There had been plenty in the earlier reigns: Xerxes had built a royal fort (βασίλεια ἐρυμνά) near Kelainai, on the road to the Halys Gates (Xen. *Anab.* I 2. 8–9: cf. Hdt. VII 26. 3); and the army which pursued the Greeks to the coast after the burning of Sardis in 498 was composed, according to Herodotos, V 102. 1, of οἱ Πέρσαι οἱ ἐντὸς Ἅλυος ποταμοῦ νομοὺς ἔχοντες. Did they remain under the Treaty? Herodotos, V 52. 1–2, describes the road to the Halys Gates[1] and mentions no fortresses till he comes to the Gates: ἐκδέκεται δὲ ἐκ τῆς Φρυγίης ὁ Ἅλυς ποταμός, ἐπ' ᾧ πύλαι τε ἔπεισι, τὰς διεξελάσαι πᾶσα ἀνάγκη καὶ οὕτω διεκπερᾶν τὸν ποταμόν, καὶ φυλακτήριον μέγα ἐπ' αὐτῷ. This may perhaps be compared with the position at the Amanos Gates, at the entrance to Kilikia from Syria. Kilikia was not indeed demilitarized, but was in alliance with (rather than subject to) the King[2] and consequently did not admit royal garrisons. When the Ten Thousand reach the Amanos Gates, they find two fortresses, τὸ μὲν ἔσωθεν τὸ πρὸ τῆς Κιλικίας Συέννεσις εἶχε καὶ Κιλίκων φυλακή, τὸ δὲ ἔξω τὸ πρὸ τῆς Συρίας

---

[1] Calder, *CR* XXXIX 7 ff., argues that this is not the Royal Road, though none the less real for that (*ib.* 8–9). Kelainai lay south of the straightest route from Sardis to the Halys Gates.

[2] The native Syennesis dynasty was ended after the younger Kyros had compelled the last of the name to rebel. For Kilikia's comparative independence, cf. Xen. *Anab.* I 2. 26; Hdt. III 90. 3. Cf. the status which Euagoras of Cyprus demands (and gets): to speak not ὡς δοῦλος δεσπότῃ but ὡς βασιλεὺς βασιλεῖ, Diod. XV 8. 3, 9. 2.

βασιλέως ἐλέγετο φυλακὴ φυλάττειν (Xen. *Anab.* I 4. 4). In both cases, the King maintains a fortress on his military frontier. What of the native levy? The commission of the younger Kyros in 407 was (Xen. *Hell.* I 4. 3) καταπέμπω Κῦρον κάρανον τῶν εἰς Καστωλὸν ἀθροιζομένων (cf. *Anab.* I 1. 2, 9. 7):[1] in the *Cyropaedia* Xenophon sets the last battle between Kyros the Great and Kroisos in Thymbrara (VII 1, 45), ἔνθα καὶ νῦν [4th century] ὁ σύλλογος τῶν ὑπὸ βασιλέα βαρβάρων τῶν κάτω (*ib.* VI 2. 11). The Kastolos plain lay some fifty miles east of Sardis, and Thymbrara is presumably the same place:[2] Kyros' commission in 407 appears to be the remilitarization of the Sardis area, the final shaking off of the treaty restrictions. Herodotos, writing whilst the treaty was in force, says (I 155–157) that Kyros the Great made the Lydians put away their armour and wear chitons, and unlearn their warlike ways: consistently, he makes the troops which pursued the Ionians from Sardis in 498 be all Persians (V 102. 1, quoted just above), though certain Lydians fought in Sardis itself (*ib.* 101. 2). But in VII 74, the Lydians serve in Xerxes' army, in their native equipment, and do not appear to have been disarmed. Is it possible that their disarming was not the work of Kyros the Great, but a consequence of the treaty with Athens? Whenever it began, the disarming of the Lydians seems to have been real. The Satrap's troops, during the period of the treaty, are mainly Greek mercenaries: when Pissouthnes revolts from Dareios II, the issue is settled by the defection of his army of Greeks (Ktesias *Pers.* 52). In his action against Kolophon (Thuc. III 34) the main troops appear to have been Arkadians: the few βάρβαροι there mentioned are no doubt Persians. Until the alliance with Sparta in 412, the Persians in the western satrapies were militarily powerless (cf. Thuc. VIII 5. 5).

If the Persians might not bring a land army west of the Halys,

---

[1] In *Anab.* I 9. 7, his style is σατράπης Λυδίας τε καὶ Φρυγίας τῆς μεγάλης καὶ Καππαδοκίας, στρατηγὸς δὲ καὶ πάντων οἷς καθήκει εἰς Καστωλοῦ πεδίον ἀθροίζεσθαι.

[2] The village of Kastolos is fixed some 60 miles east of Sardis by Ditt. *OGI* 488, cf. Robert *Études anatoliennes* 159 f.: the "plain" (n. 1 above) perhaps lay west of the village. Thymbrara is unknown: Adala, 30 miles east-north-east of Sardis, where Radet wished to site it (*Lydie* 249, 313), is the ancient Satala, according to Robert, *Villes d'Asie Mineur* 101–2.

there was presumably some reciprocal engagement by Athens: this was, probably, the dismantling of the fortifications of Ionia.[1] This is noted in general terms by Thucydides III 33. 2, ἀτειχίστου οὔσης τῆς Ἰωνίας: specifically of Klazomenai (VIII 31. 3), Knidos (*ib.* 35. 3), Lampsakos (62. 2), Kyzikos (107. 1). Ionia became a war area in 412 (perhaps sooner, see *infra*) and the treaty was broken on all sides: in Xen. *Hell.* I, we hear of the fortification by Athens of Lampsakos, Chrysopolis, perhaps Phokaia (2. 15, 1. 22, 5. 11). It was perhaps by a breach of treaty, on one side or the other, that Pygela had been fortified (2. 2):[2] many years earlier the treaty had certainly been strained by Pissouthnes' intervention at Kolophon, and the fort at Notion (Thuc. III 34) was evidently a consequence. The most instructive passage is perhaps Thuc. VIII 16. 3: a sea force and a land force of Peloponnesians both arrive before Teos in 412, and the Athenian fleet has to retire. The Teians, he says, did not at first admit the land force, until the Athenian fleet left: once admitted, this force proceeds to demolish the landward wall: τὸ τεῖχος ὃ ἀνῳκοδόμησαν οἱ Ἀθηναῖοι τῆς Τηίων πόλεως τὸ πρὸς ἤπειρον. This is a wall on the landward side, giving protection from the interior: the Athenians had *re*built it. When had it been pulled down, and when had they "rebuilt" it? It seems to me the most likely hypothesis that it was pulled down by the terms of a treaty with Persia, and had recently been "rebuilt" by Athens in contravention of that treaty: and there may be some confirmation of this in the words which follow in Thucydides: "and a few barbaroi came later and joined in the demolition of the wall, commanded by Stages, one of Tissaphernes' governors." Τῶν

---

[1] The importance of this phenomenon for the treaty was first pointed out, so far as I know, by A. J. Toynbee in a work on modern Turkey, *The Western Question* (1922), p. 221. It is confirmed in some measure by excavation, see especially Schefold *Jahrbuch* XLVIII (1933) Beiblatt 147–8; *ibid.* XLIX (1934) Beiblatt 388; von Gerkan *Milet* I 8 (1925) 113–120; II 3 (1935) 120–124. Cf. *ATL* in the Gazetteer, under Ληρισαῖοι (pp. 511–2), Ἰασῆς (492), Μιλήσιοι (520). We hear of similar dismantling of *island* fortifications, and the measure was no doubt partly intended to make control easy for Athens.

[2] Cf. Thucydides' remark on the fortification of Polichne near Klazomenai (for the site, see *ATL* 487 *s.v.* Ἐρυθραῖοι): ἐν τειχισμῷ τε πάντες ἦσαν καὶ παρασκευῇ πολέμου (VIII 14. 3).

βαρβάρων οὐ πολλοί — this help was hardly needed: was it a gesture of protest because their treaty rights had been infringed?

The land zone thus demilitarized (roughly from the Halys to the Aegean Sea) will have been exactly delimited: Isokrates' ἐντὸς Ἅλυος is no more documentary than his ἐπὶ τάδε Φασήλιδος. Since the Persian empire was essentially a road system, the line was perhaps defined by naming a point on each of the great roads: the Halys Gates were one such point. In the *Panegyrikos* 4. 120, Isokrates said ἡμεῖς φανησόμεθα τὴν ἀρχὴν τὴν βασιλέως ὁρίζοντες: this, I conceive, refers especially to the Athenian undertaking, if the King performs his part, μὴ στρατεύειν εἰς τὴν χώραν ἧς βασιλεὺς Ἀρταξέρξης ἄρχει. For this definition of the King's ἀρχή, which Athens covenanted not to attack, I am inclined to think neither the Halys line nor the Sardis line was used, but rather the Aegean coast. Two passages of Thucydides (both phrased, apparently, with reference to the treaty) speak of the King's (or the satrap's) ἀρχή as including the autonomous zone: VIII 5. 5, ἐκ τῆς ἑαυτοῦ ἀρχῆς (= ἀπὸ τῶν Ἑλληνίδων πόλεων) and VIII 56. 4, παραπλεῖν τὴν ἑαυτοῦ γῆν (= the Aegean coast). This would imply no more (and no less) than that Athens covenanted not to land troops on the Asiatic coast:[1] when in fact she does, it is perhaps as much a breach of treaty as Pissouthnes' intervention in Kolophon (e.g. Thuc. II 69, III 19, 34, and of course frequently in VIII). This concept, that the Greek cities of Asia "belonged to" the King, but were not subject to his writ, is (as Schwartz suggested, see p. 122 above) not unlike the "capitulations" once enjoyed by Europeans in the dominions of the Sultan.

For an actual fragment of the text of this delimitation of the King's dominion, see *infra, Appendix* (p. 155). Athens there recognizes the King's ownership (*sc.* covenants not to invade) the provinces of Egypt and Libya.

I would summarize the non-aggression clauses thus

A zone shall be marked out on sea, between Phaselis and Kyaneai, into (or beyond) which neither party shall send ships of war; and a

---

[1] Accordingly, when Tithraustes proposes to Agesilaos to renew the Kallias terms (Xen. *Hell*. III 4. 25; see p. 134 n. 1 and p. 147 n. 1), he requires first that Agesilaos shall withdraw his force from Asia: σὲ μὲν ἀποπλεῖν οἴκαδε.

zone on land, between the Halys and the Aegean Sea, into (or beyond) which neither party shall lead troops, nor shall they maintain fortresses in it. The King's dominions are defined, and guaranteed against Athenian attack: they include the provinces of Egypt and Libya, and the whole seaboard of Asia Minor.

The autonomy clauses then follow: —

But in the area west of Sardis, inhabited by Greeks, the King shall send no functionaries nor exercise any authority: his sole right shall be a yearly tribute, of a fixed amount based on the survey of Artaphernes in 493.

I submit that these terms are reasonable: that they cover the evidence (without assumption of forgery or lying), and do not go beyond the indications of the evidence. How do they stand in the historical context?

IV

The Historical Sequel

The first serious strain to which the Treaty was put was the Samian War of 441–439. It was a bad moment for Athens, and a temptation to the two powers with whom she was in treaty, to seize their opportunities. Both Sparta and the satrap Pissouthnes considered taking action, but neither actually did: Perikles reconnoitred towards the neutral sea-zone, but sighted no Persian fleet (Thuc. I 116. 3: cf. 115. 4–5, 41. 2, Plut. *Kim.* 13. 4). Incidents then became frequent: shortly before the Peloponnesian War Athens occupies Sinope (Plut. *Per.* 20. 1–2, *IG* I² 944), Astakos (Diod. XII 34. 5: see *ATL* in the Gazetteer, 472), perhaps a little later Pythopolis (*ib.* 544). In 430 Pissouthnes intervenes at Kolophon (Thuc. III 34). Sparta seeks many times to induce Persia to denounce the treaty (Thuc. II 7. 1, 67, IV 50), and just before Artaxerxes' death, a Persian emissary to Sparta is intercepted. Athenian embassies had no doubt been visiting Sousa during these years, cf. Arist. *Ach.* 61–125; Strabo I 3. 1; Plato *Charm.*

158a.[1] Incidents on the Athenian side are constant (Thuc. II 69, III 19, 34), culminating in the grave provocation of the Tribute assessment of 425, which not only trebled Athens' claims on the Ionian coast, but included places far beyond the neutral zone (e.g., Aspendos, Kelenderis in Kilikia, possibly Doros in Palestine), and in the interior of Karia (see *ATL* A9 II 143, 146–7, 156, and note on 155, p. 206, and Gazetteer, *s.vv.* Ἄσπενδος, Δῶρος, Ἐδριῆς, Ἰτύρα, Κελένδερις). It was no doubt to explain these matters that the embassy recorded by Thucydides, IV 50. *3*, set out fòr Sousa in the winter of 425/4, but turned back on the news of Artaxerxes' death. A year later, in 424/3, when Dareios II had disposed of his rivals, the treaty was renewed with him (section II *supra*).

This was in 423. We do not know how long it lasted, but almost certainly less than ten years, perhaps much less. Perhaps trouble was already afoot in 422 when Pharnakes, the northern satrap, "gave" Atramyttion to the Delians whom Athens had expelled from Delos.[2] It began when Pissouthnes, at a date unknown but probably early in the reign, revolted from Dareios. Faced with this delicate situation, Athens did not officially side with or against him: but the mercenary force on which he depended was commanded by an Athenian, Lykon, who decided his fate by accepting the money of Tissaphernes, sent by Dareios to supersede him: the mercenaries deserted, and Pissouthnes was captured (Ktesias *Pers. 52*). The revolt was continued by his son Amorges (Thuc. VIII 5. 5): and, for whatever reason, Athens decided to support him, officially, against Tissaphernes (Andok. 3. 29, quoted p. 128 *supra*); that is, against Dareios.

---

[1] Cf. Thuc. II 7. 1: in the Oxford text the full stop after πολεμήσοντες should be a comma.

[2] Thuc. V 1. 1. Atramyttion is on the coast, but was a Lydian town, and at the head of a deep gulf: I am not sure that the settling of Delians there was a breach of treaty. In Thuc. VIII 108. 4, it appears to be in the southern satrapy: its disposal now by the northern satrap is possibly a sign that Pissouthnes' revolt has begun.—Krateros is cited by Stephanos Byz. *s.v.* Ἀδραμύτειον for the form Ἀδραμύττιον, and it has been suggested that the name stood on one of the two assessments which Krateros transcribed (see *ATL* 203). It seems to me much more likely that the name occurred in some *decree*, e.g. the decree which recalled the Delians from Atramyttion to Delos, Thuc. V 32. 1.

When was this? I suggest not later, and perhaps not much earlier, than 414. In the expense accounts for the year 415/4, on the second day of the eighth prytany (i.e. 21 March 414), a payment is made to a strategos ἐν Ἐφ[εσοι?] (*IG* I² 302 line 69: but I quote from Meritt's text in *AFD* 163 where it is line 79).[1] A strategos in Ephesos (if this supplement be right) was, as I understand it, a breach of the treaty: and Ephesos is the natural base for a force operating against the satrap of Sardis (Xen. *Hell.* III 1. 8, 2. 11, and especially 4. 4–26). Two years later, Tissaphernes is eagerly seeking the alliance of Sparta: ὑπὸ βασιλέως γὰρ νεωστὶ ἐτύγχανε πεπραγμένος τοὺς ἐκ τῆς ἑαυτοῦ ἀρχῆς φόρους, οὓς δι᾽ Ἀθηναίους ἀπὸ τῶν Ἑλληνίδων πόλεων οὐ δυνάμενος πράσσεσθαι ἐπωφείλησεν· τούς τε οὖν φόρους μᾶλλον ἐνόμιζε κομιεῖσθαι κακώσας τοὺς Ἀθηναίους, καὶ ἅμα βασιλεῖ ξυμμάχους Λακεδαιμονίους ποιήσειν, καὶ Ἀμόργην τὸν Πισσούθνου υἱὸν νόθον, ἀφεστῶτα περὶ Καρίαν, ὥσπερ αὐτῷ προσέταξε βασιλεύς, ἢ ζῶντα ἄξειν ἢ ἀποκτενεῖν (Thuc. VIII 5. 5).

Dareios had made Tissaphernes pay the arrears.[2] These arrears cannot have run (since he could not have paid them) since 449 or even 423; they must be arrears for the last year or two, i.e. since the Athenians had begun, in breach of the treaty, to prevent his collecting the revenues. This I conceive they had done since their alliance with Amorges: we do not know its date, but I suggest the strategos in Ephesos in March 414 is already there to prevent Tissaphernes collecting tribute; and further (since the arrears were something which Tissaphernes' exchequer could still, even in 412, bear), that he had not been there in 415. The rebuilding of the landward fortifications of Teos (Thuc. VIII 16. 3: cf. p. 141 *supra*) was no doubt part of these operations.

In 414, when Athens was badly wanting money, and perhaps

---

[1] Cf. *Hesperia* V 381–2 (no. 5), for an honorary decree of the same prytany, in Ionic script: for services to this force?

[2] On this passage see Dundas, *CR* XLVIII 167, who points out the impossibility of long arrears. But I do not see why the new claim should have started in 412 (p. 168 "from this year onward"). Dundas' question "What was Dareios demanding?" suggests that πεπραγμένος means "he was asked for the money." But does it? I take it to mean "he was made to pay," as πράσσεσθαι just below means "to make them pay him": Athens could hardly prevent his "asking."

already contemplating the abolition of phoros (Thuc. VII 28. 4),
— at such a date to denounce the treaty with Dareios and support
a rebel satrap, was gambling very high: the gamble failed, and
Athens paid exceedingly heavily.

We now reach firmer ground: treaties whose actual text we have,
and negotiations reported by trustworthy contemporaries. Tissaphernes got his treaty with Sparta, and three successive forms were
sworn to, within twelve months between summer 412 and spring
411. Thucydides gives all three verbatim. Many of the clauses
refer to the conditions of alliance and the actual circumstances
of the war: I quote from the third and final form the two clauses
which are essential for our enquiry: χώραν τὴν βασιλέως, ὅση τῆς
'Ασίας ἐστί, βασιλέως εἶναι· καὶ περὶ τῆς χώρας τῆς ἑαυτοῦ βουλευέτω
βασιλεὺς ὅπως βούλεται (Thuc. VIII 58. 2):

(i) *The King's territory, so far as it is in Asia, shall belong to
the King:*

(ii) *and concerning his own territory the King may do as he
pleases.*

Against the background of the treaty with Athens, the rather surprising second clause becomes clear. Dareios may militarize the
demilitarized zone, he may put garrisons in the autonomous zone
(cf. Thuc. VIII 84. 4–5, 109). In the language of the peace of
Nikias, Ionia has sunk from the status of Argilos, Stageiros, etc.
(φερούσας τὸν φόρον αὐτονόμους εἶναι) to that of Skione, Torone, etc.
(the contracting claimant may βουλεύεσθαι περὶ αὐτῶν ὅτι ἂν δοκῇ
αὐτοῖς: Thuc. V 18. 5, 8). The King may even bring ships into the
Aegean (VIII 59, etc.); just before, in spite of her desperate need,
Athens had refused to waive that fundamental clause of her old
treaty.[1]

Once again,[2] before the end of the war, it seemed as if Persia

[1] Thuc. VIII 56. 4. Sparta does not give Dareios any islands (such as
Athens had been prepared to, *ibid.*), and Tissaphernes is still very shy of bringing ships beyond Aspendos (VIII 59, 78, 81. 3, 87–88, 99, 108. 1).

[2] At least once: how little our information is exhaustive is shown by *IG* I²
113, an undated decree (Attic script) in honour of Euagoras of Cyprus, in which
there is mention of the King and Tissaphernes (lines 38–39).

might patch up her quarrel with Athens. After his successes in the Bosporos, Alkibiades persuades Pharnabazos, probably in 408, to give five ambassadors escort up to Sousa (Xen. *Hell.* I 3. 13). At that moment, Athens came nearer to salvation than at any moment after 413: but early the next year, before they reached Sousa, they were met by Kyros, who bore a message from the King: καταπέμπω Κῦρον κάρανον τῶν εἰς Καστωλὸν ἀθροιζομένων (*ib.* I 4. 3):

> *I send down Kyros to take military command of the forces of the west:*

and the ambassadors were allowed to go no further. This was the final repudiation of all the obligations of the Kallias treaty. Dareios is using the liberty granted him in the Spartan treaty, denied to him in the Athenian: he is converting the west once more into a military area.

Soon after, Dareios died, and Kyros rebelled against the new King, Artaxerxes II. Sparta had backed Kyros rather heavily and her relations with Persia went bad: she took the remains of Kyros' forces into her service and declared war on the King. Tissaphernes is no match for Agesilaos, and treats for peace: he asks Agesilaos what his terms are: Agesilaos states them (Xen. *Hell.* III 4.5): αὐτονόμους καὶ τὰς ἐν τῇ 'Ασίᾳ πόλεις εἶναι, ὥσπερ καὶ τὰς ἐν τῇ παρ' ἡμῖν Ἑλλάδι:

> *The cities in Asia shall be autonomous, like the cities in European Greece.*

These are victor's terms, and Tissaphernes says he will lay them before the King. So bad are they, that the King orders Tissaphernes' execution: they are far worse, for Persia, than the Peace of Kallias had been. Tissaphernes' successor, Tithraustes, states the King's counter proposal: it is a compromise between the utter complaisance of Sparta in 412, and her utter defiance now: it is, in fact, the Kallias treaty[1] (*ib.* III 4. 25): — βασιλεὺς δὲ ἀξιοῖ σὲ μὲν ἀποπλεῖν οἴκαδε, τὰς δ' ἐν τῇ 'Ασίᾳ πόλεις αὐτονόμους οὔσας τὸν ἀρχαῖον δασμὸν αὐτῷ ἀποφέρειν:

---

[1] See p. 134 n. 1; and for the demand that Agesilaos shall evacuate Asia (the Kallias "non-aggression clause"), p. 142 n. 1.

> *The King thinks right[1] that Agesilaos evacuate Asia, and the cities of Asia be autonomous but pay to Persia the ancient tribute (sc. the tribute assessed by Artaphernes in 493).*

The offer was not, however, sincere. Artaxerxes had had ample warning of his danger and had prepared his counter offensive: he appointed the Athenian Konon his admiral in chief, and gave him a free hand if he would drive Sparta off the seas. It worked completely: the Spartan offensive in Asia collapsed at once, and no more is heard of any revival of the Kallias terms. That was in 395. The next we hear of negotiations is in 391. The terms offered are preserved in Didymos' commentary on Demosthenes: it is these which Andokides was recommending when he referred to the Peace of Epilykos (3. 29): Didymos says Athens would not look at them, and Andokides was exiled for his pains. The terms were sent down by the same Antalkidas who brought down the final peace five years later: and the clause quoted is τοὺ[ς τὴν ʼΑσ]ίαν οἰκοῦντας Ἕλληνας ἐν βασιλέως οἴκ[ῳ π]άντας εἶναι συννενεμημένους (Didymos *in Dem. Phil. X* col. 7, 19–23):

> *The Greeks who dwell in Asia shall all be attached to the King's household.*

Athens fought for another five years, and went some way towards recreating her empire, but Persia was now on Sparta's side, and in 386 Antalkidas brought down from Sousa the famous peace whose text is given, no doubt abridged, in Xen. *Hell.* V 1. 31.

> *The King thinks right that the cities in Asia be his, and of the islands, Kypros and Klazomenai: and that the Greek cities, great and small, shall be autonomous.*

It was a wonderful achievement for Persian diplomacy and the King's chancellery must have enjoyed drafting it. No more talk from the Greeks of Europe about how the King shall behave in Asia: no: now he prescribes how they shall behave in Europe. And that is how it struck Isokrates, 4. 120:

---

[1] Compare the formula of the Antalkidas treaty (*Hell.* V 1. 31), βασιλεὺς νομίζει δίκαιον.

"A man can see the greatness of the change, if he will read and compare the treaty which we made, and this which has just now been concluded. He will find that *we* named frontiers to the King's dominions, prescribed in some cases the amount of tribute he should receive, forbade him to sail the sea: and now it is the king who directs and prescribes the business of the Greeks, telling us what each should do, and only stops short of putting his quartermasters in our cities."

Fortunately Persia was now so decrepit that no first-class danger was to be apprehended from her. Had she been more genuinely dangerous, Greek disunion would have been healed, and Artaxerxes would not have been able to employ this tone.

Compared with this, the Peace of Kallias was glorious. In the freshness of his indignation Isokrates lets out the old treaty's most disreputable clause (4. 120): ἡμεῖς φανησόμεθα - - - - τῶν φόρων ἐνίους τάττοντες. It is never mentioned again.

V

THE DATE OF THE TREATY WITH ARTAXERXES

Diodoros makes the Treaty with Artaxerxes the immediate consequence of Kimon's last expedition to Kypros: he dates it to 449/8. The exact year is perhaps (as so often in Diodoros) wrong, but the occasion is evidently right. A treaty which in fact prescribed the relations of the two powers for the rest of Artaxerxes' reign cannot have been made before the intensive hostilities of the 'fifties; the misapprehension which led certain ancient writers to put the Treaty immediately after the Eurymedon has been noted above (p. 125).

For the exact year: I take the firm core of Pentekontaetia chronology to be that Kimon was ostracized between spring 461 and spring 451, and that the Five Years' Truce, which he made, ran from summer 451 to summer 446. Kimon's last expedition to Kypros (closely consequent on this truce, Thuc. I 112. 2) will therefore be in 450. It is not impossible *per se* that the campaign should have lasted into 449; but for the reasons following, it seems likely that the negotiations for peace occupied the winter of 450/49, and the treaty was sworn fairly early in 449.

The Treaty ended the war, and ended therefore the obligations of the allies under that assessment of 478/7, whereby the Athenians ἔταξαν ἅς τε ἔδει παρέχειν τῶν πόλεων χρήματα πρὸς τὸν βάρβαρον καὶ ἅς ναῦς (Thuc. I 96.1). It did not of course end their alliance with Athens, which was in perpetuity, ᾿Αθ. π. 23. 5:[1] but it ended their obligations to serve or pay tribute on a scale assessed πρὸς τὸν βάρβαρον. It was however evident, to Athens at least, that the League's fleet (under Athenian control) whose maintenance was the chief charge on League revenues, could not be simply discharged: on Perikles' motion, Athens invited all Greek states to send representatives to consider peace-time expenditure.[2] The agenda of this congress is given by Plutarch, *Per.* 17. 1, who evidently keeps close to the wording of the decree: the three expenditures to be discussed are (i) rebuilding the temples, (ii) maintaining the festivals started in 479, (iii) policing the seas. No one came (since Sparta, who was asked first, declined) and Athens decided to help herself. Perikles moved a second decree, that the money accumulated κατὰ τὴν ᾿Αριστείδου τάξιν (i.e. the assessment πρὸς τὸν βάρβαρον) should be used for rebuilding the Athenian temples. So at least I understand the difficult lines 3–8 of the *Anonymus Argentinensis*: see the text proposed in *ATL* p. 572, T9. This second decree was voted before the end of the year 450/49:[3] the Treaty cannot therefore be later than the early summer of 449, since Perikles' two motions, that inviting the Congress and that appropriating the reserve of Phoros, must come (in that order) between the Treaty and the end of the Attic year.

[1] Cf. Larsen, *CP* XXVIII 267; Highby *Erythrae Decree* 64.

[2] This decree is evidently the immediate consequence of the Treaty: see *JHS* LII 216 n. 47. The words καὶ τὴν εἰρήνην ἄγωσιν (Plut. *Per.* 17. 1) are presumably from the text of the decree and, if so, are a contemporary mention of the Peace.

[3] The papyrus says [ἐπ᾿ Εὐ]θυδήμο[υ] Περικλέους γνώμη[ν] εἰσ[ηγησαμένου]. The archon of 450/49 was Euthynos, but he is called Euthydemos by Diodoros (XII 3. 1). Meritt's observation (*ATL l. c.*) that the comments in this papyrus all depend on lemmata beginning with ὅτι, leaves no choice but to take this decree as part of the comment on the building of the Parthenon.

Money had thus been found for the temples. But the fleet could hardly continue to be maintained out of a capital sum, however large: the revenues had to be renewed. It is now well known that no quota-list was inscribed on the "First Stele" for one of the years between 449/8 and 447/6; it is assumed in *ATL* that the missing year is 449/8.[1] It would seem that tribute was still paid for 450/49, that the war was formally ended in the latter part of that (Attic) year, and that consequently no tribute was due for 449/8. What is certain is that after one year's interval it was re-imposed.

There is one other indication of date. Herodotos, VII 151, reports that "many years after 480" τυχεῖν ἐν Σούσοισι τοῖσι Μεμνονίοισι ἐόντας ἑτέρου πρήγματος εἵνεκα ἀγγέλους Ἀθηναίων, Καλλίην τε τὸν Ἱππονίκου καὶ τοὺς μετὰ τούτου ἀναβάντας, Ἀργείους δὲ τὸν αὐτὸν τοῦτον χρόνον πέμψαντας καὶ τούτους ἐς Σοῦσα ἀγγέλους εἰρωτᾶν Ἀρταξέρξην τὸν Ξέρξεω εἴ σφι ἔτι ἐμμένει τὴν πρὸς Ξέρξην φιλίην συνεκεράσαντο, ἢ νομιζοίατο πρὸς αὐτοῦ εἶναι πολέμιοι· βασιλέα δὲ Ἀρτοξέρξην μάλιστα ἐμμένειν φάναι καὶ οὐδεμίαν νομίζειν πόλιν Ἄργεος φιλιωτέρην. It is likely that the ἕτερον πρῆγμα for which Kallias was at Sousa, is the peace which bears his name. Now Argos had embarked on an adventurous foreign policy in 462, and involved herself on Athens' side in the war which followed between Athens and Sparta (Thuc. I 102. 4, 107. 5). Those were the years when Athens was fighting both Sparta and Persia with success. But when under the strain of the disaster in Egypt, Athens made a truce with Sparta in 451, Argos evidently felt nervous lest she might find herself isolated among stronger powers:[2] the clearest sign is her thirty-year peace with Sparta, concluded perhaps in the autumn of 451, perhaps a year later (Thuc. V 14. 4, 28. 2, 40–41: cf. Busolt *GG* III 339 n. 3). There is evidence of the same anxiety in a clause of the thirty-year

[1] *ATL* 133, 175, with references to *BSA* XXXIII 112 and Meritt *DAT* 65, 69. It should be specially noted (a) that the lists there numbered 7 and 8 are so alike that it is reasonably certain that they belong to successive years, and (b) that list "7" is unique (after list 1) in having no serial number, and a plausible explanation of this is that it was awkward to give the serial number 7 to the list which stood immediately below 5.
[2] It is much the same position as in 420: ἔδεισαν μὴ μονωθῶσι, Thuc. V 40. 1.

peace between Athens and Sparta (446/5), to the effect that while Argos was not included in this peace, it did not preclude Argive-Athenian friendship (Paus. V 23.4): it is clear that Argos had been anxious to know how this peace would leave her relations with Athens. That at the same juncture she should have enquired about her standing with Persia is likely enough.

This will not of course give us a close date. We cannot, e.g., argue that Argos is likely to have made this enquiry as soon as Athens' truce with Sparta had isolated her: for is it not caused rather by the knowledge that Athens is negotiating with Persia?[1]

VI

ESTIMATE[2]

The Persian empire revealed high qualities in its ruling nobility: courage, energy, intelligence, humanity. It was a searching test of these qualities when it encountered, in the Greeks, a higher civilization, and a creativeness almost unique in history. In

---

[1] Just so, in 446, the knowledge that Sparta was negotiating with Athens caused Argos to make the *démarche* at Athens which resulted in the clause Pausanias quotes. I note that the question "or are we considered to be enemies?" presupposes that Argos is or has been in alliance with Athens, so that the embassy cannot have been sent (as has been suggested) on Artaxerxes' accession. It has also been suggested that it went immediately after the alliance with Athens, c. 461 (and therefore that Kallias, like Antalkidas, paid two visits to Sousa, the first one unsuccessful). This seems to me incredible: both Athens and Argos felt, in 461, at the top of the world, and Persia was not formidable. But we should remember that Herodotos does not guarantee his story (152. 1).

[2] Is the fifth-century silence (but see p. 150 n. 2, p. 154 n. 2) due to shame? I think Hdt. VII 151 is euphemistic (cf. 152. 2). Demosthenes, 19. 273, says that Kallias was fined 50 talents for making the treaty: but Plutarch, *Kim.* 13. 5, reports that he was exceptionally honoured for it, and Pausanias, I 8. 2, that he was some time honoured with a statue. Diodoros, XII 7, names Kallias as one of the two chief envoys to Sparta for the thirty-year peace: if this is true, and the same Kallias, his disgrace was at least not permanent. It was no doubt his grandson who moved *IG* I² 25, for whose connection with the Treaty see p. 130; no. 24, however, was not moved (as suggested in *IG* I²) by Hipponikos (*sc.* Kallias' son), see *JHS* LI 78 n. 80.

practically all the arts of peace and war, Greece was, in virtue of this creativeness, Persia's superior — in architecture, in medicine, in naval construction, in military technique. In the clash of the two civilizations, the Persians had two advantages: their resources in material (whether accumulated or exploitable) and in men, appeared inexhaustible: and war was their essential function. Without war the Persian nobility and monarchy had comparatively little *raison d'être*: there is evident truth in the observation that Herodotos puts in Atossa's mouth (III 134. 1–2), that a Persian King must justify himself by conquests.

The Greeks were a fighting race: but since their civilization did not lack other functions also, we find in their literature, besides militarist sentiments which may sometimes surprise us,[1] much praise of peace and much sensibility to the havoc which war makes of rational felicity. This contrast is not yet poignant in Archilochos' famous couplet, *I am a servant of the Lord God of War, and I understand the lovely art of the Muses:*[2] but begins to be in the second choros of the *Septem* (288 ff.).

The fighting energy of Athens in the invasion of Xerxes and the decades following needs no argument:[3] the disparity between her energy, and that of her Ionian allies, was the profound cause of the failure of that union, conceived with such exultant hopes in 478 (cf. Thuc. I 99). Her war aims no doubt, like all war aims, varied with circumstance, but two can be picked out as fairly constant:

  (i) to win an indemnity for the damage done in 480/79, by an offensive against Persia.[4]
  (ii) to exterminate Phoenician sea power.

---

[1] Sappho α 5 (Lobel); Alkaios 119 (Lobel); Pindar fr. 66 (Bowra); Thuc. II 31, VI 41. 3; Xen. *Hell.* V 1. 17.

[2] Fr. 1 (Diehl). The translation is Yeats', *The Cutting of an Agate* 125.

[3] The casualty list of the tribe Erechtheis, of the early 'fifties, may be cited: *IG* I² 929. Athens' temper in the Kimonian period seems to me expressed very faithfully in *Hymn. Hom.* XI: Παλλάδ' Ἀθηναίην ἐρυσίπτολιν ἄρχομ' ἀείδειν,| δεινήν, ᾗ σὺν Ἄρηι μέλει πολεμήια ἔργα | περθόμεναί τε πόλης αὐτή τε πτολεμοί τε, | καί τ' ἐρρύσατο λαὸν ἰόντα τε νισόμενόν τε. | χαῖρε θεά, δὸς δ' ἄμμι τύχην εὐδαιμονίην τε. Is the poem in fact of this date?

[4] Thuc. I 96. 1, πρόσχημα γὰρ ἦν ἀμύνεσθαι ὧν ἔπαθον δῃοῦντας τὴν βασιλέως χώραν.

(The strategic point, for both aims, was Kypros.) But apart from the booty of the Eurymedon, which paid for the artificial platform on which the Parthenon later stood,[1] very little was got in the way of indemnity: and the breaking of Phoenician sea power was reserved for Alexander. But after some thirty years of encounter with Athens, Persia was wounded mortally, and her inexorable decline begins: the picture in Xenophon, *Cyrop.* VIII 8, is of the reformed marauder who has settled down to live on his *rentes* and gone soft. It was Artaxerxes' treaty with Athens which started this: by it Persia formally abjured conquest and accepted a *modus vivendi.*

The world was thus made, if not quite safe, yet safe enough, for the development of Greek civilization: not only for the arts and sciences, but for experiments in government and social order and rational felicity. It was left to Alexander to break the Persian empire. Kimon's friends believed that Athens might have secured better coöperation from her allies and from Sparta, and by more concentration of energy against Persia have done more of what Alexander was to do.[2] It may be: but to some of us, the conquest of Persia appears as the end of the especial quality of Greek civilization, and we may think that Perikles did better to bring Persia to terms than to break her.

---

[1] Plut. *Kim.* 13. 5, τὸ νότιον τεῖχος.

[2] Plut. *Per.* 12. 1–2, where the words ταύτην (*sc.* τὴν πρόφασιν) ἀνῇρηκε Περικλῆς are a reference to the Treaty; *ib.* 28. 6.

APPENDIX

A Fragment of the Text of the Treaty?

Ἐν δὲ τοῖς ψηφίσμασιν ἃ συνήγαγε Κρατερὸς ἀντίγραφα συνθηκῶν ὡς γενομένων κατατέτακται (Plut. *Kim.* 13. 5). Krateros included the text of the Treaty among his collection of documents,[1] and so presumed it genuine. The Treaty with Artaxerxes or Dareios? It is commonly said that Krateros copied from the *stele* which Theopompos had condemned as a forgery, and there is some reason to think that this *stele* held the treaty with Dareios (see p. 126). It seems to me that, for Krateros, the treaty with Artaxerxes was more interesting, and I conceive he would know which one he was copying (even though Theopompos may not have known which one he was criticizing): and my impression is that Krateros was not a στηλοκόπας but worked from the archives. So that the chances that his text was of the Treaty of 450/49 are, I think, strong.

I believe we have a fragment of it. The Townleyan scholiast on *Iliad* XIV 230, Λῆμνον δ' εἰσαφίκανε πόλιν θείοιο Θόαντος, may perhaps be restored as follows: —

πόλιν θείοιο ⟨Θόαντος: ὡς Εὐριπίδης, "Εὔβοι' Ἀθήναις⟩ ἐστί τις γείτων πόλις," ἀντὶ τοῦ "νῆσος"· οἱ δὲ ἀντὶ τοῦ "χώρα," ⟨ὡς⟩ ἐν ψηφίσματι ⟨ὃ παρα⟩τίθεται Κρατερός, "ἔστε ἐπὶ Αἴγυπτον καὶ Λιβύην τὼ πόλεε."

Lacunas explevit Meineke, modo ὡς Εὐριπίδης addidi, coll. Strab. VIII 3. 31: καρτερός ms., Κρατερός Meineke: in fragmento psephismatis, ἐστὶν ms., delevit Meineke, ἔστε ἐπὶ (sc. εστ⟨ε επ⟩ι) ego. Krech fr. 12; apud *FHG* non exstat.

This restoration is essentially Meineke's, given in his edition of Stephanos, p. 718. The scholium is evidently corrupt, but none of the restorations are vital; it is certain that we have a quotation from one of Krateros' "documents," containing the words Αἴγυπτον καὶ Λιβύην τὼ πόλεε. These words are cited to illustrate the use of πόλις in the sense of "island" or "country." This usage occurs in poetry, though rarely;[2] its presence in documentary prose needs accounting for. I have long thought that the phrase might be

---

[1] The best account of Krateros' work is in Krech, *de Crateri ψηφισμάτων συναγωγῇ*, Berlin, 1888; cf. *ATL* 203. The psephismata included various sorts of "documents" from the archives, not necessarily all decrees: though the Treaty was, quite possibly, a decree: cf. *IG* I² 26, 39, 51, 52, etc.; Thuc. IV 118. 11.

[2] See the passages cited by Strabo VIII 3. 31. The loose apposition of Σικελίαν etc. to πόλεις πολλάς in [Lysias] 6. 6 should not be cited for this usage.

from the Treaty: τότε μὲν γὰρ ἡμεῖς φανησόμεθα τὴν ἀρχὴν τὴν βασιλέως ὁρίζοντες (Isokr. 4. 120). Since Persian documents were drafted in Aramaic, I asked G. R. Driver if any Aramaic word was likely to be responsible for this curious usage in the Greek translation, and he tells me that the Aramaic *medinah*, "juridical area," is used sometimes of a city, sometimes of a province. "[*As far as?*] *the two administrative areas of Egypt and Libya.*" The King's dominions are being defined; they are to stretch, in this direction, to the areas which had rebelled under Inaros (Thuc. I 104. 1). Athens renounces her support of such rebellion.

Was the translator an Ionian? If my suggestion ἔστε ἐπὶ is right, he probably was, since ἔστε is not Attic. Perhaps the form πλέειν, for which Lindskog quotes no variant in Plut. *Kim.* 13. 4, is another Ionicism: if so, ἔνδον δὲ Κυανέων καὶ Χελιδονίων μακρᾷ νηὶ καὶ χαλκεμβόλῳ[1] μὴ πλέειν (μηδετέρους?) may be almost textual (Krateros being by then available). I do not think, even so, that a *stele* commissioned by the Poletai in 449 B.C. is likely to have been inscribed in Ionic script (see p. 126); but it becomes a little less impossible.

---

[1] Χαλκέμβολοι in Diod. XIV 59. 7 (Phoenician); Plut. *Ant.* 35. 7. In the former, are they armed merchantmen?

THE TRIBAL CYCLES OF THE
TREASURERS OF ATHENA

By William Bell Dinsmoor

BARELY more than forty years ago, when the eminent historian to whom I venture to dedicate these remarks announced the discovery of the "Ferguson Law" of tribal rotation of the secretaries of the Athenian Council, he likewise mentioned certain other offices in which such rotation was followed, among them, that of the secretaries of the treasurers of Athena.[1] To the latter, eight years ago, he devoted a special study which, though primarily of historical import, greatly extended our knowledge of the system of tribal rotation.[2] In other words, the first announcement had shown that the secretaries of the treasurers succeeded one another in sequence according to the reversed official rotation of the tribes — the earlier form — during three disconnected periods, 434–429, 416–412, and 403–389 B.C., and again in forward rotation during 351–339 B.C. The later study enlarged the third period from fourteen to twenty-six years (411–385), and suggested that this was followed by "sortition cycles" for a period of three decades and that forward rotation was eventually adopted in 355 B.C.

Meanwhile, in spite of general acceptance of the longer period of fourteen years (403–389), the two brief periods of backward rotation for five and four years (434–429 and 416–412) had been doubted by some as probably accidental.[3] Again, the extension of the longest period backward from 403 to 411 B.C. created difficulties which induced Johnson, Kolbe, and Woodward to oppose or at least to doubt it.[4] The first of the short periods, however, was corroborated by Meritt's study of the annual accounts of the statue of Athena Parthenos, showing that it should be projected back to

---

[1] Ferguson, *The Athenian Secretaries*, Ithaca, N. Y., 1898, 70–74.

[2] Ferguson, *The Treasurers of Athena*, Cambridge, Mass., 1932, 8–15, 141–152.

[3] M. Brillant, *Les secrétaires athéniens*, Paris, 1911, 58.

[4] A. C. Johnson, *American Journal of Philology*, LIII (1932), 275–276; W. Kolbe, *Göttingische gelehrte Anzeigen*, 1934, 251–252, 255; A. M. Woodward, *Journal of Hellenic Studies*, LVIII (1938), 70 n. 3, 79 n. 27.

443 B.C. and thus form an uninterrupted rotation of fourteen years.[1] On the other hand, I had extended the latest period, admittedly on very slight evidence, for twenty-seven years beyond Ferguson's final concluding date, as a substitute for the proposed "sortition cycles";[2] and now, in another connection, I am able to confirm this extension of the reversed rotation and to show that it lasted even six years longer than I had originally inferred.[3] In other words, it can now be shown that the reversed rotation of the secretaries of the treasurers continued for ninety-one years (with two interruptions of thirteen years and one year, respectively), and was then superseded by forward rotation.

The object of the present paper is to allay, if possible, some lingering doubts with regard to the existence of tribal rotation among the secretaries of the treasurers during certain portions of the period, and also to restudy the application of this principle to the financial records of the monuments of the Acropolis.

I

The authenticity of the tribal rotation for the first period of fourteen years (443–429) is certainly beyond doubt. For the last five of these years Ferguson had tabulated five unquestionable demotics in an ordered sequence which could hardly be fortuitous. Five years earlier than this group was the date which, without noting its import for the tribal cycles, I had assigned to fragment U (*IG²* I 347) of the Parthenon accounts, naming a secretary from Lakiadai (Oineis, VI).[4] It remained for Meritt to observe that this is a second support for the tribal cycle, exactly fitting the rotation projected back from Lamptrai (Erechtheis, I) in 434/3 B.C., and to demonstrate that the assumption of rotation covering

[1] B. D. Meritt, *Athenian Financial Documents of the Fifth Century*, Ann Arbor, 1932, 26–41.

[2] Dinsmoor, "The Burning of the Opisthodomos at Athens," *American Journal of Archaeology*, XXXVI (1932), 148–149, 163–165.

[3] Dinsmoor, *The Athenian Archon List in the Light of Recent Discoveries*, New York, 1939, 11 n. 69.

[4] Dinsmoor *AJA* XXV 238–240.

not only the four years after 439/8 B.C. but also the four preceding
years, back to the logical initial tribe (Antiochis, X) in 443/2 B.C.,
would be compatible with the epigraphical evidence, coming primarily from the expense accounts of the Athena Parthenos. On the
other hand, as Meritt recognized, rotation probably was not instituted before 443 B.C., since in 446/5 B.C. the secretary was Exekestos of Athmonon (Kekropis, VII), according to Parthenon
fragment S (*IG*² I 340), whereas rotation of the cycle would demand a secretary from Pandionis (III) in that year.

Adopting the cycle as thus established with a fair degree of
probability in 443 B.C., and turning to the accounts of the Athena
Parthenos, Meritt was enabled to assign to the period of pure
sortition before this initial date both *IG*² I 361, wherein the occurrence of the name Exek[estos] had already caused Bannier to
propose the date 446/5 B.C.,[1] and *IG*² I 359 with a secretary from
Philaidai (Aigeis, I1).[2] For the period after the institution of the
cycle, Meritt showed that *IG*² I 358, with a secretary from Aphidna
(Aiantis, IX),[3] should be assigned to 442/1 B.C.,[4] and that *IG*² I
355 (and 355a), with a secretary from Xypete (Kekropis, VII),
should be assigned to 440/39 B.C.[5] A chain of difficulties seemingly
raised by the last of these attributions was considered and for the
most part allayed by Meritt. First, he revised the expense record
of the Samian War (*IG*² I 293) to show that Phyromachos was not
secretary of the treasurers in 440/39 (which would have disagreed
with Demostratos of Xypete in *IG*² I 355) but rather in 441/0 B.C.,
thus displacing [Epichar]inos of Peiraieus (Hippothontis, VIII)
who would have fitted this year in accordance with the cycle[6] but

---

[1] W. Bannier *Philologische Wochenschrift* 1921, 310.

[2] The alternative, after 443, would be 435/4 B.C., which is too late because the
heavy expenditure of 34 talents for gold would have been inconceivable so long
after the dedication of the statue in 438 B.C. (cf. Meritt *op. cit.* 33).

[3] A new reading by Meritt *op. cit.* 35–38.

[4] Meritt *op. cit.* 39, 48 (pointing out that the alternative of placing it before
443 B.C. is improbable on account of resulting disagreement with two other criteria,
the diminishing number of letters per line and the simplification of the formulae in
succeeding years).

[5] Meritt *op. cit.* 40 (with similar objections to the alternative of placing it before
443 B.C.). [6] Meritt *op. cit.* 27, 48 (rejected).

must now be regarded as the first secretary of the Council for 440/39 B.C.[1] The last in turn seemingly introduced a new difficulty in that [Epichar]inos of Peiraieus as first secretary of the Council would conflict with - - - - - of Rhamnous, mentioned in the same office in *IG*[2] I 50, currently assigned to 440/39 B.C.; but Meritt found convincing reasons for postponing the latter for one year.[2] Even so, however, the Council secretary from Rhamnous seemed to conflict with fragment U (*IG*[2] I 347) of the Parthenon accounts for 439/8 B.C., wherein Meritt inferred that I had regarded the demotic [Περγ]ασῖθεν as that of the first secretary of the Council. He proposed to overcome this difficulty by restoring - - ιος at the end of the preceding line as the demotic of the first secretary of the Council, ['Ραμνόσ]ιος, and by inserting an initial line in what is now the blank upper portion of *IG*[2] I 347.[3] I cannot feel that this is justifiable: with the extra line, the prescript of 439/8 would then cover seven lines, as contrasted with five lines for 445/4, 444/3, 443/2, 442/1, and 441/0, and six lines for 440/39 and 438/7 B.C.; only in 446/5 B.C., when an exceptional clause appeared, were there as many as seven lines. Furthermore, in these Parthenon accounts the demotic of the first secretary of the Council was universally omitted. Thus no conflict exists between *IG*[2] I 50 and *IG*[2] I 347; there is plenty of room in the latter for the insertion of the 5 letters of the name of the first secretary in the former, and the demotic was omitted. As my edition had shown,[4] [Περγ]ασῖθεν is really the demotic of an *epistates*, while the letters at the end of the preceding line are merely - - os;[5] and the hypothetical first line is to be rejected. Thus the secretary cycle for the treasurers of Athena between 443 and 429 B.C. is in agreement with all the other evidence.

Inspection of the results thus attained permitted Meritt to develop two stylistic criteria. The first of these is the number

---

[1] Meritt *op. cit.* 42–48; reaffirmed in *AJP* LV 365–366, with a shorter and more reasonable length of line.

[2] Meritt *op. cit.* 48–56.

[3] Meritt *op. cit.* 54–55.

[4] Dinsmoor *AJA* XXV 238.

[5] In the *Corpus*, my bracket . . .]os was misinterpreted as ΙΟΣ.

of letters per line: 13 in IG^2 I 355, 14 in 356, 14 in 358, 21 in 359, about 28 in 360, approximately 42 in 361.[1] As arranged in the *Corpus*, therefore, the number of letters per line is successively enlarged. But the true chronological order reverses the situation, the number of letters per line gradually diminishing from about 42 in 446/5 (IG^2 I 361), 21 in 445/4–444/3 (359), 14 in 442/1 (358), to 13 in 440/39 B.C. (355). In accordance with this criterion, Meritt assigned IG^2 I 360 (with about 28 letters) to about 445/4 (between 361 and 359), and IG^2 I 356 (with 14 letters) to about 441/0 B.C. (between 358 and 355).[2]

The second of the stylistic criteria developed by Meritt was the gradual simplification of the formulae. Thus we find at first ταμίαι ἐκ πόλεος (IG^2 I 359, 360, 361), later simplified to ταμίαι (355, 358);[3] the change would seem to have occurred between 445/4–444/3 (359) and 442/1 B.C. (358). Again, the treasurers (apart from their secretary) are first named with their demotics (IG^2 I 359, 360); then in a transitional form the demotic is sometimes omitted (358); finally the names appear alone (355).[4] This change would seem to have occurred at about 442/1 B.C. (IG^2 I 358).

All three criteria unite in fitting the sequence proposed by Meritt, whose chronological table of the records of the *epistatai* of the statue may conveniently be repeated here:[5]

446/5	IG^2 I 361	442/1	IG^2 I 358
445/4?	360	441/0?	356
444/3?	359	440/39	355, 355a

The earliest of these pieces (IG^2 I 361), however, is not so definitely fixed in 446/5 B.C. as had been assumed from Bannier's identification of the name Exekestos. The record is restored in the *Corpus* as follows:

---

[1] Meritt *op. cit.* 31.
[2] Meritt *op. cit.* 40–41.
[3] IG^2 I 355a and 356 yield no evidence as to this phrase.
[4] IG^2 I 355a, 356, and 361 yield no evidence as to these names.
[5] Meritt *op. cit.* 41.

vacat o.19 m.

[λῆμμα παρὰ ταμιõν ἐκ πόλεος ho̅ῖς] Ἐχσέκ[εστος ἐγραμ]
[μάτευε Ἀθμονεύς . . . .⁸ . . . . ἀγάλμ]ατι [χρυσõι - -
[. . . . . .²¹. . . . . ἐπὶ τε̃]ς βολ[ε̃ς he̅ι - -
[. . . . . .²⁴. . . . . τα]μίαι ε̃[σαν

vacat o.085 m.

- - - - ν - - - -

But this restoration is defective in that it fails to mention the board
of *epistatai* and particularly their secretary; nor can we restore the
missing part of the prescript, which in any case should be in close
proximity to the phrase ἐπὶ τε̃ς βολε̃ς, in the vacant space of o.19 m.
above. Also the restored form of the prescript is unprecedented,
among these accounts, in starting off with the mention of the receipt from the treasurers before giving the date. If we had not
been prejudiced by the assumption that Ἐχσεκ- was the same
secretary of the treasurers of the goddess who appeared in the
Parthenon account of 446/5 B.C.,[1] we should undoubtedly have
restored it somewhat as follows:

[ἐπιστάται ho̅ῖς] Ἐχσέκ[εστος ἐγραμμάτευεν Ἀθμ]
[ονεὺς τõι ἀγάλμ]ατι [χρυσõι ἔλαβον παρὰ ταμιõν]
[ἐκ πόλεος ἐπὶ τε̃]ς βολ[ε̃ς he̅ι . . . .⁹ . . . . . ἐγραμμά]
[τευε πρõτος τα]μίαι ε̃[σαν   vacat?

The following vacant space of o.085 m. was apparently left for the
insertion of the names of the treasurers, which were never inscribed,
as in the case of *IG*² I 255 and II 1377, 1378, 1421. As for the date
of *IG*² I 361, it is now apparent that, presuming Exekestos to be the
same person who is mentioned in the Parthenon account of 446/5
B.C., the statue account could not be assigned to this same year
since Exekestos could not have held two different secretaryships
in a single year.[2] On the other hand, the prescript as thus restored

---

[1] The name Ἐχσεκ- - is incomplete both here and in the Parthenon account,
and so might also be restored as Exekestides or Exekias; but we may tentatively retain the form Exekestos which is generally adopted.

[2] The mere fact that the name [Ἀντ]ίδο[ρος] restored as first secretary of the
Council in the Parthenon account of 446/5 B.C. would also fit *IG*² I 361 is of
little significance, since Antidoros is largely hypothetical and names in 9 letters
were legion.

follows a slightly unusual order and would well serve as the initial
account of the series; it accords with all the available criteria for
such a date, having the greatest number of letters per line (though
reduced from 42 to 38) and also the more extensive formulae of the
earlier period.

In *IG²* I 360, which comes next in date, the number of letters per
line has been restored in the *Corpus* as 28, as follows:

$$[\ldots\ldots\ldots^{20}\ldots\ldots\ldots\ldots] \; \dot{\epsilon}[\pi i \; \tau \hat{\epsilon}s \; \beta o]$$
$$[\lambda \hat{\epsilon}s \; h\hat{\epsilon}\iota \ldots.^{10}\ldots\ldots \; M\upsilon\rho]\rho\iota\nu\delta[\sigma\iota os \; \pi]$$
$$[\rho \hat{o} \tau os \; \dot{\epsilon}\gamma\rho\alpha\mu\mu\dot{\alpha}\tau\epsilon\upsilon\epsilon] \qquad vacat$$
$$[\lambda \hat{\epsilon}\mu\mu\alpha \; \pi\alpha\rho\dot{\alpha} \; \tau\alpha\mu\iota\hat{o}\nu \; \dot{\epsilon}\kappa \; \pi]\acute{o}\lambda\epsilon os \; h[o\hat{\iota}s \;.]$$
$$[\ldots\ldots^{11}\ldots\ldots \; \dot{\epsilon}\gamma\rho\alpha\mu\mu\dot{\alpha}]\tau\epsilon\upsilon\epsilon \; \tau\alpha[\mu\dot{\iota}\alpha\iota]$$
$$[\delta\dot{\epsilon}\ldots\ldots^{11}\ldots\ldots \; \dot{\epsilon}\kappa \; K\epsilon\rho\alpha]\mu\acute{\epsilon}o\nu \; \iota[\ldots.]$$
$$[\ldots\ldots\ldots^{18}\ldots\ldots\ldots \; \Pi]\rho\alpha\sigma\iota\epsilon[\acute{\upsilon}s \;.]$$

It seems preferable, however, to revise this restoration in conformity with *IG²* I 358 and 359, and also, as in the earlier of these
(359), to permit the heading λῆμμα to project four spaces to the
left, over the money-column. And the restoration ἐ[πὶ τῆς βολῆς]
is in any case erroneous since the bottom of the first letter slopes,
indicating that it was Σ rather than E. Under these conditions
we may propose the following restoration with 26 letters per line
(inserting, for reasons given below, the name of Exekestos which
exactly fills the space):

$$[\dot{\epsilon}\pi i \ldots\ldots \; \gamma\rho\alpha\mu\mu\alpha\tau\epsilon\acute{\upsilon}o\nu\tau os \; \dot{\epsilon}\pi]$$
$$[\iota\sigma\tau\dot{\alpha}\tau\epsilon\sigma\iota \; \dot{\alpha}\gamma\dot{\alpha}\lambda\mu\alpha\tau o]s \; [\dot{\epsilon}\pi i \; \tau \hat{\epsilon}s \; \beta o\lambda]$$
$$[\dot{\epsilon}s \; h\hat{\epsilon}\iota \ldots\ldots \; M\upsilon\rho]\rho\iota\nu\delta[\sigma\iota os \; \pi\rho\hat{o}]$$
$$[\tau os \; \dot{\epsilon}\gamma\rho\alpha\mu\mu\dot{\alpha}\tau\epsilon\upsilon\epsilon] \qquad vacat$$
$$[\lambda \hat{\epsilon}\mu\mu\alpha \; \pi\alpha\rho\dot{\alpha} \; \tau\alpha\mu\iota\hat{o}\nu \; \dot{\epsilon}\kappa \; \pi]\acute{o}\lambda\epsilon os \; h[o\hat{\iota}s \; '\mathrm{E}\chi\sigma]$$
$$[\dot{\epsilon}\kappa\epsilon\sigma\tau os \; \dot{\epsilon}\gamma\rho\alpha\mu\mu\dot{\alpha}]\tau\epsilon\upsilon\epsilon \; \tau\alpha[\mu\dot{\iota}\alpha\iota \; \dot{\epsilon}\sigma]$$
$$[\alpha\nu \ldots\ldots \; \dot{\epsilon}\kappa \; K\epsilon\rho\alpha]\mu\acute{\epsilon}o\nu \; \mathrm{L}[\ldots\ldots]$$
$$[\ldots\ldots\ldots\ldots \; \Pi]\rho\alpha\sigma\iota\epsilon[\acute{\upsilon}s \;\ldots.]$$

Next, Woodward's idea that *IG²* I 356 formed the lower part of
IG² I 355,[1] though belonging in a different year because both pre-

---

[1] Woodward *JHS* XXXIV 282; he cites as evidence the thickness and appearance
of the two stones, a similar flaw at the left edge, and the fact that the lines begin
apparently at a similar distance from the left edge.

serve the beginnings of expenses, was doubted by Bannier;[1] and Meritt apparently reached the same conclusion. We have no analogy in this series for two annual accounts on a single stone; and another possible objection is that, while both inscriptions are *stoichedon*, IG^2 I 355 has only 13 letters per line while the other has 14 letters. Thus Meritt was perfectly free to place IG^2 I 356 before 355. But his reason for placing IG^2 I 356 after 358, because of the diminishing number of letters per line, is not cogent, since the difference between them is inappreciable. Furthermore we must notice an important change of formula: the heading Ἀναλό-ματα, employed in IG^2 I 359 but omitted in 358 (in accordance with the general tendency toward simplification), is present in IG^2 I 356.[2] For this reason we may now place IG^2 I 356 before 358.

As now charted, the four criteria as to date yield the following results:

Year	Tribal cycle	Width	Simpler formulae		Ἀναλόματα
Before 443	361 (VII)	361 (38 letters)	361		
		360 (26 letters)	360	(a)	
	359 (II)	359 (21 letters)	359		359 (present)
		356 (14 letters)			356 (present)
442/1	358 (IX)	358 (14 letters)	358	(b)	358 (absent)
440/39	355 (VII)	355 (13 letters)	355	(c)	355 (absent)
Uncertain	356, 360		356		360, 361

From this analysis it becomes apparent that IG^2 I 361, excluded from 446/5 B.C. by the fact that Exekestos could not have been secretary for two boards in the same year, is likewise excluded from any later year because it would then be impossible to insert the sequence IG^2 I 360, 359, and 356, demanding three years at least, between IG^2 I 361 and 358. In consequence, IG^2 I 361 must be dated 447/6 B.C.; and for the next three accounts we have in each case an allowable bracket of two years, until the discovery of further evidence permits greater precision, as follows:

447/6	IG^2 I 361	444/3–443/2	IG^2 I 356
446/5–445/4	360	442/1	358
445/4–444/3	359	440/39	355, 355a

---

[1] Bannier *Phil. Woch.* 1921, 311.

[2] IG^2 I 355a, 360, and 361 yield no evidence in this respect.

It may be noted that, if *IG*² I 360 were dated in the earlier of the two available years, 446/5 B.C., the secretary's name Exekestos would exactly fit,[1] and also that, if *IG*² I 359 were dated in the earlier of the two available years, 445/4 B.C., the secretary's demotic would exactly fit the cycle projected back to that year; but it seems preferable to assume that the appearance of a secretary from Aigeis (II) in 445/4–444/3 B.C. was a mere coincidence, and to agree with Meritt that the tribal cycles were initiated with Antiochis (X) in 443 B.C. In any case, it now becomes apparent that the gold-and-ivory statue was begun simultaneously with the construction of the Parthenon itself, in 447 B.C., and that the general pose and motive, if not the finer details, must represent an artistic conception already formulated in that year. It is evident, also, that the work on the statue lasted nine years,[2] until its dedication on August 17, 438 B.C.[3] The final summary of the accounts (*IG*² I 354) dating from the last year, and with no named secretary, has been discussed elsewhere.[4]

II

The tribal rotation was broken off, for some unknown reason,[5] in 429 B.C. and for thirteen years was replaced by pure sortition. Only six tribes furnished the secretaries throughout the period, Akamantis (V) in four cases — if we accept West's identification of the only uncertain secretary, Smikythos[6] — and Antiochis (X) in three. Next, for four years (416–412), we have an isolated block of four names in the reversed tribal rotation, unrelated to any system before or after them, and yet unmistakably intentional. The secretary for 412/1 B.C. again was chosen by lot. Then, as

[1] See restoration on p. 163.
[2] As I formerly suggested (*AJA* XXV 129).
[3] For the table on which this calculation is based, see Dinsmoor *Archon List* 209.
[4] Dinsmoor Ἀρχαιολογικὴ Ἐφημερίς 1937, 507–511.
[5] Ferguson's suggestion (*Treas.* 10 n. 1) that it was connected with completion of the cycle of the secretaries of the Hellenotamiai in that year is plausible.
[6] West, in Paton and Stevens, *The Erechtheum* (Cambridge, Mass., 1927), 647–648.

Ferguson has shown, the secretary during the short government of the Five Thousand in 411 B.C. was chosen from the first tribe (Erechtheis), possibly with the intention of beginning forward rotation,[1] but in any case followed in proper sequence by a secretary from the initial tribe according to reversed rotation (Antiochis, X). For, in the second year thereafter, 409/8 B.C., the date to which I had assigned the inventory *IG*² I 254 of the pronaos of the Parthenon,[2] the secretary came from Eleusis (Hippothontis, VIII), exactly fitting the rotation projected back from 403–389 B.C. Therefore, in the case of the only later pronaos inventory retaining a secretary's deme, Leukonoe (Leontis, IV), Ferguson was justified in claiming that its date must be 405/4 B.C. to fit the tribal cycle.[3]

This last inventory of the pronaos of the Parthenon is that inscribed on the lower part of the stone (EM 6774) containing the inventories of 409/8 and 408/7 B.C., namely, *IG*² I 255a (lines 323–331),[4] following an empty gap 0.10 m. high. The gap of 0.10 m. above it suggests that it may have been an appendix or later addition to the inventories;[5] and the date, in any case later than the preceding inventory of 408/7 and earlier than the adoption of the Ionic alphabet in 403 B.C., is suggested by the mention of the archon Kallias (406/5) in line 329, so that it should belong to the year before Kallias, as interpreted by Kirchhoff, Hiller, Johnson, and Kolbe;[6] or to the year of Kallias, as suggested by Bannier;[7] or to the year after Kallias, as preferred by Ferguson and myself.[8] Restorations might be devised to fit any one of these

[1] Meritt (*Ath. Fin. Doc.* 28) points out that Erechtheis (I) seems an inappropriate initial tribe for reversed rotation.

[2] *Erechtheum* 649 n. 1.

[3] Ferguson *Treas.* 8–15.

[4] The designation I 255a was applied by Ferguson, after I had shown that it belonged to a different year from I 255 (*Erechtheum* 649 n. 1).

[5] The preceding gap between *IG*² I 254 and 255 was left for the insertion of the names of the treasurers of 408/7 B.C.

[6] *IG*² I 255; Johnson *AJP* LIII 274–278; Kolbe *GGA* 251–255.

[7] Bannier *Rh. Mus.* 1915, 407.

[8] Ferguson *Treas.* 8–15; Ferguson and Dinsmoor *AJA* XXXVII 52–57. Accepted also by Meritt *The Athenian Tribute Lists* (Cambridge, Mass., 1939), p. 570, and by Schweigert *Hesperia* IX (1940) 313.

three possibilities; but such restorations would not, in themselves, be conclusive proof. The date which we are unquestionably to adopt is that which Ferguson discovered, 405/4 B.C. as required by adjustment of the deme of the secretary of the treasurers to the tribal cycle then in operation. To this I can see no alternative; and to this the restoration must be made to conform.

The restorations hitherto advanced, however, contain several inconsistencies which must be eliminated before any result can be convincing. Among these is the universal effort, in which I have participated, to supply an archon's name in an appropriate number of letters at the beginning of the inscription. I owe to Meritt (letter) the suggestion that "a board of treasurers in these records ought not to be dated by the name of the archon: (a) the board is identified normally by the name of its chairman and secretary, and inasmuch as both these names are given in lines 323–327 the restoration ἐπὶ ᾿Αλεχσίο is out of place in line 323; (b) the phrase ἐπὶ ᾿Αλεχσίο is also out of place in line 323 because we cannot insert the usual and normal ἄρχοντος after it." Noting that the difference between this inventory and those of preceding years lies in the fact that it mentions the only gold object of the older lists, but none of the silver objects, Meritt suggests that we restore ἀργυρᾶ in the first line to explain this difference, and fill out the remaining four letter-spaces with χσυν-, as follows: [τὰ τῆς θεō ἀργυρᾶ hoι χσυνά]ρχσαντες ταμίαι.

The restoration of lines 328–331 involves the entire meaning of this abnormal inventory. Continuing to employ 46 letters per line (instead of 62, 60, or 47 letters), I wish to consider certain alternative restorations which Meritt had suggested while Ferguson and I were publishing our article seven years ago, particularly ᾿Αγ[ρυλεεῖ] at the end of line 328 on the analogy of ᾿Αγρυλῆς in *IG²* I 398 and ᾿Αγκυλεεῖ in *IG²* I 301 (line 24), followed by καθάπερ ἐφσέφιστο at the beginning of line 329, as in *IG²* I 39 (line 42), 91 (line 4), 108 (line 43), 154 (line 13). As Meritt had noted in this connection, the necessary omission of [καὶ χσυνάρχοσι] at the beginning of line 329, after [hελλενοταμ]ίαις, could be paralleled by the similar omission after στρατεγοῖς in *IG²* I 324 (line 18), even though such an omission must be interpreted as a scribal error. We had listed these emendations without actually adopting them;[1] it now seems to me preferable, however, to incorporate them in the restoration, thus eliminating our proposed restoration [hὰ - - - - - - - ἔχθε], to which there has been some opposition.[2] On the other hand, Kirchhoff's old restoration κατελείφθε, which was originally retained by Ferguson and was revived by Kolbe, seems contrary to the sense, unless we assume that [ἐπὶ Κ]αλλίο ἄρχοντος begins a new sentence referring only to the gold crown, implying that the latter had already been disposed of in 406/5, and that only the silver objects remained for disposal in 405/4. The contiguity of [καθάπερ ἐφσέφιστο ἐπὶ Κ]αλλίο ἄρχοντος would certainly have resulted in ambiguity unless they belonged together; and it seems most reasonable to assume that the silver objects were turned over to the Hellenotamiai in accordance with a decree which had been voted in the archonship of Kallias, during some prytany of which the designating secretary's name is lost. The word [πρῶτος] generally restored in line 330 is probably to be replaced by the secretary's demotic, so that the number of the prytany could have been ascertained only by referring to an official list. In view of the necessity of restoring [χρυσὸς] in line 331 — an additional objection to the verb κατελείφθε, for which there would not be room — we have space for only four or five letters in the word after προνέ[ο], depending upon the presence or omission of the numeral :Ι: in line 331. Such prepositions as ἐκτός or πλέν would seem objectionable if the decree under Kallias referred only to the silver, as the probable restoration of line 323 implies. Probably, therefore, the missing word was a verb, as Meritt suggests; and he notes that [ἔμενε] would exactly fill the space. An alternative, and one which I prefer because it allows the retention of the numeral :Ι: in line 331, is the present tense [μένε], implying that in 405/4, after disposing of the silver objects according to the decree of the previous year, one gold crown *still remains* of the pronaos material. The peculiar mark before ἐκ, in such case, might have resulted from the erasure of another E resulting from dittography, as we formerly suggested,[3] but is more

---

[1] Ferguson and Dinsmoor *AJA* XXXVII 56–57.

[2] Johnson and Woodward (letters).

[3] *AJA* XXXVII 55–56.

probably to be regarded as an actual mark of punctuation, separating the silver from the gold; Meritt calls to my attention similar marks of punctuation in *IG*² I 369 + 390a.[1]

The restoration now proposed for *IG*² I 255a is the following:

[τὰ τῆς θεô ἀργυρᾶ ἧοι χσυνά]ρχσαντες ταμίαι Καλλι[. . . . .]

[. . . . . .²². . . . .] Φίλιππος Φιλεσίο Προσ[παλτι]

325 [ος . . . . .²⁰. . . . .]ευς Μενέστρατος Μενεσ[τράτο]

[Φλυεὺς . . . . .¹². . . . . 'Ελευ]σίνιος 'Αντιφôν 'Αντιφô[ρτος Κ]

[ριοεὺς ἧοῖς . . . .¹¹. . . . .]αθίο Λευκονοιεὺς ἐγρα[μμάτευ]

[εν παρέδοσαν ἧελλενοταμ]ίαις Χαριάδει Χαρίο 'Αγ[ρυλεεῖ]

[καθάπερ ἐφσέφιστο ἐπὶ Κ]αλλίο ἄρχοντος ἐπὶ τῆς βο[λῆς ἧε͂]

330 [ι . . . . .¹⁸. . . . . ἐ]γραμμάτευεν □ ἐκ τô προνέ[ο μένε]

[στέφανος χρυσôς : Ι : σταθμ]ὸν τοῦτο Δ Δ Δ Ⱶ Ⱶ Ⱶ Ι Ι Ι

The implication in the words [χσυνά]ρχσαντες ταμίαι is that the amalgamated board of treasurers had already come into existence in 405/4 B.C. With this I am now in full accord; in fact, I have long been prepared to retract my earlier argument that the amalgamation did not take place until the close of this year 405/4 B.C., an argument which was based on the erroneous reading of the demotic Προβ[αλίσιος] in *IG*² I 255a and the consequent assumption that this treasurer was identical with the one mentioned in Erechtheum fragment XXIX, referring to the separate board of treasurers of Athena. The fallacy of this identification having now been demonstrated,[2] with the result that Erechtheum fragment XXIX must be assigned to a different (and consequently earlier) year, we no longer have evidence that the separate boards of treasurers existed as late as 405/4 B.C. Thus we may now accept the testimony of Andokides (*Mysteries* I 77) as to the name of the amalgamated board in 405/4 B.C., as well as Ferguson's attribution of an inventory (*IG*² II 1502) which seemingly mentions the amalgamated board as well as golden Nikes which had been melted down by 404 B.C.,[3] and also Woodward's attribution of two successive

---

[1] Illustrated by Woodward, 'Εφ. 1937, 160.

[2] See below, p. 174.

[3] Ferguson *Treas.* 91–92, 104; the argument that *IG*² II 1502 is earlier than the early fourth century (where Kirchner placed it) and also earlier than 403/2, is

annual inventories of the Hekatompedos Neos (*IG*² II 1383 and 1382) to years before 403/2 B.C.[1] But all this carries us back only to 405/4 for the amalgamation of the boards; I still see no definite reason for assuming that it occurred in 406/5.[2] Possibly the specific use of χσυνάρχσαντες in 405/4 (*IG*² I 255a) might even be interpreted as evidence that this was the first year of the existence of the amalgamated board.[3] On the other hand, the failure to inscribe an inventory at the end of the year 407/6 B.C. might be taken as an indication of some unusual disturbance in 406 B.C., such as the amalgamation of the boards. We require additional evidence before a decision can be made.

We may, therefore, regard the dating of the last inventory of the pronaos of the Parthenon (*IG*² I 255a), in 405/4 B.C., as a fundamental basis for the ordering of the records of the end of the fifth century.

Turning now to the expense accounts of the treasurers, it is to be noted that *IG*² I 305, which had been assigned to 406/5 B.C. in the *Corpus* and was mentioned in varying degrees of uncertainty by Meritt, West, and myself,[4] was fixed in that year with almost complete certainty by Ferguson,[5] who pointed out that it can be excluded from 411–408 and from 407/6, while the single intervening year 408/7 seems too early for the Ionic lettering, and 405/4 B.C. on the other hand would be too late for the large payment of 30 talents, then falling after the surrender of Athens to Lysander.[6]

---

accepted by Woodward ('Εφ. 1937, 163), who dates it however "ca. 407/6" without noting Ferguson's arguments for regarding it as an inventory of the amalgamated board.

[1] Woodward *JHS* LVIII 70 n. 3, 73–78.

[2] As preferred by Lehner *Schatzverzeichnisse* 17; Panske *Leipz. Studien* 1890, 4; Ferguson *Secretaries* 73; *Treas.* 4, 7, 104–106; Kolbe *GGA* 1934, 250; Woodward *JHS* LVIII 70.

[3] As preferred by Johnson *AJP* LIII 277–278.

[4] Meritt *The Athenian Calendar* 96; West *Classical Weekly* XXIII (1929/30) 62; Dinsmoor *Archons* 346 n. 7.

[5] Ferguson *Treas.* 4, 23 n., 27–29, 75–77, 83, 108, 146 n., 177. Ferguson suggested (*ibid.* 26 n., 76 n.) that *IG*² I 303 and II 1687 might perhaps be combined with *IG*² I 305. I have not tested the possibilities.

[6] This fragment mentions a payment to a certain Kal - - - - in the last decade

To the next year 405/4 B.C. Ferguson assigned, with great probability, *IG²* II 1686.[1] This, as now published, consists of two pieces *a* and *b*, of which the former is 0.087 m. thick and opisthographic, while the latter is 0.04 m. thinner and has letters on one face only, according to the description by Kirchner. It seems probable, therefore, that *IG²* II 1686*b* exhibits letters solely on the front merely for the reason that the back is broken away, and that this fragment can go either below or above *a*; the latter, perhaps, is to be preferred for the reason that *a* terminates with a blank space and so is probably the end of the inscription.[2] Four additional fragments may be associated with these, two from the Agora (I 2486, 2982), a third from the north slope of the Acropolis (EM 12768), and a fourth in the Epigraphical Museum (EM 3032).[3] Of these new pieces, EM 12768 is the most important in that it may preserve part of the prescript, though this is by no means certain.[4]

Two other fragments discovered in the Agora (I 5799*a–b*) resemble *IG²* II 1686 in form and content but, as I am informed by Schweigert, "do not belong to that inscription, for the lettering is different." Nor, for the same reason, can they belong to *IG²* I 305. Meritt sends me the following measurements of the lettering:

IG² I 305   10 letters = 0.14 m.;   10 lines = 0.14 m.; upright strokes 0.011 m.

---

of Hekatombaion, 405 B.C.; but he is hardly to be identified with Kalli - - -, of the board of treasurers of Athena in 405/4 (*IG²* I 255a), in the first place because of the frequency of names beginning thus, in the second place because of chronological difficulties, and in the third because, with *IG²* I 305 forming an account of the treasurers of Athena, it is most improbable that they would have made a payment to themselves. In other words, there is no inconsistency in dating *IG²* I 305 in 406/5 and *IG²* I 255a in 405/4 B.C.

[1] *Treas.* 18, 25 n., 27–29, 77–84, 177; accepted by Johnson *AJP*, LIII 277–278.

[2] Kirchner and Ferguson (the latter for the reason that *b* has no letters on the back, *Treas.* 30) both place *b* below *a*.

[3] I owe the list of additional fragments to Meritt; a preliminary publication of EM 12768 by Broneer appears in *Hesperia* IV (1935) 165–166, no. 26.

[4] The earlier phrase [καὶ συ]νάρχ[οντες] might conceivably be restored in the dative case like the one below, then referring to some other board than that of the treasurers of Athena.

IG^2 II 1686   10 letters = 0.105 m.; 10 lines = 0.13 m.; upright
                strokes 0.009 m.

Agora I 5799   10 letters = 0.093 m.; 10 lines = 0.11 m.; upright
                strokes 0.007 m.

It is evident, therefore, that we have in these new fragments the
remains of a third annual account, of a different year from either of
the others. One of the two new pieces (Agora I 5799*b*), furthermore, is important in that it contains the top of the stone with part
of the prescript, including the name of Chariades of Ag[ryle] who
is known to us as one of the three commissioners for the building
of the Erechtheum in 409/8 B.C. (IG^2 I 372),[1] and also apparently
as chairman of the Hellenotamiai in 405/4 (IG^2 I 255a). Since
Chariades must appear in Agora I 5799*b* as a treasurer of Athena,[2]
this would seem to belong to any other year than 405/4 B.C., since
Chariades could not have served simultaneously in two annual
boards. Since 406/5 B.C. is occupied by IG^2 I 305 and the next year
(presumably in any case to be reserved for IG^2 II 1686) is unsatisfactory for Chariades as treasurer, it seems clear that Agora
I 5799*b* should be assigned to 404/3 B.C. The alternative possibility
that Chariades was mentioned in IG^2 I 255a not as Hellenotamias
but as a treasurer (the preserved letters being -ίαις), in the dative
case so that he would belong to the following board of 404/3 B.C.,
would have the effect of yielding the same date for Agora I 5799*b*
but is hardly to be recommended in view of the fact that it would
involve a complete revision of the interpretation of IG^2 I 255a as
well as some difficulties in restoration. In other words, the recently
discovered fragments of accounts are in complete agreement with
the attribution of IG^2 I 305 to 406/5, of IG^2 II 1686 (with Agora I
2486, 2982, EM 3032, 12768) and IG^2 I 255a to 405/4, and of Agora
I 5799 to 404/3 B.C.

---

[1] Caskey, in Paton and Stevens *Erechtheum* 287, 300.

[2] The alternative interpretation of Agora I 5799*b* as an account of the Hellenotamiai would be unsuitable because these officers did not publish accounts on
marble with the exception of Athena's tribute (Ferguson *Treas.* 82); another objection is the similarity to IG^2 II 1686 wherein the Hellenotamiai seem to be mentioned in an oblique case so that they were hardly the officials responsible for the
account (*ibid.* 78).

To the chronological system as thus defined by means of the treasurers of Athena we may now attempt to readjust our conclusions as to the last years of the building accounts of the Erechtheum. It may be recalled that fragment XXVIII (IG^2 II 1654b) of these accounts, previously assigned to 395/4 B.C., had been attributed by Dörpfeld to 406/5 B.C. and that when I fitted the hitherto unidentified fragment XXVII (IG^2 II 1654a) above it the equally logical date of 405/4 B.C. appeared to be required by the circumstances.[1] Next, upon the rediscovery of the forgotten fragment XXIX (IG^2 II 1655), intermediate in character between the accounts of 408/7 and those of 406/5–405/4 B.C., it seemed reasonable to assign this to the only intervening year 407/6 B.C.,[2] particularly in view of the fact that the named treasurer from Probalinthos seemed to be identical with one of the treasurers listed in IG^2 I 255a, then currently assigned to that year.[3] These conclusions as to the dates were adopted in the monograph on the *Erechtheum*;[4] but simultaneously in the new *Corpus* all three fragments were given the traditional attribution to the first decade of the fourth century.[5] When Ferguson corrected the date of IG^2 I 255a to 405/4 B.C. he nevertheless adhered to my dating of Erechtheum fragment XXIX, suggesting that the same person might have been treasurer in two different years on the ground that the boards were differently constituted (treasurers of Athena *vs.* treasurers of Athena and the Other Gods).[6] To me, however, this interpretation seemed dangerously close to the forbidden iteration of office, so that I continued, still on the assumption that the treasurers were identical, to assume that both inscriptions must refer to a single year, though this was now 405/4 rather than 407/6 B.C.; and because of this later dating it now seemed necessary to carry fragments XXVII–XXVIII down into the fourth century, presumably

---

[1] Dinsmoor *AJA* XVII (1913) 264–265.

[2] This took the place of fragment XXVI (previously designated as X, *op. cit.* 263–264), afterwards shown to have formed part of the accounts of 409/8 B.C. (*AJA* XXXVI 146–147).

[3] Dinsmoor, in Paton and Stevens *Erechtheum* 648–650.

[4] Caskey *ibid.* 416–422.

[5] Kirchner *IG²* II 1654–1655; cf. Hiller *IG²* I p. 81.

[6] Ferguson *Treas.* 49–50, 104–105.

to the year 377/6 B.C. which was indicated for the fire mentioned by Demosthenes (24. 136 and scholia).[1] Johnson, however, ascertained that the two treasurers were not identical, coming from Probalinthos and Prospalta rather than both from the former, so that there was every reason for placing them in different years rather than together.[2] His reading was corroborated by Meritt.[3] On the other hand, Kolbe insisted that Johnson's correction was erroneous and that my abandoned identification of the two treasurers was in fact verified.[4] On my own part, I reserved decision and promised a later treatment of the problem,[5] which may now be undertaken.

Taking as axiomatic the dating of IG^2 I 255a in 405/4 B.C., and accepting as unquestionable Johnson's reading of the demotic of the treasurer from Prospalta (confirmed by Meritt), it then becomes apparent that Erechtheum fragment XXIX must in any case belong to a different year, and that this other year cannot be later than 405/4 B.C. because of the mention of the separate board of treasurers of Athena. There are only two possible dates, therefore, for Erechtheum fragment XXIX, in 406/5 B.C. if the separate boards continued as late as that year, otherwise in 407/6 B.C. As for fragments XXVII–XXVIII, it would still be possible to assign both to 377/6 B.C. (as I eventually preferred on the assumption that XXIX dated from 405/4), or both to 405/4, or (with XXIX in 407/6) to the two successive years 406/5–405/4 B.C. as I originally suggested, or even both to 406/5 B.C.

A decision on this point may now be reached by means of a new fragment, XXVIIIa (EM 12910), discovered by Broneer on the north slope of the Acropolis in 1937 and published by Schweigert.[6] It does not join the two fragments (XXVII–XXVIII) previously known, but is unquestionably from the same accounts. And its particular importance lies in counteracting an impression drawn

---

[1] Dinsmoor *AJA* XXXVI 148–155.
[2] Johnson *AJP* LIII 275.
[3] Meritt, cited in *AJA* XXXVII 54 n. 2.
[4] Kolbe *GGA* 1934, 255 n. 1.
[5] Dinsmoor *AJA* XXXVII 54 n. 1.
[6] Schweigert *Hesperia* VII (1938) 268–269 no. 3.

from the two other fragments, wherein the nine names mentioned do not recur in the accounts of 409–407 B.C. and so might be regarded as belonging to a new generation of workmen;[1] for the new piece contains only three names, Prepon, Sisyphos, and Parmenon, all well known from the accounts of 408/7 B.C. and forming a connected group which would hardly be imaginable a generation later. Thus we are clearly back in the fifth century, which also agrees better with the lettering, according to Schweigert. Hence the phrase "parts of the temple destroyed by fire" (fragment XXVIII) cannot be associated with the conflagration mentioned by Demosthenes; and that of Xenophon (*Hell.* I 6. 1), which I had doubted, must be rehabilitated. The earlier fire is stated to have occurred in the archonship of Kallias (406/5), so that fragment XXVIII should date from this year or slightly later. Under these circumstances it is hardly necessary to consider my alternative restoration [θε]ν [καὶ συν]αρχόν[των];[2] the hypothetical N is more probably I, as Meritt informs me after examination of the stone, in agreement with all earlier editors. In consequence, I now return to my original restoration [ἐπ]ὶ ['Αλεξίο] ἄρχον[τος], on the assumption that this was the beginning of an annual account and that the preceding lines (fragment XXVII) must refer to the preceding year 406/5 B.C. In other words, the interpretation of these fragments in Ionic lettering which I had suggested in 1913 and amplified fourteen years later is the one which best fits the new evidence concerning the Erechtheum (fragment XXVIIIa) and the treasurers of Athena, so that they may be dated as follows: 407/6 (XXIX), 406/5 (XXVII), 405/4 (XXVIII and XXVIIIa).

The fire of Xenophon may well have occurred in the latter part of the year 406/5 B.C.; and the lines preserved in fragment XXVII, unusual in that they contain an allusion to the Council and people, may refer to emergency repairs undertaken in one of the last prytanies of the year. Fragment XXVIII seems to refer to the first prytany of the following year (405/4), and covers the third to seventh days, inclusive. Since fragment XXVIIIa seems likewise to mention the seventh day as well as a previous day, it evidently belongs to another prytany, perhaps the second.

---

[1] Dinsmoor *AJA* XXXVI 151. [2] *Ibid.* 155.

III

The cycles instituted in 411/0 B.C. continued past the turn of the century and at least as late as 390/89, when we know that the secretary came from Aphidna (IX); and so, as Ferguson has suggested, they were probably unbroken until the change in the organization of the board of treasurers in 385 B.C.[1] When we next meet a series of names of secretaries, dating from 351/0, 349/8, and 341–339 B.C., it is evident that we are concerned with forward rotation, the earliest known secretary (351/0) coming from Hippothontis (VIII).[2] During the intervening period of thirty-four years we have only one known demotic, that of the secretary in 376/5 B.C., Euthias of Kettos (IV), which disagrees with both systems. Two methods of interpreting this discrepancy have been suggested. Ferguson proposed that three sortition cycles occupied thirty years (385–355), and that forward rotation was initiated with Leontis (IV) in 355/4 B.C.[3] I offered as an alternative the theory that reversed rotation continued in use, based on Kettos (IV) as a pivot in 376/5, until it was replaced by forward rotation starting with the first tribe Erechtheis (I) in 358/7, as projected backward from the known secretary in 351/0 B.C. These reversed cycles could be attached to the earlier system by the assumption that two successive boards functioned in the single year 377/6 B.C., a year which seems to have been epochal in the history of Athena's treasury and could well be interpreted as that of the fire in the Opisthodomos to which Demosthenes referred (24. 136 and scholia). And the terminal year 358 B.C. seemed to agree exactly with the inference that the decree (*IG*² II 120) authorizing the master-inventory of the Chalkotheke, to which many of the objects in the Archaios Neos were removed, dated from the end of a Panathenaic period in 358 B.C., four years after the archonship of Molon (362/1), inclusive.[4]

We may now, I believe, reach a decision in this matter by means

---

[1] Ferguson *Secretaries* 74; *Treas.* 9, 12, 14.
[2] Ferguson *Secretaries* 74; *Treas.* 144.
[3] Ferguson *Treas.* 142–144.
[4] Dinsmoor *AJA* XXXVI 160–169.

of a new fragment of an inventory of the treasurers, found on the north slope of the Acropolis by Broneer (EM 12931) and identified by Schweigert as part of *IG²* II 1438,[1] dated just after the archonship of Thoudemos (353/2, which it mentions). By means of it Schweigert was enabled to decipher the earliest collation with the master-inventory of the Chalkotheke: [τάδε] προσεξητάσθη ὄντα ἐν τῆι χαλκο[θήκηι πρὸς τὰ ἐν τῆι στήληι λιθίνηι γεγραμμένα ἔμπροσ]θεν τῆς χαλκοθήκ[ης ἦν] Φιλοκήδης ἔστησεν ἐπὶ Θουδήμ[ου ἄρχοντος]. The comparison obviously was made with the master-inventory contained in *IG²* II 120, ἀναγράψαντα [ἐν] στήληι λιθίνηι στῆσαι ἔμπροσθεν τῆς χαλκοθήκης, which is thereby dated in 353/2 rather than in 358 B.C., which I had preferred, or 354 B.C., the other of the two alternative dates hitherto suggested.[2] And the new date is confirmed by the fact that the name of the secretary Philokedes may be restored in the decrees of 353/2 (*IG²* II 138–139), when we had hitherto known only that the secretary was . . . . . edes son of Dorotheos of Pallene (X).[3] It is clear that the last of the boards of treasurers to collaborate in drawing up the master-inventory was that of the year of the decree itself, 353/2 B.C. But the preceding boards which were likewise to collaborate were those from as far back as the archonship of Molon (362/1), inclusive. The expression is παρ[εῖ]να[ι δὲ καὶ τοὺς ταμίας] τῆς θεοῦ ὅσοι ἐταμίευσαν ἀπ[ὸ Μ]ό[λ]ω[νος ἄρχοντος]; and in such cases, as we know for instance from the lists of *thiasos* officials (*SEG* II 9: κατ᾽ ἐνιαυτὸν . . . ἀπὸ Πολυεύκτου ἄρχοντος) and of priests of Asklepios (*IG²* II 1944: Ἱερεῖς ἀπὸ ᾽Ιάσονος), as well as the Delian Amphictyonic accounts (*IG²* II 1634–1635: ἀπὸ Δημοστράτου ἐκ Κεραμέων ἄρχοντος μέχρι ᾽Αντιπάτρο, etc.), the term ἀπὸ clearly means "from the beginning of the archonship of - - - -"[4] It was reasonable, in view of the fact that 362/1 B.C. was a Panathenaic year, to assume that the period covered by the boards was limited by Panathenaic quadrennia. Now,

---

[1] Schweigert *Hesp.* VII 281–289 no. 16.

[2] Kirchner *IG²* II 120 note; Ferguson *Treas.* 119–122; I formerly adopted the date 358 (*AJA* XXXVI 164).

[3] Schweigert *loc. cit.* 286, 288–289.

[4] See Dinsmoor *Archons* 47 n. 3, 248–249; Coupry *Bulletin de correspondance hellénique* LXII (1938) 91–92.

however, we see that this was a mistaken assumption, and that the collaborating boards of treasurers were to be, not four or eight, but ten, from 362/1 to 353/2 B.C., inclusive.

The reason for going all the way back to 362/1 B.C. remains to be sought. The fact that there were ten boards is suggestive: they were to cover one complete cycle of tribal rotation. Such an interpretation would almost certainly require, however, that 362 form the beginning of a cycle and 352 the end; and such would be in conformity, furthermore, with the general practice of making inventories coincide with the limits of tribal cycles.[1] And it so happens that, in accordance with the scheme which I formerly proposed, with two successive boards in 377/6 B.C., we should require a new cycle beginning with Antiochis (X) in 362/1 B.C.[2] It is now clear that this cycle continued to rotate, not merely for one quadrennium (as I previously suggested) but for ten full years, terminating with Antigonis (I) in 353/2 B.C. Thus Schweigert's dating of *IG*² II 120 supplies the needed corroboration of my arrangement of the cycles for the period between 389 and 351 B.C.

Together with the corroboration of cyclical rotation between 389 and 351 B.C. we obtain also further evidence of a disturbance somewhere between 389 and 376 B.C., a disturbance which resulted in the shifting of the cycles by one year. The period within which the change occurred may be further narrowed by Ferguson's observation that the earlier system of rotation probably continued without interruption at least until 385 B.C.;[3] and within the nine available years an accurate selection may undoubtedly be made in view of the fact that the treasurers of the end of the year 377/6 B.C. (*IG*² II 1410) failed to name the board immediately preceding, thus implying some sort of a change.[4] It is likewise the year 377/6 B.C. that forms the occasion of numerous alterations of function, of corrections of irregularities, and of a new start in the accumulation of votive offerings.[5] And within this period 385–355 B.C. — preferably in the earlier part thereof — occurred the fire in the

---

[1] Dinsmoor *Archons* 158, 203, 234, 249, 282–284, 454; *Archon List* 12–13, 92–93, 95, 98, 105; cf. Ferguson *Athenian Tribal Cycles* 6, 43–44, 61, 90–91, 96 n. 2.

[2] Dinsmoor *AJA* XXXVI 165.   [4] Dinsmoor *AJA* XXXVI 163.

[3] Ferguson *Treas.* 12–15.   [5] *Ibid.* 161–169.

Opisthodomos to which Demosthenes referred (24. 136 and scholia).[1] Thus the corroboration of the cyclical rotation after 385 B.C. brings strong support to my earlier contention that the fire in the Opisthodomos occurred in the course of the year 377/6 B.C., and that there were two boards of treasurers in this year, — the secretaries furnished by successive tribes, Oineis (VI) and Akamantis (V) — the former being imprisoned and disgraced without executing an inventory, so that the second board on assuming office had to make a fresh start. In the light of the new evidence bearing on the year 406/5 B.C., furthermore, we must now concede, in spite of the doubts raised by Dörpfeld and myself, that the two conflagration stories associated with the Erechtheum and Opisthodomos are not to be referred to a single event either in 406/5 or in 377/6 B.C.; rather were there two distinct fires, one in each of these years, the archonships of Kallias and Kalleas, respectively.[2]

Peculiarly significant is the year 352 B.C. In that year, simultaneously with a reversed cycle of the secretaries of the treasurers, terminated the first (incomplete) forward rotating cycle of the secretaries of the Council, which had been initiated in 356/5 B.C. — the beginning of a Metonic calendar cycle — with Kekropis (VII) which happened to be the tribe selected for that year in accordance with the hitherto prevailing sortition cycle. The cycle of the council secretaries was followed as a matter of course by a new cycle beginning with Erechtheis (I) in forward rotation; and the new fashion was applied also to the priesthood of Asklepios, likewise with Erechtheis (I) in 352/1 B.C.[3] Hence the secretaries of the treasurers now adopted the new fashion; but, instead of beginning forward rotation with Erechtheis (I), which furnished at least two other annual officers in this year and had furnished the secretary

---

[1] *Ibid.* 160–161, 172.

[2] It still seems more probable to me that the Carpathian inscription *IG* XII 1, 977 (*AJA* XXXVI 155–160), refers to the later occasion. The historical conditions would be quite unsuitable for the earlier year 406/5 B.C., and an intermediate date (about 394), such as many have suggested, is entirely without foundation.

[3] For the priesthood of Asklepios, beginning a cycle ten years before 342 B.C., see *Archons* 452–457. The fundamental synchronisms for the period after 340 B.C. were of course established by Ferguson, *Priests of Asklepios*.

for the treasurers in the preceding year, the question was apparently decided by lot, resulting in the selection of Kekropis (VII) with which the secretaries of the Council had begun rotation four years earlier. Thus the secretaries of the treasurers were now regularly four tribes behind the secretaries of the Council. The situation just before and just after 352 B.C. may be illustrated by the following comparison of the three systems of cycles:[1]

	Secretaries of the		Priests of
	Council	Treasurers	Asklepios
367/6	V?	5	
366/5		4	
365/4	IV?	3	
364/3		2	
363/2	X	1	
362/1	VI	10	
361/0	IX	9	
360/59		8	
359/8		7	V?
358/7	I	6	
357/6	III	5	VIII?
356/5	VII	4	
355/4	VIII	3	
354/3	IX	2	
353/2	X	1	
352/1	I	7	I
351/0	II	VIII	2
350/49	3	9	III?
349/8	IV	X	4
348/7	5	1	V?

The forward rotation thus initiated for the secretaries of the treasurers in 352 B.C., and traced by Ferguson down to 339, probably continued — as he has suggested — down to the oligarchic period beginning in 321 B.C. This, I think, may be accepted without question.

[1] Tribes indicated by Roman numerals are given by documentary evidence, those without marks of interrogation being fixed independently of the cycles. Arabic numerals are used for those years in which we have no documentary evidence.

In conclusion, for the purpose of illustrating in detail the various periods of cycle rotation and of providing a framework for the insertion of secretaries whose names may be discovered in the future,[1] the following expansion of Ferguson's tables of the secretaries of the treasurers is offered in summary form:

447/6		422/1	I	397/6	VI	372/1	10	346/5	3
446/5	VII	421/0	IV	396/5	5	371/0	9	345/4	4
445/4	II?	420/19	X	395/4	4	370/69	8	344/3	5
444/3	___	419/8	II	394/3	3	369/8	7	343/2	VI?
443/2	10	418/7	III	393/2	2	368/7	6	342/1	7
442/1	IX	417/6	V	392/1	I	367/6	5	341/0	VIII
441/0	8	416/5	II	391/0	10	366/5	4	340/39	IX
440/39	VII	415/4	I	390/89	IX	365/4	3	339/8	10
439/8	VI	414/3	X	389/8	8	364/3	2	338/7	I
438/7	5	413/2	IX	388/7	7	363/2	I	337/6	2
437/6	4	412/1	IV	387/6	6	362/1	10)	336/5	3
436/5	3	411	I	386/5	5	361/0	9	335/4	4
435/4	2	411/0	10	385/4	4	360/59	8	334/3	5
434/3	I	410/09	9	384/3	3	359/8	7	333/2	6
433/2	X	409/8	VIII	383/2	2	358/7	6	332/1	7
432/1	IX	408/7	7	382/1	I	357/6	5	331/0	8
431/0	VIII	407/6	6	381/0	10	356/5	4	330/29	9
430/29	VII	406/5	5	380/79	9	355/4	3	329/8	10
429/8	III	405/4	IV	379/8	8	354/3	2	328/7	I
428/7	X	404/3	3	378/7	7	353/2	I)	327/6	2
427/6	VI	403/2	II	377/6	6	352/1	7	326/5	3
426/5	V	402/1	I		5	351/0	VIII	325/4	4
425/4	X	401/0	10	376/5	IV	350/49	9	324/3	5
424/3	V?	400/399	IX	375/4	3	349/8	X	323/2	6
423/2	V	399/8	VIII	374/3	II?	348/7	I	322/1	7
		398/7	VII	373/2	I	347/6	2		

In the case of the secretaries of the Council, moreover, the three years 321/0–319/8 B.C. formed a break during which the secretaries reverted to their older terms of tenths of years, while their annual functions were assumed by the registrars. During 318/7 B.C.

---

[1] Thus the new fragment Agora I 5325, a treasure list in letters of the middle of the fourth century and with a secretary from Sounion (Schweigert *Hesperia* IX [1940] 325), and so from Leontis (IV), might be dated 356/5 or 345/4, less probably 366/5 or 335/4 B.C.

the secretary of the Council resumed his normal annual term and likewise rotation at the point where it had been broken off;[1] if this analogy extended to the secretaries of the treasurers, the one elected for 318/7 B.C. should have come from Hippothontis (VIII). During the tyranny of Demetrios of Phaleron the secretaries of the Council played a very minor role, not being named in decrees, and presumably not being selected according to tribal rotation;[2] the secretaries of the treasurers may likewise be presumed to have been appointed by lot.[3] We may presume that tribal rotation recommenced for the secretaries of the treasurers, as for those of the Council and for the priests of Asklepios, in 306 B.C.; but of the system of rotation at this period we have no information.

[1] Schweigert *Hesperia* VIII 32; Dinsmoor *Archon List* 30.
[2] Meritt *AJP* LIX 498–499; LX 202.
[3] Cf. Ferguson *Treas.* 144 n. 3, with reference to *IG*[2] II 1477.

A GOLDEN NIKE FROM THE ATHENIAN AGORA

By Homer A. Thompson

IN the spring of 1932 a bronze head emerged from an ancient well immediately behind, i.e. west of the Stoa of Zeus, some 40 m. to the northeast of the Hephaisteion. When freed of grime the head proved to be essentially intact and its surface in excellent condition. Its scale is small, little more than half life; yet its admirable style and masterly craftsmanship suggest that it derives from a monument of some importance. Its whole history we shall never know; but some of its secrets have been recovered already and the gleanings of a renewed examination are presented herewith.[1]

The head is that of a girl whose hair was drawn up from all sides to a bunch at the middle of the crown. This top-knot would seem to have been cast in a separate piece with a hollow stem which was set down over a hollow peg on the top of the head and secured by a transverse pin.[2] Only the peg remains but the scheme may readily be recovered from numerous ancient representations, one of which is included here for the reader's convenience (fig. 8).[3]

[1] The head bears the Agora inventory number B(ronze) 30 and has been discussed by T. L. Shear in *Hesperia* II (1933) 519–527, pl. XV. I am grateful to Professor Shear for permission to use several new photographs of the head and to refer to various unpublished Agora materials; to Miss Alison Frantz for preparing the pictures; to Mrs. W. B. Dinsmoor for first pointing out the gold; to my wife for many helpful suggestions on the subject of the Golden Nikai of Athena.

[2] Cf. *Hesp.* II 522. The wall of the peg that remains on the head is pierced both front and back; in the back by a single hole with a bore of ca. 3.5 mm., in the front by a hole with a diameter of 3.5 mm. in its outer part, of about half that in its inner part. Inside the peg is a strip of bronze ca. 1 mm. thick which had been rolled into a cylinder and hammered in from above till it tightened (fig. 7). Since this roll blocks the back hole but was pierced by the inner, smaller part of the front hole, I infer that the back hole is the earlier and that the roll was inserted between the drilling of the two holes. Hence the pin was intended originally to be set in from behind where it would have been less conspicuous, but the craftsman blundered in driving his larger drill clear through the wall. Since this pin, like the others used on the head, required a hole of graduated bore, the workman was forced to rectify his error by inserting the little bronze tube and by drilling a second time in the front of the peg.

[3] K. Schefold, *Kertscher Vasen*, Berlin, 1930, p. 15 f., pls. 13, 14; Furtwängler-Reichhold *Griechische Vasenmalerei* pl. 68. The vase, a lidded, stemless kylix in

The head on the vase wears a wreath. So too did the Bronze
Head. This is suggested, first, by the transverse furrow in the locks
of hair above the forehead, suitably placed and shaped to support
a wreath but weakening to the profile when empty; secondly, by a
pin-hole in the middle of the back of the head, placed correctly to
support a wreath at the point where the ends of the branch over-
lapped;[1] finally, by the position of the top-knot, for in this coiffure
the top-knot ordinarily rises behind the mid-point of the top of the
head, but at the mid-point or farther forward when it is accompanied by a wreath. The girl of the Bronze Head also wore earrings,
though of them only the holes in the lobes remain.[2] Her adornment
may be completed by one or more golden necklaces.

A word next as to how our head was mounted on its torso. Apart
from minor abrasions, the lower edge of neck and V is intact and

---

Petrograd, has been dated about the middle of the fourth century, i.e. eighty years
or more after our head. It may, however, reflect an earlier style. Cf. Schefold
Röm. Mitt. XLVI (1931) 129: "fast alle Motive der Kertscher Vasen auf Keime
gerade aus der Zeit des beginnenden peloponnesischen Krieges zurückzuführen
waren." A marble head in the Metropolitan Museum may be restored with a similar
coiffure; the top-knot was cut in a separate piece of marble and pinned to the top
of the head. *Metropolitan Museum Bulletin* v (1910), 276–278; Richter, *Sculpture
and Sculptors of the Greeks*, New Haven, 1930, p. 146, fig. 443.

[1] In making this hole, as in the case of the hole in the peg, two drills were used;
the one, with a diameter of ca. 2.5 mm., was driven to a depth of ca. 3 mm., the
other, ca. 1⅓ mm. in diameter, was carried through the remaining thickness of
the bronze. It has been suggested that the pin set in this hole was intended to steady
a lock of hair trailing from the top-knot (*Hesp.* II 523). But, in keeping with
contemporary fashion, the top-knot is more likely to have been a compact mass
requiring no outside support. In the very top of the head are two other drilled holes,
one in front, one behind the peg (fig. 7). Neither carries through the "skull"; the
former has a depth of 3 mm., the latter of 5 mm. Both holes must have been covered by the top-knot and are scarcely explicable in connection with it. Since they
have precisely the same bore as the outer part of the hole in the back of the head,
we may suspect that they were made by the craftsman in trying out his drill.

[2] These holes were drilled with the same pair of tools as the hole in the back of
the head. In the case of the (proper) right ear the hole (with its greater bore toward
the front) pierced the lobe of the ear only; in the left ear the small drill, apparently
by error, was first driven through both the lobe and the entire thickness of the metal
of the neck; the error was rectified by a second application of the small drill whereby
an independent opening through the lobe alone was effected.

its shape conforms in a general way to that of bronze heads cast separately to be set into bronze torsos, i.e. the joint was undoubtedly covered by the overlapping drapery. But, whereas the ordinary bronze head was fixed permanently into its socket in the shoulders and was detached only by violence, our head was worked in a way which suggests that it could readily have been removed from and replaced on its trunk. The treatment of the underside will be reasonably clear from fig. 4. The under surface of the V and the inner surface of the neck were rasped with some care, — enough in itself to suggest the anticipation that these parts might be visible on occasion. The lateral edges of the V as also the lower edge of the neck, are smoothly dressed and are cut with a bevel to permit of their fitting snugly into their socket. After the head had been cast and its underpart given a preliminary trimming, three bronze lugs were welded to its lower edge, one on either side of the neck, one at the back of the neck. The lateral lugs are set against the inner face of the cylinder in such a way as to leave free the full width of the resting surface of its lower edge.[1] The third lug is set in the thickness of the wall of the neck so that its outer face was flush with the outer surface of the neck. It is more massive than the other two, but has approximately the same projection.[2]

The method of mounting is now apparent: the head was slipped into place from above and behind; the edges of the V fitted into a groove beneath the upper hem of the dress; the bevelled lower edge of the neck came to rest in a socket in the shoulders; the three lugs prevented lateral movement, while the weight of the head bearing down on the long V effectively prevented backward displacement. The precision with which the joint surfaces on the head are worked and the slight projection of the lugs are enough to prove that the socket was of metal rather than, let us say, wood or marble.

[1] These pieces are ca. 20 mm. long, ca. 3 mm. thick and they project downward ca. 5 mm. below the lower edge of the neck.

[2] This third lug, measuring ca. 16 x 10 x 5 mm., was cut on a larger piece of bronze which was fitted into a crescent-shaped gap in the lower edge of the back of the neck. The gap measures ca. 12 x 40 mm. Its outlines may be distinguished in fig. 5 by the fact that the surface of the inset has suffered more from corrosion than has the original bronze.

We must next consider certain curious grooves on face and neck and hair. These were cut in the cold bronze with narrow straight-faced chisels which were first tested by the craftsman on the under side of the V (fig. 4).

The marks left by these chisels in their proper employment above consist of long grooves similar to the trial cuttings, i.e. with a width of 1.5 mm. or 2.5 mm., with a depth that varies from 1 mm. to 3 mm. and averages ca. 2 mm. These channels fall into an earlier and a later set. The first served its purpose, was subsequently stripped of its original contents and was packed with bronze; the second set was obviously intended to serve the same purpose as the first, it too was eventually stripped but was never replaced.

Of the earlier set the first cuttings are to be traced in the hair (figs. 1 [frontispiece], 3, 6, 7). From either side of the hollow peg, from a point slightly back of its middle, a canal cut with the narrow chisel was carried downward to a point behind the ear. In its upper course each channel followed fairly closely the furrows of the hair; in its lower part, however, it cut boldly across the hair lines. These narrow channels were probably never used; possibly they were found to be too narrow. They were re-cut with the broad chisel; but toward the peg the broad channel was carried somewhat forward of the narrow channel over the last 10 mm. on the right side, over the last 30 mm. on the left. On the left side the narrow channel which passed well back of the ear was left unused and the broad channel was unfeelingly cut into the ear itself.

To the earlier period of channeling may be assigned also a groove of the broader sort which was carried around the back of the neck at an interval of 2 mm. to 5 mm. below the hair line. From this horizontal canal, two vertical channels of the same width were led down to the lower edge of the neck, the one falling almost exactly on the mid-line of the back of the neck, the other ca. 17 mm. forward in the direction of the left ear. It is worth noting that these vertical channels left untouched the four wisps of hair which were engraved at regular intervals on the back of the neck between the two ears, corresponding to the more deeply cut locks in front of the ears.

The earlier set of channels was completed by a broad groove that continued the line of the rear horizontal groove above the brow just below the hair line.

The earlier channels are now packed with bronze, with the exception of the groove above the brow, and of the short unused lengths of the original narrow grooves in the hair. The packing was done with commendable care: bronze was chosen of a color close to that of the head itself and it was hammered in so as to fill the whole section of the groove. On the top of the head, the surface of the inset was adjusted to the contours of the locks; on the back of the neck the new metal was polished so as to be scarcely distinguishable from the old.

The new set of channels duplicates the earlier. On top of the head the later grooves were cut, perforce, in more conspicuous positions: starting from the peg one runs down to the mid-point of the hair-line at the back of the head, the other to the mid-point of the hair-line above the brow. Both follow as closely as possible the furrows of the hair; both are ca. 2 mm. wide at their mouth, rather less at the bottom. The line between hair and exposed flesh was again marked both front and back by a groove. At the back the new groove (2 mm. wide) follows very closely the hair-line, thus avoiding for the most part the earlier cutting which ran at a lower level. Above the brow the old channel would seem to have been cleared of its temporary packing and re-used. The vertical grooves (3 mm. wide) were on this occasion carried down one on either side of the neck and were carefully ¦placed so as to be concealed by the round of the neck from a spectator standing directly in front.

What now was the purpose of this elaborate surgery? The answer is given by several masses of silver and gold that cling in the later grooves. Since these remains are slight and have been much mutilated by the chisel blows of the rifler, their interpretation will require a careful collation of their combined evidence.

In the groove above the right eye there remains a strip of silver 18 mm. long, with the thickness of heavy writing paper (figs. 9, 10). This strip is bent at right angles in such a way that half its width occupies the width of the groove and rests at the level of the mouth of the groove; the other half is turned down against the side-wall of the groove which is closer to the eye. On the upper surface of the silver traces of gold can be detected, barely with the naked eye, readily with the aid of a glass. The silver plate and the upper lip of the channel have been much battered by the chisel of the spoiler.

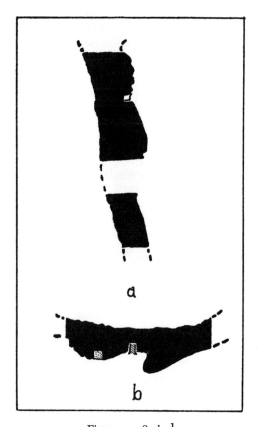

Figure 10.   Scale $\frac{1}{1}$

a. Vertical Section through Right Eye.
b. Horizontal Section through Lobe of Right Ear.

Behind each ear, where the grooves were more inaccessible, there remains in the junction of horizontal and vertical channels a mass of gold, equal in bulk to a pickle of wheat, separated from the wall of the groove on either side by a remnant of silver plate comparable in thickness with that above the right eye (fig. 10). The original surface of the gold has been entirely distorted by the chisel.

In the horizontal groove in the back of the neck, 10 mm. back of the right ear, there has survived a bit of silver, ca. 10 mm. long, now crushed out of all shape in the bottom of the groove. Blended with it is a small mass of gold. In the back horizontal channel, just

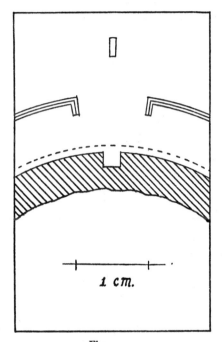

Figure 11.
Section through Neck to illustrate Second Plating.

to the left of the junction with the vertical skull channel, a particle of gold 2 mm. long clings to the bottom of the groove.

The bottom of the lower end of the back skull channel over a length of 7 mm. is covered with a thin mass of gold which again is separated from the side walls of the groove by a plate of silver. Half way up in this same channel a flake of gold 2 mm. long clings in the bottom of the groove.

In the vertical channel back of the right ear, at its lower end, I note a scrap of silver plate covered with gold; the silver being, as elsewhere, next to the wall of the groove.

From the above we may infer that in the second period of channeling the head was plated; that it was covered with sheets of gilded silver which must have been hammered until they accommodated themselves to the modelled surface of the bronze; that the edges of the sheets were next bent down into the channels and were securely keyed by a packing of solid gold; that the careful hammering of this packing and the subsequent polishing rendered the joints quite inconspicuous so that the final effect would have been that of a figure of massive gold (fig. 11).[1]

The process of plating in the first period must have been essentially the same as in the second, and, since the grooves of the two periods are of the same width, the plate must have been of the same or practically the same thickness. As to the material of the earlier plating, we have no certain knowledge. It may have been of gilded silver; it may have been of silver alone, or more probably, in keeping with contemporary practice, of gold alone.

The precious metal was removed on the last occasion by means of a straight-faced chisel 8 mm. broad. This tool has left deep scars on top of the head just behind the peg and both in front of and behind the right ear. The tops of both ears have been lopped off. In explanation of the present situation in the groove above the right eye (figs. 9, 10), I should suggest that the gold packing and the plating of the face had first been removed; the plating of the hair stuck in the groove so that its lower edge had to be cut off with a chisel and remained in the groove; the force of the chisel

---

[1] It has been suggested that the grooves were intended for a linear inlay of silver to variegate and heighten the effect of the bronze (*Hesp.* II 520). This hypothesis is rendered unlikely by the evident pains taken in both periods to make the channels inconspicuous. It becomes still more improbable with the discovery of gold together with the silver. An illuminating example of silver inlay of the fifth century is now available in the splendid bronze hydria recently acquired by the Metropolitan Museum and published by Miss Richter in the *Metropolitan Museum Bulletin* XXXII (1937) 255–259, figs. 1–2; *AJA* XLI (1937) 532–538, figs. 1–4. Here the silver is confined to the subsidiary decoration; it is applied in narrow strips which are not *inset* but *laid over* the bronze.

detached the angular strip of plate from the upper wall of the channel and drove it against the opposite wall.

The method of plating employed on the head, involving the use of a fairly thick sheet of the precious metal rather than gold leaf or amalgam, has been best known hitherto from metal vases. It was commonly used in the seventh century and is well represented among the princely furnishings of the Bernardini and Barberini Tombs, especially the bowls made of silver but covered entirely both inside and out with sheet gold.[1] For the fifth century the practice of applying sheet gold over silver is well attested for Greece and is splendidly illustrated by a number of kylikes and phialai found in graves of South Russia, Jugoslavia and Bulgaria but unquestionably of Attic origin.[2] The vases are of solid silver but the designs on their floors were overlaid with gold, usually in very thin sheets, occasionally in plates of appreciable thickness. Since vases of the latter type provide the best technical parallels for the treatment of our head, I may be pardoned for quoting in full Stephani's account of their making:

"After the design was engraved in the silver, a sheet of gold of the thickness of strong paper was laid over the whole medallion and was pressed down so hard with a blunt instrument that all the

[1] C. Densmore Curtis *Memoirs of the Amer. Academy in Rome* III (1919) p. 26, nos. 10, 11; p. 29, nos. 16, 17; p. 33, nos. 23–25; V (1925) p. 19, no. 13; p. 20, no. 14. Much of this material, notably the shallow bowls with engraved designs, is very probably of eastern origin, and the technique may well derive from the east. But such a piece as the skyphos with sphinxes seated on its handles from the Bernardini tomb was in all probability made in Etruria under Greek influence; the curious scheme of the vase is paralleled in bronze at the Argive Heraeum (*Argive Heraeum* II pl. CXVIII 2034).

[2] For the material from South Russia see *Compte-Rendu* 1876, 157 pl. IV 9 (cf. *C-R* 1881, 139); 1881, 6 ff., pl. I 1, 3 and 5; E. H. Minns *Scythians and Greeks* 206 ff., 382 ff.; M. Rostovtzeff *Iranians and Greeks in South Russia* pl. XV 3. The finds from Jugoslavia are published by B. D. Filow in *Die archaische Nekropole von Trebenischte am Ochrida-See*, Berlin and Leipzig, 1927, especially pp. 24 ff., nos. 28–30; p. 90, no. 130; and by N. Vulić in *Arch. Anz.* 1930, 276 ff., nos. 4, 8, 9, 11. For the silver-gilt objects from South Bulgaria see B. D. Filow, *Die Grabhügelnekropole bei Duvanlij in Südbulgarien*, Sofia, 1934 (superseding *Jahrb.* XLV (1930) 281–322), especially pp. 199 ff. (with numerous references to other scattered material). For a stylistic study of the silver kylikes see W. Kraiker *Röm. Mitt.* XLVI (1931) 119 ff.

individual lines became visible in the gold plate also and so could be redrawn in the gold plate with a sharp instrument. Immediately after, all those parts of the gold plate which did not serve to cover the figure and the surrounding band were cut away and removed."[1] This description applies to kylikes in which the design was lightly engraved on a flat surface. In the case of a silver phiale in which the central boss was surrounded by a ring of satyr heads hammered in high relief, Stephani notes that the same process was employed, though the gold was somewhat thicker and its adhesion was apparently assisted by soldering.[2]

In view of the perfect surface finish of our head one might question whether it had been intended originally for gilding. This intention, however, provides the only apparent explanation of the unusual provision for the ready detachment of the head from the body. The plating, moreover, required the full finishing of the bronze foundation because no modelling was to be executed in the coating of precious metal and because, as between two metals, a more perfect adhesion is possible when the contact surfaces are smooth.[3] Nor need we fear that the details, even to the engraved wisps of hair on the neck and cheeks, would have been lost in the process, for on the silver vases referred to above still more delicate engraving made itself felt through the covering of gold; and we may

[1] *Compte-Rendu* 1881, 7.

[2] *L. c.* 139. We are not here concerned with gilding by means of gold leaf or by the amalgam process, both of which were, naturally, much more commonly used than plating with thick sheets. Among the more useful discussions of gold and silver plating, first place is still taken by Hugo Blümner, *Technologie und Terminologie der Gewerbe und Künste bei Griechen und Römern*, Leipzig, IV (1887), 302 ff., especially 308 ff. See also Kurt Kluge, *Die antiken Grossbronzen*, Berlin and Leipzig, 1927, I 177 ff. For the plating of statues in particular see W. Deonna in Daremberg-Saglio, *Dictionnaire*, IV B 1492 f., *s.v. statuaria*, and a note by A. Furtwängler in *Olympia* IV 16. The numerous and frequently detailed references to metal objects of bewildering variety in the treasure lists of the Acropolis have as yet been little exploited in this connection. For discussions of the technical terms there employed see A. Böckh, *Staatshaushaltung der Athener*[3], Berlin, 1886, II 148; A. Michaelis, *Der Parthenon*, Leipzig, 1871, 313.

[3] Kluge *Die antike Grossbronzen* I 181: "Nicht nur die Blattvergoldung sondern jede Art Vergoldung kann erst ausgeführt werden, wenn das Bronzewerk vollständig fertig ist. Die Vergoldung ist der letzte Arbeitsvorgang am Erzwerk."

imagine that the artist of our head, like his fellow artist of the vases, sharpened the lines by lightly engraving the surface of the gold. The parallel of the phiale with the satyr's heads quoted above should remove all doubt as to the possibility of hammering silver and gold in this way: the heads on the phiale are worked practically in the round and they required more delicate modelling than did our head.[1]

The method used on the Bronze Head for attaching the precious metal is distinctly unusual. A parallel is suggested by a passage in Pliny (*NH* XXXIV 63) regarding a statue of Alexander the Great made by Lysippos: "The Emperor Nero was so fond of it that he ordered it to be gilded and then, when the charm of the work had been destroyed by the excessive display, the gold was removed, and the statue was counted more pleasing in this state, even though there remained the scars and the channels in which the gold had been attached (*cicatricibus operis atque concisuris in quibus aurum haeserat remanentibus*)." The picture raised by Pliny's words is, to be sure, reminiscent of the Bronze Head in its present condition, but the reference is too vague to permit one to recover the precise method. From the period of the Bronze Head I am aware of no adequate parallel for its way of fastening. In the most nearly comparable surviving works of that period, i.e. the vases noted above, adhesion was secured simply by the contact of metal with metal, or by soldering.

In explanation of the remarkable technique employed on the Bronze Head, I would venture to suggest that its designer intended the plates of precious metal to be readily removable, περιαιρετόν, to use the expression constantly employed in ancient references to the gold statue of Athena Parthenos.[2] By way of confirmation, I would point to the markedly worn state of the lips of the grooves, notably that above the brow. In view of the difference in hardness

---

[1] The skill of the contemporary artisan in hammering bronze, a less malleable material than silver or gold, is eloquently attested by, *inter alia*, the surviving pieces of armour decorated with high relief and by ancient impressions in clay taken from such articles. Cf. *Hesp.* VIII (1939) 285–316.

[2] Thucydides II 13; (= Plutarch *de vitando aere alieno* 2); Diodoros XII 40; Plutarch *Pericles* 31; Pausanias I 25. 7.

between bronze and either gold or silver, this wear can scarcely be due exclusively to the two strippings for which we have noted the obvious evidence. It implies rather that the plating had been repeatedly removed and replaced. Since the vertical channels in the neck in both periods extended down to the very bottom, the plating also must have been carried to the bottom; along the sloping sides of the V it was doubtless doubled around the edge of the bronze and thus was held securely by the overlapping drapery of the chest. In order to remove the plating from the head, one was therefore obliged first to remove the head from its socket, and, as we have seen, provision was made for its ready removal.

How are we to restore the eyes of our head? Their places are now marked by hollow sockets with smooth walls practically parallel to one another (figs. 9, 10). In keeping with contemporary practice, the various exposed parts of the eyeball, i.e. pupil, iris and white, must have been worked in a combination of glass paste, or possibly ivory, and stone of appropriate colors. These materials were undoubtedly set in a metal capsule on the outer edges of which the eyelashes would have been rendered plastically.[1] The restoration of such metal cases in the Bronze Head would, of course, give lids of normal thickness and would reduce the exposed area of the eyeball to normal proportions. On bronze statues the capsules were ordinarily of bronze. On our head they were undoubtedly of gold, — hence the pains taken to extract them on both occasions when the head was violently stripped. Each time the extraction was effected by driving a punch, rather more than 1 mm. in diameter, between the upper edge of the socket and the capsule. Hence there remain two scars on the upper edge of each socket (fig. 9). The scar closer to the nose in the right eye retains a packing of

[1] For this method, the usual one in the classical and Hellenistic period, compare the Delphi Charioteer (*Fouilles de Delphes* IV 27 f., pls. LI ff.); the Marathon Boy (*Arch. Delt.* 1924–25 (1927) 151); the bronze portrait head from Delos (*Exploration de Délos* XIII 2). Of such eyes detached from their heads a good example has been found at Pergamon (*Altertümer* VII 2, 368, no. 465; no. 466 is of similar construction but from a beast); a part of a metal capsule with plastic lashes at Delphi (*Fouilles de Delphes* V 43, fig. 131). For a general discussion consult Perdrizet *Fouilles de Delphes* V 43; Richter *Sculpture and Sculptors of the Greeks* 147. For the aesthetic aspect see Plato's comment on the eyes of the Athena Parthenos (*Hipp. Maj.* 290B).

FIGURE 3

FIGURE 2

FIGURE 4

FIGURE 5

FIGURE 7

FIGURE 6

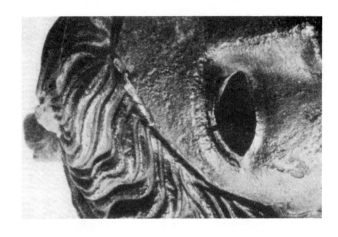

FIGURE 9

FIGURE 8

bronze comparable with that used in the long trenches of the first period.[1]

So much for the head of our figure. What of her body? From the remaining V of the chest and from the slight torsion of the neck one gathers that her gaze was turned a few degrees to her left. One may also safely maintain that she stood quietly at rest, for the muscles of throat and chest show none of the strain which accompanies striding or flying movement in contemporary sculpture.[2] Repose is indicated also by the practically level shoulders and by the drapery symmetrically disposed. The garment, pressed a very little more closely against the right than against the left side of the neck, may be taken to suggest that the right arm was slightly raised.

The disposition of the drapery is significant in another respect. We have already observed that when the head was in place the edges of the V must have been concealed by the overlapping drapery. A slight bevel on the upper surface of the V along its edges indicates that the overlap covered a width of at least 5 mm. Hence the visible part of the chest was extraordinarily narrow and the drapery pressed unusually close against the neck. Such an arrangement of the unfitted dress of the period was scarcely possible save by the wearing of wings. The point will be made clear by a glance at the winged forms of the Nike Temple Parapet and especially by figs. 506 and 507 of Miss Richter's *Sculpture and Sculptors of the Greeks*. Here one will observe that the original parapet figure of the Nike leading a bull, with the help of her wings and despite her violent agitation, has been able to maintain her dress in precisely the same orderly position as that suggested by our bronze. But as soon as she was deprived of wings by the Neo-Attic artist of the Vatican relief, her shoulder straps slipped down to the more normal position, i.e. midway between the root of the neck and the outer edge of the shoulder.[3]

---

[1] On the *ordinary* occasions of stripping assumed above, the eyes were probably left undisturbed in their sockets.

[2] Compare the Nereids from Xanthos as illustrated in M. Bieber, *Entwicklungsgeschichte der gr. Tracht*, Berlin, 1934, pls. 24–26; the Nike from the Stoa of Zeus in the Agora, *Hesp.* IV (1935) 374 ff., pl. IV.

[3] The argument, of course, works only one way. The Nike was not obliged to

The complete and detailed finish of the back of the Bronze Head leaves no doubt that the figure was worked in the round and was free-standing. We may be reasonably certain, moreover, that we have to do with an independent single figure rather than with a group, for her attention is clearly directed to the spectator rather than to any companion of her own kind.

We are faced, therefore, by a youthful female figure who is marked as a messenger goddess by her wings and by the way she has done her hair, a thoroughly practical coiffure for flying. A figure of this type when presented as an independent monument in the period to which the Bronze Head must be assigned can scarcely be other than Nike.

It will be useful at this point to define the period of our head. The bronze invites comparison with the heads of the Parthenon frieze (and still more with the little that remains of the pedimental sculpture), in general shape, in the reserved modelling of flesh parts, in the ample but firm flesh, in the clean-cut right angle between chin and throat, in the slightly arrogant pout, and in the freshness of its atmosphere. A consideration of these same points will readily show our head to be earlier than such works of the last third of the century as the small figures from the base of the statue of Nemesis at Rhamnous, the sculptures of the Argive Heraeum, the caryatids and frieze figures of the Erechtheion, the figures of the Nike Temple Parapet. A comparison has already been suggested with the heads on the coins of Syracuse,[1] which were also designed for metal by metal workers, and which have been arranged in a reasonably certain chronological framework. A reference to Plates 22 and 23 of Boehringer's *Die Münzen von Syrakus* will convince one that our head must be later than Boehringer's Group IV, Series XVIII of the mid fifth century. The heads on these coins have hair more schematic than that of the Bronze Head, faces leaner with more of archaic crispness, chins that frequently

---

exploit her wings in this manner and frequently she did not do so. See, for instance, Carpenter *The Sculpture of the Nike Temple Parapet* pls. IV, VI, 1, IX, X, XXVII. Sometimes the sculptor interfered by setting the wing through the dress, as in the Nike from the Stoa of Zeus.

[1] Shear *Hesp*. II 525.

form acute angles with the throat. More satisfactory parallels in point of sculptural style are afforded by Boehringer's Group VI (pl. 27), dated 439–ca. 435 B.C. A decisive *terminus ante quem* may be found in the earliest Syracusan issues that commemorate the victory of the Asinarius in 413 B.C.[1] The later date of these magnificent Syracusan heads is apparent from their fuller and softer flesh, from the open angle between chin and throat, from the rich and studied confusion of their hair.

A detailed study of the individual features of our head would undoubtedly confirm a date in the '30's. The treatment of the hair, for instance, is thoroughly characteristic in its deeply plastic quality and in the regular sequence of wavy ridges alternately big and little. This scheme is clearly a development from the more uniform and shallower furrowing that appears around the middle of the century on such works as the Demeter-Persephone-Triptolemos relief from Eleusis,[2] and the Girl with the Doves in New York,[3] and it as clearly antedates the impressionistic and deliberately irregular renderings of the later fifth century illustrated by a statue of a girl from the Acropolis[4] and by the Hegeso stele.[5] For our closest parallels we must turn to works of the '30's: to a splendid grave stele in the Petraki Monastery at Athens,[6] to the Berlin Amazon,[7] to the Bologna Athena.[8]

The eye, again, is distinctive: well opened, bounded above by the arc of a circle, below by a delicate double curve, with no trace of overlapping lids at the outer angle. This is a characteristic eye of the decade 440–430 and may be paralleled, for example, on cer-

---

[1] Albert Galatin, *Syracusan Dekadrachms of the Euainetos Type*, Cambridge, Mass., 1930. Cf. also G. F. Hill, *Coins of Ancient Sicily*, Westminster, 1903, p. 108, fig. 24: a Syracusan tetradrachm with head of much the same general type as ours, dated ca. 410 B.C. and stylistically more advanced than the Bronze Head.

[2] Richter *Sculpture and Sculptors of the Greeks* fig. 481; *Arch. Eph.* 1937, pls. I and II.

[3] Richter *op. cit.* figs. 205, 426.

[4] E. Buschor, *Die Plastik der Griechen*, Berlin, 1936, 78.

[5] Richter *op. cit.* fig. 429.

[6] H. Diepolder, *Die attischen Grabreliefs*, Berlin, 1931, pl. 5.

[7] Blümel *Katalog der Sammlung ant. Skulpturen im Berliner Museum* IV K 176, pl. 70.

[8] Richter *op. cit.* fig. 614.

tain heads of the Parthenon frieze,[1] of the Parthenon pediments,[2] on the Niobids of the Terme Museum and Copenhagen.[3] The same shape of eye is suggested by the more careful copies of the Pheidian Athena heads.[4] It was used also by contemporary painters.[5]

The pose of our figure, a quiet stance saved from stolidity by a slight turn of the head, is, once more, appropriate to the late Pheidian or immediately post-Pheidian period. Of many examples, the more familiar are the Dresden Athena, the Ince Athena, the goddess represented by the Berlin head K 173.

The style of our head may, therefore, be assigned with some confidence to the '30's of the fifth century.

We concluded above that the head is that of a Nike. Can the Nike be identified more closely? She can scarcely be related directly to Athena Nike of the Acropolis, for this goddess, as is well known, was represented wingless and was so described. This consideration, together with her small scale, will preclude her identification with the statue of Athena Nike which was erected to commemorate victories over the Ambraciots, the army at Olpai, the rebels in Corcyra and the Anactorians in 425 B.C., and which was repaired about the middle of the fourth century B.C.[6] Her small scale and her coating of precious metal will distinguish her also from the bronze statue of Nike which the Athenians set up on the Acropolis after the affair of Sphakteria.[7] Could she have served

---

[1] Hege-Rodenwaldt, *Die Akropolis*, Berlin, 1930, pls. 47, 53, 54.

[2] P. Johansen, *Phidias*, Berlin, 1925, 83 ff.

[3] Brunn-Bruckmann *Denkmäler* pls. 709, 713.

[4] Bologna head: Bulle *Der schöne Mensch*[3] pl. 194, 3; head of Athena Parthenos in Madrid: A. Hekler *Phidias*, Stuttgart, 1924, figs. 2–3; in Copenhagen: P. Johansen *Phidias* 38; in Berlin: C. Blümel *Katalog der Sammlung antiker Skulpturen* IV K 170, pl. 58. Compare also the Kore in the Villa Albani, A. Hekler, *Phidias* figs. 16–19.

[5] Compare the eyes of the maenads on an amphora by the Achilles Painter: Furtwängler-Reichhold *Griechische Vasenmalerei* pl. 77, 1; E. Buschor, *Greek Vase-Painting*, London, 1921, fig. 138; E. Pfuhl *Malerei und Zeichnung der Griechen* fig. 523.

[6] *IG* II[2] 403. A. M. Woodward *Arch. Eph.* 1937, 169 f.

[7] Pausanias IV 36. 6. It has been suggested that the type of this statue is reflected by a series of marble Nikai, three in Berlin, one in Paris (C. Blümel *Katalog der Sammlung antiker Skulpturen* IV 42).

as an akroterion? Her scale, her pose, her date would perhaps permit of her having been a central akroterion on the Temple of Nike Apteros. That the akroteria of the temple were gilded in whole or in part we gather from the appearance in the treasure records of the fourth century of pieces of gold plate ἀπὸ τῶν ἀκρωτηρίων τοῦ νεὼ τῆς Νίκης.[1] This identification is made improbable, however, by several considerations. In the first place, the head was clearly designed to be seen from close up and from all sides. Had the statue been intended for a roof, the delicately engraved wisps of hair on the back of the neck would have been wasted on the winds; for such a position, moreover, the straying locks in front of the ears would probably have been rendered plastically rather than by engraving. It would also seem altogether unlikely that an akroterion should have received so heavy a plating of precious metal as that implied for the Bronze Head by the manner of attachment. Finally, the fact that it had been stripped of its gold would scarcely have justified the complete discarding of the statue as an akroterion. Yet our head was thrown away as early as the third century B.C.

Another possibility must be considered. Can the Bronze Head derive from one of the Golden Nikai of Athena in which much of the gold reserve of the Athenian state was incorporated in the fifth and fourth centuries? In order to remind the reader of the qualifications to be met I shall give a brief outline of what is known from the literary and epigraphic sources about the history and the form of the Nikai.[2] The earliest surviving reference to the Nikai is a decree of 434/3 B.C., which ordered the completion of at

---

[1] *IG* II² 1415. 8; 1421. 59 ff.; 1423. 1 ff.; 1424a. 106 ff.; 1425. 101 ff.; 1428. 114 ff.; 1428 *add.* 125 ff.; 1435. 7; 1436. 66 ff.; Woodward *JHS* XXIX (1909) 186. One will recall also the gilded central akroteria in the form of Nikai made by Paionios for the Temple of Zeus at Olympia (Paus. V 10. 4; *Olympia, Ergebnisse* III 182).

[2] The original comprehensive study is by P. Foucart in *BCH* XII (1888) 283–293. The epigraphic material has been conveniently assembled by A. M. Woodward in *Arch. Eph.* 1937, 159–170, and the history of the Nikai has been summarized by W. S. Ferguson in his *Treasurers of Athena*, Cambridge, 1932, 122 n. 2. The many financial and administrative problems raised by the Nikai are best dealt with by Ferguson in this book, *passim*. See the Addenda, p. 210.

least three Golden Nikai.[1] Two others, probably distinct from the
above, were dedicated in 426/5 B.C. (*IG* I² 368); and perhaps
another pair in the neighborhood of 410 B.C. (*IG* I² 369). In the
crisis of 406/5 B.C. the Nikai with one exception were made to contribute their gold to the needs of the state. In 374/3 B.C. another
Golden Nike was dedicated; this probably means that one of the
old figures was furnished anew with gold (*IG* II² 1424. 31 ff.).
Lycurgus replaced others, probably in the years 334/3–331/0 B.C.
Apparently all were melted down by Lachares in the disastrous
year 296/5 B.C., and nothing more is heard of them.

The Nikai, being among the most precious of the treasures of
Athena, appear repeatedly in the records of her Treasurers, together with detailed accounts of their weights. For the weighing,
the figures were dismembered and the parts were weighed in
separate groups, as many as five groups to a single statue. In the
first group was included the head (described as πρόσωπον in the
earlier, as κεφαλή in the later lists) together with the ornaments of
the head: head band (στεφάνη), wreath (στέφανος ὁ ἐπὶ τῇ κεφαλῇ),
earrings (ἐνωτίδια) and one or more necklaces (ὅρμος, ὑποδερίς, περιτραχηλίδιον). In the records we find mention also of golden pins or
nails (ἧλοι), one or two of them, usually in close association with the
head. In the well-preserved lists covering the Nike which survived the crisis of 406/5 B.C. are recorded small bits of gold (χρυσίδια μικρά), usually specified as twenty in number; these too were
weighed together with the head.

In the regular records of weights, no mention is made of the supports which carried the gold. Supports of the Nikai, seven in
number (διερείσματα τῶν Νικῶν ΓΙΙ) do however appear in two lists
of the contents of the Chalkotheke.[2] These supports were presumably all that remained of the Nikai whose gold had been
melted down in 406/5 B.C. and had not yet been replaced.[3] The

---

[1] *IG* I² 92 B. The use of the plural, Νί[κας τὰς χ]ρυσᾶς, rather than the dual at
this date implies more than two objects. Meisterhans *Grammatik d. att. Inschriften*³
p. 199.

[2] *IG* II² 1424a. 378 of 369/8 B.C.; 1425 B. 382 of 368/7 B.C.

[3] Foucart *BCH* XII (1888) 292; Ferguson *Treasurers of Athena* 122 f., n. 2;
Woodward *Arch. Eph.* 1937, 168. I prefer to believe with Foucart and Ferguson

immediate contexts do not help us regarding the material or nature of the supports. On the analogy of other gilded objects (baskets and incense burners) which are referred to in the treasure lists together with χαλκᾶ διερείσματα, we may infer that the supports of the Nikai were likewise of bronze. So far as one can control the meaning of the word διέρεισμα in other contexts, it implies a rod- or beam-like object. Hence it is possible that the supports consisted of frameworks of bronze rods or straps to which were attached the sheets of gold constituting the various parts of the body and the limbs. Since the Treasurers were meticulous in the matter of specifying even slight amounts of foreign metal when it could not conveniently be detached from the gold which they were weighing, we may be sure that the supports of the Nikai were not included in their weights as recorded. Hence we must suppose that on the occasion of each weighing the various masses of gold were detached both from the supporting framework and from one another.

As for the actual weight of gold in the Nikai, it is clear from the total figures which are preserved for three of the statues and from the close correspondence in the weights of individual parts of the other statues, that the amount of gold for each Nike was fixed as closely as possible at two talents.[1]

How does our head correspond with the above data? It will be objected at once that the head suggests a statue of bronze plated with gold rather than a golden statue; and yet the Nikai are regularly described in both the epigraphic and literary sources as golden (χρυσαῖ). It may well be, however, that in the case of a head of this scale the artist considered solid bronze the most satisfactory core on which to shape his precious metal and on which to support it afterwards. In the remaining parts of our statue the gold may have been carried on a less substantial metal frame. The presence of this underpinning of baser metal beneath the heavy plating of

---

that the supports of seven Nikai are meant, rather than, with Woodward, seven supports to be divided between the Nike who survived 406/5 B.C. and her who was dedicated in 374/3 B.C.

[1] For the figures, see Woodward *Arch. Eph.* 1937, 159 ff.

gold would not have prevented the statue from being referred to as
golden; the statue of Athena Parthenos was commonly called the
golden though much of it was of ivory and though the whole of it
must have had a massive underpinning.[1]

Nor need the identification be ruled out by the use of silver
beneath the gold in the second period of the Bronze Head. The
object of its use is not obvious: possibly economy or some technical facility. In any case the silver was probably applied at a time
after the latest surviving references to our statue. In its original
form the head, as we have seen, was quite possibly clothed in solid
gold.

The procedure in connection with the weighing of the Nikai
provides a satisfactory explanation for the ready removability of
the Bronze Head. The 'little bits of gold' of the inscriptions may
be identified with the strips of gold which, as we have seen, were
used to key the edges of the gold plates on our head. It would
indeed be hard to find another adequate explanation for this item
in the treasure inventories; to suppose that the pieces were scraps
broken from the plates themselves would imply shocking carelessness in the handling of the statues. The 'golden nails' are again
precisely what was needed for securing top-knot and wreath on our
head. For the earrings we have already observed the holes of
attachment in the Bronze Head. The necklace, or necklaces, were
undoubtedly hung loosely about the throat above the gold plating,
so that no trace of them remains on the Bronze Head. But comparison with the vase paintings of the Meidias Painter or with
the heads on contemporary Syracusan coins will show that no
dainty young lady of the period could have done without her
necklace.

Could the statue represented by our head have carried two
talents of gold? If the figure is restored according to the contemporary standard of proportions, it will be found to have a full height

---

[1] The gorgoneion from the shield of the Athena Parthenos was of gold on silver
and is referred to in the treasure lists as γοργόνειον χρυσῦν ὑπάργυρον ἐπίτηκτον ἀπὸ
τῆς ἀσπίδος τῆς ἀπὸ τοῦ ἔδους. (A. M. Woodward *JHS* XXIX (1909) 179). On
the fabrication of the statue of the Parthenos see P. Johansen *Phidias* 35 f.; W. B.
Dinsmoor *AJA* XXXVIII (1934) 96 ff.

of slightly under 90 cm. without the top-knot, slightly over 90 cm. with that appendage. The height was therefore undoubtedly fixed at three feet. Now this is one thirteenth of the height of the Athena Parthenos (i.e. presumably statue + base) as reported by Pliny (*NH* XXXVI 18).[1] The weight of gold used on that work (Athena + Nike) was probably forty-four talents, twenty-two times that recorded for the individual Nike.[2] But this line of speculation is scarcely rewarding because of the large number of uncertain factors. We have no certainty, for instance, as to how much of Athena's helmet, spear and shield, of the column that supported the hand with the Nike or of the figured base may have been covered with gold; nor, if those parts were covered, can we say whether it was with thick or thin plate. In the case of the figure with which we are dealing, we are again quite ignorant of the relative thickness of the plating on the different parts. If the limbs and body, as suggested above, were supported on a frame-work rather than on a solid bronze core, those parts were probably of much more massive gold than was the covering of the head. In any case, it would seem not at all impossible that our Nike could have accounted for two talents of the precious metal.

The correspondences noted above will make reasonably probable the association of the Bronze Head with the Golden Nikai of Athena. A consideration of the history of the head will tend to confirm the identification. In view of the date established above, the piece may be associated with the earliest group of Nikai of which we have knowledge, i.e. those which were ordered to be finished by the decree of 434/3 B.C. The figure must have been designed shortly after the completion of the Athena Parthenos and the scale may well have been suggested by the proportions of Athena's Nike. According to Pausanias (I 24. 5) the Nike on Athena's hand stood about four cubits, i.e. about six feet in height,

---

[1] For the height of the base, ca. 1.26 m., see Lehmann-Hartleben *Jahrb.* XLVII (1932) 33.

[2] The weight is variously reported as forty talents (Thuc. II 13; Plutarch *de vitando aere alieno* 2), forty-four talents (Philochoros in Schol. Aristophanes *Peace* 605), and fifty talents (Diodoros XII 40). See W. B. Dinsmoor *AJA* XXXVIII (1934) 96.

just twice the height of our statue. Six feet is rather above normal
life size for the female figure and the scale was doubtless chosen
in the case of Athena's Nike to assure a monumental effect. But
the same explanation will not hold for our figure. I would suggest
that our statue, as also the other Golden Nikai, was deliberately
made one half the height of Athena's Nike, possibly to facilitate
the calculation of the amount of gold to be used.

The Golden Nikai were famous in their own day and they may
be supposed to have left some impression on contemporary art.
We have, perhaps, an indication of Pheidias' reaction to the new
creation in his free use of gilded Nikai on the throne of Zeus at
Olympia: four Nikai dancing about each leg of the throne, and
two Nikai at each of its feet (Paus. V 11. 1). The figure types of
the Olympia Nikai are lost, perhaps beyond hope of recovery, but
the very multiplicity in the representation of Nike, a new notion
in Greek art, may well have been borrowed from the first company
of Athena's Golden Nikai. The same source may have inspired
also the plurality of Nike figures on the Parapet of the Temple of
Nike Apteros. The quietly standing figures which punctuate the
scenes of activity on the Parapet suggest the influence, conscious
or unconscious, of statues of precisely the type which we have
assumed for our Nike. The probability of some connection is
strengthened by the exact correspondence in scale.[1]

The first denuding of the Bronze Head, i.e. apart from the
(hypothetical) periodical stripping for the inspection by the
Treasurers, doubtless occurred in the crisis of 406–4 B.C., and we
may be sure that our Nike contributed her share to the gold coinage
which served the Athenian state during the closing years of the
War.[2] The thoroughgoing way in which the grooves in the Bronze
Head were subsequently packed is eloquent testimony to the de-

---

[1] The upright Nikai of the Parapet stand in a frame 0.90 m. high and measure
0.88–0.89 m., without top-knots. The surviving heads of the Parapet are of precisely the same scale as the Bronze Head.

[2] On the "Minting of Temple Properties" see Ferguson *The Treasurers of Athena*
ch. IX. This inference, as also most of the rest of the history of the Bronze Head,
will be little affected by the uncertainty as to whether or not the head is really
from one of the Golden Nikai of Athena.

spair felt by the Treasurers at the time of the crisis. But the very fact that pains were taken to make the head presentable even without its gold proves that it was not consigned to the lumber room. It was, presumably, stored in the Chalkotheke, together with the διερείσματα, and it is just possibly to be identified with one of the bronze Nikai recorded as in the Chalkotheke by the treasure inventories of the mid fourth century.[1]

Of this period of comparative retirement the Bronze Head retains a record in the shape of a letter *xi* neatly engraved on the left side of the neck, a little back of the ear (fig. 6). It is sufficiently large (3.5 mm. high) to be found and read easily by those who knew where to look, but for the ordinary spectator it would have been concealed by the wing.[2] There can be little doubt that this is one of the letters placed on the temple treasures in the fourth century, chiefly in the time of Lycurgus but occasionally earlier, to facilitate the cataloguing and frequent checking of the material. These letters are constantly referred to in the published inventories: a phiale, oinochoe, etc., on which is the letter *alpha, beta, gamma,* etc.[3]

It has been observed above that the dedication of a Nike in 374/3 B.C. probably represented the re-conditioning of one of those which had suffered in 406/4 B.C.; the same is probably true of the Nikai attributed to Lycurgus. One is tempted to associate the re-plating of the Bronze Head with one or other of these activities. But the use of silver in its second period would seem to rule this out. In the records of the weighing of the Nike of 374/3 B.C. no mention

[1] *IG* II² 120. 57 (Hondius, *Novae Inscriptiones Atticae*, Leyden, 1925, p. 90); 1440. 59.

[2] The vertical joints in the sides of the neck for the plating of the second period would have been concealed by the same members.

[3] On the practice of lettering see H. Lehner, *Ueber die athenischen Schatzverzeichnisse des vierten Jahrhunderts*, Strassburg Diss., 1890, 118; *IG* II² 1469 note; Ferguson *The Treasurers of Athena* 123. It had previously been suggested that the letter on the Bronze Head may have been the initial of the artist's name (*Hesp.* II 525 ff.). This would seem unlikely in view of the pains taken to make the mark as inconspicuous as possible. From the treasure inventories it is clear that objects marked with single letters were also frequently inscribed with the names of the artist and of the divinity to whom the dedication was made.

occurs of silver or of silver gilt, and of Lycurgus' Nikai it is specifically and proudly said that they were of solid gold.[1]

Another possibility remains. On the Panathenaic amphorae of the year of Pythodelos, 336/5 B.C., a statue of Nike appears for the first time on top of one of the columns that frame the figure of Athena. Good reason has been shown for believing that this figure, like others of the same general type which now began to supplant the traditional cocks on the column tops, reflected more or less faithfully some famous statue of topical interest; and in this case it has been conjectured that the original was to be found in the Golden Nikai of Athena as re-clothed by Lycurgus.[2] Now the reverse types of the gold coins of Alexander exhibit a similar figure of Nike which is shown by its abbreviated ground line to be derived from a statue. The sculptural type of this Nike is a hundred years earlier than the date of striking of the coins: stance, proportions and drapery are close to those of the Athena Parthenos, far removed from those of other Nikai on coins of the fourth century. For our immediate purpose it is worth observing that the pose is also that which we have recovered for the Nike of our Bronze Head, further that the Nike of the coins commonly wears her hair in a top-knot like that to be restored on the Bronze Head and that she is provided with earrings and necklace. It has recently been pointed out that on certain rare gold coins which must be among the earliest issued by Alexander and which were probably struck in 336 B.C., the large Nike is accompanied by a tiny Nike identical in type and attributes with that on the Panathenaic amphorae of 336/5 B.C. Consequently it has been maintained that the Nike of the coins is based on the same prototype as that of the Panathenaic amphorae of 336/5 B.C., *viz.* one or other of the Golden Nikai of Athena as restored by Lycurgus.[3]

---

[1] [Plutarch] *Lives of the Ten Orators* 852 B: Ἔτι δὲ αἱρεθεὶς ὑπὸ τοῦ δήμου χρήματα πολλὰ συνήγαγεν εἰς τὴν ἀκρόπολιν καὶ παρασκευάσας τῇ θεῷ κόσμον Νίκας τε ὁλοχρύσους πομπεῖά τε χρυσᾶ καὶ ἀργυρᾶ καὶ κόσμον χρυσοῦν εἰς ἑκατὸν κανηφόρους.

[2] *Mon. dell' Inst.* X pl. 47b; G. von Brauchitsch, *Die panathenäischen Preisamphoren*, Leipzig and Berlin, 1910, p. 62, no. 96, 110 ff.; *CVA British Museum* III H f pl. 3, 2; M. H. Swindler, *Ancient Painting*, New Haven, 1929, fig. 347.

[3] E. Babelon *Rev. Num.* 1907, 1 ff.; P. Lederer *Zeitschrift für Numismatik* XXXIII (1922) 185 ff.; C. Seltman, *Greek Coins*, London, 1933, pp. 204 f.

The conclusion that the Nikai of both vases and coins are derived from the Golden Nikai is difficult to gainsay. But the corollary that the Golden Nikai which served as prototypes were those of Lycurgus would appear to be ruled out by the more recent evaluation of the epigraphic evidence which shows that in all probability Lycurgus' activity regarding the Nikai falls in the period 334/3–331/0 B.C.[1] It should, moreover, be remembered that the Golden Nikai were primarily a form of gold reserve and it is unlikely that Athens was putting much gold in reserve as early as 336 B.C. Yet the simultaneous appearance of the Nikai on vases and coins would seem certainly to mark some noteworthy event in the history of those statues.

As a tentative solution for the difficulty I would suggest that one or more of the Golden Nikai were actually restored in 336 B.C., not, however, by Lycurgus but by or with the help of Alexander. The historical circumstances are admittedly confused and confusing, yet a very fair case has been made out for believing that the young king even thus early was prepared to forgive the recalcitrant but venerable city;[2] he could scarcely have conceived of a more dramatic or more touching symbol of his respectful forbearance. The reader need scarcely be reminded that the treasures of Athena were certainly enriched by three hundred suits of Persian armour sent by Alexander after the battle of the Granikos in 334 B.C.[3] and by various gifts, including a gold rhyton and gold necklaces, sent by his wife Roxane, presumably between their marriage in 327 B.C. and his death in 323.[4] It would seem possible, then, that the Nike of the Bronze Head was restored in 336 B.C., replated, that is, with gilt silver. Whatever the motive behind the use of the silver, the result, to those who knew the details, must have seemed cheap indeed in comparison with an original plating of pure gold. This knowledge may well have furnished the point of the reference to Lycurgus' Nikai of solid gold, for in this respect Lycurgus' restorations were presumably in no wise superior to the original statues.

The next chapter in the history of the Bronze Head is soon recounted. In the desperate years 300–295 B.C. the "tyrant"

---

[1] Ferguson *The Treasurers of Athena* 122 n. 2.
[2] The evidence is reviewed by Lederer *l. c.*
[3] Arrian I 16. 7.
[4] *IG* II[2] 1492. 46 ff.

Lachares, in order to maintain his native and mercenary forces, was driven once more to raid the sacred treasures. On this occasion even the Athena Parthenos was obliged to surrender her golden dress; the Golden Nikai and apparently all the votives of precious metal were sacrificed.[1] There is little possibility, therefore, that the Nike of the Bronze Head should have gone unscathed. Her fate is made certain by the circumstances in which she was found in 1932, i.e. in a well which was filled in the first half of the third century B.C.[2] The ruthless way in which the chisel was úsed in the final stripping indicates that there was no intention this time of preserving even the bronze core. We may suppose therefore that the bronze was discarded shortly after this final operation: ἄχρυσος ἄχρηστος.

The sceptic is entitled to enquire why a head which is presumed to have been sacred to Athena and to have been displayed on the Acropolis should have been found at the east foot of Kolonos Agoraios. The answer is that when metal votives were to be melted down they were removed from the Acropolis to the workshops of the artisans. This is undoubtedly the explanation of an entry which recurs in the treasure lists: 'a bit of gold which was found in the home of the goldsmith.'[3] The procedure is further illustrated by the inscriptions which record the melting down of old offerings and the consolidation of the precious metals carried out in the time of Lycurgus: the votives were then taken by a goldsmith (χρυσωτής), who melted them down and returned the pure gold to the Treasurers.[4] It is well known that Kolonos Agoraios was *the* metal working region of the ancient city and the current excavations have revealed abundant traces of metal-working establishments to the west of the Stoa of Zeus and to the north of the Hephaisteion, i.e. in the immediate vicinity of the well in which the Bronze Head was found. Nor should the possibility be overlooked that the mint

[1] Ferguson *The Treasurers of Athena* 126 f.

[2] *Hesp.* II 453 f., 525; III (1934) 208. A human skeleton which was found in the lower filling beneath the Bronze Head is perhaps also to be associated with the troubles of the time of Lachares (*Hesp.* II 453 f.). For a person to fall into a well may have been no uncommon event in antiquity; but that a corpse should have been left in a well may be taken to suggest a time of confusion.

[3] E.g. *IG* II² 1388. 65 f.: ἕτερο]ν χρυσίον, ὃ παρὰ τῷ χρυσοχόῳ ηὑρέθη.

[4] *IG* II² 1495. Cf. *IG* II² 1496 note on p. 101.

(ἀργυροκόπιον) was in this region. The evidence for its position is, to be sure, slight. But, in addition to the general desirability of having the mint in the vicinity of the metal workers, it now appears that on the occasion of the standardization of currency, weights and measures in the regions under Athenian domination in the time of the Peloponnesian War, foreign money was to be turned into the mint and of the sums so collected a tithe was to be paid to Hephaistos and Athena, i.e. the divinities who were worshipped in the temple on top of Kolonos, a short stone's throw from the place of finding of the Bronze Head.[1]

If now we return to the question, did or did not the Bronze Head belong to one of the Golden Nikai of Athena, the reader may feel that the preceding argument has established little but a loosely strung sequence of probabilities. A re-consideration may suggest, however, that these probabilities are mutually strengthening. An effort has been made to compare the Bronze Head with the Golden Nikai in three respects: method of fabrication, sculptural style and history. On each of the three scores, striking correspondences have been observed which, though individually inconclusive, if taken together establish a very strong probability in favor of the identification.

Yet the reader may be inclined to leave the question of identification open. In that case he may still appreciate the Bronze Head as an historical document of but slightly lessened interest which illustrates with rare vividness the triumphs and reverses of Athens over some 140 years of her most eventful history.[2]

---

[1] The information is preserved on the copy of the decree recently found in the Chalcidice and published by D. M. Robinson in *AJP* LVI (1935) 149–154, especially 153. For other copies of the same decree see M. N. Tod, *Greek Historical Inscriptions*, Oxford, 1933, no. 67. A golden pendant (J 2) was found in a cistern some 4 m. to the west of the well of the Bronze Head in a context contemporary with that of the head (the northern chamber of the double cistern discussed in *Hesperia* II (1933) 126 ff.). Since gold ornaments are practically unknown in the domestic accumulations of the innumerable wells and cisterns around the Agora, one might be pardoned for suspecting that the piece of jewelry, like the head, had been brought to be melted.

[2] Space does not permit a detailed discussion of the sculptural type, the ornaments or attributes of our Nike. It is hoped that this may be possible in a forthcoming article by my wife.

ADDENDA

P. 199. Since this article went to press, E. Schweigert has published two inscriptions from the Excavations of the Athenian Agora which have to do with the Golden Nikai: *Hesp.* IX (1940) 309–311, Nos. 27 and 28. No. 27, dated from the style of its lettering ca. 430–425 B.C., preserves a fragmentary record of the weights of two hitherto unknown Nikai; No. 28, which is part of *IG* II² 1381 + 1386 of 401/0 B.C., gives the weights of a previously known Nike made by - - -]atides.

P. 209. Fragments of still other copies of the decree regarding currency, weights and measures in the Athenian Empire have been found at Aphytis and Kos and have been published by Segre in *Clara Rhodos* IX (1938) 161 ff.

THE OLD OLIGARCH

By A. W. Gomme

FOR nearly a century now it has been agreed that the little
work entitled in our medieval manuscripts Ξενοφῶντος ῥήτορος
(or simply Ξενοφῶντος) Ἀθηναίων Πολιτεία was written by an
Athenian, of oligarchic sympathies, at a time when Athens' empire was intact and her navy unchallenged, and when conditions of
warfare, as between Athens and her enemies, were similar to those
of the Archidamian war: therefore at some time between, say, 435
and 415 B.C., possibly a year or two earlier. There however agreement has ended. The authorship has been attributed to Thucydides the historian and to the son of Melesias, to the aristocratic
and cultured Kritias and to the uneducated and plebeian Phrynichos, to Alkibiades, to Xenophon the general who was killed at
Spartolos in 429; it has been argued from various references and
significant silences that it was written before 431, before 430 but
after 431, before 425, after 425, before the production of the
Knights and after it. Some have seen it as the work of an older man
who would curb the youthful hotheads among the oligarchs, others
as that of an extremist contemptuous of academic reformers and
moderates, ready to surrender not only the empire but his city's
independence if only the hated democracy can be got rid of; some
find in it a gay irony, others *bitterer Ernst*; to one man it is a strong
plea to fellow-oligarchs for a practical policy, to another a sophistic
παίγνιον; it is addressed to Athenians, to Spartans, to the discontented oligarchs of the empire. It is a confused jumble; only the
notes for a speech; an extempore speech; an ordered, logical whole.
Its style betrays simply the uneducated man; it can be given its
place in the orderly development of Attic *Kunstprosa*. It is not my
purpose in this paper to discuss any of these varied opinions
directly; my agreements and disagreements will appear in the
course of it. I think Müller-Strübing, Kalinka, Stail, Kupferschmid
and Gelzer have contributed most to the understanding of Pseudo-
Xenophon, since the pioneer work of Roscher; and of these I would

lay stress on the work of Müller-Strübing, which has fallen into a neglect which, in spite of much absurdity in detail, it does not deserve. (He also had a more fundamental fault: he supposed that Thucydides did not understand the Athens of his day, and that, that being so, we can; but in this respect he does not stand alone.)[1]

The question of the date of the work is so closely bound up with that of its nature and purpose that some consideration must, first of all, be given to the latter; the neglect of this has led to much purposeless argument.

No one, not even those who take X (as I shall call the author) most seriously, has denied that he exaggerates, that he is not always truthful to the letter. But exaggeration is of two kinds. There is that excellent kind that consists in emphasizing of some one fact or characteristic and ignoring minor, qualifying facts — a simplification of the picture, a heightening of the tone — which yet leaves the picture in essentials true: as the exaggeration of comedy. X has examples of this: 1. 10–12, the freedom and equality allowed to slaves and metics at Athens, οὔτε ὑπεκστήσεταί σοι ὁ

---

[1] The following books and articles are referred to by the author's name only:

W. Roscher, *Leben . . . des Thukydides*, Göttingen, 1842, pp. 526–539, 248–252 (see p. 538 n.).

A. Boeckh, *Staatshaushaltung d. Athener*,³ Berlin, 1886, p. 389 n.

A. Kirchhoff, *Abhandlungen Akad. Berlin*, 1874, *Ph. Hist. Kl.*, pp. 1–35; 1878, pp. 1–25.

H. Müller-Strübing, *Der Staat der Athener*, *Philologus* Supplementband IV, 1884, 1–188.

E. Drerup, *Untersuchungen zur älteren griechischen Prosaliteratur*, I: *Jahrb. f. class. Philologie* Supplementband XXVII, 1902, 219–351, esp. 308–314.

G. Busolt, *Griechische Geschichte*, III 2, Gotha, 1904, 609–616.

E. Kalinka, *Die pseudoxenophontische* Ἀθηναίων Πολιτεία, Leipzig u. Berlin, 1913.

G. Stail, *Ueber die pseudoxenophontische* Ἀθηναίων Πολιτεία: *Rhetorische Studien*, Heft 9, Paderborn, 1921.

M. Kupferschmid, *Zur Erklärung d. pseudoxenophontischen* Ἀθηναίων Πολιτεία: Diss. Hamburg, 1932.

U. Instinsky, *Die Abfassungszeit d. Schrift vom Staate d. Athener*: Diss. Freiburg, 1933.

K. I. Gelzer, *Die Schrift vom Staate d. Athener*: *Hermes* Einzelschriften 3, 1937.

δοῦλος. οὗ δ' ἕνεκέν ἐστι τοῦτο ἐπιχώριον, ἐγὼ φράσω· εἰ νόμος ἦν τὸν δοῦλον ὑπὸ τοῦ ἐλευθέρου τύπτεσθαι ἢ τὸν μέτοικον ἢ τὸν ἀπελεύθερον, πολλάκις ἂν οἰηθεὶς εἶναι τὸν Ἀθηναῖον δοῦλον ἐπάταξεν ἄν· ἐσθῆτά τε γὰρ οὐδὲν βελτίων[1] ὁ δῆμος αὐτόθι ἢ οἱ δοῦλοι καὶ οἱ μέτοικοι καὶ τὰ εἴδη οὐδὲν βελτίους εἰσίν.

(If X is addressing men from other Greek states which were oligarchies, especially from Sparta, this has a particular point; for every state had a δῆμος; in Sparta it was formed by the peers, and δάμῳ τὰν κυρίαν ἦμεν καὶ κράτος: but, "You must not suppose that our demos at Athens is like yours, easily distinguishable from the helots and perioikoi".)[2] Another good instance is 1.18, εἰ μὲν μὴ ἐπὶ δίκας ἤεσαν οἱ σύμμαχοι, τοὺς ἐκπλέοντας[3] Ἀθηναίων ἐτίμων ἂν μόνους, τούς τε στρατηγοὺς καὶ τοὺς τριηράρχους καὶ πρέσβεις· νῦν δ' ἠνάγκασται τὸν δῆμον κολακεύειν τὸν Ἀθηναίων εἷς ἕκαστος τῶν συμμάχων γιγνώσκων ὅτι δεῖ μὲν ἀφικόμενον Ἀθήναζε δίκην δοῦναι καὶ λαβεῖν οὐκ ἐν ἄλλοις τισὶν ἀλλ' ἐν τῷ δήμῳ, ὅς ἐστι δὴ νόμος Ἀθήνησι· καὶ ἀντιβολῆσαι ἀναγκάζεται ἐν τοῖς δικαστηρίοις καὶ εἰσιόντος του ἐπιλαμβάνεσθαι τῆς χειρός. This expresses an essential truth, that the little man was determined to have his share (or so he thought) not only of power — ἆρ' οὐ μεγάλην ἀρχὴν ἄρχω καὶ τοῦ Διὸς οὐδὲν ἐλάσσω; — but of the trappings of power, a court with the flattery of courtiers and suppliants; it is not that the generals and trierarchs and ambassadors here are aristocrats, but that they are, for the moment at any rate, eminent, and Philokleon does not intend that either Kleon or Hippokrates should have all the fun: there must be δ η μ ο κρατία.[4]

[1] This is more in keeping with the style of this work than βέλτιον of the MSS. See Kalinka.
[2] Plut. *Lyk.* 6. 2 (if this reading, due to Coraes and Sintenis, is correct, as I believe. See Ziegler *ad loc.* and his *Addenda*, vol. IV 2 p. xxv). It is interesting to note too the use of ἐπιχώριον here, a favourite word with Aristophanes, and to compare, e.g., *Clouds* 1173, *Wasps* 859, *Plut.* 47, 342.
[3] τῶν ἐκπλεόντων (Müller-Strübing, Busolt III 1, 226. 2) would be more natural in itself, for there were crews in the ships, and more consistent with the next sentence, νῦν δ' ἠνάγκασται, κ. τ. λ.; for the flattery there should be of the demos abroad, by allies in their own homes, because they know that at some time or other they may be compelled to go to Athens for a lawsuit; more consistent also with 1. 14 ἐκπλέοντες συκοφαντοῦσιν. But τοὺς ἐκπλέοντας should be kept; it is complementary to 1. 16 οἴκοι καθήμενοι ἄνευ νεῶν ἔκπλου διοικοῦσι τὰς πόλεις.
[4] It is this emphasis that Thucydides has in mind in the famous sentence ἐγίγνετό τε λόγῳ μὲν δημοκρατία, ἔργῳ δὲ ὑπὸ τοῦ πρώτου ἀνδρὸς ἀρχή.

This picture is so like that drawn in the *Wasps* (esp. 552 ff.), that some have thought that it was suggested by the comedy; and in itself, if the dates make it possible, this is likely enough. The *Babylonians* would perhaps have shown other similarities.

There are other exaggerations of this kind which may be just referred to: 1.16 ἀπὸ τῶν πρυτανείων (from the subject states only) τὸν μισθὸν δι' ἐνιαυτοῦ λαμβάνειν (τοὺς δικαστάς), *ibid*. οἴκοι καθήμενοι ἄνευ ͵εῶν ἔκπλου διοικοῦσι τὰς πόλεις, 2.12 the complete control of sea-traffic by Athens (especially οὐδὲν ποιῶν ἐκ τῆς γῆς πάντα ταῦτα ἔχω διὰ τὴν θάλατταν), 3.2 δίκας καὶ γραφὰς καὶ εὐθύνας ἐκδικάζειν ὅσας οὐδ' οἱ σύμπαντες ἄνθρωποι ἐκδικάζουσι, 3.3 the usefulness of spending money in order to get business done more quickly (Müller-Strübing, p. 29, has some sensible remarks here — it does not mean direct bribery), 3.4 choregoi at all the festivals (see Kalinka *ad loc.*) and the number of trierarchs. All these are exaggerations, but true to the character of Athens, though obviously we are warned against taking every statement in this work literally. There are, however, others which, though with some basis of fact, essentially falsify the picture; and these are important. A statement such as 2.8 φωνὴν πᾶσαν ἀκούοντες ἐξελέξαντο τοῦτο μὲν ἐκ τῆς τοῦτο δὲ ἐκ τῆς· καὶ οἱ μὲν Ἕλληνες ἰδίᾳ μᾶλλον καὶ φωνῇ καὶ διαίτῃ καὶ σχήματι χρῶνται, Ἀθηναῖοι δὲ κεκραμένῃ ἐξ ἁπάντων τῶν Ἑλλήνων καὶ βαρβάρων (note ἐξελέξαντο, as though it were a conscious process), recognized by everybody for what it is, does not much matter; but already in the passage about slaves to which I have referred, there is the sentence ἐῶσι τοὺς δούλους τρυφᾶν αὐτόθι καὶ μεγαλοπρεπῶς διαιτᾶσθαι ἐνίους, with the modification ἐνίους carefully kept to the end, and the reason given, ὅπου γὰρ ναυτικὴ δύναμίς ἐστιν, ἀπὸ χρημάτων ἀνάγκη τοῖς ἀνδραπόδοις δουλεύειν, ἵνα λαμβάνωμεν ὧν πράττῃ τὰς ἀποφοράς,[1] καὶ ἐλευθέρους ἀφιέναι. There is something in this, but no one really believes it as a description of slavery in Athens; still less the reason given for the freedom — "we give such slaves the protection of the

---

[1] For the reading see Gelzer, 111–116. I agree with him too, 118. 1, that ἐλευθέρους ἀφιέναι must mean "set free," "manumit," not "allow freedom of movement"; but I do not pretend to understand it. It is inconsistent both with what has immediately preceded and with what follows, ὅπου δ' εἰσὶ πλούσιοι δοῦλοι, κ.τ.λ.

law because a terrified slave might surrender his own property to some one else," with the result apparently that his master will not get his share, the ἀποφορά. Τρυφᾶν and μεγαλοπρεπῶς διαιτᾶσθαι are exaggerations of the same type as εὐπορία τροφῆς (on 2 obols a day) in Aristotle, Ἀθπ. 24.3, as tales of the unemployed in England motoring to Brighton for week-ends on the dole.

I. 15, εἴποι δέ τις ἂν ὅτι ἰσχύς ἐστιν αὕτη Ἀθηναίων, ἐὰν οἱ σύμμαχοι δυνατοὶ ὦσι χρήματα εἰσφέρειν. τοῖς δὲ δημοτικοῖς δοκεῖ μεῖζον ἀγαθὸν εἶναι τὰ τῶν συμμάχων χρήματα ἕνα ἕκαστον Ἀθηναίων ἔχειν, ἐκείνους δὲ ὅσον ζῆν, καὶ ἐργάζεσθαι ἀδυνάτους ὄντας ἐπιβουλεύειν, has perhaps more truth, especially in relation to the treatment of Thasos, Aigina, Samos and Mytilene; but in essentials it is false.

In the last sentence of 2.17, καὶ ἂν μέν τι κακὸν ἀναβαίνῃ ἀπὸ ὧν ὁ δῆμος ἐβούλευσεν, αἰτιᾶται ὁ δῆμος ὡς ὀλίγοι ἄνθρωποι αὐτῷ ἀντιπράττοντες διέφθειραν· ἐὰν δέ τι ἀγαθόν, σφίσιν αὐτοῖς τὴν αἰτίαν ἀνατιθέασι, the writer makes a charge against Athens which was often to be repeated, especially in the ekklesia by her democratic leaders, of refusal to accept responsibility for her own decisions (as in 413, χαλεποὶ μὲν ἦσαν τοῖς ξυμπροθυμηθεῖσι τῶν ῥητόρων τὸν ἔκπλουν, ὥσπερ οὐκ αὐτοὶ ψηφισάμενοι, Thuc. VIII 1. 1): a charge which is true. But it is introduced by another charge that, whereas oligarchies by their very nature necessarily stood by their treaties and alliances, the Athenians were always ready to repudiate theirs by putting the responsibility on to the proposer and the president of the ekklesia, each man claiming that he himself was absent or disliked the proposal, and to make every kind of excuse for refusing to do anything they did not want to.[1] This is quite untrue: Athens was,

---

[1] The text is corrupt. I believe Kalinka's reading may be right, οὐδὲ ἀρέσκει οἱ, εἴ γε μὴ συγκείμενα πυνθάνονται ἐν πλήρει τῷ δήμῳ; but we must translate, "if, that is, they learn that the agreement was not made in full assembly," with a reference to the law of the constitution, ἄνευ τοῦ δήμου πληθύοντος μὴ εἶναι πόλεμον, κ. τ. λ., re-enacted in 410 or 409 (*IG* I² 114. 36), as Müller-Strübing saw. It is interesting that X admits that a vote might have been unconstitutional. Doubtless also foreign statesmen had often been annoyed when proposals made by Athenian ambassadors, not αὐτοκράτορες, were later repudiated by the assembly.

I should note that in Kalinka's reading οἱ, εἴ γε μή is based on *C*'s εἴ γε μήν combined with *AM*'s οἱ γε (with no negative; *B* has εἴ γε). *AM* may be the

to say the least, not more unscrupulous in this respect than Sparta, and a good deal more scrupulous than Thessaly and Thebes; particularly we may remember that Athens kept strictly to the letter at least of the treaty in 433–1, and Sparta had a bad conscience afterwards that she had not.

2. 14: (if Athens were an island she would have nothing to fear), νῦν δὲ οἱ γεωργοῦντες καὶ οἱ πλούσιοι Ἀθηναίων ὑπέρχονται τοὺς πολεμίους μᾶλλον, ὁ δὲ δῆμος, ἅτε εὖ εἰδὼς ὅτι οὐδὲν τῶν σφῶν ἐμπρήσουσιν οὐδὲ τεμοῦσιν, ἀδεῶς ζῇ καὶ οὐχ ὑπερχόμενος αὐτούς. The first part of this is a commonplace, and recalls Perikles' words in Thucydides (I 143. 5), εἰ γὰρ ἦμεν νησιῶται, τίνες ἂν ἀληπτότεροι ἦσαν. But ὁ δῆμος ἀδεῶς ζῇ? This is contradicted by all that we know, at any rate of the Archidamian war, especially by Thuc. II 65. 2: ἰδίᾳ δὲ τοῖς παθήμασιν ἐλυποῦντο, ὁ μὲν δῆμος ὅτι ἀπ' ἐλασσόνων ὁρμώμενος ἐστέρητο καὶ τούτων, οἱ δὲ δυνατοὶ καλὰ κτήματα κατὰ τὴν χώραν . . . . ἀπολωλεκότες. Our author excludes the peasant-farmers from the demos; Thucydides includes them, and knows as well that the poor of Athens and of the Peiraeus too had losses to mourn. Two sentences later (2.16) X says, τὴν Ἀττικὴν γῆν περιορῶσι τεμνομένην γιγνώσκοντες ὅτι εἰ αὐτὴν ἐλεήσουσιν ἑτέρων ἀ γ α θ ῶ ν μειζόνων στερήσονται, where the subject should clearly be the demos in the narrower sense, the town thetes only, as in 2. 14; but τὴν οὐσίαν ταῖς νήσοις παρατίθενται shows that the farmers are included, thus giving away the assumption of a rift between the two classes. His ἀδεῶς ζῇ is contradicted also by what he himself says about the importance and the activities of the fleet, manned by the demos; for the latter might have retorted to the hoplites and the cavalry, "It is you who ἀδεῶς ζῆτε: except for an occasional expedition and a luxury march into Megara every year, we keep you safely within the walls. *You don't have to face the enemy in the field; we toil at the oar all the year round*" —

ὑποστένοι μέντ' ἂν ὁ θρανίτης λεώς
ὁ σωσίπολις (*Acharnians* 162–3);

and it was not the poor sailors but the well-to-do who got the

---

best MSS; but the attempt (e.g. Kupferschmid's) to explain their reading by supposing that X means, the demos reject a προβούλευμα of the boule, is surely quite mistaken.

comfortable jobs (*Knights* 1368–71). And οἱ γεωργοῦντες Ἀθηναίων ὑπέρχονται τοὺς πολεμίους μᾶλλον, "are more ready to truckle to Sparta"? The *Acharnians* and the *Knights* show us that this was not true about 425, Thucydides that it was not true in 431; nothing in any other author suggests that it is anything but false at any time (cf. *Lysistrate* 273 ff.), even though after Delion the farmers were more anxious for peace than the townsmen.

2. 18: κωμωδεῖν δ' αὖ καὶ κακῶς λέγειν τὸν μὲν δῆμον οὐκ ἐῶσιν, ἵνα μὴ αὐτοὶ ἀκούωσι κακῶς· ἰδίᾳ δὲ κελεύουσιν, εἴ τίς τινα βούλεται, εὖ εἰδότες ὅτι οὐχὶ τοῦ δήμου ἐστὶν οὐδὲ τοῦ πλήθους ὁ κωμῳδούμενος ὡς ἐπὶ τὸ πολύ, ἀλλ' ἢ πλούσιος ἢ γενναῖος ἢ δυνάμενος, ὀλίγοι δέ τινες τῶν πενήτων καὶ τῶν δημοτικῶν κωμῳδοῦνται καὶ οὐδ' οὗτοι ἐὰν μὴ διὰ πολυπραγμοσύνην καὶ διὰ τὸ ζητεῖν πλέον τι ἔχειν τοῦ δήμου, ὥστε οὐδὲ τοὺς τοιούτους ἄχθονται κωμῳδουμένους. The first sentence has entered into every discussion about the date of this work — "it must be before the *Knights*", "it can well be after it"; but before we deal with that, we should look at the next sentence, which is equally interesting. "The comic poets are encouraged to mock at any individual, for the people know that he will not be one of themselves, but rich or aristocratic or powerful; occasionally a poor man, a πολυπράγμων anxious to be distinguished from the crowd, may be mocked, and they do not mind that." Now in one sense this is true: comedy, at least good comedy, did mock τοὺς δυναμένους. Aristophanes portrayed what was important, significant:

οὐκ ἰδιώτας ἀνθρωπίσκους κωμῳδῶν οὐδὲ γυναῖκας,
ἀλλ' Ἡρακλέους ὀργήν τιν' ἔχων τοῖσι μεγίστοις ἐπεχείρει
(*Peace* 751–2)

(not, I had better add, because he was a brave man, but because he was a good dramatist). In another, but quite unimportant way also, the statement is true, in that comedy often introduced, briefly, incidentally, pen-pictures of individuals of no great stature, πλούσιοι and γενναῖοι or πολυπράγμονες and πονηροί, indifferently. But that is not the impression X wishes to convey; *he* means that comedy practically confined itself to attacks on individuals and that these individuals were almost always members of the upper classes, that it was in fact but another weapon, cleverly used, in the hands of the demos. As a statement about Attic comedy, as far as it is known to us, it is grotesque. Aristophanes' main task, not in the *Knights* only, but in the *Babylonians*, *Acharnians*, *Wasps*, *Peace*, *Birds*, *Lysistrate*, was precisely κωμῳδεῖν τὸν δῆμον; it was his business to "extract the comedy"[1] from the political situation, and the situation at that time was a democracy at war. No sane reader of Aristophanes can doubt this; and all discussion as to whether this paragraph in the Old Oligarch can be "reconciled with" the *Knights* is trivial irrelevance. He is simply saying something which is false and which he must have known to be false (if he thought at all), but which suited his mood. Yet there have been many who have treated it as serious truth[2] and have at the same time believed in an Aristophanes who was a champion of Decency and Conservatism against the demos. Some even have seen in the few men τῶν πενήτων καὶ τῶν δημοτικῶν attacked in comedy διὰ πολυπραγμοσύνην καὶ διὰ τὸ ζητεῖν πλέον τι ἔχειν τοῦ δήμου a reference to Euripides and the Sokrates of the *Clouds*, and Boeckh gravely discusses the problem whether Kritias (whom he thought to be the author of this work), as a pupil of Sokrates, would thus have spoken of his master. Of course there was *some* excuse for the paragraph — the restriction on comedy in 440 (if that had a political aim) and Kleon's attack on the *Babylonians*; and there was doubtless many an honest democrat who thought that the licence of comedy

---

[1] "The critics are sure to complain that I have not solved all the burning political problems of the present and the future in it (*Geneva*), and restored peace to Europe and Asia. They always do. I am flattered by the implied attribution to me of omniscience and omnipotence; but I am infuriated by the unreasonableness of the demand. I am neither omniscient nor omnipotent; and the utmost that I or any other playwright can do is to extract the comedy and tragedy from the existing situation and wait and see what will become of it." — Bernard Shaw, quoted in *The Times*, Aug. 9, 1938. Aristophanes would not have the same complaint to make of his modern critics; but his answer would be the same.

[2] Meyer was one of them, and I cannot refrain from quoting his words (*Forschungen* II 406): *man wird empfinden* (from *Ach.* 515 ff., and from the picture of Demos in the *Knights*), *dass Aristophanes sich der engen Schranken, die ihm gezogen waren, sehr genau bewusst war.* Somehow or other "narrow limits" seems hardly appropriate to the Aristophanes that we know.

should be curbed; but it is fundamentally false. Roscher wrote (p. 532): *kannte der Verfasser die Ritter, so durfte er nimmermehr so schreiben, ohne als Lügner offenbar zu werden.* That is just what he was, unless we assume both that he wrote before Aristophanes' first play and that all earlier comedy was quite different from the later.[1]

I. 3: ὁπόσαι μὲν σωτηρίαν φέρουσι τῶν ἀρχῶν χρησταὶ οὖσαι[2] καὶ μὴ χρησταὶ κίνδυνον τῷ δήμῳ ἅπαντι, τούτων μὲν τῶν ἀρχῶν οὐδὲν δεῖται ὁ δῆμος μετεῖναι (οὔτε ⟨γὰρ⟩ τῶν στρατηγιῶν κλήρῳ οἴονταί σφισι χρῆναι μετεῖναι οὔτε τῶν ἱππαρχιῶν)· γιγνώσκει γὰρ ὁ δῆμος ὅτι πλείω ὠφελεῖται ἐν τῷ μὴ αὐτὸς ἄρχειν ταύτας τὰς ἀρχάς, ἀλλ' ἐᾶν τοὺς δυνατωτάτους ἄρχειν· ὁπόσαι δ' εἰσὶν ἀρχαὶ μισθοφορίας ἕνεκα καὶ ὠφελίας εἰς τὸν οἶκον, ταύτας ζητεῖ ὁ δῆμος ἄρχειν. There is clearly some truth in this; and its truth is not weakened by Kleon's election to the strategia in 425 and 422 (for that was exceptional, and Kleon was a rich man and the son of a rich man, not of the demos in the sense of this passage). Compare Aristotle, 'Αθπ. 28. 1 (with its somewhat different meaning): πρῶτον γὰρ τότε (after Perikles' death) προστάτην ἔλαβεν ὁ δῆμος οὐκ εὐδοκιμοῦντα παρὰ τοῖς ἐπιεικέσιν· ἐν δὲ τοῖς πρότερον χρόνοις ἀεὶ διετέλουν οἱ ἐπιεικεῖς δημαγωγοῦντες, though we may doubt how far this is true of Themistokles; and with μισθοφορίας ἕνεκα compare Thuc. VI 24. 3 (the enthusiasm for the Sicilian expedition): ὁ δὲ πολὺς ὅμιλος καὶ στρατιώτης ἔν τε τῷ παρόντι ἀργύριον οἴσειν καὶ προσκτήσεσθαι δύναμιν ὅθεν ἀίδιον μισθοφορὰν ὑπάρξειν. But it is only a partial truth; we do not really believe that μισθοφορίας ἕνεκα καὶ ὠφελίας εἰς τὸν οἶκον was the sole motive of the masses, the only reason why humble men held humble office. Nor do we believe that aristocrats were above accepting office that would be useful financially, at least if we trust that other eminent conservative,

---

[1] What "the other Greeks" would have noted, with disapproval, was the extreme liberty of Attic comedy (which X doubtless enjoyed); they may also have asked, "why is it tolerated by the demos?" — the question which he professes to answer.

[2] This is very doubtful Greek; and it is not helped by Kalinka's argument that ἀρχαί in the first part of the sentence means "holders of office," in the second "offices." The construction of μετεῖναι just below, without its personal object (αὐτῷ), is also strange; so would be the asyndeton after it, but the insertion of γάρ is a simple remedy.

Aristophanes: *Ach.* 593–619, especially πολίτης χρηστός, οὐ σπου-δαρχίδης 595, μισθαρχίδης 597,

> ὁρῶν πολιοὺς μὲν ἄνδρας ἐν ταῖς τάξεσιν,
> νεανίας δ' οἵους σὺ διαδεδρακότας,
> τοὺς μὲν ἐπὶ Θρᾴκης μισθοφοροῦντας τρεῖς δραχμάς,
> Τεισαμενοφαινίππους Πανουργιππαρχίδας

> αἴτιον δὲ τί
> ὑμᾶς μὲν ἀεὶ μισθοφορεῖν ἀμηγέπη,
> τωνδὶ δὲ μηδέν';

ΛΑΜ. ὦ δημοκρατία ταῦτα δῆτ' ἀνασχετά;
ΔΙΚ. οὐ δῆτ' ἐὰν μὴ μισθοφορῇ γε Λάμαχος.[1]

1. 13: ἐν ταῖς χορηγίαις αὖ καὶ γυμνασιαρχίαις καὶ τριηραρχίαις γιγνώσκουσιν ὅτι χορηγοῦσι μὲν οἱ πλούσιοι, χορηγεῖται δὲ ὁ δῆμος, καὶ γυμνασιαρχοῦσι ⟨μὲν⟩ καὶ τριηραρχοῦσιν οἱ πλούσιοι, ὁ δὲ δῆμος τριηραρχεῖται καὶ γυμνασιαρχεῖται. ἀξιοῖ γοῦν ἀργύριον λαμβάνειν ὁ δῆμος καὶ ᾄδων καὶ τρέχων καὶ ὀρχούμενος καὶ πλέων ἐν ταῖς ναυσίν, ἵνα αὐτός τε ἔχῃ καὶ οἱ πλούσιοι πενέστεροι γίγνωνται.[2]

---

[1] Among the first reforms proposed in 411 was τὰς ἀρχὰς ἀμίσθους ἄρχειν ἁπάσας ἕως ἂν ὁ πόλεμος ᾖ: which, if honestly carried out, would have hit Koisyra's son as hardly as the poor dicast.

With 1. 3 Kupferschmid, p. 26. 2, well compares Isokrates 7. 20–25. The later writer's sentimentality about fifth century politics is, on the whole, more truthful than the realism of the contemporary.

[2] The first sentence of this paragraph, τοὺς δὲ γυμναζομένους αὐτόθι καὶ τὴν μουσικὴν ἐπιτηδεύοντας καταλέλυκεν ὁ δῆμος νομίζων τοῦτο οὐ καλὸν εἶναι γνοὺς ὅτι οὐ δυνατὰ ⟨αὐτῷ⟩ ταῦτά ἐστιν ἐπιτηδεύειν, has never been explained. If, with Kalinka, Stail and Gelzer, we suppose it to refer to foreigners only, we must read αὐτῶν for αὐτόθι (or ⟨αὐτῶν⟩ αὐτόθι; αὐτῶν is Müller-Strübing's suggestion, pp. 21–2, but he would restrict its reference to the slaves, which seems quite impossible). Even so it is very obscure: it appears to refer to a particular measure — "the demos has suppressed" — and gives an absurd reason; there is no other evidence to support it and much that seems to contradict it.

The last sentence of the paragraph, ἔν τε τοῖς δικαστηρίοις οὐ τοῦ δικαίου αὐτοῖς μᾶλλον μέλει ἢ τοῦ αὐτοῖς συμφόρου, is obscure in a different way. If it refers only to the action of the dicasteries in cases arising out of the leitourgiai, it is a natural thing for an oligarch to say, but it is obscurely expressed; if it refers to

2. 9–10: θυσίας δὲ καὶ ἱερὰ καὶ ἑορτὰς καὶ τεμένη γνοὺς ὁ δῆμος ὅτι οὐχ οἷόν τέ ἐστιν ἑκάστῳ τῶν πενήτων θύειν καὶ εὐωχεῖσθαι καὶ ⟨ἴσ⟩ασθαι ἱερὰ καὶ πόλιν οἰκεῖν καλὴν καὶ μεγάλην, ἐξηῦρεν ὅτῳ τρόπῳ ἔσται ταῦτα. θύουσιν οὖν δημοσίᾳ μὲν ἡ πόλις ἱερεῖα πολλά· ἔστι δὲ ὁ δῆμος ὁ εὐωχούμενος καὶ διαλαγχάνων τὰ ἱερεῖα. καὶ γυμνάσια καὶ λουτρά, κ. τ. λ. 1. 15 (see above, p. 215). And 1. 17 πρὸς δὲ τούτοις ὁ δῆμος τῶν Ἀθηναίων τάδε κερδαίνει τῶν δικῶν Ἀθήνησιν οὐσῶν τοῖς συμμάχοις· πρῶτον μὲν γὰρ ἡ ἑκατοστὴ τῇ πόλει πλείων ἡ ἐν Πειραιεῖ· ἔπειτα εἴ τῳ συνοικία ἐστίν, ἄμεινον πράττειν· ἔπειτα εἴ τῳ ζεῦγός ἐστιν ἢ ἀνδράποδον μισθοφοροῦν· ἔπειτα οἱ κήρυκες ἄμεινον πράττουσι διὰ τὰς ἐπιδημίας τὰς τῶν συμμάχων.

This is the oligarch's account of Athenian political ideas, ἰσονομία and ἐλευθερία, of the empire, of the festivals, of tragedy, comedy, and dithyramb, of the great temples: they mean nothing but the satisfying of the demos' greed, greed of belly and pocket, and petty greed at that. Democracy is all right, for there are many profitable little offices to fill; Sophokles is all right, because I can make something singing and dancing; the temples and the gymnasia are all right, because I can go into them for nothing; the navy's good, for I know how to handle an oar; and the empire's fine, it brings in money in lots of ways, an obol here, an obol there, it all helps. Truly a case of τὰ μεγάλα ταπεινὰ ποιεῖν. Does X do this consciously or unconsciously, because he had himself no feeling for music or fine building, any more than for ideas of order and freedom? He does not say: "What is the good of all this fine stuff or fine words? The demos does not appreciate it"; he implies that there is no fine stuff, that there are only *choregos* and *choregoumenos*, payer and payee, but no dramatist. (And he thereby tacitly attributes all the achievements of democratic Athens to Demos himself, to the masses, none to the individuals.) Compare with this Plutarch's account (*Perikles* 11. 4–142.). He follows in the main the oligarchic tradition; for him too the festivals, the buildings, the navy, the cleruchies are so much demagogy

dicasteries in general, it has no connexion with what precedes, and is a trite generalization, contradicted incidentally by 3. 7 διασκευάσασθαι ῥᾴδιον ἔσται πρὸς ὀλίγους δικαστὰς . . ., ⟨ὥστε⟩ πολὺ ἧττον δικαίως δικάζειν. (I prefer this emendation to Kalinka's πολὺ ἧττον ⟨δὲ⟩; it is less elegant, but more in the author's manner.)

— τῷ δήμῳ τὰς ἡνίας ἀνιεὶς ὁ Περικλῆς ἐπολιτεύετο πρὸς χάριν — to amuse the people and to give all a share in the profits (though they must do some work for their money); in particular it is the ἀσύντακτος καὶ βάναυσος ὄχλος who are the craftsmen who built the Parthenon and the Propylaia and made the statue of Athena herself. But Plutarch was a just and understanding man, though a poor historian: he says διαπαιδαγωγῶν ο ὐ κ ἀ μ ο ύ σ ο ι ς ἡδοναῖς τὴν πόλιν, he is eloquent when he describes the activities of the "crowd of vulgar," and in a few lines he has given us one of the best appreciations of the Akropolis buildings that have been written; while in the anecdote with which he ends the story of all this demagogy he agrees that the masses had some sense of its splendour — εἰπόντος οὖν ταῦτα τοῦ Περικλέους ("if you do not approve, let the expense be mine and the dedication") εἴτε τὴν μεγαλοφροσύνην αὐτοῦ θαυμάσαντες εἴτε πρὸς τὴν δόξαν ἀντιφιλοτιμούμενοι τῶν ἔργων, ἀνέκραγον κελεύοντες ἐκ τῶν δημοσίων ἀναλίσκειν καὶ χορηγεῖν μηδενὸς φειδόμενον. It seems almost absurd to pass from this to another comparison, with that other work in which we have an account of democratic Athens and her achievements — the Epitaphios of Perikles. Yet the comparison is interesting: two men, nearly contemporaries, describing the same thing, at opposite poles from each other. And Roscher, an eloquent admirer of Thucydides, yet thought that he and the writer of our pamphlet might be one and the same person.[1]

We shall not then, if we are wise, depend on X for the truth. He is an interesting writer (partly for this reason); but it is not his object to tell the truth. His object, at least in part, is τὰ μεγάλα ταπεινὰ ποιῆσαι, and to this (as is so often the case with realists) truth must be sacrificed. It is purposeless then to argue whether 2. 18 is or is not consistent with the *Knights*; he was quite capable of saying both before and after 424 that the demos will not allow itself to be mocked. It is true that ὁ δῆμος ἀδεῶς ζῇ and Thucydides II 65. 2 *unmöglich miteinander in Einklang zu bringen sind* (Instinsky p. 13); but why should we try? Thucydides was a different kind of writer. It would be just as true, and as irrelevant, to say that the whole work cannot be reconciled with λόγῳ μὲν δημοκ-

[1] Whether Thucydides is doing his best to describe Perikles' own Epitaphios or making up one of his own, does not affect the argument here.

ρατία, ἔργῳ δὲ ὑπὸ τοῦ πρώτου ἀνδρὸς ἀρχή, and therefore must have been written some time after Perikles' death. We must not say, with Kalinka, that because we read in 1. 2 ὁ δῆμος, ὁ ἐλαύνων τὰς ναῦς, the thetes therefore, πλέον ἔχει τῶν γενναίων καὶ τῶν πλουσίων, *es ist d a h e r völlig ausgeschlossen, dass die ersten drei Klassen mehr Bürger umfassten als die Theten*, as though we should give as much weight to X's words as to Thucydides. The kind of thing that he can say is διὰ τὴν κτῆσιν τὴν ἐν τοῖς ὑπερορίοις καὶ διὰ τὰς ἀρχὰς τὰς εἰς τὴν ὑπερορίαν λελήθασι μανθάνοντες ἐλαύνειν τῇ κώπῃ αὐτοί τε καὶ οἱ ἀκόλουθοι(1. 19): the careful planning and formation and training of the navy, the building of the docks and the fortification of the harbour — the whole policy of Themistokles and Perikles, aided as it was by Aristeides and Kimon — becomes the result of an accident: not a bad jest, but poor history for all that.[1] 1. 5 is typical: ἔστι δὲ πάσῃ γῇ τὸ βέλτιστον ἐναντίον τῇ δημοκρατίᾳ· ἐν γὰρ τοῖς βελτίστοις ἔνι ἀκολασία τε ὀλιγίστη καὶ ἀδικία, ἀκρίβεια δὲ πλείστη εἰς τὰ χρηστά, ἐν δὲ τῷ δήμῳ ἀμαθία τε πλείστη καὶ ἀταξία καὶ πονηρία.[2] The sophistic confusion of the ethical and political uses of πονηροί, κακοί, χρηστοί, βέλτιστοι, is common in our author (cf. 3. 10, a passage similar to this, 2. 19 φημὶ οὖν ἔγωγε τὸν δῆμον τὸν Ἀθήνησι γιγνώσκειν οἵτινες χρηστοί εἰσι τῶν πολιτῶν καὶ οἵτινες πονηροί, γιγνώσκοντες δὲ τοὺς μὲν σφίσιν αὐτοῖς ἐπιτηδείους καὶ συμφόρους φιλοῦσι, κ ἂ ν π ο ν η-ρ ο ὶ ὦ σ ι, τοὺς δὲ χρηστοὺς μισοῦσι μᾶλλον — cf. *Ach.* 595, quoted above —, 1. 6; 2. 20 δημοκρατίαν δ' ἐγὼ μὲν αὐτῷ τῷ δήμῳ συγγιγνώσκω· αὐτὸν μὲν γὰρ εὖ ποιεῖν παντὶ συγγνώμη ἐστίν· ὅστις δὲ μὴ ὢν τοῦ δήμου εἵλετο ἐν δημοκρατουμένῃ πόλει οἰκεῖν μᾶλλον ἢ ἐν ὀλιγαρχουμένῃ, ἀ δ ι κ ε ῖ ν παρεσκευάσατο καὶ ἔγνω ὅτι μᾶλλον οἷόν τε διαλαθεῖν κ α κ ῷ ὄντι ἐν δημοκρατουμένῃ πόλει ἢ ἐν ὀλιγαρχουμένῃ; yet, if it is right for a man to look after his own interests, why may not an aristocrat do well for himself by playing the δημαγωγός?);[3] a good Spartan,

---

[1] We may note that the thetes would not normally possess slaves: it is apparently the well-to-do who learn to row, — just as it was they who made money out of ἀνδράποδα μισθοφοροῦντα (1. 11, 17; above, pp. 214–15, 221).

[2] Rühl's and Kalinka's restoration of the next sentence, καὶ ἀμαθία ἡ δι' ἔνδειαν χρημάτων ἐνίοις τῶν ἀνθρώπων, is not possible. The Greek is too awkward even for this writer; and τοῖς πολλοῖς for ἐνίοις would be unavoidable.

[3] It is instructive to compare Thucydides' use of χρηστός and πονηρός, e.g. VI 53. 2.

such as Archidamos, would have had something different to say about the political effect of ἀμαθία (Thuc. I 84. 3), and Aristophanes found ἀκολασία more often among the young aristocrats than in the masses. If the opinion is right that X belonged to the extremist section of the oligarchs, prepared to surrender everything to Sparta if by that means the democracy were overthrown, the less must we be ready to believe what he says about the demos. The deeper the τομή between the parties, the less truth to be found in X.

Where, however, his political bias is not involved, his statements, and still more his implications, deserve more consideration. Instinsky, p. 33, argues that 2. 2–3, τοῖς μὲν κατὰ γῆν ἀρχομένοις οἷόν τ' ἐστιν ἐκ μικρῶν πόλεων συνοικισθέντας ἀθρόους μάχεσθαι· τοῖς δὲ κατὰ θάλατταν ἀρχομένοις, ὅσοι νησιῶταί εἰσιν, οὐχ οἷόν τε συνάρασθαι εἰς τὸ αὐτὸ τὰς πόλεις . . . .· ὁπόσαι δ' ἐν τῇ ἠπείρῳ εἰσὶ πόλεις ὑπὸ τῶν Ἀθηναίων ἀρχόμεναι, αἱ μὲν μεγάλαι διὰ δέος ἄρχονται, κ. τ. λ., cannot have been written after the successful synoecism in Olynthos in 432; and there is obviously something to be said for this. Certainly, if it was written in 430 or 425 or 415, in view of the long successful revolt of the Thraceward cities, it is inaccurate; and it is wrong to answer with Gelzer, p. 70: *soweit dieses Argument mit dem 'Synoikismos von Olynth' arbeitet, ist es hinfällig geworden, seitdem F. Hampl gezeigt hat, dass jenes ἀνοικίσασθαι ἐς Ὄλυνθον* (Thuc. I 58. 2) *gar kein staatsrechtlicher Synoikismos gewesen ist.* As though careful statement, a fine accuracy about constitutional detail were characteristic of X, and every word must be carefully considered. This passage then may be earlier than 432; and it is not likely that it was written soon after, when the successful revolt would be in everybody's mind. On the other hand to argue, as Gelzer does, p. 73, that 2. 1, τῶν συμμάχων . . . . κατὰ γῆν κράτιστοί εἰσιν, is inaccurate after the Athenian defeat at Spartolos in 429, is pedantic; the statement in general is true, and does not mean that Athenian troops could never meet with a reverse. So is 2. 5, the well-known paragraph on expeditions far afield, possible for those who control the seas, impossible for land-powers, which so many have thought could not have been written after Brasidas' expedition to Thrace in 424. Here Müller-Strübing's arguments are sound. It was true in the fifth century, in the fourth, and it has been true in all subsequent history, that land-powers find it impossible, in ordinary circumstances, to send distant expeditions and that sea-powers can; and the difficulties which Brasidas and succeeding commanders experienced (Thuc. IV 78–9, 132. 2, V 12–3) illustrate and do not contradict the statement in our author.[1] There is some exaggeration: fleets, especially fleets of triremes, cannot exactly "sail where they will"; they are not independent of the land; and armies occasionally make distant journeys; but in general the statement of the military position is true (note how the Athenians in 415 sailed along the coast of Italy "till they came to a friendly city"). The most that we can say, in view of Brasidas' brilliant successes, is that it was perhaps not written immediately after; a layman in particular might have been excused for thinking that the difficulties of land-powers had proved to be nonexistent; but it could have been written a few years later, for it was, in essence, true. Besides if the passage must be earlier than Brasidas, it should be earlier than Aristeus' expedition in 432 as well, and for that matter, than the Peloponnesian to Phokis and Boeotia in 457, when Athens controlled the Megarid and the Corinthian Gulf; the expedition of Xerxes too, as Kalinka notes, should have made X modify his statement.

A somewhat similar argument can be used about 2. 14–16. Gelzer, pp. 73–74, says: *Wir sahen schon, dass ὁ δὲ δῆμος . . . ἀδεῶς ζῆ καὶ οὐχ ὑπερχόμενος τοὺς πολεμίους nicht während der Pest geschrieben sein kann. Nach ihrem Weichen gewann der Demos das Gefühl der Immunität zwar bald wieder, wie Thukydides und die Komödie bezeugen, das ἀδεῶς ζῆ καὶ οὐχ ὑπερχόμενος traf also wieder zu wie im ersten Jahre des Krieges. Mit Instinsky (35) muss ich jedoch fragen: konnte nach der Pest die Preisgabe Attikas noch als die einzige Opfer bezeichnet werden (2. 16), das Athen seiner Festlandlage wegen auf sich nehmen musste?* The *Acharnians* does not exactly support the view that the demos (in our author's sense of the word) regained its feeling of immunity, nor that οἱ γεωργοῦντες

---

[1] Cf. Thuc. I 9. 4 (on the Trojan war), which implicitly confirms the same principle — only a sea-power could have led so large an expedition to so distant a country.

were ready to yield to the enemy; but I agree that even a cynic
like X could hardly have been indifferent to so tremendous a calam-
ity as the pestilence, and could hardly have represented the demos
as unaffected by it, and that in consequence this was probably not
written during or soon after it. But again it could have been written
as well after 421, or 418, when Athens had regained all her confidence, as before 430; all the lessons of the war had by then been
forgotten, and even the continued revolt of the Thraceward cities
was ignored (Thuc. VI 10. 5, 12. 1). There are other indications
of an early date (before 431), or one soon after 421: the apparently
peaceful trading (2. 7), the control of the trade in timber and
other raw materials valuable for a fleet against possible rivals
(οἵτινες ἀντίπαλοι ἡμῖν εἰσίν), not against enemies (2. 12);[1] the only
historical examples given to illustrate a point date from 447 or
earlier (3. 11: Athens did not support the πονηροί at Epidamnos
and Kerkyra in 433). I agree that the explanation of Athenian
strategy, 2. 16 ἐπειδὴ οὖν ἐξ ἀρχῆς οὐκ ἔτυχον οἰκήσαντες νῆσον, νῦν
τάδε ποιοῦσι· τὴν μὲν οὐσίαν κ. τ. λ. (above, p. 216), would be no news to
anyone in Greece in 425 or later, and would therefore seem to be
more natural if written in 431-0; on the other hand τάδε ποιοῦσι
should describe a regular practice, almost a habit, not a device
now used for the first time; and the apparent contentment with it
is in striking contrast with Thucydides' account of Athenian feelings in 431 (II 14-17).[2] But for whom anyhow was this written?
Not for the Spartans, who knew it well after 431; still less for

---

[1] The absence of all mention of the control of the corn supply, which was
much stricter in war-time, is also curious (especially after τὸν δὲ π λ ο ῦ τ ο ν
μόνοι οἷοί τ' εἰσίν ἔχειν τῶν Ἑλλήνων καὶ τῶν βαρβάρων: 2. 11).

The reading once more is corrupt; I do not believe that we can translate
ἄλλοσε ἄγειν, οἵτινες ἀντίπαλοι ἡμῖν εἰσίν "transport elsewhere than to us, that is,
to our rivals," though I agree that this is the general sense. Kalinka's ⟨ἤ⟩
οἵτινες . . . εἰσίν [ἤ] οὐ χρήσονται τῇ θαλάττῃ will not do; for ἤ would naturally
mean *than* after ἄλλοσε, and the subject of οὐ χρήσονται is of course the export-
ing states, not the rivals who would import. It is possible that we should read
ἄλλοσε ἄγειν οὐκ ἐάσουσιν ⟨ἤ⟩ οἵτινες ⟨οὐκ⟩ ἀντίπαλοι ἡμῖν εἰσίν, ἤ οὐ χρήσονται τῇ
θαλάττῃ.

[2] The passage does not actually imply that Athens was at war when it was
written: "as it is, in the event of war, this is what they do."

oligarchs in the subject cities, who knew it better, and who knew only too well such truth as there was in 1. 15, 16–18 (subjects compelled to come to Athens for law-suits), 2. 2–5 (advantages of a maritime empire), 2. 11–12 (Athenian control of sea-trading), 3. 5 (the four-yearly assessment of the tribute). It seems more probable on the face of it that the work was intended for Western Greeks, who had but a vague knowledge of conditions in the Aegean.[1]

There are other indications of an early date: 1. 13, the object of χορηγίαι, etc., is to supply the masses with pay and also ἵνα οἱ πλούσιοι πενέστεροι γίγνωνται; but it is curious that among the burdens of the rich X makes no mention of εἰσφορά, unless he were writing before its first imposition in 428. 1. 14, the persecution by Athens of the χρηστοί in the allied cities,[2] and her support of the πονηροί ("otherwise the people's empire would last very little time"[3]) — this would seem a mild description of the treatment of the allies after Poteidaia and Mytilene had been subdued, still more after the subjection of Skione and Melos; or was X a man who thought anything permissible in war? There is a clear relationship between this work and Perikles' two speeches (Thuc. I 140–4 and the Epitaphios: above, pp. 216, 222); if Thucydides (as I believe) records the substance of what Perikles said, this *may* be

---

[1] Busolt, p. 615. 3, has some sensible remarks on this question. It is absurd to suppose, after the plain statement in 1. 1, τἆλλα . . . ἃ δοκοῦσιν ἁμαρτάνειν τοῖς ἄλλοις Ἕλλησι, τοῦτ' ἀποδείξω, that X is simply replying to a speech of another Athenian oligarch (moderate or extremist).

[2] The simplest emendation of this passage gives, I am sure, the right sense: περὶ δὲ τῶν συμμάχων, ὅτι ἐκπλέοντες συκοφαντοῦσι καὶ διώκουσι καὶ μισοῦσι τοὺς χρηστούς, ⟨τοῦτο ποιοῦσι⟩ γιγνώσκοντες κ. τ. λ., leaving διὰ ταῦτ' οὖν to begin the next sentence, exactly as in 1. 1, 1. 12. The subject of ἐκπλέοντες is of course the Athenians, not the democrats in the allied cities, as Kalinka and Stail assume. The MSS have ὡς δοκοῦσι καὶ μισοῦσι after συκοφαντοῦσι, which is meaningless; but it is certainly difficult to see why καὶ διώκουσι should have been corrupted. Gelzer's καὶ καταδοκοῦσι (cf. Antiphon II 2. 3, 3. 7) is more ingenious than probable.

[3] Kalinka, p. 147, may be right that τοῦ δήμου τοῦ 'Αθήνησι here means the masses at Athens, not the Athenian state; but it does not follow that ἡ ἀρχή is their domination over the χρηστοί in Athens. It is obvious that in this context ἀρχή must mean the empire.

due to the fact that X was writing about the same time.[1] On the other hand 2. 17, the faithlessness of democracies to their sworn word (false as it is), if we are to allow it *any* truth, is more likely to have been written some time between 420 and 415, when Alkibiades and others were doing so much to upset the Peace of Nikias, than in 432–1 or soon after, when Sparta and Thebes were the treaty-breakers.[2] Meritt has suggested that 1. 16–17 (allies' law-suits at Athens) was written soon after 425–4 on account of *IG* I² 65. 49–50 (cf. also 3. 5 with 63. 26 ff.)[3]; but it clearly might be earlier — the Chalkis decree and Thuc. I 77. 1 would justify it sufficiently. The separation of the farmers and the demos (2. 14) has at least some truth in 421 which it had not before. The absence of all reference to ostracism as a means of oppressing the χρηστοί also makes for a late date; it practically fell into disuse after 443; and the fact that its last victim was Hyperbolos, a πονηρός, would explain why no mention was made of it, even if the work was written after 417. 3. 2, τὴν βουλὴν βουλεύεσθαι περὶ τ ο ῦ πολέμου, certainly implies that war was being waged when it was written; but as this was happening at all times between 450 and 413, except 445–0 and 439–3, it hardly helps.

The difficulty in dating the work is largely due to one cause: its academic, sophistic character. This has been stressed by most recent writers, especially by Kalinka (pp. 52–54). The argument is sound that if the object of a speech or essay is thought by some to be to urge a moderate policy on fellow-oligarchs, to be a restraining influence, by others to pour scorn on moderation and to advocate an extremist policy, we may be confident that it was neither; that is to say, that the author had no immediate practical aim. If it was a political pamphlet, it was addressed to fellow oligarchs, it was never "published,"[4] and there was no need for obscurity or

---

[1] So Schvarcz, *Die Demokratie von Athen*², 1901, pp. 231, 638 ff.: a work I only know from the reference in Instinsky, p. 7.

[2] Some have supposed a reference to the refusal of the Athenians to hand back the Spartan fleet at Pylos after the breakdown of the negotiations at Athens; but this does not, at any rate, illustrate X's point, for it was not an action by the ekklesia.

[3] *Doc. Ath. Trib.* 40–42.

[4] That it was not published is the most natural explanation of its appearance

vagueness in its purpose. It was not then a pamphlet, in this sense (as was, presumably, Andokides' Πρὸς τοὺς ἑταίρους); but neither is it simply a sophistic παίγνιον.[1] A παίγνιον was a *jeu d'esprit* intended for the display of *literary* merit — a nice arrangement of material, an effective style, with a careful rhythm and, according to taste, much or little use of rhetorical figures. This work has little or no pretension to literary merit, either in arrangement or style; it is not a display.[2] But it *is* meant to be clever; it is an essay maintaining a paradox, τὸν ἥττω λόγον κρείττω ποιῶν: "I, an Athenian oligarch, addressing oligarchs, yet will defend the democracy." The author's own political position is essential to the paradox; it has reality; that is why the essay is not simply a παίγνιον, a light work that might be written by a clever man of any political party or of none. Yet it has at the same time an academic air: it is throughout generalized. I am not referring to such γνῶμαι as αὐτὸν μὲν γὰρ εὖ ποιεῖν παντὶ συγγνώμη ἐστίν and ἐν οὐδεμιᾷ πόλει τὸ βέλτιστον εὔνουν ἐστὶ τῷ δήμῳ, ἀλλὰ τὸ κάκιστον ἐν ἑκάστῃ ἐστὶ πόλει εὔνουν τῷ δήμῳ· οἱ γὰρ ὅμοιοι τοῖς ὁμοίοις εὔνοοί εἰσι, but to the whole description of the πολιτεία. "The democracy is naturally preserved by allowing the πονηροί to counsel it"; "the empire is naturally preserved by supporting the πονηροί in the allied cities"; "the demos must get its pay, so it organizes liturgies and public works and the busy dicasteries"; the advantages of seapower in maintaining an empire; the one disadvantage — Athens is not an island (quite academically discussed); democracies can repudiate treaties. No examples are given to illustrate any of these matters, no name, no event mentioned. It is all kept on the plane of generalization. Then, in the second part (3. 1–8), we have a whole list of particulars, to explain the difficulties of getting business done quickly in Athens, which might almost come from a real Ἀθηναίων Πολιτεία;[3] and in 10–11, one of the two "notes" added

---

among Xenophon's works: Xenophon may have got possession of a copy, perhaps from his father if he too was of the oligarchic party, and kept it among his own papers. [1] Gelzer has argued this point well.

[2] ἀποδείξω, 1. 1, and ἐπέδειξα, 3. 1, are not used in the rhetorical sense (any more than Herodotos' ἀπόδεξις), but mean only "explain," "set forth."

[3] We must surely suppose a lacuna in 3. 8 after ἐγὼ μὲν τίθημι ἴσας τῇ ὀλιγίσ-

after the argument is finished, we at last get real examples, to illustrate the point that Athens has never benefited by supporting τοὺς βελτίστους in other states; but all from earlier history.[1] For much

---

τας ἀγούσῃ πόλει. ⟨ἀλλ' οὐδὲ οὕτως ἐξείη ἂν αὐτόθι πᾶσιν ἀνθρώποις χρηματίσας⟩, or the like. I should prefer an even longer one; for the next sentence, τούτων τοίνυν τοιούτων ὄντων, is a summary of the whole matter of the essay, with no immediate reference to the congestion of business in the boule and dikasteria; but that such abruptness is characteristic of X.

[1] If καὶ τοῦτό μ ο ι is kept in 3. 10 *init.*, it is not only the only instance (in spite of κ α ὶ τοῦτο) in which the author joins in the blame, but would make him stand completely apart from Athens in this case; for it is the state, not the masses, which suffered when it supported the "better side," especially in the last of the three instances.

The first example, ἐντὸς ὀλίγου χρόνου ὁ δῆμος ἐδούλευσεν ὁ ἐν Βοιωτοῖς (so Kalinka: ὁ μὲν *AM*, τοῦτο μὲν *C*: ἐν Madvig: ὁ μὲν ἐν Gelzer: perhaps τοῦτο μὲν ἐν) has not been adequately explained. Kalinka says that after Oinophyta the ruling oligarchies were overthrown and democracies set up with Athenian help; these however proved so incompetent that they were overthrown, at least in Thebes (Ar. *Pol.* V 2. 6). The oligarchs then engineered a general revolt against Athens; and as a consequence of Athens making a treaty with them after Koroneia the whole democratic, pro-Athenian movement in Boeotia was suppressed. This is a reasonable view of events; but it is far-fetched to call the treaty after Koroneia "an attempt by Athens to support the oligarchic side in a city suffering from civil war"; and the "enslavement" of the Boeotian demos was not a disaster for Athens comparable to the other two instances given. What we expect, in fact, is a direct reference to Koroneia. We must suppose, if X is truthful, that after the overthrow of the democracies (well before 447) Athens tried to work with the oligarchs, but that the only result was the enslavement of the masses *and* the consequent destruction of Athenian power in Boeotia, now that it had no internal support. Whether for this we need to assume another lacuna in the text is uncertain. Other reconstructions depend on the statement in Diodoros (XI 83. 1) that Thebes remained free after Oinophyta; but Diodoros' whole narrative of the campaign is muddled, and it is difficult to believe that Thebes maintained any real independence during the years that Athens dominated the rest of Boeotia.

Why does X instance the revolt of Miletos, not that of Samos, which was presumably a more recent and certainly a more important event, and better illustrated his point?

For the third example, it is interesting to note that another oligarch, an extremist, also criticized Kimon's readiness to support Sparta against the helots — "he put Spartan interests before those of Athens" (Kritias *ap.* Plut. *Kim.* 16. 9). But we do not know the context.

the greater part we never get away from the theoretic tone; and this is particularly noticeable in the section on "If Athens had been an island," where many scholars have thought to find the author's practical aims — the advice to his party to open the gates to the enemy, or the complaint to Sparta that she has done nothing to help her friends in Athens. It is this tone which gives almost an air of unreality to the essay (and explains why scholars before Roscher could think it a work of the fourth century and later ones should be so divided as to its purpose). The author's intention is not to write a παίγνιον, but to explain (to foreigners, I am sure) the consistency and therefore the strength of Athenian policy: "Everybody looks after his own interests, and the Athenian masses have secured theirs; hence the democracy, with anybody and everybody allowed to advise and the πονηροί in control; hence the fleet, for it is the masses who man it; hence the empire and all its advantages — they control it in this way and that"; but in doing this he is above all glad to show himself a clever essayist, to be supporting a paradox. In a sense he is objective, realistic (though not in the least impartial): a foreigner, an aristocrat, with some experience of public affairs in Athens (and in Sparta), had asked of his Athenian friends, "How can you possibly tolerate such a state of affairs? We understand a democracy, at least in theory; but this one, with such scum in control! Why allow the sailors all the influence instead of the hoplites? Why don't the people choose respectable leaders? And can such a constitution not only survive, but make the city strong enough to defy its enemies and control an empire? Why don't the decent people overthrow it, and the subject-cities break away?" "You don't understand the position," is the answer; "of course the πονηροί like having πονηροί as their leaders; they carry out their policy consistently; and their strength lies in the fleet, manned by them, not in the hoplites, and a fleet is all-powerful (and secures us all manner of comforts and luxuries besides)."[1] With a little more candour, if he had been really objective, he would have added that in the fleet the training and skill

---

[1] X is not, like Plato, averse to the material advantages of Athens' unique position (so Kalinka 61; Gelzer 76–79).

reached a higher level than among the hoplites, and probably the
discipline was better, ἀταξία (cf. 1. 5, quoted above, p. 223) commoner in the hoplite ranks and certainly in the cavalry[1] — about
which spoilt children of Athens, with their place of honour on the
Parthenon frieze, X is strangely silent. He would have confessed
that since the strategia was normally held by the χρηστοί (1. 3), to
that extent at least they and not the πονηροί were responsible for
Athenian policy; and he must have been conscious that in effect
1. 4, πλέον νέμουσι τοῖς πονηροῖς . . . ἢ τοῖς χρηστοῖς, and 3. 13, ὁ δῆμός
ἐστιν ὁ ἄρχων τὰς ἀρχάς, are quite inconsistent with 1. 3, and that
the strategoi, trierarchs and ambassadors[2] who "sailed out" (1. 18)
will have had some influence on the treatment of subject-allies
(1. 14, τοὺς μὲν χρηστοὺς ἀτιμοῦσι . . . ., τοὺς δὲ πονηροὺς αὔξουσιν· οἱ
δὲ χρηστοὶ Ἀθηναίων τοὺς χρηστοὺς ἐν ταῖς συμμαχίσι πόλεσι σώζουσι).
But he does not do anything of the kind: not only because he is
not really objective, nor in the least impartial, but because he has

---

[1] Xenophon professes to give a conversation on the subject of discipline
between Sokrates and the younger Perikles in 407–6 (*Mem.* III 5. 1, 18–19):
Μηδαμῶς . . . ὦ Περίκλεις οὕτως ἡγοῦ ἀνηκέστῳ πονηρίᾳ νοσεῖν Ἀθηναίους. οὐχ ὁρᾷς, ὡς
εὔτακτοι μέν εἰσιν ἐν τοῖς ναυτικοῖς, εὐτάκτως δ' ἐν τοῖς γυμνικοῖς ἀγῶσι πείθονται τοῖς
ἐπιστάταις, οὐδένων δὲ καταδεέστερον ἐν τοῖς χοροῖς ὑπηρετοῦσι τοῖς διδασκάλοις; Τοῦτο
γάρ τοι, ἔφη, καὶ θαυμαστόν ἐστι, τὸ τοὺς μὲν τοιούτους πειθαρχεῖν τοῖς ἐφεστῶσι, τοὺς
δὲ ὁπλίτας καὶ τοὺς ἱππέας, οἳ δοκοῦσι καλοκαγαθίᾳ προκεκρίσθαι τῶν πολιτῶν, ἀπει-
θεστάτους εἶναι πάντων.　As however Sokrates attributes the indiscipline to a
carelessness which is the result of long-continued success (13), in spite of the
previous mention of Koroneia and Delion (4), the circumstances of the conversation are quite unreal. But Xenophon may have remembered something
of what was said of the hoplites in the Peloponnesian war; or he may be
thinking only of conditions in the fourth century. In fact, we do not in
Thucydides read of any great indiscipline in the hoplite ranks, except at
Amphipolis in 422 (V 7. 2, 10. 6); the Athenians, if not quite so good
as the Spartans and the Boeotians, were at least the equals of the ordinary
Peloponnesians.

[2] Kalinka has a solemn note here: 1. 18 shows that ambassadors, like strategoi and trierarchs, were chosen from among the χρηστοί; and in view of 1. 3,
where paid posts are said to be reserved for the demos, he would not like to
say that πρέσβεις were paid their expenses — Ar. *Ach.* 65 f. was an exceptional
case, and *Ach.* 602, ἐπὶ Θρᾴκης μισθοφοροῦντας τρεῖς (!) δραχμάς geht nicht auf
πρέσβεις, sondern auf Strategen. A good example of how not to treat the evidence of X and of comedy.

caught the sophist's trick of generalization — οἱ μὲν γὰρ πένητες καὶ οἱ δημόται καὶ οἱ χείρους εὖ πράττοντες καὶ πολλοὶ οἱ τοιοῦτοι γιγνόμενοι τὴν δημοκρατίαν αὔξουσιν· ἐὰν δὲ εὖ πράττωσιν οἱ πλούσιοι καὶ οἱ χρηστοί, ἰσχυρὸν τὸ ἐναντίον σφίσιν αὐτοῖς καθιστᾶσιν οἱ δημοτικοί . . . . . εἰ μὲν γὰρ οἱ χρηστοὶ ἔλεγον καὶ ἐβουλεύοντο, τοῖς ὁμοίοις σφίσιν αὐτοῖς ἦν ἀγαθά, τοῖς δὲ δημοτικοῖς οὐκ ἀγαθά· νῦν δὲ λέγων ὁ βουλόμενος ἀναστὰς ἄνθρωπος πονηρὸς ἐξευρίσκει τὸ ἀγαθὸν αὐτῷ τε καὶ τοῖς ὁμοίοις αὐτῷ. εἴποι τις ἄν, Τί ἂν οὖν γνοίη ἀγαθὸν αὐτῷ ἢ τῷ δήμῳ τοιοῦτος ἄνθρωπος; οἳ δὲ γιγνώσκουσιν ὅτι ἡ τούτου ἀμαθία καὶ πονηρία καὶ εὔνοια μᾶλλον λυσιτελεῖ ἢ ἡ τοῦ χρηστοῦ ἀρετὴ καὶ σοφία καὶ κακόνοια. (1. 4, 6–7.) And so on. Such things are trite, not based on fresh observation or independent judgement.

X was not however himself a sophist. This is clear from the want of logical arrangement and the poor literary style of the essay. It has been the custom recently to praise the arrangement of material; for Gelzer the work (with the exception of 3. 10–13, admittedly a couple of additional notes not properly worked in) is *ein planmässig componiertes Ganzes* (p. 53). This is to exaggerate. Busolt (p. 612) judged better: *Nach einer noch ziemlich zusammenhängenden Behandlung des ersten Punktes, der inneren und Reichspolitik des Demos, und einer darauf folgenden breiteren Schilderung der Vorteile der Seeherrschaft tritt eine völlige Lockerung des Gefüges ein. Die einzelne Glieder der Darlegung stehen in der Regel ohne innere Verknüpfung nebeneinander, und der Uebergang ist nur äusserlich dadurch markiert, dass ein Stichwort oder weiterer Tadel an der Spitze des neuen Abschnittes erscheint (1. 10, 14, 2. 1, 9, u.s.w.).* But even this is flattering. As far as 1. 12 the order is good; for though the freedom and luxury enjoyed by the slaves and metics is not strictly relevant, it is an excellent point — so much do the πονηροί rule the roost in Athens that even metics and slaves are protected and cosseted: "in fact, you cannot distinguish between demos and slaves." But 1. 13, τοὺς δὲ γυμναζομένους, κ. τ. λ. whether referring only to metics or to citizens, introduces suddenly a new matter which does not follow from what has been said, nor connect with what comes after; within 1. 13 the Athenian attitude to χορηγίαι, etc., has nothing to do with the suppression of τοὺς γυμναζομένους καὶ τὴν μουσικὴν ἐπιτηδεύοντας, it belongs rather to

1. 3–4;[1] and the last sentence is only tacked on.[2] 2. 9–10 also belongs logically to 1. 13 and so to 1. 4; and 2. 11 would more naturally follow 2. 8, 3. 10–11 should follow 1. 14, and 3. 12–13 belongs, if anywhere, to 2. 19–20. In 3. 2–8 there is complete confusion of the functions of boule and dikasteria, between δικάζειν and διαδικάζειν. Even where we can see the connexion the logical structure is everywhere loose (quite apart from the false reasoning and the exaggeration), quite unlike the work of a practised sophist.[3] *Dieser mangelhaften Komposition entspricht der nicht bloss kunstlose, sondern auch lässige Stil.*[4] X has little idea of expressing connexion except by ἔπειτα . . . ἔπειτα,[5] πρὸς δὲ τούτοις, or ἐπὶ δὲ καί. He has tiresome repetition of words: so in the opening sentence ὅτι μὲν τοῦτο οὐκ ἐπαινῶ, and throughout; in 2. 14–16 he has εἰ νῆσον ᾤκουν or νῆσον οἰκοῦντες six times, θαλασσοκράτορες, ἕως τῆς θαλάττης ἦρχον and πιστεύοντες τῇ ἀρχῇ τῇ κατὰ θάλατταν, and in 15 μηδ᾽ αὖ στασιάσαι τῷ δήμῳ μηδέν, εἰ νῆσον ᾤκουν· νῦν μὲν γὰρ εἰ στασιάσαιεν, ἐλπίδα ἂν ἔχοντες ἐν τοῖς πολεμίοις στασιάσαιεν ὡς κατὰ γῆν ἐπαξόμενοι. In 2. 18 he has κωμῳδεῖν four times; in 3. 2 πολλὰ μέν followed by πολλὰ δέ four times in very short clauses.[6] His antitheses are equally simple: ἡ τούτου ἀμαθία καὶ πονηρία καὶ εὔνοια μᾶλλον λυσιτελεῖ ἢ ἡ τοῦ

---

[1] Kupferschmid, p. 34, emends to ἐν ταῖς χορηγίαις ⟨δ᾽⟩ αὖ, as 1. 10; which is an improvement, but it does not make the order more logical.

[2] See above, p. 220 n. 2.

[3] Kirchhoff saw these illogicalities most clearly, but his re-writing of the whole work has convinced nobody. At the same time, since we should most naturally suppose that the survival of the essay "among Xenophon's papers" means that it was not published before, perhaps, Alexandrian times, we must not exclude the possibility that it is only a fragment, or a rough draft, or even that the text has been disturbed.

[4] Busolt 612. Müller-Strübing's *der saloppe, durchaus banausische Stil* is not too strong.

[5] Note especially 2. 8, where we expect ἔπειτα to introduce another *advantage* of sea-power, but it does not, but only an irrelevance (the mixed dialect of Athens); and 1. 3 *init.*

[6] 2. 17 ἂν μέν τι κακὸν ἀναβαίνῃ ἀπὸ ὧν ὁ δῆμος ἐβούλευσεν, αἰτιᾶται ὁ δῆμος, κ. τ. λ.: *gewiss nicht ohne Absicht . . . wiederholt*, to make it plain that it is the same demos that votes and then grumbles — Kalinka, p. 242. That does not make it less clumsy. In 2. 20 the third μᾶλλον, which Kalinka keeps, should perhaps be bracketed.

χρηστοῦ ἀρετὴ καὶ σοφία καὶ κακόνοια.[1] There is a childlike naiveté of style which is in curious contrast with the adult cynicism of thought. But there is clumsiness as well as naiveté: 3. 8, πολὺ δ' οὐχ οἷόν τε μετακινεῖν ὥ σ τ ε μ ὴ ο ὐ χ ὶ τῆς δημοκρατίας ἀφαιρεῖν τι, followed by ὥστε μὲν γὰρ βέλτιον ἔχειν τὴν πολιτείαν, οἷόν τε πολλὰ ἐξευρεῖν· ὥστε μέντοι ὑπάρχειν μὲν δημοκρατίαν εἶναι, ἀρκούντως δὲ τοῦτο ἐξευρεῖν ὅπως βέλτιον πολιτεύσονται, οὐ ῥᾴδιον. We all know that ὁ δῆμος is often found with a plural verb; but no other example can be found quite like 2. 17: ἄσσα δ' ἂν ὁ δῆμος σύνθηται, ἔξεστιν αὐτῷ ἑνὶ ἀνατιθέντι τὴν αἰτίαν τῷ λέγοντι καὶ τῷ ἐπιψηφίσαντι, ἀρνεῖσθαι τοῖς ἄλλοις — so far good: Thucydides would have allowed himself this freedom; then — ὅτι οὐ παρῆν οὐδὲ ἀρέσκει οἱ, εἴ γε μὴ συγκείμενα πυνθάνονται ἐν πλήρει τῷ δήμῳ·[2] καὶ εἰ μὴ δόξαι εἶναι ταῦτα, προφάσεις μυρίας ἐξηύρηκε τοῦ μὴ ποιεῖν ὅσα ἂν μὴ βούλωνται. *That* simply causes confusion. A more practised hand would not have written πάσχειν δὲ μηδέν, ἕως τῆς θαλάττης ἦρχον, μηδὲ τμηθῆναι τὴν ἑαυτῶν γῆν μηδὲ προσδέχεσθαι τοὺς πολεμίους (2. 14); for the μηδέ . . . μηδέ clauses illustrate μηδὲν πάσχειν, they are not additional to it.[3] At his best X

---

[1] 1.7. Müller-Strübing's ἄνοια for εὔνοια would be an excellent suggestion, but that it is beyond the reach of our author. Thucydides might have had it (cf. VI 76. 4 οὐκ ἀξυνετωτέρου κακοξυνετωτέρου δέ); but then how differently he would have written the whole sentence.

[2] See above, p. 215 n. 1.

[3] There is however no need to add to the inelegance by the conjecture οἴεσθαι ⟨χρὴ⟩ χρῆναι 3. 5, instead of reading οἴεσθε, even though we have just below ὁμολογεῖ⟨ν⟩ δεῖ[ν] ἅπαντα χρῆναι and οἴεσθαι χρὴ καὶ ἑορτὰς ἄγειν χρῆναι. Nor do I believe that X, or anyone else, would write in consecutive sentences, 2. 19–20, ὄντες ὡς ἀληθῶς τοῦ δήμου and μὴ ὢν τοῦ δήμου to describe the same class of persons, as modern critics, with the exception of Kupferschmid (p. 49. 3), have supposed; the more particularly as in the first sentence (καὶ τοὐναντίον γε τούτου ἔνιοι ὄντες ὡς ἀληθῶς τοῦ δήμου τὴν φύσιν οὐ δημοτικοί εἰσι), with this interpretation καὶ τοὐναντίον γε has no meaning. We must transpose this to the end of 20, and the contrast is between these men of democratic origin who are not democratic by nature and the aristocrats who prefer a democracy. It is just a short note added by way of completing the picture, like that about metics in 1. 12. There is no difficulty about τὴν φύσιν: Gelzer, p. 33 n., says, *Wohl kann φύσις die Naturanlage bezeichnen, vgl. im besonderen Plut. Per. 7. 3, aber nur im Bunde, niemals im Gegensatz zur Herkunft.* But Sophokles wrote

ἀλλ' εὐγενὴς γὰρ ἡ φύσις κἀξ εὐγενῶν
ὦ τέκνον, ἡ σή· (*Phil.* 874–5)

achieves a certain Aristotelian brevity, as in 2. 5–6,[1] 12; once he attempts eloquence, with a rhetorical figure and a slight, very slight μεταβολή, variation: 2. 11, εἰ γάρ τις πόλις πλουτεῖ ξύλοις ναυπηγησίμοις, ποῖ διαθήσεται, ἐὰν μὴ πείσῃ τοὺς ἄρχοντας τῆς θαλάττης; τί δ'; εἴ τις σιδήρῳ ἢ χαλκῷ ἢ λίνῳ πλουτεῖ πόλις, ποῖ διαθήσεται, ἐὰν μὴ πείσῃ τὸν ἄρχοντα τῆς θαλάττης, ἐξ αὐτῶν μέντοι τούτων καὶ δὴ νῆές μοί εἰσι, παρὰ μὲν τοῦ ξύλα, παρὰ δὲ τοῦ σίδηρος, παρὰ δὲ τοῦ χαλκός, παρὰ δὲ τοῦ λίνον, παρὰ δὲ τοῦ κηρός. Our ears would have liked less of παρὰ δὲ τοῦ; but ἐξ αὐτῶν μέντοι τούτων καὶ δὴ νῆές μοι εἰσί, if a little crude, is lively — "we rule the seas, so we can get as much timber, etc., as we like; we get the timber, etc., and there are our ships by which we rule the seas."

Whether X purposely adopted his direct, plebeian style, that is, consciously avoided the rhetorical figures, the μεταβολή, and the rhythm of contemporary writers, or no, the result is not a success. It is usual to attribute both the looseness of structure — the poor logical order — and the inelegant style to the fact that this is so early an example of Attic prose: we must not expect the orderly arrangement of material nor the developed style that was the result of the sophists' labours.[2] But why not an orderly arrangement of material? Apart from the question of the relative dates of Attic prose writings — whether much of Thucydides and of Antiphon is not earlier than this essay — Herodotos, though using a λέξις εἰρομένη, does not show this want of order; compare especially *his* short essay on constitutions, III 80–82; nor does Aeschylus, nor Sophokles; Euripides in 431 was already a master of ῥητορική, both in arrangement and style. Our author could not manage this,

---

could not a man have said ἀλλ' εὐγενής σοι ἡ φύσις εἰ καὶ μὴ ἐξ εὐγενῶν γέγονας? Besides it is not clear that τὴν φύσιν here is to be taken with οὐ δημοτικοί, and not with ὄντες τοῦ δήμου. Here δημοτικός has a more definitely political colouring— "democratically-minded"—than in Plut. *Per.* or in Ar. 'Αθπ. 16. 8 (Peisistratos δημοτικὸς τῷ ἤθει, genial, sympathetic, not proud and reserved like Perikles).

[1] It is a mistake, I think, to assume a lacuna in the last line, ὥστε ἐκ τῆς εὐθενούσης ἀφικνεῖται τοῖς τῆς θαλάττης ἄρχουσιν. The meaning is clear in the context. If we must insert something, Müller-Strübing's ἀφ⟨θονία ὧν δεόνται ἀφ⟩ικνεῖται or ἄφθονα τὰ ἐπιτήδεια ἀφ. will do best.

[2] See especially Drerup's discussion. It ignores our author's lack of skill, which is individual to him.

and did not care to try, notwithstanding the little bit of rhetoric in 2. 11; and the reason is not his date, nor because he was writing prose and not verse, Attic and not Ionic, but because he was not the man to do it. A Greek did not have to write like Isokrates in order to write well. His value has been exaggerated, greatly exaggerated as evidence for history, but also for his place in the development of Attic prose.[1]

Yet his essay is interesting to the historian, not so much for what he asserts — for much of that is commonplace abuse of democracy — as for what he implies. This is worth examining; and it will perhaps also give us our best indication of his date. He ends with the detached note on the chances of internal revolution: the foreigner might well ask, "Why is no attempt made to overthrow the democracy by force? There must be numerous ἄτιμοι in Athens."
ὑπολάβοι δέ τις ἂν ὡς οὐδεὶς ἄρα ἀδίκως ἠτίμωται Ἀθήνησιν. ἐγὼ δέ φημί τινας εἶναι οἳ ἀδίκως ἠτίμωνται, ὀλίγοι μέντοι τινές. ἀλλ᾽ οὐκ ὀλίγων δεῖ τῶν ἐπιθησομένων τῇ δημοκρατίᾳ τῇ Ἀθήνησιν, ἐπεί τοι καὶ οὕτως ἔχει οὐδὲν ἐνθυμεῖσθαι ἀνθρώπους οἵτινες δικαίως ἠτίμωνται, ἀλλ᾽ εἴ τινες ἀδίκως. πῶς ἂν οὖν ἀδίκως οἴοιτό τις ἂν τοὺς πολλοὺς ἠτιμῶσθαι Ἀθήνησιν, ὅπου ὁ δῆμός ἐστιν ὁ ἄρχων τὰς ἀρχάς, ἐκ δὲ τοῦ μὴ δικαίως ἄρχειν μηδὲ λέγειν τὰ δίκαια ⟨μηδὲ τὰ δίκαια⟩ πράττειν, ἐκ τοιούτων ἄτιμοί εἰσιν Ἀθήνησι; ταῦτα χρὴ λογιζόμενον μὴ νομίζειν εἶναί τι δεινὸν ἀπὸ τῶν ἀτίμων Ἀθήνησιν.[2] I am not concerned with the reason for the lack of men of the true revolutionary spirit, πῶς ἂν οὖν ἀδίκως, κ. τ. λ., except

---

[1] The use of the word ῥήτωρ in our MSS in the title of course means nothing but that the work is an essay or a speech, a λόγος, not narrative history. Xenophon was a ῥήτωρ in respect of his *Agesilaos*, an enkomion, just like Theopompos (cf. Theopompos, J. 115 F 255).

[2] No really satisfactory interpretation of ἐπεί τοι καί, κ. τ. λ. has been given, but I believe the usual one, "those that have been rightly (or legally) made ἄτιμοι do not bear it in mind," i.e. do not bear a permanent grudge, will stand. Bergk's ⟨τοὺς⟩ ἀνθρώπους, "public opinion does not mind about those rightly made ἄτιμοι," i.e. only those who have suffered unjustly will have public opinion on their side, seems out of place in the context. The fact that the ordinary interpretation is contradicted in Lysias, 25. 11, is of no consequence; for it is only a piece of sophistic reasoning.

The whole paragraph is a good instance of the banausic style: note the repeated Ἀθήνησιν; and once more the use of μηδέ — cf. above, p. 235, here for ἢ μή or καὶ μή (for μὴ δικαίως = ἀδίκως).

just to note the usual cause of ἀτιμία in Athens: the normal punishment of an office-holder both for failure to obey a lawful order and for ill-success was a fine;[1] and until the fine was paid, a man was ἄτιμος (in respect of all or of some citizen rights). This class of ἄτιμοι, who might be fairly numerous at any one time, were not potential revolutionaries; they were ordinary citizens temporarily out of favour. X is thinking of oligarchs; for him ὁ ἀδίκως ἠτιμωμένος would be a man disfranchised, probably exiled, for oligarchic action (for action, that is, according to his own confession, 1. 6–7, disloyal to the state). Of these, he says, there were very few.

This admission, coming from such a source, is one of the best tributes we have to the Athenian democracy, and a cause of its preservation (ὡς εὖ διασῴζονται τὴν πολιτείαν) far more important than any mentioned in this essay. The success of a constitution after a radical change (whether made peacefully or violently) depends on the willingness of all classes to work it, unless of course all but one class is exterminated. In Athens all classes were prepared to work the constitution of Kleisthenes; even if Berve is right that Miltiades and others regarded themselves and were regarded by their followers as "princely persons" outside of the constitution, this is certainly true after 490. When Aristotle says that before Kleon all the προστάται τοῦ δήμου had been ἐπιεικεῖς, he is making a tendentious statement, but one that illustrates this point. When he gives his list of pairs of leaders, of the demos and of the γνώριμοι ('Ἀθπ. 28. 2–3), a superficial reading suggests either a regular two-party system or a permanent cleavage in the state between the masses and the few;[2] neither conclusion would be right.

---

[1] *IG* I² 63 gives good examples from this period.

[2] I believe, as Aristotle is giving *pairs* of leaders (note especially καὶ τούτῳ μὲν οὐδεὶς ἦν ἀντιστασιώτης ὡς ἐξέπεσον οἱ περὶ τὸν Ἰσαγόραν), that when he says ἔπειτα Θεμιστοκλῆς καὶ Ἀριστείδης, he means that the former was προστάτης τοῦ δήμου, the latter τῶν γνωρίμων, according to the conventional picture; that this is inconsistent with 23. 3 and 24. 3 (as well as with the facts) is not, unfortunately, proof that it is not the correct interpretation. For the same reason I am inclined to think that just above, πρῶτος ἐγένετο προστάτης τοῦ δήμου Σόλων, δεύτερος δὲ Πεισίστρατος τῶν εὐγενῶν καὶ γνωρίμων, we should emend not simply to τ. εὐγ. ⟨ὄντες⟩, but τῶν ⟨δὲ⟩ εὐγ. καὶ γν. ⟨Λυκοῦργος⟩, or ⟨Λ. καὶ Μεγακλῆς⟩; or perhaps τῶν εὐγ. ὄντες, τῶν δὲ γν. Λ. καὶ Μ.

In fact Aristeides and Themistokles, personal rivals, worked together, both during the war and immediately after and in the
formation of the League; perhaps also (if Ἀθπ. 24 is at all to be
believed) in strengthening the democracy. There was not nearly
so much difference between the policies of Kimon and Perikles as
the later conventional history depicted. Kimon was as much an
imperialist, and opposed all weakening of the bonds of the League;
Perikles supported the war with Persia, at least till 454, if not till
449.[1] If Kimon was for peace and alliance with Sparta, there is no
reason to suppose that Perikles was against this — all that we can
reasonably assert is that he saw more clearly than Kimon, or saw
after 446, that, if the empire was to be preserved, the danger was
now from the Peloponnese and no longer from Persia, and took
measures accordingly.[2] Of Thucydides, son of Melesias, it is harder
to form an opinion, for Plutarch is our only evidence: ἦν μὲν γὰρ ἐξ
ἀρχῆς διπλόη τις ὕπουλος ὥσπερ ἐν σιδήρῳ διαφορὰν ὑποσημαίνουσα δημο-
τικῆς καὶ ἀριστοκρατικῆς προαιρέσεως, ἡ δ' ἐκείνων ἅμιλλα καὶ φιλοτιμία
τῶν ἀνδρῶν βαθυτάτην τομὴν τεμοῦσα τῆς πόλεως τὸ μὲν δῆμον τὸ δ' ὀλίγους
ἐποίησε καλεῖσθαι (*Per.* 11. 3). However much exaggerated this may
be (and we must remember that the demos was suspicious of
treason before Tanagra — not, be it noted, afterwards, in spite of
the defeat), Plutarch's narrative suggests that Thucydides' opposition to Perikles was factious and unyielding, and there could be
no question of co-operation. (It is interesting to observe that this
oligarch was the first Athenian to take the part of professional
politician, not a soldier as well — Phokion's ideal — and not holding responsible office.) But though that cleavage may have been
deep, it was short-lived; it ended with Thucydides' ostracism, and

---

[1] If objection is made that we do not know that Perikles *actively* supported
the war or whether he was very influential in the fifties, that is true but only
of biographical interest. What is important is that there was little change in
Athenian policy after the ostracism of Kimon.

[2] Wilamowitz, *A. und A.* I 171. 72, says of our author: *er will belehren, aus
seiner erfahrung seinen leuten die richtschnur für ihr handeln geben "conspirirt
nicht wider den demos, es nützt nichts. transigirt nicht mit dem demos: der kann
nur die canaille brauchen"* . . . *das ist einer der* γνώριμοι, *wie sie bei Tanagra
ihre loyalität mit dem blute besiegelt haben.* The loyalty of Kimon at least was
not at all of this negative sort. Cf. Plato *Gorg.* 519A.

Perikles afterwards had only to face the inevitable personal attacks of envy and malice. After his death Kleon and Nikias are the rival pair, and there was no love lost between them; but the latter was as loyal to the demos, and each in his own way did his best to win the war — there was only, in essentials, one policy. The other γνώριμοι, Laches, Eurymedon, Nikostratos, Hippokrates, and the rest, were equally loyal, actively loyal. The hoplites of course were patriotic citizens and good democrats, for the majority of them belonged to the demos;[1] but the cavalry too were patriotic (as a body; naturally we know little of the sentiments of individuals), as we learn from Thucydides and from the *Knights*. There was no considerable body of opinion that was either opposed to the empire or in favour of a weak peace with Sparta. Nevertheless with the predominance of Kleon in the ekklesia, we see signs of a real cleavage: ἀσμένοις δ' ὅμως ἐγίγνετο τοῖς σώφροσι τῶν ἀνθρώπων, λογιζομένοις δυοῖν ἀγαθοῖν τοῦ ἑτέρου τεύξεσθαι, ἢ Κλέωνος ἀπαλλαγήσεσθαι, ὃ μᾶλλον ἤλπιζον ("expected," of course, not "hoped for"), ἢ σφαλεῖσι γνώμης Λακεδαιμονίους σφίσι χειρώσεσθαι. Thucydides was biased against Kleon, and he may be a little exaggerating here — the number of such σώφρονες (of all classes) may have been small.

---

[1] It is perhaps worth quoting Kalinka (p. 174) on τὸ δὲ ὁπλιτικὸν αὐτοῖς, ὃ ἥκιστα δοκεῖ εὖ ἔχειν ᾿Αθήνησιν (2. 1): *Das Urteil, dass in Athen nichts so schlimm bestellt sei wie τὸ ὁπλιτικόν, mag übertrieben sein; eine Ironie darin zu suchen sind wir um so weniger berechtigt, als es gerade die Gesinnungsgenossen des Sprechers, die Angehörigen der drei oberen Schatzungsklassen waren, aus denen sich die Hopliten ergänzten. So unbegreiflich es uns erscheint, dass der athenische Adel sich beim Bewusstsein seiner militärischen Minderwertigkeit beruhigte, es lag für ihn offenbar eine tiefe Befriedigung in dem unpatriotischen Gedanken, der nirgends sonst so unverhohlen zum Ausdruck kommt, dass seine athenischen Landsleute seinen lakedaimonischen Parteifreunden zu Lande nichts ernstliches anhaben konnten.* This is to misunderstand the passage entirely, which means no more than that, largely as a result of concentration on the navy, the Athenian hoplite force was comparatively weak. (The same can be, and often has been, said of England, and with the same truth.) But apart from this: Kalinka not only gives a weight to X's words that they do not deserve, but ignores Thucydides, Aristophanes, and all our other evidence, which so clearly contradict him. Even if we had no such evidence, but only the bare outline of the events of the Peloponnesian war, we could be confident that Kalinka's interpretation was false.

But the cleavage is unmistakable: Kleon's political methods had so disgusted many men that they would be glad if he disappeared even as a result of a military failure. His methods, not his policy: there is no lack of ordinary patriotism, little opposition to the war (and the success at Pylos lessened what there was); but this was the more dangerous, because more fundamental, opposition to the demos itself, not simply to its policy of the moment. When on Kleon's death it was found that not only had Athens suffered a bad defeat, but a Hyperbolos succeeded (Aristophanes proved a true prophet), and perhaps because Alkibiades was the other alternative to Nikias, the cleavage continued. With the ostracism of Hyperbolos things perhaps began to mend — *all* classes were enthusiastic for the Sicilian expedition in spite of the opposition of Nikias;[1] but the proceedings after the mutilation of the Hermai must have made many a respectable aristocrat lean towards the views of the few extremist oligarchs of the clubs. Then the defeat in Sicily discovered the incompetence, and soon the loss of confidence, of the demos, and the cleavage was deep. But it is still only in internal affairs: the winning of the war (so wantonly renewed), or an honourable peace was still the aim of all; it was indeed the principal aim of the revolutionaries, to get a more competent handling of affairs — among the first of their proposals were τὰ μὲν χρήματα τὰ προσιόντα μὴ ἐξεῖναι ἄλλοσε δαπανῆσαι ἢ εἰς τὸν πόλεμον and τὰ δὲ τοῦ πολέμου, ὅταν δέῃ, ἀκληρωτὶ προσαγαγόντας τοὺς στρατηγοὺς χρηματίζεσθαι ('Αθπ. 29. 5, 30. 5); as a result of Alkibiades' promises the oligarchs were confident αὐτοί θ' ἑαυτοῖς οἱ δυνατώτατοι τῶν πολιτῶν τὰ πράγματα . . . . ἐς ἑαυτοὺς περιποιήσειν καὶ τ ῶ ν π ο λ ε μ ί ω ν ἐ π ι κ ρ α τ ή σ ε ι ν (Thuc. VIII 48. 1; cf. 63. 4); Phrynichos was against the negotiations with Alkibiades, and especially to the offer of oligarchy to the allied states, because he knew this would not secure their loyalty — indeed the allied oligarchs would feel even more hostile to an oligarchic Athens than to the democracy,

---

[1] Thuc. VI 24, 31. Nikias, the true conservative, was suspicious of the young oligarchs' loyalty (VI 11. 7).

The nervousness of the masses about a possible *tyranny* (VI 53. 3, 60. 1, 61. 2) was rather different; it depended more on the personality of individuals — at this time of Alkibiades.

which had always to some extent protected them (VIII 48. 4–7; cf. 64. 5);[1] when in 411 Agis hoped to find the city in confusion, the cavalry, the hoplites and the light-armed were sent out against him and made a successful counter-attack (VIII 71. 1–2); even at the crisis of their affairs, the most extreme of the oligarchs would have liked to preserve the empire, or, if that were impossible, *the fleet and therewith independence,*[2] and were only ready to betray Athens if that should be the one way to save their lives (91. 3). When the unexpectedly stubborn resistance of the demos and their own blunders resulted in the fall of the 400, all but the few extremists united once more for the prosecution of the war; and it was only after the Arginousai trial and experience of an even worse demagogue, and the miseries of the last months of the war, that a large number of citizens were prepared, cowed as well by defeat and the presence of a Spartan garrison, to support or put up with an oligarchic government. The reconciliation in 403 proved that the large majority of the citizens preferred a democracy; and in spite of the many mistakes and the (as it seemed to them) oppressive taxation of the rich, there was no βαθυτάτη τομή in Athens till once more a foreign enemy defeated them and installed a garrison, in 322.

That is the story of Athens in these two centuries. We do not know enough of her internal history between 450 and 443 to judge how serious the rift then was between oligarchs and democrats; still less do we know of the private opinions of individuals; we can reasonably suppose that personal jealousy of Perikles played a large part. But to write as though the hoplites and the rich (or the

---

[1] Compare this (48.6), καὶ τὸ μὲν ἐπ' ἐκείνοις (the Athenian oligarchs) εἶναι καὶ ἄκριτοι ἂν καὶ βιαιότερον ἀποθνῇσκειν, τὸν δὲ δῆμον σφῶν τε καταφυγὴν εἶναι καὶ ἐκείνων σωφρονιστήν, with 1. 14, 15 of our essay (above, pp. 215, 232). This latter may well have some truth in it — before this time oligarchs, whether in sincere opposition to a Kleon or from factiousness, will have helped prominent men from the subject states (cf. Thuc. III 36. 5); but when in power they were not to be trusted.

[2] This is particularly interesting in comparison with X's assertion of the indissoluble connexion between the democracy and the fleet, his implication that the masses alone had any interest in either. See Miss Kupferschmid's discussion, pp. 38–42, who however ignores this passage from Thucydides.

farmers and the rich) formed one class opposed to the thetes, the demos, or even that the rich, or the aristocrats, were consistently the enemies of the demos in every way, the constitution, foreign policy, and the empire, is to falsify history, on the evidence that we have, including the evidence of Pseudo-Xenophon. In a review of my *Population of Athens* Prof. de Sanctis said he could not accept my figures for 431 B.C., c. 18,000 for the citizens of the thetic class and 25,000 for the rest, on the ground that with them we should have to suppose that an unarmed and unorganized *minority* dominated an armed and organized majority; for such a domination by the thetes is according to him the story of the Peloponnesian war. I replied that, first, it was our duty to ascertain the figures, if possible, before we interpret history; and secondly, that it was, in practice, equally difficult to understand how an unarmed and unorganized majority of 23,000 could dominate an armed and organized minority of 18,000 (his figures). To which in his turn he replied that this argument came badly from one who belonged to a country in which measures could be carried in Parliament by a majority of one, and are good law.[1] Never has a man more clearly given away his case. For Great Britain, whatever else it is, is not a country in which an unarmed and unorganized majority dominates an armed and organized minority. In one important respect its constitutional history resembles that of Athens. In the last hundred years the House of Commons has been transformed from a body closely controlled by a small landed aristocracy to one freely elected by the whole people, in which the poorer classes could, if they wished, have the dominant voice; but though there may have been individuals in 1832 who thought that Parliament was no longer the place for a gentleman, the changes have not resulted in the retirement of the aristocrats or the rich industrialists, the "governing classes," from politics. They are as content, or as eager, to govern the country by means of contested elections, by the support of the herd, as ever they were by privilege. That is one important reason for the success of our parliamentary system: no class has been driven into a disgruntled retirement, ready for violent action if the opportunity offered; and that is why measures

[1] *Riv. di filol.* XV (1937) 288-90; XVI 169-72.

can be safely carried by small majorities (not in practice very often)
— because *all* are agreed that parliamentary government must be
carried on. When I say "success," I mean of course what X means
by the success of the Athenian democracy — ὡς εὖ διασῳζόμεθα τὴν
πολιτείαν; I am not asserting that it is a good constitution in itself.
It is quite possible that with England too εἴη μὲν οὖν ἂν πόλις οὐκ
ἀπὸ τοιούτων διαιτημάτων ἡ βελτίστη, but — ἡ πολιτεία μάλιστ' ἂν
σῴζοιτο οὕτως. This is not one of the causes to which X attributes
the success of the Athenian constitution; he attributes it mainly
to the petty cunning of the masses; but he destroys his own case
by his two admissions, first that the office of strategos was generally held by the χρηστοί, and secondly that there were very few
ἀδίκως ἠτιμωμένοι and that there was no hope of revolution from
them. It was quite true: the χρηστοί had always been loyal
to the constitution, ready to work it, particularly the two men
whose political activity covered X's lifetime, Perikles, openly
προστάτης τοῦ δήμου, and Nikias, προστάτης τῶν εὐπόρων perhaps,
but not less loyal than the democrat. No *class* was excluded,
or excluded itself, from politics in Athens any more than in
England.

There was however some change after the death of Perikles,
brought about by the ascendency of Kleon and the weakness of
Nikias in opposing him. A small group of discontented oligarchs,
led apparently by Antiphon, withdrew from politics in the ekklesia
and at least thought about the possibility of revolution (Thuc.
VIII 68. 1). The last three years of the Archidamian war, carried
on without definite purpose, increased their chances; there was now
a discontented farmer class as there had not been before Delion.
The ambitious policy of Alkibiades after 420, arousing as it did the
admiration of some and the mistrust of others, and the mingled
admiration and mistrust of the majority, helped further, though
it is highly improbable that anything would have come of the
movement but for the defeat in Sicily. Whether X belonged to
this small group, his sophistic manner of writing makes it difficult
to say, though there is no doubt of his general political sympathies;
he was certainly familiar with the group, he uses its language —
οἱ χρηστοί, οἱ πονηροί, and so forth; "democracy is acknowledged

folly."[1] That is why there is (it seems to me) a definite weighing of the balance in favour of a date for his essay between 420 and 415. There are indications of an earlier date, as we have seen, but it is one difficult to fix, for while some of them point to a time before the beginning of the war, others very definitely point to one after it; and the general tone belongs to the later date, in that period of uneasy peace and much fighting which followed immediately after the peace of Nikias. This, together with the particular points given above, outweighs the arguments for an earlier date. If this is right, we can believe that the livelier passages were borrowed from the *Wasps*; and perhaps vv. 1121–1130 of the *Knights* suggested the whole —

> νοῦς οὐκ ἔνι ταῖς κόμαις
> ὑμῶν ὅτε μ' οὐ φρονεῖν
> νομίζετ'· ἐγὼ δ' ἑκών
> ταῦτ' ἡλιθιάζω.
> αὐτός τε γὰρ ἥδομαι
> βρύλλων τὸ καθ' ἡμέραν,
> κλέπτοντά τε βούλομαι
> τρέφειν ἕνα προστάτην·
> τοῦτον δ' ὅταν ᾖ πλέως
> ἄρας ἐπάταξα.

It is useless to speculate about the name of the author. His literary style shows that he was not any of the writers whose works have come down to us.[2] Therefore he is, as a writer, an unknown; and it is always best to acknowledge the fact, and to call him X or Anon. To pick out a name from the *Prosopographia Attica* and give him for author, adds nothing to our understanding.

[1] The whole of this casuistical passage from Alkibiades' speech (Thuc. VI 89. 3–6) might be contemporary with our essay, if we take into consideration difference of occasion and authorship.

[2] The above was written before I had seen John H. Finley's excellent paper on "The Origins of Thucydides' Style", *Harv. Stud. Class. Phil.* L (1939), pp. 35–84). It greatly strengthens the view that X's style is peculiar to himself, not simply the product of his age.

ATHENS AND CARTHAGE

BY BENJAMIN D. MERITT

IN the summer of 1939 Orlandos turned over to W. B. Dinsmoor squeezes and a photograph of an epigraphical fragment that had been found during work of reconstruction on the Nike-Pyrgos at Athens (fig. 1).[1] The stone is of Pentelic marble, broken on all sides, and it carries parts of twelve lines of a stoichedon text. The maximum dimensions are: height, 0.34 m., width, 0.33 m., thickness, 0.15 m. Dinsmoor has very generously placed the new document at my disposal.

The first observation to be made is that part of one uninscribed line is still preserved at the upper edge of the original face. However, it is clear that this was not the original top of the monument, for one may see in the photograph the considerable extent of marble which stretches up and to the left beyond the inscribed surface. Evidently the text belongs to an Athenian decree of the fifth century, for the letters are of the Attic alphabet, and in the opening lines the well-known formulae of a decree are recognizable. In line 1, for example, is part of the phrase [ἔδοχσεν τ͂ει βο]λ͂ει κ[αὶ τ͂οι δέμοι —], which by its projection to the left determines approximately the position of the left margin of the stone. Whether part of the margin is still preserved where the surface has been broken I do not know. If not, the preserved stone comes very close to where the original left edge must have been.

Another phrase from the preamble of the decree may be identified in line 3: [- - - - -]s ἐπεσ[τάτε - -], while in the body of the decree proper the words ἐς Σικελ[ίαν] stand out in line 9 with tantalizing clarity to indicate that in some way the decree was concerned with affairs in Sicily. But the only other restorations that come readily to hand are fragmentary snatches of the conventional [ἀ]ναγρά[φσαι - - -]- - τὸγ [γραμματέα - - - - ἐν στέλ]ει λιθίν[ει - - -] in lines 6-8.

---

[1] Both Dinsmoor and I wish to express our thanks to Orlandos for his interest in the publication of this fragment and for his kindness in making it available to us.

The stoichedon pattern of this new fragment is a square chequer for which the vertical and horizontal units each measure approximately 0.0178 m. Fortunately, this distinctive pattern can be combined with the shapes of the letters themselves, to show that the stone was once part of the inscription now published as *IG* I² 47. Both pieces have the same small omicron and theta, the same spreading upsilon, and equal measurements in corresponding strokes of other letters; there can be no doubt that they belong together.

The text of *IG* I² 47 was first published as *IG* I, Suppl. p. 25, no. 116 *n*, from a copy made by Koehler when the stone was in the museum of the Greek Archaeological Society. The right edge of the fragment is preserved, with a rather wide uninscribed margin between the final column of letters and the edge (fig. 2). Hiller's proposed text reads as follows:

$$\text{- - - - } ιλκο\text{-}$$
$$[\text{- - - } ἐ]ς\ τὸς$$
$$['Αθεναῖος\ καὶ\ τὸς\ χσυμμάχος\ ἄνδρες\ ἀγ]αθοὶ$$
$$[ἐγένοντο·\ καλέσαι\ δὲ \ldots\ldots\ldots^{14}\ldots\ldots\ldots]\ καὶ\ ἐ\text{-}$$
$$5\quad [πὶ\ χσένια\ ἐς\ τὸ\ πρυτανεῖον\ ἐς\ αὔριον].\ \textit{vacat}$$
$$\text{- - - } ρας$$
$$\text{- - - } υτ\text{-}$$

The notes on *IG* I² 47 give the shape of rho in line 6 as R, but in reality this letter is B, and there is no conflict of form between the old and the new fragments. The suggested restoration, with a stoichedon line of 35 letters, was of course conjectural.

Of more significance is the note on line 1. Hiller writes, "Laudantur aut Μ]ιλκό[ριοι aut 'Ιμ]ίλκο[ν] aliique Καρχηδόνιοι." Reference to the Milkorioi may now be rejected, for they were citizens of a small Chalcidic town in Thrace, and can have played no part in an Athenian decree relating to affairs in Sicily. On the other hand the reference to Carthage gains an added degree of probability and is made a practical certainty when one realizes that the enigmatic letters ΛΛΕΣΚΟΝ in line 10 of the new fragment spell out the name of Geskon, who was the father of Hannibal. It is a tribute to the acumen of Hiller that with so little evidence his identification yet came so true to the mark.

FIG. 1. Fragment belonging to *IG* I² 47

FIG. 2. Squeeze of *IG* I² 47

The date of the inscription must be very near the end of the century, for the name of the secretary is given with demotic in line 2. In known decrees this use of the demotic in the prescript appears first in the hitherto published texts in 405/4, where two inscriptions are preserved which name the demotics of both the secretary and the epistates.[1] It will be observed that in the present document also the amount of space necessary to the restoration makes it certain that the epistates, as well as the secretary, was named with his demotic.

The presence of Himilkon in Sicily as early as 407/6 is attested by Diodoros (XIII 80. 2), who relates that he was sent out from Carthage to accompany his kinsman Hannibal in the great expedition which began the siege of Akragas in 406 (Diodoros XIII 80. 1–2): περὶ δὲ τούτους τοὺς χρόνους Καρχηδόνιοι τοῖς περὶ Σικελίαν εὐτυχήμασι μετεωριζόμενοι, καὶ σπεύδοντες ἁπάσης τῆς νήσου κυριεῦσαι, μεγάλας δυνάμεις ἐψηφίσαντο παρασκευάζεσθαι· ἑλόμενοι δὲ στρατηγὸν ᾿Αννίβαν τὸν κατασκάψαντα τήν τε τῶν Σελινουντίων καὶ τὴν τῶν ᾿Ιμεραίων πόλιν, ἅπασαν αὐτῷ τὴν κατὰ τὸν πόλεμον ἐξουσίαν ἐπέτρεψαν. παραιτουμένου δὲ διὰ τὸ γῆρας, προσκατέστησαν καὶ ἄλλον στρατηγὸν ᾿Ιμίλκωνα τὸν ῎Αννωνος ἐκ τῆς αὐτῆς ὄντα συγγενείας.

Since Hannibal was himself an old man when the expedition set forth it is evident that the reference in line 10 cannot be to his father Geskon directly; the name appears in the inscription as the patronymic of Hannibal, and the restoration must be [᾿Αννίβαν τὸ]γ Γέσκον[ος] or perhaps [᾿Αννίβα]γ Γέσκον[ος]. The document thus names both generals, Hannibal and Himilkon, who were in Sicily together during the early part of the year 406. It is possible to be even more precise and to say with some assurance that both names appeared in lines 10–11; at any rate the restoration of at least one name besides that of Hannibal is necessary to justify what is probably the plural form αὐτός in line 11.

Hannibal and Himilkon were together until the time of Hannibal's death by plague before the walls of Akragas at the beginning of summer (Diodoros XIII 86. 3: ἀπέθανε δὲ καὶ ᾿Αννίβας ὁ στρα-

---

[1] *IG* I² 125 reads [Πο]λυάρατος Χολαργ[εὺς ἐγραμμάτευε, ...[8]. . . . ᾿Αρ]αφήνιος ἐπεστά[τε]; *IG* I² 126 reads Πόλυμνις Εὐωνυμεὺς ἐγραμμάτευε, ᾿Αλεξίας ἦρχε, Νικοφῶν ᾿Αθμονεὺς ἐπεστάτει.

τηγόs). The inscription is thus dated definitely in the year 406 and probably belongs to the archonship of Antigenes, 407/6.[1]

Repeated trials have shown that the text is probably best restored with a stoichedon line of 36 letters. There is no absolutely certain control, but the most significant restorations are those of lines 7–8 and 18–19.

407/6 B.C.   ΣΤΟΙΧ. 36

[ἔδοχσεν τε͂ι βο]λε͂ι κ[αὶ το͂ι δέμοι . . ᶜᵃ.⁶. . ἐπρυ]

[τάνευε, . . ᶜᵃ.⁶. .]s 'Αφιδ[ναῖοs ἐγραμμάτευε, . . .]

[. . . . . . ¹². . . . .]s ἐπεσ[τάτε, ...⁷. . . . εἶπε· κέρυ]

[χσι μὲν ὃs ἀφῆε]καν Κα[ρχεδόνιοι πρόσοδον ἐν]

5   [αι πρὸs τὸν δε͂μ]ον ὅτα[μπερ προ͂τον ἐκκλεσία κ]

[υρία γένεται· ἀ]ναγρά[φσαι δὲ Καρχεδονίοs εὐ]

[εργέταs 'Αθενα]ίον τὸγ [γραμματέα τε͂s βολε͂s ἐ]

[μ πόλει ἐστέλ]ει λιθίν[ει· κέρυκαs δὲ 'Αθεναῖο]

[ν αὐτίκα μάλα] ἐs Σικελ[ίαν πέμφσαι πρὸs στρα]

10   [τεγὸs 'Αννίβα]γ Γέσκον[οs καὶ 'Ιμίλκονα "Αννον]

[οs αἰτέσοντα]s αὐτὸs φ[ιλίαν καὶ χσυμμαχίαν]

[. . . . . ¹¹. . . . .] Ι [.]⁻ Λ [. . . . .]

Lacuna

[- - - - - - - - - - - - - - - - εἶπε· τὰ μ]

[ἐν ἄλλα καθάπερ τε͂ι βολε͂ι· πέμφσαι δὲ κέρυκα]

15   [s ὃs ἂν hέλονται οἱ πρυτάνεs μετὰ τε͂s βολε͂s π]

[ρὸs στρατεγὸs 'Αννίβαγ Γέσκονοs καὶ 'Ιμ]ίλκο

[να "Αννονοs· ἐπαινέσαι δὲ καὶ τὸs κέρυκα]s τὸs

['Αθέναζε ἀφιγμένοs ὅτι εἰσὶν ἄνδρεs ἀγ]αθοὶ

[περὶ τὸν δε͂μον τὸν 'Αθεναῖον· καλέσαι δὲ] καὶ ἐ

20   [πὶ χσένια ἐs τὸ πρυτανεῖον ἐs αὔριον ᵛᵛ] vac.

[- -] βάσ

[- -] υτ

- -

---

[1] It is one of the latest decrees in the old Attic script. Cf. Ferguson *Treasurers of Athena* 176–177.

This restored text is offered by way of interpretation, and it must be admitted that in no single line can the verbal accuracy of it be insisted upon. It seems clear from lines 18–20 that certain men were praised at Athens, and invited to entertainment in the prytaneion. These cannot have been the Carthaginian generals, for the Athenians had to send to Sicily to confer with them (ἐς Σικελ[ίαν] in line 9). I have assumed that they were heralds who came to Athens from the Carthaginians, and lines 3–4 have been restored so as to refer to their dispatch. The letters KANKA are a difficult combination; there may be more than one way of resolving them, but it is possible that they belong to the reading [- - - - ἀφῆ]καν Κα[ρχεδόνιοι].

The opening sentence of the decree, following the formula of motion (- - - - εἶπε), ought to be restored in such a way as to represent some positive recommendation. In this particular instance the action recommended was made contingent on some future circumstance which must have been specified in the clause beginning with ὅτα[ν] or ὅτα[μπερ] in line 5. Such phraseology is suitable to a probouleuma of the Council, in which the recommendation depends in some way on subsequent action of the Demos. Hence I have assumed that the heralds were to be presented to the Demos when the time came for the next meeting of the ἐκκλησία κυρία. The exact words used in the restoration have been determined by the stoichedon order, though it would have been appropriate to put the business over to the ἐκκλησία κυρία and not merely to the next ἐκκλησία if it involved any important question of national defense or safety.

Perhaps the heralds had brought the first news of the invasion of Sicily. Anyway it is clear from line 9 that the Athenians knew of the invasion when the probouleuma was passed, because they knew that Hannibal and Himilkon were there in the field. These must have been welcome tidings at Athens, howsoever and from whomsoever received, bringing encouragement in the dark days toward the end of the Peloponnesian war when the whole Greek world seemed to be turning against them; at the least, the invasion served to render ineffective the hostility to Athens of the western Greeks, and for this the Athenians were doubtless grateful.

Inasmuch as the formulae of the preserved portions of lines 6–8 are characteristic of honorary decrees which record on stone the names of benefactors of the Athenians, I have so restored them as to yield an expression of this gratitude toward the Carthaginians.[1]

One is on more certain ground in reading into lines 8–10 the dispatch of a mission to confer with Hannibal and Himilkon in Sicily. It is not clear that the Athenians were invited by the Carthaginian heralds to do this, nor is it clear what the purpose of the mission was. I have suggested that the Athenians asked for friendship and an alliance. As early as 414 B.C., they, or at any rate their generals in Sicily at that time, had given up any thought of imperial designs against Carthage, and had sought her friendship.[2] In the early summer of 406 the extremity of Athens and her desperate need of allies were even greater. There is no evidence that the alliance was ever consummated, though there is no reason to doubt that the Athenians hoped for the success of their overtures, whatever they may have been.

The name of Himilkon appears again in line 16. I assume, quite tentatively, an amendment which dealt with the method of selection of the Athenian heralds,[3] and provision for the praise of the heralds who had come to Athens.

The end of line 20 was not inscribed, and a new paragraph in the document begins with line 21. It is impossible here to restore either the heading of a new decree or the customary formula of amendment. Most probably the text of lines 21 ff. contained a historical record added to the decree proper. There are many possibilities, one of them being that here were listed the names of the Athenian envoys. Perhaps the letters at the end of line 21 may be restored as some form of the word [σύμ]βασ[ις]. It is tempting, of course, to read these letters as part of the name ['Αννί]βας, though it

---

[1] The whole people of a city were also named as benefactors in *IG* I² 110a (410/09 B.C.): ἀνα[γράψαι τὴν πόλιν τὴν Ἀλ]ικαρνασσέων [εὐεργέτιν Ἀθηναίων ἐν σ]τήληι λιθίν[ηι - - -].

[2] Thuc. VI 88. 6: καὶ ἔπεμψαν μὲν ἐς Καρχηδόνα τριήρη περὶ φιλίας, εἰ δύναιντό τι ὠφελεῖσθαι, - - -.

[3] One might equally well restore πρέσβες in lines 14–15. For line 15 cf. D8, lines 53–54, as published by Meritt, Wade-Gery, McGregor, *The Athenian Tribute Lists*, I, p. 167: ὃς ἂν hοι πρυτάνες με[τὰ τὲς βολὲς hέλοντα]ι.

is difficult to see how this could be done without assuming here a list of names, in the nominative, of Carthaginians who had ratified a treaty.[1] This would involve a conclusion probably not justified by the available evidence, and for the present I suggest no supplement.

There is much in the inscription that is ambiguous; what seems certain is that a mission was sent from Athens in 406 B.C. to consult with the Carthaginian generals Hannibal and Himilkon in Sicily.

[1] E.g. [Καρχεδονίον οἵδε ὄμνυον τὸν ὅρκον· ᾿Αννί]βας
[Γέσκονος, ᾿Ιμίλκον ῎Αννονος, κτλ. - - - - - -]υτ

THE UNITY OF THUCYDIDES' HISTORY

By John H. Finley, Jr.

I

THE recent revival of the old controversy on when Thucydides composed the various parts of his *History*, although designed to prove the existence of many early parts in the work which we have, has apparently tended to prove the opposite. The reason is that each new participant in the controversy, while advancing his own views, undermined those of his predecessor and hence diminished, rather than increased, the number of passages still capable of being regarded as early, with the result that it finally became possible to attack the whole position that the *History* contains many such passages. This evolution was, in brief, as follows. In 1919 Ed. Schwartz[1] seemingly opened a new era in the study of Thucydides when he urged that, of the four speeches at the council of Sparta reported in the first book, those of the Corinthians and of Archidamus were composed after the peace of Nicias, while those of the Athenians and of the ephor Sthenelaidas were added after 404 — an important observation, if true, since it would suggest that Thucydides once regarded Corinth as the cause of the war and only later saw Sparta's fear of Athens as the ἀληθεστάτη πρόφασις. A corollary was that, when in 404 Thucydides came to this new understanding of Sparta, he saw how right Pericles had been and accordingly completed his work with the purpose of vindicating the great statesman, who at that time was thought to have ruined Athens. The novelty of Schwartz's method, it will be seen, was to have identified early and late passages with the purpose of proving a development in Thucydides' thought. In the same year and the following, the method was carried further by Max Pohlenz,[2] who, however, disagreed with Schwartz's conclusions.

---

[1] *Das Geschichtswerk des Thukydides*, Bonn, 1919¹, 1929².

[2] "Thukydidesstudien," *Nachrichten von der Kgl. Gesellschaft der Wissenschaften zu Göttingen*, 1919, pp. 95–138; 1920, pp. 56–82.

After showing that the debate at Sparta in the first book is in fact a unit and thus late, he based his own view of Thucydides' development rather on his reading of the famous sentence in I 22. 1, which he took as a promise by Thucydides to report speeches exactly. Since, however, many speeches can hardly be so described, Pohlenz went on to distinguish early from late speeches by the criterion of exactitude, discovering a development not so much in Thucydides' view of the war as in his methods of historiography. And nine[1] years later W. Schadewaldt pressed the same conclusion still further. Accepting Pohlenz's literalistic reading of I 22. 1 and finding the same ideal of accuracy embodied in the Archaeology, he went on to contrast the methods seemingly adopted there with what he considered the far broader and more penetrating attitude revealed in books six and seven, both of which he argued were composed after 404. His deduction was striking: namely, that during the war Thucydides developed from an *historisierender Sophist*[2] interested only in the most literal accuracy to a historian in the fullest sense of the word, a man able to analyze the fundamental processes of state and society.

But it will be observed that in the course of this argument more and more parts of the *History* were continually being vindicated as late. The list now included books six and seven, those parts of book one which concern the rivalry of Athens and Sparta, and all passages contrasting Pericles' policies with those of his successors, a very broad topic indeed which would inevitably include all Pericles' speeches (except possibly some of the first), the estimate of him in II 65, the Mytilenean debate, the analysis of στάσις, and such parts of the fourth book as are concerned with Athens' expansionist policies. Moreover, such passages as were still called early were so described on the reading of I 22. 1 which made Thucydides seem to say that exactitude and only exactitude was the foundation of the *History*. But precisely this point was challenged in 1936 and 1937 by two young scholars, A. Grosskinsky[3] and H.

[1] *Die Geschichtschreibung des Thukydides*, Berlin, 1929.

[2] *Ibid.*, p. 30.

[3] "Das Programm des Thukydides," *Neue Deutsche Forschungen*, Abt. Klass. Phil., 1936.

Patzer,[1] whose successive studies showed beyond much doubt that Thucydides was not asserting mere accuracy as the basis of his speeches but that on the contrary, by his own words, the speeches were to contain primarily what he regarded as τὰ δέοντα, that is, the broad considerations justifying any given stand. Only secondarily were they to be limited by the ξύμπασα γνώμη of what was actually said — γνώμη meaning, in Patzer's able analysis, the essential relationship of a mind to a practical problem and thus signifying not so much the drift of one speech as the whole cast of a man's policy as revealed perhaps in several speeches. This interpretation of the first sentence in I. 22 was confirmed, so these scholars maintained, by the famous last sentence: that is, the general considerations of a social and political sort contained in the speeches (τὰ δέοντα) were to be at least a chief means of expounding the recurrent tendencies of human nature (τὸ ἀνθρώπινον), on which Thucydides squarely rested the later value of his work. But with this broader and undoubtedly more correct interpretation of I 22, the whole theory by which Pohlenz and Schadewaldt had distinguished between early and late passages fell to the ground, and when a still more recent study, that of F. Bizer,[2] concluded that a late date fits the Archaeology far better than an early one, virtually nothing remained of the whole movement which had sought to find in the extant *History* strong traces of its author's development.

That is not to say that early passages may not exist in the *History*; it is inconceivable that Thucydides did not take notes or that he failed to use them when he wrote his final work. It is merely to say that the work which we have should not be regarded as an agglomeration of passages written at widely different times and imperfectly blended together by reason of the author's premature death, but rather as composed primarily at one time with the help of earlier notes and, if broken at the end and incomplete perhaps in several places, yet possessing after all the unity which might be expected to result from a period of more or less sustained composition. But if that or anything like that is the case, then the work

---

[1] "Das Problem der Geschichtsschreibung des Thukydides und die thukydideische Frage," *ibid.*, 1937.

[2] *Untersuchungen zur Archäologie des Thukydides*, Tübingen diss., 1937.

should reveal a set of consistent ideas, organically developed from one end of the *History* to the other. Certainly, when Thucydides in the famous sentence just referred to speaks of the recurrency of historical events, he implies that the war followed some pattern and that he, as an historian, has expounded that pattern; otherwise it is hard to see what he could have imagined would be recurrent. Thus if one is to maintain that the *History* is in a fairly finished state as we have it and was composed essentially in one period of the author's life, it is not enough merely to prove how few passages imply an earlier version, valuable as that negative task is. It is necessary to show that the version which we have is in fact so complete a unit, that no part stands outside the complex of ideas known from other parts and that, since much of it is demonstrably late, all of it must accordingly have been composed or arranged at the same time — in sum, that it is the kind of work which a brilliant mind, dominated by a certain number of related ideas, would compose when those ideas were consistently before it. But it was natural that Grosskinsky and Patzer, faced as they were with the divisionistic arguments of their predecessors, should not have attempted this more positive task, and to find anything of the sort, it is necessary to return to Ed. Meyer's brilliant essay published in 1899.[1] To undertake once more so thorough an analysis as his is impossible here, but in view of the complicated nature of the controversy since he wrote, it may not be purposeless to explore again the grounds for believing in the unity of the *History*.

II

Perhaps the easiest way to do so will be to examine the leading ideas of books six and seven and then to trace these same ideas through the preceding books. For clearly, if Thucydides began composing his *History* after the end of the war or towards its close, he wrote even the first books with later events in mind, and the Sicilian narrative will consequently owe its climactic character to the fact that it draws together many strands of thought expounded previously. Now the opening books contain many passages either

[1] *Forschungen zur Alten Geschichte*, II, Halle, 1899, pp. 269–436.

certainly or probably written after 404,[1] and if one assumed that Thucydides began with the first sentence and wrote progressively to the last, then books six and seven would obviously fall towards the end of his period of authorship. There seems reason to believe that on the whole he did write consecutively. Thus in talking of Delos in V 1, he refers back to the purification described in III 104 with the words ᾗ πρότερόν μοι δεδήλωται;[2] in VI 94. 1 he refers back to VI 4 in the same way; in VI 31. 2 he compares the expeditionary army of 415 to the forces commanded successively by Pericles and Hagnon in 430, which are carefully described in II 56 and 58;[3] in introducing the account of the tyrannicides in VI 54. 1, he uses the words ἐπὶ πλέον διηγησάμενος, which may, though they need not absolutely, mean that he is conscious of having treated the subject more briefly before in I 20; and in III 90. 1 he says that he will note only the main points of the first Sicilian expedition, as if aware that it was of importance chiefly as foreshadowing the second. But even if these statements were more conclusive than they are, the probability would still remain that he would at times turn back to change or insert some passage. Thus it will not be maintained here that he wrote absolutely consecutively or that a given passage may not have been written after one that follows it (we cannot hope to follow such a delicate thing as composition with anything like complete accuracy), but only, as before said, that books six and seven are so closely knit with what precedes, that the whole work betrays a plan consistently worked out and therefore (it is natural to suppose) worked out in a period of more or less sustained authorship.

But if so, the Sicilian narrative should not have been composed at a time too far removed from the late passages in the opening books referred to above — in other words, it should not have been composed directly after the expedition itself but near or after the end of the war — and there are in fact good grounds for assuming that to be the case. The most thorough discussion of the subject

---

[1] These passages are listed by Patzer, "Problem," pp. 103–107.

[2] Similarly VIII 108. 4 refers to the moving of the Delians to Atramyttium described in V 1.

[3] In the same way VIII 15. 1 mentions the restrictions on the reserve of 1000 talents noted in II 24. 1.

is Schadewaldt's,[1] who emphasized two passages especially: VII
57. 2 where, in describing the forces at Syracuse, Thucydides lists
as Athenian by origin καὶ Αἰγινῆται οἳ τότε Αἴγιναν εἶχον, presumably
to distinguish them from the true Aeginetans restored to their
native island in 405;[2] and VI 15. 2–5, where, after noting Alcibiades'
extravagance, he goes on ὅπερ καὶ καθεῖλεν ὕστερον τὴν τῶν Ἀθηναίων
πόλιν οὐχ ἥκιστα and then explains that, through fear of his ambitions, the Athenians chose other generals and thus οὐ διὰ μακροῦ
ἔσφηλαν τὴν πόλιν. The latter verb, limited by οὐ διὰ μακροῦ, Schadewaldt took as a reference to Athens' losses from the Sicilian expedition, but the former and stronger verb, less narrowly limited by
ὕστερον, he interpreted as an allusion to her ultimate defeat.[3]
Neither passage is perhaps entirely clinching (in the first, Thucydides might possibly be distinguishing the Athenians on Aegina
from the exiles of 431 rather than from the repatriates of 405, and
in the second, the verb καθεῖλεν might imply a period late in the
war when Athens' weakness was apparent but her doom not yet
complete). Yet the obvious and probable interpretation is certainly as made by Schadewaldt, and it is confirmed by several other
passages implying a lapse of time between the actual expedition
and Thucydides' account.

The first of these is the well-known comment on Andocides'
testimony in regard to the mutilators of the Hermae (VI 60. 2),
in which, after stating the motives behind the testimony, he concludes, τὸ δὲ σαφὲς οὐδεὶς οὔτε τότε οὔτε ὕστερον ἔχει εἰπεῖν περὶ τῶν
δρασάντων τὸ ἔργον. Without going into the many discrepancies in
our accounts of the affair, it may be said that Andocides himself
in 410 admitted and in 399 denied complicity in it[4] (a point on
which Thucydides himself was doubtful, as is clear from the next
sentence to that just quoted), and that the remark in any case
posits some inquiry on the latter's part, which in view of his exile
would have been neither swift nor easy. Similar in its implications
is the account of Decelea in VII 27 and 28, formally a digression to

---

[1] *Geschichtschreibung*, pp. 8–15.
[2] Xenophon, *Hell.* II 2. 9.
[3] For further discussion of the passage, see below, p. 262 n. 5, p. 270 n. 1.
[4] *De Red.* 7 and 25, *De Myst.* 61–64. Jebb, *Attic Orators*, I, pp. 76–79.

explain why Athens could not afford to keep the Thracian mercenaries which had arrived in the summer of 413 but actually a treatment of the whole effect of Decelea on the later course of the war. Thus the tone of the passage is forward-looking: in 27. 3, the building of the fort by the assembled Peloponnesians is contrasted with its later occupation by successive garrisons; in 27. 4, it is said that at times large contingents were there (Steup appositely cites VIII 71. 1, where Agis in 411 is said to have summoned such a contingent) and at times only enough troops for raiding; in the same section Agis' continued residence there is emphasized, a passage which looks forward to VIII 5. 3 and 70. 2;[1] and in 28. 1 the new difficulties of trade with Euboea are mentioned, another passage which looks forward to the later narrative in VIII 4 and 96. 2. These references are not exact, but they undoubtedly assume a knowledge of events for some years after 413 and quite possibly to the end of the war. The same deduction must be drawn from a number of superlatives in the sixth and seventh books. These are: first, the statement that the disaster at Mycalessus was ξυμφορὰ τῇ πόλει πάσῃ οὐδεμιᾶς ἥσσων μᾶλλον ἑτέρας (VII 29. 5); then the remark on the νυκτομαχία on Epipolae, μόνη δὴ στρατοπέδων μεγάλων ἕν γε τῷδε τῷ πολέμῳ ἐγένετο (VII 44. 1); again, the judgment preceding the catalogue of peoples engaged in the great final battle, ἔθνη πλεῖστα δὴ ἐπὶ μίαν πόλιν ταύτην ξυνῆλθε, πλὴν γε δὴ τοῦ ξύμπαντος λόγου τοῦ ἐν τῷδε τῷ πολέμῳ πρὸς τὴν Ἀθηναίων τε πόλιν καὶ Λακεδαιμονίων (VII 56. 4); further, the general assertion on the Athenian defeat at Syracuse, μέγιστον δὴ τὸ διάφορον τοῦτο [τῷ] Ἑλληνικῷ στρατεύματι ἐγένετο (VII 75. 7); and finally, the crowning judgment on the expedition, ξυνέβη τε ἔργον τοῦτο ['Ελληνικὸν] τῶν κατὰ τὸν πόλεμον τόνδε μέγιστον γενέσθαι, δοκεῖν δ' ἔμοιγε καὶ ὧν ἀκοῇ Ἑλληνικῶν ἴσμεν (VII 87. 5). To say that Thucydides made these statements in ignorance of what might presently take place is to liken him to the poets and logographers whose uncritical stories he attacks in I 21; it is also to neglect several other passages where he carefully guards against extreme statement when he believes his knowledge inadequate (III 113. 6, V 68. 2, 74. 3, VII 87. 4). But indeed in the second,

[1] That Agis stayed largely at Decelea until the end of the war is clear from Xen. *Hell.* I 1. 33, II 2. 7, 3. 3.

third, and last of the passages just quoted, he is evidently referring to the whole war, and there seems no good reason not to take him at his word.

Thus a number of statements in the Sicilian narrative were in all probability composed after the end of the war, and that these passages were not inserted into an earlier draft seems to follow from the generally recognized fact that books six and seven, more than any other part of the *History*, comprise a unified and consistent whole. Schadewaldt, who has also discussed this aspect of the Sicilian narrative,[1] has shown how difficult it in fact is to detach any of its important parts from their present context, and there is perhaps no need of restating his arguments here. The advocates of an early date, on the other hand, have had to rely chiefly on Thucydides' seeming ignorance of the future in such passages as VI 62. 2 and VII 58. 2, where he writes in the present tense of Himera, although it was destroyed by the Carthaginians in 409[2] — an argument almost entirely invalidated since Patzer has shown that Thucydides elsewhere uses such historical presents even of towns the destruction of which he himself notes.[3] It is certainly his habit (itself the result of his intensity of mind) to confine himself rather strictly to what he is describing at the moment; he glances at the future for the most part only when ideas that interest him greatly are involved, as, for instance, in his estimate of Pericles in II 65 or his remarks quoted above on the magnitude of the Sicilian expedition.[4] It would therefore be unreasonable, even without Patzer's observations, to expect him always to treat the later history of what he mentions merely in passing. An argument of another sort is that of O. Rehm,[5] who found proof of incom-

---

[1] *Geschichtschreibung*, esp. pp. 10–11. For further discussion see below p. 267 and Patzer, "Problem," p. 31, n. 67.

[2] Xen. *Hell.* I 1. 37; Diodorus XIII 62. Cf. K. Ziegler, *Phil. Woch.*, L (1930), 195.

[3] "Problem," p. 14, where he quotes I 56. 2, Ποτειδεάτας, οἳ οἰκοῦσιν ἐπὶ τῷ ἰσθμῷ τῆς Παλλήνης, whence they were driven in 430/29 (II 70). Similar is II 23. 3, ἣν νέμονται Ὠρώπιοι Ἀθηναίων ὑπήκοοι, which accordingly need not have been written before 412/11 when the Boeotians took Oropos (VIII 60. 1).

[4] See below, pp. 294–297.

[5] *Philologus*, LXXXIX (1934), 133–160. His further attempt to explain all

pleteness in what he argues were blanks in VII 4. 1, 7. 1, and 43. 5 left to be filled in later with the name of a fort temporarily forgotten by Thucydides. But acute as this observation is, it proves only what would doubtless be assumed in any case, that his untimely death robbed every part of the *History*, even the most finished parts, of ultimate revision. In sum, considering the number of late passages in these books, the paucity and inconclusiveness of the supposedly early passages, and above all the inherent difficulty in imagining that so tightly woven a narrative could ever have been achieved by a process of insertion, it seems fair to assume that books six and seven were written at a time not far removed from the late passages already noted in the preceding books. But if so, we may return to the larger question set forth at the beginning of this section, namely, what are the leading ideas of the Sicilian books and how are these ideas connected with what has gone before. For if this connection could be shown to be close, then we could say that it represents, in effect, the pattern which Thucydides detected in the events of his time and on which he rested the future utility of his work. It would also justify us in believing that the *History* is not, so to speak, a notebook of passages composed at widely different times but rather a unified interpretation of the war and, as such, an interpretation possible only when his opinions were matured and the facts before him. Finally, as has been said, such a connection, if shown, would augment the valuable, if inevitably negative, work of those who have disproved many of the alleged indications of an earlier version, by suggesting in a somewhat more positive way the threads of unity in the version which we have.

Perhaps no ideas play a larger part in the Sicilian narrative than

---

late references in VI and VII as additions is unconvincing (cf. Patzer, above, p. 262 n. 1). For instance, to delete the clause in VI 15. 3 on the ruinous effects of Alcibiades' extravagance would involve deleting not only the rest of 15 but the opening of Alcibiades' speech (16), which is intended to illustrate the previous judgment. These passages, however, serve the vital purpose of acquainting the reader with the people's fears of Alcibiades which flared out during the incident of the Hermae (see also below, p. 270 n. 1). Similarly, to delete the superlatives in VI and VII would be to destroy the whole architecture of these books (see below, p. 267).

the following four: the magnitude and decisiveness of the struggle at Syracuse; the surprising nature (παράλογοs) of Athens' defeat; the fact that she was defeated by democratic Syracuse when oligarchic Sparta had proved an easy adversary; and the reasons for the defeat inherent in the character of her government and leadership. ₄ These ideas will be discussed successively in their relation to the foregoing narrative.

(1) That the Athenian attack on Syracuse produced, to Thucydides' mind, the greatest struggle in the 27-years war, appears from several passages already quoted: VII 44. 1 on Epipolae as the largest night engagement; 56. 4 on the final battle in the harbor as involving the greatest number of peoples (excepting the total number engaged in the whole war); 75. 7 on the Athenian retreat as signifying the supreme reverse ever sustained by a Greek army; and 87. 5 on the whole struggle as the greatest ἔργον in the war and probably in Greek history. In addition to these passages are: VI 31. 1, where the expeditionary force of 415 is called the most expensive and the handsomest up to that time; 31. 6, where it is observed that the undertaking constituted the farthest flight of Athenian ambition (μέγιστος ἤδη διάπλους ἀπὸ τῆς οἰκείας καὶ ἐπὶ μεγίστῃ ἐλπίδι τῶν μελλόντων πρὸς τὰ ὑπάρχοντα ἐπεχειρήθη); and VII 70. 4, where the final battle in the harbor is said to have brought together most ships in the smallest space.[1] But since these statements evidently embody two distinct ideas — first, that the expedition was on an extraordinarily large scale and second, that, such being the case, its failure inflicted a supreme blow on Athens — it may be well to consider the two ideas separately.

As for the first, there is an interesting passage in Alcibiades' first speech where he is made to say just before the expedition that the military efforts of all the Greek states had so far proved a good

---

[1] To these should be added the contested passage, VII 85. 4, on the slaughter at the Assinarus: πλεῖστος γὰρ δὴ φόνος οὗτος καὶ οὐδενὸς ἐλάσσων τῶν ἐν τῷ [Σικελικῷ] πολέμῳ τούτῳ ἐγένετο.. The deletion of Σικελικῷ, recommended by the scholiast, is supported by Marchant *ad loc.*, though opposed by Steup. The apparent reference to Herodotus, VII 170. 3, the unusual addition of two modifiers to πόλεμος, and the climactic tone of the preceding narrative seemingly argue for deletion.

deal smaller than expected (οὔτε οἱ ἄλλοι Ἕλληνες διεφάνησαν τοσοῦτοι ὄντες ὅσους ἕκαστοι σφᾶς αὐτοὺς ἠρίθμουν, ἀλλὰ μέγιστον δὴ αὐτοὺς ἐψευσμένη ἡ Ἑλλὰς μόλις ἐν τῷδε τῷ πολέμῳ ἱκανῶς ὡπλίσθη, VI 17. 5). Accepted by Hude and Marchant, the sentence was deleted by Classen on the insufficient grounds that so young a man could not have made such a statement, and by Steup because he thought that Alcibiades would not have spoken of a continuous state of war after the Peace of Nicias and before the formal revival of hostilities between Athens and Sparta in 413 (VII 18). But, as Patzer has shown in another connection,[1] a virtual state of war is assumed to exist at this time in several places, notably in the summary of the Egestians' speech (VI 6. 2 *ad fin.*), in Nicias' first speech (VI 10. 1), in Alcibiades' speech at Sparta (VI 91. 6), and by Thucydides himself in VI 73. 2, VII 28. 3, and VI 105. 1. If then the passage be accepted as genuine, we may assume that the historian and, presumably, Alcibiades as well regarded the war as only gradually gathering momentum. One reason for that view, so far at least as Athens is concerned, is several times expressed; it was, of course, the plague. Thus Nicias in warning against the expedition speaks of the city as even then only partially recovered (VI 12. 1), and Thucydides later says the same, though without Nicias' reservations (26. 2). Now, as has been pointed out already, when he comes to discuss the unparalleled scale of the original expeditionary force (VI 31. 2), he compares it to that of 430 which is carefully described in the second book (56 and 58). His point is that the earlier venture, undertaken when the plague had just begun, represented Athens' finest combined force of ships and hoplites before 415. Similarly, in speaking of the invasion of Megara in 431 (which as a land-attack could not later have been compared to the Sicilian expedition), he says, στρατόπεδόν τε μέγιστον δὴ τοῦτο ἀθρόον Ἀθηναίων ἐγένετο, ἀκμαζούσης ἔτι τῆς πόλεως καὶ οὔπω νενοσηκυίας (II 31. 2). Again, in talking of the second epidemic of 426 (III 87. 2), he says that nothing weakened Athens more than the plague.[2] Thus

---

[1] "Problem," pp. 19-20.

[2] It has been argued that this passage could not have been written after the Sicilian expedition (cf. Steup *ad loc.* but also Patzer, "Problem," p. 108). It is doubtful, however, whether the remark should be interpreted so strictly. It

these passages give a consistent answer to the question why the Athenians did not produce their full strength at once and why therefore the Sicilian expedition was the climax of the war. An explanation is likewise given for Sparta's slow beginning. In the first place, as is repeatedly stressed, the Spartans were naturally torpid and conservative (I 70, 118. 2, 132. 5, IV 55. 2, V 63. 2, VI 88. 10, VIII 96. 5); then, with the exception seemingly of a few individuals like Archidamus (I 80–81), they expected the time-honored strategy of invasion to win them a quick victory (I 121. 4, IV 85. 2, V 14. 3, VII 28. 3, VIII 24. 5). Thus they were amazed that Athens did not desist even when the revolt of Mytilene was added to the ravaging of Attica (III 16. 2), and after the defeat of Pylos they were completely shaken, feeling unable to cope with so unusual an adversary (IV 55). Hence when Brasidas, whose quite un-Spartan energy is often noted (cf. esp. IV 81. 1), attacked the Thraceward country, it was felt that they were just beginning to fight (τὸ πρῶτον Λακεδαιμονίων ὀργώντων ἔμελλον πειράσεσθαι, IV 108. 6). Both he, however, and his conquests were neglected by the home government, which after the Peace of Nicias was accordingly criticised even more fiercely for its sloth and cowardice. Hence it was that the campaign of Mantinea seemed to Thucydides so significant a turning point: not only did it clear Sparta of the charge of μαλακία, ἀβουλία and βραδυτής (V 75. 3, cf. I 122. 4) but, what is more important in the present context, it actually called forth the finest Spartan army up to that time (στρατόπεδον δὴ τοῦτο κάλλιστον Ἑλληνικὸν τῶν μέχρι τοῦδε ξυνῆλθεν, V 60. 3), with the result that the battle itself could be described as πλείστου δὴ χρόνου μεγίστη δὴ τῶν Ἑλληνικῶν καὶ ὑπὸ ἀξιολογωτάτων πόλεων ξυνελθοῦσα (V 74. 1). Thus what is said before the sixth book not only of Athens' but of Sparta's military efforts bears out the statement of Alcibiades quoted above and, by so doing, prepares the ground for the climactic descriptions of the whole Sicilian narrative.

---

merely reinforces what has been said of the plague in II 54. 1 and in Pericles' last speech (II 64. 1–3, where there is a similar juxtaposition of the idea of Athens' δύναμις). Absorbed in the period which he is describing (see below, pp. 294–297), Thucydides seems to be making a statement quite true of that time without reference to disasters of another sort which took place later.

Here then we have followed one part of that recurrent and inter-woven complex of ideas around which the *History* is built, and that Thucydides' analysis of the Spartans[1] came up in this connection (an analysis which in its entire consistency stands as one more proof that the work was conceived as a unit) suggests how a given idea is constantly invoking another, in such a way that, as the *History* advances, it draws increasingly on all that has gone before. But to confine ourselves still to the idea of magnitude, it is to be observed that these statements regarding the size of the war are not mere notes appended to the descriptions of certain events but constitute, as it were, fixed landmarks in the total structure. Thus, when in VI 31 Thucydides describes the supreme size, brilliance, and efficiency of the first Athenian flotilla and then, after retailing the later reinforcements and noting with various superlatives the growing fierceness of the struggle, rises at last to the great cata-logue of peoples engaged in the final battle (VII 57–58), he is clearly preparing for the ultimate catastrophe, a catastrophe which is itself marked by the assertions that Athens' loss was the worst ever sustained by a Greek city and that the whole ἔργον was un-matched either in the war or, to his own mind, in all Greek expe-rience (VII 87). No better proof is to be found that books six and seven were conceived as a unit than in these progressive, inter-related statements, but, what is more important, their significance cannot be limited to the Sicilian books alone. For when it is said in the first and second sentences of the *History* that the war about to be described was the greatest of all Greek wars and, in the sixth and seventh books, that it reached its climax in the struggle at Syra-cuse, the relation of these separate statements can hardly be accidental. One therefore concludes on these grounds alone (quite

---

[1] Spartan traits, other than those noted above, are: their harshness as gover-nors, I 77. 6, 95. 1, 103. 1, III 93. 2, V 52. 1, VIII 84 (but contrast Brasidas, IV 81. 2); their fear of the helots, I 132. 4, IV 41. 3, 55. 1, V 14. 3, VII 26. 2, VIII 40. 2; their religiosity, II 72. 2, III 89. 1, V 54. 2, 55. 3, VII 18; their secrecy, I 92. 1, II 39. 1, V 68. 2; their suspiciousness, I 68. 2, 90. 2, 102. 3, III 13, V 109; their justice towards one another, I 132. 5, V 105. 4; their covert pursuance of their own ξυμφέρον, I 76. 2, 102. 3, III 68. 4, V 105. 4; their dis-cipline, I 84, II 11, IV 40, V 9, 72. 3.

apart from the other indications of the Archaeology's late date),[1] that he wrote each part with the other in mind, and consequently that an orderly and consistent progression exists from the initial claim regarding the size of the war, through the various explanations why Athens and Sparta got rather slowly under way, to the full corroboration of the first claim in the Sicilian books.

With so much on the mere magnitude of the war in Sicily, we may turn to the corollary of the idea noted above, namely, the decisiveness of the struggle in the total 27-years war. Four passages already quoted perhaps best express the seriousness of Athens' loss:[2] VI 15. 3, where it is said that Alcibiades' extravagance καθεῖλεν ὕστερον τὴν . . πόλιν; VII 28, on Athens' impoverishment under the double burden of the Sicilian war and the Spartan occupation of Decelea; VII 75. 2, the famous description of the retreat from Syracuse, beginning δεινὸν οὖν ἦν . . . . ὅτι τάς τε ναῦς ἀπολωλεκότες πᾶσας ἀπεχώρουν καὶ ἀντὶ μεγάλης ἐλπίδος καὶ αὐτοὶ καὶ ἡ πόλις κινδυνεύοντες; and VII 87. 5, where after noting the magnitude of the ἔργον, Thucydides adds that it was τοῖς τε κρατήσασι λαμπρότατον καὶ τοῖς διαφθαρεῖσι δυστυχέστατον, continuing πανωλεθρίᾳ δὴ τὸ λεγόμενον καὶ πεζὸς καὶ νῆες καὶ οὐδὲν ὅτι οὐκ ἀπώλετο. It has been shown already that these statements could hardly have been written before the end of the war and, that being the case, they reveal quite clearly how important an element in Athens' ultimate defeat Thucydides considered the expedition. Thus it should be expected that the rest of the narrative, if conceived as a unit at the end of the war, should reveal this same idea, and although it is true, as observed above, that Thucydides does not commonly anticipate the future and therefore would not often refer to the expedition in the previous books, nevertheless many passages undoubtedly look to this great later event. The best known and oftenest referred to is the estimate of Pericles in II 65, where after contrasting the latter's wise leadership with that of his successors, Thucydides goes on to say that their greatest error was the Sicilian expedition, and then observes wonderingly that, even after it, the Athenians, although already in revolution, were able to hold out for several

[1] See below, pp. 274–275, 290, 295–296.
[2] See also in Nicias' speeches VII 64, 77. 7.

years against their original enemy, the latter's Sicilian reinforcements, their own revolting subjects, and Cyrus. Now it will be observed that this passage, while confirming the central importance of the Sicilian war, regards Athens' actual losses from it as only one of several factors in her ultimate defeat, the others being the blind self-interest of her politicians, the ensuing disunity of the city, and the consequent squandering of the great advantages on the basis of which Pericles had justly predicted victory. More will be said of these ideas below (pp. 284–91), but it should be noted here that, precisely by considering the expedition as the supreme evidence and result of Athens' internal faults, does Thucydides bind the whole *History* together as closely as he does. For so considered, it becomes inseparable from Pericles' warning against foreign conquests (I 144. 1, II 65. 7), from the Mytilenean debate and the description of στάσις (which merely carry further what is said in II 65 of the Athenian politicians), from Cleon's refusal of peace after Pylos (which reveals the same desire for conquest which was warned against by Pericles but supremely exemplified at Syracuse), and from the Melian dialogue. But further still, when he says in II 65 that the expedition failed for political reasons rather than because the plan was impossible, and then goes on to observe that the city, shattered though it was, could still hold out for several years, he invokes still another vital concept of the *History*, namely, that of Athens' extraordinary strength. It is this concept which forms the burden of the first book, where from the Archaeology on, Thucydides expounds the greatness of Athens' power — a power based, like that of Minos and Agamemnon, on control of the sea, therefore positing, like theirs, a great economic advance, and consequently invulnerable to an outmoded land-state like Sparta (see below, pp. 273–275). We have already seen that the superlatives of the sixth and seventh books are inseparable from the initial statements on the magnitude of the war, but it must also be noted that that magnitude itself depended on the high condition of the belligerent states, and notably that of Athens since she opposed all the others. But to the degree that the Sicilian expedition represented the highest pitch of Athens' strength, was its failure the more serious. When therefore Thucydides, while recognizing that fact, admiringly notes her ability to resist some years more, he is tying the catastrophic descriptions of the sixth and seventh books all the more tightly to the analysis of Athens' strength which had gone before. Hence II 65 sets the Sicilian expedition not only in the perspective of Athens' political weakness, of which more will be said presently, but also in that of her great initial strength which, as the burden of the first book, provides the basis of Pericles' confident prognosis (I 141. 2–144).

A word should finally be added concerning the eighth book, since this concept of the magnitude and the decisiveness of the Sicilian expedition should be expected to reveal itself there as well. Now one of the reasons[1] advanced by those who have argued that

---

[1] H. Strasburger, *Philologus*, XCI (1936), 137–152. He therefore concludes that the remark on Alcibiades' extravagance, ὅπερ καὶ καθεῖλεν ὕστερον τὴν . . πόλιν οὐχ ἥκιστα (VI 15. 3), applies to the disaster of 413, not as Schadewaldt had argued, to that of 404 (see above, p. 260). His argument is (pp. 148–49) that Alcibiades here appears as the cause of Athens' ruin, whereas in II 65 the cause is said to have lain in the nature of Athenian democracy. There can be no doubt that the latter view represents Thucydides' deeper judgment. On the other hand, it is by no means neglected in VI and VII (which accordingly were not written from a different point of view from that expressed in II 65, see below, pp. 284–91), nor is it incompatible with the above statement in regard to Alcibiades, for two reasons. First, one of the grounds given in II 65 for Pericles' ascendency is that he was χρημάτων διαφανῶς ἀδωρότατος (II 65. 8, cf. II 13. 1, where he is said to have relinquished his estates voluntarily, and below, pp. 287–88). Hence, unlike Alcibiades, he gave his opponents no handle against him. When therefore Thucydides in VI 15 stresses the latter's enormous extravagance, he is reverting to his train of thought in II 65, though with a difference of emphasis caused by the impression of Alcibiades' dissolute life. Second, it is unreasonable to claim that the words ὅπερ καθεῖλεν ὕστερον τὴν πόλιν οὐχ ἥκιστα exclude the other and deeper cause of Athens' defeat noted in II 65, since to do so is to say that Thucydides was interested only in theoretical problems. He was, however, equally interested in the effect of specific events, and the superlatives noted above show that even after 404 he continued to regard the Sicilian venture as a staggering blow to Athens. Hence when he says that Alcibiades' extravagance was "not the least" cause of Athens' ruin (οὐχ ἥκιστα, i.e. one of several causes), he is saying virtually what he says in those superlatives. His mind is on the losses which might have been avoided if Alcibiades had not been dismissed from office, and though he can elsewhere regard that dismissal as in turn lodged in the nature of democracy, still it was in itself a decisive turning-point, as he says in II 65. 11. Thus although the

books six and seven were written soon after the event is that the great emphasis there placed on Athens' defeat seemed incompatible with the offers of peace refused by her after Cyzicus in 410,[1] as again in 407 and 406. This view is of course untenable, if the foregoing arguments on the unity and lateness of the Sicilian books be accepted, but (even neglecting those arguments) it is also untenable if, as seems the case, the eighth book was written in close connection with books six and seven. It has already been observed (p. 261) that what is said in VII 28 of the strain on Athens resulting from the occupation of Decelea, of Agis' residence there, and of Athens' new dependence on sea-traffic with Euboea, certainly look to continuing passages in the eighth book. But many other parts of the latter conspicuously repeat ideas or turns of expression already familiar from what has just preceded: for instance, the remarks on the Athenian colonists on Aegina (VII 57. 2, VIII 69. 3); the repeated expressions ὀλίγον οὐδέν and ἀγώνισμα (VII 59. 3, 87. 6, VIII 15. 2; VII 56. 2, 59. 2, 86. 2, VIII 12. 2, 17. 2); Alcibiades' practice of justifying himself on the grounds of his ἰδία ξυμφορά (VI 92. 2, VIII 81. 2); the conception that soldiers in a democracy are freest in criticising their officers (VII 14. 2, VIII 84. 2); the judgment that, in preventing the Athenians on Samos from attacking the home-city, Alcibiades for the first time acted out of genuine patriotism (VIII 86. 4, a contrast to VI 15); the view that democracy at its best is a mixed government, not a domination by the poorer classes (VI 39, VIII 97. 2, to which compare the distinction drawn by Alcibiades at Sparta, VI 89. 6, between a government based on τὸ ξύμπαν and one representing the πονη-

---

statement is less profound and less general than that of II 65, it is wholly consistent with it. It is moreover the natural statement at just this point in the narrative when Alcibiades is about to speak and the whole tragic sequence of events is about to unroll. For the immediate cause of what followed at Athens, Sparta, Decelea, and Syracuse was in fact this same self-interested extravagance, and to say that Thucydides could not have spoken of it in this way after 404 is to say that he did not then consider the following events important, which we know not to have been the case. Thus καθεῖλεν does glance, though unobtrusively, at the whole later fate of Athens, a fuller diagnosis of which is given in II 65.

[1] Diodorus, XIII 53–54.

ρoί). Many more such passages could be adduced, but the above perhaps sufficiently illustrate the close continuity between the Sicilian narrative and the eighth book. But the latter was certainly written after Cyzicus, since VIII 97. 2 assumes a knowledge of the decline of the five thousand.[1] Consequently, the Sicilian books as well as the eighth book must, on any view, have been composed after the offer of peace in 410, and it cannot therefore be asserted that, in emphasizing the greatness of Athens' loss in Sicily, Thucydides failed to reckon with her partial later recovery. But the fact is that he himself explains this seeming contradiction not only satisfactorily but in a manner quite consistent with his whole narrative. His explanation falls into three parts: first, that though the Athenians were fearfully shaken after Syracuse, they once again demonstrated their great inherent strength (and once again, to their enemy's great surprise), by mustering the ability to continue (II 65. 12, IV 108. 4, VIII 2. 1–2, 24. 5, 106. 5); second, that they were enabled gradually to regain confidence because the Spartans, in spite of Agis' greater vigor, once again showed themselves unable to press home an advantage and thus remained as before the easiest possible antagonists for Athens (VIII 96. 4–5); and finally, that, so far at least as the period covered by the eighth book is concerned, the Athenians were able to transcend those revolutionary movements which, as was observed in II 65, in the long run joined with the evil consequences of Syracuse to prove their ruin (VIII 1. 3–4, 97. 2). Enough has been said on the connection of these first two concepts (those, namely, of Athens' great inherent strength and of the slowness of Sparta) with the preceding narrative, but it may perhaps be observed of the third, that the Sicilian venture had, to Thucydides mind, a certain revolutionary character. At least, as will be shown more fully below (pp. 284–291), he makes quite clear that the demos favored the expedition in the hope of more lucrative employment

---

[1] For the effect of Cyzicus in restoring democracy at Athens, see F. E. Adcock in *C.A.H.* V, pp. 343–46, and W. S. Ferguson, *ibid.*, p. 485. VIII 47. 1, where Alcibiades is said to have foreseen ὅτι ἔσται ποτὲ αὐτῷ πείσαντι κατελθεῖν, may well envisage his actual return to Athens in 407, rather than the mere rescinding of his banishment noted in VIII 97. 3.

in an extended empire, and hence that the expedition represented the expansionist policies of the extreme democrats as much as did Cleon's refusal of peace or his abortive Boeotian campaign. Thus when in the very opening section of the eighth book Thucydides observes the new reasonability and temperance of the demos and later goes on to praise the restraining constitution proposed in 411 (VIII 97. 2), he is following a line of thought which extends clear through the *History*, beginning with Pericles' plea for a moderate (that is, a non-expansionist) policy and a united people. Had he lived to describe Cleophon's refusal of peace after Cyzicus, he would doubtless have seen in it merely one more example of that extremism which had not only underlain all Athens' great reverses but, as the war advanced, had produced a condition perhaps even more fatal to empire, namely, the reaction towards oligarchy (VIII 48. 5–7). Thus, to conclude with this whole idea of the magnitude and seriousness of the Sicilian war, it is clear that Thucydides concurrently regards Athens' losses from two points of view: first, as shattering in themselves because of the mere size of the venture, and, second, as symbolizing and (by reason of the resultant poverty) to some extent producing that extremism and disunity which were Athens' supreme weakness. It is also clear that these ideas, and consequently the Sicilian books themselves, are planted firmly in the total structure of his work.

(2) A second concept which runs through the entire *History* and forms a strong band of unity within it is that conveyed by the word παράλογος. At first sight merely a term casually, if often, used by Thucydides, the word in fact conveys perhaps more neatly than any other one of his essential theses in regard to the war and therefore demands some attention. As has been observed already, Athens was expected to submit after a very few years of fighting (I 121. 4, IV 85. 2, V 14. 3, VII 28. 3, VIII 24. 5); the belief, reiterated as it is throughout the *History*, shows with how much greater a military reputation Sparta entered the war. It has also been observed that Archidamus doubted his country's ability to win on the grounds that Athens' enormous economic and naval advance had at last made her invulnerable to the old-fashioned strategy of invasion. But, as Thucydides notes (I 87. 3), he had few adher-

ents, and the Spartans evidently plunged into war in the expectation that it would soon be over. It need hardly be said, however,
that Archidamus' view fully coincided with that of Pericles, whose
first and third speeches are devoted largely to showing why Athens
had nothing to fear from a power which, though it ravaged Attica,
could in no manner affect the basis of Athens' strength in her
revenues, her access to materials, and her navy. But what most
concerns ourselves is that Thucydides also both shared and deeply
reflected on that view, so much so in fact that in the Archaeology he
projects it into the remote past and finds there the same pattern
of change which he believed exemplified in the world about him.
His argument is that Minos and Agamemnon, by establishing
centralized authority and thus transcending the previously existent
state of localism, gave rise to a stage of material civilization unlike
anything that had gone before, and that the means by which they
achieved this advance was naval power (cf. esp. I 8. 3, 15. 1).
After their fall, he continues (I 13), the process might have been
repeated by the naval states of Corinth and Samos had it not been
checked, in the one case, by the timorous policy of the tyrants
(I 17) and, in the other, by the advance of the Persians (I 16).
When, therefore, he goes on later in the first book to praise Themistocles' genius in foreseeing the future significance of Athens' navy
and in taking all practical steps to enlarge it (I 93. 3–4, 138. 3), he
is evidently harking back to the thesis of the Archaeology, that
centralism means both power and progress and that, in Greek history, the high-road to such power had always been command of
the seas. For land-states, as he specifically notes, had never been
great (I 15. 2). The conclusion therefore follows that Sparta, to
his mind, had been strong, as it were, for the negative reason that
no naval powers had come into existence in the period between the
fall of Mycenae and the rise of Athens, although, as will be observed
later (p. 290), the stability of her constitution, also noted in the
Archaeology (I 18. 1), was a factor in her strength. Accordingly,
when Pericles maintained and even extended the naval policies of
Themistocles,[1] he was, so to speak, reapplying the ancient secret of

[1] Compare the similar judgments on Attic policy attributed to the two men
in I 91. 4 and 140. 5.

power which Minos and Agamemnon had used before him. Indeed, one could almost say that, to Thucydides' eyes, he was creating a state as much stronger and more progressive than such outmoded land-states as Sparta as were the realms of Minos and Agamemnon than the communities before them. But, as has been said, not all persons realised this fact, and because Sparta had been strong, it was expected that she would continue so. Here then is the underlying meaning of the word παράλογος: it signifies the shock and surprise felt by all who (unlike Pericles and the historian himself) were unable to estimate the true sources of power and thus failed to see that the naval empire of Athens, eliciting as it had a great era of economic and technical advance, had virtually ushered in a new age of Greek history.

By this argument, then, the Archaeology stands closely woven in the texture of the *History* not only because it explains the magnitude of the war but also because it presents historical (one could almost say formal) analogies to the growth of Attic power, a power which was to visit many painful shocks upon the enemy and was to be destroyed not so much by them as by the Athenians themselves. But before we pursue this idea of surprise throughout the *History*, it may be well to note very briefly those qualities of mind which the acquisition of power, especially of naval power, had bred in the Athenians. In the first place, their skill at sea, entailing as it did an exact training in many manoeuvres, constituted an ἐπιστήμη,[1] which in turn derived from an experience (ἐμπειρία[2]) continuous since the Persian wars. (It is to be observed from the references given here and below that these ideas are brought into play continually throughout the work and thus provide one more indication of its unity.) Then, their skill and, in a larger sense, their power derived from certain inward qualities: high spirit (προθυμία[3]), courage (τόλμα, τολμηρόν[4]), capacity for innovation (νεωτεροποιία[5]),

[1] I 121. 4, 142. 6–9, II 89. 8, III 78, VI 18. 6, 68. 2, 69. 1, VII 36. 4, 49. 2, 62. 2.

[2] I 18. 3, 71. 3, 99. 3, 142. 5, II 85. 2, 89. 3, IV 10. 5, VI 18. 6, 72. 3, VII 21. 3, 49. 2, 61, 63. 4.

[3] I 74. 1–2, II 64. 6, VI 18. 2, 31. 4, 83. 1, 98.

[4] I 70. 3, 90. 1, 102. 3, II 39. 4, 88. 2, IV 55. 2, VI 31. 6, VII 21. 3, 28. 3.

[5] I 70. 2, 102. 3.

and willingness to undergo toils.[1] These qualities, noted in the famous contrast between the Athenians and the Spartans in I 70, as in several similar contrasts later (II 39, IV 55. 2, VIII 96. 5), explain the growing enmity between the two states described in the Pentecontaetia (cf. esp. I 102. 3); they also convey what the allies of Athens forfeited on substituting money for service as their contribution to the Delian league (I 99). But they are chiefly stressed perhaps in two other contexts: first, as justifying Athens' original rise to power when Sparta voluntarily retired from the war against Persia (I 74. 1–2, 90. 1, 91. 5, II 36. 4, VI 83. 1), and second, as inspiring the democratic doctrine of πολυπραγμοσύνη, the doctrine that those who deserve power should have it.[2] No concept is perhaps more central to the process of change which Thucydides is describing, and whether it be considered by itself in the speeches of Pericles (II 63–64), Alcibiades (VI 18), and Euphemus (VI 87) or in contrast to the conservative doctrine of ἡσυχία which Archidamus expounds (I 84) and with adherence to which Nicias is taxed (VI 18. 6), it connotes democracy as opposed to oligarchy, freedom as opposed to discipline, and change as opposed to maintenance of the status quo. And finally, since the above-mentioned qualities are thus connected in Thucydides' mind with the institution of democracy, it becomes of interest to note exactly how he envisages that connection. The subject will be taken up further in the next section, but it may be said here that naval power to any Greek postulated a numerous and a free demos. Hence it is that the Funeral Oration conceives of democracy as permitting free play to initiative and as thereby reaping the benefits of an enlarged commerce, an improved standard of living, and a general sense of self-trust on the part of the citizenry. Indeed, as will appear below (p. 281), Thucydides probably thought of democracy as a prerequisite of material progress, since he specifically notes that the Athenians never met their match until they encountered the Syracusans who were ὁμοιότροποι with themselves. It is of course equally true that democracy, to his mind, ran the risk of political follies, follies which in fact cost Athens the war, but that he con-

---

[1] I 70. 6, II 63, 64. 3, VI 87. 3.
[2] For further discussion, see *H.S.C.P.* XLIX (1938), 45–46.

sidered it at the same time one vital key to Athens' greatness must appear from what has just been said. Here in fact is the great dilemma of the *History*: how a state as progressive, and therefore as democratic, as Athens can nevertheless enjoy sane leadership under the stress of war and the hot demands of the populace. But for the present the important thing to notice is that the idea of παράλογος, signifying as it does the revelation of Athens' enormous vigor and enterprise, cannot be dissociated from the concept of change which, adumbrated in the Archaeology, is fully expressed in the pervasive contrast between an outmoded, oligarchic Sparta and her imperialistic, progressive, democratic rival.

Thus, to pursue this concept throughout the *History*, it takes its rise, as has been said, from the double thesis that Sparta, traditionally the great power of Greece, was expected to win but that in reality Athens (granted sane leadership) was certain of victory. References to the former idea have been given above (p. 273); the truth concerning Athens, as Thucydides saw it, is expounded early in the *History* in the Archaeology, parts of the Corinthians' and of Archidamus' speeches at Sparta, all Pericles' speeches, and the estimate of him in II 65. The first great surprise in the war (II 61. 3), namely the plague, hardly concerns the present discussion except as it weakened Athens in the way described earlier. But the next time the word is used, namely, in the description of Phormio's naval victory of 429, it carries all the connotations sketched above, since the defeat of the far larger Peloponnesian fleet presented a signal (and to the Spartans a shocking) example of their enemy's daring, skill, and experience.[1] When again in the next year the Spartans were assured that Athens was crippled by the plague (III 13.3) and thus eagerly supported the revolting Mytileneans by a second invasion in the same season, to their great surprise the Athenians dispatched a hundred ships to the isthmus without moving the fleet already at Lesbos. They wished to show, Thucydides says, that the Spartans had quite mistaken their strength. The

---

[1] II 85. 2, ἐδόκει γὰρ αὐτοῖς ἄλλως τε καὶ πρῶτον ναυμαχίας πειρασαμένοις πολὺς ὁ παράλογος εἶναι, καὶ οὐ τοσούτῳ ᾤοντο σφῶν τὸ ναυτικὸν λείπεσθαι, γεγενῆσθαι δέ τινα μαλακίαν, οὐκ ἀντιτιθέντες τὴν Ἀθηναίων ἐκ πολλοῦ ἐμπειρίαν τῆς σφετέρας δι' ὀλίγου μελέτης.

latter accordingly, ὁρῶντες πολὺν τὸν παράλογον, retired (III 16. 2).
The idea comes up several times in the fourth book, most notably
in connection with the battle of Pylos, and its identical use here and
in the seventh book provides perhaps one of the most striking
proofs of unity in the whole work. There is, first, the paradox
noted in 12. 3 and 14. 3, that in their opening assault on Demosthenes' position, the Spartans were attacking the Peloponnesus
from the water, while the Athenians were defending it from the
shore — a strange reversal of fortune, says Thucydides, since ἐν
τῷ τότε the former were reputedly a land- and the latter a sea-
power. The passage was therefore written, as has often been noted,
sometime after the Athenian navy had broken down, presumably
very late in the war or after it, and accordingly when he notes
exactly the same paradox at the height of the Sicilian narrative —
namely, that the Athenians retired from Syracuse πεζούς τε ἀντὶ
ναυβατῶν πορευομένους καὶ ὁπλιτικῷ προσέχοντας μᾶλλον ἢ ναυτικῷ (VII
75. 7) — the close connection between the two passages is ines-
capable. Similarly, the remark on the Athenians' plight before the
final attack on Sphacteria, that they were μᾶλλον πολιορκούμενοι ἢ
πολιορκοῦντες (IV 29. 2), is virtually repeated in Nicias' letter (VII
11. 4, cf. 75. 7). But the final surrender of the Spartans provided
of course the greatest surprise in this whole surprising series of
events. Thucydides accordingly comments, παρὰ γνώμην τε δὴ
μάλιστα τῶν κατὰ τὸν πόλεμον τοῦτο τοῖς Ἕλλησιν ἐγένετο (IV 40. 1),
a passage which harks back to the repeated previous assertions that,
if the Spartans had nothing else, they had at least ἀνδρεία, and
which also looks forward to the vindication of their courage at
Mantinea (V 75. 3). Finally, in reviewing the whole effect on
Sparta both of this defeat and of that which followed at Cythera,
Thucydides observes that the reverses, ἐν ὀλίγῳ ξυμβάντα παρὰ
λόγον (IV 55. 3), caused the Spartans supreme fright and adds
that they now became extremely hesitant, the more so because
they were fighting a naval war against the Athenians, οἷς τὸ μὴ
ἐπιχειρούμενον αἰεὶ ἐλλιπὲς ἦν τῆς δοκήσεώς τι πράξειν. Almost an exact
repetition of the Corinthians' remarks in I 70. 7, the words resume
the impression of both sides which has hitherto been built up. But
it is to be observed that they also coincide with what is said of the

shock to Athens after the defeat at Syracuse (κατάπληξις μεγίστη δή, VIII 1. 2; ἔκπληξιν μεγίστην, IV 55. 3) and to the judgment in VIII 96. 5, that the Spartans remained to the last a most convenient adversary, a passage also closely similar to I 70. In sum, the narrative of Pylos is tightly bound both to what precedes and to what follows, and its particularly close connection with the Sicilian narrative (a connection reinforced, as will appear presently, by what is said in both places of Athens' expansionist policies) shows that Thucydides regarded the two reverses as in many ways similar. Indeed he himself compares them in VII 71. 7. But what is to be observed especially is that neither account could have been written without an eye to the other; in fact neither account could have been written without an eye to much of the *History*, since the concept of παράλογος is both itself continuous and depends on a continuing contrast between Athens and Sparta.

But to go on, the idea comes up three times again in the fourth book: in IV 65. 4, where, after noting the punishment of the generals who had made peace in Sicily, Thucydides criticises the ignorance and folly of the Athenians for thinking that so great an island could have been subdued by a small force and adds that their unexpected success had made them too optimistic (a statement which looks back to Cleon's confident refusal of peace in IV 21 and ahead to an identical judgment on the Athenians' ignorance of Sicily in VI 1); in IV 85. 2, a passage already cited, where Brasidas speaks of the Spartans as being deceived in their hopes of a quick victory; and in IV 108. 4 where Thucydides notes that after the fall of Amphipolis many Thraceward towns deserted Athens and goes on, καὶ γὰρ καὶ ἄδεια ἐφαίνετο αὐτοῖς ἐψευσμένοις μὲν τῆς ᾿Αθηναίων δυνάμεως ἐπὶ τοσοῦτον ὅση ὕστερον ἐφάνη (a passage which confirms all that has been said hitherto of Athens' strength and of the Syracusan expedition as the climax of the war and which is also echoed in VIII 2 and 24). In the fifth book (14. 3) the statement that the ten years' war had gone παρὰ γνώμην for Sparta is repeated. But, as has been suggested, it is in the Sicilian books that the idea achieves its greatest prominence, and when at the climax the Athenians are portrayed as themselves experiencing the sense of shocked surprise which they had formerly inflicted on others, one must conclude that the entire previous narrative has worked up to this reverse, and consequently that, in this respect also, the Sicilian books are an integral part of the whole. All the superlatives hitherto noted in regard to the scale of the expedition of course bear out the notion that it was a supreme (and to many a supremely surprising) revelation of Athens' strength. Thus Thucydides prefaces his description of the first flotilla by noting that the venture seemed an ἄπιστος διάνοια (VI 31. 1), and Athenagoras is made to say in Syracuse that Athens could not conceivably attempt another war in addition to the one left unfinished in Greece (36. 4). Indeed the historian himself repeats the idea with utmost emphasis in VII 28, when he says that no one would have believed that the Athenians, while themselves besieged, could be besieging others, καὶ τὸν παράλογον τοσοῦτον ποιῆσαι τοῖς Ἕλλησι τῆς δυνάμεως καὶ τόλμης, when at the beginning they had been expected not to survive two or three invasions. But even while he is making these statements, he is also stressing the unexpected character of the resistance at Syracuse (VI 34. 6–8, VII 13. 2), until with the great battle in the harbor the complete reverse takes place. Thus he can say before the battle, οἱ μὲν Ἀθηναῖοι ἐν παντὶ δὴ ἀθυμίας ἦσαν καὶ ὁ παράλογος αὐτοῖς μέγας ἦν (VII 55. 1), and go on to observe that they had made no progress either by revolution or by arms, πόλεσι ταύταις μόναις ἤδη ὁμοιοτρόποις ἐπελθόντες, δημοκρατουμέναις τε, ὥσπερ καὶ αὐτοί, καὶ ναῦς καὶ ἵππους καὶ μεγέθη ἐχούσαις. The passage will come up again in the next section, but one must realise here that it is wholly consistent with what has gone before. For to say that the Athenians met their match only in democratic Syracuse is to revert to the whole concept of oligarchic Sparta as outmoded, of Athens as the stronger and more progressive power, and of Pericles' confident prediction that she would win if she avoided risks. When then the utter reverse pictured in VII 75 and resumed in the final chapter takes place, the reason for it is clear — the Athenians had committed errors which might have passed against Sparta but were fatal against Syracuse — and the pervading contrast to Pylos forces the mind back to the difference not only in Athens' fortune but in the nature of her antagonists and thus ultimately to the difference between democracy and oligarchy. And when in the eighth book he goes on in several passages already cited (p. 272) to note Athens' amazing recuperation (a recuperation made possible in part by the slowness of her enemy), it becomes still more clear that the work as a whole embodies a consistent and consecutive view both of the strength and of the reasons for the strength of the several states engaged in the war. Indeed the concept of παράλογος is only a striking means of showing how truth broke through opinion and thus of revealing those basic processes of national change which Thucydides thought would continually recur.

(3) We have hitherto been largely concerned with the concept of Athens' strength, a concept which in turn inspires the claims regarding the scale of the war and particularly of the Sicilian expedition, the contrast between Athens and Sparta, the explanations given for her strength in her naval empire and democratic constitution, and the repeated statements that few persons judged it correctly. Henceforth, on the other hand, we shall be dealing with the opposite and, as it were, balancing concept of Athens' weakness, a weakness traceable also to her democratic constitution and, so Thucydides thought, accentuated in war-time. As before, the method will be followed of tracing connections of thought between the Sicilian and preceding books, with a view to showing the unity of the work as a whole. But before approaching this crucial topic of Athens' weakness, it will be well to say a few last words of the actual defeat at Syracuse.

As we have seen, Thucydides several times notes that the Athenians met their match only with the Syracusans, who were ὁμοιότροποι with themselves (VI 20. 3, VII 55. 2, VIII 96. 5). The likeness which he observed between the two peoples was apparently a double one, consisting in part of their similar wealth and progessiveness and in part of certain inward traits, such as zest, vigor, and capacity for innovation (VII 21. 3–4, 37. 1, 70. 3). And that he considered these achievements and qualities the result of democracy, is shown by the fact that he joins the words ὁμοιότροποι and δημοκρατούμεναι (VII 55. 2). As has been suggested, a great city teeming with manifold activity was probably inconceivable to him except as a democracy, and it is significant that, as Pericles attributes Athens' progress to the energy of her free citizens, so Athenagoras says that the objectives of an oligarchy are ἀδύνατα ἐν μεγάλῃ πόλει κατασχεῖν (VI 39. 2). It is natural therefore that the long campaign at Syracuse should have witnessed a gradual change in position whereby the defenders slowly revealed the same qualities as the attackers, and accordingly that, in the account of this change, many motifs of the previous narrative should reappear. Thus at the start, the chief issue is between the ἐπιστήμη of the Athenians and the mere courage of their enemy (VI 68. 2, 69.1, 72. 4, VII 21. 4, 63), the same contrast that is made by the Corinthians, by Pericles, and by the Spartan generals after the naval defeat of 429 (I 121. 4, 142. 6, II 87. 4). But the fear inspired by the Athenians, like that felt towards the Spartans on Sphacteria, wore away as the contestants came to closer grips (IV 34. 1, VI 11. 4, 49. 2, 63. 2, VII 42. 3), and though the Syracusans were often beaten, it is said of them, as several times before, that their resolve at least remained unshaken (VI 72. 3, II 87. 4, V 72. 2, but contrast IV 55. 3, where after Pylos the Spartans are really shaken in γνώμη). Thus the Athenians (VII 55. 2) could make no headway either by revolution (as they had attempted to do at Megara and in Boeotia) or by arms (as they had done against the more backward and immobile Spartans). Then on the introduction of the new ship-model with heavier sides, the tide turned (VII 34. 7); the Athenians, fighting in a narrow space could no longer make use of the manoeuvres of περίπλους and διέκπλους, so terrifying formerly (VII 49. 2, II 89. 8); and perhaps the most striking symbol of their utter reverse was when they fought the final battle as a πεζομαχία ἀπὸ τῶν νεῶν, tactics called old-fashioned even at Sybota (VII 62. 2, I 49. 2).[1]

Their whole defeat then is conceived in terms of the foregoing narrative, but even in matters unconnected with the defeat,

---

[1] That Thucydides wrote the narrative of Sybota with the rest of the *History* in mind is shown by the fact that I 55. 1, the account of the Corcyrean hostages taken to Corinth, looks to III 70. 1, where those same hostages are said to have precipitated the revolution. But the account of the latter is clearly of a piece with the rest of the *History* (see below, pp. 285, 289, 294). Hence it is not surprising that the descriptions of the battles of Sybota and of Syracuse (I 50, VII 75) have much in common.

Thucydides is constantly invoking ideas expounded earlier. Thus Hermocrates refers to the fact discussed at length in the first book, that the Athenians' skill at sea was not something native to them but merely a result of the Persian wars (VII 21. 3, I 90. 1, 118. 2, 121. 4, 142. 7); like Sthenelaidas and others, he taxes the Athenians with misusing a power originally got in the name of liberation (VI 76. 3–4, I 77. 5, 86. 1, 99, III 10); and, like the Corinthians at Sparta, says that after all the Persians were not defeated by the Greeks so much as by the length and difficulty of the invasion itself (VI 33. 5, I 69. 5). Similarly, Euphemus' defense of the empire rests largely on familiar arguments: that in the Persian wars, Athens had contributed ναυτικὸν πλεῖστον καὶ προθυμίαν ἀπροφάσιστον (VI 83. 1, almost an exact echo of I 74. 1); that, leaving this argument aside (VI 83. 2, I 73. 2, V 89), it is ἀνεπίφθονον to see to one's own safety (VI 83. 2, I 75. 5); that the Spartans had always done their best to keep Athens weak (VI 82, I 91. 4 and 7, 140. 5); but that it is the latter's nature to be ever active abroad (VI 87. 3 the doctrine of πολυπραγμοσύνη, elsewhere expressed in I 70, II 63, VI 18. 2). Again, Alcibiades at Sparta, like Archidamus, refers to Athens' revenue as her supreme advantage (VI 91. 7, I 81. 4, 122), and urges Sparta to a show of energy, the lack of which had been so costly before (VI 92. 1, I 70, IV 80. 5, 108. 6, VII 1. 4). Many speeches moreover make use of familiar turns of thought: for instance, that a quarrel seemingly distant may concern one closely (VI 78. 1, 91. 4, I 68. 2, 120. 2, III 13.5, IV 95. 2, V 69. 1); that men's moods change with unexpected circumstances (VI 34. 7, I 140. 1); that what formerly had been most striven for is now freely offered (VI 10. 4, I 33. 2, III 40. 7); that one must feel καταφρόνησις towards the enemy in action but until then act with φόβος (VI 34. 9, II 11. 5, 62. 3). Such a list of recurrent motifs could be very greatly enlarged, but more significant perhaps are the passages where Thucydides himself reverts to his own previously stated ideas. For example, in I 23. 6 and VI 6. 1, he makes a similar attempt to give an ἀληθεστάτη πρόφασις, and though the former passage expounding Sparta's fear of Athens as the cause of the war is sometimes taken as later than the Sicilian books,[1] the idea

---

[1] O. Rehm, *Philologus*, LXXXIX (1934), 147.

is seemingly quite familiar there. For Nicias can speak of Sparta as a πόλιν δι' ὀλιγαρχίας ἐπιβουλεύουσαν (VI 11. 7), and as we have just seen, Euphemus describes the growth of Athens in terms quite similar to those of the Pentecontaetia, itself merely a fuller exposition of I 23.6. Other such passages are: VI 2. 1, where he glances at the stories of the poets in the same way that he does in I 21; VI 54. 1, the well-known account of the tyrannicides, which, as mentioned earlier (p. 259), may contain a reference to I 20 but in any case shows a close similarity of phrase; VII 29. 5, on the destruction of Mycalessus by the Thracians, a disaster of the sort alluded to in I 23. 2; and VII 44. 1 and 87. 4, where he talks of the difficulty of ascertaining facts in the same way as in I 22. 3, III 113. 6, V 68. 2 and 74. 3. In sum, not only the analysis of Athens' defeat but the whole texture of the accompanying narrative invoke so many elements from the preceding books, that the reader is constantly aware of dealing with the same mind, the same ideas, and the same methods. That is to say, the unity of the *History* is revealed not only by its consistent analysis of events but by a more subtle consistency of style and treatment. Hardly a page, one could almost say, fails to contain some sentence which in form or idea suggests another sentence elsewhere. The conclusion therefore follows that, by the time he wrote his *History*, Thucydides had, as it were, simplified his thought into a number of fixed, clear patterns, the more important of which centered about the great questions of the war, while others denoted the various things that men would say or do under different circumstances and still others the historian's own methods, and that it is largely from the interplay of these patterns, great and small, that the unity of the work derives.

(4) We come then, finally, to his explanation of Athens' failure, an explanation lodged in his whole estimate of Athenian democracy and thus balancing his opposite appraisal of Athens' great inherent strength. Indeed, it could be said that these two ideas together comprise the main argument of the *History*. The causes of Athens' defeat are set forth in the Sicilian book seemingly in two distinct ways: first, by direct explanation of the errors actually committed by the Athenians and, second, by a contrasting picture of the mistakes avoided by the Syracusans; and since the latter topic is the

simpler, it may profitably be treated first. In reading the Sicilian books, it is hard to avoid the impression that Athenagoras stands in the same relation to Hermocrates, as Cleon to Pericles. The parallel of course is incomplete since, in the *History* at least, Cleon appears only after the death of Pericles; nevertheless, in the portrayal of both pairs of men the same contrast is undoubtedly made between sanity and violence, restraint of the demos and popular agitation, disinterestedness and self-interest, and correct and incorrect πρόγνωσις. Thus Athenagoras, like Cleon, is scornfully introduced as πιθανώτατος τοῖς πολλοῖς (VI 35. 2, III 36. 6, IV 21. 3); like him talks with extreme passion, sometimes using very similar phrases (VI 38. 2, III 37. 1); and resembles him also in practising διαβολή (VI 36. 2, 41. 2, III 38. 2–3, 42–43, V 16. 1), though posing as a watch-dog of the people (VI 38. 4, III 38. 2). Now there is no doubt that Thucydides regarded Cleon as a revolutionary figure, since the Mytilenean debate is merely a projection of the statement made in the general description of στάσις, ὁ μὲν χαλεπαίνων πιστὸς αἰεί, ὁ δ' ἀντιλέγων αὐτῷ ὕποπτος (III 82. 5).[1] Similarly, Cleon exemplifies the concluding judgment of III 82. 8, repeated in II 65. 7 and V 16. 1, that such factional leaders, however much they spoke of the public good, were in reality acting in their own interests. Accordingly, the same judgment applies to Athenagoras, who is in fact pictured as fearing military preparations at Syracuse lest these weaken the populists (VI 38. 2). And exactly here is to be found the crucial trait common to the two demagogues, namely, their equal willingness to endanger their respective cities for their own gain. As Cleon, buoyed by the popular desire for expansion, refused peace after Pylos and went on in the campaign of Delium to risk all Athens' earlier gains — a complete rejection of Pericles' strategy — so Athenagoras closed his eyes to the menace of an Athenian attack which, according to Thucydides, had originally every chance of success because of the lack of preparation at Syracuse (VII 42. 3). There were of course still other reasons for Athens' failure; nevertheless one reason for it was that Athenagoras' views were not accepted but that the far-sighted Hermo-

---

[1] Diodotus' elaborate attempts to allay suspicion (III 42. 2–43) also illustrate the latter half of the clause.

crates carried the day. In other words, Thucydides is illustrating in the policies of both Cleon and Athenagoras the possibility, ever present under a democratic government, that politicians for their own partisan ends may jeopardise a people's military effectiveness. Now he himself says that war automatically increases the people's sufferings and thus sows the seeds of partisanship (III 82. 2), but on the other hand, there is no reason to suppose that he thought that process of degeneration irresistible. On the contrary, it was to his mind Athens' essential misfortune that she lacked a second Pericles to lead the people sanely and to check the demos, whereas by contrast it was the salvation of Syracuse to have possessed such a man in Hermocrates. Thucydides stresses his understanding in very much the words which Pericles uses of himself (VI 72. 2, II 60. 5); represents him as, like Pericles, able to rally the people when they were despondent (VI 72. 2); and above all, shows him as possessed of the supreme Periclean gift of foresight. Again, he is ready to take swift and bold action based on that foresight, and as Pericles at the start of the war had dared suggest burning and abandoning Attica, so he advocates meeting the Athenian fleet before it had even reached Italy (VI 34, I 143. 5). The portrait of Brasidas (cf. esp. IV 81. 1) and the unique little speech of Teutiaplus the Elean (III 30) also show how much Thucydides admired this capacity for incisive action. In sum, his estimate of both Athenagoras and Hermocrates bears out what he has previously said of the problem of leadership under a democracy. The conclusion therefore follows that, to his mind, one great reason for Athens' failure in Sicily was that, at the very time when her own actions were embodying the worst possible tendencies of a democracy, the Syracusans avoided those tendencies, achieving unity behind an able leader.

To turn now to his judgment of Athens' policies, it is sometimes said on the basis of II 65. 11 that he did not think the Syracusan expedition a mistake. But he says rather that it was not so great a mistake as the Athenians' subsequent failure to support it by the right decisions. Thus he saw in the expedition two cardinal errors, of which the latter was the more costly: first, ever to have undertaken a venture so contrary to Pericles' sound plan of war, and second, once it had been decided on, to have exiled the one man who might have carried it off successfully. To take up these points in order, that he considered the expedition a mistake is shown by his repeated remarks on the Athenians' ignorance of Sicily (IV 65. 4, VI 1. 1) and by Alcibiades' quite incorrect estimate of the resistance that would be met there (VI 17). As future events proved, it was Nicias who more correctly forecast the difficulty of the task ahead (VI 20–23). Now Alcibiades carried his proposal by appealing to what he called Athens' very nature as an expanding, dominating state — that is, by the democratic doctrine of πολυπραγμοσύνη (VI 18) — and when Thucydides himself sums up the motives behind the expedition, he says that the ordinary people expected so to extend the empire that they would henceforth enjoy an ἀίδιος μισθοφορά (VI 24. 3). Accordingly, he describes them as possessed of an ἄγαν τῶν πλεόνων ἐπιθυμία (VI 24. 4), and says that the entire venture was conceived ἐπὶ μεγίστῃ ἐλπίδι τῶν μελλόντων πρὸς τὰ ὑπάρχοντα (VI 31. 6, cf. VII 75. 7). There can be no doubt that he is signalizing in these statements the supreme rejection of Pericles' advice, first given in I 144. 1 and repeated in II 65. 7, that Athens should attempt no foreign conquests in the course of the war. But it is equally important to observe that he uses almost the same words in describing the popular desire for expansion in several other places, namely, of Cleon's refusal of peace after Pylos[1] (IV 17. 4, 21. 2, 41. 4), of the campaign of Delium (IV 92. 2), and of the attack on Melos (V 97). It follows that these earlier and less disastrous attempts at expansion foreshadowed to his mind the great attempt in Sicily, and that as the Sicilian books hold their true place in the narrative as relating the greatest and most intense action of the war, so do they in describing the most dangerous leap of Athenian ambition.

That ambition in turn derived from two sources — the desire of the Athenian leaders for power and the desire of the people for the profits of empire — and both of these tendencies are likewise continuously observed throughout the *History*. The danger to democracy which Thucydides recognized in the self-interested

---

[1] The people regretted this error when it was too late (V 14. 2), just as they later regretted the Sicilian expedition (VIII 1).

struggles of politicians has already been discussed in connection
with the contrast which he draws between Pericles and Hermocrates on the one hand and Cleon and Athenagoras on the other.
It scarcely needs be said that he conceived of Alcibiades also as
very largely moved by personal ambition and the need of money.
Indeed he hardly ever mentions his policies without noting the
mixed motives behind them (V 43. 2, VI 15. 2, VIII 47. 1), and it
is significant of his consistency of judgment when he says of him
in 411 that he then for the first time genuinely acted in the city's
interest (VIII 86. 4). Now Pericles in his last speech names four
qualities which a democratic leader must possess:[1] he must be able
γνῶναί τε τὰ δέοντα καὶ ἑρμηνεῦσαι ταῦτα, and must be φιλόπολίς τε καὶ
χρημάτων κρείσσων (II 60. 5), which qualities are subsumed in the
historian's judgment of Pericles in II 65. 8, κατεῖχε τὸ πλῆθος ἐλευθέρως. From the description of the later leaders both in II 65 and
throughout the *History*, it is clear that he kept these qualities in
mind, considering it, as has been said, Athens' supreme misfortune
never to have had another statesman who combined them all.
Cleon (as is evident from the Mytilenean debate) did not understand the true needs of the empire; he also enflamed, rather than
checked the people's dangerous desires. Alcibiades, though gifted
with political insight, a strong speaker, and able to lead the people,
forfeited his influence because he was neither φιλόπολις nor χρημάτων
κρείσσων;[2] and Nicias, though possessed of these two latter qualities
(it is for this reason that his ἀρετή is signalized in the end, VII
86. 5) lacked the power either of rapid action or of compelling
leadership. Only Hermocrates possessed all four essential traits.
One therefore sees in this remark of Pericles another strand of
unity running forward through the whole work; indeed it runs back
to the beginning, since in I 22 Thucydides describes his own
speeches as intended to convey τὰ δέοντα (that is, judgments of
policy of the sort which Pericles was supremely able to make) and
Themistocles too is said to have revealed the same insight (I

---

[1] Cf. G. F. Bender, *Der Begriff des Staatsmannes bei Thukydides*, Würzburg,
1938.

[2] He tries to prove at Sparta that he is φιλόπολις (VI 91. 2), but the irony
of the statement is enhanced by the contrast to Pericles (see above, p. 270 n. 1).

138. 3) in inaugurating the naval policy, the remoter background of which, as we have seen, is expounded in the Archaeology.

It remains therefore only to say a word of the self-interest and folly of the people themselves, which to Thucydides was the latent cause of all Athens' extremism and, quite specifically, of the great disaster at Syracuse. It has already been suggested that the ruinous policies of Pericles' successors described in II 65 were to his mind merely symptoms of the more fundamental social disturbance set forth in the description of στάσις in III 82–83. War, he says, is a βίαιος διδάσκαλος (III 82. 2) which inflames the people and thus makes them the prey of unscrupulous leaders. Pericles himself had warned the Athenians against their own veering moods (I 140. 1, II 61. 2), and during the plague, which is described as somewhat similar to war in its effects,[1] they were sufficiently demoralized to reject both him and his policies. On the other hand, in the course of his last speech he reassures the people by revealing the full extent of Athens' power, although, as he goes on, he had purposely never done so before for fear lest they misuse it (II 62. 1). Thus the historian's estimate of Pericles is that of a stabilizing influence against either dejection or overconfidence on the part of the people (II 65. 8). Cleon, on the contrary, in the fear inspired by the revolt of Mytilene, fostered their inevitable mood of violence, and likewise after Pylos he played on their contrasting optimism, when (so Thucydides keeps repeating) πλεόνων ὠρέγοντο.[2] The attack on Melos constituted still another departure from Periclean policy, which, as we have seen, was based on the restraint, even the concealment, of Athens' full power, not on its naked revelation. Hence, when Thucydides explains the expedition to Syracuse by saying that the people expected to gain an ἀΐδιος μισθοφορά (VI 24. 3) and that they were moved by an ἄγαν τῶν πλεόνων ἐπιθυμία (24. 4), the words come as a climax to all that has been said before of their dangerous instability and of the equally dangerous leadership to which it gave rise. Here in fact, to Thucydides' mind, is the su-

---

[1] The ἀνομία which began with the plague (II 54.) is attributed to the same destruction of ordinary habits that is noted in III 82. 2 as the cause of revolution.

[2] See above, p. 287.

preme weakness of Athens, a weakness which from the Archaeology on is often contrasted with Sparta's one great strength, a way of life which though rigid and unprogressive, was at least stable.[1] But, it must be repeated, this political weakness of Athens is merely, so to speak, the obverse of her material strength, since both were equally the product of her democratic government. Thus Athens was to Thucydides the strongest of all Greek states in his own time or in the past, because as a naval democracy she had at her command the willing, progressive energies of a multitude of free citizens. But by the same token, she was liable to the most costly errors when, under the stress of popular demands (themselves partly the result of the stress of war), self-seeking leaders held forth dangerous hopes. And when, as in Alcibiades' case, lesser politicians from equally interested motives (VI 28. 2) attacked the one man who, whatever his weaknesses, possessed the gift of leadership, the suicidal forces at work in Athens were plain. Alcibiades in Sparta could therefore contrast a democracy based on the whole people, τὸ ξύμπαν, which he said the Alcmaeonids had always striven for, with one dominated by the πονηροί (VI 89. 5–6) — the same point which Thucydides himself makes in II 65. 5 and which he has constantly in mind in comparing the temperate Athens of Pericles to the destructive city of his successors. It made no difference then if, chastened by the disaster at Syracuse, πρὸς τὸ παραχρῆμα περιδεές, ὅπερ φιλεῖ δῆμος ποιεῖν, ἑτοῖμοι ἦσαν εὐτακτεῖν (VIII 1. 4). The seeds of division were planted, and it is certain from II 65 that, had Thucydides finished his *History*, he would have followed to the end that process of disunification which he had already traced in the effects of the plague, in the policies of Cleon, in the brutalizing influence of war itself, in the conquest of Melos, and in the Sicilian expedition.

Thus if one surveys the *History* as a whole, keeping in mind the author's two theses in regard to Athenian democracy — that, on the one hand, it made Athens vastly stronger than her rival in all material ways and in the spirit of her citizens but, on the other, was forever liable to the dangers of political disunion and intemperate leadership — the unity of the work becomes clear. One could say

---

[1] I 18. 1, 71. 3, 84, IV 18. 4, 55. 1, VIII 24. 4.

that up to the death of Pericles the first thesis is dominant. It inspires the earlier history of naval power in the Archaeology, the
view of the causes of the war in I 23 and in the Pentecontaetia, the
great contrast between the two rivals in the speeches at Sparta,
the opposing forecasts of victory by the Corinthians and by
Pericles, and above all, the Funeral Oration. And as we have seen,
the same view of Athens' great strength keeps recurring thereafter
in the concept of παράλογος, to be asserted still more strongly in the
description of her huge effort at Syracuse and even in the account
of her later ability to continue. But with the analysis of the effects
of the plague, the self-defense of Pericles in his third speech, and
the comparison of him to his successors in II 65, the concept of
Athens' political weakness has already come into play. Underlying the portrait of Cleon, it is brilliantly analyzed in relation to
the more general effects of war in the description of στάσις. Again
after Pylos (itself a display of Athenian spirit and, as such, a conscious contrast to the reverse at Syracuse), the popular desire for
expansion leads to the loss of Athens' chief gains, and the same
desire, as cause of the Sicilian expedition and symptom of the
political folly by which Alcibiades was relieved of his command,
proved ruinous at Syracuse. Thus the Sicilian narrative, as an
account both of Athens' supreme strength and of her supreme folly,
draws together the vital strands of the whole preceding work.

III

As was said at the start, it is not the purpose of this paper to
discuss in detail the many passages sometimes regarded as of early
date, a task largely performed by the scholars mentioned at the
end of the first section. On the other hand, it is difficult to leave
this question of the unity of the *History* without trying to explain
why Thucydides waits until after the Peace of Nicias to expound
his view that the Archidamian, Epidaurian, Mantinean, Sicilian,
and Decelean wars comprised in fact a single struggle. For his
failure to say so at the beginning has been without doubt the principle cause of the whole controversy on when he wrote his work
and, from the time of Ullrich on, has afforded the chief argument to

those who doubted its unity. To omit minor variations, their view
has been that he began his work and had much of the first four and
a quarter books completed before he realised that the Peace of
Nicias was not the end of the war; that he continued it after 404,
going back at that time to alter what he had done in the light of
later events; but that he died before completing this process of
revision; and that consequently the first books are a medley of early
and late passages. As we have seen, it has also been thought by
some that he wrote the Sicilian books after 413, revising them at
the end of the war, and on that view one should reckon not with
two but with three periods of composition, namely, the years just
after 421, after 413, and after 404. It need hardly be said that both
of these theories are untenable, if the *History* gives anything like
as clear and unified an interpretation of the war as has been suggested above. For it is difficult to imagine any man so far-sighted
that he could anticipate by ten or fifteen years what coming events
would teach him. To take a modern example, although we can
now see in the battle of Marengo the prophecy of Napoleon's
career and in the occupation of the Rhineland the future course
of the Third Reich, it is unlikely that a contemporary observer,
however keen, would have seen in these events exactly what he
saw after Austerlitz or after the invasion of Poland. Accordingly,
if throughout the *History* Thucydides draws similar conclusions
from widely spaced events, portrays the antagonists as acting consistently, and attributes like ideas and phrases to men speaking
at very different times, it is natural to see in these continuing lines
of thought only the simplification of retrospect. As was suggested
above, by the time that he wrote his *History*, he had apparently
reduced his thought to a large, though not unlimited, number of
recurrent patterns. If so, however, these patterns inevitably betray one period of composition when the war lay clear before his
eyes and he contemplated both early and late events in each others'
light. To claim such a limited period of composition for the *History*
is not, as has been said, to claim that it was written without earlier
notes or wholly consecutively. There can be no doubt that Thucydides wrestled with his material seeking to impose order and shape
upon it, and in the struggle of writing he may at times have relied

heavily on earlier notes or have inserted new passages somewhat abruptly into a previously written narrative. We cannot conceivably follow this complicated process of authorship. But what we can, indeed must, believe, if the previous argument holds, is that no note was utilized and no passage composed before the whole war and, by consequence, the whole plan of the work were already in his mind. For only that assumption will explain the close interplay and firm consistency of his thought throughout the whole *History*.

It therefore merely remains to suggest why he may not have desired to mention the 27-years war at the start, although he was writing with it in mind. Perhaps three chief reasons could be advanced for the omission: first, that such a statement was unnecessary; then, that it would have violated his practice of confining himself to the period which he is describing; and third, that if he had made such a statement, he would normally have done so in a digression, which, however, was not called for until peace had seemingly been made in 421.

To take these points in order, the view, formerly advanced by Ed. Meyer,[1] that an initial statement regarding the length of the war was unnecessary, has great weight, if only one assume that the *History* was actually written after 404. When the Greek world had just lived through a long conflict, there could be no doubt what conflict the historian was referring to. The only escape from such a conclusion is to assume that his contemporaries did not connect the five. minor wars of the period — an assumption, improbable in itself, which is not confirmed by such references to the separate wars as have been collected from later writers.[2] For Thucydides himself can in the same breath use the word πόλεμος of the long war and of its separate phases (V 26, VII 28. 3). Accordingly, to speak as he does of an Ἀττικὸς πόλεμος or of a Μαντινικὸς πόλεμος (V 26. 2, 28. 2) did not mean that he could not also speak of a πόλεμος τῶν Πελοποννησίων καὶ Ἀθηναίων (namely, the 27-years war). Like the later Greeks, he used the word ambiguously, and there is no reason

---

[1] See above, p. 258 n. 1.

[2] F. W. Ullrich, *Beiträge zur Erklärung des Thukydides*, Hamburg, 1846, pp. 9–16, cf. Patzer, "Problem," p. 18.

to suppose that his contemporaries did not do the same. Thus, for instance, it is unnecessary to conclude with Steup that the statement in IV 48. 5 to the effect that the revolution at Corcyra stopped ὅσα γε κατὰ τὸν πόλεμον τόνδε means that Thucydides had not yet achieved the concept of a single war.[1] All one need conclude, as before said, is that Thucydides to the end used the word πόλεμος both of the long war and of any of its phases. Hence, considering the reasons advanced above (pp. 267–268, 273–275) for the late date of the Archaeology — namely, that it broaches the idea of magnitude most fully expounded in the Sicilian books and that it also reveals the historical significance of Athens' naval power — there seems not the slightest impediment to taking the first sentence in the *History* as referring to the whole war, which he in fact describes, as we have seen, in terms of the two ideas just mentioned. In 404 the sentence could hardly have connoted anything else.

The second reason for the omission is lodged in the whole nature of his thought. Few historians have doubtless ever relived so intensely the situations and scenes successively under consideration as he. Whether the explanation is to be found in his temperament, in his early identification with politics, in the quickening of memory which exile must have bred in him, or in a combination of all these and other factors, may remain uncertain; but the fact is attested on virtually every page of his work. It seems indeed a principal, if not the only, reason for his whole dramatic procedure of bringing the past vividly before the reader in speeches and descriptions. That being the case, he was undoubtedly absorbed when he began his *History* with the problems and choices confronting Periclean Athens, and was not at that time concerned with the end of the war. It is true that he digresses at times to explain why he thinks as he does about certain crucial questions; neverthe-

---

[1] Since revolution broke out again at Corcyra in 410 (Diodorus, XIII 48), the passage was written after that date, and apparently some time after, since the interval between the two revolutions is probably to be contrasted with that at Megara, which is said to have been exceptionally long (IV 74. 4). But even neglecting the latter passage, to say that Thucydides in 410 had not yet grasped the unity of the war is not only to attribute very little insight to him; it is also to say that he falsified history when he represented such a view as already existing shortly after the Peace of Nicias (see above, pp. 264–266).

less, as will appear presently, even these digressions are not primarily intended to explain the past or future, but to illustrate some vital force at work in what is to him, at that moment, the present. Here again the point may perhaps be clarified by an example. One of the passages most often adduced as of early date is that in the Archaeology (10. 2) where, after observing that the power of a vanished state cannot be judged from the mere extent of its ruins, he goes on to say that Sparta might someday be much underrated on such evidence, whereas under the same circumstances the power of Athens would be thought διπλασίαν . . . . ἢ ἔστιν. The difficulty is with ἔστιν, since, so it is argued, Thucydides would have written ἦν if he had composed the Archaeology after the end of the war. But (to say nothing of the fact that we do not know when he died and thus how much of the revival of Attic power he may have witnessed), it is unthinkable that he would have evoked the picture of Athens' defeat at the very moment when he is expounding the magnitude of the war and the high condition of the contestants. One would naturally therefore take ἔστιν as an historical present denoting the era then under consideration, particularly since, as Patzer has shown,[1] he uses such presents even of towns the destruction of which he himself notes. In sum, this passage merely brings into sharper relief the whole problem of his failure to mention the 27-years war at the start, and part of the answer to both questions must be found in the nature of his art and of his thought. A man of such absorption in the past and struggling as hard as he to analyze its dominant forces might normally be expected to confine himself (doubtless to some degree unconsciously) to the matter in hand, reserving future events for such a time as they would normally come up.

This observation leads to one final reason why he may have failed to mention the length of the war at the start, to wit, the character of his introduction. The Archaeology is not, properly speaking, an introduction but a digression confirming his statement on the magnitude of the war. When therefore Dionysius of Halicarnassus says that he should have begun his work by tracing

---

[1] See above, p. 262 n. 3.

events down from the distant past[1] — that is, by joining the
Archaeology and the Pentecontaetia — he is misunderstanding
Thucydides' method. The latter did not bring in the past to make
an imposing façade, nor does he digress on the future merely to
relieve the narrative, but when he departs from his theme, it is in
order to confirm some important statement which he has just
made. Thus although Dionysius rightly sees that the Pentecontaetia is a continuation of the Archeology, he fails to grasp the
true nature of each as corroborative notes, in the one case, on
Sparta's fear of Athens' growing power and, in the other, on the
magnitude of the war. Now there can be little doubt that Thucydides feels most free to glance at both the future and the past in
such confirmatory digressions: at the future, for example, in his
estimate of Pericles' successors (which supports the statement in
regard to his foresight, II 65. 6) his judgment of Archelaus (II
100. 2) or his remarks on Decelea (VII 27); at the past in the digressions on Cylon (I 126. 3–12), Pausanias and Themistocles (I 128. 3–
138), the history of Attica (II 15–16), or the tyrannicides (VI 54–
59). Hence if he had discussed the length of the war at the beginning, he would presumably have done so in a digression intended
to confirm some statement to the effect that this was the longest
war in Greek history. As it was, he was concerned rather with the
idea of magnitude and mentions the idea of length only in passing:
τούτου δὲ τοῦ πολέμου μῆκός τε μέγα προύβη (I 23. 1). With his interest
in chronology, he would clearly have had to go into the question of
length somewhat deeply, and therefore being, as before said, absorbed in the actual beginnings of the war and being delayed, as it
was, in explaining the nature and methods of his *History*, he de-
ferred that question until the time when it naturally came up,
that is, until the time when peace had seemingly been made.
What therefore is usually called the second introduction in V 26 is
only partly such; it is essentially a statement that he is continuing
his narrative beyond the seeming peace, together with a digression
to explain why the several smaller wars comprise one long war and
how long that war lasted. As was said earlier, there is no reason to

---

[1] *Epist. ad Pomp.* 769–770 R.

suppose that this was a unique or peculiar opinion; but, considering the ambiguity of his own and doubtless of his contemporaries' use of the word πόλεμος, it called for some discussion, as it did also from the point of view of chronology. Accordingly it is Thucydides' method, not any previous ignorance on his part, which dictates the place and nature of his remarks on the length of the war. After all, since on any theory much of the first book was written after 404, one might suppose that he would have changed the opening sentences first of all, if he knew that these did not express his full experience of the conflict. As it is, however, the omission is far more readily explained not only by the general character of his thought but, quite specifically, by his normal practice in digressions. Indeed to expect anything else is probably to imitate Dionysius in imputing methods to him which were never his own. But if that is the case, then it is possible to return with greater confidence to the facts set forth earlier and to find in the continuity and uniformity of Thucydides' thought the essential proof of the unity of his work.

THE USE OF HEMLOCK FOR CAPITAL PUNISHMENT

By Robert J. Bonner

THE date of the introduction into Athens of hemlock (κώνειον) as a means of execution in all probability falls somewhere in the latter half of the fifth century. The earliest known executions by hemlock were carried out under the rule of the Thirty.[1] Lipsius suggested that the Thirty introduced the practice in 404 B.C. "Die Hinrichtung durch den Schierlingsbecher ist übrigens, soviel wir sehen, erst durch die Dreissig in Aufnahme gekommen."[2] Lipsius supports his view by referring to some passages in the Orators to the effect that the Thirty put to death many Athenians by ordering them to drink the hemlock. Lysias in his prosecution of Eratosthenes, one of the Thirty, sought to fix upon him the responsibility for the death of his brother. "Polemarchus received from the Thirty their accustomed order to drink hemlock, with no statement made as to the reason for his execution: still less was he allowed to be tried and defend himself."[3] The words τὸ ὑπ' ἐκείνων εἰθισμένον παράγγελμα might seem at first sight to indicate that the Thirty introduced a new method of execution, namely, an order to commit suicide by taking poison. But the real charge against the Thirty was that they put men to death without giving them the semblance of a trial. The method of execution is of no significance.

There is a factor in the case that Lipsius has overlooked. In the year 405 B.C., Aristophanes[4] speaks of women committing suicide by drinking hemlock. In an earlier passage in the same play[5] he displays a knowledge of the effects of hemlock poisoning that could scarcely be gained from casual cases of suicide, which are commonly private matters. Dionysus is represented as seeking a short road to the lower world in order that he may bring back to life the best

---

[1] Glotz in Daremberg and Saglio, *Dict. Ant.*, *s.v.* κώνειον, III p. 863.

[2] *Attisches Recht* 77 n. 101.

[3] Lysias 12. 17.

[4] *Frogs* 1050–1051.

[5] ll. 123–126.

poet. He consults Heracles, who had himself once made the journey successfully. Heracles suggests hanging, a leap from a high
tower, and a draught of hemlock. The latter Dionysus rejects as
follows:

Her.   Then there's a track, a short and beaten cut,
        By pestle and mortar.
Dio.   Hemlock, do you mean?
Her.   Just so.
        No, that's too deathly cold a way;
Dio.   You have hardly started ere your shins get numbed.

> ψυχράν γε καὶ δυσχείμερον·
> εὐθὺς γὰρ ἀποπήγνυσι τἀντικνήμια.

It will be of immediate interest to quote for comparison with
these lines of Aristophanes a portion of Plato's[1] description of the
death of Socrates. After drinking the hemlock, "He walked about
and, when he said his legs were heavy, lay down on his back, for
such was the advice of the attendant. The man who had admin-
istered the poison laid his hands on him and after a while examined
his feet and legs, and then pinched his foot hard and asked if he
felt it. He said, 'no'; then, after that, his thighs, and passing up-
wards in this way he showed us that he was growing cold and
rigid (ψύχοιτό τε καὶ πηγνῦτο)."

The commentators on the *Frogs* almost invariably refer to this
passage in the *Phaedo*.[2]

Lysias[3] mentions *apotympanismos* as a method of executing
those who made traitorous signals to the enemy. From this and
several other passages it might very well be concluded that treason
was punished by *apotympanismos*. Aeschines[4] on trial for treason
says: "It is not death that men dread but it is a dishonored end.
Is he not indeed to be pitied who must look into the sneering face
of an enemy and hear with his ears his insults? But nevertheless I
have taken the risk, I have exposed my body to the peril."

[1] *Phaedo* 117B–118E.
[2] Cf. Rogers' note *Frogs* 125.
[3] 13. 67.
[4] 2. 181 f., translation by Adams.

It is not difficult to determine the kind of execution which Aeschines has in mind, when one recalls the fact that Socrates met his death in the midst of friends. We may be fairly certain that a traitor was punished by *apotympanismos*. There are two passages in Demosthenes[1] which bear on this problem. On one occasion Demosthenes says "These men who have sold themselves to Philip you should detest and execute by *apotympanismos*." On another occasion he said: "If Philip had heard that those who spoke thus at that time were put to death in this fashion as soon as they returned here, he would have done what the King of Persia did."[2] These cases look like treason but Gernet[3] properly warns us that we may have here mere rhetorical exaggeration. An ambassador who betrayed his country would of course be a traitor, but men who had sold themselves to Philip and became his hirelings to plead his cause in Athens could scarcely be regarded as traitors according to the law because Athens cherished freedom of speech. Demosthenes is in all probability trying to stir up enmity against the hirelings of Philip. If he wished to take action, the only feasible way of proceeding would be to try these men before the assembly just as the generals were tried in 406 B.C.[4]

Gernet[5] regards the manner of the execution of murderers as insoluble. Menestratus was executed as an ἀνδροφόνος by *apotympanismos* but since the question of treason was involved with that of technical homicide, the case is uncertain.[6] But the fact that the successful prosecutor of a murderer was allowed to be present at the execution of a convicted murderer[7] renders it almost certain that hemlock was not used since Socrates and others[8] died in the midst of their friends. To murderers may be added malefactors,

---

[1] 8. 61.
[2] 19. 137.
[3] *REG* XXXVII 276 f.
[4] Xenophon *Hellen.* I 7. 9.
[5] *Op. cit.* 265 n. 3.
[6] Cf. H. J. Treston, *Poine, A Study in Greek Blood-Vengeance* (London, 1923), p. 231.
[7] Demos. 23. 69.
[8] Plato *Phaedo* 116 D.

κακοῦργοι.[1] It is said that a brother of Agoratus was convicted as a clothes stealer (λωποδύτης) and garroted. As a λωποδύτης was one of five different classes of thieves known as malefactors, it is quite likely that all were garroted on conviction.

The view of Gernet[2] and of Glotz[3] that death by hemlock was "suicide par tolérance" must be based on the theory that the Thirty introduced hemlock as a means of execution, for in all other cases, notably that of Socrates, the execution was carried out by the official servants of the Eleven.

[1] Lysias 13. 67.
[2] *Op. cit.* 267.
[3] Cf. *L'ordalie* 91.

STUDIES IN HISTORICAL LITERATURE OF THE FOURTH CENTURY B.C.

By Herbert Bloch

CONTENTS

		PAGE
I.	The *Hellenica of Oxyrhynchus* and its Authorship	303
	1. Διαίρεσις	308
	2. Theopompus	317
	3. Ephorus	321
	4. Androtion	328
	5. Tradition and Preservation	334
II.	Notes on the *Atthis* of Androtion	341
III.	Theophrastus' *Nomoi* and Aristotle	355
	1. A New Fragment of Theophrastus' *Nomoi*	357
	2. An Alleged Reference to Theophrastus' *Nomoi* in Aristotle's *Politics* (E 9, 1309 b 14)	361
	3. Theophrastus' *Nomoi* and the Second Part of Aristotle's *Athenaion Politeia*	367

I

The *Hellenica of Oxyrhynchus* and its Authorship

THIRTY years have passed since the so-called *Hellenica of Oxyrhynchus*, — apart from the 'Αθηναίων πολιτεία of Aristotle the most important papyrus-fragment of a historical nature ever discovered, — was published in the fifth volume of the *Oxyrhynchus Papyri*.[1] The question of the authorship of the work, in the extant fragments of which events of the years 396/5 are related, arose at once and has not yet been satisfactorily answered. Since the discovery of the papyrus, more than a hundred books, articles and occasional notes on this problem have been published by nearly

NOTE. I am indebted to Professor W. S. Ferguson for many suggestions and to Dr. S. Dow for valuable aid in the preparation of the manuscript. Thanks are due also to Dr. A. H. Travis, who has very kindly assisted me with the English of this study.

[1] No. 842. In the remainder of this article, the *Hellenica of Oxyrhynchus* will be referred to simply as P.

304   *Herbert Bloch*

seventy scholars;[1] several of these scholars have repeatedly defined

[1] Most of the modern literature till 1926 is given in the edition of E. Kalinka, Leipzig, 1927, pp. ix–xiv. Supplementary material is presented below (it has all been incorporated in the chronological table pp. 306 f.):

1910: Ch. Dugas, "La Campagne d'Agésilas en Asie Mineure," *Bull. Corr. Hell.*, XXXIV, p. 93.

1919: Ed. Meyer, *Caesars Monarchie und das Prinzipat des Pompejus* (2nd ed.), p. 617.

1920: G. Busolt, *Griechische Staatskunde*, I, p. 81.

1921: E. M. Walker, "The Oxyrhynchus Historian," in *New Chapters in the History of Greek Literature* (J. U. Powell and E. A. Barber), pp. 124 ff.

1922: F. Jacoby, "Kratippos," *RE* XI 2 pp. 1656–1658.

     A. S. Hunt *Journ. of Egypt. Arch.* VIII 125.

     F. Kenyon *Journ. of Egypt. Arch.* VIII 130.

1926: U. v. Wilamowitz-Moellendorff, *Reden und Vorträge*, II, 4th ed., p. 224.

     W. Otto in Busolt-Swoboda, *Griechische Staatskunde*, II, p. 1577 *ad* p. 81. 2.

1927: W. K. Prentice *Class. Philol.* XXII 408.

     W. Aly *Gött. gel. Anz.* CLXXXIX 287.

     E. Cavaignac, "Sur l'attribution des fragments de papyrus," *Revue de l'Ég. anc.*, I, pp. 176–181.

     A. Körte *Hist. Zeitschr.* CXXXVI 85–90.

1928: L. Castiglioni *Gnomon* IV 18.

     G. De Sanctis *Riv. di Filol. class.* LVI 532–541.

     Ed. Schwartz *Die Antike* IV 22 (cf. F. Jacoby, *F Gr Hist* II B p. 1236) = *Gesamm. Schriften*, I, 1938, p. 77.

1931: G. De Sanctis, "Nuovi studî sulle 'Elleniche' di Oxyrhynchos," *Atti Acc. Torino*, LXVI, pp. 157–194.

     A. Momigliano, "Androzione e le 'Elleniche' di Ossirinco," *Atti Acc. Torino*, LXVI, pp. 29–49.

     A. Momigliano, "Teopompo," *Riv. di Filol. class.*, LIX, pp. 237, 354.

1932: E. Cavaignac, "Réflexions sur Ephore," *Mélanges Glotz*, I, pp. 149 ff.

1933: F. Cornelius *Klio* XXVI 29.

     E. Drerup, *Das Generationsproblem in d. griech. und griech.-röm. Kultur*, p. 64.

     J. G. Winter, *Life and Letters in the Papyri*, pp. 240–242.

1934: R. Laqueur, "Theopompos," *RE* V A 2. 2190 ff.

1935: G. L. Barber, *The Historian Ephorus*, Cambridge.

1936: M. Cary *Class. Rev.* L 64.

     P. Treves *Athenaeum* XIV 156 and note.

     G. Glotz *Histoire grecque* III 461 note 109.

1937: Ed. Schwartz *Philologus* XCII 21 note 3.

     P. Treves *Athenaeum* XV 126.

1938: S. Accame, "Le fonti di Diodoro per la guerra Deceleica," *Rendic. Acc. Linc.* ser. VI, vol. XIV, pp. 347 ff.

their position regarding it. It would be absurd therefore to return once more to the question, if it were not possible to contribute something new. The point of departure of the present treatment is not the modern literature on P, but the original work of the Oxyrhynchus historian itself, — particularly its form, its position in Greek historiography, and its fate in antiquity until the time when the papyrus of Oxyrhynchus was written (about 200 A.D.).

The following table[1] shows how far scholars still are from any agreement. Indeed, within recent years all the solutions ever proposed have found defenders. Ed. Schwartz declared three years ago (1937) that he had been firmly convinced for years that the author of P was Ephorus; several writers maintained the identity of P with the enigmatic Cratippus; even the Theopompus hypothesis, which has been practically abandoned since the war, experienced recently an unexpected resurrection (1934); and G. De Sanctis, after twenty years, restated his opinion that the papyrus was a part of the *Atthis* of Androtion (1928, 1931). F. Jacoby, rejecting in a funda-

---

1939: J. T. Shotwell, *The History of History*, 2nd ed., p. 225 note 14.
   H. E. Stier in Ed. Meyer, *Geschichte des Altertums*, IV 1, 3rd ed., p. 265.

For general works touching upon P, compare:

M. Lenchantin De Gubernatis *Aegyptus* II (1921) 23–32.

J. Kromayer, *Antike Schlachtfelder*, IV, 1926, pp. 261 ff. (Sardis).

M. Servi, "Alcibiade e le Elleniche di Oxyrhynchos," *Atene e Roma*, n. s., XIII (1932), p. 180.

H. G. Strebel, *Wertung und Wirkung des Thukydideischen Geschichtswerkes in der griechisch-römischen Literatur*, Diss. München, Speyer, 1935, pp. 8–10.

The *editio princeps* remains fundamental. The most important of the larger studies is that of L. Pareti, "Cratippo e le Elleniche di Oxyrhynchos," *Studi It. di Filol. class.*, XIX (1912), pp. 398 ff. On Ed. Meyer's book *Theopomps Hellenika* (1909), see *infra* p. 318. E. M. Walker's *The Hellenica Oxyrhynchia*, 1913, is a brilliant, but forced, attempt to defend a faulty thesis, — faulty in spite of Ed. Schwartz's support. Among more recent studies, the most interesting and original is F. Jacoby's excellent article, "Der Verfasser der Hellenika von Oxyrhynchos," *Nachr. Gött. Ges.*, 1924, pp. 13 ff.; cf. *F Gr Hist* 66. Finally, I refer expressly to G. L. Barber's sound treatment of the question in his book on *Ephorus* (1935) and to G. De Sanctis' various contributions: 1908: "L'Attide di Androzione e un papiro di Oxyrhynchos," *Atti Acc. Torino*, XLIII, pp. 331–356 (= I); 1928 (= II); 1931 (= III).

   [1] In the table, after the chief citation of an article has been made, all subsequent citations of that article are enclosed in parentheses.

	FOR THEOPOMPUS	FOR CRATIPPUS	FOR EPHORUS	OTHER AUTHORS PROPOSED	AGAINST THEOPOMPUS	AGAINST CRATIPPUS	AGAINST EPHORUS
1908	B. P. Grenfell, A. S. Hunt, Ed. Meyer, U. v. Wilamowitz, G. Busolt, H. Weil, U. Wilcken	F. Blass, V. Costanzi, W. Dittenberger, W. A. Goligher, A. v. Mess, A. J. Reinach, W. Schmid, A. W. Verall, E. M. Walker		G. De Sanctis (Androtion), C. Fuhr (Anonymous), G. E. Underhill (Anonymous)	(B. P. Grenfell) (A. S. Hunt) W. Crönert (G. De Sanctis) W. Rhys Roberts Ed. Schwartz (G. E. Underhill) (E. M. Walker)	(G. E. Underhill)	(E. M. Walker) (W. Crönert) (G. E. Underhill)
1909	Ed. Meyer, Ed. Schwartz, W. Seyffert	J. B. Bury, F. Jacoby (?)	F. Reuss		(F. Jacoby)	B. L. Foscolo, (Ed. Meyer), (Ed. Schwartz)	
1910	G. Busolt, E. Drerup, U. Kahrstedt, H. Swoboda, P. Wendland		W. Bauer		C. Dugas, A. Franz		
1911		(K. J. Beloch)	W. Judeich	H. Peter (Anonymous)			R. Laqueur
1912	E. Cavaignac, P. Wendland, U. v. Wilamowitz	K. J. Beloch, C. F. Lehmann-Haupt, (P. Maas), L. Pareti, W. Schmid		(C. F. Lehmann-Haupt) (Anonymous?)	C. F. Lehmann-Haupt, P. Maas, (L. Pareti)		(L. Pareti)
1913	E. Cavaignac, A. Körte, H. Swoboda	A. Opitz	E. M. Walker	F. Ruehl (Anonymous?)	W. Bauer, A. E. Kalischek	F. Jacoby	
1914		C. F. Lehmann-Haupt, H. Lins, A. v. Mess					(A. v. Mess)
1915		J. H. Lipsius			(J. H. Lipsius)		(J. H. Lipsius)
1916		J. H. Lipsius			B. Keil		(B. Keil)
1917		E. Kalinka, A. Körte	M. Gelzer				J. H. Lipsius
1918	W. Schubart						
1919	Ed. Meyer	T. Lenschau, J. H. Lipsius, K. Münscher	B. P. Grenfell		B. Haussoullier	Ed. Schwartz	(J. H. Lipsius)

1920	G. Busolt E. Howald	K. Münscher					
1921			E. M. Walker	W. Otto (Anonymous)		F. Jacoby	
1922		K. J. Beloch	A. S. Hunt F. Kenyon				
1923							
1924		A. Körte M. Pohlenz		F. Jacoby (Daemachus)			
1925	W. Aly				J. Geffken		
1926				F. Jacoby (Daemachus) W. Otto (Daemachus) U. v. Wilamowitz (Anonymous)			
1927	W. K. Prentice	W. Aly E. Kalinka A. Körte	E. Cavaignac				
1928			Ed. Schwartz		G. De Sanctis L. Castiglioni	(G. De Sanctis) (L. Castiglioni)	
1931				G. De Sanctis (Androtion) A. Momigliano (Androtion)			
1932		E. Drerup (?) F. Cornelius	E. Cavaignac				
1933			J. G. Winter				
1934	R. Laqueur						G. L. Barber
1935							M. Cary P. Treves
1936			G. Glotz				
1937			Ed. Schwartz				P. Treves
1938			(Ed. Schwartz) (See 1928)				S. Accame
1939	H. E. Stier (see Ed. Meyer 1909)						J. T. Shotwell

mental article all theories previously proposed, started the research along new lines (1924): it is not very important whether Daemachus of Plataea, Jacoby's candidate, was the author of P or not; the decisive point is that Jacoby abandoned the alternatives Theopompus, Cratippus, and Ephorus. He was followed in the main by U. v. Wilamowitz-Moellendorff (1926), once one of the most authoritative advocates of Theopompus, in a nearly unknown note in the last edition of his "*Reden und Vorträge.*"[1]

1. Διαίρεσις

"In the arrangement of his material he has adopted an annalistic method, evidently imitated from Thucydides, whereby events are narrated in chronological order and divided into years beginning in the 'summer' (whether spring or midsummer is not clear), and he has not grouped together according to subject events separated by any considerable distance of time." Thus, even in the *editio princeps* this most important feature of P was emphasized.[2] And this influence of Thucydides on the chronological system of P is so evident that a few examples will suffice to prove the point.

The chief passage, in spite of its mutilation, is 4. 1, where a typically Thucydidean formula of transition (from one year to another) is preserved:

$$- - - - - τὰ\ μ]ὲν\ οὖν\ ἀδρότατα\ τῶν$$
$$[- - - - - - - - - τῷ\ θέρε]ι\ τούτῳ\ συμβάντων$$

---

[1] *Loc. cit.*, p. 224: "Von den drei Fortsetzern, welche den Torso des thukydideischen Werkes ergänzten, kennen wir über Theopomp kaum etwas; der Historiker von Oxyrhynchos (von dem wir zwar wissen, dass er Theopomp, Ephoros, Kratippos *nicht* ist, aber mit Zuversicht können wir ihm keinen Namen geben) . . ." and his note: "Mehr darf man nicht sagen, auch wenn man die geistreiche Vermutung von Jacoby sehr gern glauben möchte."

[2] P. 121. For the influence of Thucydides' system of arrangement on P compare: v. Mess *Rhein. Mus.* LXIII (1908) 371; Ed. Meyer *Theop. Hell.* 55, 57, 61, 63, 121, 133, 137, 143, 148 f.; F. Jacoby *Klio* IX (1909) 113 f.; W. Judeich *Rhein. Mus.* LXVI (1911) 97 note; R. Laqueur *Hermes* XLVI (1911) 353; L. Pareti *loc. cit.* 441, 449 ff., 480; E. M. Walker *Hell. Ox.* 18; Grenfell and Hunt *Oxy. Pap.* XIII (1919), 110; F. Jacoby *F Gr Hist* II C p. 10 f.; R. Laqueur *RE* V A 2 (1934) 2196; G. L. Barber *loc. cit.* 59; H. G. Strebel *loc. cit.* 9.

[οὕτως ἐγένετο. ἀπὸ τούτου] δὲ τοῦ [θ]έρους τῇ μὲν
[- - - - - - - - - - - - - -] ἔτος ὄγδοον ἐνειστήκει.
[κατὰ δὲ τὴν 'Ασίαν τότε - - - -]αρος τὰς τριήρεις ἀπα-
[γαγὼν - - - -

Compare with this the words with which Thucydides begins his
narration of the actual war:

II 1: ἄρχεται δὲ ὁ πόλεμος ἐνθένδε ἤδη 'Αθηναίων καὶ Πελοποννησίων
- - - γέγραπται δ' ἑξῆς ὡς ἕκαστα ἐγίγνετο κατὰ θέρος καὶ χειμῶνα.

(Cf. also V 26. 1.)

Among other passages which represent such a formula compare
the following:

(a) II 70. 5: ταῦτα μὲν ἐν τῷ χειμῶνι ἐγένετο, καὶ [τὸ] δεύτερον ἔτος ἐτε-
λεύτα τῷ πολέμῳ τῷδε ὃν Θουκυδίδης ξυνέγραψεν. τοῦ δ' ἐπιγιγνο-
μένου θέρους οἱ Πελοποννήσιοι - - -

(b) IV 88. 2: ταῦτα μὲν οὖν ἐν τῷ θέρει τούτῳ ἐγένετο.

The author's synchronistic method is illustrated by the following
correspondences with Thucydides. In each of these passages there
is a shift of scene.

(a) *Hell. Ox.* 13. 5–14. 1: Βοιωτοὶ μὲν ο[ὕ]ν τοσαῦτα κακὰ ποιήσαντες
[τ]οὺς Φωκέ[α]ς ἀπῆλθον εἰς τὴν ἑαυτῶν. Κόνων δὲ - - - κατέπλευσεν
εἰς Καῦνον.

   Thuc. I 93–94: 'Αθηναῖοι μὲν οὖν οὕτως ἐτειχίσθησαν καὶ τἆλλα
κατεσκευάζοντο εὐθὺς μετὰ τὴν Μήδων ἀναχώρησιν. Παυσανίας
δὲ - - ἐξεπέμφθη - -

   Cf. *Hell. Ox.* 12. 5–13. 1 and Thuc. III 17. 4–18. 1.

(b) *Hell. Ox.* 1. 1: ὑπὸ δὲ τοὺ[ς αὐτοὺς χρόνο]υς ἐξέπλευσε τριήρης 'Αθή-
νηθεν - - -

   Thuc. VIII 20. 1: ὑπὸ δὲ τοὺς αὐτοὺς χρόνους αἱ ἐν τῷ Σπειραίῳ
εἴκοσι νῆες τῶν Πελοποννησίων - - - - ναῦς λαμβάνουσιν τῶν
'Αθηναίων - - -

   Cf. Thuc. I 100. 3, II 95. 1, III 52. 1, IV 2. 1, V 12, VII 21. 1,
VIII 99. 1.

   Hell. Ox. 4. 2: κατὰ δὲ τὸν αὐ]τὸν χρόνον Φοινίκων [παρεγενήθησαν
ἐνενήκοντ]α νῆες εἰς Καῦνον - - -.

Thuc. IV 46. 1: κατὰ δὲ τὸν αὐτὸν χρόνον, καθ' ὃν ταῦτα ἐγίγνετο, καὶ Εὐρυμέδων καὶ Σοφοκλῆς - - - ἀφικόμενοι ἐς Κέρκυραν ἐστράτευσαν - - -

Cf. Thuc. III 7. 1, 18. 1, IV 7. 1, 78. 1, V 115. 1, VI 4. 1, 61. 3, VIII 40. 1.

(c) *Hell. Ox.* 11. 1: Βοιωτοὶ δὲ καὶ Φωκεῖς τούτου τοῦ θέρους εἰς πόλεμον κατέστησαν.

Thuc. II 79. 1: τοῦ δ' αὐτοῦ θέρους - - - Ἀθηναῖοι - - - ἐστράτευσαν ἐπὶ Χαλκιδέας.

Cf. Thuc. IV 42. 1.

This method of arrangement leads us from one scene to another in such a way as to give us as true an image as possible of the actual circumstances (ὡς ἕκαστα ἐγίγνετο, according to the words of Thucydides, who was its creator). It was practically and theoretically criticized even as early as the next century. In an important study on the prooemia of Ephorus, R. Laqueur showed that Diodorus in many prooemia of his Βιβλιοθήκη copied or used ideas which Ephorus had expressed in the introductions to the books of his Ἱστορίαι.[1]

For instance, Diodorus writes, V 1: πάντων μὲν τῶν ἐν ταῖς ἀναγραφαῖς χρησίμων προνοητέον τοὺς ἱστορίαν συνταττομένους, μάλιστα δὲ τῆς κατὰ μέρος οἰκονομίας. αὕτη γὰρ - - - κατὰ τὰς ἱστορίας οὐκ ὀλίγα ποιεῖ προτερήματα τοῖς συγγραφεῦσιν; and XVI 1: ἐν πάσαις μὲν ταῖς ἱστορικαῖς πραγματείαις καθήκει τοὺς συγγραφεῖς περιλαμβάνειν ἐν ταῖς βίβλοις ἢ πόλεων ἢ βασιλέων πράξεις αὐτοτελεῖς ἀπ' ἀρχῆς μέχρι τοῦ τέλους. οὕτω γὰρ μάλιστα διαλαμβάνομεν τὴν ἱστορίαν εὐμνημόνευτον καὶ σαφῆ γενέσθαι τοῖς ἀναγιγνώσκουσιν. (2) αἱ μὲν γὰρ ἡμιτελεῖς πράξεις οὐκ ἔχουσαι συνεχὲς ταῖς ἀρχαῖς τὸ πέρας μεσολαβοῦσι τὴν ἐπιθυμίαν τῶν φιλαναγνωστούντων, αἱ δὲ τὸ τῆς διηγήσεως συνεχὲς περιλαμβάνουσαι μέχρι τῆς τελευτῆς ἀπηρτισμένην τὴν τῶν πράξεων ἔχουσιν ἀπαγγελίαν. In conformity with this view regarding the διαίρεσις of a historical work, Ephorus followed a principle opposed to the Thucydidean, — one which Diodorus adopted three hundred years later (Diod. V

---

[1] *Hermes* XLVI (1911) 340 ff.; cf. F. Jacoby, *F Gr Hist* II C p. 27; U. v. Wilamowitz *S. Ber. Berl. Ak.* 1921, 306; Barber *loc. cit.* 69 ff. The dissertation of M. Kunz, *Zur Beurteilung der Prooemien in Diodors historischer Bibliothek*, Diss. Zürich, 1935, was not accessible to me.

1. 4): Ἔφορος δὲ τὰς κοινὰς πράξεις ἀναγράφων οὐ μόνον κατὰ τὴν λέξιν, ἀλλὰ καὶ κατὰ τὴν οἰκονομίαν ἐπιτέτευχε· τῶν γὰρ βίβλων ἑκάστην πεποίηκε περιέχειν κατὰ γένος τὰς πράξεις. The studies of Volquardsen, Ed. Schwartz, R. Laqueur and F. Jacoby, confirmed recently by G. L. Barber, have demonstrated that the principle of διαίρεσις κατὰ γένος (as opposed to that κατὰ θέρη καὶ χειμῶνας) of the work of Ephorus is still recognizable in books XI–XV of Diodorus, which are taken in great part from the work of Ephorus.[1]

The criticism of Thucydides' synchronistic system by Ephorus was resumed and developed by *Dionysius of Halicarnassus*,[2] the leader of the anti-Thucydidean current in the Atticistic movement of the time of Augustus. In his treatise Περὶ Θουκυδίδου, which (as was generally the case regarding his polemics against Thucydides) exercised a remarkable influence on the entire critical tradition, Dionysius formulated his objections against the Thucydidean διαίρεσις in a most precise and detailed manner (ch. 9, I p. 336. 9 U.-R.): καινὴν δέ τινα καὶ ἀτριβῆ τοῖς ἄλλοις πορευθῆναι βουληθεὶς ὁδὸν θερείαις καὶ χειμερίοις ἐμέρισε τὴν ἱστορίαν. ἐκ δὲ τούτου συμβέβηκεν αὐτῷ τοὐναντίον ἢ προσεδόκησεν. οὐ γὰρ σαφέστερα γέγονεν ἡ διαίρεσις τῶν χρόνων ἀλλὰ δυσπαρακολουθητοτέρα [κατὰ τὰς ὥρας]. ἐφ' ᾧ θαυμάζειν ἄξιον, πῶς αὐτὸν ἔλαθεν, ὅτι πολλῶν ἅμα πραγμάτων κατὰ πολλοὺς

---

[1] Fundamental even today is Ed. Schwartz, "Diodoros," *RE* V 1 (1903), pp. 679–681; cf. Laqueur *loc. cit.* 322 ff.; *F Gr Hist* II C p. 26; Barber *loc. cit.* 17 *et passim*.

[2] Regarding Dionysius' judgment on Thucydides compare the valuable dissertation of Strebel *loc. cit.* 42 ff. He does not make sufficient distinction between the criticism of Cicero and that of Dionysius and does not attempt to characterize the pro-Thucydidean current in the Atticistic movement. Cf. moreover J. F. D'Alton, *Roman Literary Theory and Criticism*, 1931, pp. 259 ff.; J. W. H. Atkins, *Literary Criticism in Antiquity*, II, 1934, pp. 104–136. There is no value in the study of Giuseppe Pavano, "Dionisio d'Alicarnasso, critico di Tucidide," *Mem. Acc. Torino*, ser. II, vol. LXVIII, 1936. For a commentary and an English translation of Dionysius' *Epistula ad Pompeium* and the second *Epistula ad Ammaeum* cf. W. R. Roberts, *Dionysius of Halicarnassus*, 1901, pp. 27 ff., 88 ff. S. F. Bonner's interesting book *The Literary Treatises of Dionysius of Halicarnassus*, Cambridge, 1939, appeared after the present study was entirely finished. Bonner gives particular attention to the development of Dionysius' critical faculties; for the treatises on Thucydides, which he considers the most thorough of Dionysius' studies, see pp. 81 ff., 103; for the problem of the relationship between Dionysius and Caecilius of Caleacte see the noteworthy explanations, pp. 8 f.

τόπους γιγνομένων εἰς μικρὰς κατακερματιζομένη τομὰς ἡ διήγησις οὐκ ἀπολήψεται τὸ 'τηλαυγὲς φῶς' ἐκεῖνο 'καὶ καθαρόν', ὡς ἐξ αὐτῶν γίνεται τῶν πραγμάτων φανερόν. At this point he presents as an example the arrangement of events in the third book of Thucydides; he then continues (I p. 337. 18 U.-R.): πλανώμεθα δὴ καθάπερ εἰκός, καὶ δυσκόλως τοῖς δηλουμένοις παρακολουθοῦμεν, ταραττομένης ἐν τῷ διασπᾶσθαι τὰ πράγματα τῆς διανοίας καὶ τὰς ἡμιτελεῖς τῶν ἀκουσθέντων μνήμας οὐ ῥᾳδίως οὐδ' ἀκριβῶς ἀναφερούσης - - - ὅτι δὲ οὐκ ὀρθὸς ὁ κανὼν οὗτος οὐδ' οἰκεῖος ἱστορίᾳ δῆλον. οὐδεὶς γὰρ τῶν μεταγενεστέρων συγγραφέων θερείαις καὶ χειμῶσι διεῖλε τὴν ἱστορίαν. ἀλλὰ πάντες τὰς τετριμμένας ⟨ὁδοὺς καὶ δυναμένας⟩ ἄγειν ἐπὶ τὴν σαφήνειαν μετῆλθον. With this effective phrase the polemic against the διαίρεσις of Thucydides ends: *none* of the later historians adopted the disposition by summers and winters. Now we saw that in this very point the author of P follows Thucydides exactly. And Jacoby was perfectly right, when, in discussing διαίρεσις, he emphasized (although without thinking of the passage in Dionysius) this fact, — that the historian of Oxyrhynchus alone used the Thucydidean order, the *one* exception to the general aversion of Greek historians to the διαίρεσις of Thucydides.[1] But Dionysius makes *no* exception: in other words, *he does not know the work of which P is a part.*

This is proof, in the first place, that P cannot be identified with the work of Ephorus, who was at that time, as the works of Diodorus, Nicolaus, and Strabo show, a widely read historian and was also, of course, known to Dionysius.[2] The same evidence, furthermore, is of equal validity for Theopompus' *Hellenica*, especially when one considers the high estimation in which Dionysius held its

[1] *Klio* IX (1909) 114 note: "Die perpetuierliche Zeitgeschichte eines Theopomp, eines Ephoros, ja auch die Xenophons in der Fortsetzung über Thukydides hinaus wendet seine Gliederung nach Kriegsjahren nicht an. . . . An ihre Stelle tritt eine für die historia perpetua besser passende Teilung nach sachlichen Gesichtspunkten. Wenn der Historiker von Oxyrhynchos eine Ausnahme macht, so beweist auch dies, dass er dem Thukydides von allen Hellenikaschreibern zeitlich am nächsten steht."

[2] *F Gr Hist* II C p. 32; cf. 70 T 24; Barber *loc. cit.* 157; Ed. Schwartz *Philologus* XCII (1937) 21 note 3.

author,[1] whose influence is felt in Dionysius' own historical work. But a still more definite conclusion is to be drawn from the statement of Dionysius: *P cannot be the work of Cratippus*. For, a few chapters after having emphatically declared that no historian after Thucydides had adopted this chronological system by summers and winters, Dionysius introduces a long quotation from the history of Cratippus, the most detailed of the very few fragments preserved from that work (ch. 16 = *F Gr Hist* 64 F 1).

These conclusions are all the more firmly established by the fact that this violent polemic against the Thucydidean διαίρεσις represents the climax of Dionysius' criticism of Thucydides contained in the treatise Περὶ Θουκυδίδου. How aware Dionysius was, moreover, of the reaction which his attacks against Thucydides were to provoke among the Thucydideans, is shown by his own words in the prooemium (I p. 326. 22): ὑποπτεύω γὰρ ἔσεσθαί τινας τῶν ἀναγνωσομένων τὴν γραφὴν τοὺς ἐπιτιμήσοντας ἡμῖν, ὅτι τολμῶμεν ἀποφαίνειν Θουκυδίδην τὸν ἁπάντων κράτιστον τῶν ἱστοριογράφων καὶ κατὰ τὴν προαίρεσίν ποτε τῶν λόγων ἁμαρτάνοντα καὶ κατὰ τὴν δύναμιν ἐξασθενοῦντα. Finally, he challenges the φιλόλογοι with the words: εἰ δὲ ἀληθεῖς καὶ προσήκοντας ἐμαυτῷ προῄρημαι λόγους, σύ τε κρινεῖς καὶ τῶν ἄλλων φιλολόγων ἕκαστος.

We are meagerly informed about this conflict over the worth of Thucydides. It arose during the last years of Cicero's life. In the *Brutus*, in the *Orator*, and in the *De optimo genere oratorum* he turned against the *Attici*, who, under the leadership of C. Licinius Calvus, proclaimed Thucydides the great model for the orator.[2] Cicero, however, does not go so far as Dionysius; *Brutus* 287: *Thucydidem, inquit, imitamur.—Optime, si historias scribere, non si causas dicere cogitatis.* Here we see the difference: Cicero ac-

---

[1] *Ep. ad Pomp.* 6 (= *F Gr Hist* 115 T 20); De Sanctis I 335: "Di Teopompo possediamo parecchi frammenti, e si ha il giudizio datone da un altro storico che aveva letto, e accuratamente, le sue opere, Dionisio di Alicarnasso." Cf. F. Halbfas, *Theorie und Praxis in der Geschichtsschreibung des Dionysius von Halikarnassos*, Diss. Münster, 1910, pp. 16–18; Nassal, *Ästhetisch-rhetorische Beziehungen zwischen Dionysios' von Halikarnass und Ciceros rhetorischen Schriften*, Diss. Tübingen, 1910, pp. 116 ff.

[2] The most important treatment of Cicero's quarrel with the Atticists is D'Alton *loc. cit.* 208–265; cf. Atkins *loc. cit.* 34 ff.; Bonner *loc. cit.* 13, 83.

knowledges Thucydides as a model for the historian; Dionysius finds much to criticize in Thucydides even as a historian.

We do not know the names of the Greek theorists against whom Dionysius directed his attacks. In any case, the colleague of Dionysius, Caecilius of Caleacte, ὁ φίλτατος Καικίλιος (*Ad Pomp.* 3), whose position concerning Thucydides was similar to that of Cicero, is not among them.

The rhetorical system of Dionysius had an ever-increasing influence in the following period, but was not accepted without opposition. A highly interesting insight into this discussion is provided by the famous *Oxyrhynchus Commentary on Thucydides* (*Oxy. Pap.* VI 853). It belongs to that extensive find of literary papyri which produced the *Hellenica of Oxyrhynchus*. The editors noted, moreover, that P and the *Commentary* probably were written about the same time. Now the anonymous author of the *Commentary*, in explaining the words of Thuc. II 1 (quoted *supra* p. 309), replies with very effective arguments to the criticism made by Dionysius of Halicarnassus, and above all to the latter's objections against Thucydides' διαίρεσις (1. 7ff.):[1] "Dionysius of Halicarnassus in his treatise on Thucydides blames Thucydides on a few grounds, and discusses three chief points, first that he has not fixed his dates by archons and Olympiads, like other historians, but according to a system of his own by summers and winters; secondly that he has disturbed and divided the narrative and breaks up the events, not completing his accounts of the several incidents, but turning from one subject to another before he has finished with it. . . . (2. 15ff.): [it was impossible] to relate Plataean affairs from first to last, and then go back to describe all the invasions of the Peloponnesians one after the other, and Corcyrean affairs continuously, differing as they did in date. (2. 27ff.): moreover, even if he had dated by archons, he would still have been obliged to divide the events, for these occurred some under one archon, some under another; it is when a person is only writing about a single subject that his narrative is continuous throughout." Section 2. 15ff. of the *Commentary* has already been quoted by Laqueur as a proof of the influ-

---

[1] I reproduce the translation of Grenfell and Hunt, *Oxy. Pap.* VI p. 137.

ence of Ephorus' view of the διαίρεσις upon it.[1] Here, finally, we can recognize, without knowing his name, one of the Atticistic rhetors whose predecessors had been the object of Dionysius' polemic, and we must acknowledge that this anonymous commentator had a much sounder understanding of the historian than Dionysius.

The *Commentary* probably belongs to the first century A.D., in which we find still other comprehensive judgments concerning Thucydides, — namely those in the treatise Περὶ ὕψους and later in Demetrius' Περὶ ἑρμηνείας, — but without any references to the problem in question.

The problem reappears in one of the most original rhetorical works of the beginning of the second century, Theon's *Progymnasmata*; here the polemics against the διαίρεσις of Thucydides are resumed, and, while reference is made to other critics, mention of the name of Dionysius is avoided (ch. 4, II p. 80.8 ff. Sp.):[2] - - ἢ ὅταν μὴ πολλὰ ὁμοῦ διηγῆταί τις, ἀλλὰ καθ' ἕκαστον εἰς τέλος προάγῃ, ὅπερ ἐγκαλοῦσί τινες τῷ Θουκυδίδῃ. διελὼν γὰρ ἱστορίας κατὰ θέρη καὶ χειμῶνας, πολλάκις ἀναγκάζεται, πρὶν τελεσθῇ τὸ ὅλον πρᾶγμα μεταβαίνειν ἐφ' ἕτερόν τι γεγονὸς ὑπὸ τὸν αὐτὸν καιρόν. εἶτα τὸ ὑπόλοιπον τοῦ πράγματος, ἐφ' ἑτέρου χειμῶνος ἢ θέρους πραχθὲν διηγεῖται and so forth. Theon is an intelligent writer who quotes, often literally, from Ephorus and Theopompus, apparently with a first-hand knowledge of their works; if P were the work of either of these historians, why should Theon limit his objections to Thucydides, when P has the same defect? Note that he quotes Theopompus a little later, specifically in connection with his διαίρεσις.

The influence of Dionysius is clearly visible also in the rhetorical treatise of Oxyrhynchus, *Oxy. Pap.* VII 1012, which likewise belongs to the first half of the second century A.D. (and which will occupy us *infra* p. 343): this contains among other things a judgment regarding Lysias which is derived from Dionysius, and examples of the omission of πράγματα in Thucydides which recall to mind Dionysius, *De Thuc.* 14 and 15.

<hr/>

[1] *Hermes* XLVI (1911) 342; cf. Strebel *loc. cit.* 48–50.

[2] Strebel *loc. cit.* 57 did not recognize the relations between Theon and Dionysius; cf. Christ-Schmid, *Gesch. der griech. Literatur*, II 1, 1920 (6th ed.), pp. 460 f.; D'Alton *loc. cit.* 506 f.; Stegemann *RE* V A 2 (1934) 2048.

In the second century Dionysius himself became a classic: In the Τέχνη τοῦ πολιτικοῦ λόγου of the so-called Cornutus (Anonymus Seguerianus)[1] the author qualifies him (p. 50. 23 Graeven) as ὃν κανόνα ⟨ἄν⟩ τις εἴποι δικαίως τῆς περὶ ῥητορικὴν μελέτης and Hermogenes tacitly adopted about the same time not a few of the ideas of Dionysius' system.

The respect for Dionysius in the Byzantine age culminates in the words of the rhetor Doxopatres (s. XI A.D.) (VI p. 17. 9 W.):[2] Διονύσιος ὁ μέγας, ὁ τῆς ἡμετέρας τέχνης καθηγητὴς καὶ πατὴρ ἀγαθὸς γενόμενος. This is the same Doxopatres who accepted, in his commentary on the *Progymnasmata* of Aphthonius, Dionysius' criticism of Thucydides' διαίρεσις (II p. 220 W.)[3]

This history of Dionysius' judgment on Thucydides' chronological system shows that no one of the authors who after Dionysius accepted or attacked his polemics against the διαίρεσις of Thucydides mentions another historian who employed the Thucydidean type of διαίρεσις, which is the very form used by the historian of Oxyrhynchus, for us the only writer who followed Thucydides in this respect.[4]

---

[1] For the date of this book cf. A. D. Nock *RE* Suppl. V 1005.

[2] Cf. Christ-Schmid *loc. cit.* II 2. 935; Radermacher *RE* V 2. 1612.

[3] The polemics of Dionysius against Thucydides have been resumed by some modern scholars, but without reference to their ancient colleague: Wilamowitz, *Curae Thucydideae*, 1885, p. 20: "at dum scribit Thucydides, cum alii tum Hellanicus, cum monumenta vetera annalesque et sacros et publicos ederent, civilibus annis uti coeperunt, atque nos quidem lugebimus parum confisum esse patriis institutis Thucydidem, quae vel nobis tam nota sunt, ut multo accuratius indicaturi fuerimus per dies singulos res ab Atheniensibus gestas, si ad Atticos menses aut dies festos eas revocasset." Later he called Thucydides' διαίρεσις "das unglückliche Prinzip" (*S. Ber. Berl. Ak.* 1921, 306). It is very interesting to see how H. Peter, *Wahrheit und Kunst* . . . , 1911, pp. 142 f. reproaches P with the same fault, — a criticism which we should have expected from an ancient critic: "Er (P) bringt sich durch seine synchronistische, von Thucydides übernommene Anordnung um eine klare Übersicht der Entwicklung der Ereignisse, die er nach den Schauplätzen in Abschnitte sogar von Monaten zerstückelt." Cf. on the contrary F. Jacoby, *supra* p. 312 note 1. Busolt *Griech. Gesch.* III 2. 678 note 1.

[4] It is not our intention to reopen here the question of Cratippus, which already existed before the discovery of P. Only one observation need be made: those who believe that the attack of Cratippus on the speeches of Thucydides (Dionys. *De Thuc.* 16; these polemics of Cratippus were revived and followed in modern times

2. *Theopompus and the* Hellenica of Oxyrhynchus

After the analysis above presented of the new argument against the identification of P with Cratippus, Theopompus, or Ephorus, it may seem superfluous to return to the question of Theopompus, since the evidence against him is already overwhelming.[1] Whoever surveys today the literature on the *Hellenica of Oxyrhynchus* must perceive that, as a matter of fact, the hypothesis of Theopompus' authorship could have been maintained for any time at all only because of the unlimited authority which Ed. Meyer enjoyed,[2] although his arguments were unconvincing and on the whole

---

by Ed. Meyer *Forsch. zur Alten Geschichte* II 409; cf. Beloch *Griech. Gesch.* II 2. 17) cannot belong to the fourth century B.C. and that this should be an indication of the spurious character of the work of Cratippus (published according to Ed. Schwartz, *Hermes* XLIV (1909) 501, in Hellenistic time as a contemporaneous continuation of Thucydides), should take into consideration the prooemium of the twentieth book of Diodorus, the Ephorean origin of which is generally recognized (Laqueur *loc. cit.* 206; *F Gr Hist* II C p. 64; Barber *loc. cit.* 69 f.): τοῖς εἰς τὰς ἱστορίας ὑπερμήκεις δημηγορίας παρεμβάλλουσιν ἢ πυκναῖς χρωμένοις ῥητορείαις δικαίως ἄν τις ἐπιτιμήσειεν. οὐ μόνον γὰρ τὸ συνεχὲς τῆς διηγήσεως διὰ τὴν ἀκαιρίαν τῶν ἐπεισαγομένων λόγων διασπῶσιν, ἀλλὰ καὶ τῶν φιλοτίμως ἐχόντων πρὸς τὴν τῶν πράξεων ἐπίγνωσιν ⟨μεσολάβουσι τὴν ἐπιθυμίαν⟩. Jacoby's comment (*loc. cit.*): "Die Kritik des 'Kratippos' an Thucydides (64 F 1) wird man damit nicht für s. IV retten," proves only how much he himself felt the relationship between the passage of Ephorus-Diodorus and the polemics of Cratippus: we discover here the same sharp reaction against Thucydides which we find also in Ephorus' account of the Peloponnesian war: compare the exposition of the causes of the Peloponnesian war in Thucydides and in Ephorus (Diod. XI) and Jacoby's excellent characterization of Ephorus (*F Gr Hist* II C pp. 23, 30).

After all, the theory of Ed. Schwartz is founded on a hopelessly corrupt passage of the Βίος Θουκυδίδου of Marcellinus, — a passage which cannot be restored because it is not a question of simple mechanical corruptions, but of a nest of errors, due probably in large part to Marcellinus himself and to his sources, and it does not seem justifiable to base on so weak a foundation the hypothesis that the work of Cratippus is a late falsification by which Dionysius and Plutarch (who also quotes Cratippus: *F Gr Hist* 64 T 2) were taken in (cf. against Schwartz, who is followed by Jacoby, especially the study of Pareti [1912; *supra* p. 305 note]; Beloch *Griech. Gesch.* III 2. 1 ff.; Prentice [1927; *supra* p. 304 note 1]; Bux *RE* XIV 2 (1930) 1479 ff.).

[1] Cf. Jacoby *Nachr. Gött. Ges.* 1924, 13.

[2] *Ed. princeps*, p. 129: "The hypothesis that P's important work . . . is to be

insufficient, both as they appeared in the *editio princeps*, where the editors themselves reacted energetically against them,[1] and in his subsequent book *Theopomps Hellenika*. Nevertheless, Richard Laqueur in his recent voluminous article on Theopompus in the *RE* again defended this thesis, evidently basing his arguments on Meyer's book and on a strangely vague and incorrect consideration of Theopompus' style. He thus distorted completely the image of Theopompus' literary development, which the extant fragments and the ancient evaluations of his work mark with sufficient clarity.

Cicero, Dionysius of Halicarnassus, the author of Περὶ ὕψους and Demetrius Περὶ ἑρμηνείας give characterizations of Theopompus' style[2] which are entirely confirmed by the fragments preserved. His style is quite different from that of P. Confirmation of this fact in reality constituted the result of the inquiries of the editors in 1908 and of De Sanctis in the same year, and after that, of the detailed researches of A. Franz and W. Bauer.[3] The ultimate conclusions of these studies were drawn upon by P. Maas in a brief article, about which E. M. Walker justly said: "The importance of Maas's contribution is not to be measured by its length." And De Sanctis had been quite right when he asserted in the article mentioned above "che gli antichi non fanno distinzione per questo rispetto tra le Elleniche e le Filippiche, mentre Dionisio, che dà di Teopompo un giudizio diffuso e ben meditato, non poteva mancare di mettere in rilievo, se v'era realmente, una differenza così profonda."[4] It

---

identified with a known continuation of Thucydides written by a historian of the first rank, . . . possesses obvious advantages and, especially when it comes to be advocated by Meyer in his own words, is sure to find wide acceptance."

[1] Pp. 131–139.

[2] Cicero: *F Gr Hist* 115 T 26a, 36–40; Dionysius of Halicarnassus: T 20; *Auct.* II. ὕψ : T 41 f.; Dem. II. ἑρμ. : T 43 f.

[3] *Ed. princ.* pp. 136 ff.; De Sanctis I 335 ff.; A. Franz, *Ein Historikerfragment aus Oxyrhynchos*, Programm Prag, 1910; Guil. Bauer, "De sermone Hellenicorum Ox. repertorum," *Diss. philol Vindob.*, XI, 1913. The treatise of Franz is more original than Bauer's dissertation, which comes from the school of H. v. Arnim. Bauer gives a large amount of statistical material, but avoids any conclusion based upon it.

[4] De Sanctis I 337 ff.; P. Maas *Philol. Woch.* 1912, 1845 f.; Walker *Hell. Ox.* 13; cf. also D'Alton *loc. cit.* 495 note 4. Dionysius *loc. cit.* T 20. 2: Θεόπομπος - - - ἄξιος

was Maas who subsequently referred to the statement of Porphyry that Theopompus plagiarized from Xenophon and that in the eleventh book of the Hellenica he ἀργά τε καὶ ἀκίνητα πεποίηκε καὶ ἄπρακτα large portions of the negotiations between Agesilaus and Pharnabazus, which Xenophon (*Hell.* IV 1. 29–40) had described πάνυ χαριέντως καὶ πρεπόντως ἀμφοῖν.[1]

The anecdote regarding Agesilaus related by Theopompus in the *Hellenica* (*F Gr Hist* 115 F 22) and in the *Philippica* (F 106, cf. F 107) is especially typical of his method; in his characterization of Lysander (F 20) we meet the same features that are to be found in the famous characterization of Philip and his circle (F 224 f.)[2] and in the picture which Theopompus drew of Nicostratus of Argos (F 124). In this last fragment, moreover, there appears the rhetorical φανήσεται *cum participio aoristi* which is contained as well both in the passage concerning Lysander and in F 122 and 253, whereas it does not appear in P. Who could believe, after this, that Theopompus would have narrated so soberly and so prosaically the episode of Spithradates and his son (*Hell. Ox.* 16. 4)?

Laqueur avoided entering into a serious discussion of the matter. He assumed that Theopompus' style developed from an original quiet type, strongly influenced by Isocrates and employed in the *Hellenica*, to the well-known impassioned elevation manifested in the *Philippica*.[3] He does not, of course, take into consideration the two most important fragments of the *Hellenica* (F 22 and 20, indicated above) because they prove the contrary to the point he wishes to make. It is astonishing to read, a page later, that no actual stylistic

---

ἐπαινεῖσθαι πρῶτον μὲν τῆς ὑποθέσεως τῶν ἱστοριῶν (καλαὶ γὰρ ἀμφότεραι, ἡ μὲν τὰ λοιπὰ τοῦ Πελοποννησιακοῦ πολέμου περιέχουσα, ἡ δὲ τὰ Φιλίππῳ πεπραγμένα), ἔπειτα τῆς οἰκονομίας (ἀμφότεραι γάρ εἰσιν εὐπαρακολούθητοι καὶ σαφεῖς), μάλιστα δὲ τῆς ἐπιμελείας τε καὶ φιλοπονίας τῆς κατὰ τὴν συγγραφήν.

[1] *Ed. princ.* p. 132; cf. *F Gr Hist* 115 F 21. Concerning Porphyry's statements on κλοπή cf. *infra* pp. 339 f. They derive from first-class sources of the time of the great Alexandrian philologians.

[2] On the characterization of Lysander, cf. H. W. Parke *Journ. of Hell. Stud.* L (1930) 51 note 27, and W. K. Prentice *Am. Journ. of Arch.* XXXVIII (1934) 38 f.; on that of Philip and his circle D. E. W. Wormell, "The literary tradition concerning Hermias of Atarneus," *Yale Class. Stud.*, V (1935), pp. 71 f.

[3] Laqueur *loc. cit.* 2190 f., 2196, 2198.

difference exists between the *Hellenica* and the *Philippica*.[1] Thus Laqueur contradicts himself. But the absurdity of this argument culminates in the attempt to impute only to the *Hellenica* the ψυχρότης with which both the letter of Speusippus and Demetrius reproach Theopompus: Speusippus (Theop. T 7): πυνθάνομαι δὲ καὶ Θεόπομπον παρ' ὑμῖν μὲν εἶναι πάνυ ψυχρόν, περὶ δὲ Πλάτωνος βλασφημεῖν, κτλ. Demetrius (Theop. T 44): τὰ δὲ ἀντίθετα καὶ παρόμοια ἐν ταῖς περιόδοις φευκτέον· ὄγκον γὰρ ποιοῦσιν, οὐ δεινότητα, πολλαχοῦ δὲ καὶ ψυχρότητα ἀντὶ δεινότητος, οἷον ὡς ὁ Θ ε ό π ο μ π ο ς κατὰ τῶν ἑταίρων τῶν Φιλίππου λέγων ἔλυσεν τῇ ἀντιθέσει τὴν δεινότητα, 'ἀνδροφόνοι δὲ τὴν φύσιν ὄντες', λέγων, 'ἀνδρόπορνοι τὸν τρόπον ἦσαν (F 225c).' τῇ γὰρ περισσοτεχνίᾳ μᾶλλον δὲ κακοτεχνίᾳ προσέχων ὁ ἀκροατὴς ἔξω γίνεται θυμοῦ παντός. The Theopompus of the *Hellenica* ψυχρός, the author of the papyrus of Oxyrhynchus ψυχρός! Obviously one important fact escaped Laqueur, namely that Demetrius gives us, as a classical example of the ψυχρότης of Theopompus, a passage which comes from the oft quoted characterization of Philip's ἑταῖροι in the forty-ninth book of the *Philippica* (F 224 f.);[2] and in order to bring out more clearly what Demetrius is intending I quote a little more fully from the passage in question: ὅθεν δικαίως ἄν τις αὐτοὺς οὐχ ἑταίρους ἀλλ' ἑταίρας ὑπέλαβεν, οὐδὲ † στρατιώτας ἀλλὰ χαμαιτύπας προσηγόρευσεν· ἀνδροφόνοι κτλ. This makes the meaning of ψυχρότης clear. Yet it may be of value to present a rhetorical definition of this term (Dem. Περὶ ἑρμ. 114): ὁρίζεται δὲ τὸ ψυχρὸν Θεόφραστος οὕτως· ψυχρόν ἐστι τὸ ὑπερβάλλον τὴν οἰκείαν ἀπαγγελίαν and the explanation of J. Stroux:[3] "vitium ψυχρόν, quo peccat is, qui nimis

---

[1] With incomprehensible arbitrariness he declares (p. 2197) that of the *Philippica* only the colorless fragments F 30, 88, 113, 307, selected by him, could be compared with the fragments of Theopompus' *Hellenica* and that the style of those fragments corresponds to P's.

[2] Laqueur *loc. cit.* 2190 f.: "Unzweifelhaft hat sich hier [sc. in the *Hellenica*] Theopomp zu Stilfiguren gezwungen, die an sich seinem Wesen fern lagen, und dieser Zwang war in der früheren Zeit des Theop., aus der der Speusipposbrief stammt, so gross, dass man es wagen konnte, den Theop. primär als ψυχρὸς anzusprechen, in vollstem Gegensatz zu dem Bilde, das sich eine spätere Zeit auf Grund der Philippika und der Chiischen Briefe von Theop. machte."

[3] J. Stroux, *De Theophrasti virtutibus dicendi*, Leipzig, 1912, p. 107; for an earlier definition of ψυχρότης cf. Aristot. *Rhet.* III 3. L. Voit does not mention the term ψυχρότης in his dissertation, Δ ε ι ν ό τ η s *ein antiker Stilbegriff*, Leipzig, 1934.

ornamentis indulget, ita est contrarium ξηροῦ vitio eius, qui parum ornamentis utitur." Where have we such a παρέκβασις of the μεγαλο-πρέπεια in P ? The editors speak of the "plain unrhetorical composition of P"[1] and in this, as a matter of fact, they are right, although the author observes the avoidance of hiatus.[2] His style is "sober, unadorned," or "colorless"; in vain an ancient critic would have sought examples of ψυχρότης and of μεγαλοπρέπεια in the nearly thirty extant pages of the *Hellenica of Oxyrhynchus*.

Hence the recent attempt to revive the thesis of Ed. Meyer, abandoned long ago even by its original supporters,[3] is completely discredited. There is no reason to treat here the other arguments which exclude the identification of the historian of Oxyrhynchus with Theopompus, — arguments the existence of which Laqueur did not so much as mention.

3. *Ephorus and the* Hellenica of Oxyrhynchus

The discussion of the claim of Ephorus has been made easier by Barber, who in his recent book on Ephorus adopted the results of the research of previous scholars,[4] and again brought out the fact, in an examination of Walker's arguments, that P was not

---

[1] *Ed. princ.* p. 138; cf. De Sanctis I 336; Fuhr *Philol. Woch.* 1908, 199; Barber *loc. cit.* 52.

[2] More scrupulously even than Isocrates and his pupils: B. Keil *Hermes* LI (1916) 461 ff., 464; Fuhr *loc. cit.* 199; Franz *loc. cit.* 8 ff., 14; Bauer *loc. cit.* 22 ff.; D'Alton *loc. cit.* 495 f.

[3] For Wilamowitz (1908), next to Ed. Meyer the most authoritative supporter of the Theopompus thesis (*ed. princ.* pp. 127, 129), cf. *supra* p. 308 note 1; for Grenfell and Hunt: *Oxy. Pap.* XIII (1919), pp. 109 ff.; for Ed. Schwartz: *Die Antike* IV (1928) 22; A. Körte *Neue Jahrb.* XXXIX (1917) 296 f.; E. Cavaignac *Revue de l'Ég. anc.* I (1927) 179. In his lectures on Greek history (1931) U. Wilcken also abandoned his earlier position (*Hermes* XLIII (1908) 475 ff.).

[4] Barber's book is, besides H. Strasburger's *Ptolemaios und Alexander*, Leipzig, 1934 (cf. as a supplement to this book his review of E. Kornemann's *Die Alexandergeschichte des Königs Ptolemaios I. von Ägypten*, 1935, in *Gnomon* XIII (1937) 483 ff.), the most important monograph of those which appeared after the publication and under the influence of F. Jacoby's first two volumes of *F Gr Hist*. On principle he avoids entering into the problem of the authorship of P; but cf. pp. 50, 134 note 1, where he seems to incline toward Jacoby's proposal, although, like Wilamowitz (*supra* p. 308 note 1), with reservations.

directly used by Diodorus, but by Ephorus, whose work was the medium between P and Diodorus.

There is, however, a difficulty which constrains us to return to this question here, in spite of Barber's good work. For, even before Barber wrote his book and then again after its publication, Ed. Schwartz emphatically associated himself with the champions of Ephorus. In his article "Geschichtschreibung und Geschichte bei den Hellenen," *Die Antike*, IV (1928), p. 22, he writes: ". . . der sogenannte Historiker von Oxyrhynchus, den Ephorus zu nennen ich seit geraumer Zeit kein Bedenken mehr trage, zeigt auf den ersten Blick, wie die thukydideische Form gewirkt hat." And now he repeats this opinion in his study "Die messenische Geschichte bei Pausanias," *Philologus*, XCII (1937), p. 21 note 3: "Die Papyri haben bewiesen, dass das Buch (sc. des Ephorus) immer noch (sc. in der Kaiserzeit) abgeschrieben, also auch gelesen wurde. Damit schwindet für mich der einzige Grund, der davon abhalten könnte, den sogenannten Historiker von Oxyrhynchos für Ephoros zu halten; [1] ich bin seit Jahren und nach wiederholter Prüfung fest davon überzeugt."

Anyone who knows how much we owe to Schwartz's achievements in the field of ancient historiography will keenly regret

---

I do not entirely agree with the interesting review of Barber's book by P. Treves *Athenaeum* XV (1937) 125–127. In particular, I do not see what evidence he has for the statement that "questo Eforo del Barber sia ben più libresco e tedioso e umbratile e incerto che nella realtà non sia stato" (p. 127). According to Treves, Barber overlooks the most important problems (for instance: "una visione unitaria dello spirito isocrateo di Eforo") "and thinks of less important things, such as the refutation of the thesis that the *Hellenica of Oxyrhynchus* was the work of Ephorus, a thesis which, owing to the book of Walker, took root in England. The refutation is ingenious and correct, although it seems to me a little simple (lapalissiana) and, perhaps, B. himself would have considered it superfluous, if he had paid attention to our contributions" (in the note, De Sanctis III is quoted). But Treves forgets that, after the appearance of Walker's book, the Ephorus hypothesis gained the support of Grenfell and Hunt, some time later of Cavaignac and Ed. Schwartz, and eventually of G. Glotz, and was represented, therefore, by such authoritative scholars that its refutation was certainly meritorious; and an objective evaluation of the actual state of the question makes a new discussion necessary.

[1] Yet even this line of reasoning is in no way cogent; how relative the value of such considerations is will be demonstrated in chapter I, 5.

that this great scholar never offered specific reasons for his conviction, which has remained almost unknown.

An insurmountable obstacle to the claim of Ephorus is raised by mere chronological considerations. There is no question that the *Hellenica of Oxyrhynchus* was written probably before 356 B.C., certainly before 346 B.C. Ephorus wrote his fourth book after 356, books XX ff. after the publication of Callisthenes' *Hellenica* (343–335), and the twenty-fifth book after 335. How possibly, under these circumstances, could Ephorus have been the author of P, if he related the events of the years 396–395 B.C. in his eighteenth or nineteenth book? This evident dilemma cannot be resolved, especially after Barber's fair and ingenious exposition of this point, which, however, had already been cleared up by Jacoby; for all particulars I refer to them.[1]

The discovery of the Ephorus papyrus, *Oxy. Pap.* 1610 (= *F Gr Hist* 70 F 191) brought with it another argument against the identification of P with Ephorus, an argument decisive because the close agreement between the new papyrus and Diodorus is entirely different from that between P and Diodorus.[2] In order to show

---

[1] *F Gr Hist* II C pp. 24 f.; Barber *loc. cit.* 8–13, 131 f.; P. Treves *loc. cit.* 125 f. Of decisive importance is Ephorus' use of the *Hellenica* of Callisthenes in books XX ff., which is proved not only by the fundamental passage of Porphyry, *F Gr Hist* 70 T 17 (= 124 T 33), but also by the extant fragments of Ephorus' work; cf. A. Momigliano *Riv. di Filol. class.* LXIII (1935) 190 ff.

[2] Cf. now Barber *loc. cit.* pp. 53, 55, 67 note 1; Lipsius *Philol. Woch.* 1919, 958 ff.; A. Körte *Arch. f. Pap.* VII (1924), 230; Grenfell and Hunt *Oxy. Pap.* XIII (1919), p. 109: "The agreements between 842 [= P] and Diodorus . . . are less marked indeed than the correspondences of 1610 with Ephorus" (cf. *Oxy. Pap.* V p. 137, quoted in the text). The hypothesis of Jacoby that *Oxy. Pap.* 1610 might be the part of an epitome of Ephorus used by Diodorus is shown to be impossible by the relationship between Diodorus III 12–48 and Photius cod. 250, both of whom excerpted Agatharchides' work Περὶ τῆς Ἐρυθρᾶς θαλάσσης (cf. Ed. Schwartz *RE* V 1. 673). Analogous to this case is the agreement between Diodorus and Polyaenus, especially between Diod. XIV 38. 4 and Polyaenus II 21; the relationship can be explained only by the following stemma:

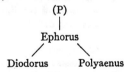

the close relationship between the Ephorus papyrus and Diodorus,
I submit two examples:

Eph. F 191. 3:

ἐκ [εῖνον] μὲν ὑπὸ τῆs πόλε[ωs]
ἠτιμασμένον, τ[ὴ]ν δὲ πόλιν
διὰ τ[ὰ]s ἐκείνου πράξε[ι]s
τῆs μεγίστηs τιμῆs ὑπὸ τῶν ῾Ελλήνων
ἀξιωθεῖσαν

Diod. XI 59. 3:

διόπερ ὅταν - - - σκοποῦντεs τὰ κατὰ
μέροs εὕρωμεν ἐκεῖνον μὲν ὑπὸ τῆs
πόλεωs ἠτιμασμένον, τὴν δὲ
πόλιν διὰ τὰs ἐκείνου πράξειs
ἐπαιρομένην εἰκότωs - - -

Eph. F 191. 8:

παραθ]αλα[ττιων καλο]υμένω[ν
πόλεων ὅσ]αι μὲν ἐκ τ[ῆs
῾Ελλά]δος ἦσα[ν ἀπῳ]κισμέ-
ναι π[αρα]χρῆμα συν[έπεισε
- - -1

Diod. XI 60. 4:

πλεύσαs οὖν μετὰ παντὸs τοῦ στόλου πρὸs
τὴν Καρίαν, τῶν παραθαλαττίων πόλεων ὅσαι μὲν ἦσαν ἐκ τῆs
῾Ελλάδος ἀπῳκισμέναι, ταύταs
παραχρῆμα συνέπεισεν ἀπο-
στῆναι τῶν Περσῶν.

It is impossible to find analogous correspondences between Diodorus and the *Hellenica of Oxyrhynchus*, and it seems to me decidedly noteworthy that the editors of P, before the discovery of
the Ephorus papyrus, wrote (*ed. princ.* p. 137): "That Diodorus
used P directly does not seem to us probable: for though the general
agreement between them is very close, the verbal coincidences are
not on the whole very striking." This is certainly true: the coincidences in P and Diodorus are never perfect. I refer simply to
Walker's own exposition [2] in which he does not succeed in eliminating the discrepancies in a satisfactory manner.

The most important of the discrepancies, all of which cannot
be treated here, is the absence in P of the episode of the devastation of Tissaphernes' gardens by Agesilaus' troops, which is preserved in Diodorus alone [3] and cannot be placed in the lacuna found

Walker *loc. cit.* 65 f. did not even take the possibility of this relationship into
consideration.

[1] Ephorus, imitated by Diodorus, employs the usual form παραθαλάττιοs, while
P has the rare word παραθαλαττίδιοs, which recurs only in Thucydides, Cassius
Dio and Didymus. Strangely, the editors of the Ephorus papyrus did not call
special attention to this discrepancy between Ephorus and P, which speaks of
course against their identification.

[2] *Loc. cit.* 54 f.; cf. Barber *loc. cit.* 179–181.

[3] Diod. XIV 80. 2: ἐπελθὼν δὲ τὴν χώραν μέχρι Σάρδεων ἔφθειρε τούs τε κήπουs καὶ

in chapter 6 of P. Walker himself was fully aware of this difficulty, but he was unable to find any acceptable solution for it. It may be suggested, then, that the *ethos* of this passage is suitable to Ephorus' moralizing, not to P's sober reporting of political fact.

The chronological confusion in Diodorus' account — stressed by Walker before his conversion (*ed. princ.* p. 137) — "is almost incredible if he [viz. Diodorus] was excerpting an author whose chronology was as clear as that of P." This confusion is easily explained by the assumption that Diodorus was using Ephorus who grouped the events by subjects. That this was the arrangement of Ephorus even in the fourth century is a fact which Walker and Cavaignac [1] in vain attempted to deny. These scholars, like the

---

τὸν παράδεισον τὸν Τισσαφέρνους, φυτοῖς καὶ τοῖς ἄλλοις πολυτελῶς πεφιλοτεχνημένον εἰς τρυφὴν καὶ τὴν ἐν εἰρήνῃ τῶν ἀγαθῶν ἀπόλαυσιν. For this passage compare Walker *loc. cit.* 56, 101; Judeich *Rhein. Mus.* LXVI (1911) 120 ff.; M. Gelzer *Philol. Woch.* 1917, 804; opposed to their view: Beloch *Griech. Gesch.* III 2. 1; Pareti *loc. cit.* 485; Lipsius *Ber. Sächs. Ges. Wiss.* 1915, 14; *Philol. Woch.* 1917, 1576.

[1] Walker *loc. cit.* 108 ff. opposed to Walker *ed. princ.* p. 137, and *Klio* VIII (1908) 362. Ed. Schwartz also, after his palinode, would not have been able to maintain, besides the identification of P with Ephorus, the thesis so emphatically stated in his famous article on Ephorus in the *RE* (VI 1. 10), namely, that of one thing we may be certain: Ephorus did not write annalistically. Cf. moreover the valuable article of N. G. L. Hammond, "The sources of Diodorus Sic. XVI," *Class. Quart.*, XXXI (1937), p. 86 note 1.

Cavaignac, *Mél. Glotz* I 149 ff., bases his exposition exclusively on Walker's book and on the presupposition that P, — for statistical reasons, — can be the work only of Theopompus or of Ephorus; concerning the latter argument cf. p. 322 n. and *infra* pp. 334 ff. G. Glotz, who previously had avoided taking any position regarding the authorship of P, maintained this reserve in the first chapter of the posthumous volume III of his *Histoire grecque* (1936, p. 25 note 2: "À qui attribuer les Helléniques d'Oxyrhynchos? La question n'est toujours pas élucidée"); but in the last pages of the same volume he decided on Ephorus, referring to Cavaignac, p. 461 note 109: "Il semble de plus en plus probable que le fragment d'Helléniques trouvé à Oxyrhynchos provient d'Ephore."

For the Pentecontaetia W. Kolbe in his important article, "Diodors Wert für die Geschichte der Pentekontaetie," *Hermes*, LXXII (1937), pp. 241 ff. (cf. especially pp. 245 f.), showed again that the older conception of Diodorus' methods and of Ephorus' chronological arrangement is right.

It is perhaps worth recalling here that the most important chronographer of antiquity, Apollodorus of Athens (2nd cent. B.C.), followed the same principles of arrangement by subjects in his *Chronicles*: "A(pollodorus) schrieb ja keine Anothers, failed to observe that Diodorus has preserved to us two chapter-headings of Ephorus; cf. Diod. XIV 81. 3: ὁ μὲν οὖν πόλεμος οὗτος ἐκλήθη Βοιωτικός and 86. 6:--ὁ πόλεμος οὗτος ἐκλήθη Κορινθιακός, καὶ διέμεινεν ἔτη ὀκτώ. A third title is perhaps preserved in 79. 1: - - Λακεδαιμόνιοι προορώμενοι τὸ μέγεθος τοῦ πρὸς Πέρσας πολέμου.

Barber is quite right in emphasizing the fundamental difference between Ephorus' well known narrative of the outbreak of the Peloponnesian War and the thorough and generally superior manner in which P explains the origin of the Corinthian War. This superiority of P in political analysis is perceptible everywhere.[1]

To these arguments we add two others. (I) A characteristic feature of the author of P is that whenever he speaks about facts already mentioned, he always refers, almost pedantically, to the earlier passage: 2. 2 καὶ τοὺς ἐν ταῖς ἄλλαις πόλεσι ταῖς προειρημέναις (referring to a lost part of the work); this is repeated in 2. 5 ἐν ταῖς πόλεσι ταῖς προειρημέναις;[2] 2. 3, 4 the political career of Timolaus and his victory over the strategos Simichus 411/10 B.C. ὥσπερ εἴρηκα καὶ πρότερον (here also referring to a lost passage);[3] 12. 1 treating the internal conflict in Thebes, he says ὥσπερ καὶ πρότερον εἴρηκα (referring to ch. 11). That the author in the very interesting excursus in ch. 12 on the situation in Thebes during the Decelean War and on the insignificance of the devastation of Attica in the Archidamian War (we return to this passage *infra*

---

nalen, sondern behandelte in fortlaufender Erzählung das sachlich Zusammengehörige, wie das ganze Leben eines Menschen oder Successionen einer Philosophenschule, auch in der Chronik zusammen." (F. Jacoby, "Apollodors Chronik," *Philol. Unters.*, XVI (1902), p. 57; cf. also *F Gr Hist* II D p. 719.)

[1] Barber *loc. cit.* 58 f. He is right, too, in asserting that it is unlikely that Diodorus would have omitted to reproduce the narration of the Boeotian constitution, if he had discovered it in his source Ephorus (*ibid.* 56).

[2] Cf. the judgment of the editors, *loc. cit.* 124: "He is decidedly careless about repeating words at very short intervals." Barber *loc. cit.* 57. A characteristic example of this carelessness in choice of words appears in ch. 16, where we read concerning Agesilaus: ὅσον μὲν χρόνον ἐβάδιζε διὰ τῆς Λυδίας, οὐδὲν κακὸν ἐποίει τοὺς ἐνοικοῦντας, and a little later: ὅσοι μὲν οὖν [τῶν Μυ]σῶν μετέχειν ᾑροῦντο τῆς στρατείας, οὐδὲν ἐποίει κακὸν αὐτούς.

[3] Th. Lenschau *RE* VI A 1 (1936) 1273 f.; Beloch *Griech. Gesch.* II 2. 267.

p. 347) does not mention a previous treatment of these problems would be incomprehensible — one might even say impossible — if he had dealt with them earlier. This excursus, as a matter of fact, has really the character of an addition — not to his own narrative, but to that of Thucydides [1] (compare the references already quoted 2. 3 and 4). This is evident proof that the historian of Oxyrhynchus wrote a continuation of Thucydides.[2] (II) The second argument is based on differences regarding the style of the two historians, Ephorus and the author of P.

Franz and Bauer, in their studies on the style of P, established the fact that the author of P — and there are remains enough to allow such a statement — never uses the conjunctions ὅθεν, διόπερ, διό, ὅταν, the particle δή, and finally, the construction διὰ τό *cum infinitivo*.[3] These remarkable peculiarities cannot be regarded as the result of chance; they are connected with the simplicity of the style of this author, who has a predilection for coordination and for the conjunctions ἐπειδή and ὡς. These latter he uses interchangeably (as he does ἅπας and πᾶς) to conform to the principle of the avoidance of hiatus.[4]

---

[1] *Ed. princ.* p. 230: "It is noteworthy that in his account of the prosperity of Attica . . . P unduly minimizes the extent of the injuries inflicted by the Lacedaemonian invasions in the Archidamian war, which, as Thucydides shows clearly [e.g., II 57, III 26], caused widespread devastation." W. G. Hardy, "The *Hellenica Oxyrhynchia* and the devastation of Attica," *Class. Philol.*, XXI (1926), pp. 346–355, is right in referring to Thuc. VII 27, where the damages caused in Attica by the Spartans in the Decelean War are described as very great (μεγάλα οἱ Ἀθηναῖοι ἐβλάπτοντο), much greater than the consequences of the Lacedaemonian invasions in the Archidamian War: πρότερον μὲν γὰρ βραχεῖαι γιγνόμεναι αἱ ἐσβολαὶ τὸν ἄλλον χρόνον τῆς γῆς ἀπολαύειν οὐκ ἐκώλυον. But this latter statement of Thucydides, written after 404 B.C., is relative and does not annul his earlier pronouncements; it cannot, therefore, be said to be consistent with the absolute assertion of the historian of Oxyrhynchus that the country had suffered but slight injury from the Lacedaemonians in the former invasions.

[2] Barber *loc. cit.* 123, and entirely independent from him S. Accame, in his thorough research on the sources of Diodorus (quoted *supra* p. 304 note 1), pp. 432 ff., showed, in an impressive manner, that Ephorus used the work of the author of Oxyrhynchus for the period 411–394 B.C., i.e. from its beginning to its end.

[3] Franz *loc. cit.* 14 f.; Bauer *loc. cit.* 32 ff.; cf. Fuhr *Philol. Woch.* 1908, 200.

[4] Franz *loc. cit.* 14; Bauer *loc. cit.* 27. For a similar use of the conjunctions

Now, among the few verbatim fragments of Ephorus extant, there are the following (*F Gr Hist* 70):

F 63: ὅ θ ε ν φασὶν ἔτι καὶ νῦν ἡμᾶς χρῆσθαι τῇ παροιμίᾳ - - -

F 71: δ ι ό π ε ρ Δερκυλλίδαν ἔπεμψαν ἥκιστα νομίζοντες ἐξαπατηθή-
σεσθαι - - - δ ι ὸ καὶ Σίσυφον αὐτὸν οἱ Λακεδαιμόνιοι προσηγό-
ρευον.

F 122a, p. 78. 9: διακριβοῦν εἰώθαμεν, ὅ τ α ν ᾖ τι τῶν πραγμάτων

F 191, 12–13: οὐ δ ὴ πολλοὶ μὲν ὑπὸ τῶν καταλειφθέντων ἐκεῖ φυλάκων
ἀπέθνη[σκον] ἐν τῇ νυκτί.

F 65f, p. 61. 14: οὐ δυνατὸν τοῦτο συμβαίνειν περὶ τὴν ἄλλην γῆν, δ ι ὰ
τ ὸ μ ή τ ε κ ο ί λ η ν ε ἶ ν α ι μ ή τ' ἐ π ί κ τ η τ ο ν - - -[1]

These differences in style between P and Ephorus are all the more important, because Bauer himself, temporarily at least, inclined toward the identification of P and Ephorus,[2] and Laqueur, in his article of 1911 on Ephorus, asserted (p. 353): "Stilistisch wäre gegen Ephorus [i.e. against identification with P] nichts einzuwenden."

4. *Androtion and the* Hellenica of Oxyrhynchus

It remains to examine the hypothesis repeatedly advanced by De Sanctis that P is a fragment of the *Atthis* of Androtion.

The starting point for De Sanctis is, as one might expect, the chronological formula in ch. 4 (cf. *supra*, p. 308). He is, of course, obliged to insert the name of the archon of the year 396/5 B.C.,

---

καθάπερ and ὥσπερ in the language of Diocles of Carystus see the interesting discussion by W. Jaeger, *Diokles von Karystos*, 1938, pp. 16 ff.

[1] Theopompus also, like Ephorus, uses ὅθεν, διόπερ, διὸ and, with great frequency, the construction διὰ τὸ *cum infinitivo*.

[2] Bauer, "Die spartanischen Nauarchen der Jahre 397 bis 395," *Wiener Studien*, XXXII (1910), p. 296 note 1. In his dissertation (cited *supra*, p. 318, note 3) one seeks in vain for the evidence upon which he bases his conclusion. Cf. also *ed. princ.* p. 126: "there is at any rate no marked discrepancy of style between the extant fragments of Ephorus and P." Walker, *New Chapters in the History of Greek Lit.*, 1921, pp. 129, 131.

Phormio, in restoring the text, which, reconstructed by him, reads as follows:

[- - - - - - - - - - - - τὰ μ]ὲν οὖν ἀδρότατα τῶν
[- - - - - - - - - - - ἐν τῷ ἔτε]ι τούτῳ συμβάντων
[οὕτως ἐγένετο· μεσοῦντος δ]ὲ τοῦ [θ]έρους τῇ μὲν
[πόλει μετὰ τὴν ἀναρχίαν] ἔτος ὄγδοον ἐνειστήκει,
[ἐν ᾧ Φορμίων ἦρξεν, ὁ δε - - -]αρος τὰς τριήρεις ἀπα-
[γαγὼν - - - -

But such a method of introducing the eponymous archon's name is impossible: the literal fragments of the Atthidographer Philochorus show that, as is natural in chronicles, the name of the archon with his demotic headed the account of the events of every year, in the form: Καλλίμαχος Περγασῆθεν· ἐπὶ τούτου - - -.[1] This form of introduction was not limited to Philochorus. A very important fragment of Androtion proves its use by that historian also. The fragment is missing in Müller's *Fragmenta Historicorum Graecorum* and is, therefore, hardly ever taken into account.[2] Discovered by Usener, it is preserved to us in an anonymous commentary on Aristotle's *Nicomachean Ethics* (*Comm. in Aristot. Graeca*, XX, Berlin, 1892, p. 232):[3] To the words of Aristotle, *Eth. Nicom.* V 10, p. 1134 b 21 f. (τὸ μνᾶς λυτροῦσθαι) the commentator writes: τοῦτο γὰρ 'Αθηναῖοι καὶ Λακεδαιμόνιοι ἐν τῷ πρὸς

---

[1] Cf. for instance fragments 144 and 146 (*FHG* I pp. 408 f.) preserved in Dionysius' treatise Περὶ Δεινάρχου (I pp. 301 f. U.-R.)

[2] L. Pareti *loc. cit.* (*supra* p. 305 note), in his polemic against De Sanctis, having referred to the fragments of Philochorus preserved in Didymus, continues thus (p. 509): "Citazioni queste simili in tutto ad altre già conosciute prima, così di Filocoro fr. 106. 132. 135 . . ., come di Androzione (Usener, *Jahrb. f. class. Philol.* 103 (1871) p. 311). E tutte le altre volte in cui si riferisce una datazione di Filocoro si ha ancora l'impressione, che il nome dell'arconte formasse come il titolo del capitolo annuo, in cui l'attidografo alludeva a quel dato fatto." It is a pity that Pareti did not lay the greatest stress upon the most important and solely decisive piece of evidence, the fragment of Androtion, which contains the solution of the whole question. The natural consequence of this is that no attention has been paid to the mention of Usener's fragment — not even by those who were most interested in the problem.

[3] For all the particulars regarding the fragment, I refer to the excellent article of Usener, now *Kl. Schriften* I 204 ff.; cf. Busolt *Griech. Gesch.* II 7 note 2.

ἀλλήλους συνέθεντο πολέμῳ, τὸ μνᾶς λυτροῦσθαι τοὺς αἰχμαλώτους. μνημονεύει τῆς συνθήκης ταύτης ᾿Ανδροτίων. "Εὐκτήμων Κυδαθήναιος· ἐπὶ τούτου πρέσβεις ἦλθον ἀπὸ Λακεδαίμονος ᾿Αθήναζε Μέγιλλος καὶ ῎Ενδιος καὶ Φιλοχαρίδας" καὶ ἐπάγει "τῶν δὲ περιγενομένων ἀπέδοσαν μνᾶν ὑπὲρ ἑκάστου λαβόντες." προείπων γὰρ ἦν ὅτι τοῦτο συνέθεντο ἐπὶ τῶν ἀλισκομένων (408/7 B.C.)." Usener alone recognized the importance of the fragment, which demonstrates that the formal arrangement of the *Atthis* of Androtion was the same as that of the work of Philochorus, and also that the demotic of the archon was not lacking. Neither then is the lacuna in ch. 4 of P sufficient to accommodate the demotic of Phormio nor could the name of the eponymous archon have been mentioned thus incidentally. This latter conclusion has all the greater weight, since the passage in question is itself a chronological formula. As such, it interrupts the narrative and stands between accounts of two entirely independent events: therefore, any attempt to argue that the author of P might have mentioned the archon incidentally at this point for stylistic reasons — that is, in order not to interrupt the continuity of his narrative — is to be categorically rejected; such a continuity not only does not exist at this point but was consciously avoided by the author.

This exposition, based on facts not considered by De Sanctis, renders his proposition untenable.[1] Since the chronological indication of the archon cannot be placed in the formula of transition from one year to another, it is impossible to identify P as part of an *Atthis*.

If we go on to discuss the other arguments of De Sanctis, we do so in order to pursue our purpose: to clarify the differences between the Thucydidean *Hellenica of Oxyrhynchus* and Androtion's chronicle of Athens. De Sanctis tried to explain the meaning of the ὄγδοον ἔτος in the passage from P quoted above by calling attention to the manner in which Aristotle in the *Athenaion Politeia* dates the anarchies of the sixth century through reference to the year of Solon's archonship (*Ath. Pol.* 13. 1): τῷ δὲ πέμπτῳ (sc. ἔτει) μετὰ τὴν Σόλωνος ἀρχὴν οὐ κατέστησαν ἄρχοντα διὰ τὴν στ[άσ]ιν.[2]

---

[1] Cf. De Sanctis' argument I 344 f.   [2] De Sanctis I 344.

There is, however, an enormous difference here: Aristotle is not writing a chronicle of Athens, but is desirous of presenting only certain selected events of Attic history; whenever he wished to give his readers an idea of the time of an event, he was compelled to connect the event he was dating with another already quoted: so he puts the first anarchy of 588/7 in the fifth year after the archonship of Solon (13. 1), the second anarchy in the fifth year after the first (13. 1), the foundation of the tyranny of Pisistratus in the thirty-second year after Solon (14. 1), the arrangement of the tribes by Clisthenes in the fourth year after the end of the tyranny (21. 2), and so forth.[1] Polybius I 6 contains a very precisely dated event of fundamental importance, the conquest of Rome by the Gauls, which is fixed exactly by reference to another well known date, the King's Peace; we have an analogous case in Thuc. II 2.1 (the date of the beginning of the Peloponnesian War) and among Roman historians in Fabius Pictor (Latinus) F 6 (I p. 113 Peter): *Quapropter tum primum ex plebe alter consul factus est, duovicesimo anno postquam Romam Galli ceperunt.*[2]

These examples are all in complete contrast to the chronological formula of P, which is a formula of transition, and the expression ὄγδοον ἔτος does not date any special event. The only real analogy for it is and remains the Thucydidean "*Jahresformel.*"

The manner in which the Spartan nauarchs are introduced in P (ch. 4. 2 and 14. 1), with the name of the predecessor of each, is impossible in an *Atthis*, — where complete lists of the Attic strategi were occasionally given, as a fragment of Androtion himself proves,[3] — but would be appropriate to a general Greek history. Now, the mention of the nauarchs had still other importance for De Sanctis' argument. Since the arrival of the new nauarch Pollis is reported immediately after the formula in ch. 4. 1; and since newly-appointed nauarchs officially assumed their

---

[1] We have an identical case, again completely different from that in P, in Philochorus F 97 (=*Schol.* Ar. *Pac.* 605), and perhaps in F 123 (=*Schol.* Ar. *Plut.* 1146).

[2] Cf. the very similar passage Liv. VII 18. 1.

[3] *Schol.* Aristid. III 485 D. = *FHG* IV p. 645, with the additions of Wilamowitz (*De scholiis Rhesi*, 1877, p. 13 = *Kleine Schriften*, I, 1935, p. 14); cf. S. Accame *Riv. di Filol. class.* LXIII (1935) 341 ff.; *Rendic. Acc. Linc.* XIV (1938) 402 ff.

duties in August, De Sanctis sees here another proof for his opinion
that the formula in ch. 4. 1 corresponds to the beginning of the
Attic year in July.[1]

He bases this conclusion on the extensive research of L. Pareti,
in which the attempt was made to establish a uniform date for the
assumption of actual command by Spartan nauarchs.[2] I have
reexamined the whole question and have found that the thesis of
Pareti, maintained only by means of forced modifications of the
text of Xenophon's *Hellenica*,[3] is entirely without foundation.
All the evidence cannot be produced here; the excursus would
be too long; we can deal only with that which concerns the
Hellenica of Oxyrhynchus. In any case, we know that Chiricrates
succeeded Pollis as nauarch in the late summer of 395 (14. 1).

[1] De Sanctis III 158 ff.

[2] L. Pareti, "Ricerche sulla potenza marittima degli Spartani," *Mem. Acc. Torino*,
LIX (1909). This thesis had already been suggested by Beloch (*Philologus* XLIII
(1884) 275), who, however, later — tacitly — withdrew it: *Griech. Gesch.* II 2. 272
ff., 282. Against Pareti cf. also the dissertation of R. Schäme, *Der Amtsantritt
der spartanischen Nauarchen*, Weida, 1915; U. Kahrstedt, *Forschungen zur Gesch.
des ausgehenden fünften und des vierten Jahrh.*, 1910, pp. 155 ff.; Jacoby *F Gr Hist*
II C p. 11.

[3] L. Pareti, "Note sulle interpolazioni cronologiche nei primi due libri delle
Elleniche di Senofonte," *Riv. di Filol. class.* XXXVIII (1910) 107 ff. Since De Sanctis, III 159 and in the attractive study "La genesi delle Elleniche di Senofonte,"
Annali R. Scuola Normale di Pisa, I (1932), p. 33, has not considered the arguments
offered by Beloch — the main representative of the interpolation theory (cf. *Griech.
Gesch.* II 2. 23, 244 ff.) — in support of his belief that Lysander and Callicratidas
began their terms in the springs of 407 and 406 (*Griech. Gesch.* II 2. 273–275), I
prefer to postpone any further discussion of the matter until an attempt is made
to refute the arguments of Beloch. J. Hatzfeld, "Notes sur la composition des
Helléniques," *Revue de philologie*, IV (1930), p. 215, is definitely against the theory
of Beloch; his objection that "on ne peut pas . . . enlever la mention de début
d'année sans admettre un bouleversement plus considérable du texte que rien
n'autorise à supposer" is insurmountable. I mention only one of the consequences
of Pareti's modifications of Xenophon's text: he reads *Hell.* II 1. 7 in the following
manner (*loc. cit.* 120): οἱ δὲ Λακεδαιμόνιοι ἔδοσαν τὸν Λύσανδρον ὡς ἐπιστολέα, ναύαρχον
δὲ Ἄρακον· οὐ γὰρ νόμος αὐτοῖς δὶς τὸν αὐτὸν ναυαρχεῖν· τὰς μέντοι ναῦς παρέδοσαν
Λυσάνδρῳ. Λύσανδρος ⟨δ'⟩ἀφικόμενος - - - -. M. MacLaren in his article "On
the composition of Xenophon's Hellenica," *Am. Journ. of Philol.*, LV (1934),
pp. 121 ff., 249 ff. (cf. especially pp. 124 f. and 251) did not undertake a new discussion of Beloch's thesis, which he obviously considers refuted.

Accordingly, Pollis was the nauarch of the year 396/5 and, in the opinion of De Sanctis, would have had to begin his term in August 396.[1] If this is right, the *"Jahresformel"* of the ninth year (395/4) lay between fragments A and B (or better B and D) of the papyrus.[2] But no one has observed that, if the beginning of the two successive ναυαρχίαι (i.e. of Pollis and of Chiricrates) had in reality fallen one in the August of 396 and one in the August of 395, we should have to expect the mention of the two events at respectively similar points of the narrative; that is, according to the example of Pollis in ch. 4, the note on the succession of Chiricrates would have to appear immediately after the supposed *"Jahresformel"* of the ninth year (395/4) and not after long accounts of the revolution in Rhodes (ch. 10), of the preparation for the Corinthian War (ch. 11–13) and of no one knows how many other incidents (related in the lost chapters before ch. 10).

Therefore, it is clear that the arrival in Asia (and with this the actual taking over of command) of the two nauarchs did not occur at the same date in two successive years, a conclusion, which is, moreover, corroborated by the following evidence, to which attention has not previously been called. The invasion of Phocis by the Locrians, reported in ch. 13, took place τοῦ σίτου ἀκμάζοντος according to Pausanias III 9. 9, that is, at the end of May or in June,[3] in any case *before* the beginning of the Attic year in July. If P were part of an *Atthis*, the *"Jahresformel"* of 395/4 would have to stand between the invasion of Phocis (May/June) in ch. 13 and the arrival of the nauarch Chiricrates (August) in ch. 14. 1. And this, obviously, is not the case, since the text here is completely preserved.

It is now firmly established that Pollis arrived in Asia in the

---

[1] De Sanctis III 160; but cf. Beloch *Griech. Gesch.* II 2. 276.

[2] De Sanctis III 161: "Accolta la data che io propongo pel principio della nauarchia di Pollide e quindi pel principio dell'anno adottato da P, dovremo ritenere che la notizia sull'inizio del nuovo anno, il nono, 395-4, cadesse o nella lacuna tra A e B o più verosimilmente nella lacuna tra B e D. . . ." Schäme, *loc. cit.* 31 note 2, is not clear.

[3] For the precise date cf. Thuc. II 19: θέρους καὶ τοῦ σίτου ἀκμάζοντος, and Busolt *Griech. Gesch.* III 2. 691. In addition, Beloch *Griech. Gesch.* III 2. 218 and *Oxy. Pap.* V p. 233.

spring of 395. The result of this series of arguments, furthermore, is a final confirmation of the fact that the chronological
proposals of De Sanctis cannot be maintained.[1]

5. *The Tradition and Preservation of the* Hellenica of Oxyrhynchus

We have now to draw the final conclusions from our discussion
on the historian of Oxyrhynchus. The result is very simple: we
do not know him.

It seemed justifiable, even reasonable, to start, after the discovery of P, with the supposition that the author was a writer
known to us. But the nearly unanimous rejection of the very
possibility that the author could be a historian whose name has
not been preserved is, to put it mildly, amazing. The argument
that any writer read and copied in Oxyrhynchus about 200
A.D. must be known to us became a dogma which was regarded
as the basis of any discussion about the authorship of P. Pages
could be filled with quotations expounding this "dogma," which
nearly every modern student of the problem has mentioned.[2]
Since our purpose is to clarify as far as possible the question of
authorship, we are obliged to examine this dogma, which has been
questioned only in occasional notes by Fuhr, Underhill, Peter, W.
Otto, Wilamowitz, Castiglioni,[3] and virtually also by Jacoby and
Barber.[4]

[1] In order not to interrupt the course of the argument, it seemed best to postpone
further consideration of the *Atthis* of Androtion to Part II. Reference is repeatedly
made there to the problem of the *Hellenica of Oxyrhynchus*.

[2] Cf. *ed. princ.* p. 139; De Sanctis I 342, II 535; Ed. Meyer *Theopomps Hell.*
124; A. v. Mess *Rhein. Mus.* LXIII (1908) 372; W. Judeich *Rhein. Mus.* LXVI
(1911) 99; M. Gelzer *Woch. klass. Philol.* 1914, 124; J. H. Lipsius, *Cratippi
Hellenicorum fragm. Oxyrhynchia . . .*, 1916, p. 4; W. Schubart, *Einführung in
die Papyruskunde*, 1918, p. 116; Beloch *Griech. Gesch.* III 2. 2; Walker, *New
Chapters* (1921) 130; R. Laqueur *RE* V A 2. 2196.

[3] Fuhr *Philol. Woch.* 1908, 149; Underhill *Journ. of Hell. Stud.* XXVIII (1908)
290; H. Peter *Wahrheit und Kunst . . .* (1911) 142; W. Otto *Hist. Zeitschr.*
CXXV (1922) 483 note 1; U. v. Wilamowitz, *supra* p. 308 note 1; L. Castiglioni
Gnomon IV (1928) 18.

[4] Jacoby *Nachr. Gött. Ges.* 1924, 13 ff.; Barber *loc. cit.* 49 ff., 134 note 1. Regarding the problem of how few names of historians of the fourth century actually

De Sanctis referred to the statistics on literary papyri which were compiled by C. H. Oldfather and which merit a revision after sixteen years of innumerable discoveries: [1] "È ovvio infatti, ed è confermato dalle analogie che ci fornisce la statistica dei papiri letterari, che in quell'angolo d'Egitto, circa il 200 d. Chr., dell'età classica non si trascrivevano se non gli autori di cui la gloria letteraria era ben assodata." On the other hand Grenfell writes: [2] "In about A.D. 200 copies of most of the Greek authors of the first rank and many of the second and third were probably still in circulation at Oxyrhynchus." This statement is correct and all the more impressive because Grenfell himself believed in the "dogma." The statistics are important only for authors who were very much read, like Homer, Hesiod, Euripides, Menander, Demosthenes, Plato, Thucydides, and so forth, not for the less popular writers. And how greatly this statistical evidence itself may change has been shown by the recent Aeschylus discoveries. A. Körte, who is also a supporter of the "dogma," [3] writes: "Unter den griechischen Klassikern, von denen uns im letzten Menschenalter der Boden Ägyptens grössere oder kleinere Handschriftenreste beschert hat, fehlte bisher Aischylos." The case of Aeschylus is not unique; there follows a list of papyri of unknown or little known authors and of unknown works of authors with whose entire literary production we thought we were acquainted:

1. *Oxy. Pap.* III no. 410:[4] Compendium of rhetoric, written in the Doric dialect, belonging to the fourth century B.C., copied in Oxyrhynchus certainly after 150 A.D. The author is completely unknown. We are even unable to propose any name.

---

are known, cf. Ed. Meyer, *Gesch. d. Altert.* III 258, 276; Wilamowitz *Aristoteles und Athen* I 286; Jacoby *Das Marmor Parium* (1904) XIV; *Nachr. Gött. Ges.* 1924, 14; *F Gr Hist* II D p. 668. 13.

[1] De Sanctis II 535; cf. also Cavaignac *Revue de l'Ég. anc.* I (1927) 176 ff.; *Mél. Glotz* I 148. C. H. Oldfather, *The Greek Literary Texts from Greco-Roman Egypt*, Madison, 1923.

[2] *Oxy. Pap.* XIII (1919) p. 110.

[3] *Hermes* LXVIII (1933) 249.

[4] *Arch. f. Pap.* III (1906) 294; Oldfather *loc. cit.* p. 42 no. 783; Fuhr, in the note cited above, has already referred to this compendium.

2. (a) *Oxy. Pap.* IV no. 665:[1] Argumentum of the fourth book of Philistus' Σικελικά, recognized as such by De Sanctis in an excellent article.[2]

(b) Coppola, *Riv. di Filol. class.* LVIII (1930) 449 ff.: Fragment of Philistus' Σικελικά, probably from Oxyrhynchus.

Both written about 200 A.D. A. Körte writes:[3] "Interessant ist auf jeden Fall, dass Philistos' Werk noch im 2. Jahrh. n. Chr. in Ägypten Leser gefunden hat."

3. *S. Ber. Berl. Ak.* 1918, 752–762:[4] Fragment of a historical work of Hellenistic times: siege of Rhodes by Demetrius Poliorcetes in 304 B.C. Written in the second century A.D.

4. *Pap. Mil.* 19:[5] 'Απολλοδώρου ζητήματα γραμματικά, from Tebtunis. Written in the second century A.D. Only the title preserved. This work of the famous Apollodorus of Athens had been totally unknown.

5. *Pap. Brit. Mus.* 2560:[6] Fragment of a tragedy: *Iphigenia in Aulis.* About 200 A.D. Poet unknown.

6. E. Lobel, "Greek poetry and life," *Essays presented to G. Murray*, 1936, p. 295:[7] Fragment of a tragedy: *Andromache.*

7. *Pap. Brit. Mus.* 186:[8] *Medea* of Neophron (??). Second or third century A.D. Let me call attention here to the list of tragic poets *Tebt. Pap.* 695, third century B.C., in which not less than three unknown poets appear.

8. *Oxy. Pap.* III no. 427:[9] Antiphanes' 'Ανθρωπογονία. The author was a contemporary of the historian of Oxyrhynchus. Written in the third century A.D. Only the title preserved. Previously we had no knowledge of this work.

---

[1] *Arch f. Pap.* III (1906) 490; Oldfather *loc. cit.* p. 24 no. 414.

[2] *Riv. di Filol. class.* XXXIII (1905) 66 ff.

[3] *Arch. f. Pap.* X (1932) 69. R. Laqueur, in his recent article on Philistus, *RE* XIX 2 (1938) 2417, denies without sufficient grounds Philistus' authorship for both papyri.

[4] *New Chapters in the History of Greek Lit.* II (1929) 66 ff.; *Arch. f. Pap.* VII (1924) p. 234 no. 627; Oldfather *loc. cit.* p. 25 no. 418.

[5] A. Vogliano *Pap. della R. Università di Milano* I pp. 174 f.; *Arch. f. Pap.* XIII (1938) 118.

[6] Milne, *Catal. of the Lit. Pap. in the Brit. Mus.*, 1927, p. 57 no. 78; *New Chapters* III (1933) 154; *Arch. f. Pap.* X (1932) p. 53 no. 727.

[7] *Arch. f. Pap.* XIII (1938) p. 100 no. 874.

[8] Milne, *Catal.* p. 53 no. 77; *New Chapters* III (1933) 152; *Arch. f. Pap.* III (1906) 1–5; E. Diehl *RE* XVI 2 (1935) 2433; Oldfather *loc. cit.* p. 48 no. 903.

[9] Milne *Catal.* p. 62 no. 87; *New Chapters* III 167; *Arch. f. Pap.* III (1906) 277; Oldfather *loc. cit.* p. 7 no. 58.

9. *Oxy. Pap.* XI no. 1399:[1] Χοιρίλου ποιήματα | Βαρβαρικά· Μηδικ(ά)· Περσ[ικά. Written about 200 A.D.

To this class of papyri P also belongs. This conclusion leads us to another question: was Oxyrhynchus really a "remote corner" of Egypt without higher intellectual interests? We have already called attention to the statement of Grenfell, which is a fact, not an opinion; we see it now confirmed. But there is still other evidence.

It may be well to recall that Heraclides Lembos of Callatis spent part of his life in Oxyrhynchus and was called therefore ὁ 'Οξυρυγχίτης,[2] and it is perhaps significant that it was in Oxyrhynchus that a fragment (written like P at the end of the second century A.D.) of his epitome of Hermippus' work Περὶ νομοθετῶν [3] was found. A part of the sixth book of Satyrus' Βίοι, containing a fragment of the life of Euripides, was discovered there, too; Satyrus and Hermippus were the most celebrated biographers of Hellenistic times and it is interesting that Heraclides Lembos, who was the former's fellow-countryman, epitomized his work as well as Hermippus'.[4]

---

[1] A. Körte *Arch. f. Pap.* VII (1924) 117: "Dass man diesen Dichter noch um 200 n. Chr. in Ägypten las, ist sehr merkwürdig."

[2] This is the most probable solution of the dilemma that Heraclides is called by Diog. Laert. V 94 Καλλατιανὸς ἢ 'Αλεξανδρεύς, but by Suidas, II p. 581 no. 462 Ad. 'Οξυρυγχίτης.

[3] *Oxy. Pap.* XI no. 1367; the title is preserved in F 2 (p. 117): 'Ηρ]ακλείδου τοῦ | [Σ]αραπίωνος ἐπ[ι]τομὴ | τῶν 'Ερμίππου περὶ | νομοθετῶν καὶ | ἑ[π]τὰ σοφῶν καὶ | Πυθαγόρου. Oldfather *loc. cit.* p. 22 no. 361. Christ-Schmid, *Gesch. der griech. Literatur*, II 1, 1920 (6th ed.), p. 85 note 3.

[4] Hunt *Oxy. Pap.* IX p. 125: "It may be noted as a curious coincidence that Heraclides, whom Suidas calls 'Οξυρυγχίτης, probably resided in the city from whose ruins the present papyrus [Satyrus!] was obtained." Since Heraclides also epitomized Sotion's Διαδοχαὶ τῶν φιλοσόφων, we see that he obviously chose for his compilations the three most important biographical works of the Hellenistic period. This is the very clear result of an analysis of the Heraclides papyrus; Crönert's theory that Suidas and Demetrius Magnes, Diogenes' authority, confused two persons (*Kolotes und Menedemos*, 1906, pp. 136 f.) was, with the discovery of the papyrus, proved untenable. R. Philippson fails completely in his attempt (undertaken without considering the document in question) to renew this theory ("Panaetiana," *Rhein. Mus.*, LXXVIII (1929), pp. 344 f.). He adhered to his opinion even

In the Empire, as in Hellenistic times, the cultural center was, of course, Alexandria, with its famous library.[1] The authority of Alexandria was so great that Domitian, in order to restock libraries which had been destroyed by fire, bought up books everywhere and sent scholars to Alexandria to correct them and to copy works which had not been found elsewhere.[2]

Emphasis, furthermore, should be laid upon the fact that at about the time P was copied Athenaeus of Naucratis, in Alexandria, composed one of the most learned works preserved from antiquity. Among the books read and excerpted by him are many of which not even the names of the authors are known to us.[3]

It is therefore clear that about 200 A.D. Alexandria was still a cultural center of the first order. Directly or indirectly, the copy P doubtless derives from an Alexandrian exemplar of a work which had been rare for centuries. But even the fact that P is a private copy was used by Ed. Meyer, Pareti, A. Körte and M. Gelzer as an argument that the *Hellenica of Oxyrhynchus* must be the work of a well-known author! We quote here a really classical passage from Ed. Meyer's book, which shows with particular distinctness how lightly the question was handled:[4] "Und der historisch interessierte Gelehrte, der sich um 200 n. Chr. diesen Text abgeschrieben hat oder abschreiben liess, hat natürlich nicht irgend einen verschollenen Autor für seinen Privatbesitz kopiert. Damit ist auch die gelegentlich geäusserte Ansicht erledigt, es sei uns hier ein gänzlich unbekannter Schriftsteller des 4. Jahrh. erhalten."

---

after being informed by A. Körte about the existence of the papyrus (*Rhein. Mus.* LXXIX (1930) 406 ff.).

For Satyrus cf. Milne *Cat.* p. 94 no. 122; Oldfather *loc. cit.* p. 55 no. 1055; *New Chapters* I (1921) 144 ff.; D. R. Stuart, *Epochs of Greek and Roman Biography*, Berkeley, Cal., 1928, pp. 163 ff., 179 ff.

[1] The following statement of Oldfather is noteworthy (*loc. cit.* 84): "The higher education, which had practically been monopolized by Alexandria, had spread into the country."

[2] Suet. *Dom.* 20: *Liberalia studia imperii initio neglexit, quanquam bibliothecas incendio absumptas impensissime reparare curasset, exemplaribus undique petitis missisque Alexandream qui describerent emendarentque.*

[3] Cf. Wentzel *RE* II 2. 2032. Athenaeus also used Satyrus directly.

[4] *Theopomps Hellenika* 124.

As a matter of fact, the direct opposite of this assertion of Meyer and his followers would seem the logically correct one: a book, in the commercial sense of the word, would be the very thing that would lead us to believe that a work was widely diffused. A copy made in Alexandria, such as P, is all the more explicable if the work could not be obtained from the public booksellers of Oxyrhynchus.

One might ask, how such a work could possibly have disappeared entirely from literary tradition. The answer is that in reality it did not entirely disappear; it is preserved to us "third-hand," so to speak, in the work of Diodorus, who made use of Ephorus, who, in turn, had had the actual work of the Oxyrhynchus historian in his hands. We are informed of the existence of scholarly literature on the plagiarisms of Ephorus. The importance of this literature was brought out effectively by F. Jacoby in developing his Daemachus thesis.[1] In those critical treatises, the historian of Oxyrhynchus certainly was mentioned. Porphyry quotes Lysimachus' work Περὶ τῆς Ἐφόρου κλοπῆς in two books, noting the names of only three authors copied by Ephorus, — Daemachus, Callisthenes, Anaximenes;[2] of course, more than three authors were discussed in the treatise of Lysimachus, but Porphyry chose to mention only three. Therefore Jacoby's proposal to identify the writer of P, who surely was among Ephorus' victims, with Daemachus is not more than a possible hypothesis. We know so little about Daemachus that it is impossible for us even to determine the chronological extent of his work.[3]

Ephorus' own history superseded the work which he had employed.[4] But that the latter did not entirely disappear even then is proved by the treatises of Lysimachus of Alexandria [5] and of

---

[1] *Nachr. Gött. Ges.* 1924, 13 ff.; *F Gr Hist* 65 f.

[2] *F Gr Hist* 70 T 17.

[3] A. Körte *Hist. Zeitschr.* CXXXVI (1927) 89; De Sanctis II 535; only W. Otto followed Jacoby: Busolt-Swoboda *Griech. Staatskunde* II (1926) 1577 *ad* p. 81. 2.

[4] Underhill *loc. cit.* 290; Peter *loc. cit.* 142. The analogy with Livy and the superseding of all the earlier annalistic literature by his work is obvious and instructive.

[5] Λυσίμαχος ὁ Ἀλεξανδρεύς (*Schol.* Soph. *Oed. Col.* 91; *Schol.* Apoll. Rhod. I 558); cf. Gudeman *RE* XIV 1 (1928) 32, 35.

Alcaeus, who are both mentioned by Porphyry (see above). Lysimachus belonged to the circle of Aristophanes of Byzantium, who with his Παράλληλοι Μενάνδρου τε καὶ ἀφ' ὧν ἔκλεψεν ἐκλογαί stands at the head of those who wrote Περὶ κλοπῆς.

The vindication of the works plagiarized by Ephorus had no reaction in a larger public. But the *Hellenica* existed in the library of Alexandria, where it had been brought by the scholars of the third century B.C., and the literature on the plagiarisms of Ephorus was still known to Porphyry, who lived two generations after our papyrus P was written. We have, incidentally, an interesting analogy: The work of Ptolemy Soter remained for centuries unused in the libraries, until Arrian brought it to light and made it the foundation of his *Anabasis*.[1] And yet the work of Ptolemy was very important and its author was a famous king. The reason for this neglect is similar to that responsible for the fate of P: the work of Ptolemy also was reduced to obscurity, although not, as in the case of P, by being plagiarized, but through the rise of another current of historiography. He was unable to prevent the triumph of the Alexander-legend against which he wrote his work in his old age. Arrian, after all, actually did nothing more for Ptolemy than the Alexandrian philologists of the time of Aristophanes had done three hundred years before (though, to be sure, in vain), for the nearly forgotten historian of Oxyrhynchus whose work had been absorbed by the work of Ephorus; but the end of the Peloponnesian War and the Corinthian War could not enlist such an interest in later times. Hence this work did not find its Arrian. Moreover, the lack of style contributed not less to its neglect. Very fortunately for us, however, at one time it interested a scholar in Oxyrhynchus, part of whose copy has been preserved.

To conclude: more important than the statement that we do not know the name of the historian of Oxyrhynchus is the inference which we have now to draw, namely, that we must stop forcing the leading historians of the fourth century B.C., Theopompus, Ephorus, Androtion, into the Procrustean bed of the

---

[1] "Natürlich muss das Buch gelesen sein, weil es sich sonst nicht so lange erhalten hätte; nur wissen wir gar nicht von wem" (Jacoby *F Gr Hist* II D p. 499. 18).

Hellenica of Oxyrhynchus. Our understanding of Greek historiography is dependent upon abandoning that practice.

II

NOTES ON THE *ATTHIS* OF ANDROTION [1]

In his masterly work *Aristoteles und Athen* U. v. Wilamowitz gave a fundamental characterization of the Attic chronicles.[2] Certainly, the discovery of Aristotle's *Athenaion Politeia*, which depended in many points on the Attic chronicles, presented him with an excellent opportunity for doing so. He established the fact that the main substance of the *Atthides* remained almost constant and that even the earliest editions of these chronicles contained detailed stories of novelistic character.[3] He fully recognized the *Atthides'* outstanding value as source-material.[4]

But neither the finding of the *Athenaion Politeia* and the study of Wilamowitz nor the discovery, made a few years later, of Didymus' *Commentary on Demosthenes* with its important new fragments of Androtion and Philochorus had the consequence of reopening the research on the *Atthis*.[5] The collection of the fragments of the Atthidographers in Müller's *Fragmenta Historicorum*

---

[1] The discussion of De Sanctis' proposal to identify the *Hellenica of Oxyrhynchus* with the *Atthis* of Androtion (*supra* pp. 328 ff.) makes it seem desirable to try to contribute something toward the clarification of our knowledge of this remarkable work. The following notes, however, deal only with certain problems.

[2] I 260–290.

[3] *Loc. cit.* I 275 ff., 284.

[4] *Loc. cit.* I 281 where Wilamowitz refers, without quotation, to his earlier study, "Aus Kydathen," *Philol. Unt.*, I (1880), pp. 121 f.

[5] The most important old-style source-study concerning the *Atthis* is Busolt's analysis of Aristotle's *Athenaion Politeia, Griech. Gesch.* II (1895) 14–55, 7–12, 57 f. and *Griech. Staatskunde* I (1920) 82 f., 91–95. See moreover regarding the *Atthis*: Ed. Schwartz *RE* II 2 (1896) 2180–2183; P. Foucart, *Étude sur Didymos*, 1907, pp. 135 ff.; F. E. Adcock, "The Source of the Solonian Chapters of the *Athenaion Politeia*," *Klio*, XII (1912), pp. 1 ff.; G. De Sanctis, *Atthis*, 1912, *passim*; A. Ledl, *Studien zur älteren athenischen Verfassungsgeschichte*, Heidelberg, 1914, *passim*; W. Graf Uxkull-Gyllenband, *Plutarch und die griechische Biographie*, 1927, pp. 69–76; R. Laqueur *RE* XIII 1 (1926) 1092–1097, XIX 2 (1938) 2434–2442.

Graecorum is still more incomplete than other parts of this work.[1]
And, while the fragments of Philochorus, also in the *FHG*, are so
numerous as to present a rather distinct picture of his work, several of the most interesting remains of Androtion are missing there.

Androtion,[2] who did not begin his political career later than the
King's Peace, became one of the most authoritative financiers of
the administration of Aristophon [3] and was attacked in vain in
two speeches of Demosthenes, *Against Androtion* (355 B.C.) and
Against Timocrates (352 B.C.). He continued to occupy a re-
spected position in Athens' political life in the following years
also. It was he who, in the year 347/6 B.C., made the motion
for the decree in honor of the sons of Leucon (Dittenberger *Syll.*[3]
206). Nevertheless, according to a notice of Plutarch, he belonged
to the group of writers who composed their works in exile; in the
case of Androtion, of course, the *Atthis*, which according to Plutarch was written in Megara,[4] is meant.

The discoveries of Didymus' *Commentary* and of another
papyrus at the beginning of this century have clarified the political
position of Androtion for the period after the two orations of
Demosthenes. This new evidence has not yet been utilized to the
fullest possible extent.

---

[1] *FHG* I pp. LXXXI–XCI, 359–427, IV pp. 645–648. See *supra* p. 329. The third
volume of Jacoby's *F Gr Hist* will contain the fragments of the *Atthides*; cf. *F Gr
Hist* I p. I and Jacoby's earlier program *Klio* IX (1909) 119 f. See now *F Gr Hist*
III A, Leiden, 1940, pp. 6*–8*.

[2] Concerning Androtion see Ed. Schwartz *RE* I 2. 2174 f.; Dittenberger *Syll.*[3]
I p. 267; F. Blass *Die att. Beredsamkeit*[2] II (1892) 19–21 and recently W. Jaeger,
Demosthenes, Berkeley, 1938, pp. 58 ff., 220 f.

[3] The existence of which was more or less denied by Beloch, *Griech. Gesch.* III
1. 240, who in his history of the fourth century omitted even mentioning Androtion
as a political personality; his reaction (already in *Att. Politik* 167 f.) against Schäfer
Demosthenes I (2nd ed.) 138 ff. was much too strong and the consequence was a
complete distortion of the picture of fourth-century Athenian history and of
Demosthenes' political development. W. Jaeger, in his book on Demosthenes, corrected earlier errors and treated the question of the party-background of Demosthenes' first political speeches with impressive clearness: the conclusion that Demosthenes began his career, if not as an immediate partisan of Eubulus, at least as a fighter
against the same opponents, is indeed inevitable (*loc. cit.* 57, 76 f., 226. 17).

[4] Plut. *De exilio* 14, p. 605 C.

In the rhetorical treatise *Oxy. Pap.* VII no. 1012 already mentioned (p. 315) we have among others a paragraph in which instances of the suppression of names in classical works are considered. And here the author refers to a passage of Aeschines (which was identified by Wilamowitz as 1. 165) with the following words: C 14 ff. : Αἰσχί]νης δὲ τὸ κατὰ γρ[αμματεῖον] πορνεύσαντος ὄνομ[α οὐκ ἡγνό]-ησε μέν, ὤκνησε δὲ [ἐξειπεῖν λέ]γων εἶναι αὐτὸ[ν τ]ῶν π[επολι]τευμένων. ἦν δὲ ᾿Ανδ[ροτίων ὡς] [Δη]μοσθένης δηλοῖ [ἐ]ν [τῷ κατὰ][᾿Αν]δροτίωνος κατὰ γραμματε[ῖ]ον αὐτὸν λέγων πεπορνευκέναι. Indeed, Aeschines, in his speech against Timarchus, says (*loc. cit.*): πόθεν οὖν ἴσχυκε καὶ σύνηθες γεγένηται λέγειν, ὡς κατὰ γραμματεῖόν τινες ἡταίρησαν, ἤδη ἐρῶ. ἀνὴρ εἶς τῶν πολιτῶν (τὸ δ᾿ ὄνομα οὐ λέξω· τὰς γὰρ ἀπεχθείας φεύγω) οὐδὲν προϊδόμενος ὧν ὀλίγῳ πρότερον ἐγὼ διεξῆλθον πρὸς ὑμᾶς, λέγεται κατὰ συνθήκας ἡταιρηκέναι τὰς παρ᾿ ᾿Αντικλεῖ κειμένας, οὐκ ὢν ἰδιώτης, ἀλλὰ πρὸς τὰ κοινὰ προσιών. There is no doubt that Aeschines here alludes to a corresponding chapter in the speech of Demosthenes *Against Androtion* (22. 21–23) — an allusion which modern scholars had not recognized before. And yet it is important because it shows us that even in the time immediately after the peace of Philocrates Androtion was so influential that Aeschines dared to manifest his hate for him only in relatively obscure language. It is perfectly clear that he was a political adversary of Aeschines and still in 346/5 B.C. stood on the side of Aristophon. In connection with this it is of great interest to note that Aristophon was introduced by Theopompus (*F Gr Hist* 115 F 166) as the most implacable enemy of any agreement between Athens and Philip in the peace negotiations.[1] Androtion, we see, in 346/5 B.C. was the same opponent of the party of Eubulus he had been ten years before, when Demosthenes still was a follower of Eubulus.

It is to be regretted that we do not know whether Androtion actually took part in the debate concerning a treaty with Persia in 344/3 B.C. or not, or, if he did, to what extent. The only thing of which we are certain is that he dealt with this matter in his *Atthis*: Didym. *In Demosth.* 8. 8: τοῦ Φιλίππου ἐπὶ ἄρχοντος Λυκίσκου ᾿Αθή-ναζε πε[ρ]ὶ εἰρήνης πέμψαντος, βασιλέως πρέσβ[ει]ς συμπροσήκαντο οἱ

---

[1] Cf. Beloch *Griech. Gesch.* III 1. 504.

'Αθηναῖοι, ἀλλὰ ὑπε[ρο]πτικώτερον ἢ ἐχρῆν διελ[έ]χθησαν αὐτ[οῖ]s. εἰρη-
νεύσειν [γ]ὰρ πρὸς 'A[ρταξέρξη]ν, ἐὰν μ[ὴ] ἐπὶ τὰς 'Ελλην[ίδας] ἴῃ [πόλεις.
ἀφηγοῦν]ται τ[αῦτ]α 'Ανδροτίων, ὃς καὶ τ[ότ' εἶπε, καὶ 'Ανα]ξιμένης· ε[ἴη]
δ' ἂν ἄμεινον [τὰ τοῦ Φι]λοχόρου παραγράψαι. F. Stähelin and Ed.
Meyer, followed recently by G. Glotz, adopted a doubtful textual
restoration (ὃς καὶ τ[ότ' εἶπε) as the basis of their theory that
Androtion himself made the motion for the psephisma and that
this later was the reason for his exile.[1] But we do not even know
whether the quotation from Androtion embraces the first sentence
of the passage of Didymus. If it does, Androtion himself criticized the reply of the Athenian people.[2] And if that restoration
is right, the sole conclusion it affords is that, sometime during the
debate, Androtion held the floor.[3]

He was more than 65 years old when he was compelled, after
344 B.C., to leave Athens.   Therefore, his *Atthis*, published in any
case before 326/5 B.C. (*terminus ante quem* for the *Athenaion
Politeia* of Aristotle[4] who made use of it [cf. *infra* p. 349 note 3])
was a work of his old age.[5] It was composed of scarcely more than
eight books (the idea of a twelfth book is untenable).[6] The his-

---

[1] F. Stähelin *Klio* V (1905) 146; Ed. Meyer *S. Ber. Berl. Ak.* 1909, 778; G.
Glotz *Hist. grecque* III (1936) 321 f.

[2] I am inclined to see with Foucart, *loc. cit.* 160, in the first sentence "une analyse
d'Androtion et d'Anaximénès, surtout du premier." P. Cloché, "La Grèce de 346
à 339 av. J.-C.," *Bull. Corr. Hell.*, XLIV (1920), pp. 125 ff. and *La politique ex-
térieur d'Athènes de 404 à 338 av. J.-C.*, Paris, 1934, pp. 252 f., did not take into consideration the problem in question.

[3] This also, apparently, is the opinion of E. Drerup, *Demosthenes im Urteile des
Altertums*, 1923, p. 19.

[4] J. E. Sandys, *Aristotle's Const. of Ath.* (2nd ed.), 1912, p. xlix. W. Jaeger,
Aristotle, Eng. trans., Oxford, 1934, p. 327 note 1. See now the note of B. D.
Meritt in *Am. Journ. of Philol.* LXI (1940) 78.

[5] Ed. Schwartz *loc. cit.*; cf. Beloch *Griech. Gesch.* III 1. 399 note 1.

[6] Ed. Schwartz, *loc. cit.*, followed by De Sanctis, I 348, and Busolt, *Griech.
Staatskunde* I (1920) 83 (opposed to his previous view, *Griech. Gesch.* II 8, where he
wrote under the influence of the faulty opinion of B. Keil, *Die solonische Verfassung
in Aristoteles Verfassungsgeschichte Athens*, 1892, p. 191) considered the twelfth
book of Androtion suspect, without presenting any argument. Harpocration *s.v.*
'Αμφίπολις - - - - πόλις αὕτη τῆς Θράκης· πρότερον δὲ 'Εννέα ὁδοὶ ἐκαλεῖτο, ὡς 'Ανδροτίων ἐν ιβ' 'Ατθίδος (= Androtion F 27). Here, there is certainly no possibility
of misinterpretation: the fragment belongs to the second book, in which Androtion

tory of the earliest period filled only one book, in which his treatment of the institution of the Areopagus was contained (S. Maximus Confessor, *Prol. in op. S. Dion. Areop.*, Migne IV p. 17); in the second he related the Clisthenian reform (Harpocr. *s.v.* ’Αποδέκται) and the history of the fifth century (cf. p. 344 note 6); in the third the Peloponnesian War, the tyranny of the Thirty and the restoration of the democracy (see *infra* p. 348 and Harpocr. *s.v.* Δέκα καὶ Δεκαδοῦχοι); in the fourth book he reached the time of his own participation in Athenian politics; in the seventh he touched upon the year 350/349 B.C. (Didym. *In Demosth.* 13. 45, 14. 36 f.): Thus he devoted three books to the history of the period before his entry into political life and five books to the history of his own time. It is clear that Androtion defended his political activity in his work,[1] as within certain limits Thucydides and, above all, Philistus had done. It is, then, more than probable that he mentioned his exile, which occurred after 344 B.C. — another argument against the identification of his *Atthis* with the *Hellenica of Oxyrhynchus*, written before 346 B.C., probably before 356 B.C.[2]

The first four books of Philochorus' *Atthis* correspond to the first

---

treated the Pentecontaetia and with this the foundation of Amphipolis: Thuc. I 100. 3: ὡς οἰκιοῦντες τὰς τότε καλουμένας Ἐννέα ὁδούς, νῦν δὲ ’Αμφίπολιν. Corruptions like EN ĪB instead of EN THI B (= EN B̄) are very frequent. I give a list of examples of similar corruptions in quotations from Atthidographers:

1. Steph. Byz. *s.v.* Ἄστυ (= Philoch. F 4) ΙΑ for Α (cf. A. Böckh *Kl. Schriften* V (1871) 406).

2. Harpocr. *s.v.* ’Οσχοφόροι (= Philoch. F 44) ἐν τῇ ιβ' for ἐν τῇ β' (Böckh *loc. cit.* 408); analogous.

3. Harpocr. *s.v.* Οἷον (= Philoch. F 76) ΙΓ for Γ (Böckh *loc. cit.* 410).

4. Hesy. *s.v.* ’Αγαμεμνόνεια φρέατα (= Clid. F 9) ἐν τῇ ιβ' for ἐν τῇ β'; analogous. We have therefore to read in Androt. F 27: ὡς ’Ανδροτίων ἐν [.]β' ’Ατθίδος.

[1] See Steph. Byz. *s.v.* ’Αρκεσίνη and Dittenberger *Syll.*³ I no. 193. It is noteworthy that he, like other Athenian orators of his time, published his speeches. Aristotle has preserved a fragment in which Idrieus, dynast of Caria, is attacked (Arist. *Rhet.* III 4. 3).

[2] De Sanctis, I 351, was therefore compelled to propose — in contradiction to the literary evidence — the hypothesis that Androtion wrote a considerable part of his work (at least the first four books) before his exile.

three books of Androtion's; because of his antiquarian interests his presentation of the earliest times, of course, was more detailed than that of the politician Androtion. In dealing with the events of the middle of the fourth century Philochorus was much briefer than his predecessor: his sixth book embraced the history of ca. 359–336 B.C., which Androtion treated in three books (VI–VIII).

How much the *Atthis* of Philochorus depended upon the earlier work of Androtion is well known.[1] The clearest testimony is provided by the two fragments concerning the ὀργάς, which Didymus *In Demosth.* 13. 44 has preserved.[2] Didymus' quotation from Philochorus begins at an earlier point than his quotation from Androtion; in Androtion, he was interested only in the conception of ὀργάς. That something else preceded this passage in the actual text of Androtion is proved by the καί which stands at the beginning.[3] But Philochorus modified a little the words of Androtion with the intention of giving a better reproduction of the oracle's reply.

Another illuminating example in which Androtion is quoted together with Philochorus is the following: *Schol.* Soph. *Oed. Col.* 698 (= Androt. F 45): ὅτι ἀπέσχοντο τῶν μορίων[4] οἱ Λακεδαιμόνιοι καὶ ἄλλοι ἱστοροῦσι καὶ Φιλόχορος ὥστε ταῖς ἀληθείαις ἐγχέων αὐτὰς φόβημα τοῖς πολεμίοις γενέσθαι.

Λακεδαιμόνιοι γὰρ ἐμβαλόντες ἐν τῇ ᾽Αττικῇ δέκα μυριάσι Πελοποννησίων καὶ Βοιωτῶν ἡγουμένου τοῦ ᾽Αρχιδάμου τοῦ Ζευξιδάμου Λακεδαιμονίων βασι-

---

[1] For correspondences between Androtion and Philochorus cf., e.g.: Harpocr. *s.v.* ῾Αγνίας, Διαψήφισις, ῾Ιερὰ τριήρης, Ξενικὸν ἐν Κορίνθῳ; Busolt *Griech. Gesch.* II 10.

[2] Foucart, *loc. cit.* 151, and De Sanctis, I 351, were right in rejecting the hypothesis of B. Keil (Didymus, ed. Teubn., 1904, p. 56) followed by Stähelin (*Klio* V (1905) 145) and Lippold (*Jahrb. d. Arch. Inst.* XXXVIII/XXXIX (1923-4) 154) that in the two versions two different political points of view are reflected. Regarding the ὀργάς see also U. Kahrstedt *Ath. Mitteil.* LVII (1932) 9, 11 and now especially Ed. Norden, "Aus altrömischen Priesterbüchern," *Acta Reg. Soc. Hum. Litt. Lund.* XXIX (1939) 22 f., 28 f., 260.

[3] The armed intervention of the Athenians was reported by him also. For the καί at the beginning compare Philoch. F 119 in *Schol.* Aristoph. *Plut.* 972 and Did. 7. 19.

[4] Latte *RE* XVI 1. 302; cf. Aristot. *Ath. Pol.* 60. 2; W. G. Hardy *Class. Philol.* XXI (1926) 351.

λέως ἀπέσχοντο τῶν λεγομένων μορίων Ἀθηνᾶν δείσαντες ὡς Ἀνδροτίων φησίν. A very interesting passage: here also, as in the case of the ὀργάς (and in a different order, upon the occasion of the negotiations with the Persian king in 344 B.C.; cf. *supra* p. 343) Didymus quoted both Philochorus and Androtion, in spite of their agreement, which secures the entire second part of the scholion for Androtion. The word γὰρ is, in the present form of the scholion, senseless and superfluous.

How is the enormous number of 100,000 invaders [1] who feared the protectress of Athens to be explained? The object of the falsification is obvious: the author wished to give the impression that even so great an army was unable to conquer Athens — and, at the same time, to imply that the enemy had such respect for the patroness of the city that he did not dare to touch her sacred olive-trees. For the rest, Attica was completely devastated: this conclusion must be drawn from the words of Androtion. [2]

To these words of Androtion the excursus in the *Hellenica of Oxyrhynchus* 12. 5 (τότε δὲ [time of the Decelean War] τῶν Ἀθηναίων ἡ χώρα πολυτελέστατα τῆς Ἑλλάδος κατεσκεύαστο· ἐπεπόνθει γὰρ μικρὰ κακῶς ἐν ταῖς ἐμβολαῖς ταῖς ἔμπροσθεν ὑπὸ τῶν Λακεδαιμονίων. This passage has been examined from another point of view *supra* p. 326) stands in complete contrast: in Androtion we have an exaggeration of the importance of the Spartan invasions; in the *Hellenica of Oxyrhynchus* an obvious tendency to minimize them. [3]

Patriotism is a primary feature of the *Atthis* in general, and in this regard Androtion's work constitutes no exception; patriotism

[1] In regard to this figure Beloch writes, "Griechische Aufgebote II," *Klio*, VI (1906), p. 78: "Die runde Zahl Androtions kennzeichnet sich schon als solche als Übertreibung." Cf. Busolt *Griech. Gesch.* III 2. 860 n. 6; G. Glotz *Hist. grecque* II (1931) 610.

[2] In the same manner we should have to conclude from Arrian's words, *Anab.* I 9. 10 — καὶ τὴν Πινδάρου δὲ τοῦ ποιητοῦ οἰκίαν καὶ τοὺς ἀπογόνους τοῦ Πινδάρου λέγουσιν, ὅτι διεφύλαξεν Ἀλέξανδρος αἰδοῖ τῇ Πινδάρου — that Thebes was destroyed — even if this passage alone were preserved.

[3] A remarkable analogy to this case is furnished by the discrepancy between Ephorus and the Atthidògrapher Phanodemus in their figures of the Persian ships involved in the battle at the Eurymedon: Ephorus speaks of 340, Phanodemus of 600 ships (Plut. *Cim.* 12 = *F Gr Hist* 70 F 192).

is, indeed, a characteristic of any local chronicle: Ephorus, who had composed an Ἐπιχώριος (the chronicle of his native city Cyme), was unable to give up the traits of local historian in his great universal history (*F Gr Hist* 70 F 236). Thus Philochorus writes upon the occasion of the συνοικισμός of Athens (Steph. Byz. *s.v.* Ἄστυ = F 4): Ἀθηναῖοι δὲ πρῶτοι τῶν ἄλλων ἄστη καὶ πόλεις ᾤκησαν and it is well known that the Atthidographers became the champions of Athens' claims against Megara: Strabo IX 1. 6 (= *F Gr Hist* 10 F 14): οἵ τε δὴ τὴν Ἀτθίδα συγγράψαντες πολλὰ διαφωνοῦντες τοῦτό γε ὁμολογοῦσιν οἵ γε λόγου ἄξιοι, διότι τῶν Πανδιονιδῶν τεττάρων ὄντων, Αἰγέως τε καὶ Λύκου καὶ Πάλλαντος καὶ τετάρτου Νίσου, καὶ τῆς Ἀττικῆς εἰς τέτταρα μέρη διαιρεθείσης, ὁ Νῖσος τὴν Μεγαρίδα λάχοι καὶ κτίσαι τὴν Νίσαιαν.[1] In a similar manner Androtion seems to have derived the old Attic king Aegeus from Cadmus.[2]

Another fragment of Androtion has been preserved, which is missing in the *FHG*, and in consequence has never been taken into account in any treatment of the *Atthis*:

Schol. Aristoph. *Pac.* 347:

ὁ Φορμίων δὲ οὗτος Ἀθηναῖος τῷ γένει, υἱὸς Ἀσωπίου, ὃς καθαρῶς στρατηγήσας πένης ἐγένετο. ἀτιμωθεὶς δὲ τῷ μὴ δύνασθαι τὰς ρ' μνᾶς τῆς εὐθύνης ἀποδοῦναι, ἐν ἀγρῷ διέτριβεν, ἕως Ἀκαρνᾶνες στρατηγὸν αὐτὸν ᾔτουν. ὁ δὲ οὐχ ὑπήκουσε φάσκων μὴ ἐξεῖναι τοῖς ἀτίμοις. ὁ δὲ δῆμος βουλόμενος λῦσαι τὴν ἀτιμίαν ἀπεμίσθωσεν αὐτὸν τῶν ρ' μνῶν † τοῦ Διονυσίου, ὡς Ἀνδροτίων ἐν γ' Ἀττικῶν.

Paus. I 23. 10:

τὰ δὲ ἐς Ἑρμόλυκον τὸν παγκρατιαστὴν καὶ Φορμίωνα τοῦ Ἀσωπίχου (*sic*!) γραψάντων ἑτέρων παρίημι· ἐς δὲ Φορμίωνα τοσόνδε ἔχω πλέον γράψαι. Φορμίωνι γὰρ τοῖς ἐπιεικέσιν Ἀθηναίων ὄντι ὁμοίῳ καὶ ἐς προγόνων δόξαν οὐκ ἀφανεῖ συνέβαινεν ὀφείλειν χρέα. ἀναχωρήσας οὖν ἐς τὸν Παιανιέα δῆμον ἐνταῦθα εἶχε δίαιταν, ἐς ὃ ναύαρχον (!) αὐτὸν Ἀθηναίων αἱρουμένων ἐκπλεύσεσθαι οὐκ ἔφασκεν. ὀφείλειν τε γὰρ καὶ οἱ πρὶν ἂν ἐκτίσῃ, πρὸς τοὺς στρατιώτας οὐκ εἶναι παρέχεσθαι φρόνημα. οὕτως Ἀθηναῖοι – πάντως γὰρ ἐβούλοντο ἄρχειν Φορμίωνα – τὰ χρέα ὁπόσοις ὤφειλε διαλύουσιν.

---

[1] For the rivalries apparent in the Attic and Megarian chronicles see Plut. *Thes.* 10 and 20; for Nisus cf. *F Gr Hist* 4 F 75 and 78 and K. Hanell, *Megarische Studien*, Lund, 1934, pp. 18 ff.; W. Kroll *RE* XVII 1 (1936) 759 f. For the discrepancies between the Atthidographers see also Plut. *Thes.* 27.

[2] *Schol.* Pind. *Isthm.* VII 13 (III p. 262 Dr. = Androt. F 28; cf. Tzetz. *ad Lyc.* 1206 p. 348 Scheer = Androt. F 30) and *Schol.* Eurip. *Phoen.* 670 (I p. 319. 1 Schwartz = Androt. F 29): the excursus on the Σπαρτοί is explained by *Schol.*

The ethical character of the little story is obvious. It is the tale of the rehabilitation of the great general who, in spite of his brilliant successes and his integrity (ὃς καθαρῶς στρατηγήσας πένης ἐγένετο) is deprived of his civil rights and lives in retirement in the country, until the people realize their mistake. It is of little importance for the present discussion that there is no possible way of completely reconciling this episode with the picture presented by our other evidence of Phormio's last years. Whether or not Androtion was influenced here by Eupolis' Ταξίαρχοι staged immediately after the death of Phormio (427 B.C.) and containing a kind of apotheosis of the general,[1] — we feel the same spirit which we sense in the parabasis of Aristophanes' *Knights* (562 f.) and in the Δῆμοι of Eupolis.[2] In regard to Androtion and the *Atthis* in general, we learn that the first part of Aristotle's *Athenaion Politeia* reflects the influence of the Athenian chronicles in the brief stories as well as in the dry notations of purely annalistic character; compare, for example, the anecdote of the disarmament of the Athenians by Pisistratus (15. 4) or the account of the psephisma of Aristion and the foundation of the tyranny of Pisistratus (14. 1).[3]

But this new fragment of Androtion has still another function:

Pind. *Pyth.* V 101 a (II p. 184 Dr. and Tzetz. *ad Lyc.* 495 p. 179 Scheer = Androt. F 37). Androtion identifies the Σπαρτὸς Aegeus with the king of Athens, — just as we do, after all, in considering him a chthonic deity (cf. De Sanctis *Atthis* (1912) 85 f.). His polemics against the chronicles of Thebes are very remarkable. — Modern scholars have not recognized these facts with sufficient clearness: Malten *Kyrene* (1911) 171 note 2; Robert-Preller *Griech. Mythologie* II 1 (4th ed., 1920) 109. But see Wilamowitz *Aristot. und Athen* II 128 note 6; A. Ledl *loc. cit.* 162 f.

[1] According to the opinion of Wilamowitz (*Philol. Unt.* I 67) followed by P. Geissler (*Philol. Unt.* XXX (1925) 32). Other attempts at explanation: A. Böckh *Staatshaushalt.* I (3rd ed., 1886) 463 f.; Busolt *Griech. Gesch.* III 2. 982 note 6; J. H. Lipsius, *Das attische Recht und Rechtsverfahren* III (1915) 964 no. 31; Adcock *Cambridge Anc. Hist.* V (1927) 211 and against him M. F. McGregor, "The last campaign of Cleon, etc.," *Am. Journ. of Philol.*, LIX (1938), p. 155 note 48.

[2] Cf. *New Chapters* III (1933) 161; W. Schmid, "Zu Eupolis' Δῆμοι," *Philologus*, XCIII (1939), pp. 413 ff.

[3] Wilamowitz *loc. cit.* I 260, 269; De Sanctis *Atthis* 271 ff. Cf. generally Busolt *Griech. Gesch.* II 33 note 1, 34 note 2. That Androtion's *Atthis* was one of the main sources of Aristotle for his *Athenaion Politeia* is a fact which should no longer be doubted; a new discussion, though badly needed, cannot be given here.

it throws light on the relationship of Pausanias to Androtion, a question which has a certain importance in connection with the *Hellenica of Oxyrhynchus*. In this case we can control a report of Pausanias which derives from Androtion. However great the textual corruption of the words of Androtion may be as they stand in the scholion, there can be no doubt that Pausanias' account is a monstrously deformed version of Androtion's narrative and that Pausanias himself did not use Androtion's *Atthis* directly. But clearly it is only by chance that Pausanias did not at this point mention the name of Androtion, which, on the other hand, appears in the story of the end of Dorieus in Paus. VI 7. 4–7 (the quotation in *FHG*, Androtion F 49 is insufficient). When Pausanias, in describing the topography of the sacred precinct of Olympia, comes to the monuments of the famous Olympic victor Dorieus, he tells of his fate as follows:

(a) χρόνῳ δὲ ὕστερον κατῆλθεν ὁ Δωριεὺς ἐς Ῥόδον· καὶ φανερώτατα δὴ ἀπάντων ἀνὴρ εἶς φρονήσας οὗτος τὰ Λακεδαιμονίων φαίνεται, ὥστε καὶ ἐναυμάχησεν ἐναντία Ἀθηναίων ναυσὶν οἰκείαις, ἐς ὃ τριήρων ἁλοὺς Ἀττικῶν ἀνήχθη ζῶν παρὰ Ἀθηναίους. (5) οἱ δὲ Ἀθηναῖοι πρὶν μὲν ἢ Δωριέα παρὰ σφᾶς ἀναχθῆναι θυμῷ τε ἐς αὐτὸν καὶ ἀπειλαῖς ἐχρῶντο· ὡς δὲ ἐς ἐκκλησίαν συνελθόντες ἄνδρα οὕτω μέγαν καὶ δόξης ἐς τοσοῦτο ἥκοντα ἐθεάσαντο ἐν σχήματι αἰχμαλώτου, μεταπίπτει σφίσιν ἐς αὐτὸν ἡ γνώμη καὶ ἀπελθεῖν ἀφιᾶσιν οὐδὲ ἔργον οὐδὲν ἄχαρι ἐργά-ζονται, παρόν σφισι πολλά τε καὶ σὺν τῷ δικαίῳ δρᾶσαι.

(b) (6) τὰ δὲ ἐς τοῦ Δωριέως τὴν τελευτήν ἐστιν ἐν τῇ συγγραφῇ τῇ Ἀτθίδι Ἀνδροτίωνι εἰρημένα, εἶναι μὲν τηνικαῦτα ἐν Καύνῳ τὸ βασιλέως ναυτι-κὸν καὶ Κόνωνα ἐπ' αὐτῷ στρατηγόν, Ῥοδίων δὲ τὸν δῆμον πεισθέντα ὑπὸ τοῦ Κόνωνος ἀπὸ Λακεδαιμονίων μεταβαλέσθαι σφᾶς ἐς τὴν βασιλέως καὶ Ἀθηναίων συμμαχίαν, Δωριέα δὲ ἀποδημεῖν μὲν τότε ἐκ Ῥόδου περὶ τὰ ἐντὸς Πελοποννήσου χωρία, συλληφθέντα δὲ ὑπὸ ἀνδρῶν Λακεδαιμονίων αὐτὸν καὶ ἀναχθέντα ἐς Σπάρτην ἀδικεῖν τε ὑπὸ Λακεδαιμονίων καταγνωσθῆναι καὶ ἐπιβληθῆναί οἱ θάνατον ζημίαν.

(c) (7) εἰ δὲ τὸν ὄντα εἶπεν Ἀνδροτίων λόγον, ἐθέλειν μοι φαίνεται Λακε-δαιμονίους ἐς τὸ ἴσον ἔτι Ἀθηναίοις καταστῆσαι, ὅτι καὶ Ἀθηναίοις ἐς Θράσυλλον καὶ τοὺς ἐν Ἀργινούσαις ὁμοῦ τῷ Θρασύλλῳ στρατηγή-σαντας προπετείας ἐστὶν ἔγκλημα.

If Pausanias in the periegesis of Elis reports an incident which took place in Athens and immediately afterwards quotes Androtion, it seems evident that the first part (a) cannot be separated from the second (b). The stupid observations of Pausanias at the end (c) show again that he had absolutely no understanding of the circumstances, — just as elsewhere (*supra* p. 348) he made the Athenians appoint Phormio a nauarch and pay his private debts. In reality, Androtion here contrasted the Spartan severity with the generosity of the Athenians. Xenophon had avoided (*Hell.* I 5. 19) mentioning the execution of Dorieus by the Spartans, for the obvious reason that their cruelty against a national hero had made a bad impression in Greece. Characteristically, Xenophon's λακωνισμὸς was too strong for his veracity. Androtion, in completing Xenophon's account with the addition of patriotic features, tacitly attacks him by including the story of Dorieus' death. In the contrast of Sparta and Athens in the tale of Dorieus we feel a reflection of the pride of Athenian freedom and humanity in the λόγος ἐπιτάφιος. This sort of praise of the Athenians reappears in another part of Androtion's *Atthis* which Aristotle has preserved: in chapter 22 of the *Athenaion Politeia*, which is more or less an excerpt from Androtion's *Atthis*,[1] we read in §4: οἱ γὰρ Ἀθηναῖοι τοὺς τῶν τυράννων φίλους, ὅσοι μὴ συνεξαμαρτάνοιεν ἐν ταῖς ταραχαῖς, εἴων οἰκεῖν τὴν πόλιν, χ ρ ώ μ ε ν ο ι τ ῇ ε ἰ ω θ υ ί ᾳ τ ο ῦ δ ή μ ο υ π ρ ᾳ ό τ η τ ι.[2]

---

[1] Harpocr. *s.v.* Ἵππαρχος: περὶ δὲ τούτου Ἀνδροτίων ἐν τῇ δευτέρᾳ φησὶν ὅτι συγγενὴς μὲν ἦν Πεισιστράτου τοῦ τυράννου καὶ πρῶτος ἐξωστρακίσθη τοῦ περὶ τὸν ὀστρακισμὸν νόμου τότε πρῶτον τεθέντος διὰ τὴν ὑποψίαν τῶν περὶ Πεισίστρατον ὅτι δημαγωγὸς ὢν καὶ στρατηγὸς ἐτυράννησεν. Except for the phrase τοῦ περὶ τὸν ὀστρ. — τεθέντος, these words agree with those of Aristotle, *Ath. Pol.* 22. 4; cf. Busolt *loc. cit.* 33 note 1, 53; J. Carcopino, "Histoire de l'ostracisme athénien," *Bibl. de la Fac. des Lettres* (Univ. de Paris), XXV (1909), pp. 104–106; De Sanctis *loc. cit.* 370 note 4; Beloch *Griech. Gesch.* I 2. 332 f. G. Kaibel, *Stil und Text der Ath. Pol. des Ar.* (1893) 174, followed by Wilamowitz, *loc. cit.* I 123 note 3, attempted to eliminate the testimony of Androtion by reading in Harpocration Ἀνδροτίων ἐν τῇ β' ⟨καὶ Ἀριστοτέλης ἐν τῇ Ἀθηναίων πολιτείᾳ⟩ φησὶν (*sic!*). For the introduction of ostracism by Clisthenes see the recent and very important article of B. D. Meritt, "An Early Archon List," *Hesperia*, VIII (1939), pp. 59 ff., esp. 63.

[2] That the attitude reflected in this passage cannot in any way be brought into harmony with Aristotle's attitude in the *Politics* is obvious. J. E. Sandys was quite

In the remains of the *Atthis* of Androtion we can recognize still other traditional features. He continues to rationalize the myths, he comments upon festivals,[1] and introduces etymologies. It is noteworthy, too, that he gave a detailed account concerning Oedipus, in which the influence of the great tragedy as well as patriotic coloring is recognizable (*Schol.* Soph. *Oed. Col.* 100 = F 31).

His euphemistic description of the Solonian σεισάχθεια[2] which culminates in the assertion that χρεῶν ἀποκοπή was alien to the πάτριος πολιτεία (Plut. *Solon* 15. 3 f.) is particularly noteworthy if one remembers Androtion's origin: his father Andron was one of the Four Hundred in 411 B.C., and he obliged his chief Theramenes, after the installation of the Five Thousand, by moving the decree of the Council against Antiphon, the most prominent member of the Four Hundred, an action with which Lysias credits Theramenes himself (12. 67), rightly, inasmuch as Theramenes was really the author of it and Andron only his instrument.[3]

The party of Theramenes produced in those years a large political literature which exercised a strong influence even eighty years later when Aristotle wrote his *Athenaion Politeia*. The 'Constitution of Draco' (*Ath. Pol.* 4) belongs to this literature.[4] How un-

---

aware of this inconsistency (*Aristotle's Const. of Athens*, 2nd ed., 1912, p. LIV), without proposing the only possible solution, namely that Aristotle has reproduced his source more or less *verbatim*.

[1] Cf. Harpocr. *s.v.* Παναθήναια (= F 1), *Schol.* Ar. *Nub.* 985 (= F 13), Athen. IX 375 b, c (= F 41, Philoch. F 64), *Etym. Mag. s.v.* Βρισαῖος (= F 59), Athen. I 9 c (= Philoch. F 63); L. Deubner, *Attische Feste*, Berlin, 1932, p. 162.

[2] According to Th. Reinach's brilliant correction (*Hermes* LXIII (1928) 239 f.), we must now read in Plut. *Sol.* 15. 4: τὴν μνᾶν πρότερον ἑβδομήκοντ' ἄγουσαν; thus the disturbing discrepancy between Plutarch and Aristotle *Ath. Pol.* 10. 2 is eliminated. Cf. also Busolt *loc. cit.* 42 note; De Sanctis *loc. cit.* 206.

[3] On Andron see Craterus in Harpocr. *s.v.* Ἄνδρων; for the decree [Plut.] *Vita X or.* 833 E, F. That it is a precious document of the régime of the Five Thousand and a clue to the constitution of Theramenes preserved in Aristotle *Ath. Pol.* 30 was proved by W. S. Ferguson in two articles: "The Constitution of Theramenes," *Class. Philol.*, XXI (1926), pp. 72–75 and "The Condemnation of Antiphon," *Mélanges Glotz*, I, pp. 349–366. Ferguson's view was accepted by U. Wilcken, *S. Ber. Berl. Ak.* 1935, 58; F. Taeger's objection *Gnomon* XIII (1937) 354 is without point.

[4] A. Ledl *loc. cit.* 18–76.

scrupulous were the methods used in the last years of the Fifth Century even by officials is shown by Lysias' speech (30) against Nicomachus, one of the redactors of the Athenian Law Code, in which the orator finally charges his opponent with the reproach that ἀντὶ μὲν Σόλωνος αὑτὸν νομοθέτην κατέστησεν (30. 2). Under such circumstances, it was easy for any political group to fake and to publish alleged 'Constitutions' of Draco or Solon. Androtion's account therefore in all probability derives from the circle around Theramenes: its original may well have been a forgery of the same kind as Aristotle's 'Constitution of Draco.'

Pisistratus appeared in his work as δημαγωγὸs and τύραννos; the more favorable judgment of *Ath. Pol.* 16. 2 and 14. 3 is Aristotle's own; it calls to mind a similar opinion regarding Solon in *Ath. Pol.* 6. 3, which Adcock[1] has rightly declared that of Aristotle himself. The passage 22. 4, quoted above, demonstrates in any case that the position of the *Atthis* was not friendly toward the successors of Pisistratus.

The fragment concerning the ὀργὰs (*supra* p. 346) shows the style of Androtion's work. The philologists were astonished when the Didymus papyrus was published. This simple language, this abundance of hiatus, did not seem to belong to the pupil of Isocrates and τεχνίτης τοῦ λέγειν (Dem. 22. 4).[2] The explanation of De Sanctis[3] that what we have preserved is the text of an inscription is not satisfactory, because the agreement with the psephisma of Philocrates is too slight, too slight also the agreement with obvious excerpts from psephismata, such as those found in Thuc. II 24.[4]

---

[1] *Klio* XII (1912) 6.

[2] F. Blass *Arch. f. Pap.* III (1906) 291; Kaibel *loc. cit.* 174. Cf. *supra* p. 345 note 1.

[3] De Sanctis I 351; Pareti *Studi It. di Filol. class.* XIX (1912) 514. Kaibel would certainly have judged differently regarding Androtion's style, if he had written after the discovery of the Didymus papyrus.

[4] Dittenberger *Syll.*³ I no. 204; Foucart *loc. cit.* 153. For the chapter of Thucydides: Wilamowitz *S. Ber. Berl. Ak.* 1915, 621. How in reality an excerpt of a law looked in the text of Androtion is shown by *Schol.* Ar. *Av.* 1541 (= Androt. F 4); cf. Wilamowitz *Ar. und Athen* I 52; W. S. Ferguson, "The Athenian Law Code and the Old Attic Trittyes," *Classical Studies presented to E. Capps*, Princeton, 1936, p. 158 note 62.

In general, it is not the documentary style, but a very sober one, like that of *Ath. Pol.* 15. 3 for instance, which derives from the *Atthis*; it is the language of the chronicles and recurs in Philochorus, whose style is entirely different from that of the contemporary historians Duris and Demochares. It was a comprehensible *petitio principii* to presuppose that the *Atthis* of the orator and politician Androtion had represented a higher achievement than that of any other Atthidographer.[1] This, however, was erroneous: for the style of Androtion's *Atthis* as well as for that of Philochorus the very clear judgment of Dionysius of Halicarnassus is valid (*Ant. Rom.* I 8. 3): σχῆμα δὲ ἀποδίδωμι τῇ πραγματείᾳ οὔθ' ὁποῖον οἱ τοὺς πολέμους ⟨μόνους⟩ ἀναγράψαντες ἀποδεδώκασι ταῖς ἱστορίαις οὔθ' ὁποῖον οἱ τὰς πολιτείας αὐτὰς ἐφ' ἑαυτῶν διηγησάμενοι οὔτε ταῖς χρονικαῖς παραπλήσιον, ἃς ἐξέδωκαν οἱ τὰς 'Ατθίδας πραγματευσάμενοι· μονοειδεῖς γὰρ ἐκεῖναί τε καὶ ταχὺ προσιστάμεναι τοῖς ἀκούουσιν.

The novelty of the *Atthis* of Androtion was not its form, but its emphasis on political implications, the result of the author's experiences; this feature is apparent even in the few extant fragments of his work.[2]

Addendum. This article had just been finished, when a new document became known which illustrates the high value of the *Atthides* as sources: in the sixteenth report on the American Excavations in the Athenian Agora T. Leslie Shear publishes "the first ostrakon of Hyperbolos which has so far been found" (*Hesperia*, VIII (1939), p. 246, fig. 47): ΥΠΕΡΒΟΛΟΣ | ΑΝΤΙΦΑΝΟΥΣ. The discovery, important for reasons pointed out by Shear, interests us here because it solves definitely an old problem. The name of the father of Hyperbolus is given by Androtion (*Schol. Luc. Tim.* 30, p. 114 Rabe = F 48): Ὑπέρβολος οὗτος, ὡς 'Ανδροτίων φησίν, 'Αντιφάνους ἦν Περιθοίδης, but by Theopompus (*F Gr Hist* 115 F 96 a = *Schol.* Luc. *Tim.* 30, p. 115 R.; cf. *Schol. Ar. Pac.* 681): ἔστι δὲ τῇ ἀληθείᾳ Χρέμητος, ὡς Θεόπομ-

---

[1] De Sanctis I 351; Wilamowitz *loc. cit.* I 277, 288; Ed. Meyer *Gesch. d. Alt.* V 339. Böckh, *Kl. Schriften* V 399, and Beloch, *Griech. Gesch.* III 1. 399, are free from this prejudice.

[2] It is interesting to note that whereas in general there is a tendency in our sources to prefer Philochorus to Androtion, in the geographical lexicon of Stephanus of Byzantium the opposed principle prevails; in a corresponding manner Philistus is there quoted much more frequently than Timaeus. Stephanus mentions

Androtion	24 times	Philistus	43 times
Philochorus	6 times	Timaeus	4 times.

πος ἐν τῷ Περὶ δημαγωγῶν. Androtion was right and we can, even today, accept the comment which Moses du Soul (Solanus) made concerning his words more than two hundred years ago in Tiberius Hemsterhusius' *Lucian* (I, Amsterdam, 1743 [the notes were written long before], p. 142 note 2): "suspicari licet, Antiphanem iocosa Comoediae libertate transformatum abiisse in Chremetem; quod Theopompum fallere potuit: nam Androtioni maior est in rebus patriis habenda fides."[1]

III

THEOPHRASTUS' *NOMOI* AND ARISTOTLE

There can be no doubt that the last edition of the fragments of Aristotle, published in 1886 by Valentin Rose, is today, after the research of half a century, entirely antiquated.[2] Whoever compares Richard Walzer's excellent edition of selected dialogues of Aristotle[3] with the corresponding parts of Rose's collection, will recognize the great progress our knowledge has made in the meantime. But the lost works of Aristotle are of so heterogeneous a character that Ettore Bignone certainly is quite right in asserting that a new edition of Rose's collection can hardly be undertaken by one scholar alone.[4]

For the fragments of the historical works we await a new edition of fundamental importance in the fourth volume of F. Jacoby's

[1] Since, moreover, Theopompus called Hyperbolus a brother of Charon in *Schol. Ar. Pac.* 681 (which is simply an excerpt from Theopompus' *Philippica* X), the proposal of Solanus is the best explanation (cf. also Kirchner *Prosop. Att.* no. 13910; Swoboda *RE* IX 1 (1914) 254). For an analogous disagreement between Androtion and Theopompus, in which also Androtion is clearly more trustworthy, compare *F Gr Hist* 115 F 91.

[2] V. Rose, *Aristotelis qui ferebantur librorum fragmenta*, Leipzig, 1886; also the same author's *Aristoteles Pseudepigraphus*, Leipzig, 1863. The two other complete editions of Aristotle's fragments by E. Heitz (*Aristotelis opera*, IV, Paris, 1869) and V. Rose (in vol. V of the Berlin edition of Aristotle, 1870) are now worthless. The need of a new collection and of a new study of the fragments of Aristotle was emphasized recently by W. Jaeger, "Vergessene Fragmente des Peripatetikers Diokles v. Karystos," *Abhandl. d. Preuss. Akad.*, 1938, Nr. 3 p. 4.

[3] *Aristotelis dialogorum fragmenta* in usum scholarum selegit R. Walzer, Firenze, 1934.

[4] E. Bignone, *L'Aristotele perduto e la formazione filosofica di Epicuro*, I, Firenze, 1936, p. xv.

Fragmente der Griechischen Historiker; but in the case of Aristotle's principal historical work, the *Politeiai*, more is wanted than a new collection of the fragments preserved to us as quotations from the *Politeiai*. Unfortunately, V. Rose advocated the strange theory that all the fragments of Aristotle are spurious; [1] moreover, his edition was published before the discovery of the *Athenaion Politeia* with which the study of the *Politeiai* entered into a new phase. Nevertheless, the questions which this work involves had received considerable clarification before that event: in two ingenious articles H. Usener and F. Dümmler gave for the first time a comprehensive interpretation of the historical and political investigations of Aristotle and his school. [2] Wilamowitz, in his *Aristoteles und Athen*, developed these new results by pointing out more clearly that in the books Δ, E, Z of the *Politics* Aristotle used the materials collected for the *Politeiai*. [3] Both the *Politeiai* and the empirical books of the *Politics* were finally assigned to their position in Aristotle's development by W. Jaeger in his *Aristoteles*: [4] they both belong to his second stay at Athens and are, consequently, works of his last years; the books Δ–Z of the *Politics* contain therefore Aristotle's latest ideas on political matters.

After these achievements no new study of the *Politeiai* can omit consideration of those parts of the *Politics* in which the influence of the *Politeiai* is discernible. The aim of a comparative study of this kind would be above all to make available for our knowledge of the *Politeiai* the evident references to this work contained in

---

[1] V. Rose *Aristot. Pseudep.*; W. Jaeger, *Aristotle* (Eng. trans.), Oxford, 1934, p. 34.

[2] H. Usener, "Organisation der wissenschaftlichen Arbeit," *Preussische Jahrbücher*, LIII (1884), pp. 1–25 = *Vorträge und Aufsätze*, ed. 2, Leipzig, 1914, pp. 69–102; see especially pp. 92–98; F. Dümmler, "Zu den historischen Arbeiten der älteren Peripatetiker," *Rhein. Mus.*, XLII (1887), pp. 179–197 = *Kleine Schriften*, II, Leipzig, 1901, pp. 463–481.

[3] I, Berlin, 1893, pp. 355–362.

[4] W. Jaeger *Aristotle* (1934) 259–275, 327–328. In the discussion which followed the publication of Jaeger's book in 1923 these statements have not been questioned (see for instance J. L. Stocks *Class. Quart.* XXI (1927) 177 ff.; E. Barker *Class. Rev.* XLV (1931) 162 ff.; W. Siegfried *Philologus* LXXXVIII (1933) 362 ff.); on the other hand, no essential contribution to the problem here to be treated has been made.

the *Politics*; [1] on the other hand, new light would be cast also upon the structure of the *Politics*. But a complete and thorough examination of all "historical" material which occurs in the *Politics* is necessary if such a study is to be conclusive. Usener had proved that work preparatory for Theophrastus' *Nomoi* was started by Aristotle himself; [2] in subsequent discussions, however, the *Nomoi* passed more and more into oblivion, until W. S. Ferguson in his article "The Laws of Demetrius of Phalerum and their Guardians," demonstrated that the legislation of Demetrius of Phalerum was largely influenced by the *Nomoi* of his teacher Theophrastus. [3] Yet study of the relationship between the *Nomoi* and Aristotle's *Politeiai* as well as his *Politics* has not been resumed. That this is an essential problem, particularly important for the task outlined above, will be shown in the following pages.

1. *A New Fragment of Theophrastus'* Nomoi

In his *Nomoi*, [4] which consisted of twenty-four books, Theophrastus treated all the branches of legislation systematically by comparing, discussing, and criticizing the laws of all Greek

---

[1] Only C. Müller, in his entirely antiquated edition of the fragments of Aristotle's historical works *FHG* II (1848) pp. 105–180, has taken the *Politics* also into account, but without drawing any conclusion from it.

[2] *Vorträge und Aufsätze* 97; see *infra* p. 361.

[3] *Klio* XI (1911) 265–276, especially 268–271; *Hellenistic Athens*, London, 1911, pp. 40–45. In his commentary to the fragments of Demetrius of Phalerum, F. Jacoby accepts Ferguson's view (*F Gr Hist* II D p. 647). There exists no sufficient collection of the fragments of Theophrastus' *Nomoi*. Wimmer's edition of the fragments of Theophrastus (Leipzig, 1862; Paris, 1866) is useless; compare now the remarks of F. Dirlmeier, *Philologus* Suppl. XXX 1 (1937) 1–3, and of W. Jaeger, *Diokles von Karystos*, Berlin, 1938, p. 114. For a preliminary collection of the fragments of the *Nomoi* see H. Hager, "Theophrastus περὶ Νόμων," *Journ. of Philol.* VI (1876), pp. 1–27, and M. Dareste, "Le traité des Lois de Théophraste," *Revue de législation ancienne et moderne*, 1870/1, pp. 262–294.

[4] That this is the correct title of the work, not Περὶ Νόμων, is proved not only by Hermippus' catalogue of Theophrastus' works, preserved in Diog. Laert. V 44. 6: νόμων κατὰ στοιχεῖον κ̄δ̄ (Usener, *Kleine Schriften*, I, Leipzig, 1912, pp. 52–70; Friedrich Schmidt, *Die Pinakes des Kallimachos*, Berlin, 1922, pp. 86–88), but also by nearly all the exact quotations from this work, see, e.g., *infra* p. 369.

states in connection with each and every legal institution. That this work contained also a chapter on ostracism [1] would be obvious even if there were not the evidence afforded by a learned scholion to Lucian, *Timon* 30 (p. 114 Rabe), which deals with the demagogue Hyperbolus. After a reference to Androtion (*supra* p. 354) and to Andocides the scholiast continues: ἐπὶ τούτου (viz. τοῦ Ὑπερβόλου) δὲ καὶ τὸ ἔθος τοῦ ὀστρακισμοῦ κατελύθη, ὡς Θεόφραστος ἐν τῷ περὶ Νόμων λέγει. More important, however, is another fragment of the same chapter which is preserved in *Schol. Aristoph. Eq.* 855 and of which the origin has not previously been recognized. The first part of this scholiast's exposition of ostracism agrees with a quotation from Philochorus, transmitted to us in three other versions, in the *Lexicon Cantabrigiense* (p. 354 Nauck), in the fragment of the *Lexicon ad Demosthenis Aristocrateam*,[2] and,

---

[1] M. H. E. Meier in Ersch u. Gruber, *Allg. Encyclopädie der Wissenschaften und Künste*, III 7 (1836), p. 177, attributed the following passage in Plutarch to this chapter:

Plutarch *Nicias* 11.10:	cf. Plutarch *Alcib.* 13.8:
οὐκ ἀγνοῶ δ' ὅτι Θεόφραστος (F 139 Wimmer) ἐξοστρακισθῆναί φησι τὸν Ὑπέρβολον Φαίακος, οὐ Νικίου, πρὸς Ἀλκιβιάδην ἐρίσαντος.	ὡς δ' ἔνιοί φασιν, οὐ πρὸς Νικίαν ἀλλὰ πρὸς Φαίακα διαλεχθείς.

Theophrastus' notice is based on the spurious fourth oration of Andocides (Ed. Meyer, *Gesch. d. Altertums* IV (1901) 492, is certainly right in this opinion, in spite of the remarks of Th. Lenschau *RE* XIX 2 (1938) 1534 f.; cf. further J. Carcopino, "Histoire de l'ostracisme athénien," *Bibl. de la Faculté des Lettres* (Paris), XXV (1909), pp. 235–243). Before I knew Meier's proposal, which has not been repeated since, I had had the same idea, but it seems more probable that Theophrastus referred to the political bargain between Alcibiades and Nicias, or Phaeax, rather in the Πολιτικὰ τὰ πρὸς τοὺς καιρούς, because the antecedents of the ostracism of Hyperbolus are really a classical example of policy πρὸς τοὺς καιρούς; it is noteworthy, moreover, that Plutarch never quotes the *Nomoi* (in *Solon* 31 he follows Hermippus), but uses the Πολιτικὰ τὰ πρὸς τοὺς καιρούς (Dümmler *Rhein. Mus.* XLII (1887) 181–189) — in fact he uses it in the very chapter (*Nicias* 10. 1) which precedes the quotation in question. If one takes into account, finally, that Theophrastus in this work treated the alleged ostracism of Theseus (Suid. *s.v.* Ἀρχὴ Σκυρία, I p. 375 no. 4101 Ad.), the probability that also *Nicias* 11. 10 derives from the Πολιτικὰ τὰ πρὸς τοὺς καιρούς, becomes a certainty.

[2] Didymus ed. Diels and Schubart, Leipzig, 1904, p. 47. 27; see also F. Blass *Hermes* XVII (1882) 159 f. and Plutarch *Aristides* 7. 5 and 6.

although abridged, in Pollux VIII 19 f.; it represents, therefore, a fourth version. This first part of the scholion ends with the words: εἰ δὲ μὴ γένοιτο ἐξακισχίλια, οὐ μεθίστατο.[1] Then the scholiast continues as follows: οὐ μόνον δὲ 'Αθηναῖοι ὠστρακοφόρουν, ἀλλὰ καὶ 'Αργεῖοι καὶ Μιλήσιοι καὶ Μεγαρεῖς. [σχεδὸν δὲ οἱ χαριέστατοι πάντες ὠστρακίσθησαν,'Αριστείδης, Κίμων, Θεμιστοκλῆς, Θουκυδίδης,'Αλκιβιάδης.] μέχρι δὲ 'Υπερβόλου ὀστρακισμὸς προελθὼν ἐπ' αὐτοῦ κατελύθη, μὴ ὑπακούσαντος τῷ νόμῳ διὰ τὴν ἀσθένειαν τὴν γεγενημένην τοῖς τῶν 'Αθηναίων πράγμασιν ὕστερον. The sentence enclosed in brackets is an insertion of the scholiast: the order of the ὀστρακισθέντες is wrong as well as the mention of Alcibiades in the place of Hyperbolus, who appears, on the other hand, in the next sentence, the best proof for the spurious character of the cancelled passage. Now, the phrase concerning Hyperbolus agrees literally with the quotation from Theophrastus' *Nomoi* mentioned above (ἐπ' αὐτοῦ κατελύθη = ἐπὶ τούτου κατελύθη).[2] The statement about the ostracism in Argos, Miletus and Megara is not found elsewhere; only for Argos we have a confirmation, and a very significant one, in Aristotle's *Politics* E 3, 1302 b 18: διὸ ἐνιαχοῦ εἰώθασιν ὀστρακίζειν οἷον ἐν "Αργει καὶ 'Αθήνησιν.[3] The arrangement in the passage of the scholion is exactly that of the known fragments of the *Nomoi*; in the longest fragment of this work which has come down to us, in the chapter περὶ συμβολαίων, laws of Pittacus, Athens, Cyzicus,

---

[1] In the passage quoted from the *Lexicon Cantabrigiense* there are added the words μόνος δὲ 'Υπέρβολος ἐκ τῶν ἀδόξων [διὰ] ἐξοστρακισθῆναι διὰ μοχθηρίαν τρόπων, οὐ δι' ὑποψίαν τυραννίδος· μετὰ τοῦτον δὲ κατελύθη τὸ ἔθος ἀρξάμενον νομοθετήσαντος Κλεισθένους etc. The passage, obviously has nothing to do with the previous quotation from Philochorus (ὀστρακισμοῦ τρόπος); its first part depends upon Thuc. VIII 73. 3; the last sentence reflects the quotation from Theophrastus given above. Theophrastus is quoted together with Philochorus also in *Lex. Cantabr. s.v.* Εἰσαγγελία = *F Gr Hist* 228 F 12 a.

[2] For this use of καταλύεσθαι in Theophrastus' *Nomoi* compare Harpocr. *s.v.* 'Αρδηττός: - - - - Θεόφραστος δ' ἐν τοῖς περὶ Νόμων δηλοῖ ὡς κατελέλυτο τὸ ἔθος τοῦτο.

[3] The statement of Busolt (in Busolt-Swoboda, *Griechische Staatskunde*, II, München, 1926, p. 885 note) that Aristotle in the passage quoted in the text refers to Megara and Miletus, too, is wrong. Although nobody has raised the question of the origin of the notice, its substantial reliability has never been doubted: see Busolt-Swoboda *loc. cit.*; W. L. Newman *The Politics of Aristotle* III (1902) p. 244; E. M. Walker *Cambr. Anc. History* IV (1926) 151.

Thurii, Aenus, Charondas and Plato are quoted.[1] An example
from the twentieth book where Theophrastus treated ἀποβατικοὶ
τροχοί may be reproduced here (Harpocration *s.v.*): χρῶνται δὲ,
φησί, τούτῳ μόνοι τῶν Ἑλλήνων Ἀθηναῖοι καὶ Βοιωτοί. Accordingly,
Theophrastus, under the heading περὶ τοῦ ὀστρακισμοῦ gave a survey of the diffusion of this ἔθος in the various Greek states, and
the second part of the scholion to Aristophanes, *Eq.* 855, represents a last extract from this chapter.

The close relationship between the new fragment of Theophrastus
and book E of Aristotle's *Politics* admits but one explanation:
Aristotle goes back in his remarks to the same material which
was discussed afterwards by Theophrastus in the *Nomoi*. He
picked out only the two most important examples, sufficient for
his purpose; Theophrastus gave a complete list.

The new fragment, moreover, is noteworthy for its political
color. The term ἀσθένεια with which Theophrastus characterizes
the Athenian democracy of the late fifth century B.C. appears
also in a passage of Aristotle's *Rhetoric* which, as shall be shown
below, is closely related to the latest parts of the *Politics*, and
particularly to book E: *Rhet.* I 4, 1360 a 25 f.: .... οἷον δημοκρατία
οὐ μόνον ἀνειμένη ἀσθενεστέρα γίνεται, ἀλλὰ καὶ ἐπιτεινομένη σφόδρα.
What δημοκρατία ἀνειμένη means, is disclosed by the following
passage from the *Athenaion Politeia* (26. 1): after the overthrow
of the Areopagus in 462/1 B.C. συνέβαινεν ἀνίεσθαι μᾶλλον τὴν
πολιτείαν διὰ τοὺς προθύμως δημαγωγοῦντας. Ostracism is regarded
by Theophrastus as an instrument suitable for strengthening
democracy (Aristotle would call it a νόμος συμφέρων τῇ δημοκρατίᾳ),
its decline as a sign of the decay of the Athenian democracy.
Similarly W. S. Ferguson in his *Greek Imperialism* associated effectiveness and failure of that institution with the prosperity and decline of Athenian democracy:[2] "By this strange device (viz.
ostracism) the Athenians saved themselves for over two generations from the procrastination and uncertainty of distracted

---

[1] For this fragment see Stobaeus IV (1909) p. 127 H.; Th. Thalheim, *Griechische
Rechtsaltertümer*, ed. 4, Freiburg, 1895, pp. 146–152; Ferguson *Klio* XI (1911)
270; Th. Gomperz, *Griech. Denker*, III, ed. 3 and 4, Berlin, 1931, p. 413.

[2] *Greek Imperialism*, Boston and New York, 1913, pp. 60 f.

counsels. It was ostracism which made possible the uncrowned kingship of Themistocles, Cimon, and Pericles; and when, after the death of Pericles in 429 B.C., this institution failed them utterly, the Athenians were pulled this way and that by rival leaders; till finally, misled by Alcibiades and Cleophon, they were convicted by disaster of being *un*sound judges of *foreign* policy."

Thus the new fragment of Theophrastus' *Nomoi* shows that critical political attitude which was emphasized by Ferguson as a characteristic feature of this work [1] and which found its practical expression in the legislation of Demetrius of Phalerum.

2. An Alleged Reference to Theophrastus' Nomoi in Aristotle's Politics (*E 9, 1309 b 14*)

In order to determine more precisely the relationship which existed between Theophrastus' *Nomoi* and Aristotle's political works we have to start from a famous passage in Philodemus' *Rhetoric* where the Epicurean philosopher criticizes the investigations of Aristotle and his pupils (*Rhet.* col. 53. 7 ff., vol. II p. 57 Sudhaus):[2] Πῶς δ' οὐχὶ θαυμασμὸν ἐνέφυσε μέγαν τῆς δυνάμεως, ἐξ οὗ τε ἀπεπήδα τῆς οἰκείας πραγματείας καὶ διὰ ταῦτ' ἐφωρᾶτο τούς τε νόμους συνάγων ἅμα τῷ μαθητεῖ καὶ τὰς τοσαύτας πολιτείας καὶ τὰ περὶ τῶν τόπων δικαιώματα καὶ τὰ πρὸς τοὺς καιρούς. Hence Aristotle not only composed the *Politeiai* together with his pupils, especially with Theophrastus, but he also suggested and actually began work on the *Nomoi* and on the Πολιτικὰ τὰ πρὸς τοὺς καιρούς, both finished and published after the master's death by Theophrastus.[3]

---

[1] *Hellenistic Athens* 35 f., 104–107.

[2] Attention was called to this important passage by Usener, *Vorträge und Aufsätze* 97 f.; see also H. Nissen, "Die Staatsschriften des Aristoteles," *Rhein. Mus.*, XLVII (1892), pp. 184–186; Th. Gomperz *Griech. Denker* III (ed. 3 and 4) 28; O. Immisch, "Der Epilog der Nikomachischen Ethik," *Rhein. Mus.*, LXXXIV (1935), p. 59; E. Bignone, *L'Aristotele perduto*, I, 1936, pp. 126–133. Immisch and Bignone do not mention the *Nomoi*.

[3] For the polemics of Timaeus against Aristotle and Theophrastus concerning the Λοκρῶν πολιτεία and Zaleucus compare the fundamental observations of Dümmler, *Rhein. Mus.* XLII (1887) 182, 190. Nissen, *Rhein. Mus.* XLVII (1892) 186, is wrong in considering as certain that Timaeus quoted both as common authors of the Λοκρῶν πολιτεία (Polyb. XII 11. 5, 23. 8). It is quite possible that Timaeus had

This testimony is supported by Aristotle's own words at the end of the *Nicomachean Ethics* (X 10, 1181 b 13) where he announces and introduces his new course of lectures on *Politics* which is based upon the material collected for the constitutions.[1] In the polemic against Isocrates' *Antidosis* 79–83 which precedes this passage he attacks Isocrates' conception of the νομοθέτης. According to Isocrates, the task of the legislator, in contradistinction to that of the rhetor, is very easy, *Antid.* 80: ... νόμους μὲν θεῖναι μύριοι καὶ τῶν ἄλλων Ἑλλήνων καὶ τῶν βαρβάρων ἱκανοὶ γεγόνασιν, εἰπεῖν δὲ περὶ τῶν συμφερόντων ἀξίως τῆς πόλεως καὶ τῆς Ἑλλάδος οὐκ ἂν πολλοὶ δυνηθεῖεν ... and 83: ... τοῖς μὲν τοὺς νόμους τιθέναι προαιρουμένοις προὔργου γέγονε τὸ πλῆθος τῶν κειμένων, οὐδὲν γὰρ αὐτοὺς δεῖ ζητεῖν ἑτέρους, ἀλλὰ τοὺς παρὰ τοῖς ἄλλοις εὐδοκιμοῦντας πειρα‐θῆναι συναγαγεῖν, ὃ ῥᾳδίως ὅστις ἂν οὖν βουληθεὶς ποιήσειε ... Aristotle, in his reply, uses even the same words, *Eth. Nicom.* X 10, 1181 a 12–17: τῶν δὲ σοφιστῶν οἱ ἐπαγγελλόμενοι λίαν φαίνονται πόρρω εἶναι τοῦ διδάξαι. ὅλως γὰρ οὐδὲ ποῖόν τί ἐστιν ἢ περὶ ποῖα ἴσασιν. οὐ γὰρ ἂν τὴν αὐτὴν τῇ ῥητορικῇ οὐδὲ χείρω ἐτίθεσαν, οὐδ' ἂν ᾤοντο ῥᾴδιον εἶναι τὸ νομοθετῆσαι συναγαγόντι τοὺς εὐδοκιμοῦντας τῶν νόμων. But as it is impossible to become a good doctor ἐκ τῶν συγγραμμάτων, without ἐμπειρία, (1181 b 6 ff.) ἴσως οὖν καὶ τῶν νόμων καὶ τῶν πολιτειῶν αἱ συναγωγαὶ τοῖς μὲν δυναμέ‐νοις θεωρῆσαι καὶ κρῖναι τί καλῶς ἢ τοὐναντίον καὶ ποῖα ποίοις ἁρμόττει εὔχρηστ' ἂν εἴη.

From the words of Isocrates the inference is that, when they were written (352 B.C.), apparently such a συναγωγὴ τῶν νόμων τῶν παρὰ τοῖς ἄλλοις εὐδοκιμούντων did not yet exist. On the other hand, the angry remarks of Aristotle, together with the very definite reference to the *Politeiai* in the following final paragraph, can be

in mind Theophrastus' *Nomoi* (W. A. Oldfather *RE* XIII 2 (1927) 1314; cf. also R. Laqueur *RE* VI A 1 (1936) 1195). Cicero's well known words *De fin.* V 4. 11 on the political writings of Aristotle and Theophrastus do not contribute to the solution of the question here discussed.

[1] Wilamowitz *Aristoteles und Athen* I 360 f.; H. Nissen *loc. cit.* 194; B. Keil, *Die solonische Verfassung*, Berlin, 1892, pp. 142–146; J. Burnet, *The Ethics of Aristotle*, London, 1900, pp. 473–475; W. Jaeger *Aristotle* (1934) 264–266; O. Immisch *Rhein. Mus.* LXXXIV (1935) 59.

understood only under the assumption that at that time both collections at least were already being commenced by Aristotle and his pupils.

There is, however, another passage of Aristotle which since Usener's article has been claimed as a kind of reference to the *Nomoi*, *Pol.* E 9, 1309 b 14: ἁπλῶς δέ, ὅσα ἐν τοῖς νόμοις ὡς συμφέροντα λέγομεν ταῖς πολιτείαις, ἅπαντα ταῦτα σῴζει τὰς πολιτείας.[1] In reality, thirty years before Usener's study was published R. Congreve in his edition of the *Politics* had proposed an interpretation of this passage which is similar to that suggested by Usener:[2] "But it seems to me rather a reference to another work of Aristotle's answering in title, though not in spirit, to the νόμοι of Plato." Since that time scholars have declared for or against an interpretation of this kind without attempting to arrive at an ultimate conclusion. Newman's comment on the passage may serve as an example of the unsatisfactory character of the conventional exegesis.[3] Nevertheless, a clear solution of the problem is possible; it can be shown that the interpretations of Congreve and Usener are untenable, although certain reasons, apparently, recommend their proposals. Examples of quotations similar to the passage in question occur; the most important analogy is found in *Eth. Nicom.* VI 3, 1139 b 26: ἐκ προγινωσκομένων δὲ πᾶσα διδασκαλία, ὥσπερ καὶ ἐν τοῖς ἀναλυτικοῖς λέγομεν and *ib.* 31: ἡ μὲν ἄρα ἐπιστήμη ἐστὶν ἕξις ἀποδεικτική, καὶ ὅσα ἄλλα προσδιοριζόμεθα ἐν τοῖς ἀναλυτικοῖς. Since further Aristotle in the second book of the *Politics* criticizes a work which has the same title as that which we are dealing with, namely Plato's *Nomoi*, it is very interesting to know in what manner he introduces this work: B 9, 1271 a 41: καὶ ὡδὶ δὲ τῇ ὑποθέσει τοῦ νομοθέτου ἐπιτιμήσειεν ἄν τις, ὅπερ καὶ Πλάτων ἐν τοῖς νόμοις ἐπιτε-

---

[1] Usener *Vorträge und Aufsätze* 97; Nissen *loc. cit.* 184 (he is speaking of a "Selbstzitat"); G. Gilbert, *The Constitutional Antiquities of Sparta and Athens*, London, 1895, p. XXXVI ("the quotation by Aristotle himself"); cf. also Busolt *Griech. Gesch.* II (1895) 44.

[2] R. Congreve, *The Politics of Aristotle*, London, 1855 (ed. 2: 1874), p. 374.

[3] *The Politics of Aristotle* I (1887) p. 537; IV (1902) p. 405. Newman follows Susemihl (*Aristoteles' Politik, Griechisch und Deutsch*, 1879, I p. 747; II p. 349 note 1633) in his interpretation. His reference to Diod. V 82. 4 and [Plut.] *De fato* 4 does not prove anything.

τίμηκεν; cf. 6, 1265 a 1: τῶν δὲ νόμων τὸ μὲν πλεῖστον μέρος νόμοι τυγχάνουσιν ὄντες; 6, 1265 b 16: ἐν δὲ τοῖς νόμοις τούτοις τοὐναντίον ἐστίν; 6, 1266 a 28: τὰ μὲν οὖν περὶ τὴν πολιτείαν τὴν ἐν τοῖς νόμοις τοῦτον ἔχει τὸν τρόπον.

The decisive evidence against any inference which could be drawn from such analogies is afforded by the context in which the supposed reference to Theophrastus' *Nomoi* appears. With the words ἀπλῶς δὲ etc. Aristotle concludes the summary of the preceding chapter which begins at 8, 1307 b 26 with a sentence in the form of a program: περὶ δὲ σωτηρίας καὶ κοινῇ καὶ χωρὶς ἑκάστης πολιτείας ἐχόμενόν ἐστιν εἰπεῖν. What follows is nothing else than a series of recommendations of legislative measures, of νόμοι, which are considered suitable for preserving or restoring the safety of the constitutions. Some examples may illustrate this: 8, 1308 a 13–16: διὸ ἐὰν πλείους ὦσιν ἐν τῷ πολιτεύματι, πολλὰ συμφέρει τῶν δημοτικῶν νομοθετημάτων, οἷον τὸ ἐξαμήνους τὰς ἀρχὰς εἶναι, ἵνα πάντες οἱ ὅμοιοι μετέχωσιν. 1308 a 31: ἔτι τὰς τῶν γνωρίμων φιλονικίας καὶ στάσεις καὶ διὰ τῶν νόμων πειρᾶσθαι δεῖ φυλάττειν. He proposes in 8, 1308 a 35 detailed measures to be taken for the regulation of the census in cases of changes caused by the increase of money. The conceptions συμφέρειν and νόμος are of primary importance in this passage. Aristotle can, therefore, say at the end of this demonstration, in a kind of recapitulation: "In short: whatever provisions in the laws we describe as advantageous to the constitutions (συμφέροντα ταῖς πολιτείαις!), are all preservative of the constitutions";[1] the clause ὅσα ἐν τοῖς νόμοις ὡς συμφέροντα λέγομεν ταῖς πολιτείαις refers evidently to the legal enactments suggested in that chapter. ὅσα ἐν τοῖς νόμοις could be translated also simply "all legal provisions" according to the following analogy: *Ath. Pol.* 26. 2: . . . οἱ ⟨δὲ⟩ ζευγῖται τὰς ἐγκυκλίους ἦρχον, εἰ μή τι παρεωρᾶτο τῶν ἐν τοῖς νόμοις.

That the interpretation given here is right is suggested by another consideration. The precepts concerning the σωτηρία of the constitutions (1307 b 26 – 1310 a 38) form, especially from the

---

[1] The translations of B. Jowett in *The Works of Aristotle translated into English*, X, and of W. Rackham, Aristotle, *Politics*, 1932, p. 433 (Loeb Classical Library) have been used.

point of view of practical politics, an essential part of book E;
Aristotle twice in other works has alluded to it, both times in the
form of a program: at the end of the *Nicomachean Ethics* quoted
above (10, 1181 b 17: εἶτα ἐκ τῶν συνηγμένων πολιτειῶν θεωρῆσαι
τὰ ποῖα σῴζει καὶ φθείρει τὰς πόλεις καὶ τὰ ποῖα ἑκάστας τῶν πολιτειῶν)
and in the fourth chapter of the first book of the *Rhetoric* where
he requires from the deliberative orator an understanding of
legislation (4, 1360 a 20). He gives only the outlines and refers
at the end, with an unmistakable hit at Isocrates, expressly to the
Politics (1360 a 37) ἅπαντα ταῦτα πολιτικῆς ἀλλ᾿ οὐ ῥητορικῆς ἔργον
ἐστίν; this passage is closely connected with the section, discussed
above, of *Politics* E, as a comparison will show:

Rhet. I 4, 1360 a 19:	*Pol.* E 9, 1309 b 14:
ἐν γὰρ τοῖς νόμοις ἐστὶν ἡ σωτηρία τῆς πόλεως,	ἁπλῶς δὲ ὅσα ἐν τοῖς νόμοις ὡς συμφέροντα λέγομεν ταῖς πολιτείαις, ἅπαντα ταῦτα σῴζει τὰς πολιτείας.
ὥστ᾿ ἀναγκαῖον εἰδέναι πόσα τ᾿ ἐστὶ πολιτειῶν εἴδη, καὶ ποῖα συμφέρει ἑκάστῃ, καὶ ὑπὸ τίνων φθείρεσθαι πέφυκε καὶ οἰκείων τῆς πολιτείας καὶ ἐναντίων.	1309 b 35: διὸ δεῖ τοῦτο μὴ ἀγνοεῖν τὸν νομοθέτην καὶ τὸν πολιτικόν, ποῖα σῴζει τῶν δημοτικῶν καὶ ποῖα φθείρει τὴν δημοκρατίαν, καὶ ποῖα τῶν ὀλιγαρχικῶν τὴν ὀλιγαρχίαν.
λέγω δὲ τὸ ὑπὸ οἰκείων φθείρεσθαι, ὅτι ἔξω τῆς βελτίστης πολιτείας αἱ ἄλλαι πᾶσαι καὶ ἀνιέμεναι καὶ ἐπιτεινόμεναι φθείρονται, οἷον δημοκρατία οὐ μόνον ἀνιεμένη ἀσθενεστέρα γίνεται ὥστε τέλος ἥξει εἰς ὀλιγαρχίαν, ἀλλὰ καὶ ἐπιτεινομένη σφόδρα ὥσπερ . . .	1309 b 20: πολλὰ γὰρ τῶν δοκούντων δημοτικῶν λύει τὰς δημοκρατίας καὶ τῶν ὀλιγαρχικῶν τὰς ὀλιγαρχίας. (cf. E 1, 1301 b 13–17)

There follows in *Rhet.* I 4, 1360 a 27, as well as in *Pol.* E 9, 1309
b 23 the same illustration, derived from the flat and aquiline nose,
which does not occur elsewhere in Aristotle's work and which,
accordingly, is noticed in the commentaries, but without any
reference to the much more extensive agreement which exists
between the two passages on the whole.[1] The νομοθέτης of the

[1] The relationship between certain parts of the *Rhetoric* and the *Politics* was
emphasized first by Chr. A. Brandis, "Über Aristoteles' Rhetorik und die griechischen
Ausleger derselben," *Philologus*, IV (1849), p. 33. Compare further L. Spengel,

Rhetoric is the νομοθέτης of *Politics* E and of the end of the *Nico-machean Ethics*; his aim consists in maintaining and improving by legislation the existing constitutions. Thus Aristotle's remarks on legislation in the *Rhetoric* are to be considered as belonging to the latest phase of this work.[1] It is therefore very significant that Aristotle, at the end of this passage, recommends not only the study of the constitutions of the past and of those in existence in other nations, but he expressly declares that for legislation (1360 a 34) αἱ τῆς γῆς περίοδοι χρήσιμοι (ἐντεῦθεν γὰρ λαβεῖν ἔστι τοὺς τῶν ἐθνῶν νόμους).[2] These words imply the program which Dicaearchus of Messene, the most ingenious of Aristotle's pupils, has realized in two epoch-making works: in the Περίοδος γῆς and in the Βίος Ἑλλάδος.

For the problem in question the conclusion to be drawn from the precedent discussion is that the parallelism between the two passages of the *Rhetoric* and the *Politics* excludes any possibility of a "quotation" of the *Nomoi* in the latter: In the *Rhetoric* the so-called quotation is given in a further abridgment.

No reference to the *Nomoi*, published afterwards by Theophrastus, occurs in the *Politics* and it is neither evident nor probable that this work was so advanced in Aristotle's last years as to be quoted by him. But Aristotle suggested it and prepared with Theophrastus the material (the συναγωγὴ τῶν νόμων; *supra* p. 362) upon which the pupil built up his work; its spiritual background — and in this Usener was quite right — remains book E of the *Politics*.[3]

Aristotelis Ars Rhetorica, II, Leipzig, 1867, p. 86; J. E. Sandys, *The Rhetoric of Aristotle*, I, Cambridge, 1877, pp. 68–71; Immisch *Rhein. Mus.* LXXXIV (1935) 60.

[1] Only the genesis and the earlier phases in the development of Aristotle's *Rhetoric* have been treated and clarified in F. Solmsen's excellent book *Die Entwicklung der aristotelischen Logik und Rhetorik*, Berlin, 1929, pp. 196–229.

[2] Aristotle's relationship to the περίοδοι γῆς which he himself consulted (*Pol.* B 3, 1262 a 19; *Meteor.* I 13, 350 a 16; II 5, 362 b 12) will be examined in another context.

[3] The same is true for the Πολιτικὰ τὰ πρὸς τοὺς καιρούς, a work which, according to Philodemus (*supra* p. 361), was also started by Aristotle. Compare the characterization of its content by Cicero, *De fin.* V 4. 11: *quae essent in re publica rerum inclinationes et momenta temporum, quibus esset moderandum, utcumque res postularet.*

3. *Theophrastus' Nomoi and the Second Part of
Aristotle's* Athenaion Politeia

We may now attempt to approach the problem from another
side. It is not surprising that the majority of the fragments of
Theophrastus' *Nomoi* deal with Athenian laws; they derive, like
most of the ancient references to the *Athenaion Politeia* and to the
Atthides, from lexica and commentaries the purpose of which was
to illustrate the classical authors of Athens. Since Aristotle in the
second part of the *Athenaion Politeia* presents an analysis of the
constitution of Athens, the relationship between it and the fragments of the *Nomoi* deserves a careful examination which, wherever
possible, has to be extended to the *Politics*.

Wilamowitz, in his fundamental treatment of the second part
of the *Athenaion Politeia*,[1] came to the conclusion that Aristotle's
account is so incomplete that it can be explained only as a kind of
epitome of another source which is identified by Wilamowitz with
an *Atthis*.[2] This hypothesis was generally rejected and a direct

---

For Theophrastus' ability to develop his master's ideas see Cicero's interesting remark in the first book of *De finibus* (I 2. 6): *Theophrastus mediocriterne delectat,
cum tractat locos ab Aristotele ante tractatos?* For the relationship between *Politics*
E and the Πολιτικὰ τὰ πρὸς τοὺς καιροὺς see Usener *Vorträge und Aufsätze* 98;
Dümmler *Rhein. Mus.* XLII (1887) 180; R. Walzer, *Magna Moralia und Aristote-
lische Ethik*, Berlin, 1929, p. 8.

[1] *Aristoteles und Athen* I 186–259. Already in 1895 V. v. Schoeffer in discussing
the book of Wilamowitz (*Bursians Jahresberichte* LXXXIII (1895) 199) emphasized
the fact that the second part of the *Athenaion Politeia* had been neglected, and he
therefore praised Wilamowitz for his treatment. This neglect has continued to
characterize the history of research on the *Athenaion Politeia* — with very few
exceptions.

[2] *Aristoteles und Athen* I 214–216, 242, 245, 256 f. In dealing with Aristotle's
treatment of the functions of the Archon and the Basileus (56–57) he writes (p. 256):
"das ist die Willkür des Epitomators; aber Aristoteles ist es, der sie sich erlaubt"
and concludes, "dass die ganze Darstellung der Verfassung nichts ist als eine stark
und ungleich kürzende, einzeln natürlich besondere Lichter aufsetzende, nament-
lich latent polemisierende, und . . . durchgehends auf den Zustand des derzeit
geltenden Rechts hin revidierte Wiedergabe fremder Arbeit." I owe to S. Dow
the knowledge of Nathan Marsh Pusey's unpublished thesis NOMOI ΤΩΝ
ΑΘΗΝΑΙΩΝ (cf. *Summaries of Harvard Ph.D. Theses*, 1937, Cambridge, Mass.,

knowledge of Athenian laws and institutions was supposed to be Aristotle's source.[1] Nevertheless, the fact of a strange incompleteness persists and requires explanation. The explanation is to be had from the fragments of Theophrastus' *Nomoi*.

Concerning the ἀγορανόμοι:[2]

Aristotle, *Ath. Pol.* 51. 1, writes:

κληροῦνται δὲ καὶ ἀγορανόμοι ⟨ι'⟩, πέντε μὲν εἰς Πειραιέα, ε' δ' εἰς ἄστυ. τούτοις δὲ ὑπὸ τῶν νόμων προστέτακται τῶν ὠνίων ἐπιμελεῖσθαι πάντων, ὅπως καθαρὰ καὶ ἀκίβδηλα πωλήσεται.

(The first sentence is quoted by Harpocration *s.v.* ἀγορανόμοι).

Theophrastus in Harpocration *s.v.*

κατὰ τὴν ἀγορὰν ἀψευδεῖν: . . . . Θεόφραστος γοῦν ἐν τοῖς περὶ νόμων φησὶ δυοῖν τούτων ἐπιμελεῖσθαι δεῖν τοὺς ἀγορανόμους, τῆς τε ἐν τῇ ἀγορᾷ εὐκοσμίας καὶ τοῦ ἀψευδεῖν μὴ μόνον τοὺς πιπράσκοντας, ἀλλὰ καὶ τοὺς ὠνουμένους.

With these passages compare:

Aristotle, *Pol.* Δ 15, 1299 b 14: ἁρμόττει δὲ καὶ τοῦτο μὴ λεληθέναι, ποίων δεῖ κατὰ τόπον ἀρχεῖα πολλὰ ἐπιμελεῖσθαι καὶ ποίων πανταχοῦ μίαν ἀρχὴν εἶναι κυρίαν, οἷον εὐκοσμίας πότερον ἐν ἀγορᾷ μὲν ἀγορανόμον, ἄλλον δὲ κατ' ἄλλον τόπον, ἢ πανταχοῦ τὸν αὐτὸν and

Pol. Z 8, 1321 b 12: πρῶτον μὲν οὖν ἐπιμέλεια τῶν ἀναγκαίων ἡ περὶ τὴν ἀγοράν, ἐφ' ᾗ δεῖ τινα ἀρχὴν εἶναι τὴν ἐφορῶσαν περί τε τὰ συμβόλαια καὶ τὴν εὐκοσμίαν.

1938, pp. 167–169). It is highly desirable that this important work should be finished and published. The very useful collection of laws which represents the main body of the thesis is preceded by a series of chapters among which the third requires our special interest. Pusey writes in *Summaries*, p. 169: "A description of the Athenian Code as it existed during the greater part of the fourth century is given in Chapter Three. It is only when this is done that the real thesis, that Chapters 42 through 69 of Aristotle's Ἀθηναίων πολιτεία constitute a virtual abstract of this code, is reached." He resumes the thesis of Wilamowitz, which, as he points out, had never been demonstrated. Until the thesis is published, it is impossible to discuss the particulars of Pusey's argument; but see *infra* p. 371 note 3.

[1] Bernhard Bursy, *De Aristotelis* Πολιτείας Ἀθηναίων *partis alterius fonte et auctoritate*, Diss. Dorpat, 1897; G. Wentzel *Gött. gel. Anz.* CLIX (1897) 616–646; V. v. Schoeffer *loc. cit.* 199 f.; J. H. Lipsius, *Das attische Recht und Rechtsverfahren*, I, 1905, p. 48 note 148; Busolt *Griech. Staatskunde* I 97 note 1.

[2] On the ἀγορανόμοι see generally Wilamowitz *Aristoteles und Athen* I 218; Lipsius *loc. cit.* I 93–95; Sandys *Ath. Pol.*, ed. 2 (1912), 197; Busolt-Swoboda *Griech. Staatskunde* II 1118; U. Kahrstedt, *Staatsgebiet und Staatsangehörige in Athen, Studien zum öffentlichen Recht Athens* I, Stuttgart, 1934, pp. 44, 46.

It is obvious that Aristotle in both passages of the *Politics* (which both belong to the latest section of this work) is thinking of Athens where officials like those described by him existed. But this description, especially the second, agrees more with that given by Theophrastus than with his own in the *Athenaion Politeia*, in which the εὐκοσμία is lacking.

In speaking of the φόνου δίκαι (under the heading ὁ δὲ βασιλεύς), Aristotle mentions the fourth of these courts in the following way:

Ath. Pol. 57. 3:	Theophrastus in Harpocr. *s.v.*
ἐὰν δὲ φεύγων φυγὴν ὧν αἴδεσίς ἐστιν, αἰτίαν ἔχῃ ἀποκτεῖναι ἢ τρῶσαί τινα, τούτῳ δ' ἐν Φρεάτου δικάζουσιν. . . .	ἐν Φρεαττοῖ: . . . ὠνομάσθαι δ' ἔοικε τὸ δικαστήριον ἀπό τινος Φρεάτου, καθά φησι Θεόφραστος ἐν ιϚ' τῶν Νόμων.

The court is mentioned by Aristotle also in *Pol.* Δ 15, 1300 b 28: . . . οἷον 'Αθήνῃσι λέγεται καὶ τὸ ἐν Φρεαττοῖ δικαστήριον. The place was called Φρεαττύς as Pausanias I 28. 11 shows (ἔστι δὲ τοῦ Πειραιῶς πρὸς θαλάσσῃ Φρεαττύς) and as is apparent from the *locus classicus* in Demosthenes' *Aristocratea* (23. 77–78).[1] Aristotle, although he gives in the *Politics* the usual form, adopts the "Peripatetic" etymology in the *Athenaion Politeia*, but without comment, leaving the elucidation to Theophrastus: that indeed is proved by the latter's words.

Aristotle, further, did not mention the νόμος ἀργίας which was attributed by Theophrastus to Pisistratus.[2]

The functions of the θεσμοθέται are treated by Aristotle in a particularly summary manner. Wilamowitz is quite right in saying that in *Ath. Pol.* 59 the enumeration of the trials for which the thesmothetae prepare the cases is incomplete even in the headings.[3] Here Theophrastus furnishes valuable supplementary material. He dealt with the important political functions which the thes-

---

[1] On the court ἐν Φρεαττοῖ see Wilamowitz *Aristoteles und Athen* I 251 note 136; Sandys *Ath. Pol.* ed. 2, pp. 228 f.; Busolt-Swoboda, *Griech. Staatskunde* II 813; W. Judeich *Topographie von Athen*, ed. 2 (1931), 436. Important for the topography: Helladius in Photius *Bibl.* p. 535 a 28 Becker.

[2] Plutarch *Solon* 31; Wilamowitz *Aristoteles und Athen* I 255 note 146; Lipsius *Att. Recht* II 1. 353 f.; Aly *RE* III A 1 (1927) 960.

[3] *Aristoteles und Athen* I 245: "Also dies Capitel gibt nicht das ganze tatsächliche Material, es gibt eine nicht einmal in den Capiteln vollständige Aufzählung der Klagen, für die die Thesmotheten den Prozess instruieren."

mothetae exercised at the annual ἐπιχειροτονία or ἐπανόρθωσις τῶν νόμων (the law regarding this procedure is preserved in the text of Demosthenes' *Timocratea*, 24. 20–23): [1] Harpocr. *s.v.* Θεσμοθέται: .... ὅτι δὲ τοὺς νόμους οὗτοι διώρθουν κατ' ἐνιαυτὸν ἕκαστον, εἴρηκεν Αἰσχίνης τε ἐν τῷ κατὰ Κτησιφῶντος (III 38) καὶ Θεόφραστος ἐν γ' Νόμων. Aristotle did not mention these functions.[2] In his description of the duties of the thesmothetai we read 59. 2: ἔτι δὲ τὰς εἰσαγγελίας εἰσαγγέλλουσιν εἰς τὸν δῆμον, καὶ τὰς καταχειροτονίας καὶ τὰς προβολὰς ἁπάσας ·εἰσάγουσιν οὗτοι, καὶ γραφὰς παρανόμων ... 3 εἰσὶ δὲ καὶ γραφαὶ πρὸς αὐτοὺς ὧν παράστασις τίθεται, ξενίας καὶ δωροξενίας, ἄν τις δῶρα δοὺς ἀποφύγῃ τὴν ξενίαν .... 6 καὶ τὰ σύμβολα τὰ πρὸς τὰς πόλεις οὗτοι κυροῦσι .... καὶ τὰ ψευδομαρτύρια ἐξ Ἀρείου πάγου. We know that Theophrastus in the fourth book of the *Nomoi* gave a very thorough analysis of the different kinds of εἰσαγγελίαι (*Lex. Cantabr. s.v.*; Harpocr. *s.v.*) which is too long to be reproduced here; [3] in the same book he treated the καταχειροτονία: Harpocr. *s.v.*: διεξῆλθε δὲ περὶ τῆς καταχειροτονίας καὶ Θεόφραστος ἐν δ' Νόμων. That in the seventh book he dealt with γραφὴ ξενίας and δίκη ψευδομαρτυριῶν is proved by *Schol. Plat. Legg.* XI 937 D (p. 369 Greene).

Passing to other chapters, the same observations can be made: Aristotle, in 58. 2, among the functions of the polemarch merely

---

[1] On ἐπιχειροτονία and ἐπανόρθωσις τῶν νόμων cf. Busolt-Swoboda *Griech. Staatskunde* II 1013.

[2] It is the merit of Bernard Haussoullier not only to have recognized this omission but to have made an attempt at least to give the correct explanation for this fact. In the introduction to the edition of the *Athenaion Politeia* published by him and G. Mathieu, Paris, (ed. 1: 1922) ed. 2, 1930, p. XXVI, he writes: "Aristote a sciemment laissé de côté tout ce qui touchait à la rédaction et à la revision des lois, réservant ce sujet à son disciple Théophraste dont le traité des *Lois* figurait au programme des travaux réglés par le maître. . . . Nous savons par Harpocration (*s.v.* Θεσμοθέται) que Théophraste parlait de l' ἐπιχειροτονία τῶν νόμων au IIIᵉ livre de ses *Lois*. . . . Aristote n'a pas voulu faire double emploi avec un livre sorti de son école." That he is not oversure of himself, is shown by the next sentence, which he introduces with the words "Quoi qu'il en soit de ces lacunes . . ." and the evidence on which he bases his explanation is indeed too small; his theory escaped my notice until this article had been written. I should like, however, to emphasize that his hypothesis is not far from the thesis developed herein.

[3] Since the purpose of this study is not to discuss juridical questions, I do not need to refer to the well known manuals.

mentions δίκαι αἱ τοῖς ἰσοτελέσι γιγνόμεναι without further explanation; Theophrastus, under the heading ἰσοτέλεια in the eleventh book, gave a detailed account of the juridical position of the ἰσοτελεῖς: Harpocr. s.v. ᾽Ισοτελὴς καὶ ἰσοτέλεια:.... ὅτι δὲ καὶ τῶν ἄλλων ὧν ἔπραττον οἱ μέτοικοι ἄφεσιν εἶχον οἱ ἰσοτελεῖς Θεόφραστος εἴρηκεν ἐν ια' τῶν Νόμων. He spoke here also of the ἰσοτέλεια conceded to entire states as Olynthus [1] and Thebes.

While Aristotle only touches upon the πομπαί (56. 4, 57. 1, 60. 1), Theophrastus must have discussed the particulars of the participation of the metics in the πομπαί (Harpocr. s.v. σκαφηφόροι, from the tenth book; Phot. and Suid. s.v. συστομώτερον σκάφης).[2]

If one takes into account the fact that scarcely thirty fragments of the twenty-four books of Theophrastus' *Nomoi* have come down to us, the evidence given above for a very close and very significant relationship between the second part of the *Athenaion Politeia* and Theophrastus' *Nomoi* seems overwhelming. It is now clear that Wilamowitz in a certain way was right when he declared that Aristotle followed and "epitomized" a detailed source (*supra* p. 367), yet this source was not a book, much less an *Atthis*: it was rather the collection of laws which Aristotle and his pupils had brought together and without which Theophrastus never would have been able to compose his work.[3] There can be no

---

[1] Mabel Gude, *A History of Olynthus*, Baltimore, 1933, p. 37.

[2] Demetrius of Phalerum treated the same subject in the third book of Περὶ τῆς ᾽Αθήνησι νομοθεσίας (*F Gr Hist* 228 F 5); cf. L. Deubner *Attische Feste* (1932) 28.

[3] Nobody disputes that in this collection the Code of 410–401 B.C. was the most important item. It does not necessarily follow that the second part of the *Athenaion Politeia* constitutes a virtual abstract of this Code (see *supra* p. 367 note 2). The discovery of fragments of the Code in the Athenian Agora has made this important document central in the discussion (J. H. Oliver *Hesperia* IV (1935) 5–32; W. S. Ferguson, "The Athenian Law Code," *Classical Studies presented to Edward Capps*, Princeton, 1936, pp. 144–151; W. S. Ferguson *Hesperia* VII (1938) 67; a new edition is being prepared by S. Dow). The fragments from the Agora attest the complicated and lengthy genesis of the Code, which is evident also from Lysias' speech against Nicomachus (Lysias 30; 399/8 B.C.). Aristotle's task, therefore, was to fuse together the different sections of the Code, taking into consideration also the numerous laws published after the year of Euclides (403/2 B.C.; Dem. 24. 42; see Ferguson *Class. Stud. Capps* 147). Under these circumstances,

doubt that this collection of laws, derived from the archives of the various states as well as from literary sources, especially local chronicles, formed the background for the second part of the *Politeiai* in general. Aristotle had no reason at all to anticipate in this work the discussions reserved for the *Nomoi*, he often gave only a survey or, so to speak, the headings of topics which were to be treated in detail in the other work and did not strive for completeness in the headings.

Nevertheless, he offered in the *Athenaion Politeia* itself an excellent example of a really minute account in the concluding chapters (63–69) on the law courts. The literary form of this portion of the treatise is that of the excursus and it belongs to 59. 7:

<table>
<tr><td align="center">59. 7:</td><td align="center">63. 1:</td></tr>
<tr><td>τοὺς δὲ δικαστὰς κληροῦσι πάντες οἱ ἐννέα ἄρχοντες, δέκατος δ' ὁ γραμματεὺς ὁ τῶν θεσμοθετῶν, τοὺς τῆς αὐτοῦ φυλῆς ἕκαστος.</td><td>τὰ δὲ δικαστήρια κληροῦσιν οἱ θ' ἄρχοντες κατὰ φυλάς, ὁ δὲ γραμματεὺς τῶν θεσμοθε- τῶν τῆς δεκάτης φυλῆς.</td></tr>
</table>

The fact that scholars generally failed to recognize the true character of these chapters was certainly one of the chief reasons for the lack of understanding in the interpretation of the text. Two of the most authoritative scholars, Wilamowitz and Kaibel, went so far in the misunderstanding of the structure of the book as to bracket 59. 7 although the passage is quoted in *Schol.* Ar.

---

the importance of the Code of 410–401 B.C. for the *Athenaion Politeia* can easily be overestimated.

Besides the Peripatetic νόμων συναγωγή, a work has to be mentioned with a strikingly similar title: Craterus' Ψηφισμάτων συναγωγή. Long ago it has been pointed out that this work cannot be separated from the group of collections of political and juridical documents which were so characteristic of the productions of the school of Aristotle (B. Keil *Hermes* XXX (1895) 217; F. Jacoby *RE* XI 2 (1922) 1618; see also B. D. Meritt, H. T. Wade-Gery, M. F. McGregor, *The Athenian Tribute Lists*, I, Cambridge, Mass., 1939, pp. 203 f.). It is obvious that Craterus, in the time of Theophrastus, published the psephismata *because* they were unpublished, just as Aristotle and his pupils collected the laws because they were not yet collected (see the quotation from Isocrates' *Antidosis, supra* p. 362). There is no evidence for any such activity before Aristotle.

Vesp. 775.[1] And the same Wilamowitz who in his works more than any other scholar took advantage of the literary form of the excursus denied to Aristotle this right, denied that he had any feeling for uniformity of style and composition.[2] And even when a pupil of Wilamowitz, Th. Teusch, called the last chapters of the *Athenaion Politeia* an "appendix," [3] neither he nor other scholars abandoned their bias. It still occurs in Hommel's study *Heliaia*,[4] which shows very well the other defects of the previous attempts to understand Aristotle's exposition. This account, very recently, has been clarified by S. Dow in an article which may be considered as one of the most important and essential contributions to the interpretation of the *Athenaion Politeia* in general.[5] His identification of the kleroteria with the Greek allotment machines and the analysis of the text of Aristotle he gave successively entitled him to attribute to these chapters "a tone of special clarity and fulness"; [6] up to the present time the opinion had been universally held that Aristotle's description of the courts is, as a consequence of his diffuseness, obscure and ambiguous. The effect of Dow's study as a whole is, indeed, completely to vindicate Aristotle. We need no longer imagine, with Wilamowitz,[7] that Aristotle sent

---

[1] In their first two editions (Berlin, 1891); cf. G. Kaibel, *Stil und Text der ʼΑθ. πολ.*, Berlin, 1893, pp. 247 f. In *Aristoteles und Athen* I 243 f. Wilamowitz withdrew the rejection of the passage, but without a satisfactory explanation of the problem. The same is true also of B. Keil *Die solonische Verfassung* 52.

[2] *Aristoteles und Athen* I (204–) 205: "Aristoteles der Schriftsteller hat somit auch hier wie in allen erhaltenen Schriften bewiesen, dass er auf Gleichförmigkeit des Stiles und der Composition kein Gewicht legte, vielleicht wenig Gefühl dafür hatte." On ancient excursus technique see A. S. Pease, "Book and Style," *Italica*, XV (1938), pp. 129–131.

[3] *De sortitione iudicum apud Athenienses*, Göttingen, 1894, p. 10.

[4] *Philologus* Suppl. XIX (1927) 29, 31 note 67.

[5] "Aristotle, the Kleroteria, and the Courts," *Harvard Stud. in Class. Philol.*, L (1939), pp. 1–34.

[6] *Loc. cit.* 2, 18.

[7] *Aristoteles und Athen* I 205. In the two pages into which Wilamowitz compresses his treatment of the excursus there is hardly one sentence which can be accepted. Remarkable is the following statement: "Die geltende Praxis ist ersichtlich nach dem Leben copiert, nicht nach dem Schema des Gesetzes" (p. 204). In reality, the excursus is a reconstruction of the procedure of the dicastic courts, based upon observations in the Heliaia as well as upon laws.

some student of the Peripatos to the Agora and into the Heliaia
in order to write down this account of the law courts. Aristotle's
own spirit is in this careful description, it is the spirit of the
famous "program for research and instruction in the Peripatetic
school" in the introduction to his work *On the Parts of Animals*.[1]
It is obvious that Aristotle, if he had had the intention to do so,
would have been able to describe the whole constitution of Athens
in the same detailed manner, exhausting the collected material
to a larger extent. He selected the procedure of the dicastic courts,
well aware of the importance which the courts had in the political
life of Athens, but probably also in order to give a model of an
elaborate exposition of this kind.[2] The style of this excursus reappears therefore in that work in which such an influence is after
all to be expected, in Theophrastus' *Nomoi*:

<table>
<tr><td>

Aristotle, *Ath. Pol.* 63. 3:

ἐὰν δέ τις δικάζῃ οἷς μὴ ἔξεστιν, ἐνδείκνυται
καὶ εἰς τὸ δικαστήριον εἰσάγεται. ἐὰν
δ' ἁλῷ, προστιμῶσιν αὐτῷ οἱ δικασταί,
ὅ τι ἂν δοκῇ ἄξιος εἶναι παθεῖν ἢ ἀποτεῖσαι,
etc.

</td><td>

Theophrastus (in the fifth book)[3]
in *Schol.* Dem. p. 665. 1 Dind.:

Θεόφραστος ἱστορεῖ λέγων οὕτως· Ἀθή-
νησιν οὖν ἐν τοῖς δημοσίοις ἀγῶσιν,
ἐὰν μὴ μεταλάβῃ τις τὸ πέμπτον μέρος,
χιλίας ἀποτίνει, καὶ ἔτι πρόσεστί τις
ἀτιμία οἷον τὸ ἐξεῖναι μήτε γράψασθαι
παρανόμων μήτε φαίνειν μήτε ἐφηγεῖσθαι.

</td></tr>
</table>

But also the *Politics* shows that Aristotle disposed of more
material than that which is found in the second part of the *Athenaion Politeia*, that he rests, in other words, on a large collection
of laws, and not only on those mentioned in the treatise. The case

---

[1] To which W. Jaeger, *Aristotle* (1934) 337–339, has called attention and which
Hommel, *Heliaia* 31 note 67, already has mentioned in connection with this section
of the *Athenaion Politeia*. Wilamowitz, however, is speaking of "Redseligkeit über
Bagatellen" (p. 204).

[2] It is noteworthy that all ancient notices which refer to the subjects treated in
this excursus (and in the chapter 42 concerning the Ephebes) rest on Aristotle,
that, in other words, the grammarians did not find these topics discussed except
in the *Athenaion Politeia* (cf. Wilamowitz *Aristoteles und Athen* I 204, 193). Is it
not more than probable that Theophrastus in the *Nomoi* followed the same practice
which Aristotle had observed with respect to the *Nomoi*, avoiding repetitions of
Aristotle's detailed exposition?

[3] This is proved by *Lex. Cantabr. s.v.* Πρόστιμον; for the restoration of the passage see also *Schol.* Dem. p. 664. 16 Dind.; Harpocr. *s.v.* ἐάν τις and Poll. VIII 53.

of the ἀγορανόμοι is an instructive example (*supra* p. 368). It is simply not true that Theophrastus composed his work with the material which Aristotle had produced in the *Politeiai*. Both works go back to the same extensive body of material which had been collected at the instigation of Aristotle. It was first arranged according to the geographical principle, by cities, and it served in this form as the basis for the *Politeiai*; at the same time Theophrastus began to arrange it according to subjects also; he prepared his *Nomoi* on a comparative basis and discussed the laws much more in detail than Aristotle had done in his *Politeiai*, which were addressed — this should not be forgotten — to the world at large.[1]

There is in the literary production of Theophrastus a striking analogy to the *Nomoi*, it is the work which more than any other of Theophrastus' writings has influenced the whole tradition: the Φυσικῶν δόξαι in eighteen books. In this work the systems of the philosophers were not presented one after the other, but the material was arranged in the same manner as in the *Nomoi*, by subjects, by problems; περὶ ἀρχῶν, περὶ αἰσθήσεων, etc.[2] The sources were in this case of course more easily available: they were the writings of the philosophers themselves which had to be excerpted; the excerpts had to be distributed among the various headings.[3] Aristotle had felt that before the larger comparative study of the laws could be undertaken, a description of the constitutions of the single states was needed: similarly Theophrastus felt the need of monographs on single philosophers (he chose Anaxagoras, Anaximenes, Archelaus, Democritus, Diogenes, Empedocles, Metrodorus, Plato, and Xenocrates)[4] as a basis for the great comparative history of philosophy. These monographs correspond actually to the *Politeiai*.

---

[1] Sandys *Ath. Pol.* (ed. 2) p. lx; W. Jaeger *Aristotle* (1934) 24.

[2] H. Diels, *Doxographi Graeci*, ed. 2, Berlin, 1929, pp. 103, 153.

[3] Like the *Nomoi*, it was not an impersonal exposition, but a work in which Theophrastus "quid male quid recte quid proprie cogitassent ad Aristoteleam normam diiudicaret" (Diels *Doxogr. Graeci* p. 103). See H. Cherniss, *Aristotle's Criticism of Presocratic Philosophy*, Baltimore, 1935, p. XIII; W. Jaeger *Am. Journ. of Philol.* LVIII (1937) 355.

[4] Usener *Kleine Schriften* I 52 f.; Diels *Doxogr. Graeci* pp. 103, 479.

As to the *Nomoi*, it is quite natural that ancient scholars interested in the antiquities and institutions of Athens preferred in general to consult Aristotle's *Athenaion Politeia* which was easy to handle; on the contrary, in the *Nomoi* the material regarding Athens was dispersed over all the twenty-four books. The *Athenaion Politeia* remained therefore the starting point for any research — that is proved by the survival of more than eighty quotations [1] — ; for further investigation, it was then relatively easy for ancient scholars engaging in such researches to pass from the single constitution to the *Nomoi* and to study in the work of Theophrastus the particulars of topics which Aristotle had only touched upon.

In conclusion it can be said that the correlations between Aristotle's *Politeiai*, the empirical section of the *Politics*, and Theophrastus' *Nomoi*, are very close. All three works have a common background. The problems of the *Nomoi* are already present in book E of the *Politics*, as the discussion of the new fragment of Theophrastus' *Nomoi* has shown. The structure of the second part of the *Athenaion Politeia* implies that Aristotle when he wrote it already had in mind the great work on the laws. This is fully proved by the connection between the extant fragments of the *Nomoi* and the second part of the *Athenaion Politeia*.

At the end of the *Nicomachean Ethics*, after the collection of laws and constitutions had been built up — as we can now say — Aristotle had declared [2] that collections of laws and constitutions would be useful to those who are capable of examining and deciding what is right or wrong, and what is suitable to particular cases. In fulfillment of this principle, Aristotle and Theophrastus relied primarily on these collections, when they set about to reconcile political theory with political reality.

[1] Cf. Sandys *Ath. Pol.* (ed. 2) pp. lxiv–lxv.

[2] See the Greek text *supra* p. 362.

TWO ATTIC TREASURE-RECORDS

By Arthur M. Woodward

THE contribution which is here offered, on the subject of two Attic *Traditiones* belonging to the fourth century B.C., will, I believe, be thought appropriate to the occasion, for no student of these documents can ignore the services rendered to their study by W. S. Ferguson, in his *Treasurers of Athena*. There is however a further reason for my choice, since the first of the two texts here discussed was studied in close collaboration with Allen West, whose tragic death deprived the study of Attic epigraphy of one of its leading figures; and my notes on it owe much both to his scholarly grasp of the problems, large and small, which it involves, and to his unselfish cooperation.[1] Had he lived he would assuredly have enriched the present volume with an outstanding contribution.

I. The Inventory of the Treasurers of Athena for 385/4 B.C.

The *Traditio* of the "Treasurers of the Goddess" for 385/4 B.C. (*IG* II² 1407) is presumed to be the first list compiled by them after the board of the "Treasurers of the Other Gods" had been again constituted as a separate body, independent of the "Treasurers of Athena." This record, which is known only from a copy made by Richard Chandler during his residence in Athens in 1765–6,[2] since when the original has disappeared, contains 48 lines, and is complete above and on the left, but, as will be seen *infra*, the portion which he copied comprises less than a third of the original width of the stele. His copy seems to be on the whole remarkably accurate, apart from a few slight errors to be men-

---

[1] The substance of this article was included, in very summary form, in a paper on Attic Treasure-Records of the fourth century B.C. read to the Epigraphical Congress at Amsterdam, on Sept. 1, 1938.

[2] *Travels in Greece*, etc. (1776), p. 57 f. (= 1821, II 71 f.), quoted by Dinsmoor in *AJA* 1913, 243 f.

tioned later, but we may regret that he was not sufficiently in advance of his time to record either the dimensions of the stone
or the height of the letters. Before considering its contents we may
with advantage note an important feature, plainly visible in his
copy, namely that whilst the text as a whole is engraved strictly
στοιχηδόν, each group of the signs for numerals, whether signifying
weights or numbers, is preceded and followed by a vacant space;
and whilst the signs for one drachma and its multiples each occupy
a letter-space, the obol-signs are sometimes compressed so that
two or even three occupy a single space.[1] The original width
of the stele can be calculated with almost absolute certainty from
the restoration of the details of the familiar list of twenty-seven
silver hydriai of Athena Polias which we find in ll. 14–20, giving
us apparently 118 letters to each line.

Turning now to the contents: it is impossible to restore the text
completely throughout, since many of the items of which the
description is only partly preserved are not recognisable elsewhere;
and, moreover, we find that, after all the legitimate restorations
have been inserted, several gaps are left, especially from l. 34
onwards, which defy completion. Our task is made more difficult
by the fact that, as is well known, a new system of arranging the
entries is found in this list for the first time, by which they are
grouped according to type,[2] at any rate as far as l. 37, though
there are occasional exceptions; but it is, I think, clear that the
sacrificial vessels are all entered before the crowns and miscellaneous dedications. The order, from l. 8 onwards, where the inventory begins, is this: (1) Νίκη χρυσῆ, in five ῥυμοί. (2) θυμιατήρια.
(3) ὑδρίαι ἀργυραῖ. (4) κανᾶ. (5) οἰνοχόαι. (6) πίνακες(?). (7) another οἰνοχόη. (8) φιάλαι χρυσαῖ and χρυσίδες. (9) ὑδρία χρυσῆ.
(10) κρατῆρες and their supports (ὑπόστατα). (11) σκάφαι χαλκαῖ(?).
(12) στέφανοι. (13) φιάλαι ἀργυραῖ, followed by miscellaneous
smaller items, in no particular order. As far as they can be recognised, the great majority of these items were listed as in the Hekatompedon under the régime of the joint board of Athena and the

---

[1] Certain exceptions appear in Chandler's text, some of which *may* be due to
inaccurate copying, but this must not be assumed too confidently.

[2] Cf. most recently, Ferguson *Treasurers* 111 f.

Other Gods, and the remainder as "from the Opisthodomos," although actually stored in the Hekatompedon. No single item, on the other hand, can be recognised as having been previously listed among the objects "from the Parthenon" in the same period, but the absence of such items has been accounted for by the suggestion that they were recorded on the lost lower portion of the stele.[1] There is no difficulty in accepting this explanation, but is it necessary to assume with equal certainty that this lower portion is in fact lost? It had naturally occurred to me to enquire whether any of the other fragmentary lists which are seen by the nature of their contents to belong to the same category as II² 1407, and by their arrangement to antedate the columnar system which began in 374/3 B.C., might possibly prove to be our missing lower portion. It was easy to eliminate all these, with the single exception of II² 1414, which reached the British Museum with the Elgin Marbles,[2] and in the light of the evidence which is set out *infra* I believe that it is not merely possible, but absolutely certain that this is our missing lower portion.

We must start with a few details concerning its present condition. It is complete on the left and below, and has suffered extensive damage to the surface by being used at some time as a step, for in many places the lettering is entirely worn smooth, especially towards the left margin, from l. 7 onwards; moreover, a faulty vein in the marble, and other surface-injuries, have destroyed many of the other letters. Nevertheless we can see that the writing is στοιχηδόν, with a few exceptions towards the end where it shows signs of more crowded and careless cutting; that there are vacant spaces before and after the numerals and weight-signs; that the obol-signs are compressed, and that the unit-sign sometimes occupies less than a space, e.g. in l. 8, where IIII twice over occupies only three spaces. In addition to its resemblance in these details to II² 1407, the orthography seems identical.[3] When we

---

[1] Cf. W. Bannier *Rhein. Mus.* 1911, 41 f., followed by Kirchner in his commentary on II² 1407.

[2] *Greek Inscriptions in the British Museum* I no. 32; *IG* II¹ 675.

[3] E.g. the genitive singular, second declension, ending in -o, and χρυσôν for χρυσοûν.

turn to examine the contents, we find in the first place that no single one of the items found in 1407 occurs in 1414, or vice-versa; secondly, that the latter begins (ll. 1–7) with just such a miscellaneous assemblage of coins and small pieces of gold plating as are found in the last few lines of 1407; and thirdly, and to my mind most convincingly, we find in ll. 22 ff. the regular list of Parthenon items (surviving in many cases from before the end of the fifth century) which begins with the *protomai* of gryphon and lion. It is true that already, in l. 12, some of the items of furniture from the same source (δίφρος στρογγυλόπος, etc.) have been recorded. It remains to see if the lines of 1414 are of the requisite length. Unfortunately this can only be tested in l. 22 f., but the restoration of these objects from the Parthenon, in the order normally found in the earlier fourth century lists, fits convincingly into a line of 118 letters in length.

These points of resemblance seem to leave us with no reason to doubt the proposed combination of these two stones, and when we look at the width of the surviving portion of the lower half, we seem to find fresh confirmation. In 1407 the number of letters preserved ranges between 35 (ll. 2–6, 17, 18) and 28 (ll. 42 and 47), though nothing after the 20th letter has survived in the last line (l. 48); in 1414 the number never exceeds 36 and at no point falls below 29 (except that the fracture in l. 1 leaves only 14). It is hard to avoid the conclusion that the original stele was first split vertically into three or four long strips, of a width convenient for use as steps, and that the horizontal fracture which separated 1407 from 1414 occurred subsequently, at some unknown date prior to Chandler's visit to Athens. How much is missing from between the two pieces cannot be calculated, but in view of the fact that objects of the same type continue from the upper to the lower piece, it may be reasonably concluded that very little is lost; and the transcript (given below) of four lines on each side of the break points to a clean-edged fracture, involving the loss perhaps of only one line, or possibly of none at all.

IG II² **1407.** I do not propose to reprint the text in full, but a few suggestions and comments will, I hope, contribute towards an im-

proved text and a fuller understanding of some obscure passages.
L. 5. As restored in the *Editio Minor*, this line is excessively
long. In Kirchner's words, *si in lacuna tria nomina quaestorum
exstabant, versus iusto longior evadit*. If we allot altogether for
the demotic of the ταμίας of the eighth tribe (Hippothontis) and
for the names and demotics of those of the ninth and tenth tribes
a total of 37 letters (equal to the number occupied by the two
names and demotics plus one name for the sixth, seventh, and
eighth tribes), plus ca. 30 letters for the phrase οἷς - - - - ἐγραμμάτευε,
we reach 104 letters, leaving room for only 14 to complete the line.
Kirchner, however, proposed to restore here [τὸ ἄγαλμα ἐν τῶι
'Εκατομπέδωι ἐντελὲς κατὰ τὴν στήλην τὴν] | χαλκῆν, requiring 47 letters
before the end of the line. In other words, from his total of 151
we should have to cut out much more than the name and demotic
of one ταμίας to reduce the line to the ascertained length of 118
letters. A possible, but rather drastic, solution would be to sacrifice the names and demotics of two ταμίαι; and almost equally
undesirable would be to cut out the entry referring to the γραμμα-
τεύς. So I would suggest that a simpler solution would be to cut
out the name of one ταμίας and his demotic, and in addition the
words ἐν τῶι 'Εκατομπέδωι. The words τὸ ἄγαλμα must be retained,
to account for the participle ὁμολογόμενον in l. 6, and ἐντελὲς is
required to account for [κατὰ τὴν στήλην τὴν] χαλκῆν. The proposed
restoration would therefore read - - Δε[ξ]ιθέ[ωι - -, - - - -, οἷς - -
- - ἐγραμμάτευε, τὸ ἄγαλμα ἐντελὲς κατὰ τὴν στήλην τὴν] | χαλκῆν.

L. 7. The last five letters ΤΑΣΤΑ point to τὰ στα[θμία], presumably with reference to the process of weighing the separate parts
of the chryselephantine statue of Athena Parthenos, and the whole
phrase may have run thus: [τὸ χρυσίον καὶ τὸν] | ἐλέφαντα παρέδομεν,
πρὸς ἀργύριον τὰ στα[θμία ἀντιστήσαντες,[1] i.e. weighing them on the
scales against silver.

Ll. 8–11. In restoring the details of the golden Nike in these
lines, which Kirchner leaves uncompleted, it is to be observed
that the version contained in the Hekatompedon list of 398/7
B.C. (II² 1388) proves to be too short for the space available

---

[1] Or perhaps δοκιμάσαντες or ἐξισώσαντες. Cf. the list of synonyms connected
with the process of weighing given by Pollux IV 171–172.

here. In 1407 exactly three lines (= 354 letter-spaces) are required from the beginning of the entry to the end of the fourth of the five ῥυμοί into which the Nike is divided, as against 300 letter-spaces in 1388.[1] Obviously, to account for this increase, certain items must be either added or described more fully; but it is clear that this does not apply to the first ῥυμός, for in 1388 the words Νίκης χρυσῆς πρῶτος ῥυμός, κ.τ.λ., down to the end of its weight inclusive, occupy 121 spaces, as against just one line of 118 in 1407. Actually, the difference is not three but four, since we must allot one space of our 118 for a *vacat* before the weight; a second one after it proves to be unnecessary, as the last weight-sign falls in the 118th space. Following the example of a list of about fifteen years later (*IG* II² *Addenda* 1424a l. 8), I would read χρυσία μικρά (as against χρυσίδια μικρά in 1388) and omit the word δύο from the phrase ἥλω δύο χρυσώ. On the other hand, we must presumably restore χείρ here for χέρ in 1388, giving us 121 − 2 − 3 + 1 letters, plus one *vacat* before the weight, = 118. The second and third ῥυμοί together occupy 107 letters in 1388, as against 118 + 39 = 157, including two *vacat*s, in 1407. In the former, the second ῥυμός comprises only θώραξ and στρόφιον, but in the latter the second word is followed by περιτρα[χηλίδιον], and we can again complete the description with the aid of 1424a, which gives us θώραξ, στρόφιον, περιτραχηλίδιον, στολίδε δύο, μικρὰ χρυσία, an addition of thirty-eight letters, and the words χρυσίδια μικά (*sic*), preserved at the end of the third ῥυμός, in line 10, give us the additional twelve, to make up the difference to fifty letters. These further items must represent only a fuller description, and not additional parts of the statue, since the weights should be, apparently, restored as in 1388.

In the fourth ῥυμός there appears to be no room for the word στέφανος, which is included in it in 1388, 1400 and 1424a, and I am inclined to ascribe its omission to oversight. The available space again permits of a restoration for which 1424a is our guide, τέταρτος ῥυμός, χείρ δεξιά, ἀμφιδέα, κατωρίδε δύο, χρυσία μικρά, σταθμὸν τούτων v. ΧΓΗΗΗΓΔΔΔΔΗΗΗΗ. This seems preferable to the

---

[1] Cf. my article, "The Golden Nikai of Athena," Ἀρχαιολογικὴ Ἐφημερίς, Centenary volume, 1937, 159 ff., especially 165.

alternative χρυσίδια μικρά, which would leave us twelve spaces for the weight, and enable us to restore it as ΧΓΗΗΗΗΓΔΓΗΗ (= 1968 drs.) as in II² 1388. If on the other hand we reject the χρυσία μικρά and retain the στέφανος we have three vacant spaces to account for, and there is no justification for suggesting a third variant, three spaces longer, for the weight.

The fifth ῥυμός requires 71 spaces, including two *vacat*s, since we know that the next entry, the θυμιατήριον dedicated by Kleostrate, requires the last 47 letters of the line. Again we follow 1424a, and insert χρυσία μικρά, reading πέμπτος ῥυμός, ἀκρωτήριον ὀπίσ[θ]ιον, σκέ[λη δύο, χρυσία μικρά, σταθμὸν τούτων *v.* ΧΧΧΧΗΗ||| *v.*

L. 12. After the θυμιατήριον dedicated by Kleostrate we should expect to find that dedicated by Aristokritos, as in II² 1425, ll. 110–12, which is also recognisable in 1412 ll. 13–14, and 1413 ll. 3–4 (both slightly later in date than 1407). This will exactly fill the available space if we omit his demotic, 'Ανακαιεύς, as in 1425.

L. 13. After the θυμιατήριον ἵνα ἡ Νίκη, weighing 1448 drs., it is tempting to insert its cover, as in 1396 ll. 31–33 (cf. 1397 ll. 4–5) τὸ θυμιατήριο τούτο καλύπτρα ἀργυρᾶ, σταθμὸν ΓΔΓΗΗ, though if the weight is the same it leaves us with two vacant spaces unaccounted for. In l. 14, before the list of silver hydriai which begins with the 86th space, there are fifty spaces free after the weight of the "gilt θυμιατήριον with the crooked leaves" which we should naturally expect to be followed by the similar vessel "with the straight leaves," as in the Opisthodomos lists II² 1396, 1398 and 1399, but it can only be described in a shortened form, so I suggest ἕτερον ὑπόχαλκον ἵνα τὰ ὀρθὰ φύλλα, σταθμὸν *v.* ΧΧΓΗΗΗΗΔΔΔ *v.·* ὑδρίαι ἀργυραῖ, κ.τ.λ.

Ll. 14–20. It does not seem necessary to restore in full the details of the whole list of twenty-seven silver hydriai, for the completion of l. 15 will suffice to confirm the length of line as 118 letters, as stated above.[1] It may be assumed that σταθμὸν followed the word πρώτης, though it is omitted from the description of the other twenty-six. We may now transcribe ll. 8–15 in the light of the restorations suggested above, as follows:

[1] P. 378.

Νίκης χρυσῆς πρῶτος ῥυμός, κεφαλή, στεφά[νη, ὅρμος, ἐνωιδίω, ὑποδερίς, ἦλω χρυσώ, χεὶρ ἀριστερά, ἀμφιδέα, χρυσία μικρά, σταθμὸν τούτων
v. ΧΧΔΔΔΔⱵⱵⱵⱵ|||·]

δεύτερος ῥυμός, θώραξ, στρόφιον, περιτρα[χηλίδιον, στολίδε δύο, χρυσία
μικρά, σταθμὸν τούτων v. ΧΧΔ v.· τρίτος ῥυμός, ἀπόπτυγμα, περόνα
δύο, πόδε δύο, χρυ-](119)

10 σί[δ]ια μικά, σταθμὸν τούτων v. ΧϜΗΗΗΗΔΔΔΓ[ⱵⱵⱵ||| v.· τέταρτος
ῥυμός, χεὶρ δεξιά, ἀμφιδέα, κατωρίδε δύο, χρυσία μικρά, σταθμὸν τούτων
v. ΧϜΗΗΗϜΔΔΔΔⱵⱵⱵ·]

πέμπτος ῥυμός, ἀκρωτήριον ὀπίσ[θ]ιον, σκέ[λη δύο, χρυσία μικρά, σταθμὸν
τούτων v. ΧΧΧΧⱵⱵ||| v.· θυμιατήριον ἀργυρὸν ὃ Κλεοστράτη ἀνέθηκε
Νικηράτο, χαλ-]

κᾶ διερείσματα ἔχον, σταθμὸν σὺν τῶι χα[λκῶι v.ΧΗΗΗΔΔv.· ἕτερον θυμιατήριον ἀργυρὸν ὃ Ἀριστόκριτος ἀνέθηκε, σταθμὸν v.ΧΧΗΗΗΔΔΔv.·
θυμιατήριον ἀρ-]

γυρὸν ὑπόξυλον ἵνα ἡ Νίκη, σταθμὸν v.ΧΗΗΗ[ΗΔΔΔΔΓⱵⱵv.· τὸ
θυμιατήριο τούτο καλύπτρα ἀργυρᾶ, σταθμὸν v.ϜΔΓⱵⱵvvv. θυμιατήριον χρυσὸν ὑπόχαλκον]

ἵνα τὰ καμπύλα φύλλα, σταθμὸν v.ΧΧϜΗΗΗΗ[ϜΔv.· ἕτερον ὑπόχαλκον
ἵνα τὰ ὀρθὰ φύλλα, σταθμὸν v.ΧΧϜΗΗΗΗΔΔΔΔv.· ὑδρίαι ἀργυραῖ·
πρώτης σταθμὸν v.ϜΗΗΗΗϜ-]

15 ΔΔΔΔΓⱵⱵv.· δευτέρας v.ϜΗΗΗΗ[Ϝ]ΔΔΔΔⱵv.· τρίτ[ης v.ϜΗΗΗΗϜ-
ΔΔΔⱵv.· τετάρτης v.ϜΗΗΗΗϜΔΔΔΔΓⱵⱵv.· πέμπτης v.ΧⱵⱵⱵⱵ|||v.·
ἕκτης v.ϜΗΗΗΗϜΔΔΔΓⱵⱵ|||v.· ἑβδόμης v.ϜΗΗ-]
ΗΗϜΔΔΔΔⱵⱵv.·κ.τ.λ.

L. 20. The weight of the twenty-seventh hydria brings us to
the 58th letter-space. Allowing for a *vacat*, the next item begins
in the 60th space, and is no doubt to be restored as the κανὸν χρυσὸν
ὑπόχαλκον, ἵνα ὁ Ἀπόλλων, weighing 3596 drs., which would naturally
accompany the similar vessel ἵνα ὁ Ζεύς, which follows it here.
The six vacant spaces presumably are to be filled with the word
ἕτερον. After the second κανοῦν we have a gap extending from the
45th space to the end of the line, towards the end of which comes
an uncertain object described as unweighed (ἄστατον). Here we
may expect to find more vessels of the same type, so I would propose to restore κανὸν ὑπόχαλκον χαλκᾶ διερείσματα ἔχον, ἄστατον· v.

κανὸν ἀργυρὸν ἵνα τὰ ἐλεφάντινα ζῶια,] | ἄστατον. The former will be identical with the vessel which bears also the epithet κατάχρυσον, and is likewise unweighed, in 1424a, ll. 85–86, and the latter appears as one of two unweighed items in the list of silver objects later in the same inventory, ll. 190–91.

In l. 22 it is possible, as I suggested *supra* (p. 378), that the next items are the three silver πίνακες (1424a ll. 171–3), but the weight of the last one, which has survived at the beginning of l. 23, is 816 drs. whilst it is given in 1424a as 719½ drs.[1] The difference is a formidable objection to the suggested identification, but on the other hand, there seems no other gap in our text large enough to hold these three πίνακες and their weights, and experiment shows that they would exactly fill the space available, if we read (from the 48th space onwards) [πίναξ ἀργυρὸς μέγας, σταθμὸν *v*.ΧΧΔΔΓⱵⱵⱵ²*v*·* πίναξ ἀργυρὸς, σταθμὸν *v*.ΧΔΔΓⱵⱵⱵ||*v*·* πίναξ ἔτε]|ρος, σταθμὸν *v*.ΓΗΗΗΔΓⱵ*v*·* οἰνοχόη, κ.τ.λ.

L. 23. After the οἰνοχόη, of which the weight has been correctly restored as 652 drs., the remainder of lines 23 and 24 present an intriguing problem, which I hope to discuss elsewhere, in connexion with the occurrence of the same phrase - - ἄγει ἡ ὑπάργυρος ΗⱵⱵⱵⱵⱵⱵ|||, in II² 1400 l. 39.

L. 25. The unidentified object of which the weight is preserved as 649 drs., 3 obols is almost certainly to be recognised as [χρυσίδες τρῆς καὶ κονδυλωτὸν ἐν ἇ Στέφανος Θάλλο Λαμπτρεὺς ἀνέθη] | κεν, which will thus have begun in the 64th space of l. 24, leaving us with a gap of 29 spaces, for which I have no suggestion to offer, after the last weight-sign of the previous item. It must be noted that this group of objects weighs three obols more than it does in two earlier lists, II² 1386, ascribed to 401/0 B.C.[3] and 1388 (398/7 B.C.),[4] but this small difference need cause no hesitation.

---

[1] Partly restored, but the same weight is fully preserved in 1415 l. 1; the date of the latter is put by Ferguson, *op. cit.* 184, after 378/7 B.C. It may very likely belong to the year 375/4, i.e. the last of the pre-columnar lists.

[2] This weighs 2027 drs., 3 obols in 1424a, but must be restored as 2028 drs. in 1428.

[3] Cf. *JHS* 1938, 86.

[4] Cf. *JHS* 1931, 140 f. for a new fragment which continues 1388 and enables this item to be restored in ll. 50–52, with a weight of 649 drs.

Ll. 27–34. We now come to the long list of crowns, all of gold, except one which is of silver, and we find that the first half of the list involves many difficulties. It must be admitted that the restorations printed in the *Editio Minor* prove an untrustworthy guide, since l. 27 is made to contain about 135 letters, as against 85 in l. 28, as a result of needlessly inserting the names of the archons in whose years the first two gold crowns were dedicated. Since there is no doubt that the weight 245 drs., 1½ obols (l. 28 *init.*) is that of the crown dedicated as ἀριστεῖα τῆι θεῶι in 398/7 B.C.,[1] we may confidently follow previous editors in restoring immediately before it the corresponding crown of 402/1 B.C., weighing 272 drs., 3½ obols. This is, it is true, open to the objection that it leaves us with no room for the vacant spaces which we should expect before and after the weight of the first crown, or for those accompanying the weight of the σκάφαι χαλκαῖ H which directly precede it, but this need not invalidate the proposed restoration. Then follow, in l. 28, the crowns of the years of Eubolides (394/3) and Demostratos (390/89), the weight of the latter, 232 drs., 5 obols, being preserved in l. 29. This seems a much simpler solution than that offered by Kirchner in the *Editio Minor*, for, following Lehner,[2] who relied on Boeckh, he tries to crowd into l. 28 the crown of the year 386/5 as well, but only by means of omitting both the weights and the words χρυσοῦς and ἀριστεῖα τῆι θεῶι from the description of each of the crowns which precede it. But there seems no objection to restoring the crown of 386/5 in the extensive space available in l. 29, where, if we insert ἄρχοντος after Μυστιχίδο, and allow twelve spaces, including two *vacats*, for the weight, we reach the 92nd space, leaving twenty-six letters for the entry of the item which ends, according to Chandler's copy, in l. 30 with the words ΟΝΥΞ, σταθμὸν *v.*ΗΗΡΔΔΓΗϹ *v.* This item affords a puzzle, hitherto not merely unsolved, but to my knowledge entirely neglected.

It is, to say the least, surprising to find an onyx inserted in the middle of a list of gold crowns, and one may well ask if a crown

---

[1] It is entered among the ἐπέτεια of that year in 1388 B l. 66.

[2] *Über die athenischen Schatzverzeichnisse des vierten Jahrhunderts*, Strassburg, 1890, p. 49.

adorned with an onyx is a satisfying solution. Certainly no such object occurs in any of the Attic *Traditiones*, though a στέφανος χρυσὸς διάλιθος weighing 46 drs. is found in the Parthenon lists, e.g. II² 1376 l. 7 f., 1377 l. 14 f. Nor does it seem very likely that an onyx would be weighed, either by itself or in combination with other objects, for the parallel afforded at first sight by the entry in 1388 B l. 62 f. ὄνυξ μέγας τραγελάφο πρια[πίζοντος, στα]|θμὸν ΔΔΔⱵ is almost certainly based on a false reading, and seems to conceal two distinct objects.[1] May not the true explanation be that Chandler's ΟΝΥΞ is a mistake? I feel sure that it is, and that he has misread all four letters. On a somewhat worn stone,[2] with the rather small letters which are indicated for 1407 by the identification of 1414 as the lower portion of the stele, it would be easy to misread ΘΗΚΕ as ΟΝΥΞ, especially if the letters in question looked like ΟΙΙΥΞ. Having thus disposed of the "Onyx" we may surely restore this entry as [στέφανος χρυσὸς ὃν . . . . ἀνέ] | θηκε, σταθμὸν v.ΗΗℙΔΔΓⱵC. Unfortunately this cannot be identified elsewhere, but this is equally true of the silver crown which follows it,[3] and of the crown(?) of which the weight ends in the figures −73 drs., 3 obols, at the beginning of l. 31. After this comes a familiar series of crowns, calling for little comment as the weights are all known from earlier lists, particularly II² 1388. The order is: (1) the crown on the head of the Nike, then those dedicated by (2) Lysander, (3) Aristomache, (4) Gelon, (5) Hierokles, (6) the city, as νικητήρια τὸ κιθαρωιδό. Nos. 3 and 5 are certain restorations which exactly fit the spaces available, but it is to be noted that if we restore the crown of Nike as ἄσταθμος it leaves us with seven vacant spaces before the beginning of the next crown; but it would be rash to suggest that it may have been weighed on this occasion, for it is always "unweighed" both in earlier and in later lists.[4]

---

[1] I hope to discuss this item elsewhere, and to justify the restoration ὄνυξ μέγας· τραγελάφο πρ[οτομὴ χρυσῆ, στα]θμὸν ΔΔΔⱵ.

[2] This seems to account for such errors as Ξ for Ε (l. 3), ΟΛ for ΟΜ (l. 6), Ω for Δ (l. 10), ΟⱾΩΙ for ΘΕΩΙ (l. 29), to note only a selection.

[3] Perhaps to be identified with the [στέφα]νος ἀργυ[ροῦς] restored in 1420 l. 5, a list of uncertain category.

[4] West suggested - - ἄσταθμος· v. ἕτερος στέφανος, κ.τ.λ., which is certainly preferable to leaving an unfilled gap.

We may now accordingly transcribe ll. 27–34 as follows: —

27 μεγάλο ἀπὸ τῆς χειρὸς τῆς Νίκης· σκάφαι [χαλκαῖ Η· στέφανος χρυσôς ἀριστεῖα τῆι θεῶι, σταθμὸν ΗΗ𐅄ΔΔ⊢⊢I͜IIC· στέφανος χρυσôς ἀριστεῖα τῆι θεῶι, στα-]

28 θμὸν *v.*ΗΗΔΔΔΔΓΙC*v.*· ἐπ' Εὐβολίδο στέφανο[ς χρυσôς ἀριστεῖα τῆι θεῶι, σταθμὸν *v.*ΗΗ . . . . *v.*· ἐπὶ Δημοστράτο ἄρχοντος στέφανος χρυσôς ἀριστεῖα τῆι]

29 θεῶι, σταθμὸν *v.*ΗΗΔΔΔ⊢⊢I͜IIII*v.*· στέφανο[ς χρυσôς ἐπὶ Μυστιχίδο ἄρχοντος ἀριστεῖα τῆι θεῶι, σταθμὸν *v.*ΗΗ . . . . *v.*· στέφανος χρυσôς ὃν - - 8 - - ἀνέ-]

30 ⟨θηκε⟩, σταθμὸν *v.*ΗΗ𐅄ΔΔΓ⊢C*v.*· στέφανος ἀργ[υρôς - - - - - - - - - 81 - - - - - - - - -]

31 𐅄ΔΔ⊢⊢⊢.I͜II*v.*· στέφανος χρυσôς ὃν ἡ Νίκη ἔχ[ει ἐπὶ τῆς κεφαλῆς, ἡ ἐπὶ τῆς χειρὸς τô ἀγάλματος τô χρυσô, ἄσταθμος· *v.* ἕτερος(?) στέφανος χρυσôς, ὃν Λύσανδρος]

32 Ἀριστοκρίτο Λακεδαιμόνιος ἀνέθηκε, σ[ταθμὸν *v.*𐅄ΔΓ⊢I͜II͜II*v.*· στέφανος χρυσôς θαλλô ὃν Ἀριστομάχη Ἀριστοκλέος ἀνέθηκε, σταθμὸν *v.*ΔΔΓ⊢I͜II*v.*· στέφανος]

33 χρυσôς θαλλô ὃν Γέλων Τλησωνίδο ἀνέθη[κε, σταθμὸν *v.*ΔΓ⊢⊢I͜II*v.*· στέφανος χρυσôς θαλλô ὃν Ἱεροκλῆς Φασηλίτης ἀνέθηκε, σταθμὸν *v.*𐅄Γ⊢⊢⊢⊢*v.*· στέφανος]

34 χρυσôς θαλλô ὃν ἡ πόλις ἀνέθηκε νικητή[ρια τô κιθαρωιδô, σταθμὸν *v.* 𐅄ΔΔΔΓ*v.*· - - - 30 - - - τραγελάφο προτομὴ χρυσῆ (?), σταθμὸν]

35 [Δ]ΔΔ⊢⊢*v.*· φιάλη, κ.τ.λ.

Passing over the list of φιάλαι and other objects in lines 35 to 40, we may note that the description added to the twelve bronze balances ἃ ὁ δῆμος σηκῶσαι ἐψ[ηφίσατο] - - is not paralleled in any other list and cannot be fully restored, but that, after a gap which it is impossible to fill, we have a recognisable entry, [παρακαταθήκη Μελητάδο Ἐρχιῶς· ἐπιτήκτο ἀργυρίο ἀ]|σήμο ΔΔΔ*v.* This is followed by παρακαταθήκ[η] Ἀθηναίας· [στλεγγὶς χρυσῆ, as in 1400 l. 50, and for the dedicator's name, West's suggestion, Προκλῆς, as in 1382 l. 25, seems very tempting, especially as this article is followed by the relative ἥμ - - in 1400 *l.c.*[1] After this comes, pos-

[1] Cf. *JHS* 1938, 76 f.

IG II² 1414

Two Attic Treasure-Records 389

sibly, [γοργονεῖον χρυσὸν ὑπάργυρον ἀπὸ τῆς ἀσπίδος τῆς ἀπὸ τὸ νεώ,] | ἄστατον·, but this would leave us with only four spaces, including two *vacat*s, for the weight of the στλεγγίς, if recorded, whereas in 1382, if correctly identified this scraper weighs at least 70 drs. Between this entry and the end of 1407 come several other recognisable items, but in no instance can we complete a whole line. The final letters . . σου . . . χρυσὸν Βοιωτι[κόν] are most enigmatic. West suggested to me that we should restore [ἀ|πὸ] Σου[νίο]·, comparing ἀπὸ Σουνίο παρακαταθήκη in 1400 l. 48, in reference to a silver φιάλη. If so, the change of word-order is rather unusual, but it is also conceivable that the "Boeotian gold," if it was rightly read by Chandler, was also transferred from a sanctuary at Sunium to the treasury of Athena. Even so, it would be a numismatic curiosity.

IG II² 1414. See photograph on page opposite. To show the presumed relationship of the two portions of the stele, I append a transcript of the last four lines of 1407 and the first four of 1414.

```
|ΔΟΣΕΓΙΤΗΚΤΑΥΓΑΡΓΥΡΑΣΤΑΘΜΟΝΗΗΗΡ*
|ΔΔΙΙΙ  ΣΤΑΘΜΟΝ  ΔΔΔΔΓΗΗΗΙΑΙΓΙΝΑΙΟ
|  ΕΓΙΤΗΚΤΟΝΓΑΡΑΔΗΜΟΚΛΕΟΣΣΤΑΘ
|  ΣΟΥ    ΧΡΥΣΟΝΒΟΙΩΤΙ
(? One line lost)
        ΝΕΩΤΟΕΚΑΤΟ[ΜΓ]ΕΔΟ
        ΣΟΝΑΓΗΝΕΓΧΘΗΣΤΑΘΜΟΝ ΗΗΙΙ
|  ΑΓΑΛΜΑΤΟΣΣΤΑΘΜΟΝ ΓΗΗΗΙΙΙ  ΑΡΓΥΡ
|ΓΕΑΟΧΡΥΣΟΝΑΓΟΤΟΗΛΟΑΡΓΥΡΙΟΝ ΣΥΜΜΕΙΚ
```

* I have corrected Chandler's Γ to Ρ.

L. 1. The *Editio Minor* reads, after 19 spaces, ο . εαι . . . . δο, which I have deciphered as - - 15 - - νεὼ τὸ 'Εκατο[μπ]έδο, but I cannot identify the object referred to.

L. 2. - - 8 - - σον ἀπηνέγχθη, not ἀπήνεγκον.

L. 3. The weight is ΓΗΗΗΗΙΙΙ, not ΓΗΗΗΙΙΙ.

L. 6 *init.* ΔΕ ΙΙ, not ΕΣ ΙΙ.

L. 7. Φαληρέω[ς ἀν]έθηκε, wrongly corrected to Φαληρε[ύς, in II² *Appendix* p. 799.

L. 8 *init.* Apparently ΜΕ̣[ΝΑΙ?] *v.* ΓΙΙΙΙ.

L. 15. - - 8 - - [κα]ὶ̣ [κρί]ο κεφαλή, κ.τ.λ. This is surely the item from the Parthenon, cf. 1377 l. 10 f., ὅρμος χρυσὸς διάλιθος ὁ μέζων ἀριθμὸς ῥόδων εἴκοσι καὶ κριὸ κεφαλή, σταθμὸν τοῦτο ΔΔΔ. The faint traces of the third symbol of the weight on our stele look more like Γ or Ⱶ than the Δ we should expect, but, if this appearance is not deceptive, the weight as recorded here may quite possibly have been slightly under thirty drs.

L. 16. The weight should read ⲢΔΔΔΔΓⱵΙΙΙ., 96 drs., 3½ or 4 obols.

L. 21. After ὄφεως ἀργυρὸ read ἥμ̣[ι]σ̣υ, rather than [ἥμισυ] as restored in II² *Appendix* p. 799. The following items cannot be restored, but before the end of the line we clearly have the beginning of the group of unweighed objects from the Parthenon, which occur so regularly in the same order that we may confidently restore lines 22–25 as follows:

21 - - - - - - - 62 - - - - - - - γοργονεῖον, κάμπη κατάχρυσα, ἴ-]
22 [ππος, γρύψ, γρυπ]ὸς προτομή, γρὺ[ψ] ὁ [μέγας, λέοντος κεφαλή, δράκων ἐπίχρυσος, κλῖναι Χιοργὲς *v.*ΓΙΙ*v.*, ξιφομάχαιραι *v.*ΓΙⳫ*v.*, ἐγχειρίδιον, ξίφη *v.*Γ *v.*, θώρακες *v.*]
23 [ΔΓΙ *v.*, πέλτη χα]λκ[ῆ], λύρα κατάχρυσος, λύρ[αι ἐλεφάντιναι *v.*ⳫⳫ *v.*, λύραι ξύλιναι *v.* ⳫⳫ*v.*, κράνη χαλκᾶ *v.*ⳫⳫ*v.*, ἀσπίδες ὑπόξυλοι ἐπίχαλκοι *v.* . . . *v.*, κράνος 'Ιλλυρικὸ-]
24 [*v.*, ἀσπὶς ἐγ Λέσ]βο̣ ἐπίσημος, - - - - - - - 93 - - - - - - - -, ἀλαβ-]
25 [αστοθήκη ἄλυσι]ν ἀργυρᾶν ἔχοσα, κ.τ.λ.

L. 27. The reading of the name as [Γλα]ύκωνος [γυ]νή is mistaken, for the name definitely ends with νσωνος, and faint traces of Ε are visible before the Υ. We must accordingly read [Σπ]ε̣ύσωνος [γυ]νή,[1] followed almost certainly by ἀνέ[θ]ηκεν, though the middle of the word is almost effaced.

L. 29. Apparently [. . . . . . ἄνευ ἐπ]ι̣θήμα̣τ[ο]ς· ἀσπί[δ]ες, κ.τ.λ.

L. 30 *fin.* Not εν[. . ἀ]σπίδ[ες], but ἐν τ[ῶι] ἐπὶ Λ, presumably ἐν τῶι ἐπὶ δ[εξιᾷ] or ἐπὶ ἀ[ριστερᾷ].

---

[1] For this rare name cf. *IG* I² 950, l. 184 (= Kirchner *Prosopographia Attica* 12848).

L. 31. The *Editio Minor* reads here - - 15 - - κπ . . ν . σ . . μ .
φορ. Hicks, in the British Museum Catalogue,[1] restored the final
letters as [ἀ]μφορ[εῖς], but after the *rho* is plainly an *eta*, and, as
Hicks rightly saw, there is no gap between the *mu* and the *phi*,
so we may confidently read [ἀ]μφορῆ[s].[2] The word before this is
exceptionally puzzling, as a prolonged scrutiny suggests the letters
to be μεκπ . . νασ., which it would be rash to emend.

L. 34. Not οβολο but θεολο . . ντ. Can this be e.g. [τῆς] θεὸ λό[φο]ν
τ - (or even ἔ[χον, *vel sim.*)? Another possibility would be - - θέο
ἀ⟨ρ⟩[χο]ντ[os], in which case [ἐπὶ Δεξι]θέο ἄρχοντος (385/4 B.C.)
would be the obvious restoration.

L. 37. Though the curious reading παιστο ἐλαιο seems to be confirmed by a photograph, I believe that, working from West's suggestion . . αι δύο, we should restore [μικρ]αὶ δύο, ἐλαιο - -, and expect
the name of a vessel to follow. That this item should be identified
with the ἀμφορεὺς ἐλαιηρός of 1425 l. 345 is unlikely, as the following
letter seems not to be *alpha*, but perhaps *kappa* or *nu*.

L. 38. - - - ιαι πέντε. L. 39. [- - - τριπο]δίσκος ἄνευ ὑποστάτο.

L. 42. - - - θερμαστρίς ΗΤΙΙΝΛ, which must be θερμαστρὶς ἢ τὴν
ἄ[λυσιν ἔχει], and not ἡ ἐτ[έ]ρα ἄλυσιν ἔχει, as in 1424a, l. 287.

L. 46. Certainly [- - - 'Α]ργολικαί, κ.τ.λ., the first letter is alone
illegible.

L. 47. The reading is clearly Ρ/ϝ ιΓ⅌ΤΙΗΡΙΟ κλεὶς ἑτέρα πα[λαιά?];
presumably [κλεὶς τὸ] β[ο]υλευτηρίο,[3] κ.τ.λ.

L. 48. - - - παρὰ] Θεοδότο, παρὰ Τηλεμάχο.

Ll. 50–54. The *Editio Minor* gives quite a misleading idea of the
positions of the surviving letters in these lines, of which the correct version is as follows:

```
50-- -- 14 - - - - - τ α μ ι α ι s τ ῆ s θ ε ὸ ν ο μ ι σ μ α - - -
--7-- ε δ ọ . ạ ρ έ δ ο μ ε ν ἱ ε ρ ὸ ν ἀ ρ γ ύ ρ ι ο ν - - - -
-- - 10 - - - ε ἱ δ η ι κ α ὶ σ υ ν ά ρ χ ο σ ι  ν Χ Χ - - - - -
-- - - 13 - - - - - - α υ τ ο τ ο ῖ s ἀ π ο δ έ κ τ [α ι s - - -
-- -9 - - - ἱ ε ρ ὸ ἀ ρ γ υ ρ ί ο δ π α ρ έ δ [ο μ ε ν (?)
```

---

[1] I 32.   [2] For this form of the plural cf. II² 1440 B l. 57.

[3] Note that the engraver, instead of cutting a cross-bar to the Η, has joined
the right hasta of it to the Ρ.

In l. 51 it is tempting to read [Ἑκατομπ]έδρ [π]αρέδομεν, κ.τ.λ. As in l. 52 the seventh letter was apparently M, preceded by traces of H, and the last five letters of the name were obviously - ειδηι, the restoration must be clearly [. . . . Δ]ημ[οκλ]είδηι, and it is reasonable to identify this Demokleides with the man whose name is found in connexion with a list of envoys concerned with the alliance between Athens and Chios in *IG* II² 34 l. 37 (384/3 b.c.).[1] In l. 53 the restoration [ἐνι]αυτô is not confirmed by the traces on the stone, which suggest more definitely δι αὐτο, and before the *delta*, I seem to see Λ., which might be the end of - - ἐδοσ]α[ν. In l. 54 the vacant nine spaces would exactly and appropriately contain the word κεφάλαιον, but there are absolutely no traces of any letters preserved.

Even these additional readings do not enable us to restore any continuous sense in the passage, but there is nothing to impair Ferguson's interpretation of l. 53 as showing that the Tamiai had disbursed some of the sacred money to the Apodektai;[2] it is indeed confirmed, if we regard Demokleides and his colleagues as another party receiving a further payment from the same source, and the word κεφάλαιον in the last line becomes even more appropriate as summing up all the payments in cash by the Tamiai during this year.

Before leaving this document we may with advantage ask whether it sheds any fresh light on the dating of any of the other lists whose date is still uncertain, notably nos. 1412, 1413 and 1415. Ferguson is clearly right[3] in placing these three in the period between 384/3 and 374/3, the latter being the year of the first of the columnar lists (1421, etc.), and in recognising that 1415 should be put nearest to the end of the period. In fact there seems no objection to dating it to 375/4, since 377/6 and 376/5 are represented by 1410 and 1411 respectively, with neither of which can it be combined. The most striking features of 1412 and 1413, as Ferguson has pointed out,[4] are the abandonment of the ordered

---

[1] Kirchner *PA* 3476.

[2] *Op. cit.* 128 note 2; but in another place, p. 140 note 2, he is less confident, "we cannot tell whether it was expenditure, *epeteia*, or balance."

[3] *Op. cit.* 114 note 1, 180–184.   [4] *Ibid.*

arrangement seen in the greater part of 1497, and also the inter-polation in the midst of other votive objects of the lists of silver hydriai of various other deities, Nike, Demeter and Kore, the Anakes, etc., which are accessions of later date than 385/4, since there is no trace of them in our reconstructed stele. The occurrence in 1412 l. 17 of the unexplained phrase καὶ συ]νάρχοσι just before the entry of the first hydria seems to indicate a rubric relating to their original dedication, or perhaps rather their reception from some other body of officials, in which case we would naturally think of the ἐπιστάται τῶν πομπείων.[1] As this rubric is not found in the corresponding place in 1413, we may, *pace* Ferguson, suggest that 1412 is the earlier of these two, but we are no nearer to assign-ing an exact date to either. Nevertheless, in view of the plentiful evidence from earlier lists, to which West and I have drawn atten-tion,[2] that changes of arrangement are more likely to be found in the first year of a Panathenaic period, there are grounds for pro-posing that the addition of the other hydriai may have taken place in 382/1, and thus that 1412 might be tentatively assigned to that year. But this suggestion does not help us to understand either why the order in which these hydriai are entered varies extensively between these two lists, or why there is an equally great diver-gence between the objects inventoried before and after the hydriai in them, or, which is more intriguing still, why the logical and orderly system of 1407 was so completely abandoned within a few years.

It is almost equally surprising to see how complete a contrast in arrangement is presented by 1414, where, except for the recognis-able group of items from the Parthenon which we have restored in ll. 22–25, the list does not agree at all with either earlier or later Parthenon-inventories. No doubt there were numerous accessions which we cannot trace earlier than the year 385/4, and which dis-appeared again before the date when we can reconstruct an almost complete inventory from the columnar lists, such as the χιτων στύππινος (l. 26) and the dedication by the wife of Speuson (l. 27), but it is disappointing not to be able to trace elsewhere such a large

---

[1] Ferguson *op. cit.* 15, 108 note 1; and 180 *ad fin.* in reference to this rubric.

[2] *JHS* 1938, 72; Ferguson *op. cit.* 14, 118 note 1.

proportion of the items in 1414. And it is also to be regretted that we can do so little towards completing the list of the bronze objects, given in ll. 38–49, which presumably is our first record of the contents of the Chalkotheke.[1] It is at any rate of some interest to have established the fact that from 385/4 onwards the Treasurers of the Goddess are responsible for these objects, though we remain in ignorance as to where they had been kept, and how, if at all, they had been recorded before this date.

II. THE INVENTORY OF 341/0 B.C.

The inventories belonging to the second half of the fourth century are for the most part so fragmentary, and include so few to which an exact date can be assigned, that we cannot hope either to establish the full contents of the list for any single year, or to arrange the undated lists in even an approximate chronological order. Nevertheless, despite their incomplete form there is a good deal more that can be done in the matter of combining fragments and restoring their contents than appears at a first inspection. The difficulties of decipherment, due not only to the characteristic small lettering but also to the damaged surfaces of the stones and the not infrequent inaccuracies of the engravers no doubt help to explain why the published versions are seldom entirely satisfactory.

From this series I select for brief study *IG* II² 1455, of which the date (341/0) is fixed by the presence of the name of the Archon Theophrastos in line 4, at the head of the list of the incoming Tamiai. It consists of three fragments which Köhler originally published under separate numbers as *IG* II¹ 703, 704, and 705, though he ascribed them to the same list; and this attribution is followed by Kirchner in the *Editio Minor*, in spite of the doubts of Lehner,[2] who had not seen the stones. Not only is Kirchner correct, but actually fragment *a*, containing the names of the Tamiai and sixteen lines of one column of the inventory, joins with a perfect contact to fragment *c*, in such a way that *c* line 1 continues *a* line 16, though the nature of the break is such that a few letters, ranging from three to six, are lost at the point of con-

---

[1] Cf. Ferguson *op. cit.* 112.   [2] *Schatzverzeichnisse* 119.

tact. The following transcript shows the relation of the first five lines of *c* to the right hand edge of *a*.

a, l.15
```
- - - K H Φ I Ƨ o δ ω ρ o δ o κ ι
- - - T H I δ η μ o σ ι A I σ φ ρ    c, l. 1
- - T A M ι a ι o ι ε Γ I Θ ε μ ι
- - - A P χ ο ν τ ε Ƨ Δ A K T υ λ
- - κ ε φ a Λ η N E X Ω N Θ H ραι    ?
- - - χ a Λ K A Δ[Δ] Γ I I K P a ν
```

Moreover, since *c* preserves part of the right-hand edge of the stele (as is pointed out by Kirchner), we can calculate exactly how much is lost from the right-hand side of *a* in lines 1–6 which contain the heading running across the whole width of the stele, namely ten letters in ll. 1 and 2, nine in l. 3 and eight in ll. 4 and 5. L. 6 stops short some distance from the edge. Now that the position of the edge of the stele has been fixed, we may feel pretty sure that the column of inventory preserved is the third, as we have no parallel for a four-column stele in these *Traditiones*, and no certain example, till a much later date,[1] of one with two only. Moreover, the restoration of the preamble fits well with a length of line approximately equal to the width of three columns, set very close together and containing ca. 39 to 41 letters each. I have assumed that the lines of the heading contained 124 letters each; it can scarcely have had as few as 120, but certainty is not attainable.

The combination of *a* and *c* gives us thirty-four lines in all. Below *c*, at an uncertain distance, comes *b*, also complete on the right, and giving us thirty-two more lines. The shape of the fractured top of *b* shows that it must fall not less than six lines below *c*, but the interval may be considerably larger, and the contents do not help us to place it exactly. In addition to these three, there is another substantial fragment to be ascribed to this stele, belonging, as will be seen below, to the second column. This is published in the *Editio Minor* as no. 1444. The marble — Hymet-

---

[1] *IG* II² 1492 had apparently three columns on the front and two on the back: it would, I feel sure, repay further study. (Date 307/6–305/4.)

tian, blue in the fracture but weathered to buff on the dressed surfaces—is exactly similar to that of 1455; the thickness (o.124 m.; *Ed. Min.* incorrectly gives o.12 m. for both) is identical, and the writing has all the characteristics of style and of spacing both vertical and lateral seen in 1455. The surface has suffered a very similar degree of weathering, and the fractures at the sides run in an oblique direction resembling those of the other fragments, *a, b,* and *c.* Unlike them, however, it is not opisthographous, and must be presumed to have come from a place lower down on the stele than fragment *b,* of which the back is inscribed for its whole height. I will return later to the contents of the reverse face, for they are not so completely illegible as Kirchner indicates.[1] Meanwhile we may glance briefly at 1444, before turning to the restoration of our third column. It contains, in 34 lines, part of the inventory of silver vessels, most of which are familiar from earlier lists. First come the last eleven of the 27 silver hydriai of Athena, followed by those of Athena Nike, Artemis Brauronia, Demeter and Kore, Aphrodite, and the Anakes,[2] and then after three or four of uncertain ownership [3] we have *oinochoai,* two *chernibeia* and lastly three *pinakes.* It must be noted that the list of the hydriai shows several omissions, namely nos. 1 and 4 of Athena Nike, no. 3 of Artemis Brauronia, and no. 1 of the Anakes, and that many of those of Athena earlier in the list are described as leaky (ῥέοσα). This raises a difficulty which cannot be ignored, for in 1437 col. II ll. 43 ff., many of these hydriai are described as having been repaired (αὕτη καινή γέγονεν), and the original weight is given as well as that after the repairs were carried out, whereas in our list there is no mention of repairs, and where the weights can be recognised they seem to be the old ones. As 1437 is several years earlier than 1455 [4] it is not easy to explain this anomaly,

---

[1] *Lapis fuit opisthographus, sed quae in parte aversa fuerunt, in tribus fragmentis oblitterata sunt, nec iam dispiciuntur,* Kirchner *ad loc.*

[2] A certain restoration. For the full lists of these hydriai cf. 1425 ll. 182–5, 1437 col. II ll. 67–72.

[3] Probably the "new hydriai of Athena Polias"; cf. 1425 ll. 165–8.

[4] "1437 must fall after 350/49, but not many years later." E. Schweigert *Hesperia* VII 288.

but there seems to be some connexion between these repaired vessels and those missing from our list, since the two of Athena Nike (nos. 1 and 4), which it lacks, are the two described as repaired in 1437, as also is no. 1 of the Anakes, together with no. 3, but our list in 1444 is too much damaged to indicate whether no. 3 of this batch is also missing. On the other hand, whilst no. 3 of Brauronia is omitted from our list, it is no. 4 that is described as having been repaired in 1437. It looks, at any rate, as if some of the repaired hydriai had been moved, either to another place in the list, or possibly had been taken out of the custody of the Tamiai in the interval between the drawing up of the two lists. We can only hope that some further discovery may shed light on their history, which does not after all affect our immediate enquiry, namely, the place of 1444 in the stele. It is reasonable to assume that the list of the silver vessels followed that of the golden ones, as was the practice in the columnar records of the earlier series (374/3 B.C. onwards), and hardly less likely that those of bronze or silver plated with gold came in between these two categories. Moreover, when we see that in 1443 col. II ll. 154–165 (of 344/3 B.C.), the plated vessels follow directly after the golden ones, it would be strange if the order was altered in our list of three years later. We shall see frequently *infra* how close is the parallel between our third column and the third column of 1443, and it is reasonable to assume that if the latter were complete below we should find these silver vessels towards the end of col. II.

We may, however, go a stage further towards fixing the place of 1444 in our second column, again by means of a comparison with 1443. In column III of the latter we have the remains of a list of miscellaneous dedications, among which, in ll. 203–204 of the text (= l. 47 f. of the column) is an item correctly restored as [γραμματεῖ]|ον σε[σημασ]μένον ὑ[πὸ τῆς βουλῆς τῆς ἐξ Ἀρείου πάγου], which is identical with the first item in column III of 1455, and is followed in both lists by the ὄνυξ κατεαγώς, familiar in the Heka-tompedon lists from the very beginning of the fourth century.[1]

---

[1] 1388 B l. 62; 1400 l. 57 (restored). It is not described as broken in the former list, but this is added in 1415 l. 20 (375/4 B.C.: cf. *supra* p. 392).

This coincidence extends much further, as we shall see, and justi-
fies the view that the items recorded in the 9th–55th lines of 1443
col. III must have been included at the foot of col. II in 1455.
As the lines of 1443 contain on an average forty-two letters, these
objects, if entered in the same form in every instance, may have
occupied slightly more than 47 of the lines in 1455 col. II if, as
seems probable, they were shorter by one or two letters. The
difference is unimportant, but it may, I think, be reasonably
claimed that at least 48 lines were inscribed in column II after the
list of the silver vessels recorded in 1444. We may now reckon
approximately the minimum length of column II, as follows:
we saw above that $a + c$ gave us 34 lines, that at least six are lost
between c and b, which contains thirty-two; further that 1444
is not inscribed on the back, whereas b is, and so must be placed
after l. 72 of its column, and that as it contains 34 lines, and in
turn was followed by at least 48 to correspond to the contents of
1443 col. II ll. 9–55, we must allot at least 154 lines to the second
column of 1455. This implies that the first column was no shorter,
though we cannot safely conclude that this was true of the third.
There is no difficulty in accepting a stele of the height needed to
contain this number of lines, for its width was, as we have seen,
sufficient to contain lines of 124 letters in length in the heading,
where they are so spaced that twenty, plus one interval, measure
.168 m. laterally ($124 \times \frac{168}{20} = 1.042$ m.); allowing .02 m. for
margins, we obtain a stele 1.062 in width, and as the vertical spacing
of twenty lines plus one interval is apparently identical with the
lateral spacing, 154 lines would require a stele not less than 1.293
m. in height. This is not an improbable proportion of width to
height, but it is easy to believe that it may have been taller still,
possibly containing as many as 200 lines in each column, which
would give us approximately a proportion of height to width of
$1\frac{2}{3}$: 1.

We may now turn to the contents of the third column, in which,
as the result of prolonged study of the stone and of a squeeze,[1]

---

[1] I studied the stone itself in Athens in 1931 and the squeeze on many occasions
since that date.

I have managed to decipher a good deal more than is given in the version in the *Editio Minor*, as will be seen from the transcript that follows. Occasional eccentricities of spelling (cf. ll. 7, 16, 31) are kept.

[Τάδε ταμίαι οἱ ἐπὶ Νικομάχου ἄρχοντος - - - - ca. 53 - - - -]ατος
Φρεάρριος, Δημόφιλος Δημοκλε[..........]
[- - - - - - - - - - - - - - - οἷς ἐγραμμάτευε - - -]ιμάχου Ἐλευσίν(ιος), πα-
ραλαβόντες παρὰ [ταμιῶν τῶν ἐ-]
[πὶ Σωσιγένους ἄρχοντος - - - - - - ca. 66 - - - - - - - -]ος Αἰσχίνου
Περιθοίδο, Ἱεροφῶντος Σωκ[.........]
[- - - - - - - - - - - - - - - - - -'- - - - οἷς ἐγραμμάτευε - - - - -]ς, παρέδομεν
ταμίαις τοῖς ἐπὶ Θεοφράσ[του ἄρχον-]
5 [τος - - - - - - - - - - - - - - ca. 81 - - - - - - - - - Νι]κοστράτωι Νικιάδο Ἁλι-
μοσίωι, Μεναίω[ι.......]
[- - - - - - - - - - - - οἷς ἐγραμμάτευε - - - - -]ράτος Τρικορύσιος. (vacat)]

Col. III. Γραμματεῖον σησημασμένον ὑπὸ τῆς βολῆ[ς τῆς ἐξ Ἀ-]
ρέο πάγο· ὄνυξ κατεαγώς· φιάλη χαλκῆ, ἣν Κ[αλλίας Πλ-]
ωθεεὺς ἀνέθηκεν· σφ[ρ]αγίδιον ἐλεφάντιν[ον μικ-]
10 ρὸν δακτυλί[δ]ιον ἔχον· κρανίδ[ι]ον μικρὸν [ἐπίχρυ-]
σον ἀπὸ τοῦ βάθ[ρ]ο παρε[ι]ὰς [ο]ὐκ ἔχον· πρὸς τ[ῶι τοίχ-]
ωι τοῦτο πρόσκειται· φιάλιον χαλκὸν ἔλυτ[ρον οὐ-]
[κ] ἔχ[ο]ν· [στ]άχυς ἐπίχρυσος ὑπόχαλκος ὃν ἀ[νέθεσαν]
ο[ἱ] τ[αμί]αι οἱ ἐπὶ Κη[φι]σοδώρο· σφραγίδιον ἀργυρίω[ι δεδεμέ-]
15 ν[ο]ν ὃ [ἀν]έ[θε]σαν [ο]ἱ ταμίαι οἱ ἐπὶ Κηφισ[οδώρο· δοκι-]
μεῖα ἐν [κ]ιβωτίωι, σησαμασμένα τῆι [δημοσί]αι [σφρ-] = 1455 c, l. 1.
αγῖδι|.|·τάδε προσπαρέδοσαν ταμ[ίαι οἱ ἐ]πὶ Θ[εμι-]
στοκλέος Λεπτίνης καὶ οἱ συνάρ[χοντε]ς· δακτ[ύλι-]
ος χ[α]λκο[ῦς ὑπά[ρ]γυρος ἵππου κ[εφα]λ[ὴ]ν ἔχων· θη[ραι(?)-]
20 ο[ς κα]τ[ε]αγώ[ς]· κ[ρά]νη Γ· κραγ[ί]δι[α χα]λκᾶ Δ[Δ]ΓΙΙ· κρ[άν(?)-]
[η Δ(?)]ΓΙΙ· .... ΓΚ.ΟΜΛ.ΙΛ..Υ...[χα]λκᾶ· προκνημί[δων]
ϛ[ε]ύγη [Δ]ΔΙΙΤΙ..Ι.ϛευγ........ΔΙΙΙ· ἀσπίδες ἐπί[σ-]
[ημοι......ca. 16.......γράμμα]τα ἔχει Ἀθηναῖο[ι]
[.........ca. 17......ἀσπίδες ἐ]πίσημοι δράκον-
25 [τα ἔχουσαι - · ἀσπίδες ἐπίχαλκοι πομπικαὶ - -]Δ· ἀσπίδες ἐπίσημοι ΔΔΓ·
το[ύτ]ων
..........ca. 23........., μία δὲ ἐπίσημον οὐ[κ]

[ἔχει· ἀσπίδες ἐν τοῖς μετακι]ονίοις ἐπίχρυσοι [ὑ-]

[πόξυλοι . . . .· ἀσπίδες] ἐπίσημοι Δ Γ· ἀσπίδε[s]

[. . . .· μάχαιρα ὁλοσίδηρος τὸ] κολεὸν ἐλ[ε]φάντιν[ον]

30 [ἔχουσα· . . . . ca. 15 . . . . . .]· ἀσπὶς ἐπίχρυσος· κν[ημ-]

[ιδ . . . . ca. 18 . . . . . .] ἀνήθηκε πρὸς τῶι νε[ώι·]

[. . . . . ca. 14 . . . . . . ἀσπὶs ἐ]πίχρυσος ἐν τοῖ[s μετακ-]

[ιονίοις ἀσπίδες ἐκ Παν]αθηναίων τ[ῶ]ν μεγ[άλων.]

[- - - - - ca. 21 - - - - - -] Ο.Τ . . . . Λ - - - - - - - - -

Ll. 12–13. After φιάλιον χαλκὸν the next letters seem to have been ΕΛΥΤ . . . . . and at the start of l. 13 .ΕΧ.Ν, giving us ἐλυτ[ρον οὐ|κ] ἔχ[ο]ν. Then comes a six-letter word with the epithets ἐπίχρυσος ὑπόχαλκος, masculine, in view of the ὃν which follows, and as it apparently ended in ΑΧΥ⩽ we need not hesitate to restore [στ]άχυς. This is confirmed by 1443 III, l. 211, where the copy gives ⩽ΤΑ.⩽ΕΓ[Ι]ΧΡΥ⩽Ο[⩽].[1]

L. 14. Kirchner, following Köhler, reads ΟΤΑ . . . .⁽¹⁰⁾. . . . ΡΟ, but several of the letters in the gap are faintly visible, and obviously crowded, and enough can be read to ensure the restoration ο[ἱ] τ[αμί]αι οἱ ἐπὶ Κη[φι]σοδώρο. This crowding is due to the correction of an omission, apparently of the words ταμίαι οἱ, since the original incorrect version ὃν ἀ[νέθεσαν] | οἱ ἐπὶ Κηφισοδώρο will exactly fit into a stoichedon arrangement with the lines above and below. Here again we have the support of 1443 III, l. 212, which begins ι οἱ [ἐπὶ Κ]ηφ[ι](σ)[οδώρο, and the insertion of ἀνέθεσαν following ὃν at the end of l. 13 exactly fills the gap in 1443.

Ll. 17–20. After [σφρ] | αγῖδι there is room for three symbols before the word τάδε, and I suspect a number, either Γ[Ι]Ι or |[Ι]Ι, probably the former, as the first *hasta* visible is to left of centre, and there is room for a unit-sign between it and the last one of the group. The junction of a + c as described above leaves no doubt as to the completion of ll. 17–18, and in l. 19, where Kirchner prints only . . . .⁽⁹⁾. . . . Υ . . [ἀρ]γυρὸς Ι, I have deciphered ος χ . λκο . . ὑπά[ρ]γυρος ἵππου κ⫽⫽⫽, which combines with the letters λ[η]ν ἔχων on fragment c to give us δακτ[ύλι]ος χ[α]λκο[ῦς] ὑπά[ρ]-

---

[1] The spacing of the isolated letters in 1443 III betrays frequently an unskilled copyist.

γυρος ἵππου κ[εφα]λ[ὴ]ν ἔχων, an item not hitherto known elsewhere.

In 1443 we have δα̣(κ)τ[υ]λ[ι]ο - - - and κων for χων at the beginning of the next line, but the entry seems to have been longer by two letters; perhaps we should restore ἱππικήν. Then follows θή[ραι]ͅο[ς κα]τ[ε]αγώς, after which comes the first of several groups of helmets. For Kirchner's . . ΛΡΗΓ . . Λ . . Δ - - ⸦ΤΑ⸪[.]ΓΙͺ κρ . . read κ̣[ρά]νη Γ· κ̣ρα̣ν[ί]δι[α χα]λκ̣ᾶ Δ[Δ]ΓΙΙ· κρ[άν|η] κ.τ.λ. It would take us too long to consider whether some of these helmets can be traced in earlier lists,[1] as is very probable.

L. 21. After κρ[άν|η Δ(?)]ΓΙΙ comes a passage where little can be deciphered, and to which 1443 gives no clue as the corresponding letters are lost. I seem to see . Λ . ͺΓΗ. ΟΜ . . ΙΛ . Υ . . . . . ΛΚΑ. The Υ is in the wrong place for restoring ὑ[πόχα]λκα, but ⟨ς⟩[ε]ύ[γη . χα]λκᾶ seems quite possible, and if my Μ is an illusion the real reading may have been [π]α̣[ρ]α̣γν[α]θ⟨ί⟩[δω]ν̣, likely enough in the context, but too speculative without corroborative evidence.[2]

L. 22. For Kirchner's ὑχ υγιε . ΔΓ read clearly ς[ε]ύγη . ΔΓ, completing the previous line as προκνημί[δων], the Ν apparently added in the margin; apart from ςεύγ[η] towards the middle of the line I cannot complete the remainder. Here we part company with fragment *a*, and have a list of shields, extending over several lines, but it is impossible to restore the entries in full, though occasionally we get confirmation, or even a clue, from 1443.

L. 25, as stated above, is, as far as it is preserved, written in much smaller letters, presumably again rectifying an omission, and seems to have contained not less than sixty letters, instead of ca. 39. In the gap after [ἀσπίδες ἐ]πίσημοι δράκο[ν|τα ἔχουσαι -] we must insert [ἀσπίδες ἐπίχαλκοι πομπικαί(?)-]Δ, which are followed by ἀσπίδες ἐπίσημοι ΔΔΓ· τούτων, κ.τ.λ. Πομπικαὶ is suggested by [ἐπίχ]αλκοι πο - - in the corresponding entry in 1443 (l. 222), which however contained also some additional word about ten letters in

---

[1] E.g. κρανίδια ΔΓΙΙ in the Chalkotheke (1424a l. 134), possibly transferred and increased by ten, to appear in our list as ΔΔΓΙΙ (27).

[2] In 1461 l. 16 (not before 330/29 B.C.) we have παραγναθί[δες or -δων ςεύγη], but this does not prove that my suggestion is correct, especially as many changes in the order of the list had been made in the interval.

length for which 1455 has not room. After τούτων must have come a statement that all(?) of these had devices, with the single exception recorded.

In l. 27, where Kirchner gives ο . . οἷς? ἐπίχρυσοι[.], the first five letters preserved are plainly ονιοις and the restoration indicated is [ἔχει· ἀσπίδες ἐν τοῖς μετακι]ονίοις ἐπίχρυσοι [ὑ|πόξυλοι - -], for which the clue is supplied by 1461 l. 9, - - ς μετακιονιο - - which we can in turn restore to resemble our item in 1455. Μετακιόνια, which we should apparently restore again in l. 32 f., is the word used to describe the inter-columnar spaces in the Erechtheion building-record, IG I² 373 l. 252 (διαφάρχσαντι τὰ μετακιόνια), and in our stele it may be assumed to refer to the intercolumniations of the inner order of the "Hekatompedos Neos" of the Parthenon.

L. 29. Kirchner reads only - - - -.⁽¹¹⁾- - - - - - ον εχ . . Δ . . . ν . ., but the chi is clearly lambda, and the delta might be alpha, so we may read without hesitation ἐλ[εφ]ά[ντι]ν[ον], and closer study reveals traces of all the letters except the third and the last two. As, moreover, I have deciphered ΚΟΛΕ before the ΟΝ, we see that we have to deal with some weapon with an ivory sheath. Towards identifying it we get only . . . ΕΟ in 1443, presumably the remains of [κολ]εό[ν], but in 1461 ll. 6–7 we have - - - η· μάχαιρα ΟΛ | [- - - - κολ]εὸν ἔχουσα, and in 1481 ll. 5–6, [μάχαιρα ὁ]λοσίδη-ρ[ος - - -]τὸ κολειὸ[ν ἔχουσα]. Since in both these lists the μάχαιρα follows various groups of shields, it is extremely probable that we have the same item in each, and that we should restore ll. 28–30 of our stele as - - ἀσπίδε[ς] . . . · μάχαιρα ὁλοσίδηρος τὸ] κολεὸν ἐλ[ε] φάντιν[ον| ἔχουσα· - -⁽¹⁵⁾- -]ἀσπὶς ἐπίχρυσος.

In l. 31, the objects which someone ἀν⟨έ⟩θηκε πρὸς τῶι νε[ώι] seem to be the κνημίδες(?), of which the first two letters survive towards the end of l. 30. We again find this in 1443, identifying it from the letters [ἀνέθ]|ηκεν π[ρὸς - -] but it is not to be traced for certain elsewhere. Then comes, after a gap of thirteen letters, [ἀσπὶς ἐ]πίχρυσος ἐν τοῖ[ς - -] where again we may supply μετακιο-νίοις as in l. 27 above. The entry in 1443 raises a difficulty, for (if correctly copied) the epithet is in the plural — . οι ἐν τοῖς —, and certainly dedications of single shields are much rarer than of shields in groups, but whatever be the explanation of the divergence — whether an error of the engraver of 1455 or of the copyist of 1443 — I believe that the same object (or objects) is meant. L. 33. After the word Ἀθηναίων the squeeze seems to show τ[ῶ]ν μεγ, i.e. τ[ῶ]ν μεγ[άλων], and not T.IMO ....., (as Kirchner reads), for I am sure that the O is wrong, and E probable. This leads to the restoration [Παν]αθηναίων τ[ῶ]ν μεγ[άλων], and applies to shields dedicated after a celebration of the Great Panathenaea. For this we have two parallels in 1424a l. 130, ἀσπίδες ἐπίχαλκοι ἐκ Παναθηναίων ΔΙΙ (in the Chalkotheke), and l. 332, ἀσπίδες ἐκ Παναθηναίων ἐπίχαλκοι Δ (under the heading ἐκ τοῦ Παρθενῶνος), and as there is room for seven letters between the word μετακιονίοις and the words ἐκ Παν-, the insertion of ἀσπίδες is obvious. Moreover, it is not unlikely that the date of the festival was inserted here (τῶν ἐπὶ - - ἄρχοντος), in view of a suggestive entry in 1461 ll. 18–19, where we should, I think, read ἀσπίδες - - ἐκ Παναθηναί[ων τῶν μεγάλων τῶν ἐπὶ Ἀριστ]οφῶντος ἄρχο|[ντος - -]. This gives us a line of the required length, 34 letters, which is certainly correct, since 1461 is from the same stele, and apparently from lower down in the same column, as 1460, of which the line-length is established as 34 letters; and, of course, the year of Aristophon (330– 29) was a Great Panathenaic year.[1]

We may call attention in passing to a few improved readings in fragment *b* (retaining the numbering of the lines in the *Editio Minor*); note that the edge of the stone is incorrectly indicated for ll. 23–29, as there are two, or in some cases three, more letters on the right of those shown as ending these lines. L. 23, - - - - ιον [ἐ]τε[ρ]ον μα ..; l. 24, - - ε[s] περι[κεχρ]υσωμ[ένα]ι. L. 25, κε[κρύ-]| φαλος; l. 27,- - - - - καὶ δράκων (perhaps an ἐπίσημον ?).[2] Ll. 29–30, σφραγ[ὶs] περίχρυσο[s· χλι|δώνια δύο· χ]ρυσίδ[ι]α τ[ρί]α ὑπάργυρ[α] ... ΙΛ .... ΛΙΙ ·. L. 32, read [ἴνη· δακτύλι]ος ἀρ[γυρο]ῦs ἀπείρων,

---

[1] I suggested this combination of 1460 + 1461 in my paper at the Amsterdam Congress. I would add that an earlier entry in 1461 will permit of a similar restoration. Ll. 10–12 Kirchner reads [- -ο]χ ὑγιεῖς· δικασ|[ταὶ - - - - ἐ]πὶ Ἀρχίου ἄρχο-| [ντος - -]. But no similar dedication by δικασταί is known, and as the *kappa* is not certain, I would read [οὐ]χ ὑγιεῖς ΔΙΙ· ἀσ|[πίδες ἐκ Παναθηναίων τῶν ἐ]πὶ Ἀρχίου ἄρχο|[ντος] (340/39, again a Panathenaic year).

[2] I can make no sense of the letters preceding the καί.

χρυσίον Φωκαῖο||ν ἔχει·] i.e. a continuous silver ring with a gold Phocaean coin attached. This recurs in 1457 l. 5, where it is given as δ. ἀργ. ἀπείρων· χρυσίον Φωκαϊκόν· E.LIΔ^., but clearly we again have ἔ[χ]ει, followed by δα[κτυλι - -]: |||: καὶ χαλκοῦν:|:. As we require a neuter noun, I would restore δα[κτυ|λίδια ἀργυρᾶ]: |||: καὶ χαλκοῦν:|:, and this is the reading which fits what I have deciphered in *b* l. 11.[1]

It will have already been seen that wherever we can compare the contents of our two conjoined fragments with those of 1443 there is a very close resemblance both in the descriptions and in the order of arrangement. We might therefore expect that the lines lost after the end of *c* would agree with the contents (mostly scattered letters which defy restoration) of the ensuing lines of 1443.[2] It is to be noted that none of these fragmentary entries can be recognised as present in the opening lines of our fragment *b*, which would indicate that the gap separating it from *c* was perhaps longer than the minimum of six lines suggested above (p. 395). But this leads to a more pertinent query: since 1455 *a + c* so closely resemble 1443, did the latter include, lower down, the contents of 1455 *b*? There is little doubt that several lines are lost from the foot of 1443, as we saw above in regard to column II. But the contents of *b* definitely include property τῶν ἄλλων θεῶν, which ought not to appear in 1443 if the accepted view is correct that in the interval between the engraving of these two stelai (1443 in 344/3 and 1455 in 341/0) a change of administration had taken place, by which the Treasurers of the Other Gods had been again incorporated into one board with the "Treasurers of the Goddess." The date for this change is not exactly agreed upon: Kirchner would put it in 342/1 or the following year,[3] Ferguson in 342/1,[4] whilst Lehner, who was not convinced that our fragment *b* belonged to the stele, preferred to put it after 340,[5] ascribing it to the activities of Lycurgus, in about 338. As this last view is surely ruled

[1] [- - ἀ]ρ[γυρᾶ |||] καὶ χ[α]λκοῦν |· σφραγῖ|[δες - -].
[2] Kirchner omits these, but they will be found in *IG* II[1] 701.
[3] 1455, commentary.
[4] *Op. cit.* 117 note 2.
[5] *Schatzverzeichnisse* 119.

out by the dating of *b*, no date later than 341/0 can be tenable. On the other hand the evidence for dating the change to 342/1 or 341/0 is more slender than is generally realised, and must be briefly restated. Whilst fragment *b*, which contains various items belonging to "The Other Gods," shows that they had passed back into the hands of the Treasurers of the Goddess by 341/0, and so supplies a *terminus ante quem*, there is no direct mention of the former board after 357/6,[1] though, as Ferguson rightly points out, its existence is implied by the reference in Demosthenes' speech against Timocrates, for 352 B.C.[2] Within this interval, the crucial evidence is supposed to be furnished by II² 1454, a fragmentary list of exceptional type, of which the contents are given in the *Editio Minor* as follows:

[τάδε παρέδο]σαν τ[αμ]ίαι τῶ[ν ἄλλων θεῶν - -]
[. . . . . . ο]ἱ βουλευτ[αὶ] οἱ Ἀκ[αμαντίδος - - - -]
[. . . τῆς] βουλῆς ἐπὶ Πυθοδό[του ἄρχοντος - -].

From this it is assumed that the ταμίαι τῶν ἄλλων θεῶν were still in existence in the year of Pythodotos, 343/2. But (1) the length of line is quite uncertain, so we need not assume that the ταμίαι in l. 1 are those of that year, for these may be two quite distinct entries. (2) For τάδε it would be equally easy to restore a relative pronoun, making this sentence refer to some item described in the previous line, since the stone is *undique mutilum* and the *Editio Minor* conveys unintentionally the misleading impression that we have the beginning of the text preserved in l. 1; and (3) the restoration τῶ[ν ἄλλων θεῶν] is a conjecture, for which τῶ[ν τῆς θεοῦ] is, as Ferguson points out,[3] an equally possible alternative. On such slender evidence as this we ought not to state categorically that the Tamiai of the Other Gods were still existing in 343/2.

Until, therefore, some more convincing evidence is found, it seems preferable to argue from the similarity in the contents and style of arrangement of 1443 and 1455 that no change of régime had taken place in the interval between the years to which they

[1] Ferguson *loc. cit.*
[2] *Ibid.*
[3] *Loc. cit.*

respectively belong. Since a date after 341/o is excluded, as we have just shown, we must consider it possible, and in my opinion probable, that the fusion took place earlier than 344/3, to which conclusion other factors seem to point. In favour of dating the change to 346 three pieces of evidence may be adduced: (1) the passing of the decree, of which two copies have survived, *IG* II² 216 and 217, enacting that steps be taken to inspect and record the ἄγαλμα, the πομπεῖα, the στέφανοι καὶ τὰ ἄλλα τὰ ἐν τῆι Ἀκροπόλει; and it is possible, though not conclusive, that the use of the phrase τοὺς ταμίας τοὺς νέ[ους] in line 5 of 217 might imply a change of régime. (2) In favour of the new date suggested for the change is the altered style of the arrangement of the inventory, with its three columns of continuous text. As far as we know, 1443 is the earliest example of this style, and the latest of the earlier style of columnar list, in which each item begins with a fresh line, is 1441, which includes a crown dedicated in the year of Themistokles (347/6), and may very well belong to that year.[1] (3) It is much more likely than not that such a change took place in a Panathenaic year, a requirement which 346/5 fulfils. These considerations seem to reinforce each other in support of the new date suggested for this important change in the administration of the Treasurers of Athena and the Other Gods.

It remains to mention the contents of the reverse face which the *Editio Minor* describes as illegible. The writing is very small and faint, and in many places nothing at all can be seen, but near the top of *a* I have made out the following:

L. 1 .... λκους .ικρος ο.ρ.ν ο - - - -
.... χει .... οσυ .... ρο ... ΓΛ - -
ονω .. [χαλ]κοῦν μι[κρὸν - -]
ΔΔΔΓΙ θ[υ]μιατηριο ..... ο - -
L. 5   μ]ικρὸς ὑπόστατον κ[ρα]τῆρος χαλκο

This is sufficient to show us that we have a portion of the list of the contents of the Chalkotheke, for there can be little doubt that in l. 1 we have [ἵππος χα]λκοῦς [μ]ικρὸς ο[ὐ]ρ[ὰ]ν ο[ὐκ ἔχων], as

---

[1] There are no στέφανοι ἐπέτειοι for 346/5 at the end of the list of crowns, which suggests 347/6 as a more likely date than the following year.

in II² 120 l. 47 and 1440 l. 54 (restored). The θυμιατήριον and the ὑπόστατον κρατῆρος are very likely to be those in the same lists, ll. 50–51 and 55–56 respectively, in which case we may restore l. 4 θυμιατήριο[ν μέγα] ο[ὐχ ὑγιές]. But as the length of the lines is uncertain, further attempts at restoration would be unwise. If, moreover, the bronze horse without its tail is the first item, the order has been completely changed, since 1440 was engraved shortly before;[1] but it is also possible that the list of the Chalkotheke began on the obverse face and that some considerable number of items was included on it.[2] If so the order may not have been changed so extensively. Nothing continuous could be recognized on the reverse faces of *b* and *c*, and it is not worth trying to transcribe isolated letters, especially as the contents of *a* have been safely identified as contents of the Chalkotheke.[3]

---

[1] Its date may be 350/49 or just later.

[2] In 1440 there are ca. 700 letters (8 lines × 87) of bronze objects before the bronze horse.

[3] It might be possible to make out something more on the reverse of both *b* and *c*, but it would require infinitely more patience and stronger eye-sight than I can claim to possess; but I doubt if the labour would be adequately rewarded by the results.

THE DATE OF ISOCRATES' *AREOPAGITICUS* AND THE ATHENIAN OPPOSITION

By Werner Jaeger

FOR many centuries Isocrates was considered mainly as a great moralist and the author of the Demonicea, a paraenetic speech, which was probably a product of one of his pupils and certainly is not an authentic work of the Athenian rhetorician. It was widely read in schools in the late ancient period, as the papyrus finds have proved, during the Byzantine era, and even in the centuries following the revival of learning in Italy. It was the first work of the Isocratean corpus to be translated into the elegant Latin of the humanists in the 15th century, long before the first printed edition of the Greek speeches was published; and during the Middle Ages, it was the only part of the preserved collection of Isocrates' writings known to the occidental world by means of an earlier Latin translation. When, in the 19th century, with the awakening of the historical sense which is one of its main characteristics, the interest in Isocrates turned from the moral to the political side of his oratory, it was his Panhellenic ideal and its development from the *Panegyricus* (380) to the *Philippus* (346) which primarily attracted the attention of modern historians. But there is still another line of Isocrates' political thought which is no less significant and historically important, although in a different sense, than his persistent attempt to bring about the unification of the Greek city-states under the leadership of one or a few states by means of a common national war against the Persian empire: this second line is his criticism of his native Athenian state as it was during the period of decadence of both its classical democracy and its international position as a leading power of Greece. The two representative documents of that criticism are the speech *On Peace* and the *Areopagiticus*. It seems quite natural in a collection of essays, which, like the present one, are dedicated to one of the world's most eminent scholars in the field of Athenian history, to deal with Isocrates' politics from the

Athenian viewpoint rather than from the Panhellenic one, which has been discussed so often in recent times.

Turning from the bright visions of the Greek future as revealed in his Panhellenic manifestoes to the tragically gloomy reality of the present conditions pictured by the two speeches concerned with the decline of the Athenian state, we cannot fail to observe that the *Areopagiticus* and the oration *On Peace* are closely related to each other. Modern scholars have recognized this and connected both of them with the events and the end of the so-called Social War (357–355). Some of Isocrates' criticisms of the radicalism of Athenian demagogues, the degeneration of the people, the poor methods of Athenian warfare, and the financial disruption of the state occur in both speeches, though not at the same length. Thus they appear to be only two different aspects of one and the same tragedy, the *Areopagiticus* representing it from the viewpoint of internal politics, the speech *On Peace* from that of Athens' international position. The pessimistic resignation of the author seemed to be essentially the same in both speeches. At first sight this may seem true, but on closer consideration the pessimism of the speech *On Peace* appears to be more passive and negative, whereas that of the *Areopagiticus* is more active and culminates in a positive political and moral demand. This observation may pave the way to a more precise differentiation of the time when, and the situation for which, each of these speeches was written.

The *Areopagiticus* takes its name from the proposal set forth in it: to restore the political authority and the constitutional rights of the Areopagus as the supreme court of the Athenian state. Isocrates conceived it as a sort of counterbalance and control of the power of the masses. This view of the high importance and the political function of the Areopagus was shared, as is generally known, by other contemporaries. Aristotle, in his *Constitution of Athens*, represents the development of Athenian democracy as the history of the various attempts to break down the authority of the Areopagus during the 5th century. The philosopher derives the political degeneration of the Athenian state from the progressive elimination of the retarding influence of this august body. The moral power of the Areopagus was even greater than the political one. But Isocrates would rather insist on calling this moral paideia of the citizens under the watchful supervision of the Areopagus the very essence of a sound political life. As the head of a famous school, he was concerned with the problem of higher education, and rhetoric, as he understood it, meant political culture in the broadest sense based on strictly ethical norms. All his political speeches are models of that new education. They illustrate a "philosophy" which pretends to be useful for human life but, on the other hand, they do not make rhetoric a mere tool of the individual who knows how to make use of it to his own advantage. His speeches are dedicated to actual problems of the political community; they want to set up standards of political judgment and action suited to the needs of their time. The *Areopagiticus* is a fine example of this new Isocratean ideology which takes its place on the boundary line between theoretical education and practical politics.

The question as to when Isocrates published the *Areopagiticus* [1] has been discussed by scholars since the 16th century, when Hieronymus Wolf tried to fix the date of this oration in the footnotes of his learned edition.[2] His opinion that the speech was rather late and that Isocrates wrote it at the age of ninety was taken up by some of the later editors.[3] Modern scholars, who studied the question more thoroughly, have discussed this thesis repeatedly but, on the basis of a more detailed knowledge of the historical facts of the 4th century, they arrived at a different date. Wolf's attempt to date the *Areopagiticus* was indeed a very primitive and rough one. Isocrates mentions in §2 that there is peace at the present time, and in §9 he says that the Athenians

---

[1] I have outlined briefly my view on the present problem in my *Demosthenes: The Origin and Growth of his Policy* (Berkeley, 1938), Sather Classical Lectures, vol. XIII, pp. 50–52.

[2] Cf. his main edition of Isocrates of the year 1570, pp. 477 ff. The bibliographical material has been carefully collected by F. Kleine-Piening, *Quo tempore Isocratis orationes quae περὶ εἰρήνης et Ἀρεοπαγιτικός inscribuntur compositae sint*, Diss. Muenster (Paderborn, F. Schoeningh, 1930), p. 43.

[3] Auger, *Isocratis opera omnia*, II, p. 91. Bergman, *Isocratis Areopagiticus*, Lugduni Batavorum, 1819, p. 59 ff.

have lost all the cities in Thrace (τὰς πόλεις τὰς ἐπὶ Θρᾴκης). Wolf referred this to the cities of the Chalcidian League, the Χαλκιδεῖς ἐπὶ Θρᾴκης. Their destruction by Philip of Macedon followed the conquest of Olynthus (348). Wolf said he could think of no other event by which they were lost for Athens and therefore placed the date of the *Areopagiticus* after the peace of Philocrates in 346.[1] Modern scholars have objected that, if the speech were written after the catastrophe of Olynthus, the Macedonian danger should somehow have been mentioned or there should be an indication, at least, of the existence of the Macedonian problem. The *Philippus* shows that, after the peace of Philocrates, Isocrates was as much concerned with this problem as Demosthenes or Aeschines, even though he was looking for another solution of it. The *Areopagiticus*, however, knows only two urgent problems of Athenian foreign politics: the distrust of the Athenian allies and the enmity of the Persian king.[2] Neither problem was actual after the peace of Philocrates.

Most scholars of the 19th century, therefore, were inclined to think that the *Areopagiticus* was written at an earlier date.[3] Like

---

[1] Some scholars have argued that the *Areopagiticus* must be later than the *Antidosis* (353) because it is not quoted there, cf. Kleine-Piening, *loc. cit.*, p. 43. But the selection of specimens taken from his former speeches which Isocrates gives in the *Antidosis* does not pretend to be complete. He may have had good reason for not quoting, in a political self-defense, a speech which he had not even published without great hesitation since he was afraid it might be interpreted as a document of anti-democratic sentiment, cf. *Areop.* 56 ff. and this article p. 441 (cf. also p. 428). It was probably for similar reasons that he omitted the statesman Androtion in the long list of his famous pupils in the *Antidosis*, cf. my *Demosthenes*, p. 219. There he felt obliged to defend even Timotheus, whom he could not omit, against the reproach of having been a μισόδημος. Cf. *Antid.* 131 ff.

[2] *Areop.* 10.

[3] Cf. the complete survey of the literature in F. Kleine-Piening, *loc. cit.*, pp. 43–44. I do not reproduce his list and beg to refer the reader to his dissertation for bibliographical purposes even though I do not agree with the views of the author on the problem in question. Of the literature of the last years since 1930, the year in which Kleine-Piening's work appeared, I quote Arnaldo Momigliano, "Per la storia della pubblicistica sulla κοινὴ εἰρήνη nel IV secolo A. C." in: *Annali della R. Scuola Normale Superiore di Pisa*, Bologna, 1936, pp. 115–117, who also places the *Areopagiticus* shortly after the Social War, close to the parallel speech *On Peace*. Cf. the same author, *Filippo il Macedone*, Firenze, 1934, pp. 188–189.

Hieronymus Wolf, they took as their point of departure mainly the two passages of the speech where Isocrates mentions the present state of peace and the loss of the Thracian cities. But the peace preceding that of Philocrates seemed to fit in much better with the situation described by the orator in the first pages of his pamphlet. This was the peace which ended the Social War in 355. It sealed the doom of the second maritime confederacy of Athens, since it acknowledged the secession of her most important allies, Chios, Cos, Rhodes, and Byzantium, from the confederacy, and the loss of a large number of the other allies who had belonged to it at the time of its greatest expansion after the strategy of Timotheus. Isocrates mentions the almost immediate decline of the Athenian confederacy and the loss of the allies after the *strategia* of Timotheus,[1] and this was understood to refer to the secession of the allies in the Social War.

Consequently, the enmity of the Persian king, of which Isocrates speaks as the other permanent danger to Athenian politics, was interpreted to mean the friction with Persia during the Social War, caused by the alliance of the Athenian mercenary general, Chares, with the rebellious Persian satrap, Artabazos, and the military assistance given him by the Athenian army, which invaded Persian territory in Asia Minor in 355/4 and attacked the troops of the Persian king. Diodorus tells us that the king sent the Athenians a menacing ultimatum and that the peace between Athens and the allies, concluded in the same year, was the effect of the Persian threat to enter the Social War on the side of the allies against Athens.[2] At the end of the *Areopagiticus*, Isocrates points again, as he does in the introductory part where he pictures the present situation, to the hatred of the Athenian allies and the hostility of the Persian king as the two sources of danger, and mentions the letters sent by the king, [3] even though he does not disclose their contents. It is obvious, however, that they are not of a friendly nature. They therefore were identified by scholars with the ultimatum of Persia, which was the reaction to Chares' military interference in Asia Minor, in 355.

---

[1] *Areop.* 12.   [2] Diod. XVI 22. 2.   [3] *Areop.* 81.

Isocrates, moreover, speaks of more than 1,000 talents, which the Athenians had spent in vain for their mercenary armies. This, too, seemed to fit in with the situation after the Social War which had been conducted, like most of the Athenian wars during those decades, by mercenary forces.

There is one more allusion in the same passage of the speech (§§ 9–10) which furnishes most of our information about the historical background of the *Areopagiticus*: Isocrates complains that the Athenians had been compelled to rescue the friends of the Thebans, i.e., their most hated enemies, whereas they had lost their own allies. Thinking of the year 355/4 as the presumable date of the speech, modern commentators connected this with the defensive alliance of Athens with Messenia, which must have been concluded about this time.[1] The Messenian state was a product of Epaminondas' attempt to keep Sparta in permanent weakness by establishing a Theban protectorate over the two recently created anti-Spartan states in the Peloponnesus, the Messenians and the new democratic Arcadian state. Demosthenes, in his speech for the Megalopolitans, which was written a few years after the Social War, reports [2] that the Messenians had anticipated the possibility that their Theban protectors might become engaged in a war in Central Hellas and consequently might not be able to give them assistance against a Spartan attempt to reconquer Messenia. They therefore had entered an alliance with Athens, which obliged Athens to come to their help in case of a Spartan attack.

For all these reasons, most modern scholars have placed the *Areopagiticus* soon after the peace, of 355, i.e., the end of the Social War. There was only one thing in which the supporters of this chronology agreed with Hieronymus Wolf and his followers, who had adopted the later date after the peace of Philocrates in 346: they both took as their starting point the remark of Isocrates in §2 that Athens was enjoying peace at present. In this view modern commentators, who were mostly philologists, acquiesced. It was an historian who struck a note of dissension in this rare

---

[1] *Ausgewählte Reden des Isokrates* erklärt von Rauchenstein-Reinhardt, 5th ed., Berlin 1882, p. 122. Cf. Schaefer, *Demosthenes*, I², p. 511.

[2] Demosth. *Megal.* 8–9; cf. my *Demosthenes*, pp. 83 ff.

unanimity of opinion. Eduard Meyer wanted to place the *Areopagiticus* in the time not *after* but *during* the Social War, i.e., after the victory of Chares in Asia Minor over the Persian troops and after the letter of the Persian king threatening Athens with war, but before peace was restored.[1] Meyer did not give his reasons for this date, but he apparently did not take the words of §2 about the prevailing peace as seriously as did his predecessors. Miltner has advocated[2] Meyer's chronology by pointing out the fact that the very words about the present state of peace on which former scholars had unanimously based their conclusions were obviously qualified by the orator himself, who says that the Athenians are enjoying peace at present in and around their country (εἰρήνην δὲ καὶ τὰ περὶ τὴν χώραν ἀγούσης). From this Miltner concluded that in reality there was no peace but war outside of Attica, and he thought this date was confirmed by the remark of the proem that Athens was still controlling the sea. After the catastrophic outcome of the Social War, the situation of Athens and the power of her confederacy could not be pictured that way.

One can hardly agree with Miltner's somewhat artificial interpretation of the words of §2 about the present state of peace, by which he turns that statement into its contrary, a state of war which affects all the world except Attica. We know how the condition of Athens during the Social War would normally be described from the famous words[3] with which the general, Iphicrates, inveighed against his persecutor, the demagogue Aristophon, in the famous law suit against the generals who had commanded the navy at Embata: "What do you do, man, who persuade the city to consult about me instead of with me *while war surrounds us* (πολέμου περιεστῶτος)!" If that description of Athens' situation in those desperate years is correct, the *Areopagiticus* cannot have been written during the Social War, and Isocrates could not describe in it the present as a time of "peace around the country." [4]

---

[1] Cf. *Geschichte des Altertums*, V, pp. 493–494.
[2] Cf. *Mitteilungen des Vereines Klassischer Philologen in Wien* I (1924), p. 46.
[3] Plut. *Apophth.* (Iphicr. 4), 187 B.
[4] On the other hand, Miltner may be justified in feeling that the words εἰρήνην δὲ.

I agree, however, with Miltner and Eduard Meyer that the general picture of the political situation given by Isocrates at the outset of the speech does not fit with the conditions of the peace after the Social War. They could not possibly be described the way Isocrates does, even by the greatest optimist. The contrast of the bright picture painted in the proem as the view of the average Athenian with the actual conditions at the time after the war in which scholars wanted to place the oration had puzzled scholars like Sittl and Blass even before Eduard Meyer and Miltner. But instead of changing the chronology of the whole speech, they set forth the hazardous theory [1] that the only way out was to amputate the proem and to suppose that at least this part was written before the war, whereas the rest of the speech belonged to the time after the war.

The main difficulty in placing the speech is the ambiguity of the historical allusions which it contains. This ambiguity has become apparent only in the course of the successive attempts to identify those allusions with a specific historical situation. At first that situation seemed to be unmistakably clear, as is evident from the very words of the first scholar who tried to date the speech: Hieronymus Wolf said he could not think of any other event, by which the Athenians had lost the cities in Thrace, but Philip's conquest of Olynthus in 348.[2] Later scholars were quite as sure that the allusion to the loss of the allies was to be interpreted as the Social War, in which the Athenians lost other

---

καὶ τὰ περὶ τὴν χώραν ἀγούσης (scil. τῆς πόλεως) imply a certain restriction. Probably there was a sort of war farther removed from Athens when Isocrates wrote these words. But this description would fit much better the time before the Social War when the Athenians had declared war against Philip but did not display any military activity in the Northern Aegean.

[1] Sittl, *Geschichte der griechischen Literatur bis auf Alexander den Grossen* (Munich 1886) II, p. 113. Blass, *Geschichte der attischen Beredsamkeit* (Leipzig, 1892) II², p. 305, n. 2.

[2] Cf. Hieronymus Wolf, *loc. cit.*, p. 477: "Tamen urbium Thraciae amissionem nullam egoquidem aliam novi nisi eam cum Olyntho expugnata etiam caeterae in eius (Philippi) potestatem ceciderunt." But, again, on p. 480 Wolf seems to be afraid that he might be accused of δεινὴ ἀνιστορησία for he feels that he cannot really solve all the chronological difficulties which the speech offers.

important allies, and that the menacing "letters" of the Persian king, which Isocrates mentions,[1] were identical with the embassy sent by Artaxerxes Ochos shortly before the end of the Social War. As a matter of fact, the "cities on the Thracian coast," however we may interpret this phrase,[2] were lost several times. The cities of the Chalcidian League under the leadership of Olynthus, who had joined the second maritime confederacy a few years after it was established in 378, had seceded from it again after the peace of Sparta of 371, when the confederacy was still at the peak of its power.[3] Most of the cities of the Thracian coast were lost during the 'sixties of the fourth century, when the decline of the confederacy began, and only part of them were regained by Timotheus' campaign in the years 365–360 in the northern waters of the Aegean.[4] One might say that they were lost definitely when Philip of Macedon succeeded to the throne and seized Amphipolis and Pydna, and Olynthus, with the rest of the Chalcidian cities, entered an alliance with him against Athens, i.e., in 357, sometime before the outbreak of the Social War.[5] Thus the allusion to the loss of the Thracian cities fits more than one situation.

The allusion to a letter of the Persian king [6] is no more individual. It is true that he sent a threatening ultimatum [7] to put an end to the Social War in 355. But he had ended every Greek war during the 4th century by threatening letters. Isocrates does not even speak in the *Areopagiticus* of *one* letter which was sent in a special situation; he wants to characterize a permanent

---

[1] *Areop.* 81.
[2] *Areop.* 9 ἁπάσας μὲν τὰς πόλεις τὰς ἐπὶ Θράκης ἀπολωλεκότες.
[3] Beloch, *Griechische Geschichte* III I², pp. 195 ff.
[4] Cf. Beloch, *loc. cit.* Timotheus regained Methone and Pydna, but Amphipolis, Olynthus, and the cities of the Chalcidian League (Χαλκιδεῖς ἐπὶ Θράκης), with the exception of Torone and Potidaea, remained independent.
[5] Cf. my *Demosthenes*, p. 112 and the new inscription of the treaty of alliance between Philip and Olynthus: D. M. Robinson *T.A.P.A.* LXV (1935) 103 ff.
[6] *Areop.* 81 ὡς δὲ βασιλεὺς ἔχει πρὸς ἡμᾶς, ἐκ τῶν ἐπιστολῶν ὧν ἔπεμψεν ἐδήλωσεν.
[7] I do not insist on the fact that Diod. XVI 22. 2 does not speak of a *letter* at all but of the *embassy* which the king sent to Athens in 355. Such embassies used to bring with them a written message with the seal of the king, as we learn from Xen. *Hell.* V 1. 30–31 and VII 1. 36–39.

state of Athenian weakness that extends over a long period of
gradually decreasing power and, therefore, speaks of the "letters"
of the Persian king (in the plural) as typical indications of that
state of Athenian weakness with regard to the barbarians.[1] The
weakness of the "present" time is contrasted with the period of
Athenian power after the Persian wars of the 5th century, when
the Persians did not dare to interfere with Greek affairs, as early
as in the *Panegyricus* (380), i.e., 25 years before the Social War.[2]
Not only the peace of Antalcidas (386) but also the peace treaties
of Sparta in 374 and 371 were concluded with Persian interference, and in 366 the king had sent a letter to Athens, menacing
them with war if they did not accept his peace dictate at once.[3]

[1] *Areop.* 81.

[2] Cf. p. 437 n. 3 about the more typical character of Isocrates' picture of Athens'
weakness in the present period and the parallel passage of the *Panegyricus.*

[3] Persian embassies who presented letters from the king: at peace of Antalcidas
(386) cf. Xen. *Hell.* V 1. 31; at peace of Sparta (374) Diod. XV 38. 1; at peace
of Sparta (371) Diod. XV 50. 4; at the peace conference in Susa (366) a letter of
the king was sent through the Greek ambassadors who were present at Susa, cf.
Xen. *Hell.* VII 1. 36 ff. Isocrates speaks in *Areop.* 81 of the "letters of the king"
as a sign that the Athenians are no longer the protectors of Hellas as they had
been after the Persian wars. The "letters of the king" must be those which concerned the so-called κοινὴ εἰρήνη of which Persia had become the guarantor. Isocrates does not speak, by the way, of letters which the king had just sent to the
Athenians but only of letters which he had sent in the past, and supposes they
are known to everyone. This phrase obviously includes all the famous ἐπιστολαὶ
βασιλέως from the peace of Antalcidas up to the present time, regardless of whether
they were addressed expressly to the Athenians or to all the Greeks, for they all
proved that the Athenians were no longer the protectors of the liberty of Greece.
These letters even forced the Athenians to recognize that the Greek cities in Asia
were now the slaves of the barbarians.

The only other scholar who has come to the conclusion that the identification of
the "letters of the king" *Areop.* 81 with the ultimatum after Chares' victory in 355
cannot be maintained seems to be A. Momigliano in his article on the κοινὴ εἰρήνη
in the 4th century: *Annali della R. Scuola Superiore di Pisa*, Bologna 1936, p. 116.
This is all the more interesting since he still clings to the time after the Social War
as the probable date of the *Areopagiticus.* He therefore thinks of a letter sent
by the king during the tension of Athenian relations with Persia after the Social
War which Demosthenes describes in his speech *On the Symmories*, but we do not
hear of any embassy or letter of the king at that time. The excitement in Athens
was caused by the mere rumor of huge military preparations of the king for an

The most individual feature of the situation, as described by Isocrates in the *Areopagiticus*, seemed to be the loss of Athens' allies, for it seemed to point to the dissolution of the confederacy in the Social War. But, as a matter of fact, the words of Isocrates, in which he mentions this event,[1] are by no means an unmistakable description of a specific situation, for he does not say of which allies he is thinking. Allies had seceded from the confederacy ever since Euboea and the Chalcidian cities broke away from it about 370. There was a gradual secession of allies from Athens during the 'sixties of the 4th century and at the beginning of the 'fifties, long before the Social War started. Consequently, the statement about the loss of the allies, which scholars have made the basis of their attempt to identify the historical situation of the speech, is much too commonplace to justify any such conclusion.

Moreover, not only does this allusion fit in just as well with several other situations but it even seems rather improbable that Isocrates should have mentioned the events of the Social War in such a manner. Would he have passed in silence the all-important fact of the rebellion of Chios, Cos, Rhodes, and their alliance with Byzantium (a city which had seceded from the confederacy even before the war), if the *Areopagiticus* was written after the beginning of the Social War or after the end of it? In the speech *On Peace*, which was written after the secession of these powerful allies, they are named explicitly, as everybody would expect.[2] Why does Isocrates, in the *Areopagiticus*, mention explicitly [3] only the secession of the Thracian cities which had happened before the Social War if, in the meantime, the secession of Athens' main allies had become a fact, an event which was so much more important?

But after closer consideration, the identification of the lost allies in §10 with the rebellion of those most powerful Athenian allies in the Social War becomes still more doubtful. Isocrates counts

---

unknown purpose. I cannot agree with this explanation for the reasons mentioned above, but Momigliano has paved the way for a real understanding of the "letters of the king" by his analysis of the problem of the κοινὴ εἰρήνη in the 4th century.

[1] *Areop.* 10.
[2] *De Pace* 16.
[3] *Areop.* 9.

up some of the less favorable aspects of the seemingly bright situation of the present time: We have lost the cities on the Thracian coast. We have spent more than 1,000 talents in vain for our mercenaries. We are unpopular with the rest of the Greeks and we are considered as enemies by the barbarians. We have been compelled to rescue the friends of our enemies, whereas we have lost our own allies.[1] The sentence structure of the last statement, which is divided into two cola, contrasted with μέν and δέ, is typically Isocratean, and it is more than doubtful whether the second colon ("whereas we have lost our own allies") is meant to add a new fact at all. Obviously Isocrates wants to say that it is the height of irony that the Athenians had to come to the assistance of the allies of their enemies, whereas they could not keep their own allies (as he had said before, when he mentioned the loss of the cities on the Thracian coast). The loss of the allies is mentioned here again only for the sake of the antithesis, as it is so often the case in Isocrates' antithetic and rhetorical style; it is unthinkable that he should have introduced the most important of all the facts, which he counts up, in such a casual manner if he meant the Social War.[2] The next sentence confirms clearly that the part of the preceding sentence which really matters is not the loss of the allies, but the paradoxical fact that the Athenians were compelled to rescue the allies of their enemies, for he goes on: "and in honor of such deeds we have already twice given thanks to the gods." This they certainly had not done because they had

---

[1] *Areop.* 10 ἔτι δὲ τοὺς μὲν Θηβαίων φίλους σώζειν ἠναγκασμένοι τοὺς δ'ἡμετέρους αὐτῶν συμμάχους ἀπολωλεκότες (cf. 9, ἁπάσας μὲν τὰς πόλεις τὰς ἐπὶ Θράκης ἀπολωλεκότες).

[2] In ordinary non-antithetic prose the sentence would read: "And we who were not even able to keep our own allies (see above §9) were compelled (by our silly alliance policies) to come to the assistance of the allies of our enemies!" In other words, the second part of the sentence with δέ has only the syntactic value of a relative clause. The fact that the Athenians had lost (part of) their own allies which was mentioned before in §9 is mentioned here again in a somewhat generalized form only for the sake of the rhetorical antithesis in order to make even more evident the silliness of a policy which compelled them to rescue the allies of their enemies. That Isocrates only wants to remind the reader of the loss of the Thracian cities which he had mentioned before as the most striking one of this kind is apparent also from the verb ἀπολωλεκότες which he repeats here from §9 (see above n. 1).

lost their allies, but in order to celebrate the victories won by Athenian troops in rescuing the allies of their enemies. Last, but not least, the rhetorical analysis of the sentence structure makes it clear that the generality of the statement, "whereas we have lost our own allies," which has induced scholars to think of the final secession of the Athenian allies in the Social War, is conditioned by the generality of the preceding clause, "we have been compelled to rescue the friends of our enemies." No one will conclude from the rhetorical exaggeration of this general statement that the Athenians have rescued *all* the allies of their enemies; but this had evidently happened twice, since the Athenians have given thanks to the gods twice for such paradoxical victories. Consequently, the generality of the antithesis, "whereas we have lost our own allies," must not be taken any more seriously. We cannot infer from it that Isocrates could speak thus only after Athens had lost *all* of her allies. Incidentally, this did not happen even after the lost Social War.

The critical examination of all the statements in the *Areopagiticus*, which point to historical events and on which modern scholars have based their conclusions, should have made it clear that it is wrong to pick out of the context of the speech some isolated historical data and to refer them to a specific situation without taking into account the general picture of the situation, as represented in the rest of the speech.

For historical thinking, it seems to be more suitable to go in the opposite direction and to ask first which historical situation agrees best with the one painted in the oration, and then to see whether or not the historical details mentioned in the speech confirm the hypothesis. Eduard Meyer and Miltner have tried to do this and, therefore, objected to the traditional chronology which places the speech after the Social War. But their suggestion is not possible, as we have seen above, because of their misinterpretation of the words εἰρήνην δὲ . . . ἀγούσης.[1] It seems most natural then, if the speech fits neither the time after the war nor during the war, to attribute it to the period of peace preceding the Social War, and we have to ask ourselves whether this time fits any

---

[1] Cf. *Areop.* 2 and this article, p. 415 ff.

better the situation pictured by Isocrates throughout the whole speech and especially the condensed description in the introductory part of the conditions as they were.

At the outset of the speech, Isocrates apologizes, as is fitting for a good proem, for coming forward with a proposal aimed at the salvation of the Athenian state in a situation which, to the average citizen and politician, must appear to be a condition of great power and complete security for their city. He tries first to look upon the situation with the eyes of the majority of the Athenian people, who, Isocrates tells us, are rather optimistic about the political prospects of their country in the near future. He presumes that no one will understand why he should be concerned about the future since everything is running smoothly and there seems to be no real danger which Athens might fear. She has more than 200 warships to defend herself against any attack from the outside; she is enjoying peace all around her country; she rules the sea; she has many allies who are ready to come to her assistance if need be, and many more allies to pay their taxes and to obey her orders. For all these reasons, Isocrates says, an optimist might think it natural to have confidence and to believe that the Athenians are far from danger, and that her enemies must fear her and be concerned about their own salvation. Isocrates, therefore, is afraid that the Athenians may despise the advice which he is going to give them because they are confident that they will be able to coerce all Hellas by their present power.[1]

It is true, of course, that Isocrates himself holds a view very different from this sanguine optimism, for the reasons which he will set forth in his speech. The symptoms of weakness which he discovers in the present state of affairs are, in fact, disquieting for an introspective mind. But the rôle of the warner, which Isocrates assumes in the *Areopagiticus*, would lose much of its dramatic effect if the danger to which he points were so obvious that even a simple mind could see it without his guidance. Indeed, after the catastrophic outcome of the Social War and even during the war, after the lost battle of Embata, where Eduard Meyer and Miltner

---

[1] *Areop.* 1–3.

want to place the speech, the general optimism depicted by Isocrates in §§1-2 would be unthinkable; and what we know from contemporary sources about the mood in which the Athenians found themselves in those years does not entitle us to suppose that Isocrates could have described it in terms similar to those used in this speech. It would have been impossible then for an Athenian to pretend that Athens was ruling the seas and that she had a large number of allies who would come to her assistance if need be with all their power, military and financial. The Social War had reduced the confederacy to a very small number of unimportant islands which made up about a third of the territory which it had dominated in better times.[1] The distinction between allies who, in the event of war, would willingly come to Athens' assistance and a second group of allies who would be glad to pay their contributions and to obey the orders of Athens appears to be identical with the two classes of allies mentioned by Thucydides.[2] Only a few allied states had preserved their right to have an independent navy and lend military support to the Athenians in case of war. The majority were only tax-paying members of the confederacy and had no ships of their own. It is difficult to see who were the many allies who would have come to Athens' assistance with military contingents or ships of their own after or during the Social War, for the only important ally of this category was Chios, and this island had seceded from Athens at that time.[3]

[1] The territory of the confederacy was reduced by the Social War to less than a third of its original extent (from 20,000 qkm. to 6,500 qkm.: cf. Beloch, *op. cit.* III 2², p. 165). Demosthenes, *Cor.* 234 describes the weakness of Athens after the Social War when he began his political career in the following way: δύναμιν ... εἶχεν ἡ πόλις τοὺς νησιώτας, οὐχ ἅπαντας ἀλλὰ τοὺς ἀσθενεστάτους· οὔτε γὰρ Χῖος οὔτε Ῥόδος οὔτε Κέρκυρα μεθ' ἡμῶν ἦν. χρημάτων δὲ σύνταξιν εἰς πέντε καὶ τετταράκοντα τάλαντα, καὶ ταῦτ' ἦν προεξειλεγμένα ... ὃ δὲ πάντων καὶ φοβερώτατον ... οὗτοι παρεσκευάκεσαν τοὺς περιχώρους πάντας ἔχθρας ἢ φιλίας ἐγγυτέρω, Μεγαρέας, Θηβαίους, Εὐβοᾶς.

[2] *Areop.* 2; cf. Thuc. VI 85, VII 57.

[3] Thuc. VI 85. 2 mentions only Chios and Methymna as the allies who under the first confederacy assisted Athens with ships of their own. Χίους μὲν καὶ Μηθυμναίους νεῶν παροκωχῇ αὐτονόμους, τοὺς δὲ πολλοὺς χρημάτων βιαιότερον φορᾷ, ἄλλους δὲ καὶ πάνυ ἐλευθέρως ξυμμαχοῦντας. Cf. VII 57. 3 τῶν δὲ ἄλλων οἱ μὲν ὑπήκοοι, οἱ δ' ἀπὸ ξυμμαχίας αὐτόνομοι; 57. 4 τούτων Χῖοι οὐχ ὑποτελεῖς ὄντες φόρου, ναῦς δὲ

Isocrates' description of the confederacy fits in only with the time preceding the Social War when at least the appearance of a powerful confederacy still existed. At that time an optimist might still overestimate the fear of Athens' enemies and the devotion of her allies to the common cause. Isocrates, in his speech *On Peace* which was published at the end of the Social War, and Xenophon, in his essay *On Revenues* written soon after that war, both suppose that Athens has lost her domination of the sea and discuss the problem of whether or not she ought to regain it.[1] They both strongly advise the Athenians not to make any such attempt, and indeed at that time the majority of the people were convinced that it was impossible to do so. They were so far from aspiring to the domination of the seas that they did not even dare to interfere on single occasions, which offered them a chance of partly reconstructing the dissolved confederacy.[2]

We know from the speech *On Peace* that the events of the Social War and the disruption of the second maritime confederacy, which had been built up largely by the efforts of his friend and pupil, Timotheus, made a tremendous impression on Isocrates' mind. We cannot answer the question as to how the *Areopagiticus* fits the situation about the end of or after that war without examining carefully the relationship of the *Areopagiticus* to the speech

---

πάρεχοντες αὐτόνομοι ξυνείποντο; 57. 5 Μηθυμναῖοι μὲν ναυσὶ καὶ οὐ φόρῳ ὑπήκοοι. Thus there was still a difference between the Chians and the Methymnaeans as to the degree of their independence. Only the Chians were autonomous, the Methymnaeans were not in spite of the fact that they had their own ships. About the second confederacy we have no special information on this point, but Isocr. *Areop.* 2 proves that the same distinction of two categories of allies still existed at that time.

[1] *De Pace* 69. Xen. *De Vectig.* 5, 5.

[2] Even Demosthenes advocated a policy of peace and non-intervention in his speech *On the Symmories* which he delivered soon after the Social War and in doing so won the support of the majority of the Athenian people as he tells us *Rhod.* 6. Only a small group of adventurers, Aristophon, Chares, and their followers, dreamed of restoring the lost ἀρχή and their own lost reputation by planning a "national war" against Persia, as suggested by Isocrates in his *Panegyricus* twenty-five years before. But neither Isocrates nor the majority of the Athenians believed any longer in such a possibility at that time and the young Demosthenes ridicules the project because there is no money and no navy at present.

On Peace. Already during the war Isocrates must have arrived at the conviction that Athens had irrevocably lost the command of the sea, which she had obtained during the period of her greatest power after the Persian Wars and which she had tried to rebuild with surprising success after the Peloponnesian War under the second maritime confederacy. Isocrates there argues that it is not enough to make peace with the allies who have seceded from Athens, and to give them up definitely.[1] Athens cannot recover, and she will never enjoy real peace if she does not resign, once and for all, her historical ambition to rule the sea. For this is the cause of all her troubles and Isocrates therefore wants to prove that this domination (ἡ ἀρχὴ ἡ κατὰ θάλατταν) is neither just nor possible nor useful.[2] As long as the Lacedaemonians maintained that rule over the Greeks, he says, the Athenians unceasingly complained about the injustice of the tyranny of one city over all the others, and advocated the principle of autonomy of the single states.[3] But under the present conditions the Athenians would not even be able to regain their former position, for how could they, in their present poverty, gain a domination which they were not able to

[1] *De Pace* 16; 25 ff.; 29; 64. The speech *On Peace* is placed by most scholars either during or immediately after the Social War. The conclusion of Kleine-Piening, *op. cit.*, 17 ff., that it must have been written early in the war because it does not mention the battle of Embata (356) does not convince me. Isocrates would not have set up this program of resignation as long as his admired friend and pupil Timotheus still was the commander of the Athenian navy and the ardent hopes of all patriots were with him and his "Tyche." This speech is based on the literary fiction that Isocrates delivers it in the assembly in the presence of the ambassadors of the rebellious allies who are offering peace. This would have been out of place at a time when the Athenians were preparing for the great offensive by which they were sure to smash the coalition of their former allies. The speech apparently belongs to the time when peace negotiations were actually taking place or even shortly after the war when the general situation was being discussed. The speech is concerned not so much with the problem whether or not the Athenians should make peace, as with the question of the nature of that peace, i.e., the problem whether they ought to continue the imperialistic policies of the second confederacy which had caused the downfall of the Athenian empire or adopt a new course. The resignation which Isocrates advocates would not have been possible before the downfall of Timotheus after the battle of Embata.

[2] δίκαιον *De Pace* 67, δυνατόν 69, συμφέρον 74.

[3] *De Pace* 67.

preserve even at the time of their greatest financial power. This is all the more impossible since the Athenians do not possess the character any longer through which they won that domination, but only the qualities through which they lost it.[1] He teaches his fellow-citizens that the ambition to rule an empire is not essentially different either with a democracy or with the tyranny of one man alone, which they pretend to hate.[2] Playing with the Greek word for domination, which at the same time means "beginning," Isocrates says that the ἀρχή of the sea became for the Athenians the ἀρχή of all evils, since power is the worst of all educators.[3] Making a somewhat artificial distinction, he contrasts domination (ἀρχή) and hegemony, and since he does not want to discourage entirely the hopes of those patriots who cannot forget the old glory of Athens, the queen of the sea, he suggests, instead of a domination based on mere power, a hegemony, which ought to be founded on the confidence and friendship of the other states.[4] He compares this sort of dignity with the authoritative position which the Spartan kings admittedly hold in their country under a constitution which does not give them any material power whatever. If such a moral authority is possible among individuals within a state, why should it not be possible among individual states within a community of free nations?

How far all this is from the ideas which Isocrates had expressed in his *Panegyricus* a quarter of a century ago! He had written that famous speech in order to prove the historical and moral right of Athens, the greatest spiritual power in Hellas, to share with Sparta the domination of Greece. The natural part of Athens in Greek history, according to that program, was the domination of the sea, which she had lost in the Peloponnesian War and which all Athenian patriots ardently hoped to restore in the near future.[5]

---

[1] *De Pace* 69.
[2] *De Pace* 115.
[3] *De Pace* 101 (cf. 77).
[4] *De Pace* 142 ff.
[5] Whereas in *De Pace* 16 Isocrates advises the Athenians to return to the peace of Antalcidas which guaranteed the autonomy of the single states, he had argued *Paneg.* 115 that the much hated ἀρχή of the Athenians in the 5th century was much better than the so-called autonomy of the present peace, i.e. that of Antalcidas.

This was written at the time when the second maritime confed-eracy was morally and intellectually prepared. Only the tragic experiences of the history of that second confederacy during its later phase could bring about a change of mind as radical as the transition of Isocrates' political thought from the high pretensions of the *Panegyricus* to the absolute resignation of the speech *On Peace*. It is therefore interesting to ask which attitude Isocrates adopts in the *Areopagiticus* with regard to the problem of the domination of the sea, with which he deals in the *Panegyricus* and the speech *On Peace* in such a different way. If the *Areopagiticus* were written after the Social War and after the speech *On Peace*, as is now generally assumed, we should expect him to have kept in line with the program of resignation, which he had set forth with so much moral emphasis a short time before in the speech *On Peace*. Even in his *Panathenaicus*, the last product of Isocrates' political speculation, which he published a few years before his death, he did not return to the old dream of Athenian domination although his subject was a last glorification of his native city, which pro-vided him with ample opportunity to voice similar ideals. But after he had written his *Philippus* (346), in which he had offered the king of Macedonia the historical rôle originally destined for Athens and Sparta, he could hardly change the position which he had taken in the speech *On Peace*. The *Areopagiticus*, however, does not yet show any trace of a definite liquidation of the Athe-nian demand for domination. This fact, which has been entirely neglected in the discussion about the chronology of this speech, places it unmistakably in a time when the pretense of Athenian imperialism still existed and the will to dominate the seas was still unbroken.

In the *Areopagiticus* Isocrates tells us that the optimistic view of the majority of the Athenian people is founded on the fact that they possess a strong navy, a powerful confederacy, and that they com-mand the sea. He uses there the same word ἀρχή, which he re-jects in the speech *On Peace* as a false ideal and a tyrannic ambition. One might object that the characterization of Athenian power which he gives in this passage (§§1 and 2) of the *Areopagiticus* is not Isocrates' own view but that of foolish optimists who do not see the dangers of the present situation. But modern scholars have overemphasized the folly of those optimists in thinking that they still believed that Athens held the command of the sea after she had actually lost it. It is easy to show that in the *Areopagiticus* not only the optimists, of whom Isocrates speaks at the outset of the oration, but also Isocrates himself still clings to the ideal that Athens should rule the sea. In §§62 ff., he praises the Athenian democracy in order to show his democratic conviction and, since he cannot praise without restriction the present form of democracy, which he wants to improve, he compares it with the rule of the thirty tyrants after the Peloponnesian War. For such a comparison makes the present regime appear as a paradise despite its weaknesses. After the defeat of Aegospotami, the democrats in Athens were ready to sacrifice everything to avoid the Spartan dictates, and thought it unbearable to see the city that had ruled the Greeks fall under the domination of others. But the oligarchs readily tore down the walls and bore serfdom. As long as the people were in power, we guarded the acropolises of the other cities, but after the Thirty took over the government, our enemies guarded the acropolis of Athens. At that time the Lacedaemonians were our masters, but after the democrats returned and dared to fight for our liberty and Conon won the sea battle at Cnidus, ambassadors came from Sparta and offered us the domination of the sea. Everyone knows that it was democracy which decorated the city with public buildings, sacred and profane, so many that even now every visitor thinks our city to be worthy to rule not only all the Greeks but also the rest of the world, whereas the thirty oligarchs neglected and robbed and destroyed her and wasted her riches. At the end of this long comparison (§69) Isocrates sums up his thesis. In a word, the basic difference of their views is this. The oligarchs thought it right to dominate their fellow-citizens, and to obey the enemies; the democrats, however, wanted to dominate the other Greeks, but they were willing to share equally with their own citizens. This then is Isocrates' ideal in the *Areopagiticus*. The entire speech is dedicated, as we have seen, to proving the thesis that, in order to maintain her predominant position abroad, Athens ought to restrict the extreme liberties of her present democracy, because she would not be able to preserve that power for a long time if the radical elements within the state continued to determine its course. But this conservative policy is still far from the mere resignation of the speech *On Peace* at which Isocrates arrived through the experience of the Social War. On the contrary, in the *Areopagiticus* it is still the main merit of democracy that it has proved so closely connected with Athenian domination in Hellas. This is not only a memory of a glorious past, but Athens there appears as still worthy (ἔτι καὶ νῦν) of that political predominance,[1] and Isocrates does not distinguish domination and hegemony, as in the speech *On Peace* where he condemns domination, but unhesitatingly speaks of domination (ἀρχή) over the other Greeks as a supreme ideal, as he had done in the *Panegyricus*.[2] The *Areopagiticus* falls between the *Panegyricus* and the speech *On Peace*.

It now becomes clear that Isocrates' attitude in the *Areopagiticus* with regard to Athenian imperialism, i.e., the policies of the second maritime confederacy, does not differ from the views of the foolish optimists which he attacks in §§1 and 2 in that he considers Athenian domination either unethical or impossible to retain. He differs radically from them only in that he believes that it cannot be retained without a reorientation of the course of action in a more conservative sense and the restoration of the Areopagus as the highest juridical and moral authority in the state. He thus sees the future of Athens' empire and of the confederacy tied up with the problem of the inner structure of the state. This had been the conviction of the conservative elements of Athens for a long time. But, whereas these circles were led to believe, by the experience of the downfall of the Athenian confederacy in the Social War, that Athens ought to give up on principle her traditional imperialis-

---

[1] *Areop.* 66 ὥστε ἔτι καὶ νῦν τοὺς ἀφικνουμένους νομίζειν αὐτὴν ἀξίαν εἶναι μὴ μόνον τῶν Ἑλλήνων ἄρχειν ἀλλὰ καὶ τῶν ἄλλων ἁπάντων.

[2] In the *Areopagiticus* Isocrates still uses both words as synonyms: cf. ἀρχή and ἄρχειν *Areop.* 1, 7, 64, 65, 66, 69; ἐπρωτεύσαμεν τῶν Ἑλλήνων *Areop.* 6 might seem to point more in the direction of ἡγεμονία which occurs 17. But ἁπάσης τῆς Ἑλλάδος ὑπὸ τὴν πόλιν ἡμῶν ὑποπεσούσης . . . μετὰ τὴν Τιμοθέου στρατηγίαν 12 is undoubtedly the ideal of ἀρχή, and a phrase like 65 ἡμᾶς τὰς τῶν ἄλλων ἀκροπόλεις φρουροῦντας would be impossible as a praise of Athens in *De Pace*.

tic policies, Isocrates in the *Areopagiticus* still recommends his proposal to strengthen the position and the conservative influence of the Areopagus by arguing that this is the only means to maintain the empire. The Athenian democracy, it is true, has proved itself able to expand its foreign influence and to establish its domination over all Greece, partly through the favor of fortune, partly through the merits of a few great personalities; and here he mentions his favorite pupil, the general Timotheus, and his father, Conon, as the founders of the second empire. But we have not been able, he says, to maintain that fortunate position even for a short time; instead, we have soon ruined it again because we do not have the constitution able to preserve it.[1]

From all we have proved thus far it is clear that Isocrates is not speaking here of the final collapse and the annihilation of the confederacy and Athens' domination, but of the gradual decline of the Athenian power after the retirement of Timotheus. Unless we refer his words to the period from the end of his *strategia*, which Isocrates explicitly mentions, until the outbreak of the Social War, we cannot understand his criticism of the views of the political optimists in §§3–7. He is aware that if the Athenians adopt their point of view they must necessarily despise what he is going to tell them, and they must be confident that they will be able to coerce all Greece by their present power. But this confidence is just what makes him afraid. "For I see that those cities who think they are in the best condition are the most ill-advised, and those who are most confident run into most dangers. The reason for this is that no good or evil comes to man by itself, but with abundance and power there is always connected and associated wantonness and with it intemperance, but with poverty and humbleness, much moderation and temperance. Thus it is hard to decide which of these lots you would choose to leave to your children. For you can see that from seemingly worse conditions human action as a rule progresses towards the better, whereas from seemingly better conditions it usually turns towards the worse. I can give many examples for this from private life, for there such changes are most frequent. But more important and better known to my listeners.

[1] *Areop.* 12.

are those examples which I can take from Athenian and Lacedaemonian history. For when our city was destroyed by the barbarians, because of our fear we won . . . the leadership of the Greeks. But when we thought we had an invincible power, we almost fell into serfdom. The Spartans, who originally began their history with weak and inconspicuous cities, became the masters of the Peloponnesus because they lived a moderate and soldier-like life. But later on when they became wanton and had won domination on land and sea, they came into the same dangers as we."

Isocrates applies here the wisdom of Greek tragedy that "satiety bears wantonness" to the present situation of Athens. According to this doctrine he ought to be optimistic if the speech were written, as is usually supposed, after the downfall of the Athenian empire in or after the Social War, for, from poverty and weakness, moderation and self-discipline originate, and human action improves.[1] What Isocrates expects is just the opposite. He fears that the present seemingly good conditions may fill the Athenians with wantonness and fallacious over-confidence, and, therefore, their present power may lead suddenly towards a catastrophe. The examples by which he illustrates this tragic fear [2] are the downfall of the first Athenian empire from the peak of its might in the Peloponnesian War and the analogous catastrophe of the Spartan realm, which succeeded the Athenian empire, at Leuctra, for this is the event to which he apparently refers. In both cases he compares the present condition of Athens, not with the lowest but with the highest grade of Athenian and Lacedaemonian power, with their domination on land and sea. And he thinks that too much confidence on the part of the Athenians is all the more self-delusive since their present power is not the same as it was under the first maritime confederacy, and the hatred of the Greeks and the enmity of the Persian king, which were then the causes of Athens' fall, have revived again.[3] This tragic prophecy would be out of place during or after the Social War but fits in exactly with the situation which preceded it. In the

---

[1] *Areop.* 4.   [2] *Areop.* 6. 7.   [3] *Areop.* 8.

opinion of Isocrates, it is no mere emotional apprehension, but he gives it the form of a logical conclusion which is based not on mathematical certainty but on empirical observation. It is this empirical character [1] of his statement which is stressed by the words ὡς ἐπὶ τὸ πολύ and εἰθισμένας μεταπίπτειν (§5). Isocrates often says that the political paideia which he teaches to his pupils does not pretend to be infallible, like that of Plato, but is founded on experience.[2] But for that very reason he thinks it to be more useful to human life. The experience on which it is based is represented by the historical examples to which he refers. It is the function of history in Isocrates' political thought to supply analogies for every situation as it arises.[3] It would be silly for Isocrates to give his warnings the form of a probable empirical conclusion about the future if the collapse, which he predicts will be the necessary effect of the premises of a given situation, had already happened when he wrote his speech.

After we have clarified the situation contemplated in the speech not only by means of the direct description which Isocrates gives of it but also through the political analogies of the past, by which he illustrates it, we can exclude with certainty the time during and after the Social War as possible dates. The *Areopagiticus* must have been written before the war, and this is confirmed by the allusions to single events which it contains, if we re-interpret

---

[1] Cf. my *Diokles von Karystos. Die griechische Medizin und die Schule des Aristoteles* (Berlin, 1938), p. 31 ff., where I have commented on the phrases ὡς ἐπὶ τὸ πολύ, εἴωθε συμβαίνειν, τὰ εἰθισμένα γίγνεσθαι and their connection with the empirical conception of knowledge. They occur in medical as well as political and rhetorical literature about the same time and for the same reason. Isocrates' conclusions in *Areop.* 3–7 are of a *prognostic* character. The words εἰθισμένας μεταπίπτειν (*Areop.* 5) refer to the medical theory of the contraries which convert into each other. This experience has its analogy in the social world.

[2] Isocrates stresses the empirical character of his political "philosophy" *Soph.* 14–15, *Hel.* 5, *Antid.* 187, 188, 191, 192.

[3] Cf. G. Schmitz-Kahlmann, "Das Beispiel der Geschichte im politischen Denken des Isokrates," in *Philologus*, Suppl. Bd. 31, Heft 4, a dissertation of the University of Berlin which was started on my suggestion. Thucydides had gone ahead in applying medical analogies to historical processes in the political field. Isocrates, on the other hand, made use of historical examples for political diagnosis and prognosis.

them in the light of our general conclusions. As a *terminus post quem*, Isocrates gives the end of Timotheus' *strategia*, after which, he says, the decline of the confederacy set in almost immediately.[1] We may think either of Timotheus' first *strategia* (ending 373) during the ascending curve of the second maritime confederacy or his second *strategia* (365–360), by which he tried to repair the losses which Athens had suffered since the end of his first *strategia*. The singular μετὰ τὴν Τιμοθέου στρατηγίαν does not help us to decide this question since Isocrates uses the same singular in his *Antidosis* when he speaks of events of both periods of Timotheus' activity.[2] Although the singular need not have the same meaning in the *Areopagiticus*, it is at least possible, and I think probable, that Isocrates speaks in both speeches of the first and the second *strategia* together. The general distrust of the allies and the hatred of the Greeks fit better the years after the end of Timotheus' second *strategia* (360) until the outbreak of the Social War (357/6).

The statement that the Athenians were compelled to rescue the friends of the Thebans — their most embittered enemies — whereas they were not able to keep their own allies together, must refer to some definite actions by which they had given military assistance to the protégés and allies of Thebes. It is, therefore, impossible to think of the alliance of Athens with the Messenians,[3] concluded during the Phocian War (about 355), because Demosthenes tells us only that the Athenians were obliged to help the Messenians in case of a Spartan attack, but the *casus foederis* never became actual. The statement in the following sentence (§10) that the Athenians had already twice offered thanks to the gods for such deeds (πράξεις) must refer to *two* definite military *actions* in favor of some Theban allies who had requested Athenian help. This happened for the first time in the 'sixties of the 4th century. At that time Lycomedes, the statesman who founded, under Theban protection, the new Arcadian state of Megalopolis, asked Athens

---

[1] *Areop.* 12.

[2] *Antid.* 127, after having mentioned the most famous events of both periods of Timotheus' strategy, that before 373 and that from 365 to 360, speaks of both as ἐπὶ τῆς ἐκείνου στρατηγίας.

[3] Cf. *supra* p. 414.

to conclude a defensive alliance with Arcadia [1] although Athens was an ally of Sparta and Arcadia belonged to the Theban confederacy (366). Xenophon tells in the *Hellenica* that the *casus foederis* became effective in 364, when the Athenian cavalry came to the assistance of the Arcadians in their war against Elis.[2] In his essay *On Revenues*, Xenophon mentions two expeditions of Athens into the Peloponnesus, one, of which we do not know, under Lysistratus, and the second under Hegesileos, who was the leader of the Athenian troops in 362 in the battle of Mantinea.[3] The expedition of Lysistratus, which preceded it, can be identified with much probability as the expedition in aid of the Arcadians [4] in 364. Xenophon explicitly tells us that there was much dispute in Athens before this alliance with Arcadia was concluded, since it seemed paradoxical to lend assistance to the friends of the Thebans. This is just what Isocrates criticizes.[5] The Athenians did not send troops for a second time to help the Peloponnesian allies of Thebes but, as we have seen, there must have been a second expedition to help another Theban ally, and I cannot think of any other event of this sort except the expedition to Euboea in 357. Euboea had seceded from the Athenian confederacy shortly after the Theban victory over Sparta at Leuctra and had joined the Thebans, and since that time she had been lost for Athens. When in 357 internal controversies broke out in Euboea, one group of

[1] Xen. *Hell*. VII 4, 2. The perfect congruity of the situation with that described by Isocrates has not been noticed thus far, for scholars were preoccupied by their idea that the *Areopagiticus* was written after the Social War. Xenophon says that Lycomedes concluded an alliance with Athens at a moment when he saw that the Athenians were angered because their own allies had recently refused to assist them on several occasions (Oropus, Sicyon), cf. VII 4. 1 τοῖς δ' Ἀθηναίοις οὐδεὶς τῶν συμμάχων ἐβοήθησεν. This fits in with Isocrates' description of the paradoxical situation.

[2] Xen. *Hell*. VII 4. 29.

[3] Xen. *De Vectig*. 3, 7.

[4] Xenophon, *loc. cit.*, says that the expedition under Lysistratus was made in order to help the Arcadians (ὅτε Ἀρκάσιν ἐβοήθει).

[5] Xen. *Hell*. VII 4. 2–3 τὸ μὲν οὖν πρῶτον ἐδυσχέραινόν τινες τῶν Ἀθηναίων τὸ Λακεδαιμονίοις ὄντας φίλους· γενέσθαι τοῖς ἐναντίοις αὐτῶν συμμάχους, ἐπειδὴ δὲ λογιζό-μενοι ηὕρισκον οὐδὲν μεῖον Λακεδαιμονίοις ἢ σφίσιν ἀγαθὸν τὸ Ἀρκάδας μὴ προσδεῖσθαι Θηβαίων οὕτω δὴ προσεδέχοντο τὴν τῶν Ἀρκάδων συμμαχίαν.

the Euboeans turned to Athens and the Athenians sent an expedition which won an easy victory.[1] We are not able to verify Isocrates' statement that the Athenians "had already twice offered thanks to the gods for such actions," which accentuates the paradox of these policies, for we do not learn anything of this sort from our sources, which are very incomplete in their narrative.

But we can exclude with almost complete certainty the interpretation which has been given by modern scholars to the offerings of thanks mentioned by Isocrates. They found in them a reference to Chares' victory in Asia Minor in 355, but the offering after it rests on mere conjecture.[2] As we have seen, the close relation of the two offerings (εὐαγγέλια θύειν) to the preceding two lines does not allow us to refer them to the facts mentioned before those lines,[3] especially since Isocrates speaks only generally of the "hostility" of the Persians [4] but does not mention concrete military actions (πράξεις) like those in favor of the Theban allies.

The rest of the facts, which are summarized in §10, cannot be

---

[1] Diod. XVI 7; Dem. *Chers.* 74 and other passages; Aesch. *Ctes.* 85.

[2] Diod. XVI 22. 1–2 does not know anything about an offering of thanks made by the Athenians after Chares' victory in Asia. In Dem. *Ol.* III 31 ἀγαπῶντες ἐὰν μεταδιδῶσι θεωρικῶν ὑμῖν ἢ Βοηδρόμια πέμψωσιν οὗτοι (sc. οἱ πολιτευόμενοι) apparently the Βοηδρόμια of which our best manuscripts speak have nothing to do with an offering of thanks made for a victory. But there is a variant βοΐδια in the vulgar manuscripts, a word which must have originated from Βοηδρόμια by mechanical corruption, since it makes no sense at all. Already Dionysius of Halicarnassus, Hermogenes, and the author of our Demosthenes-scholia found it in their manuscripts. The scholia on Dem. *Ol.* III 31 misunderstood πέμψωσιν which in connection with Βοηδρόμια means to make the procession at the festival of Boedromia and referred it to the otherwise unknown fact that Chares after his victory ἔπεμψεν Ἀθηναίοις βοῦς ἃς διείλοντο κατὰ φυλάς. A. Schaefer, *Demosthenes und seine Zeit* I² p. 171 n. 2 audaciously referred this distribution of cattle among the Athenian people to the offerings of thanks mentioned by Isocr. *Areop.* 29. But this is a mere conjecture, since this scholiast does not say that the cattle were used for an offering. Schaefer made his conjecture in order to support another conjecture: the alleged identity of the events referred to by Isocrates with the victory of Chares. But there is no reference to an Athenian victory over the Persians in Isocrates. As we have seen before, his words δὶς ἤδη εὐαγγέλια τεθύκαμεν clearly refer to the assistance given to the allies of the Thebans.

[3] See the end of n. 2 above and p. 420 ff.

[4] Cf. p. 436, n. 1.

verified because they are too general. The Athenians have spent, we are told, more than 1,000 talents in vain for their mercenaries, but they are looked upon with distrust by the Greeks and considered as enemies by the barbarians. As to the latter statement we have seen before that it can be referred to the years of gradual decline of the second confederacy even better than to the Social War and the time after it.[1] There was tension in the relations with Persia ever since the king had sent in 366 a letter to the Athenians threatening them with war unless they called back their navy and kept peace. This intervention was made in favor of Thebes and against the Spartan-Athenian alliance.[2] The distrust of the Greeks increased ever since the 'sixties of the fourth century when Epaminondas tried to undermine the Athenian confederacy and Athens was compelled to take steps against disobedient allies. In those years the unfortunate policy of centralization, which had caused the disruption of the first confederacy and led to the Peloponnesian War, was revived, and the allies who seceded from the confederacy later on at the outbreak of the Social War — Chios, Rhodes, Cos — and Byzantium were already in sympathy with Thebes and

---

[1] *Areop.* 10 καὶ τῷ βαρβάρῳ πολέμιοι γεγονότες indicates "unfriendly relations." The relations of Athens with the king were of such a nature long before the invasion by Chares of Asia Minor in 355 or the time of Demosthenes' speech *On the Symmories*, cf. Beloch, *op. cit.*, III 1² p. 194, A. Schaefer, *op. cit.*, II 455 ff. To the events recorded by Schaefer (Athenian interference in Egypt and Asia Minor in the 60's) we may add the expulsion of the Persian garrison from Samos by Timotheus after a siege of 10 months in 365 and the support which he gave the rebellious satrap Ariobarzanes, cf. Dem. *Rhod.* 9. In compensation for such services Ariobarzanes returned to Athens the fortified places Sestos and Crithote on the Thracian Chersonese, which he had held until then, and the Athenians conferred upon him the rights of citizenship, cf. Dem. *Arist.* 141, 202. All these were decidedly acts by which the Athenians were πολέμιοι τῷ βαρβάρῳ γεγονότες. It is true that they had sent Timotheus to help Ariobarzanes and to expel the Persian garrison from Samos μὴ λύοντα τὰς σπονδὰς τὰς πρὸς τὸν βασιλέα, cf. Dem. *Rhod.* 9. But that in reality the situation was very close to war is shown by Isocr. *Antid.* 111: speaking of that campaign he says it did not cost the Athenians a penny, since Timotheus financed it entirely by taking the money out of the land of the enemy (ἐκ τῆς πολεμίας χώρας).

[2] Xen. *Hell.* VII 1. 36 (message of the king to the Athenians) Ἀθηναίους ἀνέλκειν τὰς ναῦς, εἰ δὲ μὴ πείθοιντο στρατεύειν ἐπ' αὐτούς. εἰ δέ τις πόλις μὴ ἐθέλοι ἀκολουθεῖν, ἐπὶ ταύτην πρῶτον ἰέναι. By sending this message the king definitely sided with Thebes.

negotiated with Epaminondas.¹ On the other hand the words τοὺς δὲ ἡμετέρους αὐτῶν συμμάχους ἀπολωλεκότες with which Isocrates describes this situation are too weak and indefinite to be referred to a time when the main allies had left the confederacy.² Isocrates seems to weigh, in §§10 ff., the entire policies of the second Athenian confederacy up to the present time.³ Much money had been spent on their mercenaries during that period, and the spending was not confined to the Social War. We do not know the exact figures, but the sum which Demosthenes gives shortly after the Social War, 1,500 talents, surpasses the amount given by Isocrates by 50%. It is probable that these huge sums are supposed to cover the entire period of almost continual wars and expeditions which Athens had to undergo during the decline of the second confederacy.⁴

¹ Cf. Diod. XV 79. Isocr. *Phil.* 53. Beloch. *op. cit.*, III 1² p. 197. Byzantium seceded several years before the Social War as a consequence of the negotiations with Thebes mentioned in the text. Besides Byzantium such powerful allies as the Thracian cities, Euboea, and Corcyra had abandoned the confederacy long before the Social War.

² Cf. p. 419 ff.

³ *Areop.* 78 summarizes the contents of the entire speech by saying that if the Athenians continue pursuing a policy like the present one (ὥσπερ νῦν) the results will be the same ἅπερ ἐν τῷ παρόντι καιρῷ καὶ τ ο ῖ ς π α ρ ε λ θ ο ῦ σ ι χ ρ ό ν ο ι ς. It is this time which Isocrates describes as a unified period of decline throughout his speech. He contrasts it with the policies of the ancestors to which he wants the Athenians to return. He repeats and sums up in the epilogue the main features of decay which he has criticized in the speech and contrasts this sad picture with the ideal conditions prevailing at the time of the ancestors. As in the speech *On the Peace*, he includes in this picture of the "present" misery the entire period of decline of the second confederacy and even some features pertaining to the decline of the first confederacy. Cf. *Areop.* 82 and *De Pace* 77 where the same features are referred to the times of the Peloponnesian War. In *Areop.* 80 he complains that the Persians as long as the Athenians were powerful did not dare to go with their ships beyond Phaselis (on the southern coast of Asia Minor) whereas "now" (81) they despise the Athenians and send them menacing letters. This all sounds as though it were actual at the present moment, but Isocrates had made the same complaint in the *Panegyricus* 118 ff. The word "now" must therefore not be taken at face value. The criticism can hardly refer to an individual situation of the year 355, since it was taken over from a previous speech of Isocrates written a quarter of a century earlier.

⁴ Dem. *Ol.* III 28 criticizes the policy of the Athenian demagogues of the second

The most significant event which has happened thus far and to which Isocrates therefore refers explicitly is the loss of the Thracian cities. We think primarily of Olynthus and the cities of the Chalcidian League. They had seceded from the Athenian confederacy about 370, as we have seen before. But if we are correct in referring the two expeditions made by the Athenians, in order to help unnamed allies of Thebes, to Arcadia in 364 and Euboea in 357, it seems most natural to think also of the recent events of the year 357 when Olynthus and the Chalcidian cities made an alliance with Philip and thereby were definitely lost for Athens.[1] The words πόλεις ἐπὶ Θρᾴκης may, however, imply more than the cities of the Chalcidice alone and may include the other cities on the northern coast of the Aegean. The Athenians had lost Amphipolis long before: when Philip beleaguered the town in 357 and the Amphipolitans, shortly after the Athenian victory on Euboea, sent an embassy to ask for Athenian help, the Athenians had to decline the appeal.[2] They sent Chares with a fleet to the Dardanelles because the Thracian Chersonese was menaced by Cersobleptes, king of Thrace, and the loss of this strategic point involved a still greater danger than that of Amphipolis and Pydna, a city which they lost soon after Philip conquered Amphipolis. The successful expedition to Euboea was made in the summer of 357 early in the archonship of Agathocles, beginning in July, and, since it took only thirty days, was finished in August. When the Athenians returned from Euboea, they found in Athens the

---

confederacy in much the same way as Isocrates does, *Areop.* 9–10. He even seems to have before his eyes and to indicate the very passage of Isocrates, but since he writes the Olynthiac orations in 349/8 he is likely to include the time of the Social War. It is, therefore, interesting to observe that he gives a total amount of 1,500 talents instead of the thousand talents of which Isocrates speaks in the *Areopagiticus*. This apparently is not just another somewhat exaggerated calculation but the higher figures are due to the fact that he there covers another period. Since Isocrates does not tell us which years his calculation includes, his figures do not help us to identify the situation, for mercenaries had been used in large numbers during the entire period of the second confederacy.

[1] Cf. above p. 416 ff.

[2] Philip takes Amphipolis Diod. XVI 8. 3. The embassy of the Amphipolitans to Athens Dem. *Ol.* I 8.

ambassadors of Amphipolis, Hierax and Stratocles. Thus the siege of Amphipolis took place at the same time. The expedition of Chares to the Chersonese came immediately after these events, as Demosthenes tells us. It happened in the fall of 357. It is hard to say whether there remains time enough before the outbreak of the Social War for the capture of Pydna by the new Macedonian king, but we must admit over-emphasis in Isocrates' rhetorical style, which is always inclined to exaggeration, when he says that "all" the Thracian cities were lost. Practically they were. The Social War did not start, according to the prevailing chronology, before the winter of 357/6, perhaps not even before the spring [1] of 356. At any rate there remains sufficient time in which Isocrates could write his speech. There is, indeed, a strong probability for the second part of the year 357 as the date of the *Areopagiticus*.[2] It fits best in the time immediately preceding the outbreak of the Social War. But although this precise identification of the historical situation rests on the interpretation of some facts which cannot be identified with absolute certainty, one thing is beyond doubt: the *Areopagiticus* belongs to the last period of the second maritime confederacy *before* the beginning of the Social War.

If the conclusions which we have established are sound, the *Areopagiticus* becomes a document of much greater importance for the historian than has been assumed hitherto. It has always been acknowledged that this speech is the most adequate expression of Isocrates' attitude with regard to the problems of internal politics. It contains his criticism of Athenian democracy as it was during the phase of its decline in the 4th century. But now the connection of his program for a conservative reform of the state with

[1] Cf. Beloch, *op. cit.*, III 2², p. 259–260. The first dated event of the war is as late as May 356 (IG II² 123). The inscription concerns measures to protect the island of Andros.

[2] I follow the now prevailing chronology, cf. Beloch, *loc. cit.*, p. 261, who tries to prove that Diod. XVI 21–22 has placed all the events of 357 one year too early, under the archonship of Cephisodotus 358/7. If, however, Diodorus is correct about the date of the conquest of Amphipolis and Pydna and Philip's alliance with Olynthus and has placed only the beginning of the Social War one year too early, all the better. In this case the interval between the last events mentioned in the *Areopagiticus* and the war would be somewhat increased (from 358 until the end of 357).

Athenian foreign politics receives new light. If the speech were written after the Social War, Isocrates would have used the accomplished fact of the disruption of the Athenian confederacy in order to prove the necessity of setting up a strong Areopagus to counterbalance the power of the masses and the demagogues. But if the speech was written as a warning before the Social War broke out, with a view to teaching the Athenians how closely the inner structure of the leading state and its healthiness was tied up with the destiny of the confederacy, the speech has an immediate bearing upon the vital problems of the Athenian empire. Hitherto, the *Areopagiticus* appeared more as the work of a moralist and educator than that of a politician. Ferdinand Duemmler has gone so far as to see in it an advertisement for Isocrates' school [1] written only to attract the sons of the propertied class and the moderate democrats by the authoritative ideal of education which it sets forth. Even if Isocrates had hoped for such an incidental effect, this interpretation underrates the political meaning of the speech. The problem of the interaction of Athenian inner politics and the strength and vitality of the empire must have been the concern of the more far-sighted Athenian statesmen. During the years after 378 when the second maritime confederacy was built up by such men as Timotheus and Callistratus, there was no talk of inner reforms of the Athenian democracy. On the contrary, the democratic liberties of Athens were a great asset when they made a new attempt to call forth the Greek cities against the unbearable tyranny of Sparta. But now, after the tyranny of the Athenian demos had replaced that of the Spartans and the political downfall of the founders of the confederacy had caused the rapid decline of its power, the problem of the inability of the masses to rule a vast empire rose again [2] and with it the memory of the tragic experiences of the Periclean time.

Isocrates tells us that he had discussed the idea of a strong

[1] Ferdinand Duemmler, "Chronologische Beiträge zu einigen platonischen Dialogen," in *Kleine Schriften*, I 98 ff. This opinion is rightly criticized by G. Mathieu, *Les idées politiques d'Isocrate*, p. 144.

[2] The thesis had been set forth by the Athenian demagogue Cleon (Thuc. III 37) but for other reasons.

Areopagus as an anchor of the democratic constitution of Athens even before he wrote the speech.[1] Like Plato, who reveals in his seventh letter that he had advocated the main ideas of his *Republic* two decades before he published that work,[2] Isocrates is likely to have pronounced his views on internal politics for many years in the oral teaching of his school. There he had praised the democracy of the forefathers [3] (πάτριος πολιτεία), under which the Areopagus had still exercised on the citizens an educational influence in the highest sense. Every reader of Isocrates knows that this contrast of the present and the past pervades all his political thought, and the idealization of the past supplies the normative element in it. What then caused Isocrates finally to publish these thoughts and to insist with all his moral authority on the necessity of an inner reorganization of Athenian political life in spite of his own hesitations and the warnings [4] of some of his friends? Even before the *Areopagiticus*, most of his political pamphlets were written not only with a definite political aim but in direct contact with, or on the instigation of, practical politicians.[5] We would conclude from Isocrates' praise of his famous pupil Timotheus in the *Antidosis* [6] that he must have been in close contact with him and in agreement with his political ideals even if we did not learn from Pseudo-Plutarch's biography that he had accompanied Timotheus during his generalship and written for him the bulletins of his victories and political actions which he sent to the demos of Athens.[7] It is in the *Areopagiticus* that Isocrates names Timotheus for the first time in his writings. He speaks of him with particular emphasis and dates the decline of the second Athenian empire, as mentioned above, from the end of his *strategia*.[8] After his retirement in 360, Timotheus lived in Athens without public office. He must have watched the political

---

[1] *Areop.* 56 ff.

[2] Plat. *ep.* VII 326 A.

[3] He avoids however repeating the somewhat discredited slogan but paraphrases it, cf. *Areop.* 30. 59.

[4] *Areop.* 57.

[5] Such were Plataicus, Nicocles, Euagoras, Archidamus, perhaps also the Panegyricus.   [7] [Plut.] *vit. X or.* 837 C.

[6] *Antid.* 101–139.   [8] *Areop.* 12.

development with increasing apprehension and may have waited for a last opportunity to take over once more the leadership of the threatened empire, to whose establishment he had contributed more than anyone else. We are entitled to conclude this from the fact that he willingly accepted the appointment as one of the admirals of the Athenian fleet a year later in the Social War, although at that time it was too late. It seems to be not too audacious to conjecture, but an almost unavoidable thought, that Isocrates' demand in the *Areopagiticus* for a conservative reform of the Athenian democracy in the spirit of the πάτριος πολιτεία cannot have been raised at that time in public without Timotheus' approval. It is the same reproach of hostility towards the demos, against which Isocrates defends Timotheus a few years later after the latter's death, and of which he himself is afraid in the *Areopagiticus* because of his severe criticism of the present radicalized form of democracy.[1] This was the position in which the circle of Timotheus and his followers must have found themselves permanently during those decisive years. From their pessimistic point of view the problem of the Athenian empire was largely a problem of internal politics. Isocrates' proposal in the *Areopagiticus* was an attempt to sound out public opinion with regard to this fundamental problem. Undoubtedly it was made when it was too late, if there ever was a prospect of realizing the hopes of this group. The outbreak of the Social War and the third downfall of Timotheus after the battle of Embata convinced Isocrates and the entire group, whose views he had expressed in the *Areopagiticus*, that Athens should now give up definitely all her imperialistic ambitions, which he still had maintained in the *Areopagiticus*, and the speech *On Peace* is the announcement of this resignation.[2]

The ideas of the *Areopagiticus* were not exclusively Isocrates' own. With his tendency to restrict the radical democracy, the theorist stands in a long tradition which we can pursue through

[1] *Areop.* 57 εἶναι δ' ἔφασαν ἐμοὶ καὶ κίνδυνον μὴ τὰ βέλτιστα συμβουλεύων μ ι σ ό-δ η μ ο s εἶναι δόξω καὶ τὴν πόλιν ζητεῖν εἰς ὀ λ ι γ α ρ χ ί α ν ἐμβαλεῖν. Cf. the same reproach against Timotheus and Isocrates' explanation of it, *Antid.* 131.

[2] Cf. above p. 424-426.

several generations even though it naturally does not come much
to the foreground in the political life of anti-oligarchic Athens.
The slogan of the πάτριος πολιτεία, which recommends the restriction of the rights of the masses by transferring the ideal from the
future to the past and picturing the glorious period of Athenian
history as the true realization of a moderate democracy — this
slogan had been used before by Theramenes and his conservative
group during the Peloponnesian War when they made their various attempts to bring about a change of the constitution. Isocrates,
who was born in 436, and belonged to the propertied class of the
city, had observed the revolutions of 411 and 403, in which
Theramenes took part, and, although he never became himself
an active politician, he must have shared in the discussions about
the character and the aims of this much-criticized statesman,
which find a repercussion in Aristotle's *Constitution of Athens*.[1]
The restoration of the Areopagus was one of the main items of
Theramenes' program. One of the revolutionary measures which
were taken under the rule of the Thirty was the abolition of the
laws of Ephialtes and Archestratus.[2] It was these laws by which
the retarding influence of the Areopagus on the constitutional life
of Athens had been eliminated.[3] Consequently these anti-Areop-
agitic laws were repealed at once in the early phase of the régime
of the Thirty, i.e., at a time when Theramenes still exercised a
leading influence in that committee. Aristotle praises the measure
as we should expect him to do, for he distinguishes throughout
Theramenes and his policies from the rest of the Thirty,[4] and tries
to prove that the usual condemnation of this statesman by the
Athenian democrats of the fourth century was undeserved. He
places Theramenes among the best statesmen of Athens after
those of the earlier period, i.e., along with Nicias and Thucydides
son of Melesias, the great antagonist of Pericles.[5] Isocrates

---

[1] Ar., *Resp. Ath.*, 28, 5.   [2] *Ibid.*, 35, 2.

[3] *Ibid.*, 25, 1–2. Cf. Wilamowitz, *Aristoteles und Athen* I 68, 40.

[4] Ar., *op. cit.*, 35. 2 stresses the moderate and reconstructive character of the
first phase of the Thirty. He characterizes it mainly by the restoration of the
Areopagus and the laws of Solon, and identifies it with the period of Theramenes'
influence, cf. 36. 1 ff.   [5] *Ibid.*, 28, 5.

would agree with this historical picture of the development of the Athenian democracy, but it is not at all the conventional view of the democratic majority. We may rather take it as a specimen of a radical revaluation of the constitutional history of Athens from a point of view substantially identical with that of Isocrates in his *Areopagiticus*.[1]

But Isocrates' program in the *Areopagiticus* shows more than one resemblance with the policies of Theramenes. Not only the reconstruction of the Areopagus but also the elimination of the mechanical election method of the lot,[2] and the return to the true laws of Solon which Isocrates recommends were original demands of Theramenes.[3] In 403 he tried to abolish all the so-called laws of Solon whose origin was disputed.[4] Under his rule the senators and other state officials were elected ἐκ προκρίτων.[5] That is exactly the procedure which Isocrates postulates in his *Areopagiticus*.[6] Both Isocrates and Theramenes wish to bar the pernicious influence of the sycophants and denouncers and to restore lawfulness.[7] According to Aristotle this was Theramenes' true motive and for this reason he was killed by his own comrades. He was called the "cothurn," because he always seemed to go with the stronger party, but Aristotle thinks that this was a misunderstanding which will always be the lot of the lawful man who hates the crime regardless of whether it comes from the left or the right. He can go with either side but only so far as his strict sense of justice permits him.[8] In reality he fits into no system. Isocrates sees his own position in a similar light. He hates the radicalism and injustice of the demagogues and the intrigues of

---

[1] The relationship of Aristotle's *Constitution of Athens* to Isocrates' ideas in the *Areopagiticus* is a problem that becomes urgent in the light of our conclusions. I plan to take it up in a special article which will follow later.

[2] Isocr. *Areop.* 22.

[3] *Areop.* 16.

[4] Ar., *op. cit.*, 35, 2.

[5] *Ibid.*, 35, 1.

[6] *Areop.* 22.

[7] Ar., *op. cit.*, 28, 5; 35, 3, cf. Isocr. *De Pace* 123, 133 and the passages Preuss, *Ind. Isocr.* 81.

[8] Ar., *op. cit.*, 28. 5.

the sycophants, but at the same time he feels that he wants to mark his distance from the oligarchs as well, to whom he prefers even the extreme form of democracy then prevailing.[1] This was exactly the situation of Theramenes which therefore was bound to impress not only Isocrates but also Aristotle, the philosopher of the right mean.

We are now prepared to understand the ancient biographical tradition which explicitly includes Theramenes among Isocrates' teachers. Little attention has been paid thus far to that brief statement to be found in Dionysius of Halicarnassus, Pseudo-Plutarch, and Suidas,[2] although it is not a little interesting in this connection that beside the school rhetoricians, Gorgias and Tisias, and the theorizing sophists, Protagoras and Prodicus, the name of a practical Athenian statesman appears. We can verify that tradition only by comparing Isocrates' views with those of Theramenes. Modern critics mostly failed to combine the facts of Isocrates' political ideology with the biographical tradition about him. Blass [3] enumerates Isocrates' teachers where he discusses the historical value of the ancient biographical tradition and mentions Theramenes among them, but he does not try to control that tradition by analyzing Isocrates' political ideas. He only vaguely suggests that that tradition might be correct because Isocrates as well as Theramenes pursued a middle course, avoiding both extreme oligarchy and extreme democracy. Mathieu,[4] on the other hand, sees that there must be a connection between Isocrates' ideas on internal politics as set forth in the *Areopagiticus*, and the moderate democrats of 411 and 403, but he does not pay attention to the fact that Theramenes is mentioned in our biographical tradition of Isocrates as his teacher and model. If I have not overlooked anything important, Mathieu does not even note in his two extensive chapters on Isocrates' internal politics that such a tradition exists. He infers that Isocrates might have taken over the

---

[1] Cf. *Areop.* 62 ff.
[2] Dionys. Hal. *Isocr.* 1, p. 54, 14 Us.-Rad.; [Plut.], *vit. X or.*, 836 F; Suid. s.v. Isocrates.
[3] Blass, *op. cit.*, II², p. 12.
[4] Mathieu, *op. cit.*, p. 137.

ideal of the πάτριος πολιτεία from the program of the revolutionaries of 411 and as such he quotes Clitophon.[1] But Aristotle
names Theramenes as the true leader of the group to which Clitophon belonged.[2] He remarks that Theramenes had been the outstanding leader of the γνώριμοι ever since the death of Nicias.[3]
In another passage Mathieu [4] thinks of names like Anytus and
Phormisius as Isocrates' sources. It is true that Aristotle mentions both of them [5] as members of Theramenes' group besides
Clitophon and Archinus, but they were after all men of second
rank as compared with Theramenes. One of the ancient biographies names a certain Erginus as Isocrates' political teacher
besides Theramenes, and Ruhnken's conjecture may be correct in
changing this unknown name into Archinus.[6] At any rate Isocrates'
ideas on the best constitution for Athens must be traced back to
the circle of Theramenes and the biographical tradition must be
combined with the program of the *Areopagiticus* which confirms it.

The ancient biographies may be correct in the literal sense that
Isocrates had personal relations with Theramenes which determined
his course for his lifetime. Athens was, after all, a small city, and
the propertied class (οἱ γνώριμοι) to which Isocrates belonged and
whose interest Theramenes represented was even smaller. Theramenes' ideas on a change of the constitution in a more conservative
sense must have been discussed in this group for many years
during the final period of the Peloponnesian War. But even if we
do not assume a personal acquaintance of Isocrates with Theramenes, his views apparently had influenced him a great deal. The
relation of teacher and pupil as understood by the ancient biography certainly implies more than mere classroom contacts. The
struggle of Theramenes throughout the critical phase and after
the catastrophic outcome of the war must have revealed to Isocrates for the first time the problem which he discussed himself

[1] Cf. Ar., *op. cit.*, 29, 3.
[2] Ar., *op. cit.*, 34, 3.
[3] *Ibid.*, 28, 3.
[4] Mathieu, *op. cit.*, p. 139.
[5] Ar., *op. cit.*, 34, 3.
[6] Blass, *op. cit.*, p. 13.

later in the *Areopagiticus*: the connection of the fate of the Athenian empire with the internal political structure of the state and its pathology, and it must have made a lasting impression on his mind. For obvious reasons Isocrates never mentions Theramenes explicitly in his speech, as he apparently avoids his slogan of the return to the "constitution of the ancestors"[1] because, for many good democrats, it had the connotation of the oligarchy into which Theramenes' attempt to realize it had finally developed. But there is no doubt that Isocrates derived his basic ideas on the constitutional problem from this source.

The fate of Theramenes' ideas after his fall now appears in a new light, and a perfect historical continuity in their transmission and development becomes visible to us. After the restoration of the Athenian democracy and the downfall of the Thirty in 403, these ideas were silenced in public but they obviously did not die out in theoretical and private discussion and were automatically revived in the declining years of the second maritime confederacy. At that time Isocrates' school was a center of these political tendencies. But we can hardly confine them to one definite year of his life or one of his publications only, for the *Areopagiticus* apparently is representative of his attitude toward internal politics in general if the decisive impressions underlying it were formed as early as we have shown. Such pupils of Isocrates as Timotheus and Androtion undoubtedly were brought up with these ideas and their lack of popularity in spite of their merits was largely due to that reason. We are accustomed to think of Isocrates' school and political paideia primarily as a focus of the Panhellenic ideology, but simultaneously there were focused in it those contemporary forces which aimed at rebuilding the democratic constitution of Athens. We may define this conservative ideal of democracy, at least in Isocrates' sense, as the right mean between the hated oligarchy of the "Thirty Tyrants" and the radicalized democracy of the fourth century. Isocrates takes pains in his *Areopagiticus* to distinguish his ideas from those of the Thirty, but Aristotle's distinction between Theramenes and the other members of that committee shows that Isocrates' rejection

[1] Cf. above p. 441.

of the Thirty as a bad extreme does not mean that he identified Theramenes with them.

Isocrates' school was, however, not the only channel through which the ideas of Theramenes were diffused during those decades. We remember that Xenophon in his *Memorabilia* pictures Socrates, too, as a believer in the same ideas. Like Theramenes and Isocrates he criticizes the mechanization of the Athenian method of electing the most important state officials by lot.[1] Moreover, he emphasizes the lack of discipline in the lives of Athenian citizens and in the Athenian army and praises the Areopagus as the highest moral authority in the state.[2] This picture of Xenophon's is in agreement with Plato's view of Socrates; only the high praise of the Areopagus is peculiar to Xenophon's report. It is very probable that Xenophon added this feature out of his own conservative conviction with an eye on the controversies of his own day. This would be only another evidence of the continuity of the Areopagus problem during the period of the second confederacy, independent of Isocrates' *Areopagiticus*. At the time when Xenophon wrote these pages in which he pictured Socrates as a member of the opposition against the radical trends in the constitutional life of Athens, the problem of the Areopagus must have been again under discussion. But this does not exclude the historicity of Xenophon's statement, and the historical Socrates may, indeed, have been in sympathy with Theramenes' views. We must not forget that Plato also sided at first with the Thirty, as he tells us in the seventh letter, hoping that they would bring about a sound reform of the state, and that he turned his back to them only when they forbade Socrates to teach. Plato's own criticism of the Athenian democracy is not centered around the question of the Areopagus, but the more basic problem of knowledge and its function in political life. But in his *Laws* the institution of the νυκτερινὸς σύλλογος as the highest authority of his state proves his awareness of the problem which was so passionately discussed in his time. Also the demand of Isocrates to give up the character of Athens as the dominating sea power finds a parallel in Plato's *Laws*, for he conceives his new

[1] Xen. *Mem.* III 9. 10; cf. III 5. 20.
[2] *Ibid.*, III 5. 20.

state as a conservative land power that should be cut off as much as possible from the sea.

We have pointed out before that the program of Isocrates' school in the field of internal politics could not be realized at the time when he published his *Areopagiticus*, but like his Panhellenic ideas it found a partial realization, at least temporarily, under the Macedonian rule. Following the short rise of democracy after Alexander's death, when "order" had been restored by Antipater in the Lamian War, an oligarchic constitution was established at Athens.[1] Its main features remained the same even under the somewhat more moderate rule of the Peripatetic scholar and statesman Demetrius of Phaleron who governed the Athenian state under the protection of a Macedonian garrison from 317 to 307. One of the reforms of those years was the restoration of the Areopagus and it is very probable that the reform program which was then realized with the coöperation of Demetrius was taken over from the old program of Isocrates set forth in his *Areopagiticus*. Isocrates had always advocated the rights of the propertied class and demanded a strengthening of their influence on the administration of the state.[2] It was in line with this policy that Demetrius and Antipater confined the rights of citizenship to Athenians with a certain amount of income. Another characteristic measure which was taken over from Isocrates and Theramenes was the abolition of election by the lot. One might doubt whether Demetrius and his colleagues adopted these policies from Isocrates, whose political views had been carefully studied by Aristotle and his school, or went farther back to the constitution of Solon and Clisthenes as Isocrates and Theramenes had claimed. But we learn from Diodorus [3] that Antipater offered to the poor citizens, who had lost their citizenship by the new laws, an opportunity to emigrate and settle in Thrace far from their city, and this makes

---

[1] Formerly the restoration of the Areopagus was generally ascribed to Demetrius of Phaleron but now the reform is mostly placed under the oligarchy set up by Antipater after the Lamian War, cf. De Sanctis in Beloch, *Studi di storia antica*, II p. 4 and W. S. Ferguson, *Hellenistic Athens*, p. 24.

[2] Isocr. *Areop.* 32; *De Pace* 13, 128, 131, 133.

[3] Diod. XVIII 18. 4.

it sure that there is a direct connection between the new legislative measures of that time and the program of Isocrates. The problem of the poor and unemployed part of the population became more and more acute during the years of the second Athenian confederacy when great numbers of them entered military service as mercenaries in order to earn a living. They soon formed an element of permanent unrest in Greece and the problem of establishing a lasting peace could not be solved without offering them an opportunity to work and a place where they could make a home. In his speech *On Peace* Isocrates had proposed [1] to solve this question by an agreement with the king of Thrace who should offer such an opportunity to the unemployed people of Greece, and it was this idea that was taken up by Antipater. His and Demetrius' legal measures were based on the learned studies of the Peripatetic school on the earlier history of Athenian constitution and legislation, as is well known, but at the same time they represent the actual demands of the Athenian political opposition which had been kept alive for a century by continual discussion and finally were realized with the assistance of the foreign power of Macedonia.

[1] Isocr. *De Pace*, 24.

ATHENAEUS AND THE SLAVES OF ATHENS

By William Linn Westermann

IN THE calculation of the population of the Athenian state made by Demetrius of Phalerum "the returns for the slave population . . . have not come down to us, but the number of the slaves perhaps equalled the citizens and aliens combined." [1] Many years have passed since Professor Ferguson suggested this ratio as a possible proportion between slaves and free in the city-state of Athens late in the fourth century B.C. It would mean that bond and free were about equal, one to one. Since that time his views may well have changed. As at the time when it was penned, this view would even now be regarded as a judiciously balanced estimate, characteristic of the good judgment and temperance which have been so consistent a quality of that scholarship which the friends and pupils of Professor Ferguson have wished to honor through these studies. If the more drastic estimate which eventually is presented in this paper differs from his own, it is offered without polemical intent, as a problem vital to the consideration of the history and culture of the city-state of Athens which has so long enlisted the interest and scholarly ability of Professor Ferguson.

Inquiries into the number of slaves in Attica have been made many times.[2] There is little new evidence contemporary with the special period of the fifth and fourth centuries before Christ [3] to

---

[1] W. S. Ferguson *Hellenistic Athens* (1911) 54. Through combination of Diodorus XVIII 74. 3 with the report of this population estimate as it has come down to us, Felix Jacoby, *Fragmente der griechischen Historiker*, II D 245, p. 813, under *Stesikleides*, would date the ἐξετασμός of Demetrius in 317–316 B.C. Ferguson placed it shortly after 311 B.C. Because of an obvious mistake in the text a positive conclusion as to date is not possible.

[2] For a summary of the modern attitudes and discussions of the numbers of slaves see Rachel L. Sargent, *The Size of the Slave Population at Athens*, University of Illinois Studies in the Social Sciences XII no. 3 (1924), 13–43.

[3] It is one of those disappointments inherent in the luck of excavations that the American excavations of the Agora at Athens have thrown no new light upon the slave system of the city.

present and evaluate. In discussing the slave problem in Greece Alfred Zimmern has said: "the same evidence is marshalled; the same references and footnotes are transferred, like stale tea-leaves, from one learned receptacle to another."[1] Partly true; but it should be said in praise of the persistence of pedantry — not in blame. Every ambitious actor must at some time stage his own conception of Hamlet. In like manner every student of the greatness of Athens, of the causes which made its people so vibrant a force in the moulding of Greek culture, must make his own decision, so far as he can, upon this matter of the numerical relation of the slave population to the free. For upon that decision, in some degree, depends an important judgment regarding the total character of Athenian society and its vaunted individual freedom and liberty. Was it a slave state, in its total spirit, or was it really free? One cannot evade the issue or conjure it away by re-defining Greek slavery upon general assumptions regarding its nature and its effects. Every slave system is an integral part of that social and economic organism in which it is embedded. In every social system of which it is a part slavery determines in some measure the nature of that system and is itself, in some degree, modified by the total social system. In no two state organisms is it ever quite the same.

In one of his assumptions Zimmern was not well informed. As a matter of record there was available when he wrote a large amount of new information upon ancient slavery. This information has been considerably increased since he wrote his article.[2] It consists of documentary and contemporary evidence upon slavery itself and upon related forms of bondage, which derives

---

[1] Alfred Zimmern, *Solon and Croesus* (1928), p. 106.

[2] Cf. Zimmern's statement of ten "distinctive features" of a slave system of labor, *op. cit.* 110–113. Five may be accepted as correct, so far as generalizations are correct; but the remaining five are either incorrect or questionable. Who needs to be told in these days that theoretical economics do not guide us to an understanding of society's problems? Zimmern's distinction between chattel-slavery and apprentice-slavery (p. 120) has no meaning to me. Slavery is a system under which some human beings are chattels. Where this fundamental legal and social fact does not exist another relationship between human groups has arisen which is not slavery.

from the lands and peoples of the pre-Greek cultures and from the extensions of Greek civilization, in hybrid forms of cultural expression, into the Hellenistic and Roman phases of antiquity.[1] Refreshed with new knowledge and new points of view one moves backward from the later period into the two centuries of Athenian leadership. So doing, one may question with revived interest the old facts and the old falsehoods; and one finds that they have taken on new meanings. The old tea-leaves, quite suddenly, are no longer stale.

In 1423 the ardent Italian collector of Greek manuscripts, Giovanni Aurispa, brought back the one manuscript of the *Deipnosophists* of Athenaeus which is the source of all later manuscripts and editions of that work.[2] It was this, our good luck, which introduced into the study of ancient slavery all the difficulties which face us regarding the relative proportion of enslaved and free in antiquity. Were it not for the rambling and antiquarian table-talk of these dining-club professors of Athenaeus we would have had to deal, predominantly, with comprehensible and credible numbers of slaves — fifties, hundreds, and thousands, instead of thousands, myriads and hundreds of thousands.

Athenaeus, a "culture Greek"[3] of Naucratis in Egypt, put together this work, of the symposium type, somewhere near the close of the second century of our era. Despite obvious and demonstrable blunders in copying made by Athenaeus or by his amanuensis[4] it is impossible to dismiss him summarily. So much of his material

---

[1] The new materials from Hellenistic and Roman times will be found in synthetic presentation, interwoven with the old, in the article "Sklaverei" in Pauly-Wissowa-Kroll, *Realencyclopädie*, Supplementband VI, cols. 893–1068. A large amount of new information upon slavery in the Neo-Babylonian Kingdom has been assembled at the Oriental Institute of the University of Chicago. At the time of this writing it has not yet been published.

[2] Wilhelm von Christ — Wilhelm Schmid, *Geschichte der griech. Literatur*, 5th ed. (1913) II 2. 628.

[3] The phrase was coined, so far as I know, by W. W. Tarn in his *Hellenistic Civilization*.

[4] E.g. in XI 500 c Dercyllidas is called a "Scythian." Actually he was called a "Sisyphus." *Vide* Xen. *Hell.* III 1. 8 and Jules Nicole in *Bibl. de l'École des Hautes Études, Sciences Phil. et Hist.* LXXIII (1887) p. 29. In II 44 c where Athenaeus should be speaking of a certain Sostratus he places instead Philinus who

is right that one must specifically prove him to be wrong or fantastic if one wishes to discard his alleged facts at any point. In Book VI 272–273 a, Athenaeus cites several passages upon the number of slaves owned by individuals in the past and of slaves resident in certain city-states. Among these is this statement: "Ctesicles says, in the third book of his *Chronica*, that during the one hundred and ——teenth [1] Olympiad an investigation [2] was held at Athens by Demetrius of Phalerum of those inhabiting Attica; and the Athenians were found to be 21,000, the metics 10,000 and the servants (οἰκετῶν in the text) forty myriads (400,000)." The context makes it certain that by οἰκέται Athenaeus means slaves; and we would not be warranted in doubting that the numbers were correctly copied from Ctesicles' *Chronica*. If we are to accept this number the enslaved persons of the Athenian state about 317–308 B.C. surpassed the free by about four to one. About the same ratio, according to further citations given by Athenaeus, would hold for Corinth and Aegina. The entire group of his quotations dealing with slave numbers is presented with the obvious intent of proving this single point, that the slaves in ancient Greece, that is 500 years before his time, greatly outnumbered the free. To discredit his proofs one must necessarily analyze ʼhe entire set of citations, because one must concede that they make a formidable group of alleged facts, which in their totality become impressive through the array of their numerical similarities.

Timaeus of Sicily is first cited as stating that it was not customary among the Greeks to possess slaves. Probably Timaeus said that the Greeks, in olden times (presumably referring to Homeric times, as shown by τὸ πάλαιον), did not use purchased slaves as personal attendants. [3] Athenaeus then points out that

---

was, in reality, the source of the information about Sostratus. See K. Funk in *Philologus*, Supplementband X (1905–1907) 641 n. 233.

[1] There is a lacuna in the text at this point. The manuscript has only καὶ δεκάτηι πρὸς ταῖς ἑκατόν.

[2] The word used is ἐξετασμός, from ἐξετάζειν, not ἀπογραφία, which would be used to designate a formal census.

[3] See Athenaeus VI 264 c. Polybius, book XII, is quoted by Athenaeus, VI

Timaeus' statement is inconsistent with another of his statements that Mnason of Phocis owned more than 1,000 slaves, and with still another citation, from the third book of the "Histories" of Timaeus, to the effect that Corinth was so prosperous that it possessed forty-six myriads of slaves (460,000). After this follows the quotation from Ctesicles about Demetrius of Phalerum and his 400,000 slaves at Athens. From a monograph of Aristotle upon the *Polity of the Aeginetans*, which is now lost, comes the information that there were 470,000 slaves in their state. Out of Sicilian and Italian history of the second and first centuries B.C., without statement of his sources, Athenaeus offers the information that more than a million slaves were put to death in the slave revolts, and that Spartacus caused "a large number" of slaves to rise and that daily they "poured in" to join him.

The numbers which he advances for individual property in slaves are so chosen that they consistently support the general idea of these masses of enslaved persons in the Greek city-states. There is the affirmation, quoted above, about Mnason of Phocis and his more than 1,000 slaves. From the pamphlet *Upon the Revenues*, ascribed to Xenophon,[1] Athenaeus quotes a reference to the effect that Nicias (the general of the Sicilian expedition) had a thousand slaves and leased them for work in the silver mines to Sosias, a Thracian, on an arrangement by which each rented slave brought in an obol a day.[2] The slave investment of Nicias is later supported by a quotation from Posidonius regarding a slave revolt in Attica which occurred about 103–102 B.C.[3] Posidonius "says that they murdered the guards at the mines, captured the fortress at Sunium

---

272 b, in refutation of the first statement. This part of the twelfth book of Polybius is lost except in the citation by Athenaeus.

[1] The question of the authorship, whether actually written by Xenophon or not, does not vitally affect the discussion of slave numbers given in the *Revenues*. I however, have not been favorably impressed with the contention of W. Schwahn in *Rheinisches Museum* LXXX (1931) 258–259, that it is not from Xenophon's hand, nor by his arguments which would assign it to Eubulus, finance minister at Athens, or to one of his followers. See Adolf Wilhelm's able discussion of the *Revenues* of Xenophon in *Wiener Studien* LII (1934) 18–19, 37–38.

[2] The statement is a fairly exact abridgement of Xenophon, *Upon the Revenues* 4.14.

[3] W. S. Ferguson in *Klio* IV (1904) 12 and in *Hellenistic Athens* 427 n. 4 and 428 n. 1.

and caused havoc in Attica for some time."[1] This incident might easily have been caused by a total of 500 or 1,000 slaves if they were a determined lot. In fact a similar riot of the slaves in the Attic mines had occurred about thirty years earlier (ca. 130 B.C.) and their numbers are given as "over one thousand."[2] As a figure derived from an ancient source this is fairly definite. At best the slave revolt at Athens, as taken from Posidonius, has no validity as proof that Nicias three hundred years earlier owned a thousand slaves.

It is these "Attic myriads of slaves who worked the mines" which bother Athenaeus, as they have, since his time, bothered everybody who is interested. He returns to the task of bolstering up his Attic myriads. "Each of the Romans . . . has owned prodigious numbers of them. For very many have owned ten thousand and twice ten thousand" which they keep as attendants when they go out. If we begin with the numbers given by Athenaeus about the slaves of the time nearest his own life it becomes immediately apparent that this clipper of interesting data, a bookworm living in Egypt, had no personal knowledge of the Roman Empire in its western part. It is also significant that his dining professors, as they talk about their own time, do not cite references.

Let us begin with those numbers which have actually been transmitted to us by ancient authorities other than Athenaeus for the period of the empire. The writers of the Augustan Histories were credulous enough, in all conscience. But even their credulity never swallowed more than two or three thousand slaves in any one man's possession. Proculus, a robber chieftain of the Maritime Alps in the Ligurian district when he was declared Imperator in 280 A.D. "is said to have armed 2,000 of his own slaves."[3] He was a robber chieftain and might well have armed 2000 followers. But one doubts that they were slaves, because the Emperor Tacitus himself, when he manumitted all the slaves of his urban household, nevertheless kept within the provisions of the Caninian Law which did not permit the freeing of more than one hundred slaves

---

[1] Athenaeus VI 272 f.

[2] Diodorus XXXIV 2. 19: καὶ κατὰ τὴν Ἀττικὴν ὑπὲρ χιλίων.

[3] *Scriptores Historiae Augustae, Firmus* 12. 2.

by any one person.[1] The actual evidence as to numbers of slaves owned by the most powerful families of the Empire, as recorded in the ancient literature and as estimated from epigraphical sources, has been assembled in Pauly-Wissowa-Kroll *Realencyclopädie* Supplementband VI 1000–1002. These data indicate that Seneca's description of a household of conspicuous wealth, where it mentions the "trained cohort of slaves,"[2] sets the upper limit of slave numbers which one can ascribe even to the richest Romans of the early Empire. Taking the legion at its full complement of 6,000 this would place the highest number of slaves in individual possession at about 600.

So much for Athenaeus' ten and twenty thousand slaves owned by the Romans of his time. If we turn to the west at the time of the Republic he betrays his gullibility much more quickly. The total numbers of slaves and poor free persons engaged in the great slave revolts in Sicily and Italy, according to the ancient authorities, are as follows. In Sicily in the revolt of 135–132 B.C. the total numbers ran to 70,000,[3] in the uprising of 104–101 B.C. 3,500 in Italy[4] and certainly not more than 50,000 to 100,000 in Sicily;[5] under Spartacus in Italy in 72–71 B.C. possibly 120,000 men.[6] Out of a total number of slaves and free, in the major slave uprisings, which did not surpass 300,000, Athenaeus has relentlessly slain a million.[7]

[1] *Script. Hist. Aug.*, *Tacitus* 10 .7.

[2] Seneca *Epistulae Morales* 110. 17. I reject the 4,116 slaves which Isidorus, a freedman of Gaius Cornelius, is alleged to have enumerated in his will at his death in 8 B.C., Pliny *N. H.* XXXIII 135. The number of small cattle there ascribed to Isidorus, namely 257,000, is somewhat more than one-half of the total of sheep and goats owned in the province of Umbria at the present time. Furthermore it would require about 400 square miles of grazing land to feed Isidorus' sheep and goats alone.

[3] This total recorded by Livy *Epitome* LVI, is more credible than the 200,000 given by Diodorus XXXIV–V 2. 18.

[4] Diodorus XXXVI 2. 6.

[5] The suppression of this revolt was carried out by a Roman army of 17,000 men: Diodorus XXXVI 8. 1.

[6] Appian *Bella Civilia* I 14. 117. The number handed down in the text of Velleius Paterculus II 30. 6 has obviously been corrupted in transmission.

[7] Athenaeus VI 272 f.

Athenaeus may be entirely credible on fish and cakes, but it does seem sensible to eliminate him as an independent source upon the institution of slavery. We must grant, however, that his direct quotations, where he gives his sources, may be quite accurate as quotations, though not so as to fact. For, as we have seen, his quotation about the thousand slaves owned by Nicias is given substantially as it stands in Xenophon *Upon the Revenues*. Let us first dispose of the four hundred and seventy thousand slaves of the Aeginetans. The number purports to come from Aristotle's *Polity of the Aeginetans*. Wherever the mistake lay [1] this figure is jettisoned by common sense and by common consent. Aegina is eight miles long by six miles wide. In 1928 it boasted 8,832 inhabitants.[2] A rough calculation, if we were to accept the number, would give Aegina, in Aristotle's time, a population density of almost twelve thousand to the square mile, counting slaves alone.[3] The most rational guess that we have of the population in the Cyclades islands in antiquity — that of Julius Beloch — allows them about one hundred twenty-five persons per square mile.[4]

Athenaeus is completely out of the picture as an independent witness for masses of slaves owned by wealthy men of Roman times or for the tens of myriads of slaves whom he places among the populations of the Greek city-states of the fourth century B.C. The statement ascribed to Aristotle regarding the 470,000 slaves in Aegina must be disregarded as physically impossible. For the slave numbers in hundreds of thousands we are forced back upon three witnesses of the Hellenistic and earlier Greek periods: first, upon Ctesicles in the *Chronica*, or the investigation of Demetrius of Phalerum, for the 400,000 in Attica; second, upon Timaeus of Sicily for the thousand owned by Mnason of Phocis and the 460,000 possessed by the Corinthians; third, upon the Xenophontic pamphlet *Upon the Revenues* for a thousand slaves

---

[1] It is as difficult to imagine that this number actually appeared in the Aristotelian study as to suppose that Demetrius of Phalerum actually reported that there were 400,000 slaves in Attica.

[2] *Annuaire Statistique de la Grèce* IV, Athens, 1933, p. 43.

[3] Rachel L. Sargent *Slave Population* 20 note 60, 31.

[4] 48 to the square kilometer, as given by Beloch, *Bevölkerung der griechisch-römischen Welt* 506; cf. 84–85.

personally owned by Nicias, six hundred belonging to Hipponicus, and three hundred to Philemonides.

Professor Ferguson himself, in *Hellenistic Athens* p. 54 and note 3, briefly but completely disposed of the slave figures which reputedly go back to the investigation of Demetrius, by assuming that the numbers of the slaves actually recorded in the ἐξετασμός of the Phalerian have not come down to us. If Athenaeus used the very text of Ctesicles' *Chronica*, rather than a quotation from it culled from some later author, and if this text was sound, the fault lay with Ctesicles. There is no possibility of checking upon the reports from Timaeus about Mnason of Phocis and the slaves of Corinth. But if the numbers for Athens are of no value, those for Corinth must be discarded with them. Setting aside for the moment the *Chronica* of Ctesicles and its four hundred thousand Attic slaves, let us approach the statement about the private ownership at Athens of one thousand, of six hundred, and of three hundred slaves by Nicias, Hipponicus, and Philemonides respectively. The first two of these slave owners were well known as exceedingly rich men according to the standards of wealth of their time.[1]

Known instances of family fortunes of the time make it quite certain that capital sums in private hands were sufficient to enable single men of outstanding wealth to purchase as many as a thousand slaves if they concentrated upon this form of investment. According to the reputed wealth of Nicias his investment in slaves would have constituted a third of his entire fortune.[2] Such a fortune must, of course, be regarded as highly exceptional.[3]

---

[1] Xenophon *Upon the Revenues* 4. 14–15. Regarding Hipponicus, note the Athenian jibes directed at him and several of his ancestors because of the sources of their fortunes, in Pauly-Wissowa-Kroll *Realencyclopädie* VIII 1907–1909, *Hipponikos* 1, 2, 3.

[2] According to Lysias, 19. 47–48, the fortune of Nicias was thought to have been 100 talents, that of Callias 200 talents. It should be noted in both of these cases that the evidence available to Lysias was not entirely convincing even to himself. This is apparent from his use of προσεδοκᾶτο in the one case, and ὥς φασι in the other.

[3] The ancient information upon the size of fortunes in Attica in the fifth and fourth centuries in relation to alleged investment in slaves will be found conveniently stated in Sargent *Slave Population* 49–56, 96–100.

If we were to accept at face value the statement of these amazing numbers of slaves owned by Nicias, Hipponicus and Philemonides, as handed down *only* in Xenophon's plan for increasing the state revenues,[1] we would still be unable to arrive at any figure for the total slave population which would make their number exceed that of the free residents of Attica. For it is clear that Xenophon has selected and grouped the highest numbers that he could find and that he regards them as rare and extraordinary cases. Athenian slave labor was predominantly used in the mines at Laurium or as skilled labor in handicraft shops in the city. Intrinsically, under the conditions of economic use of slave labor in Attica, the maintenance by single persons of so many unfree workmen is not credible. Under the plantation system in the southern sections of the United States, which made actual sustenance of the slaves a relatively easy matter, I have found but few instances of ownership of more than 700 negroes by any one planter, whether his main crop was tobacco, cotton or sugar.[2] The slaves owned and employed upon the Brazilian sugar plantations, exclusive of the military forces used as guards on these estates, averaged about 300.

If the evidence of Xenophon in regard to private ownership of

---

[1] The number does not appear in Plutarch *Nicias* 4. Plutarch contents himself with a πλῆθος ἀνδραπόδων. Probably he doubted Xenophon's thousand slaves as much as I do.

[2] In South Carolina just before the Civil War a planter named Burnsides is reputed to have owned more than 1,000 slaves; but this figure is not established by a census report. Where great slave concentrations in single ownership occur they are likely to be on several non-contiguous estates. The numbers of slaves actually owned by the outstanding plantation proprietors in the United States may be illustrated by the following list: In 1790 in South Carolina, William Blake, 695; Ralph Izard, 604; Nathaniel Heyward, 433; William Washington, 393; and three members of the Horry family, respectively, 340, 229 and 222 slaves. See Ulrich Phillips, *American Negro Slavery*, New York, 1918, pp. 95–6. At Mt. Vernon in 1821 Bushrod Washington had 90 slaves. In 1832 the larger plantations in Virginia customarily maintained from 50 to 100 slaves. See Fr. Bancroft, *Slave Trading in the Old South*, Baltimore, 1931, pp. 15–6. This was a sufficient number on any plantation to stamp the owner as an aristocrat, a large planter of honored position, Bancroft pp. 345–6. In 1858 the wealthiest cotton grower in Georgia, Joseph Bond, owned 566 slaves, *ibid.* 353. Compare the 235 slaves of General Gadsden sold in 1859 at Charleston, South Carolina, according to Bancroft, p. 182.

slaves is open to doubt on general consideration of the difficulties of slave maintenance, it is still further weakened upon close analysis of his text. He is arguing that the Athenian state could buy up a large number of slaves and help to replete the state income by renting them out, as the "wage-earning" slaves (μισθοφοροῦντα σώματα) were constantly leased to entrepreneurs by private owners. In citing his examples of large incomes derived from the slave-renting system he betrays the scanty nature of his information. "For long ago, I presume, we who have been interested have heard that Nicias, son of Niceratus, owned in the silver mines a thousand men which he leased out to Sosias, the Thracian, on the basis that he pay an obol per day net for each slave and keep the number always equal.[1] Hipponicus also owned six hundred slaves let out in the same manner who brought in a mina net per day, and Philemonides three hundred who brought in a half mina. And others owned slaves in accordance, I suppose, with their (financial) ability."[2] No source is given. So far as Xenophon is concerned it is hearsay from a long time ago (πάλαι; and note the doubting δήπου). What has he to say of the silver-mine workers of his own time? "But why speak of matters of long ago? For now there are many men in the mines rented out thus." Either the numbers of rented slave laborers in the Laurian mines in his day were too few to suit his argument, or he had no knowledge of the number. In either case why believe him on hearsay about matters of fifty-five years earlier?

Two hundred years ago the number of four hundred thousand slaves for Athens was summarily rejected by the French scholar, Charles Rollin, who reduced them to forty thousand by the arbitrary method of assuming an error in the text of Athenaeus.[3] In 1752 David Hume in his essay upon *The Populousness of Ancient*

---

[1] The modern editions read here παρέχειν instead of παρεῖχεν of the manuscripts. See Rudolph Herzog in *Festgabe für Hugo Blümner*, Zürich, 1914, pp. 475–6. Herzog's idea, that Sosias was a slave bailiff, owned by Nicias, may be correct.

[2] Xenophon *Upon theRevenues* 4. 14–15. The rate of interest on investment, namely an obol net per day on each slave, is the same throughout.

[3] In the edition of his *Histoire ancienne des Egyptiens, des Carthaginois, des Assyriens*, etc., IV 409, published at Amsterdam in 1735, Rollin merely states that the 400,000 of Athenaeus are "a manifest error." See also the English translation

Nations adopted this drastic reduction of Rollin and gave ten reasons for so doing.[1] Hume's arguments are thoroughly sound although his reasoning is entirely general and *a priori* in character. In 1817 the great German classicist August Boeckh came to the defense of Athenaeus. His authority was great enough to re-establish faith in the traditional four slaves at Athens to every free person and the corresponding predominance of slaves over the free at Corinth and Aegina.[2] In support of this reaction he advanced a difficult fragment from the Athenian fourth century orator Hyperides[3] in which Hyperides urged that "more than 150,000 from the silver mines and those throughout the rest of the country, then those indebted to the public treasury, the disfranchised and the metics" should be conscripted for military service; but this fragment, which appears in a quotation by the tenth-century lexicographer Suidas,[4] is so late and the text in

---

The Ancient History of the Egyptians, Carthaginians, Assyrians etc., of the same year (London 1735), IV 302, where the note appears with the phrase as just quoted.

[1] *Essays Moral, Political and Literary*, edited by T. H. Green and Grose, London, 1898, I 419–21.

[2] August Boeckh, *Die Staatshaushaltung der Athener*, 3rd ed., Berlin, 1886, I 47–52. He assumes that the relation of the free to the slave population can be placed at 27 to 100, or about 1 to 4 (p. 49). His next statement, that the same relation on the American sugar plantations stood at one free to six slaves, may be true of single plantations; but the comparison between American sugar plantations and the ancient city-states is entirely misleading. In 1850 in the state of Louisiana, where sugar culture was most highly developed in the United States, there were 100 free persons to every 96 slaves. In South Carolina the ratio was 140 slaves to 100 free and in Georgia 124 to 100 free. These are the highest slave numbers known to me in any of the states of the South. See *U. S. Bureau of Census: A Century of Population Growth*, Washington, 1909, p. 140.

Boeckh was followed in England by H. F. Clinton, *Fasti Hellenici*, Oxford, 1841, II 480, and in Germany by B. Büchsenschütz, *Besitz und Erwerb im griechischen Altertume*, Halle, 1869, pp. 140–2, and by the eminent German classicist, Friederich Blass. See his essay upon the *Soziale Zustände in Athen im 4ten Jahrhundert*, Kiel, 1885, p. 9. Jakob Burckhardt, *Griechische Kulturgeschichte*, Berlin, 1898, I 158, although he found it difficult to adjust his conception of Greek culture to such a preponderance of slaves, could not bring himself to an outright break with the statements of Athenaeus.

[3] In the third edition of *Hyperidis Orationes Sex* by C. Jessen, Leipzig, 1917, it appears as fragment 7. 29.

[4] Suidas I 1, p. 279. 22–25 (ed. Adler, Leipzig, 1928).

itself so doubtful that it should not be regarded as admissible evidence in an attempt to determine, even roughly, the ratio of slaves to free in Attica.[1] The passage of Athenaeus regarding the relatively vast number of slaves in Greek city-states must be dropped *in toto* and, with it, any attempt to re-establish the results of the investigation of the population of Attica, so far as it relates to the numbers of the slaves, except as estimates based upon contemporary indications. The alleged numbers of the slaves privately owned by Nicias, Hipponicus and Philemonides are also, in my judgment, of no historical value, other than to prove that these three were wealthy men who were reputed to have had heavy investments in "wage-earning slaves" ($\mu\iota\sigma\theta\circ\phi\circ\rho\circ\hat{\upsilon}\nu\tau\alpha$ $\sigma\acute{\omega}\mu\alpha\tau\alpha$). The one hundred fifty thousand slaves from the mines of Attica, supposedly recorded by Hyperides, must go. With these figures all of the testimony is exhausted, which would warrant the conclusion that Greek society in the fifth and fourth centuries, and particularly that of Athens, was predominantly slave ridden. There were no slave revolts in Greek lands until the second half of the second century B.C., such as marked the history of western plantation slavery from 200 B.C. to 71 B.C. The two revolts which did occur, in 130 B.C. at Delos and Athens and 103–102 B.C. in Athens alone, were backwashes of the great western slave outbreaks of the same periods. The Greek insurrections do not give the impression that large numbers were involved.[2] There is no piece of Greek city-state legislation which betrays any great fear of slave revolts

---

[1] This number of 150,000 slaves is rejected by Beloch, *Bevölkerung* 98–9 (who would amend it to 40,000 or 50,000) and by Ettore Cicotti, in *Rendiconti dell' Istituto Lombardo*, Series II vol. XXX (1897), pp. 657–9. Attempts to make use of this fragment by arbitrary emendation are unsatisfactory, as stated by Cicotti in the study cited above, p. 668, and by A. W. Gomme, *Population of Athens* 21–2, in criticism of Beloch's emendation.

The story need not be retold of the growing tendency among modern scholars since 1890 to abandon Athenaeus' figures and cut down the estimates of the ratio of slaves to free in Greece, including Athens. See Sargent *Slave Population* 35–42.

[2] These revolts are dealt with, much in this sense, by Professor Ferguson in *Hellenistic Athens* 378–9 and 427–8.

such as lurks constantly in the consciousness of every society in which the slaves equal the free or exceed them in number.

There is one instance known to me from the classic Greek world in which a public fear of revolution involving the emancipation of slaves and their use in class warfare has been predicated. This was in the League of the Hellenes established by Philip II of Macedon at Corinth in 338 B.C. The constitution of the League provided that the central organization and its policing force should see to it that, among the constituent members, there would be "no executions and banishments contrary to the laws established in the city-states, no confiscations of property nor redistributions of land, no abolition of debts and no freeing of slaves for the furthering of revolutionary movements." [1] These were provisions designed by Philip of Macedon for the preservation of social order, as against revolutionary disorder, within the separate city-state members of the League. It is true that the separate state entities gave over to a police force of the federation the power of enforcement of order and obviously with the object of preserving the propertied interests of each community against radical changes. But it is going too far toward modernism to see, back of these conservative proposals, the threatening "horrors of class warfare." [2] Class warfare was, admittedly, a constant factor in the political life of the city-states of the fourth century which had to be met or endured. So far as the slaves were concerned the city-states merely agreed to make it illegal to permit slave-owners to manumit their slaves for enlistment in the contending ranks in local revolutions. It is not an indication of unrest among the slaves as servile groups — rather, in fact, the contrary.

The most exact information available upon the number of the slave population at Athens toward the close of the fifth century lies in a remark made by Thucydides. It is the more trustworthy because it has no intention of proving that the slave numbers were either large or moderate. As observer he was careful; and, above all, he was rational in his outlook and sober in his judgments;

---

[1] Demosthenes *On the Agreements with Alexander*, 17. 15.

[2] This is the attitude of Robert von Pöhlmann in his *Geschichte der sozialen Frage und des Sozialismus* (2d ed., 1912) I 420–1.

and he knew his Athens. He tells us that the permanent occupation by the Spartans in 413 B.C. of a fortified place at Decelea near Athens did great damage to the Athenians, and that, because of the destruction of property and loss of men which this occupation brought about, the war turned out badly for them. In describing the damage which the Decelean garrison caused by its constant presence *through the remaining years of the war* he states that more than 20,000 slaves "had deserted"[1] and that the greater part of these were handicraftsmen. This has no further meaning than that Thucydides had heard this estimate of the number of the runaway slaves during an eight year period. There is no way of knowing whose estimate it was; but, obviously, Thucydides thought it a reasonable one. The majority of these, he believed, were handicraftsmen. Possibly we may assume that the artisans among them numbered 13,000 or 14,000, as Gomme has suggested.[2] It seems reasonable enough that the majority were

[1] Thucydides VII 27. 5: πλέον ἢ δύο μυριάδες ηὐτομολήκεσαν, καὶ τούτων πολὺ μέρος χειροτέχναι. It is clear from the tenor of this entire section that Thucydides has in mind the gradual and constant attrition of Athenian strength down to the end of the war. This is expressed in the imperfect tense, πολλὰ ἔβλαπτε τοὺς Ἀθηναίους and in the aorist, ἐκάκωσε τὰ πράγματα, "it brought their affairs to a bad end." The pluperfect, ηὐτομολήκεσαν, is retrospective, from the standpoint of the end of the war. Cf. Eduard Schwartz *Das Geschichtswerk des Thukydides* (2d ed., 1929) 200, and W. Schadewaldt *Die Geschichtsschreibung des Thukydides* (1929) 8, 21. Failure to note this fact has vitiated Rachel Sargent's use of the passage (*Size of the Slave Population at Athens*, p. 88), when she assumes that, *at the time of the occupation* of Decelea, 20,000 slaves deserted, all in the single year 413 B.C. Also her statement that the majority of these were from the mines is not warranted by the promise of Alcibiades in Thuc. VI 91. 7. Alcibiades stated that slaves would come over and that the Athenians would lose the revenues of the Laurian mines. There is no suggestion that these two results of the occupation of Decelea were to be connected one with the other.

This evidence of Thucydides received a surprising confirmation in 1908 through the publication of a newly discovered fragment of an historian of the fourth century B.C. which states that, after they had joined the Spartans in the occupation of Decelea, the Thebans became prosperous through taking over slaves and other war booty at a low price. See Grenfell and Hunt, *Oxyrhynchus Papyri* V (1908) no. 8 col. 13. 28–33, reprinted by F. Jacoby, *Fragmente der griechischen Historiker*, Berlin, 1923–1930, II A p. 26 (no. 66 col. 12. 4).

[2] A. W. Gomme *The Population of Athens in the Fifth and Fourth Centuries B.C.* 20.

handicraftsmen, in view of the war situation and the constant need, before and after Decelea, of the manufacturing of war materials, both offensive and defensive. Distributed over the eight years from the first occupation of Decelea to the end of the war the slave desertions would be at the rate of about 2,500 per year.

In two cases the numbers of slaves owned by individual residents of Athens at about this time are known. In 414 B.C. the property of a resident alien named Cephisodorus was confiscated. He owned sixteen slaves.[1] In 404 B.C., when their properties were confiscated in the oligarchic revolution, the orator Lysias and his brother owned one hundred and twenty slaves including their domestic servants, attendants, and handicraftsmen employed in a shield-making establishment which they ran.[2]

For the fourth century we are only a little better off in respect to slave numbers, if at all, than in the fifth century. In elaborating his project for increasing the revenues of the Attic state Xenophon proposed, among other ideas, that the Attic state should make an immediate purchase of 1,200 slaves whom it was then to lease out to the owners of the silver mine pits at Laurium as mining laborers. Out of the profits of the enterprise these were to be increased by gradual purchase over a space of five or six years until a total of 6,000 should be reached, with the idea, contemplated under the plan, of an eventual total of 10,000 state-owned slaves.[3] Most important is Xenophon's dream that eventually the state would own three slaves for every Athenian citizen.[4] This implies that Xenophon could conceive a total of about 60,000 to 65,000 slaves in public ownership, when those in private ownership must necessarily have shrunk to a small number because of the competition of the state's slaves. Xenophon, therefore, thought of the slaves in terms of about a third or a quarter of the total

---

[1] The information is exact since it is from an original document of that year: Dittenberger *Sylloge Inscriptionum Graecarum* (3d ed.) I no. 96.

[2] Lysias 12 *Against Eratosthenes* 8, 19. See Hasebroek *Trade and Politics in Ancient Greece* 72–3 (= *Staat und Handel* 76).

[3] Xenophon *Upon the Revenues* 4. 23–4. For the gradual process of purchasing, *ibid.* 4. 38.

[4] *Ibid.* 4. 17.

population.[1] For the slave population of Syracuse in Sicily we have a confirmation of this estimate. This is found in a statement of Diodorus that Dionysius I in 396 B.C. freed enough slaves in that state to man sixty war vessels.[2] Julius Beloch has estimated that this number indicates that the Syracusan territory had at least 12,000 slaves capable of bearing arms. His conclusion as to the entire population of the Syracusan territory resulted in an approximate total of 250,000 inhabitants.[3] This would indicate for Syracuse also a ratio of slaves to free population of about one to four.

In the eyes of Plato about fifty would be the limit of the number of slaves owned by a wealthy citizen of Athens. In the *Republic*, when discussing the constant terrors which surround tyrants, he has Socrates says: "Suppose that one of the gods should snatch up out of the state a man who had fifty slaves or more and place him, with his wife and children and his slaves and the rest of his property, in a desert place where no free man could help him. How terrible and how great his fear would be for himself, his children and his wife that they would be killed by his slaves?"[4] Plato's idea of the number of slaves which a wealthy man might be expected to possess is borne out with singular exactness by the actual number owned by the orator Demosthenes. In his prosecution of the guardian of his estate he disclosed to the court that his father had left him an establishment for the manufacture of knives and swords with thirty-two or thirty-three slaves and a workshop for making couch frames with twenty slave workmen

---

[1] The number of the citizens in 355 B.C. is not known. Beloch's doubtful figure of 21,000 citizens in 400 B.C. (*Bevölkerung* 74) or Gomme's equally questionable 22,000 (*Population of Athens* 26) have been taken arbitrarily as the basis of this ratio.

[2] Diodorus XIV 58. 1.

[3] Beloch *Bevölkerung* 280-1.

[4] Plato *Republic* 578 e. The statement that it is to be a *wealthy* citizen appears in 578 d. In Plato's State of the *Laws*, which was designed as an agrarian society, supported primarily by slave labor in agricultural production, one-third of the food produced was to be assigned to the slaves, one-third to the artisans and alien residents, the other third to the free men, *Laws* VIII 848 a. This implies that about one-third of the population would be servile in status.

trained to this trade.[1] Another Athenian of the same time, a certain Timarchus, had inherited eleven or twelve slaves, including nine or ten leather workers, a woman linen weaver and a leather embroiderer.[2]

The observation that a considerable part of the Attic population had no slaves at all is even more important than the figures given above in proving that the exaggerated numbers which Athenaeus gives must be abandoned.[3] The statement should be obvious for the poorer classes of the city;[4] and it is definitely proven for the disabled citizen workman for whom Lysias wrote a speech in defense against an action which was brought for the withdrawal of a state dole formerly received by him. The cripple asserted that he could not afford to keep a slave to help him in his trade.[5] It is also to be proven in the case of people of enough means so that they became involved in litigation over estate inheritances. One case will be enough to illustrate the fact. One member of the group involved in the complicated litigation did not inventory any slaves in his property. Stratocles, a brother of the defendant in the case, inherited through the death of a daughter a property valued at two and a half talents, or 15,000 drachmas in silver. It is listed as consisting of real estate, sixty sheep, a hundred goats and other equipment; but no slaves appear.[6] The inventory

---

[1] Demosthenes 27 *Against Aphobus* I 9 for the knife makers and 24 for the twenty couch makers. In Demosthenes, 37 *Against Pantaenetus* 4, a loan was made to a mine owner on the security of his mine pit and thirty slaves which he owned.

[2] Aeschines 1 *Against Timarchus* 97.

[3] Sargent, *Slave Population* 101, evidently recognized the value of this negative evidence, but applied the method only with reference to the slaves in handicraft shops.

[4] A. W. Gomme, *Population of Athens* 21, has correctly concluded that the number of domestic slaves in the homes of the lowest class, the thetes, would be negligible because of the expense of keeping them.

[5] Lysias 24 *In Defense of the Cripple* 6. In the property inherited by the Athenian, Diodotus, in Lysias 32 *Against Diogeiton* 5, amounting to the considerable sum of 7 talents, 40 minas, and 2,000 drachmas, no slave is mentioned.

[6] Isaeus 11 *On the Estate of Hagnias* 40–1. The defendant and his brother had sufficient means to care for themselves, but not enough to subject them to the liturgical services which fell upon the well-to-do. Since the number of the sheep and goats inherited by the daughter of one of the two men is enumerated, I judge

of his estate at the time of his death is also given. The estimated total then was put at 33,000 drachmas, made up of real property, interest-bearing loans, furniture, sheep, barley, wine, and nine hundred drachmas in silver. Not a single slave appears.

Two extracts from the literature of the period may serve to clinch the argument. In the *Ecclesiazusae* of Aristophanes, produced in 392 B.C., in her proposal for collective ownership of property the feminist Praxagora wants to put an end to a situation in which one person has many slaves and another has not even a single attendant.[1] In respect to the working classes of the population Xenophon makes the significant remark — "*those who can do so* buy slaves so that they may have fellow workmen."[2]

All of the evidence which is really significant points toward the conclusion that in Attica the slaves did not comprise more than a third of the total population, possibly not more than a fourth. It must be granted that this statement is no more than a reasonable suggestion. For the Peloponnesus, outside of Sparta and its Helot population, a much smaller ratio of slaves must be postulated because of the statement ascribed to Pericles[3] that the Peloponnesians, in contrast to the Athenians, did their own work. Even Athenaeus, who is responsible for the long-established belief in the huge masses of slaves at Corinth, Aegina, and Athens, else-

---

that if the estate had possessed slaves they would be given. I am assuming that the slave inventory of the estate, if there were any slaves, would not be included under the item of "remaining equipment." Cf. the further enumeration of the items in the property, *ibid.* 43. Some of the property, it is true, was not declared in the inventory. Again, however, I do not believe that slave holdings could be concealed in the declaration.

No slaves appear in the modest property holding of Dicaeogenes in Isaeus 5. 22–3, 29, nor in the dowry of a daughter in 8 *On the Estate of Ciron* 8. In the *Cyropaedia* I 1. 1 Xenophon says that some families kept in their homes a considerable number of slaves, others very few. There is no way of determining what proportion of the families in Athens had some slaves and what part owned "very few."

[1] Aristophanes *Ecclesiazusae* 593.

[2] Xenophon *Memorabilia* II 3: 3.

[3] Thucydides I 141. 3. From Thucydides III 15 it becomes clear that the Peloponnesian allies of Sparta were loth to undertake military operations during the harvest season because their citizens would at that time be engaged in getting in their crops.

where states that the most of the Greeks, except the Chians, originally tended to use conquered Greeks in helotage rather than have slaves.[1] No Greek writer of this period has uttered any complaint against a supposed influx of slaves such as was expressed so freely at Rome in the first century of the Christian era. For Chios we have the authority of Thucydides that it contained more slaves than any other Greek state except Sparta.[2] It should be clear that Thucydides' comparison is between the number of *slaves* at Chios and the number of *Helots* at Lacedaemon. Actually we know very little about the number of the Helots. The best guess available puts the minimum at 60,000. If this be somewhere near the truth, Beloch's rough estimate of about 100,000 slaves at Chios may be near the mark.[3] It is fairly certain that in other Greek communities than those which were centers of handicraft production the slave ratio fell considerably below any percentage which may be established for Athens.

Without question the Greek city-states of the fifth and fourth centuries B.C., and among them notably Athens, used slave labor upon a fairly large scale. But the slaves were employed at the same work as the free, usually side by side with them, and apparently without prejudice or friction. In any sense which implies either that the enslaved population predominated over the free or that the Greek city-states displayed the mentality of a slave-ridden society, Greek culture was not founded upon slavery.

[1] Athenaeus VI 265 b, c.

[2] Thucydides VIII 40. 2.

[3] For the Helot figures see Beloch *Bevölkerung* 147; for the Chian slaves, *ibid.* 2. The total population of Chios was estimated in 1932 at about 80,000.

LES RAPPORTS D'ATHENES ET DE L'AITOLIE AU IIIᵉ SIECLE AVANT J.-C.

PAR R. FLACELIÈRE

CERTAINS noms semblent prédestinés: l'archonte d'Athènes Polyeuctos, le "très désiré," a beaucoup préoccupé les savants, qui souhaitèrent longtemps en vain lui assigner une date fixe. Cet archontat forme en effet comme le pivot ou la charnière de la chronologie delphique et de la chronologie attique du IIIᵉ siècle, à l'établissement de laquelle nul érudit n'a travaillé plus efficacement que celui à qui est offert le présent volume. Les recherches menées sur ce point ont donné un bon exemple de cette collaboration internationale qui est de règle dans nos études: M. Ferguson ayant montré que Polyeuctos avait été archonte soit en 255-4, soit en 243-2,[1] les épigraphistes français qui essayaient de construire la chronologie delphique ont choisi entre ces deux dates la plus récente,[2] et leur choix a été récemment confirmé par la découverte d'une inscription attique dans les fouilles américaines de l'Agora.[3]

Grâce à la fixation de cet archontat en 243-2, on a pu classer avec une approximation suffisante les inscriptions delphiques du IIIᵉ siècle, qui nous fournissent tant de renseignements sur la Confédération aitolienne, alors maîtresse de la ville d'Apollon Pythien,[4] et aussi sur les différents peuples amphictioniques, parmi lesquels figure Athènes. C'est en utilisant surtout ces textes delphiques que je voudrais essayer de répondre à la question suivante: parmi tant de conflits où nous voyons Athéniens et Aitoliens tantôt s'affronter, tantôt lutter côte à côte, est-il possible de

---

[1] W. S. Ferguson, *Athenian Tribal Cycles in the Hellenistic Age* (1932), part I: "The Third Century B.C."

[2] P. Roussel *Rev. ét. anc.* 1924, 97-111; L. Robert *Rev. ét. anc.* 1936, 5-23; R. Flacelière, *Les Aitoliens à Delphes* (1937), chapitre IV.

[3] B. D. Meritt *Hesperia* VII (1938) 121 no. 24.

[4] Cependant Delphes ne faisait pas partie juridiquement de la Confédération aitolienne et restait théoriquement autonome.

déterminer quelle fut la ligne de conduite *dominante* de la politique étrangère d'Athènes à l'égard de la Confédération aitolienne?

Ce m'est un plaisir d'offrir ces quelques pages en respectueux hommage à celui qui a tant contribué à éclairer l'histoire d'Athènes et des autres Etats grecs à cette époque.

*　　*　　*

Dans la guerre lamiaque (323), Athéniens et Aitoliens, unis, avaient été les principaux champions de la révolte contre la Macédoine, et nous les trouvons ensuite le plus souvent côte à côte jusqu'à la bataille d'Ipsos (301). C'est ainsi qu'Athènes, assiégée par Cassandros en 305, fut délivrée par les Aitoliens.[1] Il est très probable aussi qu'en 301, peu avant Ipsos, un contingent aitolien aida les troupes athéniennes du stratège Olympiodoros — partisan convaincu de l'alliance aitolo-athénienne — à dégager la ville d'Elatée, qui était alors assiégée par le même Cassandros.[2] Mais celui-ci revint à la charge un peu plus tard et finit par emporter la place de Phocide.[3] Comme Ipsos avait beaucoup changé le rapport des forces en présence, les Athéniens ne se sentirent plus capables de résister au roi de Macédoine et conclurent la paix avec lui.[4]

Quand Démétrios Poliorcète eut mis fin à la tyrannie de Lacharès en s'emparant d'Athènes (294), la ville dut suivre, bon gré mal gré, la politique de son "libérateur," qui était très hostile à l'Aitolie. Aux Grandes Eleusinies de 291, un poète à gages dénonçait, dans un *ithyphallos* qui nous a été conservé, les méfaits de l'Aitolie, cette nouvelle sphinge, plus funeste que l'ancienne, qui enlevait les habitants de l'Attique (dont les pirates aitoliens ravageaient alors les côtes), et il suppliait Démétrios de la châtier.[5] L'année suivante, année pythique (290), comme Delphes était occupée par la Confédération de l'ouest, Démétrios fit célébrer les *Pythia*, par une

---

[1] Pausanias I 26. 3; cf. W. S. Ferguson *Hellenistic Athens* 114.

[2] Pausanias X 18. 7; cf. *Les Ait. à D.* 52–4.

[3] Le fils de Cassandros, Philippos, mourut en 297 à Elatée: Eusèbe I 231 (éd. Schöne); cf. *Les Ait. à D.* 54–55.

[4] *Syll.*³ 362.

[5] F. Jacoby *FGH* 76 (Duris von Samos) fr. 13; cf. *Les Ait. à D.* 73–5.

hardie innovation, à Athènes.[1] Mais le roi ne put venir à bout des
Aitoliens, alliés à Pyrrhos d'Epire; il fut chassé de Macédoine en
288; peu après, en 287, Athènes lui fit défection et dut renouer
alors de bonnes relations avec l'Aitolie. En tout cas, au cours de la
période 300–280, d'assez nombreux Athéniens reçurent la proxénie
à Delphes,[2] et il est certain que les rapports d'Athènes et de
l'Aitolie ne furent pas toujours aussi mauvais qu'entre 294 et 287.
Très probablement, les hostilités contre Athènes, de la part des
Aitoliens, avaient été surtout dirigées contre Démétrios, maître de
la ville; à Athènes même, à côté du parti pro-macédonien dans
lequel se rangeait l'auteur de l'*ithyphallos*, les amis de l'Aitolie,
tels que le stratège Olympiodoros, devaient être nombreux et puis-
sants, et ils relevèrent la tête assurément dès 287. Nous n'avons
conservé malheureusement, pour cette période, aucune liste amphictionique, en sorte que nous ignorons si Athènes envoyait alors
un hiéromnémon à Delphes, où l'influence aitolienne était prépondérante depuis une année voisine de 300;[3] mais, sauf évidemment pendant la période 294–287, nous ne voyons pas pourquoi
elle se serait abstenue de se faire représenter au Conseil amphictionique.

* * *

En 279–8, Athéniens et Aitoliens allaient se trouver côte à côte
aux Thermopyles en face d'un ennemi imprévu: les Celtes de
Brennos. Les Aitoliens fournirent le contingent le plus nombreux
de toute l'armée grecque: quinze mille hommes environ. Quant
aux Athéniens, ils contribuèrent à la défense commune au moyen
d'un corps d'ἐπίλεκτοι et d'un corps de cavaliers[4] — quinze
cents hommes au total — sans parler de leur flotte, qui, probablement, ne resta pas inactive.[5] Si l'honneur de commander en chef

---

[1] Plutarque *Démétrios* 40. 7–8.

[2] Exactement trois avant 294 (*Les Ait. à D.* App. II 2 *a* et *b*[5], 5 *a*) et cinq après
287 (*ibid.* App. II 14 *b*[1,2,3] et 16 *a*[2] (deux noms)).

[3] Cf. *Les Ait. à D.* 50–68.

[4] Décret d'acceptation des Sôtéria, daté de l'archontat de Polyeuctos: *Syll.*[3] 408.
11–2.

[5] Cf. W. W. Tarn *JHS* 1934, 35.

devant les barbares fut vraiment attribué, comme l'affirme Pausanias, à l'Athénien Callippos,[1] on peut penser que celui-ci le dut surtout à l'amitié des Aitoliens pour sa cité.

Dès que la Grèce fut sauvée de l'invasion, au printemps de 278, les Amphictions, voulant assurer l'éclat des *Pythia* et aussi, peut-être, de la nouvelle fête qu'ils instituaient pour commémorer le salut de Delphes et de l'Hellade (les *Sôtéria*), s'adressèrent aux artistes dionysiaques d'Athènes à qui ils garantirent l'*atélie* et l'*asylie* à titre perpétuel.[2]

Mais beaucoup plus significative pour l'histoire des relations d'Athènes et de l'Aitolie est la présence à Delphes d'un hiéromnémon athénien, au moins à partir de la session de printemps de l'année 277.[3] Alors que de nombreux peuples restaient volontairement à l'écart d'une Amphictionie dominée par les Aitoliens, Athènes tint à se faire représenter au Conseil, ce qui équivalait à une reconnaissance implicite de la situation des Aitoliens à Delphes. Et ce fait est d'autant plus remarquable que les Athéniens entretenaient alors des rapports étroits avec Antigonos Gonatas: on a même pu écrire que cette période fut "l'âge d'or des relations d'Antigonos avec Athènes."[4] Ce prince, en homme d'Etat avisé et profond, entendait laisser aux Athéniens une certaine part de liberté et, par ailleurs, soucieux avant tout de consolider sa position en Macédoine, il évitait à cette époque tout conflit direct avec l'Aitolie: cette constatation suffit à expliquer qu'Athènes ait pu être alors en bons termes à la fois avec lui et avec les Aitoliens, mais elle ne doit pas cependant nous porter à croire que les Athéniens, en se faisant représenter à Delphes, se conformaient à un ordre ou à une suggestion du roi; tout indique au contraire qu'ils prirent cette décision de leur plein gré et qu'Antigonos se contenta de n'y pas mettre obstacle.

---

[1] Pausanias X 20. 5. Mais le fait est très douteux: cf. *Les Ait. à D.* 96 n. 4.

[2] *IG* II[2] 1132. 1–39 = *Syll.*[3] 399.

[3] Il est surprenant de constater l'absence du hiéromnémon athénien au printemps de 278, à cette même session au cours de laquelle les Amphictions accordèrent des privilèges aux artistes dionysiaques d'Athènes; il doit s'agir d'une absence purement fortuite, à moins que, peut-être, comme on l'a soutenu, la liste amphictionique gravée en tête de ce décret ne nous soit parvenue sous une forme incomplète.

[4] W. W. Tarn *Antigonos Gonatas* 217 sqq.; cf. *CAH* VII 206.

Il est possible aussi qu'aux environs de l'année 274 Athènes et
l'Aitolie soient allées plus loin dans la voie de l'amitié par la conclusion d'un traité d'alliance ou, à tout le moins, d'une convention
d'*asphalie*.[1] En tout cas le trop mince fragment qui nous reste
d'un tel document présente une écriture qui s'accorde beaucoup
mieux avec cette date qu'avec celles de 228 environ ou 219.[2] Mais
il faut ajouter aussitôt que, si une συμμαχία fut réellement conclue
à cette époque entre Athènes et l'Aitolie, elle ne pouvait être que
défensive, puisqu'elle ne contraignit pas les Aitoliens à participer
à la guerre de Chrémonidès.[3]

En effet, si légère que fût alors à Athènes, semble-t-il, la domination des Macédoniens, les patriotes, fidèles à l'idéal de l'autonomie
absolue, obtinrent que la ville se rangeât, aux côtés de l'Egypte
et de Sparte, à la tête de toute une coalition contre la Macédoine,
en 267. Les Aitoliens furent certainement sollicités de se joindre
à cette tentative de libération πρὸς τοὺς καταδουλοῦσθαι τὰς
πόλεις ἐπιχειροῦντας.[4] C'est même très probable que des ambassadeurs athéniens vinrent en Aitolie et firent valoir, non seulement
la grandeur et la beauté de l'entreprise, mais aussi l'attitude amicale
d'Athènes à l'égard de la Confédération et, bien entendu, l'alliance
aitolo-athénienne, si elle avait été vraiment conclue vers 274.
Mais rien n'y fit: les Aitoliens restèrent sourds à tous les appels
et, plutôt que de s'engager dans un conflit qu'ils jugeaient sans
doute prématuré, ils préférèrent rester neutres et profiter de cette
neutralité pour opérer sans coup férir — le roi de Macédoine étant
trop occupé par ailleurs — d'importantes annexions.

Les Athéniens, engagés dans la guerre de Chrémonidès, con-
tinuèrent, tant qu'ils le purent, à se faire représenter à Delphes;
peut-être espéraient-ils encore que l'Aitolie allait se décider, quoi-

---

[1] *Klio* XV (1918) 7 nos. 35 (décret athénien) et 36 (décret aitolien *IG* IX 1²,
176). C'est M. Segre qui pense qu'il s'agit peut-être seulement d'une convention
d'*asphalie*: cf. *Les Ait. à D.* 190 n. 3.

[2] Dates proposées par G. Klaffenbach et H. Pomtow.

[3] D'ailleurs il en va de même si ce traité fut conclu en 219 ou quelques années
auparavant, puisque les Athéniens restèrent neutres lors de la guerre des Alliés
(219–217).

[4] Ce sont les termes mêmes du décret athénien rendu sur la proposition de Chrémonidès: *Syll.*³ 434. 11–2.

que tardivement, à prendre les armes. A l'automne de l'année 265 un hiéromnémon athénien put encore se rendre à Delphes,[1] mais ce fut probablement le dernier,[2] car, peu après sans doute, Antigonos vint mettre le siège devant Athènes, qui résista longtemps, mais finit par se rendre en 262.

On comprend aisément qu'après ce conflit, l'attitude d'Antigonos à l'égard d'Athènes soit devenue toute différente: il installa une garnison au Mouseion et ne permit pas qu'Athènes fût de nouveau représentée à l'Amphictionie. En effet, bien que les Aitoliens ne fussent pas intervenus militairement contre lui, leurs accroissements successifs les rendaient dès lors trop redoutables à la Macédoine pour que le roi acceptât volontiers de fortifier ainsi indirectement leur situation morale à Delphes. Même quand Athènes eut recouvré par la suite une certaine indépendance,[3] elle ne fut pas représentée davantage au Conseil des hiéromnémons; c'est qu'Antigonos, qui restait maître du Pirée, de Munichie, du Sounion et de Rhamnonte, la tenait tout de même de plus près, malgré la restitution officielle de l'autonomie, qu'avant la guerre de Chrémonidès.

En fait, dans les listes amphictioniques conservées, nous ne trouvons aucun hiéromnémon athénien entre les années 265 et 216, c'est-à-dire pendant cinquante ans.

*   *   *

La période de trente-cinq années environ qui suit la fin de la guerre de Chrémonidès est l'une des plus mal connues de toute l'histoire grecque. Elle correspond sensiblement à l'apogée de la puissance aitolienne, mais les Athéniens, toujours inféodés à la Macédoine — d'une manière plus ou moins étroite, d'ailleurs, suivant les moments, — n'ont pas une politique étrangère autonome et ne peuvent donc manifester leurs sentiments, en tant que peuple, à l'égard de la grande Confédération.

---

[1] *Les Ait. à D.* App. I no. 15.

[2] *Ibid.* no. 16, il faut donc sans doute supprimer la restitution ['Aθηναίων Εὐθυδίκου].

[3] En 256–5 ou 255–4: Eusèbe II 120 (éd. Schöne).

Quelques faits seulement nous sont connus, d'importance très inégale: l'acceptation des Sôtéria "aitoliennes" par Athènes en 243-2, les hostilités entre Athènes et l'Aitolie pendant la longue crise de la guerre démétriaque (239-29) et, par ailleurs, le nombre relativement élevé des Athéniens qui furent honorés de la proxénie delphique entre 245 et 226.

Les Aitoliens, désirant faire reconnaître par la Grèce entière leur situation prédominante à Delphes, réorganisèrent en 243 la fête des Sôtéria, célébrée jusque-là sous la présidence des Amphictions, de façon à lui imposer délibérément leur patronage. Athènes ne se fit pas prier pour accepter l'ἀγών ainsi transformé, ou plutôt institué par les Aitoliens, qui se donnaient l'apparence de le fonder à nouveau; son décret, rendu précisément sous l'archontat de Polyeuctos, rappelle fièrement que ses ἐπίλεκτοι et ses cavaliers ont collaboré eux aussi, avec les Aitoliens, au salut commun de la Grèce que commémorent les Sôtéria.[1] Et sans doute de telles acceptations de fêtes, si fréquentes à l'époque hellénistique, n'ont-elles à peu près aucune signification politique.[2] Il n'en reste pas moins intéressant de voir Athènes, à une époque où elle n'est plus libre, semble-t-il, d'envoyer à Delphes un hiéromnémon, témoigner ainsi de ses sentiments, fût-ce sous cette forme convenue et banale, à l'égard de la Confédération aitolienne.

Au début de l'année 239 la mort du sage souverain que fut Antigonos Gonatas provoque en Grèce un renversement des alliances et ouvre vraiment une époque nouvelle. Aitoliens et Achéens se liguent contre la Macédoine, au sort de laquelle Athènes — de force assurément, et non de plein gré — reste attachée. Les temps de Démétrios Poliorcète paraissent revenus sous Démétrios II, et de nouveau l'Attique doit souffrir des incursions de pirates aitoliens, qui ravagent les côtes des pays ennemis. Un décret d'Athènes rappelle en effet que l'Aitolien Boucris, "au cours de ses incursions en Attique, enleva et emmena en Crète un assez grand nombre de citoyens et de gens résidant sur le territoire athénien."[3]

---

[1] *Syll.*³ 408.

[2] Cf. L. Robert *REA* 1936, 18-19.

[3] *Syll.*³ 535. 5-7. Sur Athènes pendant la guerre démétriaque, cf. P. Roussel *BCH* 1930, 268-282. Il est possible, comme l'a fait remarquer A. Wilhelm, *Sitz-*

Il ne semble pas, cependant, que d'aussi mauvais souvenirs aient empêché des Athéniens de se rendre à Delphes à titre individuel, dès que la paix fut revenue. Entre 245 et 226 en effet on compte jusqu'à huit Athéniens qui furent honorés de la proxénie delphique;[1] deux d'entre eux au moins étaient des poètes: Eratoxénos, ποιητὴς ἐπῶν, et Cléocharès, ποιητὴς μελῶν, qui avait écrit à Delphes pour la fête des Théoxénies un προσόδιον, un péan et un hymne. A cette époque même la version attique de la légende d'Apollon, qui attribuait un rôle important à Pallas, était en honneur à Delphes.[2]

* * *

L'indication que semblent donner ces décrets de proxénie ne peut être accueillie qu'avec prudence;[3] il est pourtant très probable que des rapports amicaux existèrent entre Athènes et l'Aitolie avant comme après la guerre démétriaque. Cependant Athènes, qui obtenait en 228 le retrait de la garnison macédonienne du Pirée et recouvrait ainsi son autonomie complète, attendit au moins cinq ans, et peut-être davantage,[4] pour reprendre sa place au Conseil amphictionique dominé par les Aitoliens. C'est que, si certains citoyens, dans la chaleur de leurs sentiments pro-aitoliens, avaient rapidement oublié les incursions de Boucris et de ses pirates, d'autres probablement, qui avaient la mémoire plus longue, s'opposaient à la reprise officielle de relations amicales avec l'Aitolie. Pour cette raison, et surtout pour d'autres, Athènes, mal remise de luttes longues et épuisantes et craignant pour son indépendance à peine reconquise, ne se soucia pas d'affronter Philippe V aux

---

ungsb. Akad. Wien 1925 fasc. 202. 2. 57–58, que les décrets mutilés *IG* II² 746 et 858 doivent être rapportés à ces mêmes événements.

[1] Voir la liste de ces Athéniens, *Les Ait. à D.* 272 n. 1.

[2] Voir les strophes III et IV de l'hymne d'Aristonoos à Apollon, qui date des environs de 237–6: *Fouilles de Delphes* III 2. 191.

[3] Parce que les proxènes reçoivent cet honneur à titre privé: cf. *Les Ait. à D.* 88.

[4] En effet le hiéromnémon athénien manque certainement dans la liste *Les Ait. à D.* App. I 38, qui date de 223 environ; il ne figure pas non plus dans la liste 38 *bis*, mais celle-ci est trop mutilée pour que l'on puisse affirmer l'absence de l'Athénien cette année-là (220–19 environ).

côtés de l'Aitolie lors de la guerre des Alliés (219–7) et garda prudemment la neutralité.[1] C'est vers 216 au plus tard que le siège amphictionique d'Athènes fut occupé à nouveau,[2] ce qui marque sans doute la victoire définitive du parti pro-aitolien. Entre 226 et 200, d'ailleurs, c'est encore Athènes qui, comme dans la période précédente, semble avoir fourni le plus grand nombre de proxènes delphiques.[3]

Malgré sa sympathie pour les Aitoliens et la cause qu'ils représentaient, Athènes ne prit non plus aucune part à la première guerre de Macédoine (212–05), où la Confédération, toujours remuante et belliqueuse, continua à user progressivement ses forces; la ville se contenta de jouer, avec d'autres cités neutres, le rôle de médiatrice.[4]

Mais, lors de la seconde guerre de Macédoine (200–196), ce furent au contraire les Athéniens, attaqués par les Acarnaniens et Philippe, qui entrèrent en guerre les premiers aux côtés de Rome. Ils eurent même beaucoup de peine à décider leurs alliés d'Aitolie[5] à prendre les armes à nouveau. Ceux-ci finirent par se laisser persuader, et l'on vit encore Athéniens et Aitoliens combattre dans le même camp contre la Macédoine, mais s'agissait-il alors vraiment de la défense de la liberté comme au temps de la guerre lamiaque? Il s'agissait seulement de savoir qui, des Macédoniens ou des Romains, seraient les maîtres de la Grèce.

Dans la dernière liste amphictionique conservée qui date de l'époque de la domination aitolienne à Delphes, celle de 193–2, l'absence du hiéromnémon athénien ne prouve aucunement qu'Athènes était alors hostile à l'Aitolie, mais seulement qu'elle appréhendait de se compromettre aux yeux de Rome en envoyant à Delphes un représentant:[6] c'était l'époque, en effet, où la Con-

---

[1] Cf. W. S. Ferguson *Hellen. Athens* 248.

[2] *Les Ait. à D.* App. I 39: archonte Polycleitos, 216–5 env.

[3] Cf. *Les Ait. à D.* 331 n. 2.

[4] M. Holleaux *Rome, la Grèce et les monarchies hellénistiques* 118 et n. 1, 119 n. 1.

[5] Cf. M. Holleaux, *ibid.* 266 n. 3, qui énumère les textes de Pausanias, de Tite-Live et de Polybe montrant "qu'à la fin du IIIe siècle et au début du suivant les relations sont fort amicales entre les deux peuples [athénien et aitolien]."

[6] Cf. *Les Ait. à D.* 353 et n. 2.

fédération s'engageait follement dans cette lutte contre les Romains, qui devait la conduire à sa perte en 189.

* * *

Il est possible maintenant de répondre à la question que je posais au début de cette rapide enquête.

J'ai dit ailleurs [1] qu'à mon avis la situation prépondérante des Aitoliens à Delphes ne fut jamais acceptée unanimement par la Grèce et que c'est là certainement la raison pour laquelle l'Amphictionie, pendant tout le IIIe siècle, eut des réunions incomplètes. J'ajoutais: "Envoyer un hiéromnémon aux Thermopyles ou à Delphes, c'était reconnaître une continuité légitime entre l'Amphictionie d'autrefois et celle où dominaient maintenant les Aitoliens; les peuples hostiles ou simplement indifférents à l'égard de la Confédération n'avaient aucune raison de le faire; seuls y étaient amenés ceux que leurs intérêts ou leurs sympathies inclinaient vers cette puissance."

Evidemment Athènes ne doit pas être comptée parmi les Etats qui refusèrent de reconnaître la situation créée par la domination aitolienne à Delphes, puisqu'elle se fit représenter à l'Amphictionie à peu près à toutes les époques où elle fut en mesure de le faire, c'est-à-dire, chaque fois qu'elle était indépendante de la Macédoine ou que, du moins, l'influence de cette puissance n'était pas assez lourde pour lui enlever en cette matière son pouvoir de décision. Comme exception certaine à cette règle, nous ne pouvons noter que la période de cinq ans au moins, de douze ans au plus, qui commence en 228 et pendant laquelle Athènes, quoique absolument autonome, ne fut pas représentée à Delphes. Ce fait isolé s'explique probablement, je l'ai dit, par les mauvais souvenirs qu'avaient laissés aux Athéniens les attaques aitoliennes de la guerre démétriaque.

D'où vient donc qu'Athènes, dont le nom seul suffit à évoquer la plus pure et la plus ancienne tradition de l'Hellade, ait eu à l'égard de ce peuple nouveau et grossier, et qui n'était qu'à moitié grec, l'indulgence que beaucoup d'autres états amphictioniques,

[1] *Les Ait. à D.* 372-373.

ordinairement moins délicats sur ce point, lui refusèrent? En 290, Démétrios Poliorcète, lors qu'il faisait célébrer à Athènes les jeux pythiques, avait probablement l'intention, en flattant les Athéniens dans leur orgueil national, de les amener en plus grand nombre à penser que le "foyer commun de la Grèce" ne pouvait plus demeurer dans la ville de Delphes, que souillait la domination de ces intrus, et devait être transporté dans leur cité, reine de l'Hellade. Si la plupart des Athéniens ne consentirent pas, par la suite, à prendre à leur compte cette politique anti-aitolienne que leur indiquait alors le roi de Macédoine, c'est qu'au IIIe siècle encore l'amour de la liberté et de l'autonomie était plus fort dans leur cœur que tout autre souci. La Confédération aitolienne, depuis la guerre lamiaque, leur apparaissait comme le meilleur champion, dans la Grèce centrale, de l'opposition à l'hégémonie macédonienne, et c'est pourquoi le parti pro-aitolien, quand du moins Athènes fut libre de ses décisions, l'emporta plus souvent que le parti adverse.

Pourtant cette politique de l'alliance aitolo-athénienne ne fut pratiquée sans défaillance ni à Athènes ni, d'autre part, en Aitolie, puisque, pour des raisons de circonstances, les Aitoliens jugèrent bon de s'abstenir dans la guerre de Chrémonidès, et les Athéniens, à leur tour, dans la guerre des Alliés et dans la première guerre de Macédoine. Malgré ces abstentions parallèles et malgré le consentement forcé qu'Athènes dut donner à plusieurs reprises à la politique anti-aitolienne des Macédoniens, auxquels elle se trouvait rivée malgré elle, le sens de l'union nécessaire des démocraties contre la domination étrangère — encore que fréquemment émoussé ou obscurci — subsistait chez beaucoup de citoyens, et c'est lui assurément qui explique, en dernière analyse, que la tendance dominante de la politique étrangère d'Athènes au IIIe siècle avant J.-C. ait été favorable à l'Aitolie.

PHTHIA — CHRYSEIS

By W. W. Tarn

THE information contained in Athenian inscriptions about the Macedonian royal house, which was the suzerain of Athens in the mid-third century, information which bears on the history of Athens itself, has not always been easy to elicit. In 1924 I wrote an article [1] to prove that Phthia and not Chryseis was the mother of Philip V, a view which has had some acceptance.[2] The article was based on a system of my own of filling out the gaps in four Athenian inscriptions where statements relating to some Macedonian king had been chiselled out. I would have taken the obvious view that Phthia and Chryseis were the same woman,[3] but for my belief that the Eleusinian garrison decree *IG* II² 1299 showed that Phthia predeceased her husband Demetrius II, while Chryseis, as is known, survived him; therefore, perforce, I made Chryseis Philip's mother by adoption.

In 1937 Messrs. Sterling Dow and C. F. Edson (whom I refer to as "the authors") wrote an important paper called *Chryseis*.[4] The first part, dealing with the royal style of the Antigonid kings, and the fourth, on Antigonus III, do not concern me here; but the second and third parts sought to prove that Demetrius' wife Phthia was not Philip's mother, and that his mother Chryseis was not Demetrius' wife but his concubine. Though I regard both conclusions as unacceptable, the paper in some respects marked a

[1] "Philip V and Phthia," *Class. Quart.*, XVIII (1924), 17–23.

[2] See M. Cary, *History of the Greek World from 323 to 146* (1932), 159 n. 2; G. H. Macurdy, *Hellenistic Queens* (1932), 72; J.V.A. Fine, "The Mother of Philip V of Macedon," *Class. Quart.* XXVIII (1934), 99. F. Jacoby in *F. Gr. Hist.* II D no. 260 p. 862 called my view *ansprechend* but thought there was no certainty. P. Treves, *Athenaeum* XII (1934), 408, thought Philip was Phthia's son, but (rightly, as it turned out) doubted the idea of Chryseis as his mother by adoption; his own view involves too drastic a use of the knife.

[3] *Op. cit.* 18: "her death precludes us from adopting the otherwise simple hypothesis that Phthia and Chryseis were two names of the same woman".

[4] "Chryseis", *Harvard Stud. in Class. Philol.* XLVIII (1937), 127–180.

considerable advance and cleared much ground. For the Athenian inscriptions, which are fundamental, I had had to rely on the erasures as given in *IG²*; the authors carefully re-examined the actual stones and re-estimated the gaps. Naturally I accept their results; it follows that my scheme of filling the gaps cannot stand. Another thing that they showed is that *IG* II² 1299 gives no information, one way or the other, about Phthia's death; I have been over all that again very carefully, and am certain that they are right, so I need not trouble the reader further. It follows that the idea that Chryseis was Philip's mother by adoption is now either unnecessary or impossible (we shall see that it is impossible), and by getting rid of it the authors have cleared the way for the identification of Phthia and Chryseis, which is what I hope in this paper to prove. As I shall have to controvert a good deal of what they have said, I would acknowledge here, once for all, my great obligations to their paper.[1]

I

PHTHIA

THE inscription that is material to the enquiry is the first decree for Aristophanes, *IG* II² 1299, passed at latest in July 235; in this, by some fortunate chance, the reference to the Macedonian king has not been chiselled out, and we have to examine the statement (l. 10) that Aristophanes had offered sacrifice for the Athenian People and for king Demetrius and queen Phthia and their ἔγγονοι, — ὑπὲρ τοῦ δήμου τοῦ Ἀθηναίων καὶ τοῦ βασιλέως [Δημητρίου κ]αὶ τῆς βασιλίσσης [Φθίας] καὶ τῶν ἐγγόνων αὐτῶν. (The name Δημητρίου is restored from l. 36; Φθίας has long been recognised as certain by everybody). This, *prima facie*, means that in 235 Demetrius and Phthia had at least two living children.[2] The authors however, contend that the words καὶ τῶν

---

[1] The present paper has been read in MS by both authors. They have written me that they agree with my essential points.

[2] I do not see how to distinguish between ἔκγονοι and ἔγγονοι, words which both began by meaning 'foetus' and were finally expanded to mean 'descendants'.

ἐγγόνων αὐτῶν are only a formula, which could be used even if there were no children.[1] I will leave the matter of a formula for a moment, till I have cleared the ground; for the first point is that the authors, in the passage quoted, have confused two things, a grant and a sacrifice, or rather, to be precise, a grant and a prayer; for a sacrifice to a god on behalf of somebody was not only in itself a prayer for him, but was sometimes — possibly always — accompanied by a formal prayer.[2] In the same way, a dedication to a god for somebody was in effect a prayer for him. I drew the distinction before, but briefly, as being obvious:[3] I fear I must now elaborate it.

In Greek law, as in English, and I suppose in every law, you could and did grant an estate or an honour to a man and his issue, his ἔκγονοι or ἔγγονοι, when he had none; it was extremely common in Greek grants of proxeny or citizenship; it meant, as it means today, that the thing granted was heritable.[4] But you could not sacrifice, i.e. pray, for persons who had no existence, or

---

At Athens, ἔκγονοι was used till near the end of the fourth century B.C. and ἔγγονοι usually in the third, ἔκγονοι subsequently reappearing; Liddell and Scott⁹ say (*s.v.* ἔγγονος) "ἐγγ — may represent ἐκγ —," and ἔκγονοι continued to be used in many places. The dictionaries (that is Hesychius) distinguish ἔκγονος, child, from ἔγγονος, grandchild, and there are sufficient instances of both; but some grammarians — Zonaras, and the 'others' mentioned by Eustathius — reversed the meaning, with instances: ἔγγονος ὁ υἱός, ἔκγονος δὲ ὁ τοῦ υἱοῦ υἱός (see Dindorf's Stephanus *s.v.* ἔγγονος). In *IG* II² 448 (318/7 B.C.) ἐγγόνων (l. 74) is practically synonymous with παῖδες (l. 83), and in *IG* II² 832 (Heliodorus' year, 229/8 B.C.) it includes θυγατέρες.

[1] *Chryseis* 148. 'Phrases referring to offspring are not to be pressed for specific meaning, if their language is not specific. The phrase καὶ τῶν ἐγγόνων αὐτῶν means "and of such children as they may have", or, more in our legal idiom, "and of the (actual or hypothetical) heirs of their bodies" — a general quasi-legal term, that is, covering whatever may be the actual situation. It does not imply that there were then living children.'— This statement is true of *grants*, but of them only.

[2] Instances of the actual prayer are Michel 490 (Ephesus); Holleaux *BCH* XXVIII (1904) 354 (Panamara).

[3] *Op. cit.* 18.

[4] Similarly, if a treaty was meant to be permanent, it was expressed to be made with the king and his ἔκγονοι, whether he had any or not, merely to show that it was not intended to lapse on his death, as it would otherwise have done. There are many cases: *IG* II² 105 and 236 will serve as instances.

make a dedication to the gods for (ὑπέρ) such non-existent persons, such a dedication being in effect a prayer. The sacrificial prayer at Athens, in its fullest form, was a prayer for the health and safety, ἐφ' ὑγιείᾳ καὶ σωτηρίᾳ, of the Council and the People, their wives and children, and their friends and allies, though sometimes only Council and People are named. [1] But you could not ask the gods to give good health to people who did not exist, or to keep them in safety; it would have had no meaning. (In reciting in a decree what happened, the words 'for the health and safety of' were sometimes, for brevity's sake, replaced by ὑπέρ, 'for,' [2] which is also used in dedications made to a god 'for' somebody: this does not of course affect the sense.) After the sacrifice was offered, the next step was that the priest announced that the god or gods had accepted the sacrifice and that the blessings prayed for had enured to the people for whom the sacrifice was offered; decrees therefore, after reciting the sacrifice, continue, 'be it resolved to accept the blessings which have enured in the sacrifice offered for so-and-so' — δεδόχθαι, τὰ ἀγαθὰ δέχεσθαι τὰ γεγονότα ἐν τῇ θυσίᾳ κ.τ.λ.; and blessings could not 'have enured' to non-existent persons. If then, as sometimes happened, a special person or persons were named as objects of the sacrifice in addition to the Council and People, etc. — which in practice, at Athens anyhow, usually meant a king,[3] with or without his family — that special person or persons had to be in existence; therefore in *IG* II² 1299 the special persons named in addition to the People, that is, Demetrius, Phthia, *and* their children, had all to be in existence.

The same thing is shown by the latter part of this decree, where (ll. 35–6) Aristophanes is given a crown and a statue for his consistent good service (ἀρετή) to, and goodwill (εὔνοια) towards, the People and king Demetrius καὶ τοὺς ἐγγόνους αὐτοῦ (that is merely, as the authors say, a shortened form — there are others in the

---

[1] References collected in the Index to *IG* II² part IV, 1, under σωτηρία.

[2] A good instance to show the exact equivalence is *IG* II² 1039 I. But ὑπέρ is very common.

[3] Other special objects were occasionally included: *IG* II² 410, the other possessions of the Athenians; *ib.* 668, the crops. *Ib.* 772, the State doctors sacrifice twice a year for themselves and their patients.

inscription — and does not imply that Phthia was dead). This also means living children, the same children previously mentioned, those of Demetrius and Phthia; for you cannot give good service to, or feel goodwill towards, persons who do not exist.

On this interpretation of the inscription *IG* II² 1299, then, Phthia had two children living in 235. But I must examine the authors' contention that the phrase καὶ τῶν ἐγγόνων αὐτῶν is a formula, which could be used even if there were no children at all. To be a formula, an expression must at least recur several times, but there is no other instance of these words in a sacrifice or dedication — at least the authors give none, and I have not succeeded in finding one: and it seems clear from their language in the passage I quoted that they took their belief from *grants*, which are legion but which have no bearing on the matter. They do however claim three cases of the use of these words in a sacrifice, in their filling up of three out of the four inscriptions I mentioned where a king's name had been chiselled out. All three belong to the reign of Antigonus Gonatas. In *IG* II² 775, shortly before 248/7, they restore [καὶ τοῦ βασιλέως Ἀντιγόνου καὶ τῶν ἐγγόνων αὐτοῦ], though they add that it might be [καὶ τοῦ βασιλέως Ἀντιγόνου καὶ τῆς βασιλίσσης Φίλας]. In *IG* II² 780, 246/5, they restore [καὶ τοῦ βασιλέως Ἀντιγόνου καὶ τῆς βασιλίσσης] Φ[ίλας καὶ τῶν ἐγγόνων αὐτῶν]. For *IG* II² 776 they take a date c. 240, and accordingly restore it with the names Antigonus and Phila or Demetrius and Phthia as alternatives. The date is shortly after, perhaps the year after, the year of the archon Alcibiades. Professor Dinsmoor in *Archons of Athens* dated this archon in 255/4, with a query. Professor W. S. Ferguson, in *Athenian Tribal Cycles*, in scheme A dated him 242/1 with a double query, and in scheme B left him undated. Professor B. D. Meritt, in his list *Hesperia* IV (1935) 585 put him in 242/1; but, with the increasing probability (some would say certainty) that 242/1 was Hieron's year, Meritt's latest list in *Hesperia* VII (1938), p. 135, (later than *Chryseis*) puts Alcibiades in 251/0. Consequently one must take the authors' restoration of *IG* II² 776 as that for the reign of Gonatas [καὶ τοῦ βασιλέως Ἀντιγόνου κ]αὶ τῆς βασιλίσης (*sic*) [Φίλας καὶ τῶν ἐγγόνων αὐτῶν].

These restorations, however, can give no support to the idea that the phrase καὶ τῶν ἐγγόνων αὐτῶν was a formula, because in the absence of precedents, which apparently do not exist (for to use *IG* II² 1299 would be arguing in a circle), no one can say that they are right. It would be possible to fill in καὶ τοῦ ἐγγόνου αὐτῶν, citing the inscriptions in which Ptolemy V is called the ἔκγονος of his parents, Ptolemy IV and his wife Arsinoe;[1] for Gonatas and Phila had a son (Demetrius II) and so far as is known no other children. One could go further, which might be preferable, and fill in καὶ τοῦ υἱοῦ Δημητρίου; this would fit just as well,[2] and there are a number of cases of the omission of αὐτῶν which the authors admit to be immaterial,[3] there being no question whose son Demetrius was; moreover it would have the support, not merely of the Delian dedication *IG* XI, 4, 1215,[4] but of a whole group of inscriptions relating to Ptolemy IV, who like Gonatas had one legitimate son and no other known children.[5] For this son of Ptolemy IV (Ptolemy V) is specifically mentioned by name after his parents in three dedications,[6] and specifically mentioned, though without

---

[1] *OGIS* 90 (the Rosetta Stone) 1. 3: ἐκγόνου Θεῶν Φιλοπατόρων. So in 91, a decree from Xanthus in Lycia.

[2] In *IG* II² 775 and 776 it would be exact, taking the authors' reckoning of iota as only half a letter in inscriptions which are not *stoichedon*. In 780, which is *stoichedon*, it would be one letter longer than their reckoning for the total gap, 62 letters; but there appear on their showing to be various irregularities, with some lines on the stone one letter too long.

[3] *Chryseis* 147 n. 2. Beside the instance there given, see *OGIS* 101; *ib*. 153, compared with 155, 156, 158; *IG* II² 844.

[4] [ὑπὲρ βα]σιλέως Ἀν[τιγόν]ου καὶ βασιλίσσης [Φίλας κ]αὶ Δημητρίο[υ] οἱ θεραπευταὶ οἱ ὑπ' αὐ [τ]αττόμενοι [Σαρά]πι Ἴσι. Ἀντιγόνου is certain, for no Antiochus had a queen with a name short enough to go into the gap. Demetrius should be the crown prince. Roussel *ad loc.* doubted this; he read αὐτόν instead of αὐτῶν or αὐτούς, and suggested that he was an official. But we *have* a dedication in honour of a king and queen, Ptolemy II and Arsinoe II, and an official, Callicrates the Nauarch (*OGIS* 29); it shows that in such a case the official's office is stated, and it is hard to believe that the priests would have called a commoner by his bare name without mentioning his office, though there can be no certainty.

[5] Had there been another child, it must have been mentioned by Polybius in his minutely detailed account of what happened to the known child when his father died.

[6] *OGIS* 86, ὑπὲρ βασιλέως Πτολεμαίου καὶ βασιλίσσης Ἀρσινόης καὶ Πτολεμαίου

his name, in a sacrificial inscription.¹ It is therefore impossible to say for certain what is the right restoration at the end of the gaps in the three inscriptions in question; consequently the authors' restorations cannot be used as evidence, and it is impossible to argue that the phrase in *IG* II² 1299, καὶ τῶν ἐγγόνων αὐτῶν, which is unique in a sacrifice, is only a formula.²

For completeness I give the fourth inscription considered in *Chryseis*, *IG* II² 790, 235/4 B.C. on Meritt's dating; that is, it belongs to the reign of Demetrius II and is a little later than *IG* II² 1299. The authors (p. 147) take the gap as 53, 54, or 55 letters, with a strong preference for 54; they restore it as [καὶ τοῦ βασιλέως Δημητρίου καὶ τῆς βασιλίσσης Φθίας καὶ . . . . . .], and say they can think of nothing better for these 7 letters than τοῦ υἱοῦ. If they contemplate this, it would seem difficult for them to argue that Philip was not Phthia's son.³ There seems, however, to be another possible restoration, Φιλίππου (which makes 55 letters if it be *stoichedon*, 54 otherwise;⁴ the *stoichedon* arrangement is said to be irregular), citing Δημητρίου in the Delian dedication *IG* XI

τοῦ υἱοῦ, θεῶν Φιλοπατόρων· *ib.* 87, ὑπὲρ β. Π. καὶ β. 'Α. θεῶν Φιλοπατόρων καὶ Πτολεμαίωι τῶι υἱῶι αὐτῶν· *ib.* 88 has the variant καὶ τοῦ ὑοῦ (*sic*) αὐτῶν Πτολεμαίου.

¹ Decree of Eresos, 'Αρχ. Δελτ. IX (1924–5), Παραρτ. 53, Θυσιάσαις . . . . . τῶ τε βασίλει καὶ τᾶ βασιλίσσα καὶ τῶ παιδὶ αὐτῶν.

² I note that in the sacrifices at Eresos (*above*) and Panamara (set out, *Chryseis* p. 130) the forms correspond to the known children; and one cannot distinguish καὶ τῶν τέκνων αὐτῶν at Panamara from καὶ τῶν ἐγγόνων αὐτῶν of *IG* II² 1299, see p. 484 n. 2 (above).

³ They suggest (p. 147) that αὐτῶν might have been omitted for accuracy, since Philip was a bastard; but in fact it is omitted in precisely the same way after the same words τοῦ υἱοῦ in *OGIS* 86, quoted above, and the legitimacy of Ptolemy V is unquestioned. On the other hand, there *is* a known case of a king and queen whose presumptive successor was a bastard, and there the matter is expressed very differently: *OGIS* 319 l. 14, (so again *ib.* 329 l. 38), sacrifice for king Attalus II and queen Stratonice (who were childless) καὶ 'Αττάλου (afterwards Attalus III) τοῦ υἱοῦ τοῦ βασιλέως Εὐμένου; and Stratonice had been Eumenes' wife, which disposes of a suggestion which has been made (not by the authors) that αὐτῶν was omitted to spare Phthia's feelings. She would probably not have known what that meant.

⁴ Taking the authors' reckoning that in *stoichedon* inscriptions iota counts as a whole letter, in others as a half.

4. 1215 already considered. But naturally I do not rely in any way upon *IG* II² 790.

Phthia then in 235 had two children living [1] and the dates show that her eldest child must have been Philip V. Antigonus Gonatas died in 240/39,[2] and Demetrius II therefore became king at latest before July-August 239, and possibly late in 240.[3] Olympias of Epirus applied to him after his accession for protection against Aetolia; she must have done so at once, partly because the Aetolians would move the moment Gonatas died, as they did again the moment Doson died, and partly because the inducement to Demetrius was the hand of her daughter Phthia and had she delayed he might have married someone else; an unmarried Hellenistic king normally married on his accession. It is admitted that the marriage preceded his war with Aetolia (the Demetriean war), because it was the reason for the war; and that war began in the Athenian year of the archon Lysias, 239/8.[4] Owing to the abiding nuisance of the Athenian year bisecting the campaigning season, the natural Greek reckoning,[5] it cannot be said whether the war began in early spring 238 or with an autumn campaign in 239; if the latter, the marriage was in the first half of 239; if the former, it was in winter 239/8 (or possibly late autumn 239),

[1] We are badly informed about daughters in any of the dynasties. Two Seleucid princesses, unknown to literary sources, have been recovered by deduction from numismatic evidence: Tarn, *The Greeks in Bactria and India* (1938), pp. 73 with 448, 169. I suppose that Fine's suggestion, *op. cit.* 102 n. 6, that the other child might be Apama, Demetrius' daughter by his first wife Stratonice, is possible, and that a child and a stepchild could be called "their children".

[2] Beloch *Gr. Gesch.* IV 2. 112; the date is independent of the Athenian archon-list.

[3] Beloch *ib.* thought of the *end* of the year 240/39, because he took the king A—— of *IG* II² 833 (a decree of 20 Thargelion of Heliodorus' year) to be Antigonus and the year of Heliodorus to be 240/39. But Heliodorus is really later (232/1 Dinsmoor, 229/8 Ferguson, *Tribal Cycles* scheme B p. 27, and Meritt, *Hesperia* VII 137) and the king is certainly Attalus I. So we do not know whether Antigonus died early or late in 240/39.

[4] *IG* II² 1299. 57. Lysias' date seems now certain; see Meritt's table in *Hesperia* VII.

[5] Historians who desired accuracy, like Thucydides, and Hieronymus of Cardia, dated by campaign years.

that winter being the *latest* date possible. Philip's age (in years, not months) is known: he was born in 238/7. The authors (p. 158) put his birth at latest in winter 238/7, though Polybius' phrase does not exclude early spring 237. There was then, at the least, about a year between the marriage and Philip's birth; and several months more is just as likely. Philip therefore was Phthia's son.

This is amply confirmed by Trogus-Justin, in an important passage which I omitted to notice in 1924. Long ago, by a detailed analysis of Trogus' *Prologues*,[1] I showed that Trogus, when a new character came on the scene, always 'introduced' him, that is, put in something to show the reader that he *was* a new character, as was necessary when there were so many people with the same names; where this was *not* done, the name ran on, and the last mentioned bearer of the name was still meant. For its then purpose that analysis was conclusive and has never been questioned. Justin of course had the benefit of Trogus' system, and in fact he never leaves it doubtful which bearer of any name he means. Now in XXVIII 1, 2 he records Demetrius' marriage to Phthia, and has much to say about it; and from the marriage he goes straight to XXVIII 3, 10 (for what comes between are two digressions on other subjects), where he says that Demetrius died leaving a young son Philip, and 'Antigonus (III) . . . *accepta in matrimonium matre pupilli*,' etc. There can be no doubt that by *mater pupilli* he means Phthia, otherwise the '*mater*' would be introduced, for no one except Phthia who *could* be the '*mater*' has been mentioned; and as the '*mater*' is not introduced, Phthia's name runs on.[2] *Mater pupilli* is as clear as *pater pupillorum* in XX 1, 1. Justin, i.e. Trogus, therefore says that Phthia was mother of Philip, survived Demetrius, and married Antigonus III. As Justin is the only extant writer who records Phthia's name, Trogus at this point was following good information.

I must end this section by re-emphasing the point I made at

[1] *JHS* XXIX (1909) 265–7.

[2] Jacoby, who did not know my analysis of Trogus, nevertheless took this to be the natural reading of Justin's text, as it is in any case: *F.Gr.Hist.* II D p. 862, 'Nach Justin XXVIII, 1, 1–4 . . . sollte man glauben dass Philippos V Sohn Phthia's war.'

length before,[1] that Phthia's inherited blood will explain why
her son was, as everyone has seen, so unlike an Antigonid, and
nothing else will. The authors seek to minimise this by saying
that Polybius on Philip (I assume that they mean his later life)
is tendencious. It may be so; but, tendencious or not, Polybius
did not invent Philip's proceedings at Abydos.

II

CHRYSEIS

PHILIP then was the son of Demetrius' wife Phthia; *IG* II²
1299 and Trogus-Justin seem conclusive. But what little other
literary evidence exists — it is all set out in full by the authors —
states clearly that he was the son of Chryseis: Antigonus III
married Philip's mother (Plutarch and *Etymologicum Magnum*)
and Antigonus' wife's name was Chryseis (Polybius and *Et. Magn.*)
As Phthia was alive long after Philip's birth, and as (everyone
agrees) Demetrius could not have had two legitimate wives at
once, the authors, since they argue that Phthia was not Philip's
mother, are forced to argue also that Chryseis was not Demetrius'
wife but only his concubine. Their reasons for this boil down to
three: Eusebius, whom I shall come to; the name Philip, previously unknown in the Antigonid house; and the alleged failure of
every writer to say that Chryseis was Demetrius' wife (though in
fact Eusebius does say it). The last two arguments, I think, have
no validity. Demetrius may have had a dozen reasons unknown
to us for naming his son after his (supposed) great ancestor; and
as to Chryseis' not usually being called Demetrius' wife, not only
are there too few writers to prove a negative, but also no Greek
writer would ever have dreamt that anyone could suppose that
she was anything else. Any writer knew that her son in due
course became king, that Antigonus married her, and that Hellenistic kings did not marry other people's concubines; why (he would
think) should he waste ink on anything so obvious?

Before coming to Eusebius, there is one thing to be said about

[1] *CQ* XVIII 23.

this. Polybius gives two firm facts, that Antigonus III married Chryseis and that he adopted Philip as his son.[1] This last no doubt was to fulfil a promise made to Demetrius, though we are not told so. But why did he marry Chryseis? There are four possibilities and no more: (1) because he wanted to; (2) Plutarch's story that the Macedonian nobles made him do so, i.e. as a security for Philip; (3) that he had promised Demetrius to do so, as additional security for Philip; (4) to strengthen his own position. Now suppose that Chryseis *was* Demetrius' concubine: every one of these reasons at once becomes impossible. As a concubine, she was nothing at all; for all purposes of State she had no existence. To marry her would not have strengthened Antigonus' position, though it might have weakened it. It could give Philip no additional security; his security lay in Antigonus' adoption of him. I do not see Demetrius asking his cousin, the legitimate heir to the throne (since *ex hypothesi* Philip was illegitimate),[2] to marry his mistress; neither do I see Macedonians compelling their future king to marry someone else's concubine (in fact, as I showed before,[3] Plutarch's story is more than doubtful on its merits). And most certainly I do not see a king of Macedonia, and one of much force of character, with the world to choose from, marrying for choice someone else's concubine, a thing not done by any Hellenistic king even at their worst. If, on the contrary, Chryseis was Demetrius' wife, it is all plain enough: Antigonus married her, possibly because he had promised Demetrius, possibly on account of Philip, but certainly to strengthen his own position. For he was not in the direct line; and at all times and in all countries it has been common enough for a ruler not in the direct line — conqueror, usurper, collateral, or what not — to strengthen his position by marrying his predecessor's widow, i.e., by stepping into his shoes.

---

[1] For Polybius' evidence see Tarn, *CQ* XVIII 21; Fine *op. cit.* 102–3.

[2] The authors appear to have forgotten their own hypothesis when (p. 157) they call Philip 'heir to the throne'; for that the Macedonian army could, and once did, crown a bastard has nothing to do with heirship. Perhaps they meant that Demetrius had proclaimed Philip as his heir.

[3] *CQ* XVIII 22.

I come to the evidence on which the authors really rely, Eusebius. They say (p. 155) 'Scholars have as a rule neglected to examine this statement of Eusebius'; I agree, particularly as regards myself. The statement is not of course Eusebius' own; neither, if it did come through Porphyry,[1] was it Porphyry's own. There is no means of knowing who first made it, nor does it much matter; I will call the writer of it 'Eusebius' source.'

Eusebius, Schöne I 238: ὃν διαδέχεται υἱὸς Δημήτριος, ὃς καὶ πᾶσαν τὴν Λιβύην ἔλαβε Κυρήνης τε ἐκράτησε καὶ κατέσχεν ἐτῶν δέκα. γήμας δέ τινα τῶν αἰχμαλώτων καὶ Χρυσηΐδα προσειπών, Φίλιππον ἐξ αὐτῆς ἔσχε τὸν πρῶτον πολεμήσαντα Ῥωμαίοις καὶ κακῶν αἴτιον Μακεδόσι γενόμενον. Next follows the story of Antigonus III.

I translate. "(Antigonus Gonatas) was succeeded by his son Demetrius (II), who took all Libya and made himself master of Cyrene and held it (or 'them') for ten years. But having married one of the captives and named her Chryseis, he had by her (a son) Philip, who was the first (Macedonian) to go to war with Romans and became a cause of evils to Macedonians." I note in passing that no interpretation of this passage can be convincing which does not explain why the writer, who is only giving very brief accounts, brings in Philip's wars with Rome out of place between Demetrius II and Antigonus III.

To take the passage in order. Gonatas' son Demetrius II was never in Africa, and it is a commonplace that the statement about his conquest of Libya and Cyrene relates to the rule of Demetrius the Fair; the first sentence is a mix-up of the two.[2] What has not been seen is that the mix-up runs on into the second sentence, in the words 'But having married one of the captives'. The subject of this clause is still Demetrius II; but who are 'the captives'? There is only one thing they *can* be, either in grammar or sense: captives taken in the only war which has been mentioned, that in Africa, which, if ever waged at all, was *not* waged by Demetrius II. This has usually been obscured by loose statements that Deme-

---

[1] Jacoby *F. Gr. Hist.* II B no. 260 fr. 3 (13) makes it Porphyry.

[2] E. Schwartz (see Jacoby *op. cit.* 862) made Eusebius himself author of the confusion. We shall see that it came from his source.

trius married 'a captive', but it is perfectly plain, and with it
the whole story of the captive falls to the ground; there never was,
or could have been, any such captive, for Demetrius II never
waged any such war. With the captive there of course vanishes
also the statement that Demetrius named her Chryseis; if there
was no captive, he could not name her.

Next, the word γήμας, 'having married'. It seems strange that
the authors should, as evidence for Chryseis as a concubine, rely
on a passage which says that Demetrius married her; they say
however (p. 154 n. 2.) that 'the use of γήμας by Eusebius cannot
be taken to mean a formal marriage' (why not?) 'for γαμέω is used
of quite informal unions.' I have collected all the cases of this I
can get. Liddell and Scott⁹ give three; but of these *Odyssey* I
36 is quite uncertain, for in Homer's story there is no reason why,
once Agamemnon was dead, Clytemnestra should not have formally married Aegisthus; Dindorf's Stephanus accordingly does
not give this reference. In Euripides *Troades* 44 ¹ the meaning
is certain from the context — the common fate of the captive
woman; and the unpleasant passage in Lucian *Asinus* 32, a fanci-
ful story of a man who turned into an ass, is also certain from the
context. Dindorf's Stephanus gives three other cases. The
scholium on Aristophanes *Plutus* 1082 is a long passage where
the word has to be interpreted from the context and probably,
though not certainly, means an irregular union. *Anthologia Graeca*
V 94, ἡμίθεος δ'ὁ φιλῶν, ἀθάνατος δ'ὁ γαμῶν, probably, from the context, means marriage. Lastly, Callimachus, *Hymn to Delos* l. 241,
where Hera is abusing Leto,

> Οὕτω νῦν ὦ Ζηνὸς ὀνείδεα, καὶ γαμέοισθε
> λάθρια καὶ τίκτοιτε κεκρυμμένα —

this is certain from the circumstances and from ὀνείδεα (here =
light-o'-loves). What these passages show, then, is this. Γαμέω,
even in poetry, can only mean an irregular union if the context
makes it quite clear. There is no case of that meaning in ordinary

---

¹ Of Cassandra: Apollo had spared her, but

> τὸ τοῦ θεοῦ τε παραλιπὼν τό τ' εὐσεβὲς
> γαμεῖ βιαίως σκότιον 'Αγαμέμνων λέχος.

prose narrative, like that of Eusebius; and there is no case at all in which γαμέω means the continuing relation of a man and his mistress. Γήμας in the passage in question has therefore its natural meaning, and means, as the Armenian translator took it to mean,[1] formal marriage.

As there was no captive, the authors' view (p. 155 n. 1) that "Demetrius gave Chryseis her name because she was a captive" falls to the ground; Eusebius' source invented the captive from the name Chryseis, which means that it *is* a Homeric allusion, as Beloch suggested. I am coming to the reason why Eusebius' source did this and brought in Homer; but I must first note that, though the authors also believe in a Homeric allusion, they have not got it right. They say (p. 154) "In the Iliad the captive Chryseis was the mistress of Agamemnon, and by giving the name Chryseis to his mistress, also a captive, Demetrius II of course implied that she stood in the same relationship to himself, the Macedonian king, as Homer's Chryseis to Agamemnon, ruler of the Achaeans." There is nothing whatever in the Iliad to show, or suggest, that Chryseis was Agamemnon's mistress. Certainly, when her father comes to ransom her, Agamemnon cries out in a rage that he will not release her; sooner than that (πρίν) he will take her back to Argos with him, to grow old weaving at the loom and sleeping with him.[2] But that does not bear on the point, for it is in the *future*; and it is to be remembered that, after Agamemnon had taken Briseis in her place and was subsequently forced to return her to Achilles, he swears a great oath to Achilles that he has not touched her (Briseis).[3] Of course later writers made Chryseis bear Agamemnon a son;[4] but Eusebius' source, by his use of the word γήμας, shows clearly enough that he is not thinking of that story, and also that he is not thinking, or suggesting, that either the first or the second Chryseis was anybody's mistress. That is not his point at all. What his point was we shall see if we

---

[1] *Uxorem duxit* in the old Latin verson, *heirathete* in the modern German translation.

[2] *Il.* I 29–31.

[3] *Il.* IX 132.

[4] For these stories see Tümpel, *Chryses* (1) in PW III, cols. 2496–2498.

read what he has written; and as he *has* brought in Homer's Chryseis, we had better first recall what Homer's story was. Chryseis, daughter of Chryses, priest of Apollo, was captured by the Greeks with other women and allotted to Agamemnon as his γέρας, his portion of honour. Thereon [1] her father came to ransom her; Agamemnon refused; her father appealed to Apollo, who sent a great pestilence on the Greeks, and to save them from destruction Agamemnon had to let the girl go. He consoled his wounded pride by taking from Achilles *his* captive, Briseis; Achilles in wrath retired to his tent, Hector almost drove the Greeks into the sea, and to save them from destruction a second time Agamemnon had to give back Briseis. Chryseis, that is, brought just about as much evil on her captors as one woman could; twice, through her, they came near to destruction. Eusebius' source, some literary man who knew his Homer better than his history,[2] saw his way, over the rare name Chryseis, to a clever literary parallel, so clever that he could not refrain from drawing it; enough of it has reached us to enable us to see what it was. He made the second Chryseis a captive, like the first, for the sake of his parallel, and also said that Chryseis was not her original name because Alexandrian learning had said the same about Homer's Chryseis,[3] and, this done, he had his parallel to his hand: as the first Chryseis had been a cause of evils, κακῶν αἰτία, to her captors, the Greeks, when they fought against Rome's ancestors, the Trojans, so the second Chryseis, through her son Philip, had been κακῶν αἰτία

[1] *Il.* I 370, αὖθ'.

[2] To him is due, not only the confusion of Demetrius II with Demetrius the Fair and the consequent 'captive', but also, in the following section on Antigonus III, the horrible story that Antigonus for Philip's sake killed all his own children by Chryseis. As this story is also told (Plut. *Mor.* 184 B, 489 F) of Attalus II and Stratonice, for the benefit of Attalus (III), Stratonice τεκοῦσα πολλάκις being at the time about 50, neither version can be true; it is a bad literary cliché, which apparently some people admired as Buddhists admired the conduct of the king in the *Sibi-Jataka*, and which was invented to explain why neither king left a son. See also, on the Antigonus story, Treves *op. cit.* 409 and his deduction from Livy XL 54. 4.

[3] Her original name was said to have been Astynome: Schol. *Il.* I 392; Tümpel *op. cit.* It was disputed whether Chryseis was a patronymic (so the Scholiast) or an ὄνομα κύριον (Suidas, Χρυσηΐς).

to *her* captors, the Macedonians, when they fought against Rome itself.[1] That is why the passage which has come down to us drags in, out of place, Philip's wars with Rome.

That is all there is to Eusebius, and I hope (though with little confidence) that no one will ever quote this passage again as evidence for anything. The theory that Chryseis was Demetrius' concubine, when tested, breaks down at every point.

III

Φθία ἡ καὶ Χρυσηΐς

PHTHIA then was wife of Demetrius and mother of Philip, and Chryseis was also wife of Demetrius and mother of Philip; and as a man cannot have two mothers, Phthia and Chryseis are merely two names for the same woman, who in the ordinary phraseology would have been Φθία ἡ καὶ Χρυσηΐς. It accords with this that Trogus-Justin makes Phthia survive Demetrius and marry Antigonus III, while in Polybius the name of Antigonus' wife is Chryseis. All that now remains is to consider the double name of the woman who was successively the wife of Demetrius II and of his successor.

These double names occur by the thousand in the Hellenistic and Graeco-Roman periods [2] — nicknames, pet names, second names which were neither; there are cases, like Adeia-Eurydice, wife of Philip III, where it cannot be said which name was the real one. In many cases they are names in two different languages, Greek and non-Greek; but the name Phthia occurs fairly often in the mythology, and is not therefore likely, I suppose, to be non-Greek, though subsequently confined to Epirus and Thessaly. Phthia, which alone occurs in official documents,[3] was her real

---

[1] It may have gone a little further; Homer's Chryseis had *twice* brought evils upon the Greeks, and Philip had fought *two* wars with Rome.

[2] A great collection was made by M. Lambertz, "Zur Ausbreitung des Supernomen oder Signum im römischen Reiche", Part I, *Glotta* IV (1913), 78; Part II, *ib.* V (1914), 99.

[3] *IG* II² 1299; Durrbach, *Inscriptions de Délos, Comptes des Hiéropes* (nos. 372-

name; Chryseis, never used officially, was her second name, which (except fortunately for Trogus-Justin) ousted the real name from literature, just as in the East the nicknames of many cities completely ousted the official names, even for Polybius.[1]

There is no reason to suppose that Demetrius gave Phthia her second name; there is no evidence,[2] and no cause is apparent. There are two cases, one certain one probable, of a Macedonian king's giving his wife a second name, but in each case there was a special reason: Antiochus III named his bride from Chalcis Euboea[3] as a political manifesto, and if it was Philip II who named his wife Myrsale Olympias, it was inevitable in the circumstances.[4]

Armies or peoples often gave their kings nicknames, either friendly ones or, like the Alexandrian nicknames of the later Ptolemies, derogatory. Kings in literature were often called by the nickname alone, as can be seen at large in Trogus-Justin; even Antigonus II could be called merely 'the Gonatas';[5] in one case, Caesarion, the real name vanished completely from literature and has only been recovered from papyri and coins. But I think there is no known case of army or people nicknaming a woman.

There can be no real doubt that Chryseis was Phthia's name ἐν τῇ συνηθείᾳ, that is, 'in familiar usage', 'in the circle of her intimates' — possibly a pet name come down from childhood.[6]

---

498) (1929), no. 407 1. 20, no. 461 Bb 1. 46, dedication of a vase; see A. Wilhelm *B.Ph.W.* 1912, 314.

[1] Tarn *Bactria and India* 13–16.

[2] Eusebius has been dealt with; but I note that late Greek and Latin writers often say that a king gave some city its nickname when we know he did not.

[3] Polyb. XX 8. 5: ἔθετο δὲ καὶ τῇ παιδὶ ὄνομα Εὔβοιαν.

[4] Olympias, never previously (and seldom subsequently) used as a woman's name (doubtless because of its suggestion of divinity), must be derived from the Olympia, as the common woman's name Pythias was from the Pythia. Philip II (Plut. *Alex.* 3) received at the same time two messages, that he was an Olympic victor and that his wife had born him a son (Alexander); and it was presumably he who made of her an 'Olympic victor' also. She was indeed.

[5] The Philodemus fragment in *P.Herc.* 339 col. V (text given in *Philol.* LXXI 226).

[6] A number of 'nursery' names in Lambertz *op. cit.* II 141.

It is not likely to have had anything to do with Homer; [1] it is
probably 'Goldilocks' and was given her, as the Armenian translator of Eusebius thought,[2] from her golden hair,[3] probably rare
in Epirus; second names given from personal traits are common
enough.[4] Generally, with double names, we only get A ὁ καὶ B, or
some equivalent, but occasionally the inscription explains what
the second name is. The two best cases of this which I have met
are two given by M. L. Robert:[5] one, a girl from Olympus in Lycia,
'Kyrathūs, familiarly known as Agoraste', Κυραθοῦνι, ἐν τῇ συνηθείᾳ
'Αγοράστῃ; [6] the other a man from Celenderis in Cilicia — his
parents named him Synegdemos, 'but everyone else called him
Billos', οἱ δ'ἄλλοι πάντες ἐπωνόμασαν Βίλλον.[7] There are plenty of

---

[1] It is to be remembered however that, though Homer's Chryseis brought much
evil on her captors, she brought none on her own family or people. The name also
occurs twice in the mythology: *Hom. Hymn Dem.* 421, Hesiod *Theog.* 359.

[2] The old Latin version translates *Oskeak* by *Aureolam*, the modern German by
'*die güldene.*'

[3] Mr. Edson suggested to me in a letter that, if so, the name should have been
Χρύση, not Χρυσηΐs. But Χρύση is just as rare a woman's name as Χρυσηΐs, and there
was a very good reason for not giving it to the girl: it was the name of a goddess.
Chryse was the goddess of Lesbos, graecised as Aphrodite Chryse; she must have
been more important than our tradition suggests, for she may have been the
origin of Homer's epithet 'Golden Aphrodite' (Tümpel, *Chryse* (13) in PW), and
the hold of her name upon Lesbos was so strong that a generation ago, some sixteen
centuries after she had ceased to be a goddess, it was stated that every girl child
in the island bore that name as a pet name, Ξό, i.e. Χρυσό (P. Kretschmer, cited by
Lambertz *op. cit.* I 83). On the other hand, when we find sea-nymphs (a Nereid
and an Oceanid) called Chryseis, the name *must* mean, 'the golden'.

[4] Lambertz *op. cit.* I 133, ὁ καὶ Φαλακρίων, 'Bald-head' (said to be common);
II 138, ὁ καὶ Στράβων, 'Squint-eye'; p. 111, a whole list from Egypt, including ὁ
(*sic*) καλούμενον Κῶφον, 'Deaf' or 'Dumb', and ὁ καὶ Μέλας, 'Black-hair' or 'Raven-
locks', cf. Cleitus the Black and Cleitus the White (? an albino) in the Alexander-
story; some others p. 116 n. 2. Add the Seleucid Antiochus VIII Γρῦπος, 'Hook-
nose' (query, if II 136 ὁ καὶ Γρεῖπος be not a mis-spelling of Γρῦπος rather than
of Γρῖπος, the explanation given of γρῖπος (a fishing net) being far-fetched).

[5] In '*Études épigraphiques et philologiques*, 1938.

[6] *BCH* 1892, 215 n. 11; Robert, *op. cit.* 188, who translates ἐν τῇ συνηθείᾳ by
'*dans l'usage familier*'. Agoraste was a common Pisidian name, Lambertz *op. cit.*
II 138 n. 2.

[7] *CIG* III 4322 and Add.; Robert *op. cit.* 166. For some other cases see Lambertz I 83, 136.

men and girls in England today whose baptismal names have been completely ousted by a 'to-name'; and the phenomenon is very old.

I hope that we are now really at the end of what has been a long road.

ARCHON DIOMEDON

Von † Johannes Kirchner

NÄCHST dem Archon Polyeuktos, dessen Jahr durch einen glücklichen Fund auf der athenischen Agora jetzt für das Jahr 243/2 festgelegt ist (vgl. Meritt *Hesp.* VII [1938] 121), gibt es wohl kaum einen athenischen Archon aus der Mitte des dritten Jahrhunderts v. Chr., dessen Jahr so umstritten ist wie das des Archon Diomedon. Im Jahr dieses Archon war nach *IG* II² 791 Schreiber Φορυσκίδης 'Αριστομένου mit einem Demotikon von 10 Stellen, von dem nur der Anfangsbuchstabe überliefert ist. Von diesem *einen* Buchstaben, dessen Lesung strittig ist, hängt die Fixierung des Archon Diomedon ab.

Das Demotikon in *IG* II² 791₄ war von Koehler *IG* II 334 nach einer Abschrift Velsens A - - - - - ? - - - - gegeben worden. Lolling Δελτ. 1892, 48 bemerkt, dass der betreffende Buchstabe ihm eher ein Λ als A zu sein scheine und ergänzt Λ[ευκονοεύς] als einziger mit Λ anfangender Demotikon mit 10 Buchstaben. Auch Wilhelm 'Εφημ. 1892, 139³ erklärt sich für Λ[ευκονοεύς] auf Grund der von ihm ergänzten Inschrift *IG* II 2314 [Φορύ]σκος ['Αριστ]ομένους [Λευκ]ονοεύς. Lollings Lesung schliessen sich an: der Unterzeichnete *Gött. gel. Anz.* 1900, 448; Ferguson, *The Priests of Asklepios,* 1906, 155; Kolbe, *Att. Archonten,* 1908, 66. Dagegen kommt Johnson *Amer. Journ. Philol.,* 34 (1913), 386 nach Untersuchung des Steines wieder auf die von Koehler gegebene Lesung Velsens zurück und ergänzt 'Α[γνούσιος]. Vgl. dazu Dittenberger Syll.³ 542 Anm. 9. Die im Jahr 1913 in *IG* II² 791 aufgenommene Ergänzung Λ[ευκονοεύς] wird in den Add. *ib.* S. 66 F durch Leonardos bestätigt. Auch 'Εφημ. 1918, 87 hat sich Leonardos im Gegensatz zu Johnson zu dieser Feststellung bekannt. Bisher handelte es sich nur darum, ob der Anfangsbuchstabe A oder Λ lautete. Als aber im Jahr 1923 das Thiasotendekret von Salamis (Keramopullos 'Ο ἀποτυμπανισμός in der Βιβλιοθήκη τῆς ἐν 'Αθήναις ἀρχ. ἑταιρ. 1923, 113 = *Suppl. ep. gr.* II 9) entdeckt war, das für den Archon Diomedon als Nachfolger des Hieron einen Schreiber aus der Phyle Kekropis verlangt, schlug De Sanctis *Rivista di filol.* 1923, 172 die Ergänzung Δ[αιδαλίδης] = Kekropis IX vor. Eingetreten ist für diese Lesung nach Prüfung des Steines Roussel *Rev. ét. anc.* 1924, 100 (vgl. auch *Rev. ét. anc.* 1932, 198⁹). Dagegen hielt Beloch *Gr. Gesch.*² IV 2 (1927) 82 an Λ[ευκονοεύς] fest, ebenso Dinsmoor *Archons* 1932, 97. Klaffenbach hat dann auf meine Bitte im Jahr 1934 die Lesung einer nochmaligen Untersuchung unterzogen und mir mitgeteilt, dass das Λ über allen Zweifel erhaben sei; die angeblich vorhandene horizontale Linie des Δ erweise sich als Absplitterung des Steines. Für Λ erklärt sich auch St. Dow bei Ferguson *The Tribal Cycles* 1932, 17, während Ferguson selbst ebenda 18 die Frage unentschieden lässt. Im Jahr 1935 bin ich im Verein mit Leonardos nach abermaliger Prüfung zum Ergebnis gelangt, dass kein anderer Buchstabe als Λ in Frage kommt. Dem gegenüber kommt Meritt *Hesp.* VII 1938, 136 in der von ihm aufgestellten Archonliste wieder auf die Ergänzung Δ[αιδαλίδης] zurück, bezeichnet aber das Δ als unsicher.

Das ist das Schicksal, das der Anfangsbuchstabe des Demotikons des Schreibers Φορυσκίδης 'Αριστομένόυ im Jahr des Archon Diomedon gehabt hat. Für Deutung des Buchstaben als Λ und für die Ergänzung Λ[ευκονοεύς] treten nun als wesentliches Moment die verwandtschaftlichen Beziehungen des Schreibers hinzu. Darauf hat, wie oben erwähnt, bereits Wilhelm hingedeutet, und Dinsmoor hat unter Hinzuziehung weiterer Familienglieder, ohne allerdings die chronologischen Daten in Rechnung zu ziehen, einen Stammbaum mit den Voreltern des Phoryskides aufgestellt. Des Phoryskides Bruder ist *IG* II² 1299 'Αριστοφάνης 'Αριστομένου Λευκονοεύς, στρατηγός in den Jahren 239/8 und 237/6. Als des Phoryskides Urgrossvater ist zu betrachten *IG* II 2314 = *IG* II² 6750 [Φορύ]σκος ['Αριστ]ομένους [Λευκ]ονοεύς auf einem grossen Monument unbekannter Art, das mit Koehler unter die Grabsteine aufgenommen worden ist. Dieses Phoryskos Bruder ist *IG* II² 1632₉₃ 'Αριστοφάνης Λευκονοεύς, τριήραρχος in einer Seeurkunde vom Jahr 323/2. Zur gleichen Familie gehören *IG* II² 2382₉ Φο[ρ]ύσκος Τιμοκρά[τ]ους Λευκονοεύς in einem Katalog der Leontis um 360–350 und — bei Dinsmoor nicht erwähnt — dessen Enkel

’Εφημ. 1918, 74 (Inschr. aus dem Amphiaraion) Φορύσκος Τιμοκράτους Λευκονοεύς, Ephebe kurz vor dem Jahr 323/2. Der Stammbaum wird also folgendermassen zu gestalten sein:

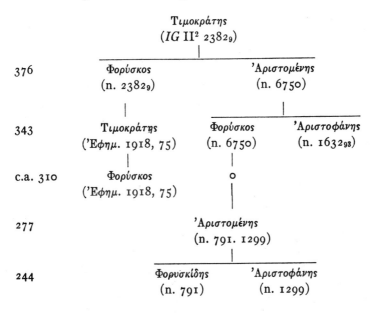

Τιμοκράτης
(*IG* II² 2382₉)

376   Φορύσκος   ’Αριστομένης
       (n. 2382₉)   (n. 6750)

343   Τιμοκράτης   Φορύσκος   ’Αριστοφάνης
      (’Εφημ. 1918, 75)   (n. 6750)   (n. 1632₉₃)

c.a. 310   Φορύσκος   ○
      (’Εφημ. 1918, 75)

277   ’Αριστομένης
              (n. 791. 1299)

244   Φορυσκίδης   ’Αριστοφάνης
         (n. 791)   (n. 1299)

Zeigt diese Zusammenstellung deutlich die Zugehörigkeit des Phoryskides zu den Λευκονοεῖς, so muss für jeden, der unschlüssig ist, ob der erhaltene Rest des ersten Buchstabens des Demotikons mit 9 darauffolgenden Stellen als Λ oder Δ zu deuten sei, ein Zweifel an der Richtigkeit der Ergänzung Λ[ευκονοεύς] schwinden.

Ausgehend von der Lesung Λ[ευκονοεύς] habe ich *Gött. gel. Anz.* 1900, 448, sofern die Λευκονοεῖς der Leontis (IV) angehören, nach der Schreiberfolge den Archon Diomedon dem Jahr 232/1 zugewiesen. In diesem Jahr amtierte nach *IG* II² 791₂ Εὐρυκλείδης Μικίωνος Κηφισιεύς als ταμίας στρατιωτικῶν. Hierauf nimmt das zu Ehren des Eurykleides bald nach dem Jahr 229 d. h. der Befreiung Athens durch Diogenes abgefasste Dekret *IG* II² 834 Bezug, in dem vor Erwähnung der Verdienste um die Befreiung der Stadt in Z. 1 der Tätigkeit des Eurykleides als ταμίας στρατιωτικῶν gedacht ist. Aus dem Vergleich der Dekrete II² 791 und II² 834 ist zunächst zu schliessen, dass der Archon Diomedon in die Jahre vor 229/8 gehört. Vgl. *Hermes* 28 (1893), 140[1]. Für die Ansetzung Diomedon = 232/1 treten aber die Worte II² 791₁₀ aus dem Frühsommer dieses Jahres ein: [ἵνα κατὰ τὸν κ]ατάλοιπ̣ον χρόνον τοῦ ἐνιαυτοῦ συνκ[ομισθῶσιν οἱ ἐκ γῆς κ]αρποὶ μετ' ἀσφαλείας. Aus ihnen ist zu entnehmen, dass die Ernte im Umkreis von Athen kurz zuvor verwüstet war, und Ferguson *Hellenist. Ath.* 203 hat diese Stelle mit Recht mit den Kriegszügen im attischen Lande zu Ende des Demetrischen Krieges im Jahr 232 in Verbindung gebracht. Auf die gleiche Zeit wird auch von Beloch *Gr. Gesch.*², IV 2, 530, 636 der Passus aus dem Ehrendekret für Eurykleides *IG* II² 834₇ bezogen: τῆς χώρας κατὰ] τοὺς πολέμους ἀργοῦ καὶ ἀσπόρου οὔ[σης αἴτιος ἐγέ]νετο τοῦ ἐξεργασθῆναι καὶ σπαρῆναι [χρήματα πορί]σας. Den letzten Worten entspricht, dass Eurykleides *IG* II² 791₃₄ unter den ersten ἐπιδόντες εἰς τὴν σω[τηρίαν τῆς πό]λεως καὶ τὴν φυλακὴν τῆς [χώρας] genannt wird.

Nach dem oben erwähnten Thiasotendekret aus Salamis (*Suppl. ep. gr.* II 9) ist für das Jahr 241/0 der Archon Diomedon als Nachfolger der Archonten Polyeuktos (243/2) und Hieron (242/1) gesichert. Vgl. Meritt *Hesp.* VII (1938), 136. Wir haben demnach zwei Archonten mit dem Namen Diomedon anzunehmen, wie ich es *Philol. Wochenschr.* 1924, 871 vorgeschlagen und Ferguson *Tribal Cycles* 88 in Erwägung gezogen hat: Diomedon I ohne überlieferten Ratsschreiber vom Jahr 241/0, *Suppl. ep. gr.* II 9, und Diomedon II mit dem Schreiber Φορυσκίδης ᾿Αριστομένου Λ[ευκονοεύς] aus dem Jahr 232/1, *IG* II² 791. Letzterer ist ohne nachfolgendes Distinktiv (sei es durch beigefügtes Demotikon oder durch ὁ δεῖνα μετὰ τὸν δεῖνα) überliefert, ebensowenig wie Archon Eubulos II vom Jahr 259/8 (*Hesp.* VII [1938], 135) vom Archon Eubulos I vom Jahr 272/1 durch ein Distinktiv unterschieden ist.

Wenn wir für Diomedon II nach dem Schreibercyklus das Jahr 232/1 in Anspruch nehmen, so steht dem entgegen, dass nach dem Thiasotendekret aus Salamis als Nachfolger des Archon Kydenor (233/2) für das Jahr 232/1 Eurykleides aufgeführt wird, somit das Jahr 232/1 bereits besetzt erscheint. Dazu ist zu sagen, dass,

wie die von Keramopullos der Thiasoteninschrift beigegebene
Photographie (auch bei Dow *Amer. Journ. Arch.* 40 [1936], 68)
zeigt, die Aufzeichnung des Eurykleides in schärferen Schrift-
zügen, ohne ἐπιμεληταί hinter dem Archontennamen und ohne
beigefügten Ölzweig, sich als späterer Zusatz erweist. So sind wir
nicht gezwungen, Eurykleides für den unmittelbaren Nachfolger
des Kydenor zu halten. Ich möchte ihn, da das Jahr 231/0 durch
Jason besetzt ist, dem noch freien Jahr 230/29 zuweisen. Archon
Eurykleides ist der bekannte Staatsmann aus Kephisia, dem wir
im Jahr 232/1 als ταμίας στρατιωτικῶν begegneten. Über die
führende Stellung, die Eurykleides und sein Bruder Mikion nach
ihrer Beteiligung an der Befreiung Athens in der auf das Jahr
229/8 folgenden Zeit eingenommen haben, hat Ferguson *Hell.
Ath.* 243 ff. ausführlich gehandelt.

Wenn in den letzten vier Jahrzehnten erhebliche Fortschritte
in der Erforschung der attischen Archonten im Zeitalter des
Hellenismus erzielt worden sind, so verdanken wir das in erster
Linie den weitfördernden Arbeiten William Scott Fergusons.
Mögen dem rastlos tätigen, verdienstvollen Gelehrten, der sich
bereits in jungen Jahren durch die Aufstellung der "lex Ferguson"
ein bleibendes Denkmal auf dem Gebiet der attischen Chronologie
gesetzt hat, noch viele glückliche Jahre der Forscherarbeit zu
Nutz und Frommen der Altertumswissenschaft beschieden sein.

ΑΜΦΙΘΑΛΗΣ

PAR LOUIS ROBERT

J'AVAIS promis d'étudier ici des "Inscriptions attiques relatives à des fêtes." Les circonstances ne m'ont pas permis encore d'achever ce travail, et je prie M. Ferguson d'agréer l'hommage de cet 'Αμφιθαλής; il y est peu question d'inscriptions attiques, mais les institutions religieuses ont toujours retenu l'attention de M. Ferguson, comme il l'a montré encore récemment dans son beau commentaire sur "The Salaminioi of Heptaphylai and Sounion."

En partant de l'inscription dionysiaque du Latium publiée naguère par F. Cumont,[1] un récent article, dû à A. Oepke, dans *Archiv für Religionswissenschaft*,[2] a traité des 'Αμφιθαλεῖς *im griechischen und hellenistischen Kult*, du rôle religieux des enfants qui ont encore leurs père et mère. Oepke, constatant l'absence d'un travail complet sur ce sujet, a voulu d'abord réunir les textes, puis élucider le rôle des ἀμφιθαλεῖς dans les cérémonies du culte. Une fois de plus, les documents épigraphiques n'ont été exploités que très insuffisamment. Oepke, après Cumont, a cité ces inscriptions, qui étaient déjà enregistrées dans la nouvelle édition du dictionnaire de Liddell-Scott.

1. Magnésie du Méandre. *Sylloge*[3] 589. 18–21. Décret sur le culte de Zeus Sôsipolis et l'ἀνάδειξις d'un taureau:[3] ἀποστέλλειν δὲ τοὺς παιδονόμους παῖδας ἐννέα ἀμφιθαλεῖς, ἀποστέλλειν δὲ καὶ τοὺς γυναικονόμους παρθένους ἐννέα ἀμφιθαλεῖς. 196 a. C. n.

2. Thyatire. *BCH* 1886, 415 n° 23,[4] τοῦ Σωτῆρος 'Ασ[κληπι]οῦ λαμπρῶς καὶ πολυδαπάνως, δεκαπρωτεύσαντα καὶ ἐφηβαρχήσαντα καὶ ἀμφιθαλέα γενόμενον τῶν μεγάλων 'Αντωνίων.[5]

---

[1] *AJA* 1933, 215–263.

[2] XXXI (1934) 42–56.

[3] Cf. E. Bikerman *Mélanges Boisacq* 123 n. 5.

[4] Clerc, Περὶ τῶν τῆς πόλεως Θυατείρων (1900), 141 n° 55.

[5] Il s'agit de fêtes en l'honneur, non point d'Antoine (par ex. O. Seeck, *Klio* I (1901) 150 n. 4: "es versteht sich von selbst, dass diese Spiele den Tod des Antonius nicht überdauert haben"), mais d'un Antonin, Caracalla ou Elagabal. Dans plusieurs inscriptions les 'Αντωνίνεια sont appelées 'Αντώνεια (un exemple caractéristique à Laodikeia du Lykos *IGR* IV 850: 'Αντωνῆα Γετεῖα 'Ολύμπια).

3. Thyatire. *BCH* 1886, 415 n° 24,[1] ʽΗ βουλὴ καὶ ὁ δῆμος ἐτείμησεν Ληναῖον Μενάνδρου Θυατειρηνόν, ἐνδόξως παλαίσαντα καὶ ἀνφιθαλεύσαντα τὰ μεγάλα ᾽Ασκληπιεῖα, ὑπὸ ἐπιστάτην Διόφαντον Εὐνόμου.

4. Thyatire. *BCH* 1887, 105 n° 26 ll. 26–8: ἀδελφὸν - - ἀμφιθαλέων.

5. Dans l'inscription dionysiaque du Latium sont nommés deux ἀμφιθαλεῖς, Λάτριος et Μένανδρος. II° siècle p. C. n.

Il faut ajouter les inscriptions suivantes.[2]

6. Pergame. *Ath. Mitt.* 1910, 408 l. 19. Vers la fin du II° siècle av. J.-C., un des décrets pour l'évergète Diodoros Pasparos dit de lui, dans un contexte mutilé: [π]ροσήκειν ἀρχιερατικὴν τιμὴν ἀμφιθαλοῦς αὐτοῦ - -.

7. Athènes. *Ath. Mitt.* 1898, 26–7 (Michel *Recueil* 1544; *IG* II² 4991). [᾽Επὶ] Μηδείου τὸ δεύτερον (a. 91–90) · ἀμφιθαλὴς Φιλῖνος Φιλίνου Εὐωνυμεὺς. ᾽Επὶ Μηδείου · ἀντὶ τοῦ ἀμφιθαλοῦς Νικίας Καλλιμάχου Διραδιώτ[ης]. Plus loin, [Καλλί]μαχος Δειρα. ἀμφιθαλής.

8. Athènes. *IG* II² 3190. En 126 ap. J.-C., Καρπόδωρος (Καρποδώρου) ʽΑλαιέως υἱὸς ἀμφιθαλής, καθίσας, θύσας τοῖς θεοῖς [ἀνέστη]σεν (?)[3]

9. Tralles. Boeckh, *CIG* 2932, a publié ainsi le texte, d'après la copie de Sherard.

```
    [- - - - - - ἐτεί]-
    [μη]σαν Τρυφω(ν)ιανὸ[ν]
    . . ννίου ʽΕλένου υἱόν,
    . . ᾽Αμφιθαλέα, τ(ὸ)ν δεί[κτ]-
  4 [ην] καὶ εἰσαγω(γ)ὸν τῶν [ἱ]-
    [ερ]ῶν ε(ἰ)σελαστικῶν
    [εἰ]ς τὴν οἰκουμένην
    [Πυ]θίων [- - - - ἀγών]-
  8 [ω]ν, πρῶτον μετὰ τὴν ἀνανέ[ω]-
    σιν κτλ.[4]
```

---

[1] Clerc *loc. cit.* 141 n° 24; mais cf. l'addendum *BCH* 1887, 98 n. 1.

[2] J'en avais déjà réuni plusieurs dans *Rev. Phil.* 1929, 141 n. 3.

[3] Restitution de P. Graindor, *Athènes sous Hadrien* (1934) 117 n. 1. — Je dois dire que le sens du mot καθίσας (lecture de Dittenberger, Graindor, Kirchner) m'est impénétrable. Peut-on penser à καθ' ἴσας (avec l'aspiration de ἴσος fréquente dans la *koinè*, dans la formule ἐφ' ἴσηι καὶ ὁμοίαι), dans le sens de: "également des deux côtés"?

[4] Sur les Pythia de Tralles et sur leur ἀνανέωσις, cf. *Études anatoliennes* 428–429.

Ligne 2, la copie de Sherard donne: ΤΡΥΦΩΣΙΑΝΟ. Il n'y faut rien corriger. Deux Τρυφωσιανός sont connus dans la ville voisine, à Nysa.¹ — Ligne 3, la copie de Sherard donne ΤΩΝ. Il est clair que ἀμφιθαλέα n'est pas un nom propre, mais un titre de fonction, suivi d'un nom de fête: [τὸν] ἀμφιθαλέα τῶν Δεί[ων]² plutôt que ('Α)λεί[ων]³.

10. Ephèse. *Ephesos* III p. 105 n° 14. πανηγυρίαρχος 'Εφεσήων καὶ ἀμφιθαλε[ύσας ?]. J. Keil signale là deux fragments inédits qu'il a bien voulu me communiquer.

11. Ephèse. Agora. Fragment brisé à droite et au bas, trouvé en 1902.

ἀγων[οθετ - -

ΟΥ - - -

ἀμφι[θαλ - - -

12. Ephèse. Dans la Double Eglise. Fragment brisé de tous côtés, trouvé en 1914.

[- - - ἀγωνο]θέτι[ν - -

[- - - - ἀ]μφιθα[λ - -

13. Milet. E. A. Gardner a publié, *JHS* 1885, 350 n° 98, cette inscription de Didymes copiée par Cockerell:

'Αγαθῇ τύχ[η].　　　　　7 φη(β)ον καὶ ἀμ[φι]-
'Η βουλὴ καὶ [ὁ]　　　　　θαλῆ, νικήσα[ν]-
δῆμος ἐτε[ί]μ[η]-　　　　τα παίδων π[ά]-
4 σεν Μάρκον [Αἴ]-　　　10 λην τὰ μεγά[λα]
λιον Αὐρήλι[ον]　　　　Διδυμεῖα ἐν [τῷ]
Δόμνον τὸν [ἔ]-　　　　ἱερῷ.

Ligne 7, la copie de Cockerell porte ΡΗΓΟΝ. Il ne faut rien corriger, et je restitue: [χο]ρηγόν; cette fonction est connue par plusieurs inscriptions milésiennes.⁴

¹ Cf. Münsterberg, "Beamtennamen auf gr. Münzen," *Numism. Zeitschr.* 1912, pp. 79–80; 1914, p. 57 (pp. 143–4, 233 du tirage à part); von Diest *Nysa ad Maeandrum* 102. Des Τρυφωσιανός à Thyatire: cf. Keil et von Premerstein *IIᵉ Reise in Lydien* n° 47.

² Ainsi J. Keil *Ephesos* III p. 105 *ad* n° 14.　　　³ *Rev. Phil. loc. cit.*

⁴ *Rev. Phil.* 1897, 42 n° 16: χορηγὸς πασῶν τῶν χορηγιῶν; n° 17: τετελεκὼς δὲ κ[αὶ τὰ]ς ἐν παισὶ λιτουργίας, χο[ρηγί]αν καὶ ἀγωνοθεσίαν τὰ[ς —] θεοῦ, πατρὸς λιτουργοῦ κτλ. (à rapprocher spécialement de notre texte, pour l'âge du personnage);

14. Aussi, dans deux graffites d'éphèbes du type νίκη, à Milet, ἀμφιθαλ — me semble être, plutôt qu'un nom propre,[1] comme on l'a transcrit,[2] un substantif.[3] Voici le texte de l'éditeur:

A. Νίκη
 Ληναίου
 Ἀμφιθαλ(οῦς) Μοιραγένου
 Νικομά(χου?) [4]
  Ἐπικράτ(ου)
 Μενε   νίκη

B. Ἱεροκ-
 λέους
 Ἀγ[ί]ου
 Ἀμφιθαλ[οῦς]
 νίκη

Enfin je retrouve des ἀμφιθαλεῖς dans des inscriptions inédites de Didymes trouvées par B. Haussoullier dans ses fouilles de 1895 et 1896.[5]

15. [Ἀγ]αθῇ [τύ]χῃ.
 Ἡ βουλὴ καὶ ὁ δῆ-
 μος ἐτείμησεν
4 Αὐρ. Ἄλυπον β′,
 τὸν ἀμφιθαλέ-
 α τῶν μεγάλων

16.   Ἀγαθῇ τύχῃ.
 Ἡ βουλὴ καὶ ὁ δῆμος ἐ-
 τείμησαν τὸν ἀμφιθαλέ-
4 [α τῶν] μεγάλων Διδυμεί-

7 Διδυμείων Κομ-
 μοδείων, νεική-
 σαντα τὰ μεγά-
 λα Διδ[υμ]εῖα παί-
11 [δων - -] ἐπὶ
 - - - - -
5 [ων Κ]ομμοδείων Ὑγι-
 [ανὸν - -]ιον Ῥουφι-
 [νὸν - - - - -] ΒⱵ

Il me semble que, dans un mince fragment de Didymes, on doit rétablir la mention de l'ἀμφιθαλεύς d'après notre n° 13. La copie de B. Haussoullier donne: [6]

Milet, Südmarkt p. 336 n° 265: une gymnasiarque, paidonome, χορηγὸς πασ[ῶν χορηγι]ῶν, agonothète; cf. *Delphinion* p. 395 n° 174: χορηγήσαντα τὰς χορηγίας πάσας καὶ νικήσαντα.

[1] Il est connu à Délos; cf. Bechtel *HP s.v.*

[2] *Milet, Thermen und Palestren* p. 192 n° 386 *c* I ll. 9 sqq. et *b* I ll. 3 sqq.

[3] De même, au n° 387, νίκη Τύχω(νος) Φιλοπόν(ου), est-il assuré que Φιλοπόνου soit un nom? Ne serait ce pas l'adjectif φιλόπονος? La φιλοπονία est une qualité des éphèbes; elle est récompensée par un prix; au gymnase de Pergame, il y a les groupes des εὔτακτοι, des φιλόπονοι et des εὐέκται (cf. E. Ziebarth *Aus dem gr. Schulwesen*[2] 142–144).

[4] On peut penser aussi à Νικομᾶ, l'hypocoristique Νικομᾶς étant attesté.

[5] Les carnets sont conservés à la bibliothèque de l'Institut.

[6] Le marbre est brisé partout, sauf en bas.

I / \ I
I M O N
H Γ O N I
Ξ A N T AT
?N Π Λ Λ H
feuille

J'écrirais: ['Η βουλὴ καὶ ὁ δῆμος ἐτίμησεν τὸν δεῖνα τὸν χορ]ηγὸν ϙ[αὶ ἀμφιθαλέα, νεική]σαντα τ[ὰ μεγάλα Διδυμεῖα παίδ]ων πάλη[ν].

Parmi ces inscriptions il en est où ἀμφιθαλής est un adjectif signifiant: "dont les parents sont vivants", ce qui permet d'être désigné pour certaines fonctions religieuses; ainsi les nᵒˢ 1 et 6. Dans la plupart ἀμφιθαλής est devenu un substantif, un titre de fonction, ὁ ἀμφιθαλής. Ma restitution du nᵒ 13, qui respecte la copie de Cockerell, y dégage nettement ce sens, τὸν χορηγὸν καὶ ἀμφιθαλῆ. En plusieurs cas même, ἀμφιθαλής est si bien un nom de fonction qu'on a créé un nom d'agent en εύς, ἀμφιθαλεύς; ainsi dans les inscriptions nᵒˢ 2, 4, 9, 10, 15 et 16, tout au moins. D'où la création du verbe ἀμφιθαλεύειν, au nᵒ 3. On doit donc se demander quelles étaient les fonctions précises de l'ἀμφιθαλής,[1] de celui qui ἀμφιθαλεύει. Sans pouvoir préciser leur rôle, F. Cumont a supposé qu'il s'agissait de "jeunes acolytes", d' "enfants de chœur", qui, par exemple, lisent un texte sacré.[2] Oepke[3] donne à ἀμφιθαλής dans les inscriptions de

---

[1] J'emploie dans la suite de cette étude la forme ἀμφιθαλής, pour désigner aussi bien l'ἀμφιθαλεύς.

[2] *Loc. cit.* 256: "L'enfant dont les parents étaient tous deux en vie, appartenait à une famille bénie des dieux, à une maison que n'avait pas souillée une mort, et le παῖς ἀμφιθαλής était seul apte à remplir nombre de fonctions sacrées en Grèce, comme à Rome certains prêtres ou *camilli* devaient être *patrimi et matrimi*. De l'adjectif ἀμφιθαλής on forma un substantif ἀμφιθαλεύς, qui désigna le ministère de ces enfants de chœur. Nous connaissons à Thyatire un ἀμφιθαλεὺς τῶν μεγάλων Ἀντωνίων et dans la même ville un ἀδελφὸς ἀμφιθαλέων. Mais, sauf erreur, on n'avait pas encore constaté la présence d'ἀμφιθαλεῖς dans le clergé de Bacchus et nous ignorons le rôle que le rituel des mystères réservait à ces jeunes acolytes. On a supposé que l'enfant nu, lisant un texte sacré, dans la première scène de la grande composition qui décore la Villa Item était un παῖς ἀμφιθαλής et cette interprétation est vraisemblable. D'ailleurs nous savions déjà que des enfants étaient admis à l'initiation. Nous reviendrons sur ce point à propos de l'ἀρχινεανίσκος."

[3] *Loc. cit.* 50–1.

Thyatire et du Latium le sens technique de "Opferdiener, Minis-trant". Puis, entrainé, semble-t-il, par un contre-sens sur le fran-çais "enfant de chœur", employé par F. Cumont, il se demande si l'ἀμφιθαλεύς ne serait pas le χοροδιδάσκαλος d'un chœur formé par des ἀμφιθαλής. Il s'appuie sur un contre-sens sur le grec ἐπιστά-της, qui, selon lui, peut, dans l'inscription de Thyatire n° 3, désigner le "chef du temple", un supérieur de l'ἀμφιθαλεύς chef des choristes.[1]

Parmi les inscriptions réunies ci-dessus, un bon nombre — dix en tout — présentent un caractère commun; elles sont relatives à des concours. Domnos de Milet (n° 13) vient d'être vainqueur aux Didymeia παίδων πάλην, ce pourquoi on lui a érigé une statue dans le sanctuaire de Didymes où s'est déroulé le concours. Alypos de Milet (n° 15) est amphithaleus des Didymeia Kommodeia et a remporté la victoire; de même Hygianos (n° 16). A Ephèse, l'ἀμφιθαλής a été aussi soit panégyriarque des Epheseia, soit agono-thète (n°⁸ 10–12). A Tralles, Tryphosianos a été ἀμφιθαλής d'un concours et εἰσαγωγός, "introducteur", [2] d'un autre, les Pythia (n° 9). A Thyatire, l'un des ἀμφιθαλής a exercé sa fonction pour les μεγάλα Ἀντώνια (n° 2), Lenaios (n° 3) pour les Asklepieia, et, comme Domnos de Milet, il a concouru lui-même à la lutte (ἐνδόξως παλαίσαντα); c'est une formule agonistique bien connue sur les bases de statues d'athlètes que ὑπὸ ἐπιστάτην; il ne s'agit pas d'un "Tempeloberst", mais du maître de gymnastique et entraîneur de l'athlète.[3] L'inscription de Thyatire n° 4 [4] nous mène dans le

---

[1] *Ibid.* 50 n. 3: "Cumont deutet ἀμφιθαλεύς ebenfalls als terminus technicus im Sinne von 'Chorknabe'. Man könnte erwägen, ob es nicht den χοροδιδάσκαλος der ἀμφιθαλεῖς — von ἀμφιθαλής abgeleitet — bezeichnet. Dann würde sich die Reihen-folge der Aufzählungen leichter erklären. Die zuletzt zitierte Inschrift spricht nicht dagegen, da ἐπιστάτης den Tempelobersten, also einen Vorgesetzten des ἀμφιθαλεύς in dem angegebenen Sinn, bezeichnen kann (*IG* I 32. 18–19). ἀδελφὸς — ἀμφιθαλέων in einer Inschrift aus Selendi bezeichnet nicht ein Glied der Kultbruder-schaft, sondern betrifft Familienbeziehungen."

[2] J'ai étudié cette fonction agonistique dans *Rev. Phil.* 1929, 140–2; cf. *Études anatoliennes* 419 n. 2.

[3] Matériel assez abondant et interprétation dans *Études anatoliennes*, 60–1 et 139 n. 1; *Anatolian Studies W. H. Buckler* 232 n. 1.

[4] Publiée aussi, moins bien, dans le *Mouseion* de Smyrne, 1886, 45, et insérée dans *IGR* IV 1273.

même milieu; le personnage dont on mentionne qu'il est le frère d'ἀμφιθαλεῖς est honoré à cause de ses générosités comme agonothète des Tyrimneia: Γ. Σαλλούστιον — πιανὸν Ἀριστέφανον,[1] [πατρ]ίδος[2] ἀρχικόν, δεκαπρω[τεύσ]αντα, ἀγωνοθετήσαν[τα τῶν] μεγάλων Σεβαστῶν [Τυρι]μνήων ἀγώνων θυμελ[ικῶν] καὶ γυμνικῶν θέμασιν [καὶ] τειμήμασιν παρ' αὐτοῦ[3] ἀξ[ιολόγ]ως, πάσας τὰς εἰς τὸν θεὸ[ν καὶ] εἰς τοὺς κυρίους αὐτοκρά[τορ]ας[4] εὐχὰς καὶ θυσίας κα[ὶ τὰ]ς εἰθισμένας τοῖς πολεί-[ται]ς καὶ τοῖς συνπανηγυρ[ίζου]σιν δωρεὰς ἀφθόνως [καὶ] μεγαλοπρεπῶς πεπλη[ρωκό]τα, ἀλείψαντα ἐν τῷ [ἄνω]θε[ν?] γυμνασίῳ τοὺς π[ανηγυ]ρί-ζοντας πολείτας [καὶ τ]οὺς ἐπιδημοῦντας π[άντας] ἐκτενῶς, σειτωνήσα[ντα ἀγ[νῶς καὶ πολυδαπάνω[ς, υἱὸν] Γ. Σαλλουστίου στεφ[ανηφόρου καὶ σ]τρατηγοῦ καὶ φ[ιλοτίμ]ου ἐν πᾶσιν γεγονότο[ς εἰς] τὴν πατρίδα, ἀδελφὸ[ν —] Σαλλουστίου Ἑρμωνια[νοῦ ἀ]μφιθαλέων. Il faut joindre à ce groupe de textes un passage de Malalas, XII 287, relatif aux Olympia d'Antioche de Syrie. Ce chapitre de Malalas contient des renseignements authentiques, mêlés à de ridicules déformations qui nous montrent ce qu'était un concours antique aux yeux d'un Byzantin.[5] Malalas mentionne comme dignitaires du concours l'alytarque et le secrétaire, ce en quoi il suit une bonne source,[6] puis il ajoute: ἡ αὐτὴ δὲ βουλὴ καὶ ὁ δῆμος πάλιν προεβάλοντο ἀμφιθαλὴν ὀνόματι Κάσιον

---

[1] J'y reconnaîtrais un nom propre, plutôt que, comme les éditeurs, un mot ἀριστέφανος, dont je ne vois pas le sens.

[2] Le supplément ne me paraît guère acceptable, et je proposerais: [ἀπὸ πα]ιδός.

[3] Pour le don des prix par l'agonothète dans les fêtes de Thyatire, cf. *Rev. Phil.* 1913, 324 n° 16: ἀγωνοθετήσαντα τοῦ Σωτῆρος Ἀσκληπιοῦ σεμνῶς καὶ πολυδαπάνως, δόντα παρ' ἑαυτοῦ τὰ ἔπαθλα; *BCH* 1887, 460 n° 22 (aux Sebasta Tyrimneia): τά τε τῶν ἀγωνισμάτων θέματα καὶ τὰς ἐπιδόσεις τῶν ἐπιδειξαμένων ἐκ τῶν ἰδίων ποιησάμενον (cf. *Mélanges syriens Dussaud* 737); 464 n° 29: ἀγωνοθετήσαντα τοῦ πρὸ πόλεως Ἀπόλλωνος Τυρίμνου λανπρῶς καὶ ἐνδόξως θέμασιν καὶ τειμήμασιν πρὸς τοὺς ἀγωνιστάς. Dans *CIG* 3493, texte connu par Spon et Wheler, Boeckh a restitué (suivi par Clerc *loc. cit.* 126 n° 17): κοσμήσαντα τὴν πατρίδα ἔν τε τῷ θυμελικῷ καὶ γυμνικῷ ἀγῶνι θέμασιν ἀσυνκρίτως οἴκοθεν καὶ ἐμ (π)ᾶσιν (copie: καιτεμνασιν) πρὸς πά[ντ]ας τοὺς ἀγωνιστὰς κατά(ξιο)ν (ἑαυτ)οῦ (copie: κατασταναθεου) καὶ τοῦ πατρὸς Λαιβιανοῦ; j'ai revu et photographié la pierre à Thyatire en 1932; j'ai lu: θέμασιν ἀσυνκρίτοι[ς] οἴκοθεν καὶ τειμήμασιν πρὸς πάν[τ]ας τοὺς ἀγωνιστὰς κατ' ἀξίαν τοῦ θεοῦ κ.τ.λ.

[4] Marc Aurèle et Lucius Verus, ou Septime Sévère et ses fils; cf. Keil et von Premerstein *loc. cit.* 34.

[5] Cf. provisoirement *Études épigraphiques et philologiques* 61 n. 1.

[6] Cf. *ibid.* 60-1.

Ἰλλούστριον, φοροῦντα ὡσαύτως στολὴν ἄσπρον ὁλοσηρικὸν καὶ στέφανον
πεπλεγμένον ἀπὸ δαφνίνων φύλλων καὶ ἐν τῷ μέσῳ στηθάριν χρυσοῦν ἔχον
τὸν Δία · ὄντινα ἀμφιθαλὴν ἐτίμων καὶ προσεκύνουν ὡς τὸν Ἑρμῆν, καθὼς
ὁ σοφὸς Δομνῖνος ὁ χρονογράφος πάντα ταῦτα συνεγράψατο. Nos dix inscriptions mentionnant un ἀμφιθαλής agonistique assurent la valeur
du renseignement de Malalas;[1] il y avait à Antioche un ἀμφιθαλής
(ou εὑς) τῶν Ὀλυμπίων.

Cet ἀμφιθαλής agonistique est un jeune homme. Plusieurs des
inscriptions le laissent reconnaître facilement. Domnos et Alypos
de Milet viennent de remporter une victoire dans la catégorie des
παῖδες. Le jeune âge de Tryphosianos de Tralles est attesté par sa
fonction d'εἰσαγωγός.[2] Le n° 2 a été éphébarque. Ce sont des
jeunes gens du gymnase à qui les inscriptions du n° 14 souhaitent
la victoire, ou la saluent. Les fonctions de *décaprote*, d'agonothète,
de panégyriarque, remplies par les n°ˢ 2, 4, 10, 11 et 12, n'indiquent
nullement que ce ne sont pas des jeunes gens;[3] à l'époque impériale,
même les enfants, dans les familles riches, sont titulaires de magistratures.[4] Dans le n° 4, le frère des ἀμφιθαλεῖς est encore tout jeune;
il a été seulement *décaprote* et agonothète; son père a été stéphané-
phore éponyme et stratège.

Il me semble que, quand il s'agit d'un ἀμφιθαλής agonistique,
nous pouvons préciser son rôle. Ce doit être un rôle très précis,
comme celui d'alytarque ou de secrétaire, comme celui d'*eisagôgos*.
Or nous avons des mentions d'un ἀμφιθαλής à Olympie même et à
Delphes, dans les scholies de Pindare.[5] Voici pour Olympie: τὸ

---

[1] Aucune n'est connue de A. Schenk von Stauffenberg dans son commentaire,
Die römische Kaisergeschichte bei Malalas (1931), 436.

[2] Cf. l'article auquel renvoie, plus haut, la note 2 de la page 514.

[3] Oepke dit à tort, *loc. cit.* 51, au sujet des inscriptions de Thyatire: "Die Aufzählung schreitet von der Gegenwart zur Vergangenheit fort. Der Umstand, dass
man bei einem Erwachsenen das von ihm früher bekleidete Amt eines Ministranten
der Erwähnung noch für wert hielt, bezeugt die Bedeutung, die man diesem Dienste
beimass."

[4] Cf. Is. Lévy *REG* 1899, 257–258. D'où ma restitution (plus haut, p. 515,
n. 2) : [ἀπὸ πα]ιδὸς ἀρχικόν.

[5] Ces textes ont souvent été signalés dans les études sur l'ἀμφιθαλής, pêle-mêle
avec les autres; cf. par ex. Stengel dans PW *s.v.*; Oepke *loc. cit.* 46: "Gross ist
die Fülle von sakralen obzwar noch nicht eigentlich priesterlichen Funktionen,

Πάνθειον, ἐν ᾧ πεφύτευται ἡ ἐλαία, ἣν δρέπει ἀμφιθαλὴς παῖς χρυσῷ δρεπάνῳ, κλάδους ιζ' τέμνων, ὅσα καὶ τὰ ἀγωνίσματα.[1] A Delphes, μέχρι δὲ πολλοῦ ἡ εἰς τοὺς τῶν νικώντων στεφάνους χωροῦσα δάφνη ἐντεῦθεν (de Tempe) ἐκομίζετο ὑπὸ παιδὸς ἀμφιθαλοῦς.[2] Dans les concours de l'époque impériale, organisés ordinairement sur le modèle des Olympia et des Pythia, pour les fonctionnaires, les classes d'âge et les récompenses,[3] l'ἀμφιθαλής a dû avoir pour charge de couper, et d'apporter sur le lieu du concours,[4] les couronnes de feuillage destinées aux vainqueurs.[5]

D'autres textes relatifs à des fêtes mettent en relation des ἀμφιθαλεῖς avec le port de feuillages. Aux Pyanepsia d'Athènes la branche d'olivier de l'εἰρεσιώνη est accrochée à la porte du temple d'Apollon par un ἀμφιθαλής.[6] Selon un scholiaste de Nicandre, aux Oschophories ce seraient des παῖδες ἀμφιθαλεῖς qui luttent à la course pour porter du sanctuaire de Dionysos à celui d'Athena Skiras des rameaux de vigne.[7] Aux Daphnéphories de Thèbes, décrites par Proklos, c'est un ἀμφιθαλής qui marche en tête du cortège processionnel: ἄρχει δὲ τῆς δαφνηφορίας παῖς ἀμφιθαλής.[8]

welche nur Amphithalen übertragen werden. Die Zweige, welche in Olympia die Sieger krönten, schnitt ein solcher, usw."

[1] *Ol.* III 60 (Drachmann I 122).

[2] *Pyth.*, *Hypothesis* (Drachmann II 4). Cf. A. Severyns *Recherches sur la Chrestomathie de Proclos*, Première partie, tome II (1938), 212–13; H. Jeanmaire, *Couroi et Courètes* (1939), 389–90.

[3] Cf., provisoirement, notamment *Études épigraphiques et philologiques* 60–1.

[4] D'où, peut-être, le rapprochement avec Hermès messager, indiqué par Malalas. Il ne peut être question d'une "adoration" de l'ἀμφιθαλής (Oepke, *loc. cit.* 47: "Zur Zeit des Commodus kam es, wenn wir eine verworrene Notiz des Johannes Malalas ernst nehmen und so deuten dürfen, in Antiochien zur Anbetung eines Amphithalen als Hermes."

[5] Aux Didymeia de Milet, les couronnes étaient certainement, comme à Olympie, coupées à un arbre du sanctuaire. Cf. *OGI* 227. 11–12 (Welles *Royal Correspondence* 22): des ambassadeurs milésiens apportent à Seleukos II τὸν ἱερὸν στέφανον τὸν ἐκ τοῦ ἀδύτου ὧι ἐστεφανώκει ἡμᾶς ὁ δῆμος.

[6] On a mis cela en rapport avec l'ἀμφιθαλής athénien de n° 7.

[7] Mais, sur la valeur du renseignement, cf. A. Severyns *loc. cit.* 250. — Sur les Oschophories et Pyanepsies, cf, en dernier lieu H. Jeanmaire *loc. cit.* 338–363; sur les Oschophories, W. S. Ferguson *Hesp.* 1938, 36–41.

[8] Voir la discussion approfondie de A. Severyns, *loc. cit.* 218–29, avec les auteurs cités.

Ce rôle de l'ἀμφιθαλής, ses fonctions dans les concours ont dû faire
établir un lien entre le nom de l'ἀμφιθαλής, ὁ ἀμφοτέροις τοῖς γονεῦσι
θάλλων, et les rameaux, θαλλοί, θαλεία, qu'il coupait et portait; ou
peut-être ce rapprochement a-t-il eu quelque influence sur la
spécialisation agonistique de l'ἀμφιθαλής.

Peut-être les précisions que nous avons acquises sur l'ἀμφιθαλής
agonistique peuvent-elles nous aider à faire une conjecture — seulement une conjecture — sur les ἀμφιθαλεῖς de l'association dionysiaque du Latium. On a pensé à les rapprocher de l'ἀρχινεανίσκος
nommé aussi dans cette inscription. "Les νεανίσκοι ne peuvent
avoir compris seulement deux ἀμφιθαλεῖς," dit F. Cumont.[1] Oepke
écrit:[2] "Ob die beiden ἀμφιθαλεῖς zu seinen Pflegebefohlenen
[de l'*archineaniskos*] gehörten, lässt sich nicht sagen. Sicher ist,
dass ausser ihnen noch ein grösserer Kreis von Jugendlichen zur
Gemeinde gerechnet worden ist." Mais il faut remarquer que les
ἀμφιθαλεῖς et l'ἀρχινεανίσκος sont tout à fait séparés dans la liste.
"On voit à première vue," écrit F. Cumont, "que la liste commence
par les plus hautes [charges] et se termine par les plus modestes.
Mais il n'y a aucun indice d'une hiérarchie rigide, dont on devrait
successivement franchir les degrés, comme les sept grades des
mystères de Mithra ou le *cursus honorum* des magistratures ro-
maines. Bien que nous n'en ayons pas de preuve certaine, toutes
les probabilités sont pour que la préséance accordée soit celle à
laquelle chacune des catégories de prêtres ou de mystes avait
droit dans les processions, qui formaient partout une partie essen-
tielle du culte bacchique, au même titre que les sacrifices. L'importance que ce cortège avait pour la confrérie de Torre Nova se
traduit par la multiplicité des titres composés avec -φόρος. Après
les dignitaires les plus élevés de la communauté, le héros, la dadou-
que, les prêtres et prêtresses, le hiérophante, vient la statue divine
portée par les *théophores*. Elle est suivie des ministres d'un rang
inférieur, parmi lesquels des *cistaphores*, des *liknaphores*, une *phallophore* et deux *pyrphores*."[3] J'adhère entièrement à cette opinion.
Or l'ἀρχινεανίσκος vient à cinq rangs après les ἀμφιθαλεῖς; il ne peut

[1] *Loc. cit.* 255. [2] *Loc. cit.* 56. [3] *Loc. cit.* 233.

être leur chef. Il vient juste avant les ἀρχιβασσάραι, les βουκόλοι et la foule des membres de la communauté classés en ἀπὸ καταζώσεως, βάκχοι et βάκχαι ἀπὸ καταζώσεως, ἱεροὶ βάκχοι, ἀντροφύλακες, βάκχαι et σειγηταί. Les deux ἀμφιθαλεῖς au contraire se placent juste avant les "porteurs de vans", la phallophore, les porteurs du feu sacré. Ne seraient-ils pas des porteurs du feuillage sacré, des "thallophores", exactement des "kissophores", porteurs du lierre dionysiaque?

JULIA DOMNA AS ATHENA POLIAS

By James H. Oliver

IN 1913 A. von Premerstein published an Athenian inscription which Ad. Wilhelm, B. Leonardos and he had assembled from ten fragments in the Epigraphical Museum at Athens. Since then O. Broneer contributed four new pieces, which had been identified with the aid of the Museum technician Stavros Kondes, and here I add two more small fragments of the same inscription.[1] It contains an amended version of a decree assigning divine honors to Julia Domna.

The stele of Pentelic marble, 0.07 m. thick, with a smooth back and beautifully formed letters 0.017 m. high, originally stood on the Acropolis. Two of the fragments cannot be placed in respect to the others, but thanks to the labors of Premerstein and Broneer all the rest join as three pieces whose relative position has been determined through an examination of the subject matter.[2] The preserved height of this part is 1.42 m., and the restoration calls for a width of ca. 0.85 m.

---

[1] The second new fragment, found February 1939 in a modern fill in the American Excavations of the Athenian Agora, was recognized by the writer in August when he came to Athens through the financial aid granted by the Committee for Research in the Social Sciences at Columbia University and just as the manuscript was ready to go to press. It has the inventory number Agora I 5680. Thanks are here offered to T. L. Shear and B. D. Meritt for permission to include it in the publication. All the other fragments are in the Epigraphical Museum at Athens. Those published by Premerstein have the following numbers in the Museum catalogue: EM 8369, 8370, 8371, 8372, 8373, 8374, 8375, 8376, 8377, 8379. Those added by Broneer are: EM 3144, 4646, 12731, 12751. The new fragment discovered there by the writer has the number EM 3490.

[2] The main group (EM 8369, 8370, 8375, 8373, 8374 and 8379) constitutes a piece 1.23 m. high, 0.40 m. wide, broken away above, below and at either side. The group at the lower left corner (EM 4646, 8371, 8372, 3490, 8377) constitutes a piece 0.80 m. high, 0.32 m. wide, entirely broken away above and at the right but preserving part of the bottom and part of the left side. The third piece (EM 8376 + EM 12751 + Agora I 5680), 0.25 m. high and 0.185 m. wide, is broken away above, below and at either side. Several of the fragments present evidence of a reworking subsequent to the destruction of the monument.

EDITIONS: A. von Premerstein, "Athenische Kultehren für Kaiserin Iulia Domna," *Jahreshefte des österreichischen archäologischen Institutes*, XVI (1913), 249–270; J. Kirchner *IG* II² (1916) 1076; [R. Cagnat and M. Besnier *Revue archéologique* XII (1920) 365, No. 53]; O. Broneer, *Hesperia* IV (1935) 178–184. ADDITIONAL COMMENTARY: P. Graindor, *Marbres et textes antiques d'époque impériale*, Ghent, 1922, 52–66; A. D. Nock *Harvard Studies in Classical Philology*, XLI (1930), 34–35; U. von Wilamowitz-Moellendorff, *Der Glaube der Hellenen*, Berlin, 1932, II, 473; L. Deubner, *Attische Feste*, Berlin, 1932, 236–237; Louis Robert, *Études Anatoliennes*, Paris, 1937, 14, note 2.

The document does not consist of many formulae, and the restoration of it, therefore, is a very difficult matter. Premerstein made a bold attempt in presenting a reconstructed text, for which he has deservedly received grateful recognition from later students of the document, but he neglected to take the simple precaution of actually drawing in the restorations to see that they conformed to the available space. When Broneer took the trouble to do so, he found that Premerstein's widely accepted restorations did not always fit. Furthermore, the discovery itself of new fragments forced Broneer to revise the wording and sometimes even the sense of Premerstein's text.

The first new fragment which I have recognized, E['pigraphical] M[useum] 3490, effects a direct join with an old piece in a section edited by Premerstein as follows:

30   τὰς δὲ ἱ]ερείας καὶ τὴν το[ῦ νέου ἔτ]
[ους β]ασίλισ[σαν πάσας] τὰ εἰσι[τήρι]α τῆς ἱερω[σύνης]
[ποι]εῖν τῆι Ἀ[θηνᾶι Πολι]άδι· [παρεῖναι] δὲ καὶ τὰς [παρ]
[θέν]ους τὰς [ἐλευθέρα]s καὶ δᾶ[ιδα ἱσ]τᾶν καὶ σ[υνά]
[γειν] καὶ χόρ[ον καὶ ἑορ]τήν, κτλ.

Against this restoration Graindor objected that the law of syllabic division was violated at the end of line 30, that the word πάσας in line 31 seemed to be hanging in the air, and that in line 33 the word ἐλευθέρας suggested by Wilhelm to Premerstein was unconvincing; and Graindor replaced with another restoration the name of Athena Polias in line 32. Broneer, however, at this point returned

to Premerstein's restoration of the name of the goddess, and my
new fragment proves him right. In line 31 Broneer replaced the
offensive adjective πάσας with the two words θύειν καί, and here
again he seems to have achieved literal accuracy. In line 33 Broneer
replaced the adjective [ἐλευθέρα]s, which did not fit the space, with
the participle [ἀρρηφορούσα]s, which in turn was rejected by Louis
Robert in favor of [καταλογείσα]s. The new fragment, however,
gives the text τὰς ἀπολυ[. . ⁵ . .]s, which practically forces us to the
verb ἀπολύω, namely ἀπολυ[ομένα]s or ἀπολυ[θείσα]s. So Broneer's
text did not recover the actual wording of this passage, but his
interpretation in my opinion is quite correct. If so, we must
reword the phrase to read τὰς [ἀρρη|φόρ]ους τὰς ἀπολυ[ομένα]s. For
ἀπολύω in the meaning *discharge from service* or *release from duty*,
see Preisigke's *Wörterbuch, s.v.*

Pausanias (I 27. 3) relates that two maidens called by the
Athenians ἀρρηφόροι dwelt near the temple of Athena Polias, and
received their board in the sanctuary of the goddess. They were
obliged to remain there some time; and when the festival was
celebrated they carried at night certain sacred objects down from
the Acropolis, and later they carried something else up again.
Then at last they were released (τὰς μὲν ἀφιᾶσιν ἤδη τὸ ἐντεῦθεν), and
another pair of maidens was inducted into the sacred office (ἑτέρας
δὲ εἰς τὴν Ἀκρόπολιν παρθένους ἄγουσιν ἀντ' αὐτῶν).

At the ceremonies, accordingly, there were two pairs of ἀρρηφόροι,
the outgoing and incoming pairs. The rider in my interpretation
specifies that it is the outgoing pair of ἀρρηφόροι who must set up
the torch and dance. The expression αἱ ἀρρηφόροι αἱ ἀπολυόμεναι
corresponds to Pausanias' phrase τὰς μὲν ἀφιᾶσιν.

Other sections of the inscription, moreover, seem to me un-
convincingly restored or still capable of further elucidation.
According to Broneer's text and drawing, commemorations or
sacrifices are to take place:

21   ἐν ᾗ ἡμέρᾳ τὸν /[. ⁼⁴.]
22   [. . .]λον αὐτῇ[ι τῆι Ἰουλίαι] ἀνῆκαν αἱ Ἀθῆναι.

For stylistic reasons I am unwilling to accept a restoration of the
article before the name Ἰουλία, which moreover is always followed

in this inscription by the word Σεβαστή. Names of persons are never accompanied by the article in the official language, even when the names are well known and have been mentioned before.[1] Instead of the phrase τῆι Ἰουλίαι I would substitute another restoration or leave the lacuna. But the main question still remains, what Athens dedicated to Julia Domna. It is mentioned in the other lacuna between lines 21–22. It was no ordinary dedication if the day was henceforth to be celebrated annually.

To this we shall return by and by. The next sections of the inscription call for sacrifices to the μήτηρ στρατοπέδων and for the erection of her cult statue (ἄγαλμα) in the Parthenon [too]. "The priestesses," continues the rider, "and the queen of the king archon shall sacrifice and on entering office shall make their inaugural offerings (εἰσιτήρια τῆς ἱερωσύνης) to Athena Polias. Also the retiring *arrephoroi* shall sacrifice and set up a torch and dance at the festival in order that when these things are done our piety toward Julia Domna the savior of Athens may be apparent."

From this passage I draw the inference that Julia Domna was not associated but identified with Athena Polias. The piety toward Julia Domna could have been partly expressed in the sacrifices to Athena Polias only if Athena Polias represented one aspect of Julia Domna. Sacrifices, accordingly, were made to the latter as μήτηρ στρατοπέδων, and again as Athena Polias.

In consequence of this opinion I cannot accept Premerstein's restoration above in lines 15–16, as adapted by Broneer:

καὶ τὰ εἰ]σιτήρια τῆι [Ἰουλίαι Σεβασ]
[τῆι ποιεῖν καθὼς καὶ τῆι] Ἀθηνᾷ Πολιά[δι.

For that would imply not an identification but a mere association of Julia Domna with Athena Polias. There exist also other objections to this restoration. The word καθὼς (or καθάπερ) does not produce a satisfactory sense, because according to the only information we have, the εἰσιτήρια were previously offered not to Athena Polias but to Athena Soteira.[2] We cannot well restore the name Ἰουλίᾳ

---

[1] Meisterhans-Schwyzer, *Grammatik der attischen Inschriften*[3], Berlin, 1900, 223, §5.

[2] See L. Deubner, *Attische Feste*, Berlin, 1932, 175.

Σεβαστῇ immediately after the article, because names of persons are never accompanied by the article in the official language, even when the names are well known and have been mentioned before.[1] Similarly the style of the official language admits the usages Ἀθηνᾷ Πολιάδι and τῇ Ἀθηνᾷ τῇ Πολιάδι, but not τῇ Ἀθηνᾷ Πολιάδι [2] as here restored. Therefore, I reject that reconstruction, and since an identification of Julia Domna with Athena Polias is here to be expressed, I would restore rather

καὶ ποιεῖν τὰ εἰ]σιτήρια τῆι [σωτείρᾳ τῶν]
['Αθηνῶν 'Ιουλίᾳ Σεβαστῆι] Ἀθηνᾷ Πολιά[δι.

This type of nomenclature to express an identification is very common, e.g. *Fouilles de Delphes* III 2. 65: [ἐ]πὶ Α[ὐ]τοκράτορο[ς] Καίσαρο[ς Σεβ]αστοῦ Δ[ομ]ιτιανοῦ Γερμανικοῦ Διὸς Ἐλευθε[ρ]ίου ἄρχοντο[ς ἐ]ν Ἀθήναις.[3] The old goddess is not reduced to the humiliating status of a mere companion to a more important Julia Domna (so Wilamowitz on the basis of Premerstein's text), but rather Julia Domna is recognized and worshipped as a living incorporation of Athena Polias. The inaugural offerings are made to Julia Domna because the Athenians have recognized in her a living incorporation of the Soteira too, the savior of Athens. Julia Domna is Athena herself and not her rival. It is, nevertheless, true that much of the vitality had long since gone out of the devotion to the old goddess: indeed the seventh article of the decree itself seems to attest the waxing indifference of the Athenians.

The cult of Athena Polias at an earlier period was attached to the "Ancient Temple" (ἀρχαῖος νεώς), of which the latest mention under that name occurs in Strabo IX 16. If Julia Domna was really identified with Athena Polias, then the temple of the goddess was dedicated to Julia Domna as Athena Polias, and I suggest that for the passage in lines 21–22 where Athens is said to have dedicated something to her we adopt the solution that what Athens dedicated was the "Ancient Temple." Not only does the restoration τὸν

[1] Meisterhans-Schwyzer, *Grammatik der attischen Inschriften*[3], Berlin, 1900, 223, §5.
[2] Meisterhans-Schwyzer, *op. cit.* 222–223.
[3] For other cases see P. Riewald, *De imperatorum Romanorum cum certis dis et comparatione et aequatione*, Dissertation, Halle, 1911.

ἀ[ρχαῖ|ον ν]αὸν exactly fit the space, but it also receives a strong support in its conformity with the requirement of syllabic division at the end of a line. There is of course no stylistic objection to the phrase, because after 250 B.C. the common Greek form ναός appears more frequently than the old Attic νεώς in Athenian inscriptions.[1] Concerning the identification of this temple agreement has not yet been reached, but those who identify it with the Erechtheum seem to me personally to have the better argument.[2] Into this problem we need not enter here, for W. Judeich,[3] the chief supporter of Dörpfeld's theory that the Ancient Temple was the Pisistratid building, presumes that the Ancient Temple continued in use throughout the second century of the Christian era and longer still. For our purposes that is enough.

The date of the inscription, as Premerstein observed, cannot be earlier than 195 A.D., when Julia Domna received the title *mater castrorum*. The occasion of her assistance, mentioned in line 6, may have been the audience of an Athenian embassy to the emperor, but in the text all supposed references to the embassy have disappeared with Broneer's restoration of the inscription, unless a very slight indication remains in the word ἀποδ[ημίαν in line 11. On the basis of a passage in the *Vita Severi* (3. 7) Premerstein pointed out that Septimius Severus was angry at the Athenians because of their treatment of him at a time well before his accession, and he suggests that Julia Domna helped to avert some of the emperor's vengeance. Between 195 and 198 A.D. Julia Domna was being honored at Eleusis (*IG* II² 3415).

The photograph (Figure 1) shows the relation of EM 3490 to the other fragments which can be located in respect to each other. A glance at Broneer's drawing will enable the reader to satisfy himself that the restorations adopted in the following text do actually meet the requirements of space and letter traces, and the drawing should always be consulted as a control before any new suggestions. An inaccuracy occurs there in line 14 where Broneer has duplicated

---

[1] Meisterhans-Schwyzer, *Grammatik der attischen Inschriften*³, Berlin, 1900, 127.

[2] W. B. Dinsmoor, "The Burning of the Opisthodomos at Athens," *AJA*, XXXVI (1932), 143-172, 307-326, but particularly 307-312.

[3] *Topographie von Athen*², Munich, 1931, 261-270.

a letter. I read $_{| \backslash}\overset{\wedge}{\wedge}\overset{\mathsf{N}}{\mathsf{N}}$ instead of $_{\backslash / \backslash}\overset{\wedge}{\wedge}\overset{\mathsf{N}}{\mathsf{N}}{}^{1}$ and present in evidence the photograph Figure 2. This entails a slight readjustment between the sections above and below. Lines 1–13 on the main piece should be shifted in the drawing one letter space to the left. It is this determination which has induced me to return to a discarded restoration by Premerstein in lines 9 and 12.

Three other disputed points call for brief comment. I prefer Premerstein's restoration $\psi\eta\phi\acute{\iota}\zeta o\mu a]\iota$ in line 8 to Broneer's restoration $\delta\epsilon\delta\acute{o}\chi\theta a]\iota$, because line 9 with the phrase $\acute{o}$ $\sigma vv\epsilon]\rho\gamma\acute{o}s$ μov shows that the text is here reported in the actual words of the proposer. See W. Larfeld, *Griechische Epigraphik*[3], Munich, 1914, 404–405, on the gradual adoption of direct address in the language of Greek decrees. There is room for this change if we discard the engraver's punctuation mark which Broneer has postulated at a place where in my opinion no colon or period belongs. Secondly, the article in lines 20–21 contains an epigraphical formula, and since Premerstein's restoration, which Broneer unjustly suppressed as purely conjectural, is the only familiar version of the formula to fit the space, we can accept it with considerable confidence. Lastly, I believe with Premerstein that the word $\sigma vv\theta\rho ov[$ in line 19 implies that the new cult statue with the features of Julia Domna was to be enthroned along with the ancient wooden statue of Athena Polias, the one that was said to have fallen from heaven.

The decree, accordingly, contains the following proposals: (1) that the archons each year sacrifice to Agathe Tyche on the birthday of Julia Domna; (2) that inaugural offerings be made each time to Julia Domna as Soteira and Polias; (3) that a cult statue of Julia Domna as Athena Polias be placed in the sanctuary beside [the old statue of the goddess]; (4) that the date on which the "Ancient Temple" was dedicated to Julia Domna as Athena Polias [be celebrated]; (5) that the polemarch sacrifice annually on the first day of the Roman year to Julia Domna as $\mu\acute{\eta}\tau\eta\rho$ $\sigma\tau\rho a\tau o\pi\acute{\epsilon}\delta\omega v$, patron deity of the Roman army, and that the priestess of Athena Polias participate in these ceremonies and receive the perquisites; (6) that a gold cult statue of Julia Domna be erected in the Parthenon too;

---

[1] The letter traces could be interpreted as $\mathring{\eta}\rho[\eta]\kappa\mathring{a}v$, but other readings are doubtless possible.

(7) that at the festival of Athena all the chief representatives of the state, namely the hoplite general, all the archons, all the priests, the herald of the Areopagus, the priestesses, the queen of the king archon and the retiring ἀρρηφόροι, shall always be on hand and perform their parts as a mark of respect and devotion to Julia Domna; (8) that these articles be engraved and erected beside the altar of the Augusti on the Acropolis.

```
     [- - - - - - - - - - - - - - - - - - - - -]ιε ιι[- - - - - -]
     [- - - - - - - - - - - - - - - - - -]ι των εὐσεβει[- - - -]
     [- - - - - - - - - - - - - - - - -]ως οὖν ἀπὸ τῆς [- -]
     [- - - - - - - - - - - - - - - -] τετυχηκὼς δ[- - - -]
 5   [- - - - - - - - - - - - - - - - τ]ῆς ἐνφύτου αὐ[τ- - -]
     [φι]λανθρ[ωπίας - - - - -] συνεργούσης [- - -]
     [. .] πᾶσιν τ[- - - - - τῆς] σωτείρας τῶν ['Αθηνῶν]
     ['Ιου]λίας Σεβ[αστῆς, ψηφίζομ]αι τὰ μὲν ἄλλα π[άντα]
     [πρ]άττεσθαι [καθὼς ὁ συνε]ργός μου τῆς ἐ[πιμελη]
10   [τεί]ας 'Ελπιδηφ[όρος . .⁼⁶. . .]άδου Παληνε[ὺς κατὰ]
     [τὴ]ν ἐμὴν ἀποδ[ημίαν ἐψηφί]σατο〉 θύειν δ[ὲ πάντας]
     [το]ὺς κατ' [ἔ]τος [ἔκαστον ἄρ]χοντας 'Αγαθῆ[ι Τύχηι]
     [ἐν ἧι ἱερωτάτηι ἡμέραι 'Ιουλία] Σεβαστὴ ἐγ[εννήθη]
     [- - - - - - - - - - - - - - - - -]α ηι[.]καν τ υ[- -]
15   [- - - - - καὶ ποιεῖν τὰ εἰ]σιτήρια τῆι [σωτείρᾳ τῶν|
     ['Αθηνῶν 'Ιουλίᾳ Σεβαστῆι] 'Αθηνᾷ Πολιά[δι - - -]
     [- - - - - - - - - τὸν ἐπὶ τοὺς ὁπ]λείτας στρατ[ηγὸν -]
     [- - - - - - - - - - - - - - - τὸ]ν δὲ ἄρχοντα τη[- -]
     [- - - - - - - - - - - - - - - -]λφωι ἵνα συνθρον[-]
20   [- - - - - εἶναι δὲ ἱερὰν τὴν τ]οῦ Θαργηλιῶνος μ[ηνὸς]
     [. . .⁼⁶. . . ἡμέραν ἱσταμέ]νου, ἐν ᾗ ἡμέρᾳ τὸν ἀ[ρχαῖ]
     [ον ν]αὸν αὐτῆ[ι ὡς Πολιάδι] ἀνῆκαν αἱ 'Αθῆναι〉 τ[ὸν]
     [δὲ π]ολέμαρχο[ν τῆι μητ]ρὶ τῶν στρατοπέδων [θύειν]
     [τῆι π]ρώτηι ἡμέ[ραι τοῦ κ]ατὰ 'Ρωμαίους ἔτους, κα[τ]
25   [ἀρχε]σθ[α]ι δὲ [κ]αὶ [τούτω]ν τῶν θυσιῶν τὴν ἱέρεια[ν]
     [τῆς 'Α]θηνᾶς [τῆς Πολιά]δος καὶ τὰ γέρα φέρεσθ[αι〉]
     [ἀναστ]ῆσαι [δὲ αὐτῆς καὶ] ἄγαλμα χρυσοῦν ἐν τ[ῶι]
     [Παρθ]ενῶν[ι· τὸν δὲ στρατηγ]ὸν 'Αγαθῆι Τύχη[ι προθύ]
     [ειν κ]αὶ τοὺ[ς ἄρχοντας καὶ ἱ]ερεῖς πάντας [καὶ τὸν]
```

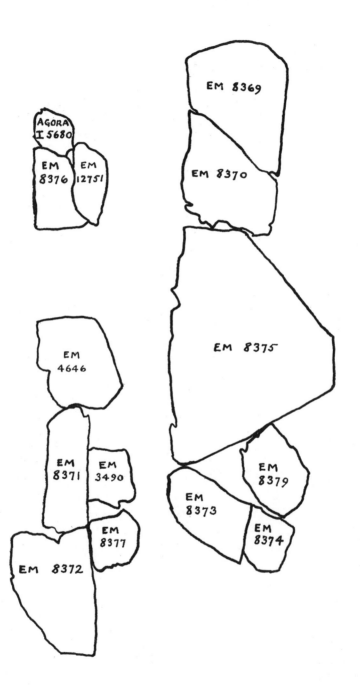

Figure 1. Photograph by H. Wagner of those fragments to which a definite place can be assigned in the inscription.

Figure 2. Photograph (by Janet Oliver) of squeeze showing the disputed letters in line 14 and the relations between the fragments concerned.

Julia Domna as Athena Polias 529

30 [κήρυκ]ᾳ σπέν[δειν, καὶ τὰς ἱ]ερείας καὶ τ[ὴ]ν τοῦ [ἄρχον]
    [τος β]ασίλισϲ̣αν θ[ύειν καὶ] τ̣ὰ εἰσ[ιτήρι]ᾳ τῆς ἱερω[σύνης]
    [ποιε]ῖν τῆι Ἀθηνᾶι [τῆι Πολι]άδ[ι, θύειν] δὲ καὶ τὰς [ἀρρη]
    [φόρ]ους τὰς ἀπολυ[ομένα]ς καὶ δᾷ[ιδα ἱσ]τᾶν καὶ σ[υνά]
    [γειν] καὶ χορεύειν τ[ὴν ἑορ]τὴν ἵνα κα[ὶ το]ύτων γ[εγε]
35 [νημ]ένων ἐ[πιφανὴς ἡ εἰς] τὴν σώτειραν τῶν ['Αθη]
    [νῶ]ν̣ Ἰουλίαν Σεβα[στὴν εὐ]σέβεια ὑπάρχῃ [ἀνα]
    γράψαι δὲ καὶ τὴν [τούτων εἰ]σήγησιν ἐν στ[ήληι]
    καὶ ἀναθε[ῖ]ναι πα[ρὰ τὸν ἐν Ἀκροπό]λει βωμὸν [τῶν]
    Σεβαστῶν ☾   vacat

EM 3144	EM 12731
τελ[- -	- -]αιθ[- -
γεν[- -	- -]ρμ[- - -
σιλ[- -	- -]οιτ[- -
π[- - -	- -]ω ⟩ ρ[- -
	- -]εβα[- -

RESTORATIONS: — 3, εὐτυχ]ῶς, Premerstein. 3–4, ἀπὸ τῆς τ[ρεσ|βείας ἐπ-
ανῆλθεν ὁ name, Premerstein. 4–6, δ[ιαπρε|πῶν δώρων παρὰ τοῦ Σεβαστοῦ ἐκ τ]ῆς
ἐνφύτου αὐ[τῶι φι|λανθρωπίας καὶ εἰς ἡμᾶς εὐνοίας], Premerstein. 6–8, συνεργούσης
[καὶ εἰς| ταῦτα τῆς Ἰουλίας Σεβαστῆς τῆς] σωτείρας τῶν [Ἀθηνῶν|· διὰ ταῦτ]ᾳ γ[οῦν
ἐγὼ ψηφίζομα]ι, Premerstein; συνεργούσης [δὲ εἰς| ταῦτα τῆς εὐεργέτιδος καὶ] σωτείρας
τῶν [Ἀθηνῶν| Ἰουλίας) Σεβ[αστῆς· δεδόχθα]ι, Broneer. 8–9, π[άντα οὔ|τως πρ]
άττεσ[θαι, Premerstein; π[άντα! πρ|άττεσ[θαι, Broneer. 9, συνε]ργός, Ditten-
berger (IG III 24); καθὼς ὁ συνε]ργός, Premerstein; καθάπερ ὁ συνε]ργός, Broneer.
9–10, τῆς ε[ἰς Ῥώμην| πρεσβε]ίας Ἑλπ[ιδηφόρος?, Premerstein; τῆς ἐ[πιμελη|τεί]ας,
Broneer. 10–11, Παληνεὺ[ς ἄριστα| κατὰ τὴ]ν, Premerstein; Παληνε[ὺς κατὰ| τὴ]ν
ἐμὴν ἀποδ[ημίαν, Broneer. 11, ἐψηφί]σατο, Dittenberger (IG III 24). 11–12,
ἄρ]χοντας ἀγαθῇ [τύχῃ, Dittenberger (IG III 24); θύειν δ[ὲ πάν|τας το]ὺς κατ[ὰ
ἔτος ἕκαστον ἄρ]χοντας, Premerstein; θύειν δ[ὲ πάντας| το]ὺς κατ᾽ [ἔ]τος [καὶ τοὺς
νῦν ἄρ]χοντας, Broneer. 13, [τῆι εὐτυχεῖ ἡμέρᾳ ἐν ἧι Ἰουλί]ᾳ Σεβαστὴ ἐγ[εννήθη],
Premerstein; [ἐν ἧι ἱερωτάτηι ἡμέραι Ἰουλία] Σεβαστὴ ἐγ[εννήθη], Broneer. 15–16,
καὶ ποιεῖν τὰ εἰ]σιτήρια τῇ Ἰ[ουλίᾳ Σε|βαστῇ τῇ σωτείρᾳ τῶν Ἀθηνῶν καὶ] Ἀθηνᾷ
Πολιά[δι, Premerstein; καὶ τὰ εἰ]σιτήρια τῆι [Ἰουλίαι Σεβασ|τῆι ποιεῖν καθὼς καὶ
τῆι] Ἀθηνᾷ Πολιά[δι, Broneer; καὶ ποιεῖν τὰ εἰ]σιτήρια τῆι [σωτείρᾳ τῶν] Ἀθηνῶν
Ἰουλίᾳ Σεβαστῆι] Ἀθηνᾷ Πολιά[δι, Oliver. 16–20, ποιή|σαι δὲ ὡς τάχιστα τὸν ἐπὶ
τοὺς ὁ]π̣λείτας στρατη[γὸν ἄ|γαλμα τῆς Ἰουλίας Σεβαστῆς, τὸ]ν δὲ ἄρχοντα τῆ[ι Πολι|
άδι συνιδρῦσαι ὑπὸ τῶι αὐτῶι ὀρό]φωι, ἵνα σύνθρον[ος ᾖ| τῆι θεῶι, Premerstein; ἵνα
σύνθρον[α ᾖ τὰ| δύο ⟩ aut simile, Oliver. 20–21, εἶναι δὲ ἱερὰν τὴν] τοῦ Θαργηλιῶνος
μ[η|νὸς . . . . ἡμέραν ἱσταμέ]νου, Premerstein; ἱερὰν δὲ ἀναδεδεῖχθαι τὴν] τοῦ
Θαργηλιῶνος, Graindor. 21–22, τὸν ἀ[ρχαῖ|ον ν]αὸν αὐτῆ[ι ὡς Πολιάδι] ἀνῆκαν,

Oliver. 22–23, τ[ὸν δὲ π]ολέμαρχο[ν, Broneer. 23, τῆι μητ]ρί, Premerstein. 23–24, θύειν τῆι, Premerstein; π]ρώτηι ἡμέ[ραι, Broneer; τοῦ κ[ατὰ, Premerstein. 24–25, κα[τ|εύχε]σθ[α]ι δὲ [κ]αὶ [τούτω]ν, Broneer; ἱερεια[ν], Premerstein. 26, τῆς Ἀθηνᾶς Πολιά]δος, Premerstein; [τῆς Ἀ]θηνᾶς [τῆς Πολιά]δος, Broneer. φέρεσθ[αι], Premerstein. 27–28, [καθιερῶ]σα[ι δὲ τῆς Σεβαστῆς] ἄγαλμα χρυσοῦν ἐν τ[ῶι], Premerstein; [ἀναστ]ῆσαι [δὲ καὶ Ἰουλίας] ἄγαλμα, Broneer; [ἀναστ]ῆσαι [δὲ αὐτῆς καὶ] ἄγαλμα, Oliver. 28, Premerstein. 29, Premerstein. 29–30, κα[ὶ τὸν κή|ρυκ]α σπέν[δειν, Premerstein; κα[ὶ τοὺς πο|λίτ]ας πέμ[πειν, Graindor. 30, τὰς δὲ ἱ]ερείας, Premerstein; καὶ τὰς ἱ]ερείας, Oliver. 30–31, β]ασίλισ[σαν, Premerstein; τότ[ε ἐσομέ|νην β]ασίλισ[σαν, Graindor; τοῦ [ἄρχον|τος β]ασίλισ[σαν θύειν καί, Broneer. 31, τὰ εἰσι[τήρι]α, Premerstein. ἱερω[σύνης], Dittenberger (*IG* III 3840). 32, [ποι]εῖν τῆι Ἀ[θηνᾶι Πολι]άδι· [παρεῖναι] δὲ, Premerstein; τῆι Ἀ[θηνᾶι τῆι Πολι]άδ[ι· θύειν] δὲ, Broneer. 32–33, τὰς [παρ|θέν]ους τὰς [ἐλευθέρα]ς, Wilhelm (*apud* Premerstein); τὰς [παρ|θέν]ους τὰς [ἀρρηφορούσα]ς, Broneer; τὰς [ἀρρη|φόρ]ους τὰς ἀπολυ[ομένα]ς, Oliver. 33, δᾳ[ῖδα ἱσ]τᾶν, Premerstein. 33–34, σ[υνά|γειν], Premerstein; σ[υντε|λεῖν], Broneer. 34, ἑορ]τὴν ἵνα κα[ὶ το]ύτων, Premerstein. 34–35, γ[εγε|νομ]ένων, Broneer. 35, ἐπ[ιφανὴς, Premerstein; ἐ[κφανὴς, Kirchner; *cetera*, Premerstein. 36–37, Premerstein. 38, ἐν πό]λει (Acropolis), Premerstein; ἐν τῆι Πό]λει, Kirchner; ἐν Ἀκροπό]λει, Broneer; *cetera*, Premerstein.

INDEX LOCORUM

This index includes those passages which are restored, emended, reinterpreted, dated, or otherwise significantly discussed.

Aeschines 2 *falsa leg.* 181–182: 300–301.

Agora Excavations: see Athens.

American Journal of Archaeology XXXVII (1933) 215–263: 509, 513, 518–519.

Andocides 1 *de myst.* 77: 169.

3 *de pace* 29: 127–131.

Androtion: 328–334, 341–355.

frag. 4: 353 n. 4.

5: 351 n. 1.

27: 344 n. 6.

frags. 28–30: 348 n. 2.

frag. 31: 352.

37: 348 n. 2.

45: 346–347.

46: 352.

48: 354, 358.

49: 350–351.

in schol. Aristophanes *Pax* 347: 348–349, 351.

in *Comm. in Aristot. Graec.* XX 232: 329–330.

Anthologia Palatina V 94: 495.

VII 258: 100 n. 1.

296: 102–104.

Ἀρχαιολογικὴ Ἐφημερίς 1918, 74: 505.

Aristides 28 *paraph.* 64 Keil: 103, 107 n. 2.

46 *pro quatt.* 209–210 Dindorf: 103–104, 107 n. 2.

Aristodemus (*F Gr Hist* 104) frag. 13. 2: 133 n. 2.

Aristophanes, schol. *Equites* 855: 358–361.

schol. *Pax* 347: 348–349, 351.

Plutus 1082: 495.

Aristoteles *Eth. Nic.* X 10, 1181 a 12–b 23: 362, 365, 376.

Pol. Δ 15, 1299 b 14: 368.

1300 b 28: 369.

E 3, 1302 b 18: 359.

8, 1307 b 26 — E 9, 1310 a 38: 364–366.

9, 1309 b 14: 363–366.

Z 8, 1321 b 12: 368.

Resp. Ath.: 367–376.

4: 352–353.

13. 1: 330–331.

22. 4: 351.

25: 443–444.

26. 1: 360.

28: 238 and n. 2, 443–444.

35: 443–444.

51. 1: 368.

57. 3: 369.

59: 369–370.

59. 7: 372.

63–69: 372–374.

63. 1: 372.

Rhet. I 4, 1360 a 19 ff.: 365–366.

25 f.: 360.

Comm. in Aristot. Graec. XX 232: 329–330.

Athenaeus VI 264 c: 454–455.

VI 272–273 a: 454–463.

Athenische Mitteilungen XXXV (1910) 408: 510, 513.

LI (1926) 27: 116–120.

Athens, Agora Excavations, inventory no.

I 2486: 171.

2982: 171.

5325: 182 n. 1.

5680: see *IG* II² 1076.

5799 a–b: 171–172.

Athens, Epigraphical Museum, inventory no.
  3032: 171.
  3144, 3490, 4646, 12731, 12751: see
    IG II² 1076.
  12768: 171.
  12910: 174–175.
  12931: 177.

Bulletin de correspondance hellénique XI
  (1886) 415 no. 23: 509, 513–514,
  516.
  XI (1886) 415 no. 24: 510, 513–514.
  XII (1887) 105 no. 26: 510, 513–516.

Callimachus *Hymn. Del.* 241: 495.
Callisthenes (*F Gr Hist* 124) frags. 15–
  16: 123 ff.
Collitz *Sammlung der griech. Dialekt-
  Inschr.* 2656: 63 n. 1.
Corpus Inscriptionum Graecarum 2932:
  510–511, 513–514.
  3493: 515 n. 3.
Cratippus (*F Gr Hist* 64) frag. 1: 313,
  316 n. 4.

Demosthenes 3 *Olynth.* III 31: 435 n. 2.
  3 *Olynth.* III 28: 437 n. 4.
  8 *Chers.* 61: 301.
  18 *corona* 141: 51.
  19 *falsa leg.* 137: 301.
  22 *Androt.* 21–23; 343.
  24 *Timocr.* 136: 176–179.
  schol. 665. 1 (Dind.): 374.
  Didymus *in Demos.* 8. 8: 343–344, 347.
    13. 44: 346–347,
    353.
Didyma, three inscriptions hitherto unpublished: 512–514.
Didymus: see under Demosthenes.
Diodorus Siculus V 1: 310–311.
  XI 29. 3: 125 n. 1.
  59–60: 324.
  62.3: 102–104, 105 n. 1, 106–107.

XII 4. 4–5: 121–156, *passim.*
  4. 5: 121 n. 2, 133 and n. 2, 134.
XIII 80: 249.
XVI 1: 310.
  21–22: 439 n. 2.
Dionysius Halicarnassensis *Antiquities
  Rom.* I 8. 3: 354.
  Ep. ad Cn. Pompeium 769–770 R.:
  296.
  Thuc. 9: 311–313.
    16: 313, 316 n. 4.
Dittenberger, *Orientis graecae inscrip-
  tiones selectae* 86–88: 488 n. 6.
  Sylloge inscriptionum graecarum, ed.
  3, 589: 509, 513.

Ephesos III 105 no. 14: 511, 513–514,
  516.
Ephesus, two inscriptions hitherto un-
  published: 511, 514, 516.
Ephorus (*F Gr Hist* 70): 321–328.
  frag. 17: 339–340.
  191: 323–324.
Epigraphical Museum: see Athens.
Erechtheum frags.: see Stevens.
Eusebius *Chron.* I 238 (Schoene): 494.

Flacelière, *Les Aitoliens à Delphes,* ap-
  pendix I no. 16: 476 n. 2.
Fouilles de Delphes III 1, 83: 67 n. 1.
  III 2, 76: 66 n. 1.
F Gr Hist = F. Jacoby *Die Fragmente
  der griech. Historiker:* see Aris-
  todemus, Callisthenes, Cratippus,
  Theopompus.

GDI: see Collitz.

Harpocratio *s.v.* Ἀμφίπολις: 344 n. 1.
  s.v. ἀποβατικοὶ τροχοί: 360.
    Ἀρδηττός: 359 n. 2.
    ἐν Φρεαττοῖ: 369.
    θεσμοθέται: 370.
    Ἵππαρχος: 344 n. 1.
    ἰσοτελὴς καὶ ἰσοτέλεια: 371.

GREEK HISTORY

AN ARNO PRESS COLLECTION

Aeschinis. **Aeschinis Orationes.** E Codicibus Partim Nunc Primum Excussis, Edidit Scholia ex Parte Inedita, Adiecit Ferdinandus Schultz. 1865.

Athenian Studies; Presented to William Scott Ferguson (*Harvard Studies in Classical Philology,* Supplement Vol. I). 1940.

Austin, R[eginald] P. **The Stoichedon Style in Greek Inscriptions.** 1938.

Berve, Helmut. **Das Alexanderreich:** Auf Prosopographischer Grundlage. Ersterband: Darstellung; Zweiterband: Prosopoghaphie. 1926. 2 volumes in one.

Croiset, Maurice. **Aristophanes and the Political Parties at Athens.** Translated by James Loeb. 1909.

Day, John. **An Economic History of Athens Under Roman Domination.** 1942.

Demosthenes. **Demosthenes,** Volumina VIII et IX: Scholia Graeca ex Codicibus Aucta et Emendata, ex recensione Gulielmi Dindorfii. 2 volumes. 1851.

Ehrenberg, Victor. **Aspects of the Ancient World:** Essays and Reviews. 1946.

Finley, Moses I. **Studies in Land and Credit in Ancient Athens, 500-200 B.C.:** The Horos Inscriptions. 1952.

Glotz, Gustave. **La Solidarité de la Famille dans le Droit Criminel en Grèce.** 1904.

Graindor, Paul, **Athènes Sous Hadrien.** 1934.

Grosmann, Gustav. **Politische Schlagwörter aus der Zeit des Peloponnesischen Krieges.** 1950.

Henderson, Bernard W. **The Great War Between Athens and Sparta.** 1927.

Herodotus. **Herodotus: The Fourth, Fifth, and Sixth Books.** With Introduction, Notes, Appendices, Indices, Maps by Reginald Walter Macan. 1895. 2 volumes in one.

Herodotus. **Herodotus: The Seventh, Eighth, and Ninth Books.** With Introduction, Text, Apparatus, Commentary, Appendices, Indices, Maps by Reginald Walter Macan. 1908. 3 volumes in two.

Jacoby, Felix. **Apollodors Chronik.** Eine Sammlung der Fragmente (*Philologische Untersuchungen,* Herausgegeben von A. Kiessling und U. v. Wilamowitz-Moellendorff. Sechzehntes Heft). 1902.

Jacoby, Felix. **Atthis:** The Local Chronicles of Ancient Athens. 1949.

Ledl, Artur. **Studien zur Alteren Athenischen Verfassungsgeschichte.** 1914.

Lesky, Albin. **Thalatta:** Der Weg der Griechen Zum Meer. 1947.

Ollier, Francois. **Le Mirage Spartiate.** Etude sur l'idéalisation de Sparte dans l'antiquité Greque de l'origine Jusqu'aux Cyniques and Etude sur l'idéalisation de Sparte dans l'antiquité Greque du Début de l'école Cynique Jusqu'à la Fin de la Cité. 1933/1934. 2 volumes in one.

Ryffel, Heinrich. ΜΕΤΑΒΟΛΗ ΠΟΛΙΤΕΙΩΝ Der Wandel der Staatsverfassungen (*Noctes Romanae.* Forschungen Uber die Kultur der Antike, Herausgegeben von Walter Wili, #2). 1949.

Thucydides. **Scholia in Thucydidem:** Ad Optimos Codices Collata, edidit Carolus Hude. 1927.

Toepffer, Iohannes. **Attische Genealogie.** 1889.

Tscherikower, V. **Die Hellenistischen Städtegründungen von Alexander dem Grossen bis auf die Römerzeit** (*Philologus,* Zeitschrift fur das Klassische Alterum, Herausgegeben von Albert Rehm. Supplementband XIX, Heft 1). 1927.

West, Allen Brown. **The History of the Chalcidic League** (*Bulletin of the University of Wisconsin,* No. 969, History Series, Vol. 4, No. 2). 1918.

Woodhouse, William J. **Aetolia:** Its Geography, Topography, and Antiquities. 1897.

Wüst, Fritz R. **Philipp II. von Makedonien und Griechenland in den Jahren von 346 bis 338** (*Münchener Historische Abhandlungen.* Erste Reihe: Allgemeine und Politische Geschichte, Herausgegeben von H. Günter, A. O. Meyer und K. A. v. Müller. 14, Heft). 1938.

II² 1437: 396–397.
  1438, new frag.: 177.
  1440: 205 n. 1, 391 n. 2, 407.
  1443: 397–398, 400–404.
  1444: see II² 1455.
  1454: 405.
  1455 + 1444: 394–407.
  1457: 404.
  1460 + 1461: 403 n. 1, 401–403.
  1461: see II² 1460.
  1481: 402.
  1492: 207, 395 n. 1.
  1495: 208.
  1502: 169 and n. 3.
  1654 a (= Erechtheum frag.
    XXVII): 173–175.
  1654 b (= Erechtheum frag.
    XXVIII): 173–175.
  165|5 (= Erechtheum frag.
    XXIX): 169, 173–175.
  1686: 171–172.
  3190: 510.
  3415: 526.
  4991: 510.
Inscriptiones Graecae
  XI 4, 1215: 488.
    1298: 50 n. 1.
  XII 1, 977: 179 n. 2.
Inscriptions, hitherto unpublished:
  Didyma, three: 512–514.
  Ephesus, two: 511, 514, 516.
Isaeus 11 *Hagn.* 40–41: 468 n. 6.
Isocrates 4 *Panegyr.*: 426–427.
  4 *Panegyr.* 120: 132 ff., 148–149.
  7 *Areopagit.*: 409–450.
    80: 136.
  8 *de pace*: 424–427.
  12 *Panath.* 59: 136.
  15 *Antid.*: 412 n. 1, 441.
    79–83: 362.

Joannes Malalas XII 287: 515–516.
Journal of Hellenic Studies VI (1885)
  350 no. 98: 511, 514.
Justinus XXVIII 1. 2, 3. 10: 491.

Lucianus, schol. *Tim.* 30: 354, 358.
Lycurgus *Leocr.* 81: 125 n. 1.
Lysias 12 *Eratosth.* 17: 299.
  23 *Pancl.* 67: 300.
  30 *Nicom.* 2: 353.

Meritt, B. D., *et al.*, *Athenian Tribute
  Lists* D8: 252 n. 3.
Milet, Thermen u. Palestren 192 no.
  386 *b* I, 386 *c* I: 512, 516.
  192 no. 387: 512 n. 3.

OGIS: see Dittenberger, *Orientis.*
Oxyrhynchus Papyri VI 853: 314–315.
  VII 1012: 315, 343.
  XI 1367: 337.
  XIII 1610: 323–324, 328.

Pausanias I 19. 4: 20.
  I 23. 10: 348–349.
    27. 3: 523.
    41. 6, 44. 3: 20.
  III 9. 9: 333.
  VI 7. 4–7: 350–351.
Philochorus frag. 4: 348.
Philodemus *Rhet.* col. 53. 7 ff.: 361,
  366 n. 3.
Pindarus, schol. *Ol.* III 60 (I 122 Dr.):
  516–517.
  schol. *Pyth.*, hypoth. (II 4 Dr.): 517.
Plato, schol. *Legg.* XI 937 D: 370.
Plinius *Hist. Nat.* XXXIV 63: 193.
Plutarchus *Alcib.* 13. 8: 358 n. 1.
  Cim. 12: 109–114, 347 n. 3.
    13. 4: 123 ff.
    19. 4: 123 n. 1.
  Nic. 11. 10: 358 n. 1.
  Sol. 15. 3–4: 352.
[Plutarchus] *Vit. X Or.* 833 E–F: 352
  n. 3.
  Vit. X Or. 852 B: 206.
Pollux IV 171–172: 381 n. 1.

Scriptores Historiae Augustae *Firmus*
  12. 2: 456–457.

s.v. κατὰ τὴν ἀγορὰν ἀψευδεῖν: 368, 375.
καταχειροτονία: 370.
σκαφηφόροι: 371.
Hellenica Oxyrhynchia: 303–341.
4. 1: 308–309, 328–333.
12: 326–327, 347.
13: 333.
14. 1: 332–333.
Herodotus I 192. 1: 137.
V 73. 1: 78.
97. 3: 80, 82.
VI 121, 123–124: 86.
VII 151: 151.
170. 3: 264 n. 1.
Hesperia IV (1935) 165–166 no. 26: 171.
VIII (1939) 246: 354.
IX (1940) 325: 182 n. 1.
Hiller von Gaertringen, *Historische griech. Epigramme* 53: 100 n. 1.
Homerus *Ilias* I 29–31, IX 132: 496–497.
schol. Townleian. *Il.* XIV 230: 155–156.
[Homerus] *Hymn. Demet.* 123–134: 19.

Inscriptiones Graecae (ed. min.)
I² 25: 129–131.
47 + new frag.: 247–253.
87: 129–131.
92 B: 200.
110 a: 252 n. 1.
145: 129–131.
255 a: 166–170, 170 n. 6, 172–174.
302: 145.
305: 170–171.
324: 130–131.
347: 160.
355: 163–164.
356: 163–164.
358: 164.
359: 165.
360: 163–165.
361: 161–164.
368: 200.
369: 200.

I² 373: 402.
950: 390.
II² 8: 128–131.
34: 392.
120: 176–178, 205 n. 1, 407.
138: 177.
139: 177.
216: 406.
217: 406.
775: 487–488.
776: 487–488.
780: 487–488.
790: 489.
791: 503–507.
833: 490 n. 3.
834: 505–506.
1076 + six new frags.: 521–530.
1299: 483–487.
1376: 387.
1377: 387, 390.
1382: 170, 388–389.
1383: 170.
1386: 385.
1388: 208, 381–383, 385–387, 397 n. 1.
1396: 383.
1397: 383.
1398: 383.
1399: 383.
1400: 382–383, 385, 388–389, 397 n. 1.
1407 + 1414: 377–394.
1410: 178, 392.
1411: 392.
1412: 383, 392–394.
1413: 383, 392–394.
1414: see II² 1407.
1415: 385 n. 1, 392–394, 397 n. 1.
1420: 387 n. 3.
1421: 392.
1424: 200.
1424 a (Addenda pp. 800–805): 382–383, 385, 391, 401 n. 1, 403.
1425: 200, 383, 391, 396 n. 2.
1428: 385 n. 2.

Sophocles, schol. *Oed. Col.* 698: 346–347.
Stevens, G. P., *et al.*, *The Erechtheum*
  frag. XXVII: see *IG* II² 1654 a.
  XXVIII: see *IG* II² 1654 b.
  XXVIII a: see Athens, Epigr.
    Mus. 12910.
  XXIX: see *IG* II² 1655.
Stobaeus IV 127 H.: 359–360.
Strabo IX 1. 6: 348.
  IX 16: 525.
Suetonius *Dom.* 20: 338.
Supplementum Epigraphicum Graecum
  II 9: 503, 506.
Sylloge: see Dittenberger, *Sylloge*.

Theon *Progymnasm.* 4: 315.
Theophrastus *Legg.*: 355–376.
  Phys. sent.: 375.
Theopompus (*F Gr Hist* 115): 317–321.
  frag. 7: 320.
    44: 320.
    96 a: 354.
    113: 137.
    153–155: 125–127.
    166: 343.
    224–225: 319–320.
Thucydides: 255–297.
  I 4: 21–22.
    100: 99–100.
    100. 3: 345 n. 1.
  II 1: 309, 314.
  VI 17. 5: 265.
    88. 6: 252.
  VII 27: 327 n. 1, 465 and n. 1, 466.

Xenophon *Hell.* I 5. 19: 351.
  Hell. I 6. 1: 175.
  II 1. 7: 332 n. 3.
Mem.: 448.
  III 5. 1, 18–19: 232 n. 1.
Oec. 4. 6: 137.
Vect.: 424, 434.
  4. 14–15: 459–461.
[Xenophon] *Resp. Ath.*: 211–245.
Resp. Ath. 1. 1: 229 n. 2.
  1. 2: 223.
  1. 3: 219 n. 2, 232 n. 2.
  1. 5: 223 n. 2.
  1. 13: 220 n. 2.
  1. 14: 227 nn. 2 and 3.
  1. 16–17: 228.
  1. 18: 213 n. 3, 232 n. 2.
  2. 1: 240 n. 1.
  2. 1–3, 2. 5: 224.
  2. 6: 236 n. 1.
  2. 12: 226 n. 1.
  2. 14–16: 225.
  2. 14: 228.
  2. 17: 215 n. 1, 228 and
    n. 2.
  2. 18: 217.
  2. 19–20: 235 n. 3.
  2. 20: 234 n. 6.
  3. 1: 229 n. 2.
  3. 2: 228.
  3. 5: 235 n. 3.
  3. 7: 220 n. 2.
  3. 8: 229 n. 3.
  3. 10: 230 n. 1.
  3. 12–13: 237 n. 2.